STUCK RUBBER BABY

BY HOWARD CRUSE

OTHER BOOKS BY HOWARD CRUSE

WENDEL

WENDEL ON THE REBOUND

DANCIN' NEKKID WITH THE ANGELS

EARLY BAREFOOTZ

STUCK RUBBER BABY

BY HOWARD CRUSE

PARADOX PRESS

NEW YORK

DEDICATION

FOR KIM,

FOR PAM,

AND

(AS ALWAYS)

FOR EDDIE

DC Comics, 1700 Broadway, New York, NY 10019.
A Warner Bros. Entertainment Company.
Printed in Canada. Third printing.
ISBN: 1-56389-255-3

Cover illustration by Howard Cruse.
Cover design by Suzanne Noli.
Author photograph by Tim J. Luddy.

INTRODUCTION

by TONY KUSHNER

I first encountered book-length comic book art when I was ten or eleven years old, browsing the shelves of my synagogue library: a history of the Soviet Union, told in black and white drawings and word balloons. I remember neither its title nor its author, only that its pages teemed with burly, gap-toothed, Mongol-faced, furhatted greatcoated or butcher-aproned Ivans. This was a cold war history produced entirely from a right perspective, so the Ivans were invariably drawn steeped to their swollen upper biceps in blood — the blood rendered simply, and appropriately, in smears and swaths of black ink, slathered generously in practically every panel.

The effect was thrilling, alarming, faintly nauseating: in addition to the dark pools of gore it was meant to evoke, the flat black called to mind mud, excrement, and the burnt bones that are the source of a carbon soot pure enough for India ink. The technique more than successfully intimated sensational levels of depravity and bestiality. As I read the book I imagined its author in the grim ecstasy of graphically depicting the uncountable crimes of the Stalin era; with his oversoaked, ink-logged brushes dripping midnight, murder, and despair, the righteously aroused and enflamed cartoonist-historian-ideologue winds up as smudged and stained as the sadistically grinning commissars he is depicting, indicting. In this image there is a suggestion of some sort of disquieting complicity between the accuser and the accused: the accuser as creative artist, through the act of representing, having created the accused. I remember feeling extremely uncomfortable and impressed. The image of the inkstained artist, muddied up to his elbows with the grime he's busily, inexactly but passionately slinging about, will to this day flash through my mind on any occasion when I encounter a troubling, stirring example of the exuberant, complicitous outrage of the writers and the artists of the political right.

The cartoon history of the USSR, with its ardent, serious, political intentions, its screaming for justice and the world's attention, was similar to but also different from the super-hero comics I devoured monthly the instant they appeared on the local 7-Eleven magazine racks. Comic books were an important part of my transition to adulthood. My childhood, like most, was preoccupied with magic and enchantment, with day-dream versions of the world, in which the Terrors with which one would eventually come to terms were expressed in a guise sufficiently metaphorical to countenance unflinchingly. Comic books paved the path up to the portals of adulthood, offering sexy and dangerous fantasies in which the sex was present but still subliminal (muscular men in BVDs), the danger grand and improbable enough to be intensely gratifying and yet manageable for a neurotic, rather cowardly gay boy entering early adolescence. The super-heros were, like me, full of anxieties of being unmasked, rendered powerless, and destroyed. Unlike me they were beautiful and irresistibly strong, able to participate fearlessly in the violence that seemed increasingly to be the true language of the world.

My parents worried about the growing stacks of comic books in my room, believing that my addiction to pictures would keep me from becoming the adult reader I ought to become. I pointed out that the comic books I read were strewn with literary references, mostly unattributed quotes from the Bible, Shakespeare, Milton, and Coleridge; and the villains especially possessed an ambitious vocabulary — I remember learning "meretricious" and "invidious," among other useful words. My parents, unimpressed, continued to worry. Perhaps it was my unmistakable fascination for the muscular men in their BVDs.

I no longer remember when or even why I stopped reading comic books. I completed the transition they had helped me through, I suppose. Having found the nerve and the necessity, I turned to a literature that addressed sex and danger costumed as I was encountering them in real life, the drab drag of the quotidian.

But I never stopped adoring the drawing and word-balloon form. An adult now, free enough to indulge in all manner of parentally banned activities, I read the daily comic strips in the newspaper. I find that when the news is awful, as it almost always is, it's only the promise of the comic strips that keeps me wading through the pages of holocaust, catastrophe, psychosis, abuse, and chicanery that are, they tell me, the proper business of an adult.

Playwrights work within many of the same drastic economies of dialogue and image as comic book artists; both have to grapple, albeit in differ- ent ways, with severe limitations and pressures of time and space. So my admiration for the artists who produce good comic strips is unbounded, and yet I still detect in myself a certain furtiveness when I'm reading these strips out in the open, on the subway. Shame, an unavoidable residue of any successful transformation, attaches itself to the comics, as if reading them were age-inappropriate. The generic name, "comics" (or its earlier version, "funnies"), is no help in this regard.

My appetite for longer narratives in comic book form was left largely unsatisfied, and guiltily repressed, till the day I first purchased *The Advocate*. In the Pink Pages section at the back of the magazine, I discovered (along with many other forbidden delights) a picaresque novel, meted out in one-page installments in every issue. It was complicated, politically-minded, gently humorous and psychologically sophisticated. It was called *Wendel*, and for the next several years I followed its recountings of the lives of lesbians and gay men, while at the same time becoming acquainted with the previous work of its author, Howard Cruse, and with the author himself.

Howard Cruse is a pioneer in the field of lesbian and gay comics, an important participant in the underground comics movement, and in my opinion one of the most talented artists ever to work in the form. His short pieces are wonderful examples of narrative compression, politically and emotionally complex, provocative and moving. In short and longer works, like *Wendel*, Howard demonstrates a quicksilver intelligence and imagination that can shift, with lightning speed, from the hallucinatory and visionary to the gnarly and grotty, from the sexy and sublime to the downright revolting, from the comic to the tragic, and from one side of a political argument to the other. One part of this ability he owes to his region; such graceful, wry, apparently effortless chameleoning is a Southern virtue. The other part is attributable to sheer talent and a serious commitment to art that is unafraid of its usefulness in a political fight.

Howard was a body-and-soul participant in the '60s revolution, which made him an anarchist, or left-libertarian. His politics are the antithesis of doctrinaire; I find his opinions, as expressed in his work, irresistibly attractive, even when I disagree.

Howard told his friends a few years ago that he was stopping work on *Wendel* to devote himself to writing and drawing a graphic novel: the result of that labor you are holding in your hands.

It is ever the conundrum of the introducer of something really good that the thing itself needs no introduction, it needs only to be read. Its readers will surely find in *Stuck Rubber Baby* all manner of richness and depth and value, only one aspect of which is political. But as political art this book is timely. It articulates a crying need for solidarity, it performs the crucial function of remembering, for the queer community, how essential to the birth of our politics of liberation the civil rights movement was. The point, it seems to me, is not that one movement co-opts the energy or the nobility or the history of another; not that one people, rising to an angry knowledge of how it has been abused, competes for status of "most abused" with any other; but rather that we need to know the genealogies of our movements, and with that knowledge come to understand the interdependence of all liberation struggles. We must finally accept and practice what we've been saying for decades, for centuries: Freedom is only possible when it's everyone's freedom, and slavery anywhere means slavery everywhere.

To overcome the perils of the present moment will require all the human force and power and collective will we can bring to bear. Our political leaders these days seem more and more like the caricatures political cartoonists draw. Even a supremely gifted political cartoonist will have trouble exaggerating the malevolence of Gingrich, the manifest instability of Dole, the dithering and waffling of Clinton, the satanic flatulent eructations of Limbaugh. They're all bespattered with the inky muck of extremism, heartlessness, and criminality.

Here is a book drawn in a finer, more scrupled and scrupulous, more rigorous style. In the beauty of its details, in the subtlety of its narrative, its heart is manifest: Its author addresses his work to the labyrinthine internal politics one encounters in trying to be a good person in the world. This book is quiet, elegiac, and turned toward the past. In reconstructing a memory of a time when one struggle lit up the path for another, and an oppressed people gave instruction, through example, in the ways of resistance to the entire watching world, Howard Cruse offers us something deeply important and fortifying, something we need.

"The antonym of *forgetting*," says the Jewish historian Yosef Hayim Yerushalmi, "is not *remembering*, but *justice*."

*Tony Kushner is the author of **Angels in America: A Gay Fantasia on National Themes**, among other plays.*

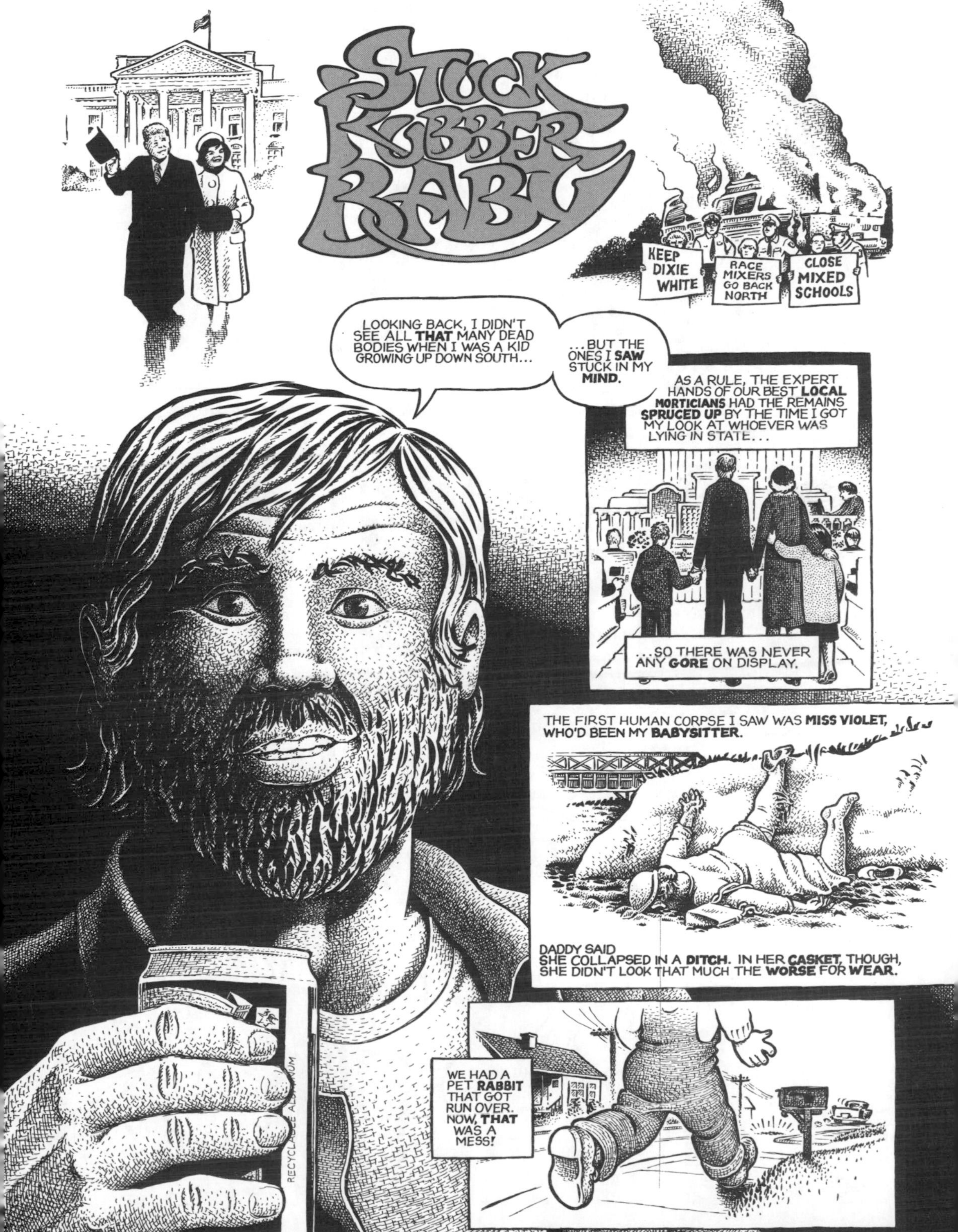
STUCK RUBBER BABY
KEEP DIXIE WHITE
RACE MIXERS GO BACK NORTH
CLOSE MIXED SCHOOLS
LOOKING BACK, I DIDN'T SEE ALL **THAT** MANY DEAD BODIES WHEN I WAS A KID GROWING UP DOWN SOUTH...
...BUT THE ONES I **SAW** STUCK IN MY **MIND**.
AS A RULE, THE EXPERT HANDS OF OUR BEST **LOCAL MORTICIANS** HAD THE REMAINS **SPRUCED UP** BY THE TIME I GOT MY LOOK AT WHOEVER WAS LYING IN STATE...
...SO THERE WAS NEVER ANY **GORE** ON DISPLAY.
THE FIRST HUMAN CORPSE I SAW WAS **MISS VIOLET**, WHO'D BEEN MY **BABYSITTER**.
DADDY SAID SHE COLLAPSED IN A **DITCH**. IN HER **CASKET**, THOUGH, SHE DIDN'T LOOK THAT MUCH THE **WORSE** FOR **WEAR**.
WE HAD A PET **RABBIT** THAT GOT RUN OVER. NOW, **THAT** WAS A MESS!
RECYCLABLE ALUMINUM

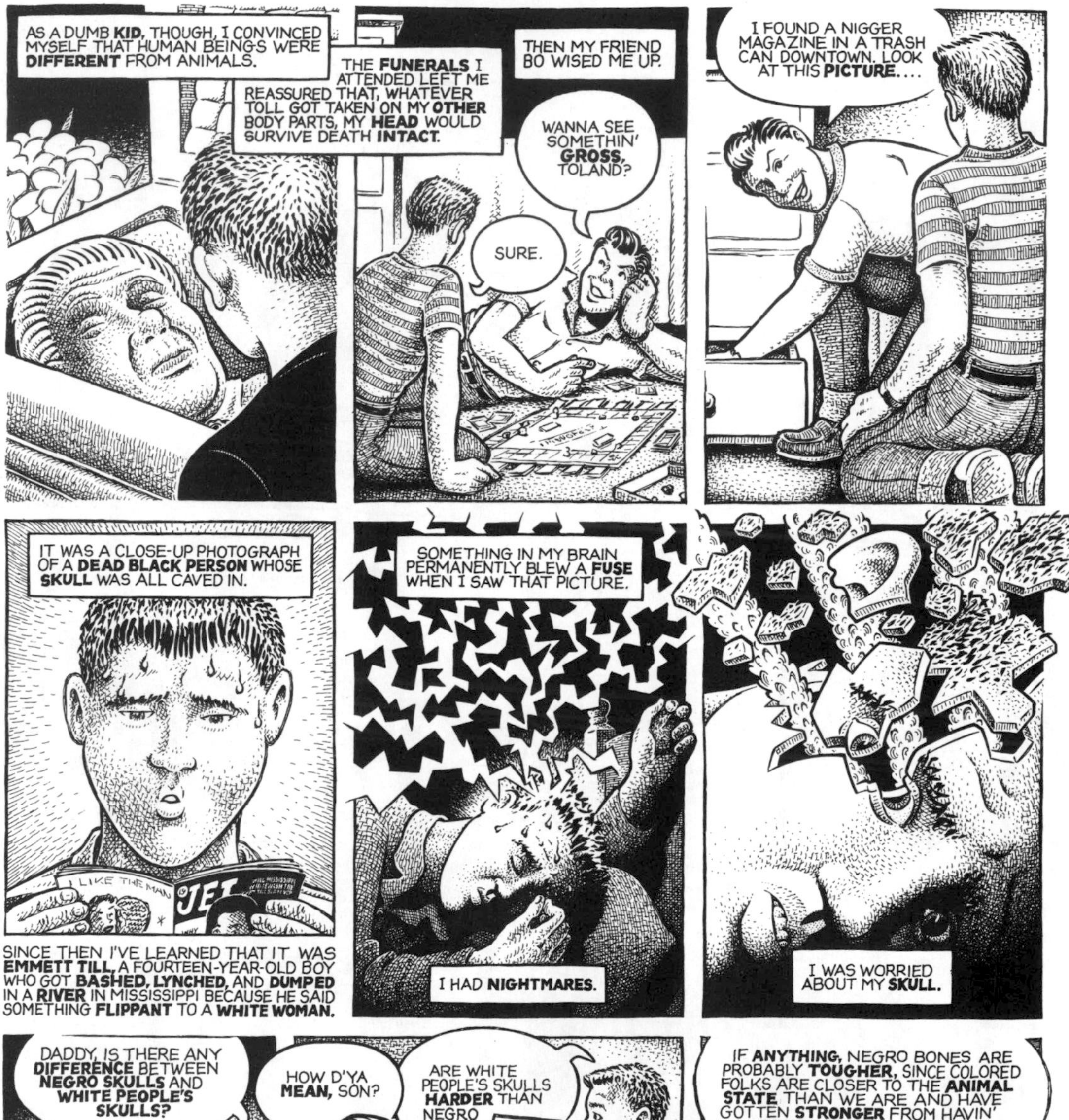

AS A DUMB KID, THOUGH, I CONVINCED MYSELF THAT HUMAN BEINGS WERE DIFFERENT FROM ANIMALS.
THE FUNERALS I ATTENDED LEFT ME REASSURED THAT, WHATEVER TOLL GOT TAKEN ON MY OTHER BODY PARTS, MY HEAD WOULD SURVIVE DEATH INTACT.
THEN MY FRIEND BO WISED ME UP.
WANNA SEE SOMETHIN' GROSS, TOLAND?
SURE.
I FOUND A NIGGER MAGAZINE IN A TRASH CAN DOWNTOWN. LOOK AT THIS PICTURE....
IT WAS A CLOSE-UP PHOTOGRAPH OF A DEAD BLACK PERSON WHOSE SKULL WAS ALL CAVED IN.
I LIKE THE MAN
JET
SINCE THEN I'VE LEARNED THAT IT WAS EMMETT TILL, A FOURTEEN-YEAR-OLD BOY WHO GOT BASHED, LYNCHED, AND DUMPED IN A RIVER IN MISSISSIPPI BECAUSE HE SAID SOMETHING FLIPPANT TO A WHITE WOMAN.
SOMETHING IN MY BRAIN PERMANENTLY BLEW A FUSE WHEN I SAW THAT PICTURE.
I HAD NIGHTMARES.
I WAS WORRIED ABOUT MY SKULL.
DADDY, IS THERE ANY DIFFERENCE BETWEEN NEGRO SKULLS AND WHITE PEOPLE'S SKULLS?
HOW D'YA MEAN, SON?
ARE WHITE PEOPLE'S SKULLS HARDER THAN NEGRO SKULLS?
OH, I DOUBT IT, TOLAND. I DOUBT IT SERIOUSLY.
IF ANYTHING, NEGRO BONES ARE PROBABLY TOUGHER, SINCE COLORED FOLKS ARE CLOSER TO THE ANIMAL STATE THAN WE ARE AND HAVE GOTTEN STRONGER FROM HAVIN' TO GET BY IN THE WILD.

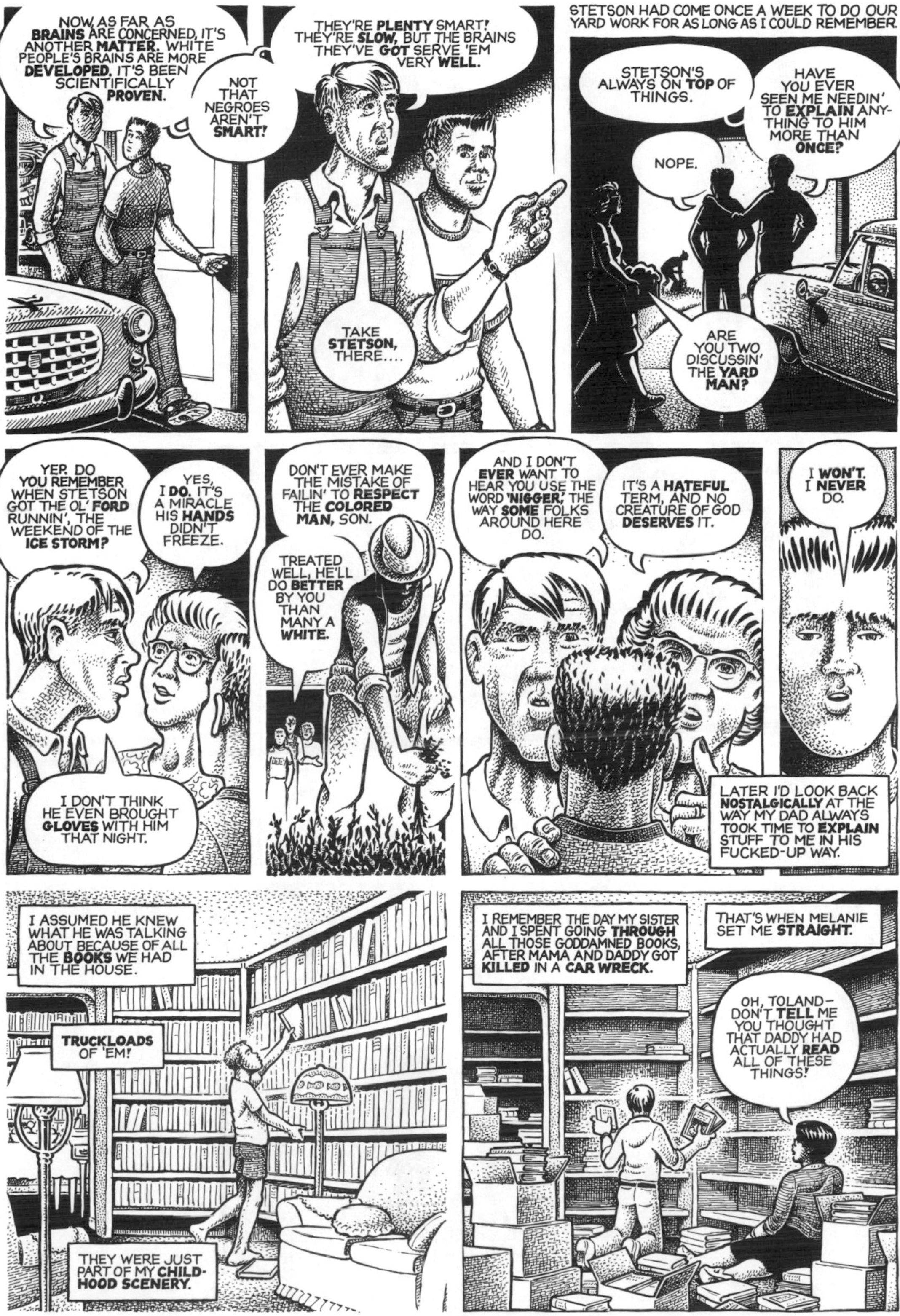
NOW, AS FAR AS **BRAINS** ARE CONCERNED, IT'S ANOTHER **MATTER**. WHITE PEOPLE'S BRAINS ARE MORE **DEVELOPED**. IT'S BEEN SCIENTIFICALLY **PROVEN**.
NOT THAT NEGROES AREN'T **SMART!**
THEY'RE **PLENTY** SMART! THEY'RE **SLOW**, BUT THE BRAINS THEY'VE **GOT** SERVE 'EM VERY **WELL**.
TAKE **STETSON**, THERE....
STETSON HAD COME ONCE A WEEK TO DO OUR YARD WORK FOR AS LONG AS I COULD REMEMBER.
STETSON'S ALWAYS ON **TOP** OF THINGS.
HAVE YOU EVER SEEN ME NEEDIN' TO **EXPLAIN** ANYTHING TO HIM MORE THAN **ONCE?**
NOPE.
ARE YOU TWO DISCUSSIN' THE **YARD MAN?**
YEP. DO **YOU REMEMBER** WHEN STETSON GOT THE OL' **FORD** RUNNIN', THE WEEKEND OF THE **ICE STORM?**
YES, I **DO**. IT'S A MIRACLE HIS **HANDS** DIDN'T FREEZE.
I DON'T THINK HE EVEN BROUGHT **GLOVES** WITH HIM THAT NIGHT.
DON'T EVER MAKE THE MISTAKE OF FAILIN' TO **RESPECT** THE **COLORED MAN**, SON.
TREATED WELL, HE'LL DO **BETTER** BY YOU THAN MANY A **WHITE**.
AND I DON'T **EVER** WANT TO HEAR YOU USE THE WORD **'NIGGER,'** THE WAY **SOME** FOLKS AROUND HERE DO.
IT'S A **HATEFUL** TERM, AND NO CREATURE OF GOD **DESERVES** IT.
I **WON'T**. I **NEVER** DO.
LATER I'D LOOK BACK **NOSTALGICALLY** AT THE WAY MY DAD ALWAYS TOOK TIME TO **EXPLAIN** STUFF TO ME IN HIS FUCKED-UP WAY.
I ASSUMED HE KNEW WHAT HE WAS TALKING ABOUT BECAUSE OF ALL THE **BOOKS** WE HAD IN THE HOUSE.
TRUCKLOADS OF 'EM!
THEY WERE JUST PART OF MY **CHILDHOOD SCENERY**.
I REMEMBER THE DAY MY SISTER AND I SPENT GOING **THROUGH** ALL THOSE GODDAMNED BOOKS, AFTER MAMA AND DADDY GOT **KILLED** IN A **CAR WRECK**.
THAT'S WHEN MELANIE SET ME **STRAIGHT**.
OH, TOLAND– DON'T **TELL** ME YOU THOUGHT THAT DADDY HAD ACTUALLY **READ** ALL OF THESE THINGS!

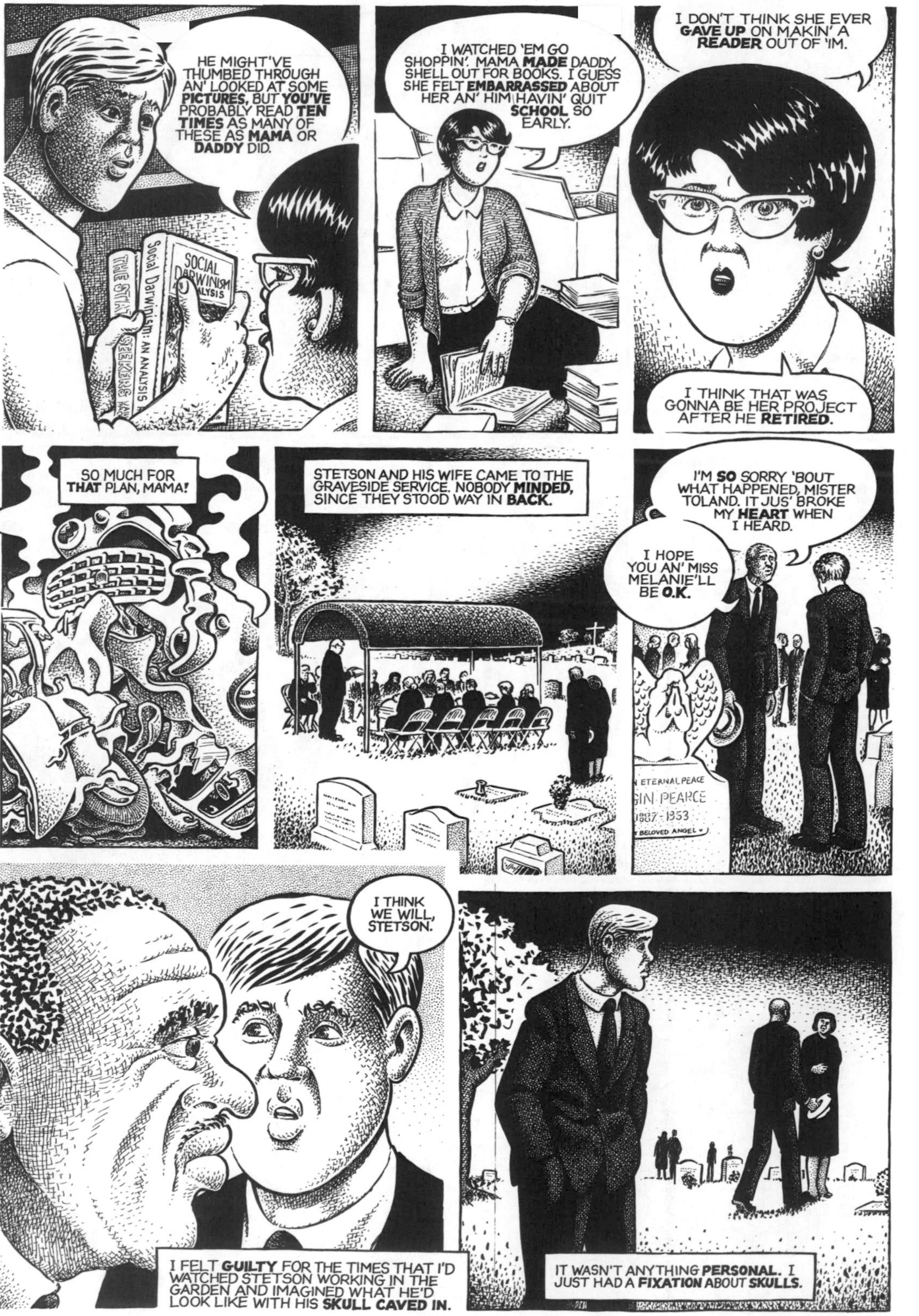
HE MIGHT'VE THUMBED THROUGH AN' LOOKED AT SOME PICTURES, BUT YOU'VE PROBABLY READ TEN TIMES AS MANY OF THESE AS MAMA OR DADDY DID.
SOCIAL DARWINISM ANALYSIS
Social Darwinism: AN ANALYSIS
I WATCHED 'EM GO SHOPPIN'. MAMA MADE DADDY SHELL OUT FOR BOOKS. I GUESS SHE FELT EMBARRASSED ABOUT HER AN' HIM HAVIN' QUIT SCHOOL SO EARLY.
I DON'T THINK SHE EVER GAVE UP ON MAKIN' A READER OUT OF 'IM.
I THINK THAT WAS GONNA BE HER PROJECT AFTER HE RETIRED.
SO MUCH FOR THAT PLAN, MAMA!
STETSON AND HIS WIFE CAME TO THE GRAVESIDE SERVICE. NOBODY MINDED, SINCE THEY STOOD WAY IN BACK.
I'M SO SORRY 'BOUT WHAT HAPPENED, MISTER TOLAND. IT JUS' BROKE MY HEART WHEN I HEARD.
I HOPE YOU AN' MISS MELANIE'LL BE O.K.
I THINK WE WILL, STETSON.
I FELT GUILTY FOR THE TIMES THAT I'D WATCHED STETSON WORKING IN THE GARDEN AND IMAGINED WHAT HE'D LOOK LIKE WITH HIS SKULL CAVED IN.
IT WASN'T ANYTHING PERSONAL. I JUST HAD A FIXATION ABOUT SKULLS.

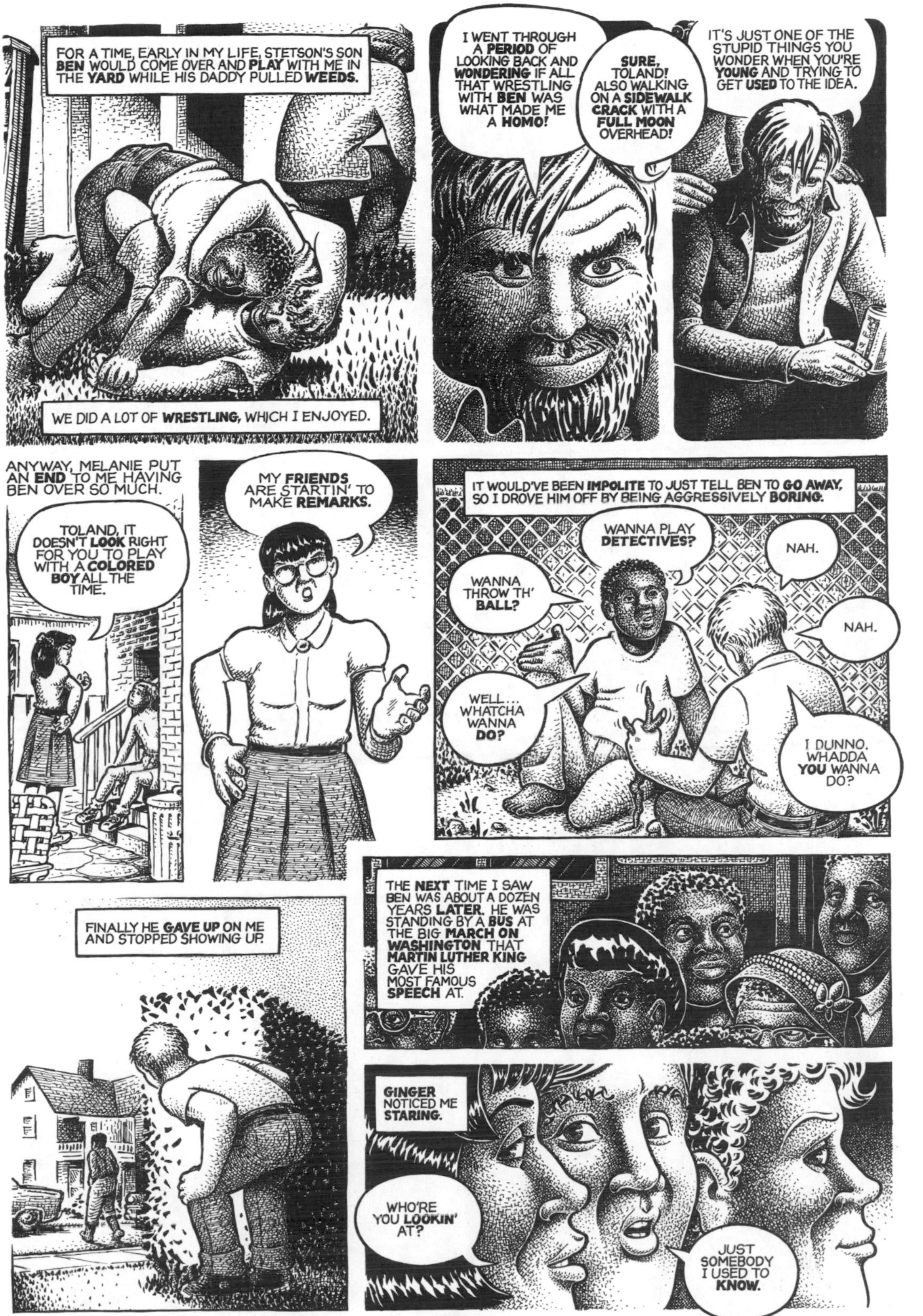

FOR A TIME, EARLY IN MY LIFE, STETSON'S SON BEN WOULD COME OVER AND PLAY WITH ME IN THE YARD WHILE HIS DADDY PULLED WEEDS.
WE DID A LOT OF WRESTLING, WHICH I ENJOYED.
I WENT THROUGH A PERIOD OF LOOKING BACK AND WONDERING IF ALL THAT WRESTLING WITH BEN WAS WHAT MADE ME A HOMO!
SURE, TOLAND! ALSO WALKING ON A SIDEWALK CRACK WITH A FULL MOON OVERHEAD!
IT'S JUST ONE OF THE STUPID THINGS YOU WONDER WHEN YOU'RE YOUNG AND TRYING TO GET USED TO THE IDEA.
ANYWAY, MELANIE PUT AN END TO ME HAVING BEN OVER SO MUCH.
TOLAND, IT DOESN'T LOOK RIGHT FOR YOU TO PLAY WITH A COLORED BOY ALL THE TIME.
MY FRIENDS ARE STARTIN' TO MAKE REMARKS.
IT WOULD'VE BEEN IMPOLITE TO JUST TELL BEN TO GO AWAY, SO I DROVE HIM OFF BY BEING AGGRESSIVELY BORING.
WANNA PLAY DETECTIVES?
NAH.
WANNA THROW TH' BALL?
NAH.
WELL... WHATCHA WANNA DO?
I DUNNO. WHADDA YOU WANNA DO?
FINALLY HE GAVE UP ON ME AND STOPPED SHOWING UP.
THE NEXT TIME I SAW BEN WAS ABOUT A DOZEN YEARS LATER. HE WAS STANDING BY A BUS AT THE BIG MARCH ON WASHINGTON THAT MARTIN LUTHER KING GAVE HIS MOST FAMOUS SPEECH AT.
GINGER NOTICED ME STARING.
WHO'RE YOU LOOKIN' AT?
JUST SOMEBODY I USED TO KNOW.

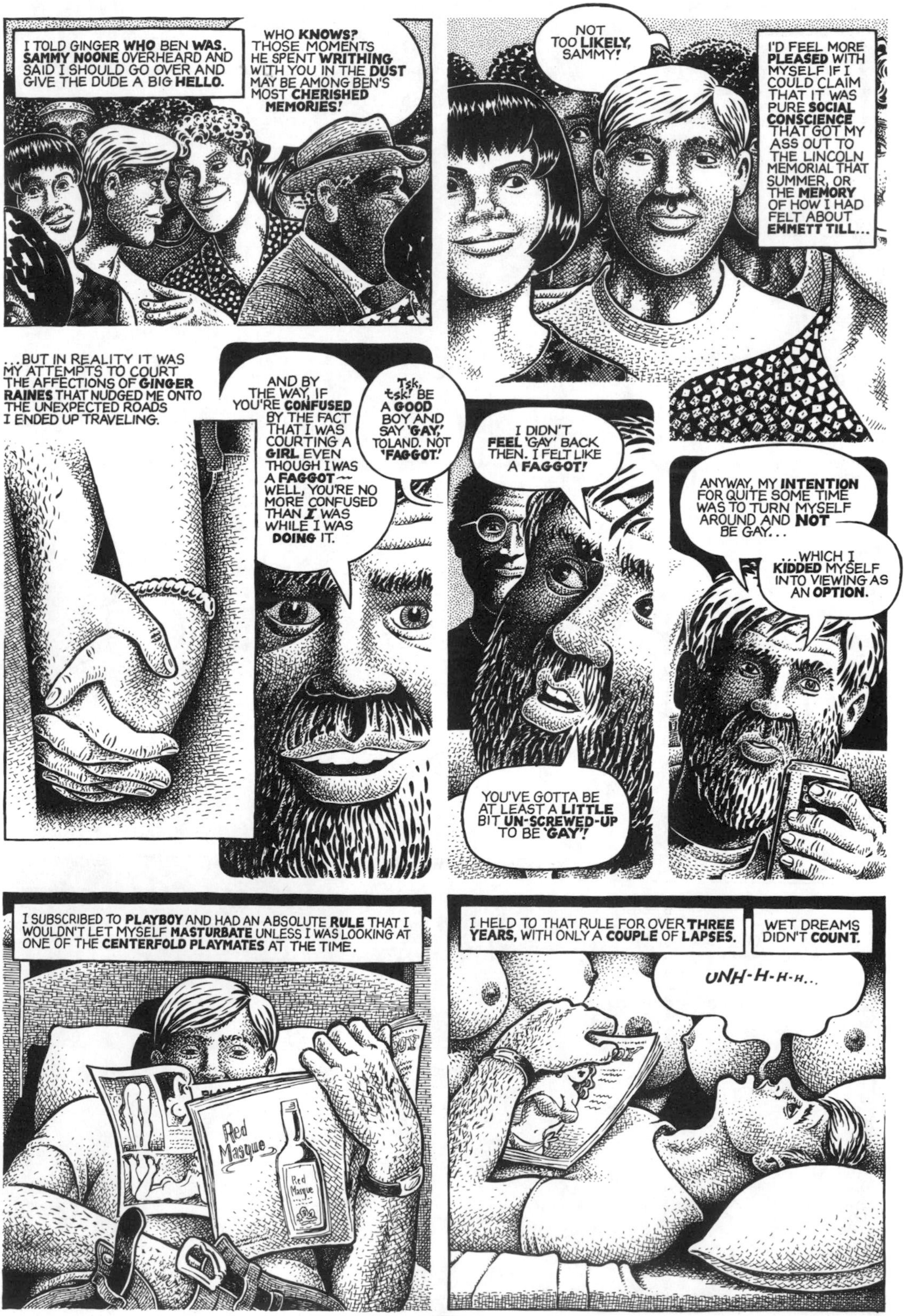
I TOLD GINGER WHO BEN WAS. SAMMY NOONE OVERHEARD AND SAID I SHOULD GO OVER AND GIVE THE DUDE A BIG HELLO.
WHO KNOWS? THOSE MOMENTS HE SPENT WRITHING WITH YOU IN THE DUST MAY BE AMONG BEN'S MOST CHERISHED MEMORIES!
NOT TOO LIKELY, SAMMY!
I'D FEEL MORE PLEASED WITH MYSELF IF I COULD CLAIM THAT IT WAS PURE SOCIAL CONSCIENCE THAT GOT MY ASS OUT TO THE LINCOLN MEMORIAL THAT SUMMER, OR THE MEMORY OF HOW I HAD FELT ABOUT EMMETT TILL...
...BUT IN REALITY IT WAS MY ATTEMPTS TO COURT THE AFFECTIONS OF GINGER RAINES THAT NUDGED ME ONTO THE UNEXPECTED ROADS I ENDED UP TRAVELING.
AND BY THE WAY, IF YOU'RE CONFUSED BY THE FACT THAT I WAS COURTING A GIRL EVEN THOUGH I WAS A FAGGOT— WELL, YOU'RE NO MORE CONFUSED THAN I WAS WHILE I WAS DOING IT.
Tsk, tsk! BE A GOOD BOY AND SAY 'GAY,' TOLAND. NOT 'FAGGOT.'
I DIDN'T FEEL 'GAY' BACK THEN. I FELT LIKE A FAGGOT!
YOU'VE GOTTA BE AT LEAST A LITTLE BIT UN-SCREWED-UP TO BE 'GAY'!
ANYWAY, MY INTENTION FOR QUITE SOME TIME WAS TO TURN MYSELF AROUND AND NOT BE GAY...
...WHICH I KIDDED MYSELF INTO VIEWING AS AN OPTION.
I SUBSCRIBED TO PLAYBOY AND HAD AN ABSOLUTE RULE THAT I WOULDN'T LET MYSELF MASTURBATE UNLESS I WAS LOOKING AT ONE OF THE CENTERFOLD PLAYMATES AT THE TIME.
Red Masque
Red Masque
I HELD TO THAT RULE FOR OVER THREE YEARS, WITH ONLY A COUPLE OF LAPSES.
WET DREAMS DIDN'T COUNT.
UNH-H-H-H...

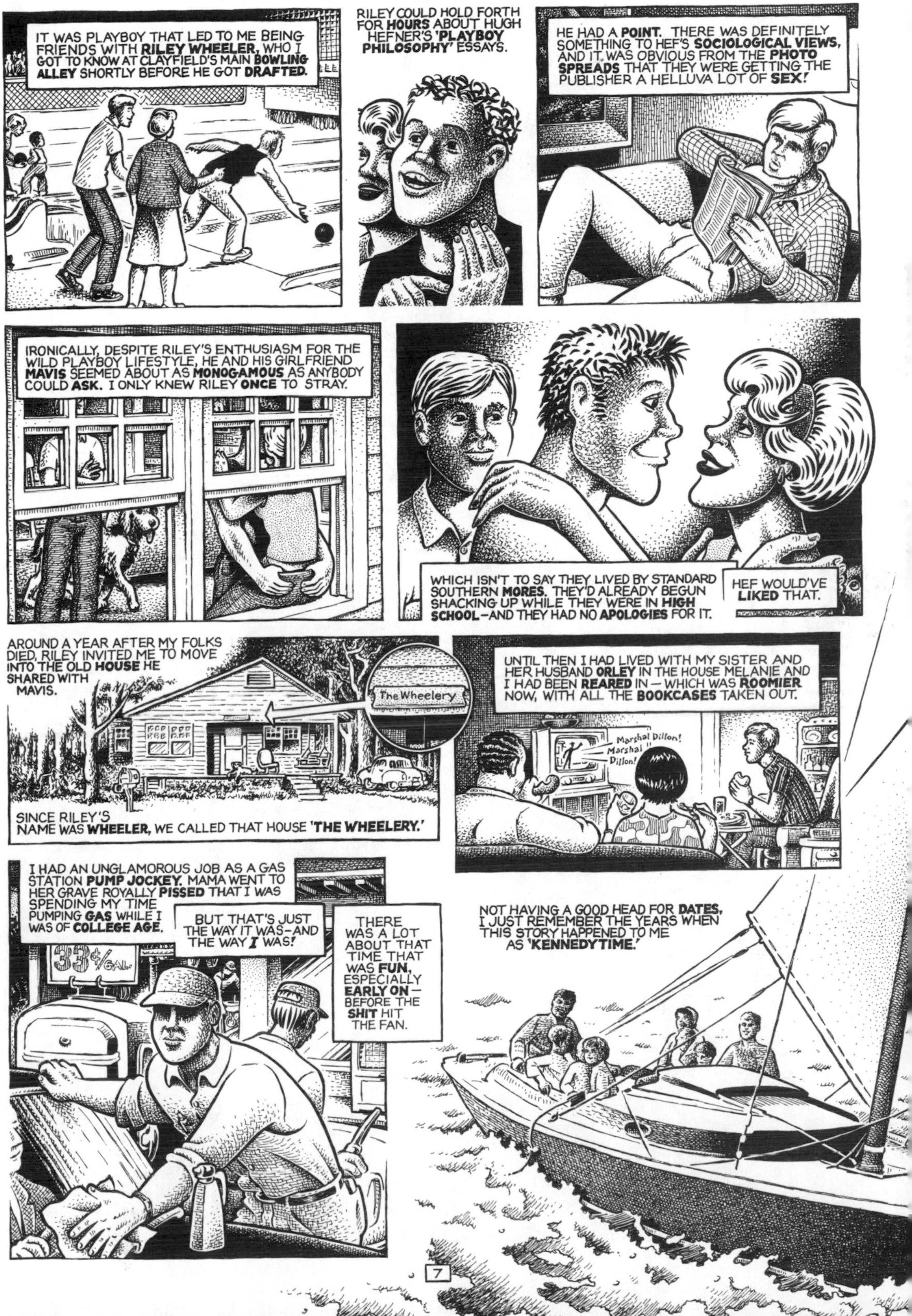
IT WAS PLAYBOY THAT LED TO ME BEING FRIENDS WITH **RILEY WHEELER**, WHO I GOT TO KNOW AT CLAYFIELD'S MAIN **BOWLING ALLEY** SHORTLY BEFORE HE GOT **DRAFTED**.
RILEY COULD HOLD FORTH FOR **HOURS** ABOUT HUGH HEFNER'S **'PLAYBOY PHILOSOPHY'** ESSAYS.
HE HAD A **POINT**. THERE WAS DEFINITELY SOMETHING TO HEF'S **SOCIOLOGICAL VIEWS**, AND IT WAS OBVIOUS FROM THE **PHOTO SPREADS** THAT THEY WERE GETTING THE PUBLISHER A HELLUVA LOT OF **SEX!**
IRONICALLY, DESPITE RILEY'S ENTHUSIASM FOR THE WILD PLAYBOY LIFESTYLE, HE AND HIS GIRLFRIEND **MAVIS** SEEMED ABOUT AS **MONOGAMOUS** AS ANYBODY COULD **ASK**. I ONLY KNEW RILEY **ONCE** TO STRAY.
WHICH ISN'T TO SAY THEY LIVED BY STANDARD SOUTHERN **MORES**. THEY'D ALREADY BEGUN SHACKING UP WHILE THEY WERE IN **HIGH SCHOOL**—AND THEY HAD NO **APOLOGIES** FOR IT.
HEF WOULD'VE **LIKED** THAT.
AROUND A YEAR AFTER MY FOLKS DIED, RILEY INVITED ME TO MOVE INTO THE OLD **HOUSE** HE SHARED WITH MAVIS.
The Wheelery
SINCE RILEY'S NAME WAS **WHEELER**, WE CALLED THAT HOUSE **'THE WHEELERY.'**
UNTIL THEN I HAD LIVED WITH MY SISTER AND HER HUSBAND **ORLEY** IN THE HOUSE MELANIE AND I HAD BEEN **REARED** IN — WHICH WAS **ROOMIER** NOW, WITH ALL THE **BOOKCASES** TAKEN OUT.
Marshal Dillon! Marshal Dillon!
I HAD AN UNGLAMOROUS JOB AS A GAS STATION **PUMP JOCKEY**. MAMA WENT TO HER GRAVE ROYALLY **PISSED** THAT I WAS SPENDING MY TIME PUMPING **GAS** WHILE I WAS OF **COLLEGE AGE**.
BUT THAT'S JUST THE WAY IT WAS—AND THE WAY **I** WAS!
33¢/GAL.
THERE WAS A LOT ABOUT THAT TIME THAT WAS **FUN**, ESPECIALLY **EARLY ON**— BEFORE THE **SHIT** HIT THE FAN.
NOT HAVING A GOOD HEAD FOR **DATES**, I JUST REMEMBER THE YEARS WHEN THIS STORY HAPPENED TO ME AS **'KENNEDYTIME.'**

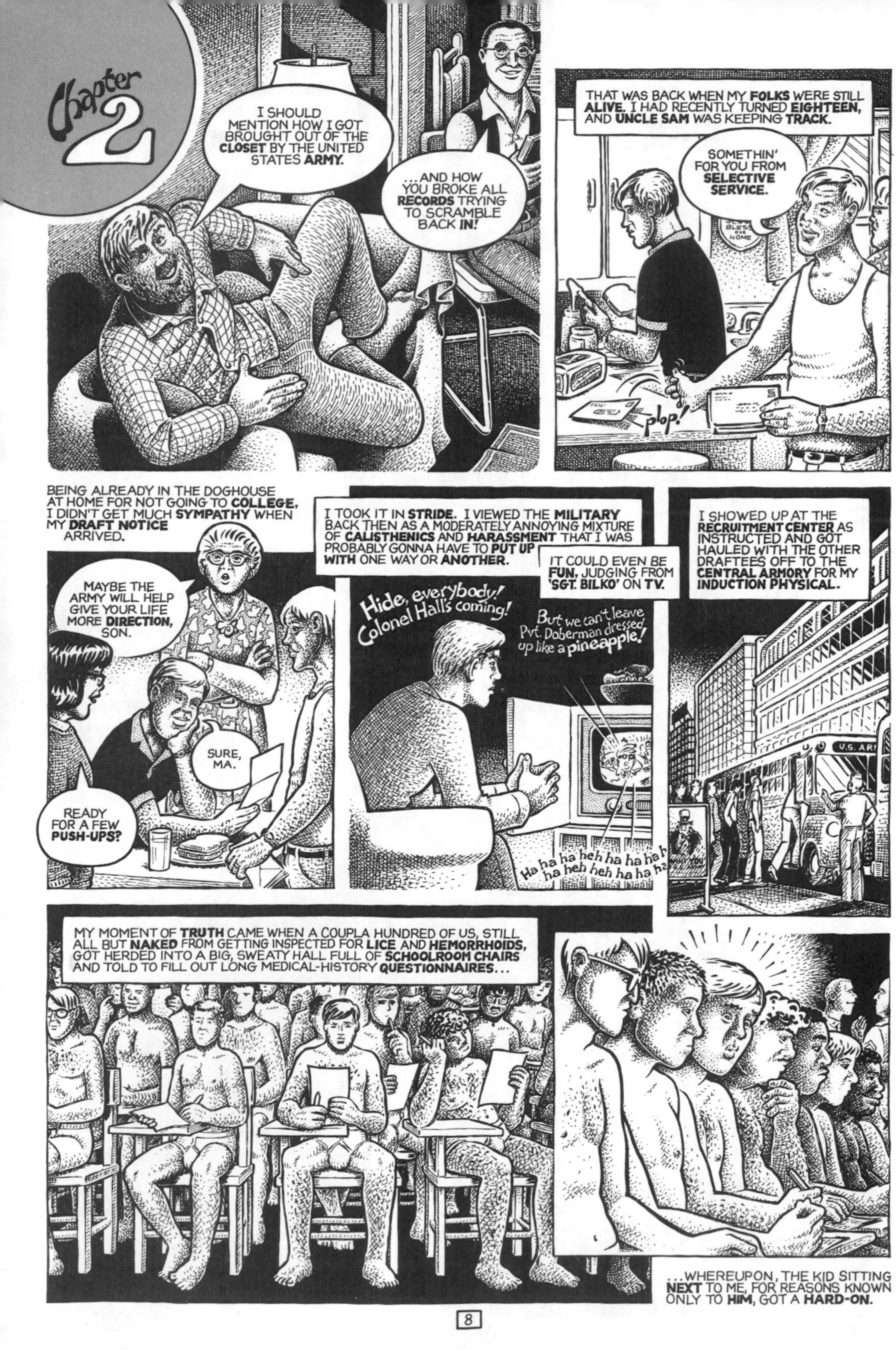
Chapter 2
I SHOULD MENTION HOW I GOT BROUGHT OUT OF THE CLOSET BY THE UNITED STATES ARMY.
...AND HOW YOU BROKE ALL RECORDS TRYING TO SCRAMBLE BACK IN!
THAT WAS BACK WHEN MY FOLKS WERE STILL ALIVE. I HAD RECENTLY TURNED EIGHTEEN, AND UNCLE SAM WAS KEEPING TRACK.
SOMETHIN' FOR YOU FROM SELECTIVE SERVICE.
plop!
BEING ALREADY IN THE DOGHOUSE AT HOME FOR NOT GOING TO COLLEGE, I DIDN'T GET MUCH SYMPATHY WHEN MY DRAFT NOTICE ARRIVED.
MAYBE THE ARMY WILL HELP GIVE YOUR LIFE MORE DIRECTION, SON.
SURE, MA.
READY FOR A FEW PUSH-UPS?
I TOOK IT IN STRIDE. I VIEWED THE MILITARY BACK THEN AS A MODERATELY ANNOYING MIXTURE OF CALISTHENICS AND HARASSMENT THAT I WAS PROBABLY GONNA HAVE TO PUT UP WITH ONE WAY OR ANOTHER.
IT COULD EVEN BE FUN, JUDGING FROM 'SGT. BILKO' ON TV.
Hide, everybody! Colonel Hall's coming!
But we can't leave Pvt. Doberman dressed up like a pineapple!
Ha ha ha heh ha ha ha h ha heh heh ha ha ha
I SHOWED UP AT THE RECRUITMENT CENTER AS INSTRUCTED AND GOT HAULED WITH THE OTHER DRAFTEES OFF TO THE CENTRAL ARMORY FOR MY INDUCTION PHYSICAL.
MY MOMENT OF TRUTH CAME WHEN A COUPLA HUNDRED OF US, STILL ALL BUT NAKED FROM GETTING INSPECTED FOR LICE AND HEMORRHOIDS, GOT HERDED INTO A BIG, SWEATY HALL FULL OF SCHOOLROOM CHAIRS AND TOLD TO FILL OUT LONG MEDICAL-HISTORY QUESTIONNAIRES...
...WHEREUPON, THE KID SITTING NEXT TO ME, FOR REASONS KNOWN ONLY TO HIM, GOT A HARD-ON.

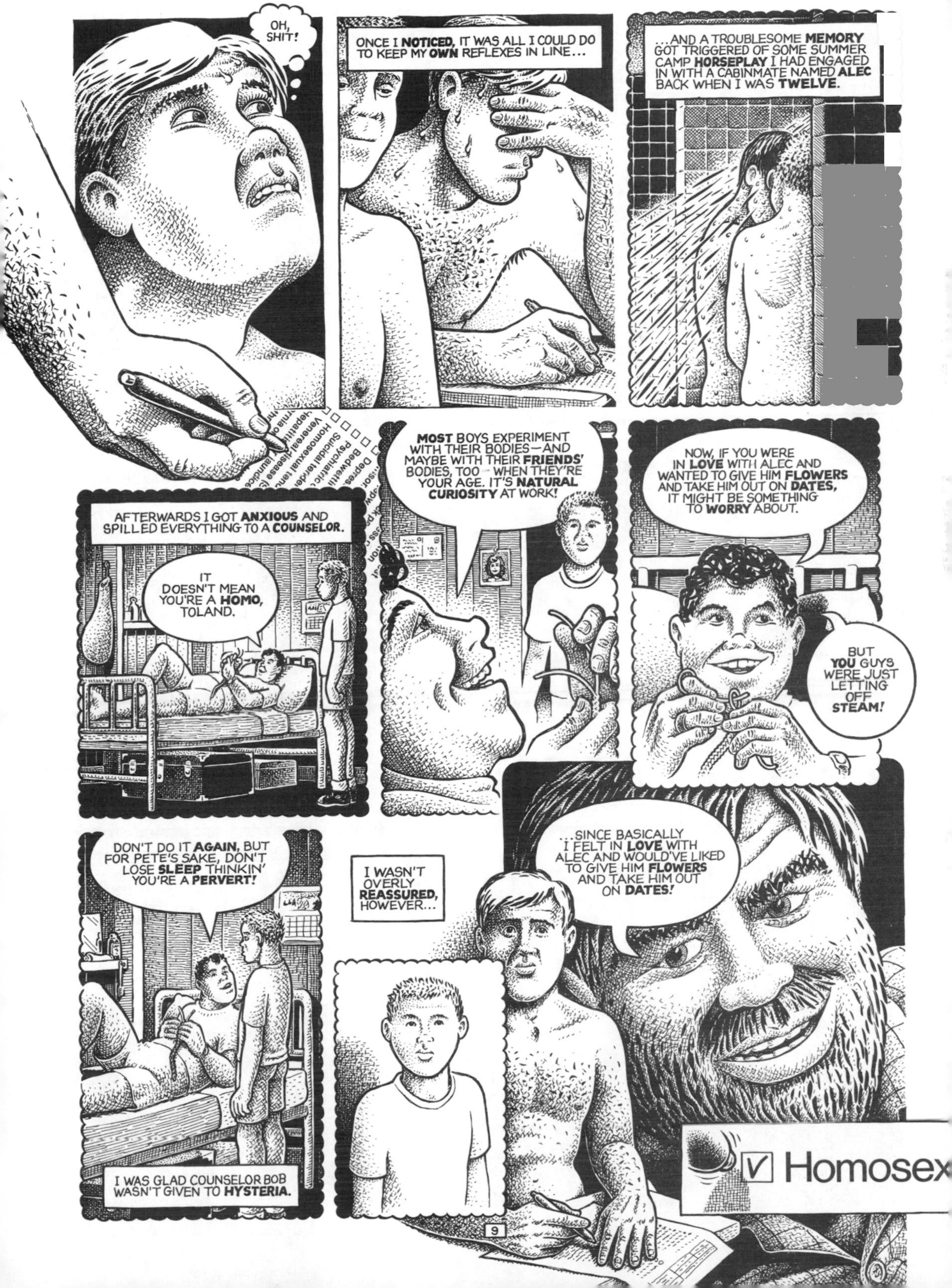
OH, SHIT!
ONCE I NOTICED, IT WAS ALL I COULD DO TO KEEP MY OWN REFLEXES IN LINE...
...AND A TROUBLESOME MEMORY GOT TRIGGERED OF SOME SUMMER CAMP HORSEPLAY I HAD ENGAGED IN WITH A CABINMATE NAMED ALEC BACK WHEN I WAS TWELVE.
AFTERWARDS I GOT ANXIOUS AND SPILLED EVERYTHING TO A COUNSELOR.
IT DOESN'T MEAN YOU'RE A HOMO, TOLAND.
MOST BOYS EXPERIMENT WITH THEIR BODIES—AND MAYBE WITH THEIR FRIENDS' BODIES, TOO—WHEN THEY'RE YOUR AGE. IT'S NATURAL CURIOSITY AT WORK!
NOW, IF YOU WERE IN LOVE WITH ALEC AND WANTED TO GIVE HIM FLOWERS AND TAKE HIM OUT ON DATES, IT MIGHT BE SOMETHING TO WORRY ABOUT.
BUT YOU GUYS WERE JUST LETTING OFF STEAM!
DON'T DO IT AGAIN, BUT FOR PETE'S SAKE, DON'T LOSE SLEEP THINKIN' YOU'RE A PERVERT!
I WAS GLAD COUNSELOR BOB WASN'T GIVEN TO HYSTERIA.
I WASN'T OVERLY REASSURED, HOWEVER...
...SINCE BASICALLY I FELT IN LOVE WITH ALEC AND WOULD'VE LIKED TO GIVE HIM FLOWERS AND TAKE HIM OUT ON DATES!
✓ Homosex

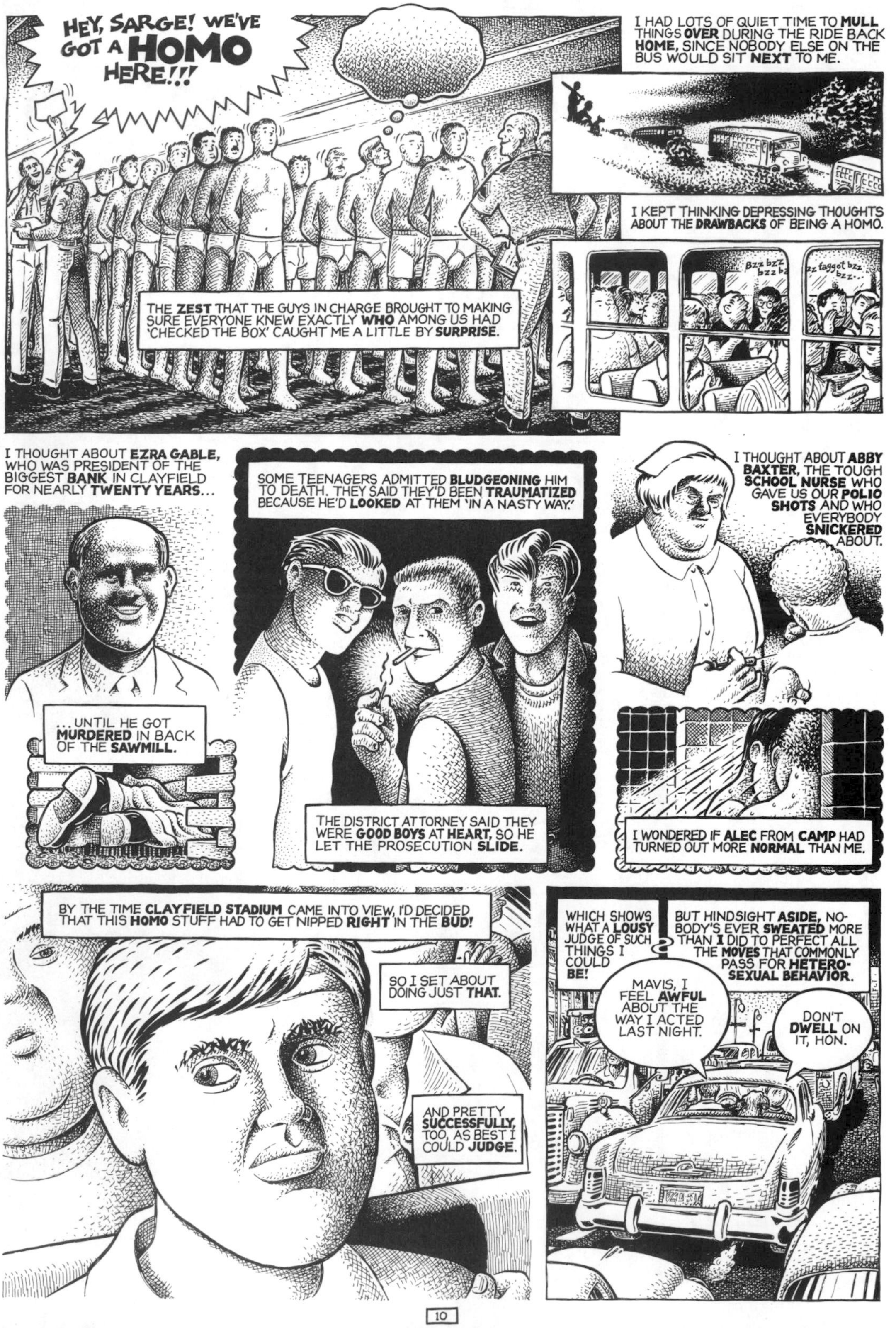
HEY, SARGE! WE'VE GOT A HOMO HERE!!!
THE ZEST THAT THE GUYS IN CHARGE BROUGHT TO MAKING SURE EVERYONE KNEW EXACTLY WHO AMONG US HAD 'CHECKED THE BOX' CAUGHT ME A LITTLE BY SURPRISE.
I HAD LOTS OF QUIET TIME TO MULL THINGS OVER DURING THE RIDE BACK HOME, SINCE NOBODY ELSE ON THE BUS WOULD SIT NEXT TO ME.
I KEPT THINKING DEPRESSING THOUGHTS ABOUT THE DRAWBACKS OF BEING A HOMO.
Bzz bzz bzz b
zz faggot bzz bzz...
I THOUGHT ABOUT EZRA GABLE, WHO WAS PRESIDENT OF THE BIGGEST BANK IN CLAYFIELD FOR NEARLY TWENTY YEARS...
...UNTIL HE GOT MURDERED IN BACK OF THE SAWMILL.
SOME TEENAGERS ADMITTED BLUDGEONING HIM TO DEATH. THEY SAID THEY'D BEEN TRAUMATIZED BECAUSE HE'D LOOKED AT THEM 'IN A NASTY WAY.'
THE DISTRICT ATTORNEY SAID THEY WERE GOOD BOYS AT HEART, SO HE LET THE PROSECUTION SLIDE.
I THOUGHT ABOUT ABBY BAXTER, THE TOUGH SCHOOL NURSE WHO GAVE US OUR POLIO SHOTS AND WHO EVERYBODY SNICKERED ABOUT.
I WONDERED IF ALEC FROM CAMP HAD TURNED OUT MORE NORMAL THAN ME.
BY THE TIME CLAYFIELD STADIUM CAME INTO VIEW, I'D DECIDED THAT THIS HOMO STUFF HAD TO GET NIPPED RIGHT IN THE BUD!
SO I SET ABOUT DOING JUST THAT.
AND PRETTY SUCCESSFULLY, TOO, AS BEST I COULD JUDGE.
WHICH SHOWS WHAT A LOUSY JUDGE OF SUCH THINGS I COULD BE!
BUT HINDSIGHT ASIDE, NOBODY'S EVER SWEATED MORE THAN I DID TO PERFECT ALL THE MOVES THAT COMMONLY PASS FOR HETEROSEXUAL BEHAVIOR.
MAVIS, I FEEL AWFUL ABOUT THE WAY I ACTED LAST NIGHT.
DON'T DWELL ON IT, HON.

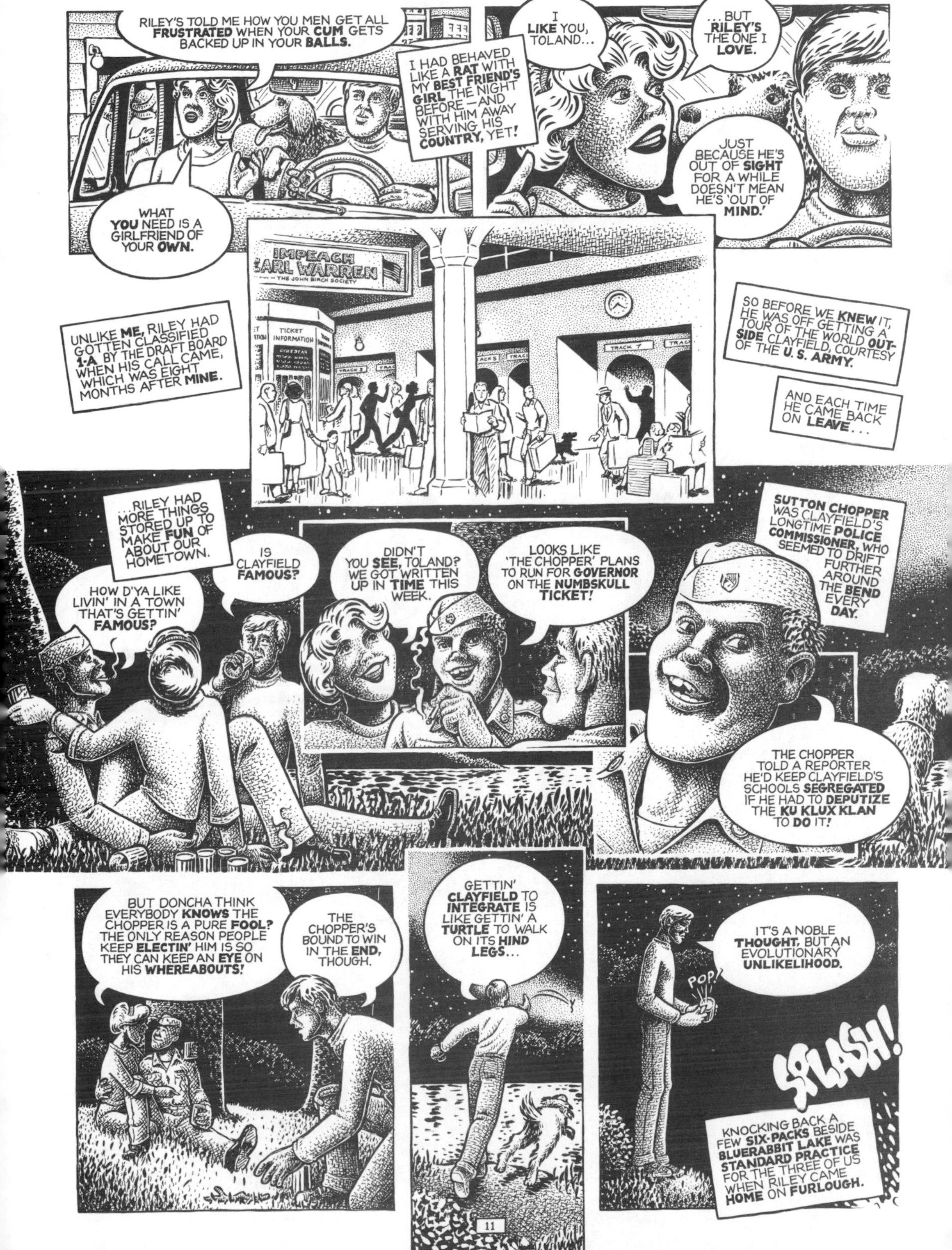

RILEY'S TOLD ME HOW YOU MEN GET ALL FRUSTRATED WHEN YOUR CUM GETS BACKED UP IN YOUR BALLS.
WHAT YOU NEED IS A GIRLFRIEND OF YOUR OWN.
I HAD BEHAVED LIKE A RAT WITH MY BEST FRIEND'S GIRL THE NIGHT BEFORE—AND WITH HIM AWAY SERVING HIS COUNTRY, YET!
I LIKE YOU, TOLAND...
...BUT RILEY'S THE ONE I LOVE.
JUST BECAUSE HE'S OUT OF SIGHT FOR A WHILE DOESN'T MEAN HE'S 'OUT OF MIND.'
UNLIKE ME, RILEY HAD GOTTEN CLASSIFIED 1-A BY THE DRAFT BOARD WHEN HIS CALL CAME, WHICH WAS EIGHT MONTHS AFTER MINE.
IMPEACH EARL WARREN
THE JOHN BIRCH SOCIETY
TICKET INFORMATION
TRACK 7
SO BEFORE WE KNEW IT, HE WAS OFF GETTING A TOUR OF THE WORLD OUTSIDE CLAYFIELD, COURTESY OF THE U. S. ARMY.
AND EACH TIME HE CAME BACK ON LEAVE...
...RILEY HAD MORE THINGS STORED UP TO MAKE FUN OF ABOUT OUR HOMETOWN.
HOW D'YA LIKE LIVIN' IN A TOWN THAT'S GETTIN' FAMOUS?
IS CLAYFIELD FAMOUS?
DIDN'T YOU SEE, TOLAND? WE GOT WRITTEN UP IN TIME THIS WEEK.
LOOKS LIKE 'THE CHOPPER' PLANS TO RUN FOR GOVERNOR ON THE NUMBSKULL TICKET!
SUTTON CHOPPER WAS CLAYFIELD'S LONGTIME POLICE COMMISSIONER, WHO SEEMED TO DRIFT FURTHER AROUND THE BEND EVERY DAY.
THE CHOPPER TOLD A REPORTER HE'D KEEP CLAYFIELD'S SCHOOLS SEGREGATED IF HE HAD TO DEPUTIZE THE KU KLUX KLAN TO DO IT!
BUT DONCHA THINK EVERYBODY KNOWS THE CHOPPER IS A PURE FOOL? THE ONLY REASON PEOPLE KEEP ELECTIN' HIM IS SO THEY CAN KEEP AN EYE ON HIS WHEREABOUTS!
THE CHOPPER'S BOUND TO WIN IN THE END, THOUGH.
GETTIN' CLAYFIELD TO INTEGRATE IS LIKE GETTIN' A TURTLE TO WALK ON ITS HIND LEGS...
IT'S A NOBLE THOUGHT, BUT AN EVOLUTIONARY UNLIKELIHOOD.
POP!
SPLASH!
KNOCKING BACK A FEW SIX-PACKS BESIDE BLUERABBIT LAKE WAS STANDARD PRACTICE FOR THE THREE OF US WHEN RILEY CAME HOME ON FURLOUGH.

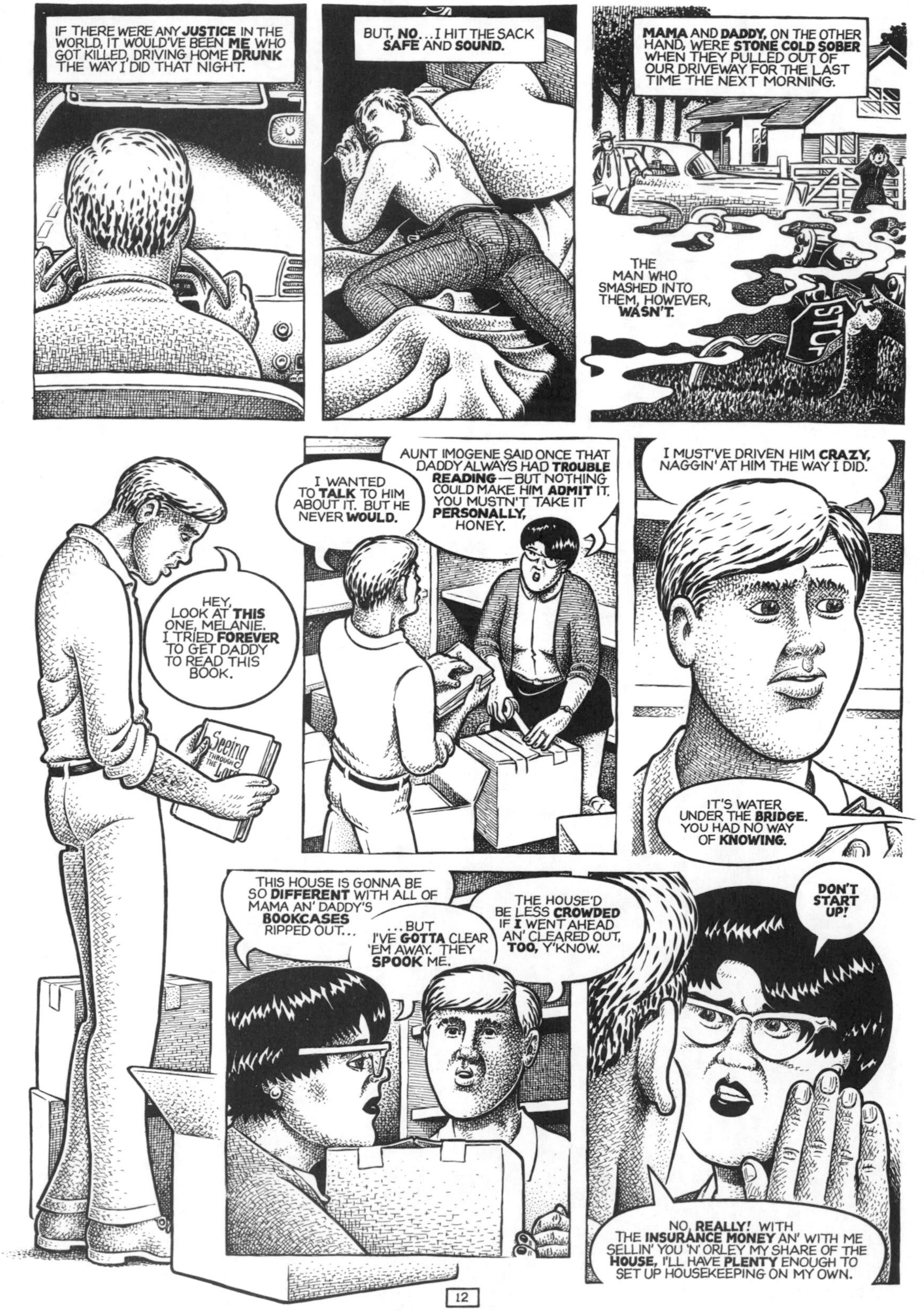
IF THERE WERE ANY **JUSTICE** IN THE WORLD, IT WOULD'VE BEEN **ME** WHO GOT KILLED, DRIVING HOME **DRUNK** THE WAY I DID THAT NIGHT.
BUT, **NO**...I HIT THE SACK **SAFE** AND **SOUND**.
MAMA AND **DADDY**, ON THE OTHER HAND, WERE **STONE COLD SOBER** WHEN THEY PULLED OUT OF OUR DRIVEWAY FOR THE LAST TIME THE NEXT MORNING.
THE MAN WHO SMASHED INTO THEM, HOWEVER, **WASN'T**.
STOP
HEY, LOOK AT **THIS** ONE, MELANIE. I TRIED **FOREVER** TO GET DADDY TO READ THIS BOOK.
I WANTED TO **TALK** TO HIM ABOUT IT. BUT HE NEVER **WOULD**.
AUNT IMOGENE SAID ONCE THAT DADDY ALWAYS HAD **TROUBLE READING** — BUT NOTHING COULD MAKE **HIM ADMIT** IT. YOU MUSTN'T TAKE IT **PERSONALLY**, HONEY.
I MUST'VE DRIVEN HIM **CRAZY**, NAGGIN' AT HIM THE WAY I DID.
IT'S WATER UNDER THE **BRIDGE**. YOU HAD NO WAY OF **KNOWING**.
THIS HOUSE IS GONNA BE SO **DIFFERENT** WITH ALL OF MAMA AN' DADDY'S **BOOKCASES** RIPPED OUT...
...BUT I'VE **GOTTA** CLEAR 'EM AWAY. THEY **SPOOK** ME.
THE HOUSE'D BE LESS **CROWDED** IF **I** WENT AHEAD AN' CLEARED OUT, **TOO**, Y'KNOW.
DON'T START UP!
NO, **REALLY!** WITH THE **INSURANCE MONEY** AN' WITH ME SELLIN' YOU 'N' ORLEY MY SHARE OF THE **HOUSE**, I'LL HAVE **PLENTY** ENOUGH TO SET UP HOUSEKEEPING ON MY OWN.

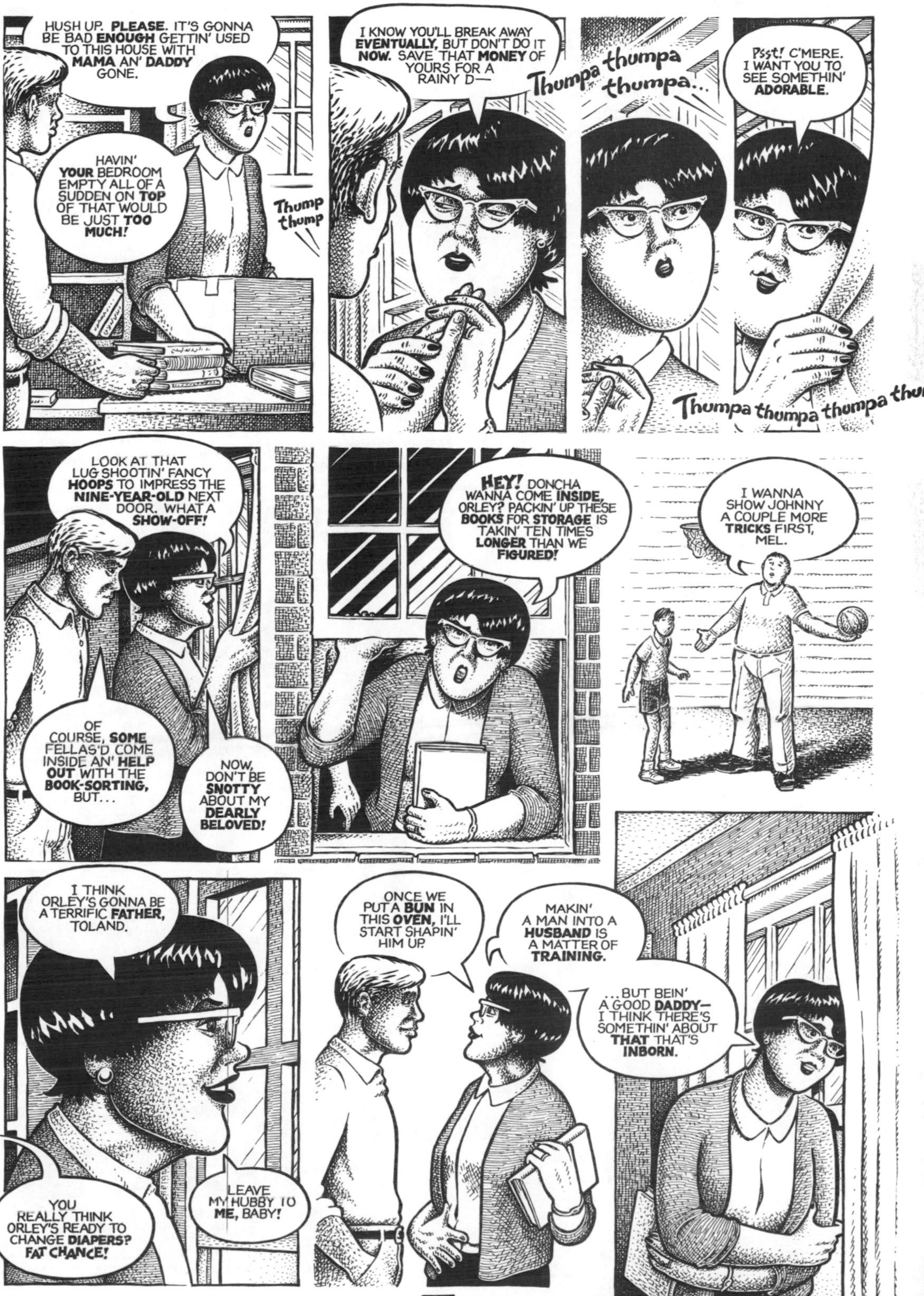
HUSH UP. PLEASE. IT'S GONNA BE BAD ENOUGH GETTIN' USED TO THIS HOUSE WITH MAMA AN' DADDY GONE.
HAVIN' YOUR BEDROOM EMPTY ALL OF A SUDDEN ON TOP OF THAT WOULD BE JUST TOO MUCH!
Thump thump
I KNOW YOU'LL BREAK AWAY EVENTUALLY, BUT DON'T DO IT NOW. SAVE THAT MONEY OF YOURS FOR A RAINY D—
Thumpa thumpa thumpa...
Psst! C'MERE. I WANT YOU TO SEE SOMETHIN' ADORABLE.
Thumpa thumpa thumpa thu
LOOK AT THAT LUG SHOOTIN' FANCY HOOPS TO IMPRESS THE NINE-YEAR-OLD NEXT DOOR. WHAT A SHOW-OFF!
OF COURSE, SOME FELLAS'D COME INSIDE AN' HELP OUT WITH THE BOOK-SORTING, BUT...
NOW, DON'T BE SNOTTY ABOUT MY DEARLY BELOVED!
HEY! DONCHA WANNA COME INSIDE, ORLEY? PACKIN' UP THESE BOOKS FOR STORAGE IS TAKIN' TEN TIMES LONGER THAN WE FIGURED!
I WANNA SHOW JOHNNY A COUPLE MORE TRICKS FIRST, MEL.
I THINK ORLEY'S GONNA BE A TERRIFIC FATHER, TOLAND.
YOU REALLY THINK ORLEY'S READY TO CHANGE DIAPERS? FAT CHANCE!
LEAVE MY HUBBY TO ME, BABY!
ONCE WE PUT A BUN IN THIS OVEN, I'LL START SHAPIN' HIM UP.
MAKIN' A MAN INTO A HUSBAND IS A MATTER OF TRAINING.
...BUT BEIN' A GOOD DADDY— I THINK THERE'S SOMETHIN' ABOUT THAT THAT'S INBORN.

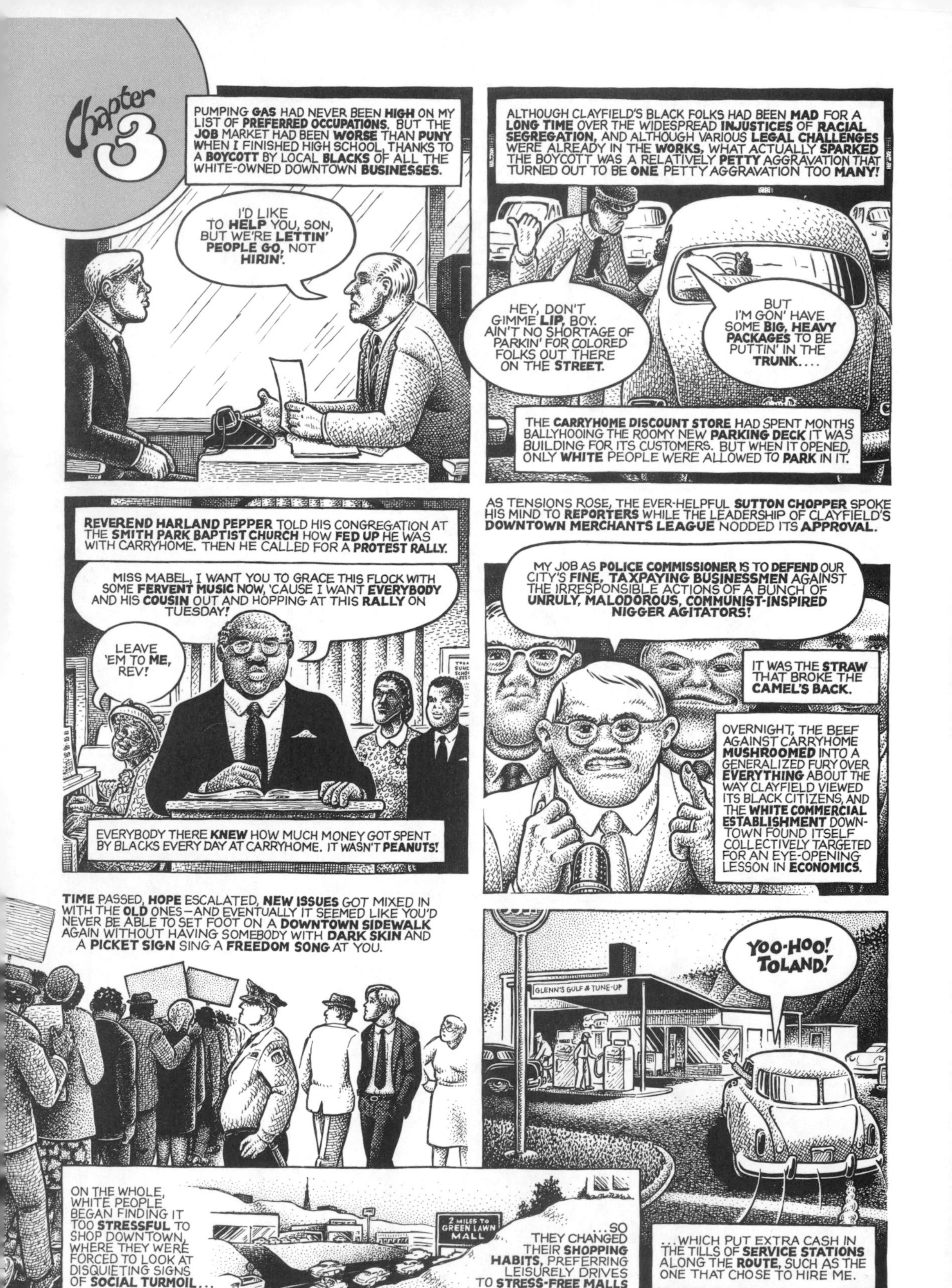
Chapter 3
PUMPING GAS HAD NEVER BEEN HIGH ON MY LIST OF PREFERRED OCCUPATIONS. BUT THE JOB MARKET HAD BEEN WORSE THAN PUNY WHEN I FINISHED HIGH SCHOOL, THANKS TO A BOYCOTT BY LOCAL BLACKS OF ALL THE WHITE-OWNED DOWNTOWN BUSINESSES.
I'D LIKE TO HELP YOU, SON, BUT WE'RE LETTIN' PEOPLE GO, NOT HIRIN'.
ALTHOUGH CLAYFIELD'S BLACK FOLKS HAD BEEN MAD FOR A LONG TIME OVER THE WIDESPREAD INJUSTICES OF RACIAL SEGREGATION, AND ALTHOUGH VARIOUS LEGAL CHALLENGES WERE ALREADY IN THE WORKS, WHAT ACTUALLY SPARKED THE BOYCOTT WAS A RELATIVELY PETTY AGGRAVATION THAT TURNED OUT TO BE ONE PETTY AGGRAVATION TOO MANY!
HEY, DON'T GIMME LIP, BOY. AIN'T NO SHORTAGE OF PARKIN' FOR COLORED FOLKS OUT THERE ON THE STREET.
BUT I'M GON' HAVE SOME BIG, HEAVY PACKAGES TO BE PUTTIN' IN THE TRUNK....
THE CARRYHOME DISCOUNT STORE HAD SPENT MONTHS BALLYHOOING THE ROOMY NEW PARKING DECK IT WAS BUILDING FOR ITS CUSTOMERS. BUT WHEN IT OPENED, ONLY WHITE PEOPLE WERE ALLOWED TO PARK IN IT.
REVEREND HARLAND PEPPER TOLD HIS CONGREGATION AT THE SMITH PARK BAPTIST CHURCH HOW FED UP HE WAS WITH CARRYHOME. THEN HE CALLED FOR A PROTEST RALLY.
MISS MABEL, I WANT YOU TO GRACE THIS FLOCK WITH SOME FERVENT MUSIC NOW, 'CAUSE I WANT EVERYBODY AND HIS COUSIN OUT AND HOPPING AT THIS RALLY ON TUESDAY!
LEAVE 'EM TO ME, REV!
EVERYBODY THERE KNEW HOW MUCH MONEY GOT SPENT BY BLACKS EVERY DAY AT CARRYHOME. IT WASN'T PEANUTS!
AS TENSIONS ROSE, THE EVER-HELPFUL SUTTON CHOPPER SPOKE HIS MIND TO REPORTERS WHILE THE LEADERSHIP OF CLAYFIELD'S DOWNTOWN MERCHANTS LEAGUE NODDED ITS APPROVAL.
MY JOB AS POLICE COMMISSIONER IS TO DEFEND OUR CITY'S FINE, TAXPAYING BUSINESSMEN AGAINST THE IRRESPONSIBLE ACTIONS OF A BUNCH OF UNRULY, MALODOROUS, COMMUNIST-INSPIRED NIGGER AGITATORS!
IT WAS THE STRAW THAT BROKE THE CAMEL'S BACK.
OVERNIGHT, THE BEEF AGAINST CARRYHOME MUSHROOMED INTO A GENERALIZED FURY OVER EVERYTHING ABOUT THE WAY CLAYFIELD VIEWED ITS BLACK CITIZENS, AND THE WHITE COMMERCIAL ESTABLISHMENT DOWNTOWN FOUND ITSELF COLLECTIVELY TARGETED FOR AN EYE-OPENING LESSON IN ECONOMICS.
TIME PASSED, HOPE ESCALATED, NEW ISSUES GOT MIXED IN WITH THE OLD ONES—AND EVENTUALLY IT SEEMED LIKE YOU'D NEVER BE ABLE TO SET FOOT ON A DOWNTOWN SIDEWALK AGAIN WITHOUT HAVING SOMEBODY WITH DARK SKIN AND A PICKET SIGN SING A FREEDOM SONG AT YOU.
GLENN'S GULF & TUNE-UP
YOO-HOO! TOLAND!
ON THE WHOLE, WHITE PEOPLE BEGAN FINDING IT TOO STRESSFUL TO SHOP DOWNTOWN, WHERE THEY WERE FORCED TO LOOK AT DISQUIETING SIGNS OF SOCIAL TURMOIL...
2 MILES TO GREEN LAWN MALL
...SO THEY CHANGED THEIR SHOPPING HABITS, PREFERRING LEISURELY DRIVES TO STRESS-FREE MALLS IN THE SUBURBS...
...WHICH PUT EXTRA CASH IN THE TILLS OF SERVICE STATIONS ALONG THE ROUTE, SUCH AS THE ONE THAT CHOSE TO HIRE ME.

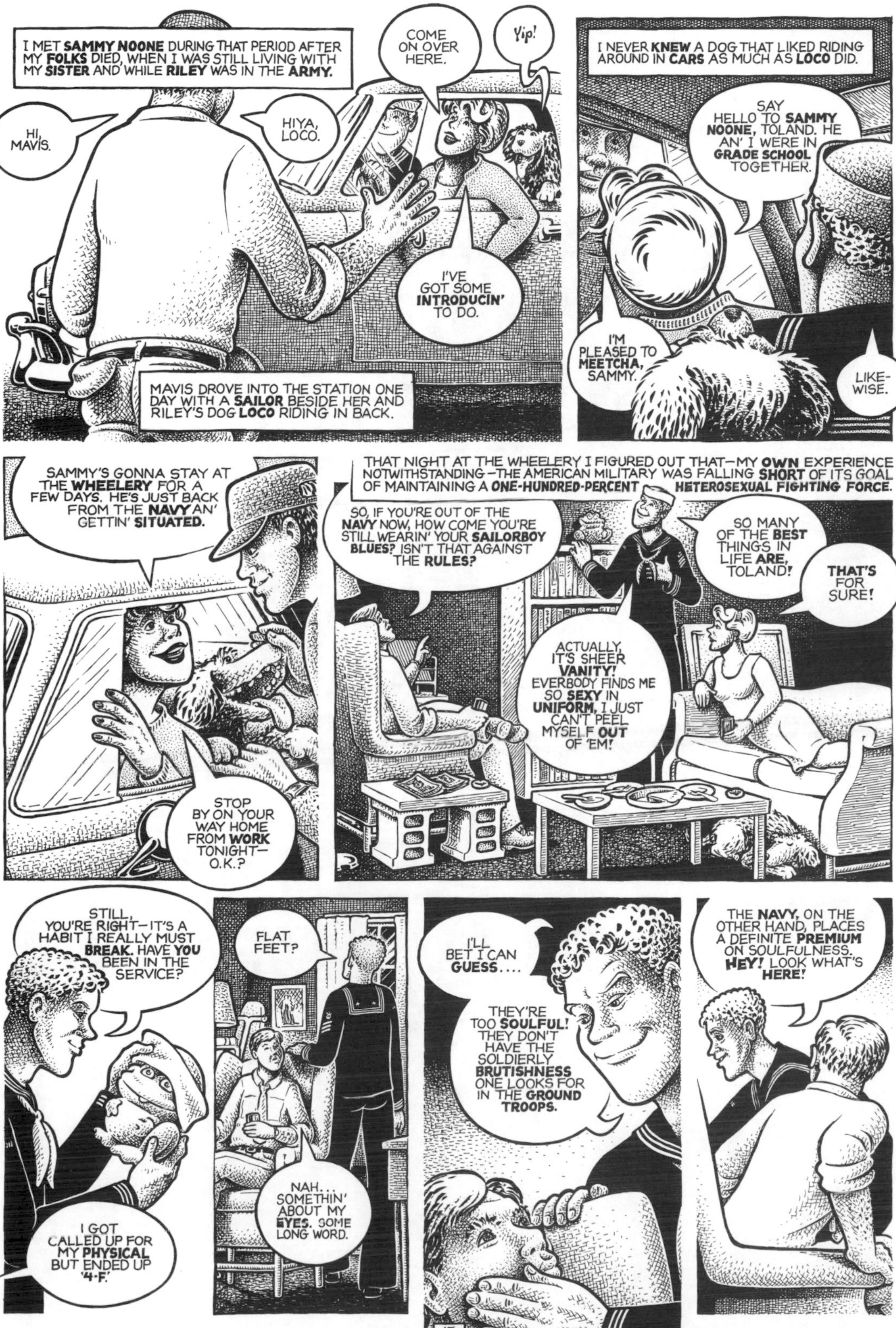
I MET **SAMMY NOONE** DURING THAT PERIOD AFTER MY **FOLKS** DIED, WHEN I WAS STILL LIVING WITH MY **SISTER** AND WHILE **RILEY** WAS IN THE **ARMY.**
HI, MAVIS.
HIYA, LOCO.
COME ON OVER HERE.
Yip!
I'VE GOT SOME **INTRODUCIN'** TO DO.
MAVIS DROVE INTO THE STATION ONE DAY WITH A **SAILOR** BESIDE HER AND RILEY'S DOG **LOCO** RIDING IN BACK.
I NEVER **KNEW** A DOG THAT LIKED RIDING AROUND IN **CARS** AS MUCH AS **LOCO** DID.
SAY HELLO TO **SAMMY NOONE,** TOLAND. HE AN' I WERE IN **GRADE SCHOOL** TOGETHER.
I'M PLEASED TO **MEETCHA,** SAMMY.
LIKE-WISE.
SAMMY'S GONNA STAY AT THE **WHEELERY** FOR A FEW DAYS. HE'S JUST BACK FROM THE **NAVY** AN' GETTIN' **SITUATED.**
STOP BY ON YOUR WAY HOME FROM **WORK** TONIGHT— O.K.?
THAT NIGHT AT THE WHEELERY I FIGURED OUT THAT—MY **OWN** EXPERIENCE NOTWITHSTANDING—THE AMERICAN MILITARY WAS FALLING **SHORT** OF ITS GOAL OF MAINTAINING A **ONE-HUNDRED-PERCENT HETEROSEXUAL FIGHTING FORCE.**
SO, IF YOU'RE OUT OF THE **NAVY** NOW, HOW COME YOU'RE STILL WEARIN' YOUR **SAILORBOY BLUES?** ISN'T THAT AGAINST THE **RULES?**
ACTUALLY, IT'S SHEER **VANITY!** EVERBODY FINDS ME SO **SEXY** IN **UNIFORM,** I JUST CAN'T PEEL MYSELF **OUT** OF 'EM!
SO MANY OF THE **BEST** THINGS IN LIFE **ARE,** TOLAND!
THAT'S FOR **SURE!**
STILL, YOU'RE RIGHT—IT'S A HABIT I REALLY MUST **BREAK.** HAVE **YOU** BEEN IN THE SERVICE?
I GOT CALLED UP FOR MY **PHYSICAL** BUT ENDED UP **'4-F.'**
FLAT FEET?
NAH... SOMETHIN' ABOUT MY **EYES.** SOME LONG WORD.
I'LL BET I CAN **GUESS....**
THEY'RE TOO **SOULFUL!** THEY DON'T HAVE THE SOLDIERLY **BRUTISHNESS** ONE LOOKS FOR IN THE **GROUND TROOPS.**
THE **NAVY,** ON THE OTHER HAND, PLACES A DEFINITE **PREMIUM** ON SOULFULNESS. **HEY!** LOOK WHAT'S **HERE!**

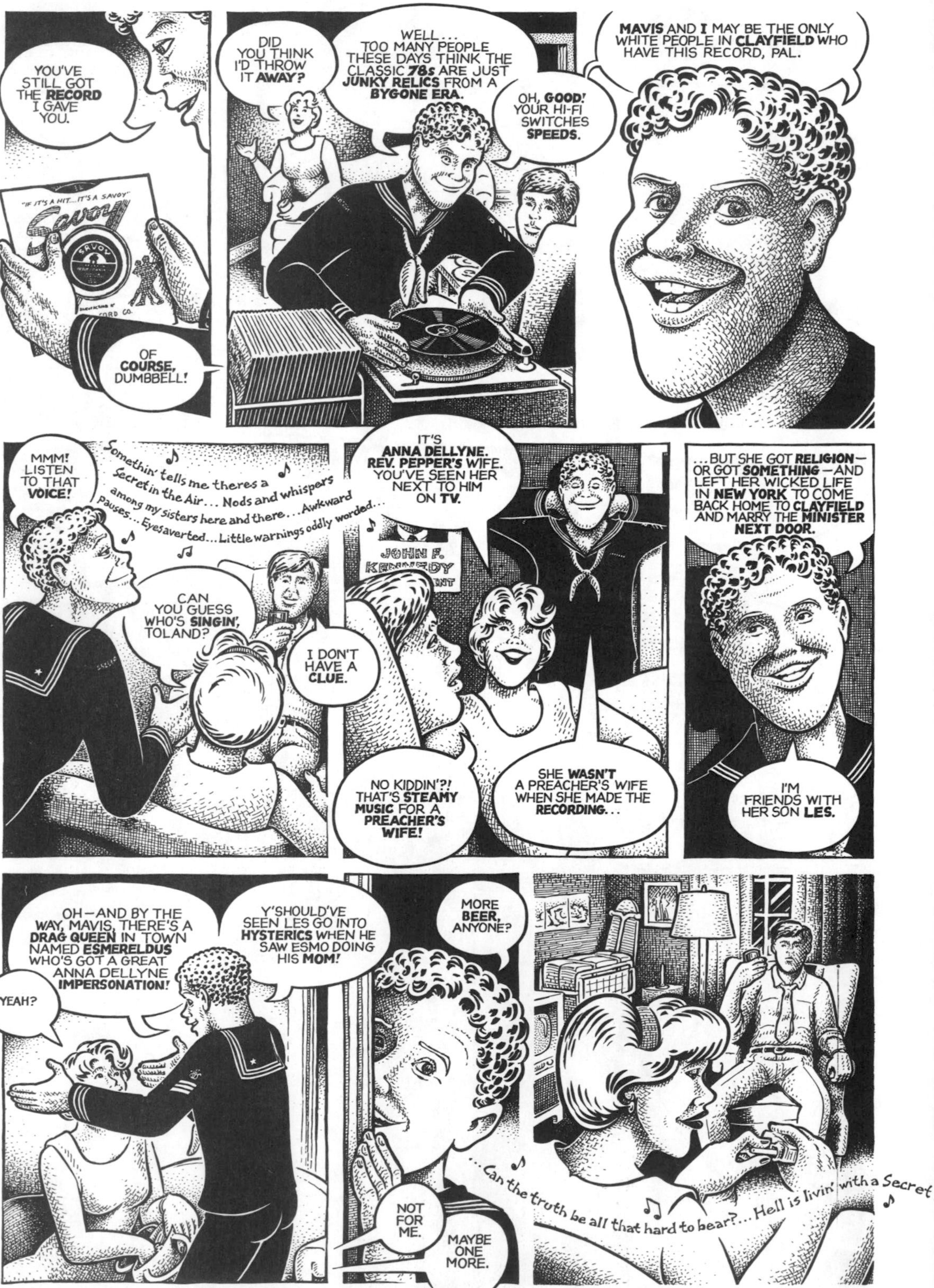
YOU'VE STILL GOT THE RECORD I GAVE YOU.
"IF IT'S A HIT... IT'S A SAVOY"
Savoy
SAVOY
OF COURSE, DUMBBELL!
DID YOU THINK I'D THROW IT AWAY?
WELL... TOO MANY PEOPLE THESE DAYS THINK THE CLASSIC 78s ARE JUST JUNKY RELICS FROM A BYGONE ERA.
OH, GOOD! YOUR HI-FI SWITCHES SPEEDS.
MAVIS AND I MAY BE THE ONLY WHITE PEOPLE IN CLAYFIELD WHO HAVE THIS RECORD, PAL.
MMM! LISTEN TO THAT VOICE!
Somethin' tells me theres a Secret in the Air... Nods and whispers among my sisters here and there... Awkward Pauses... Eyes averted... Little warnings oddly worded...
CAN YOU GUESS WHO'S SINGIN', TOLAND?
I DON'T HAVE A CLUE.
IT'S ANNA DELLYNE. REV. PEPPER'S WIFE. YOU'VE SEEN HER NEXT TO HIM ON TV.
JOHN F. KENNEDY
NO KIDDIN'?! THAT'S STEAMY MUSIC FOR A PREACHER'S WIFE!
SHE WASN'T A PREACHER'S WIFE WHEN SHE MADE THE RECORDING...
...BUT SHE GOT RELIGION— OR GOT SOMETHING —AND LEFT HER WICKED LIFE IN NEW YORK TO COME BACK HOME TO CLAYFIELD AND MARRY THE MINISTER NEXT DOOR.
I'M FRIENDS WITH HER SON LES.
OH—AND BY THE WAY, MAVIS, THERE'S A DRAG QUEEN IN TOWN NAMED ESMERELDUS WHO'S GOT A GREAT ANNA DELLYNE IMPERSONATION!
YEAH?
Y'SHOULD'VE SEEN LES GO INTO HYSTERICS WHEN HE SAW ESMO DOING HIS MOM!
MORE BEER, ANYONE?
NOT FOR ME.
MAYBE ONE MORE.
...Can the truth be all that hard to bear?... Hell is livin' with a Secret

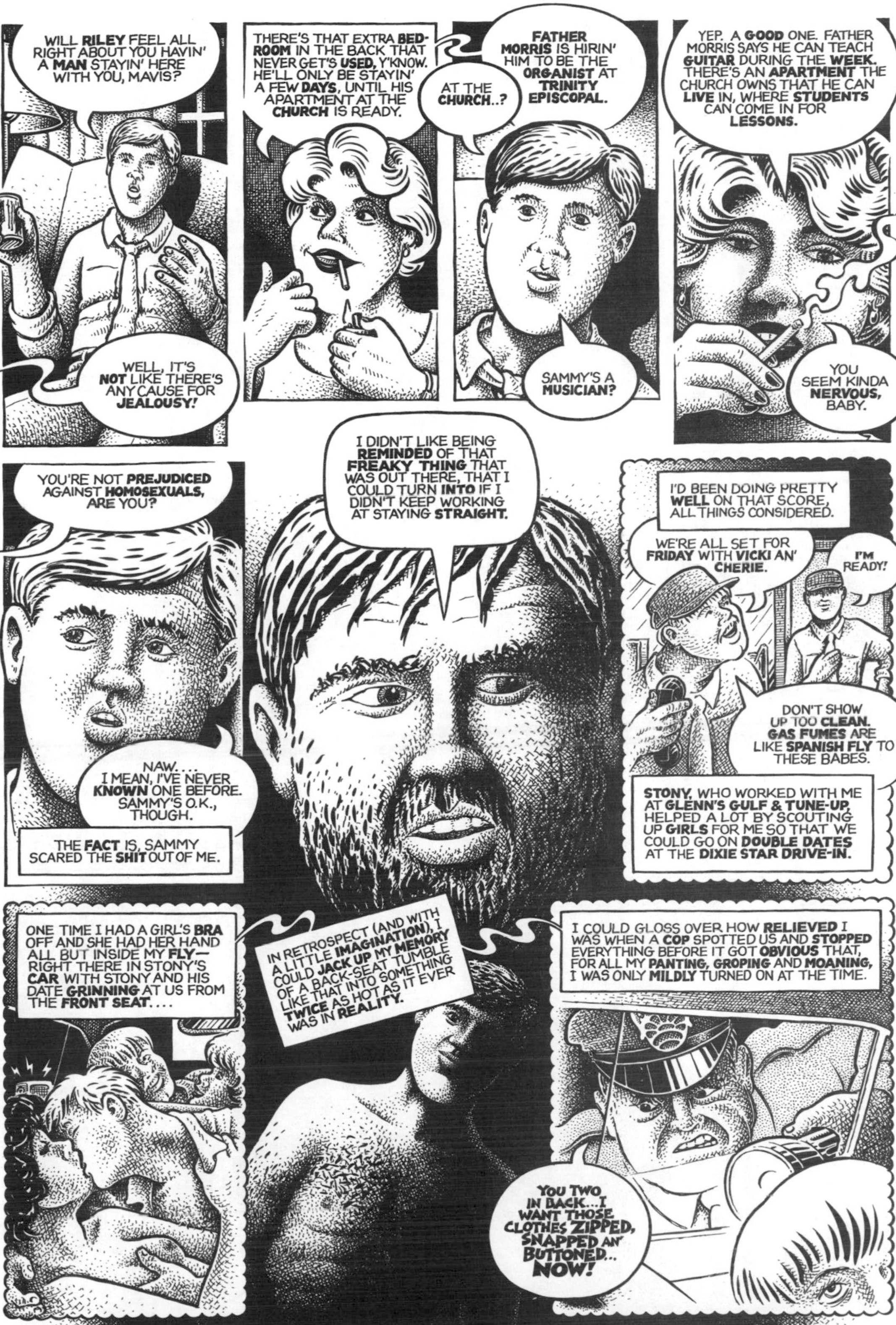
WILL RILEY FEEL ALL RIGHT ABOUT YOU HAVIN' A MAN STAYIN' HERE WITH YOU, MAVIS?
WELL, IT'S NOT LIKE THERE'S ANY CAUSE FOR JEALOUSY!
THERE'S THAT EXTRA BED-ROOM IN THE BACK THAT NEVER GET'S USED, Y'KNOW. HE'LL ONLY BE STAYIN' A FEW DAYS, UNTIL HIS APARTMENT AT THE CHURCH IS READY.
AT THE CHURCH..?
FATHER MORRIS IS HIRIN' HIM TO BE THE ORGANIST AT TRINITY EPISCOPAL.
SAMMY'S A MUSICIAN?
YEP. A GOOD ONE. FATHER MORRIS SAYS HE CAN TEACH GUITAR DURING THE WEEK. THERE'S AN APARTMENT THE CHURCH OWNS THAT HE CAN LIVE IN, WHERE STUDENTS CAN COME IN FOR LESSONS.
YOU SEEM KINDA NERVOUS, BABY.
YOU'RE NOT PREJUDICED AGAINST HOMOSEXUALS, ARE YOU?
NAW.... I MEAN, I'VE NEVER KNOWN ONE BEFORE. SAMMY'S O.K., THOUGH.
THE FACT IS, SAMMY SCARED THE SHIT OUT OF ME.
I DIDN'T LIKE BEING REMINDED OF THAT FREAKY THING THAT WAS OUT THERE, THAT I COULD TURN INTO IF I DIDN'T KEEP WORKING AT STAYING STRAIGHT.
I'D BEEN DOING PRETTY WELL ON THAT SCORE, ALL THINGS CONSIDERED.
WE'RE ALL SET FOR FRIDAY WITH VICKI AN' CHERIE.
I'M READY!
DON'T SHOW UP TOO CLEAN. GAS FUMES ARE LIKE SPANISH FLY TO THESE BABES.
STONY, WHO WORKED WITH ME AT GLENN'S GULF & TUNE-UP, HELPED A LOT BY SCOUTING UP GIRLS FOR ME SO THAT WE COULD GO ON DOUBLE DATES AT THE DIXIE STAR DRIVE-IN.
ONE TIME I HAD A GIRL'S BRA OFF AND SHE HAD HER HAND ALL BUT INSIDE MY FLY— RIGHT THERE IN STONY'S CAR WITH STONY AND HIS DATE GRINNING AT US FROM THE FRONT SEAT....
IN RETROSPECT (AND WITH A LITTLE IMAGINATION), I COULD JACK UP MY MEMORY OF A BACK-SEAT TUMBLE LIKE THAT INTO SOMETHING TWICE AS HOT AS IT EVER WAS IN REALITY.
I COULD GLOSS OVER HOW RELIEVED I WAS WHEN A COP SPOTTED US AND STOPPED EVERYTHING BEFORE IT GOT OBVIOUS THAT, FOR ALL MY PANTING, GROPING AND MOANING, I WAS ONLY MILDLY TURNED ON AT THE TIME.
YOU TWO IN BACK...I WANT THOSE CLOTHES ZIPPED, SNAPPED AN' BUTTONED... NOW!

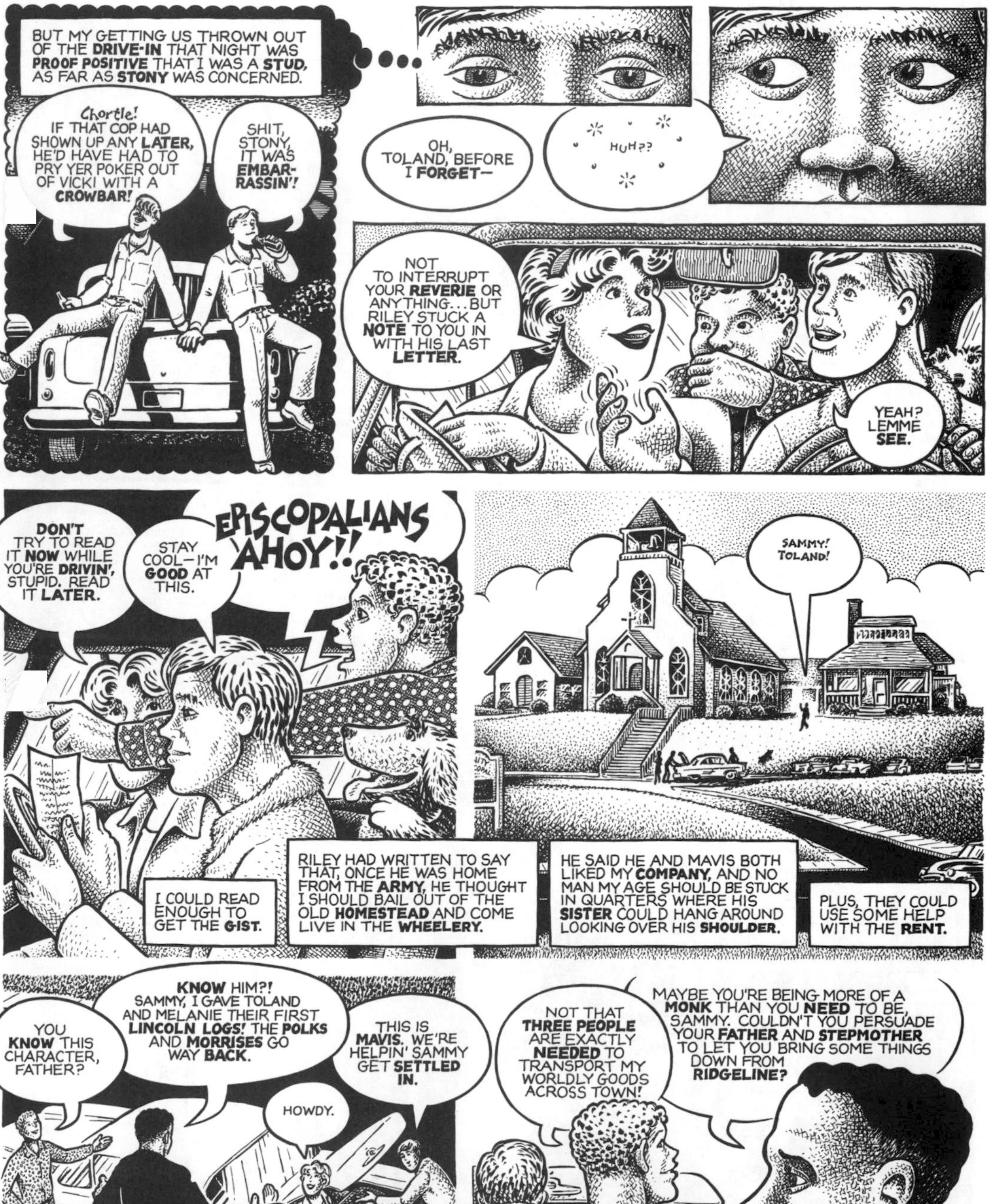

BUT MY GETTING US THROWN OUT OF THE DRIVE-IN THAT NIGHT WAS PROOF POSITIVE THAT I WAS A STUD, AS FAR AS STONY WAS CONCERNED.
Chortle! IF THAT COP HAD SHOWN UP ANY LATER, HE'D HAVE HAD TO PRY YER POKER OUT OF VICKI WITH A CROWBAR!
SHIT, STONY, IT WAS EMBAR-RASSIN'!
OH, TOLAND, BEFORE I FORGET—
HUH??
NOT TO INTERRUPT YOUR REVERIE OR ANYTHING... BUT RILEY STUCK A NOTE TO YOU IN WITH HIS LAST LETTER.
YEAH? LEMME SEE.
DON'T TRY TO READ IT NOW WHILE YOU'RE DRIVIN', STUPID. READ IT LATER.
STAY COOL—I'M GOOD AT THIS.
EPISCOPALIANS AHOY!!
SAMMY! TOLAND!
I COULD READ ENOUGH TO GET THE GIST.
RILEY HAD WRITTEN TO SAY THAT, ONCE HE WAS HOME FROM THE ARMY, HE THOUGHT I SHOULD BAIL OUT OF THE OLD HOMESTEAD AND COME LIVE IN THE WHEELERY.
HE SAID HE AND MAVIS BOTH LIKED MY COMPANY, AND NO MAN MY AGE SHOULD BE STUCK IN QUARTERS WHERE HIS SISTER COULD HANG AROUND LOOKING OVER HIS SHOULDER.
PLUS, THEY COULD USE SOME HELP WITH THE RENT.
YOU KNOW THIS CHARACTER, FATHER?
KNOW HIM?! SAMMY, I GAVE TOLAND AND MELANIE THEIR FIRST LINCOLN LOGS! THE POLKS AND MORRISES GO WAY BACK.
THIS IS MAVIS. WE'RE HELPIN' SAMMY GET SETTLED IN.
HOWDY.
NOT THAT THREE PEOPLE ARE EXACTLY NEEDED TO TRANSPORT MY WORLDLY GOODS ACROSS TOWN!
MAYBE YOU'RE BEING MORE OF A MONK THAN YOU NEED TO BE, SAMMY. COULDN'T YOU PERSUADE YOUR FATHER AND STEPMOTHER TO LET YOU BRING SOME THINGS DOWN FROM RIDGELINE?
SAMMY LET OUT A BIG SNORT AT THAT SUGGESTION.

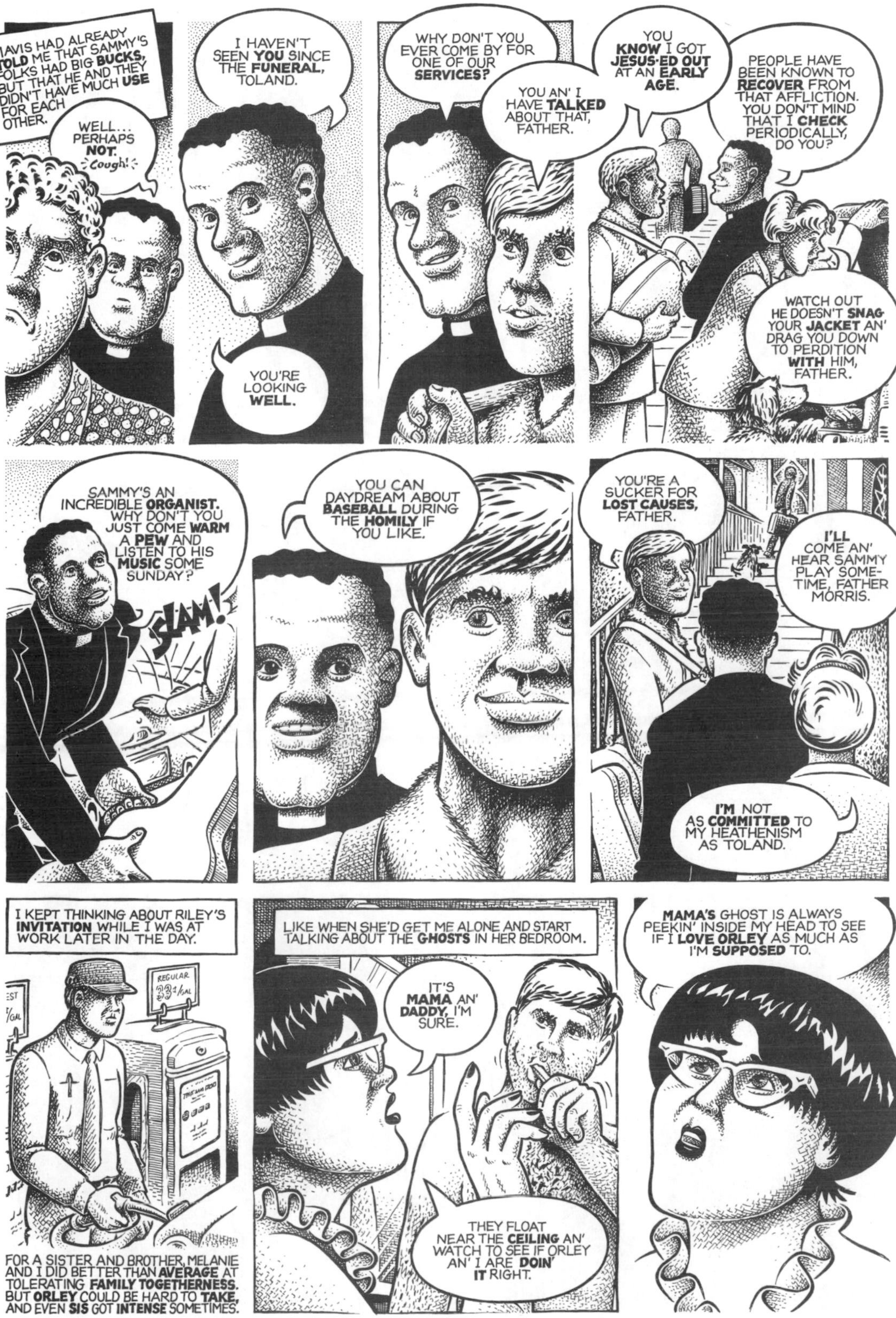

MAVIS HAD ALREADY TOLD ME THAT SAMMY'S FOLKS HAD BIG BUCKS, BUT THAT HE AND THEY DIDN'T HAVE MUCH USE FOR EACH OTHER.
WELL... PERHAPS NOT. Cough!
I HAVEN'T SEEN YOU SINCE THE FUNERAL, TOLAND.
YOU'RE LOOKING WELL.
WHY DON'T YOU EVER COME BY FOR ONE OF OUR SERVICES?
YOU AN' I HAVE TALKED ABOUT THAT, FATHER.
YOU KNOW I GOT JESUS-ED OUT AT AN EARLY AGE.
PEOPLE HAVE BEEN KNOWN TO RECOVER FROM THAT AFFLICTION. YOU DON'T MIND THAT I CHECK PERIODICALLY, DO YOU?
WATCH OUT HE DOESN'T SNAG YOUR JACKET AN' DRAG YOU DOWN TO PERDITION WITH HIM, FATHER.
SAMMY'S AN INCREDIBLE ORGANIST. WHY DON'T YOU JUST COME WARM A PEW AND LISTEN TO HIS MUSIC SOME SUNDAY?
SLAM!
YOU CAN DAYDREAM ABOUT BASEBALL DURING THE HOMILY IF YOU LIKE.
YOU'RE A SUCKER FOR LOST CAUSES, FATHER.
I'LL COME AN' HEAR SAMMY PLAY SOMETIME, FATHER MORRIS.
I'M NOT AS COMMITTED TO MY HEATHENISM AS TOLAND.
I KEPT THINKING ABOUT RILEY'S INVITATION WHILE I WAS AT WORK LATER IN THE DAY.
REGULAR 33¢/GAL
FOR A SISTER AND BROTHER, MELANIE AND I DID BETTER THAN AVERAGE AT TOLERATING FAMILY TOGETHERNESS. BUT ORLEY COULD BE HARD TO TAKE, AND EVEN SIS GOT INTENSE SOMETIMES.
LIKE WHEN SHE'D GET ME ALONE AND START TALKING ABOUT THE GHOSTS IN HER BEDROOM.
IT'S MAMA AN' DADDY, I'M SURE.
THEY FLOAT NEAR THE CEILING AN' WATCH TO SEE IF ORLEY AN' I ARE DOIN' IT RIGHT.
MAMA'S GHOST IS ALWAYS PEEKIN' INSIDE MY HEAD TO SEE IF I LOVE ORLEY AS MUCH AS I'M SUPPOSED TO.

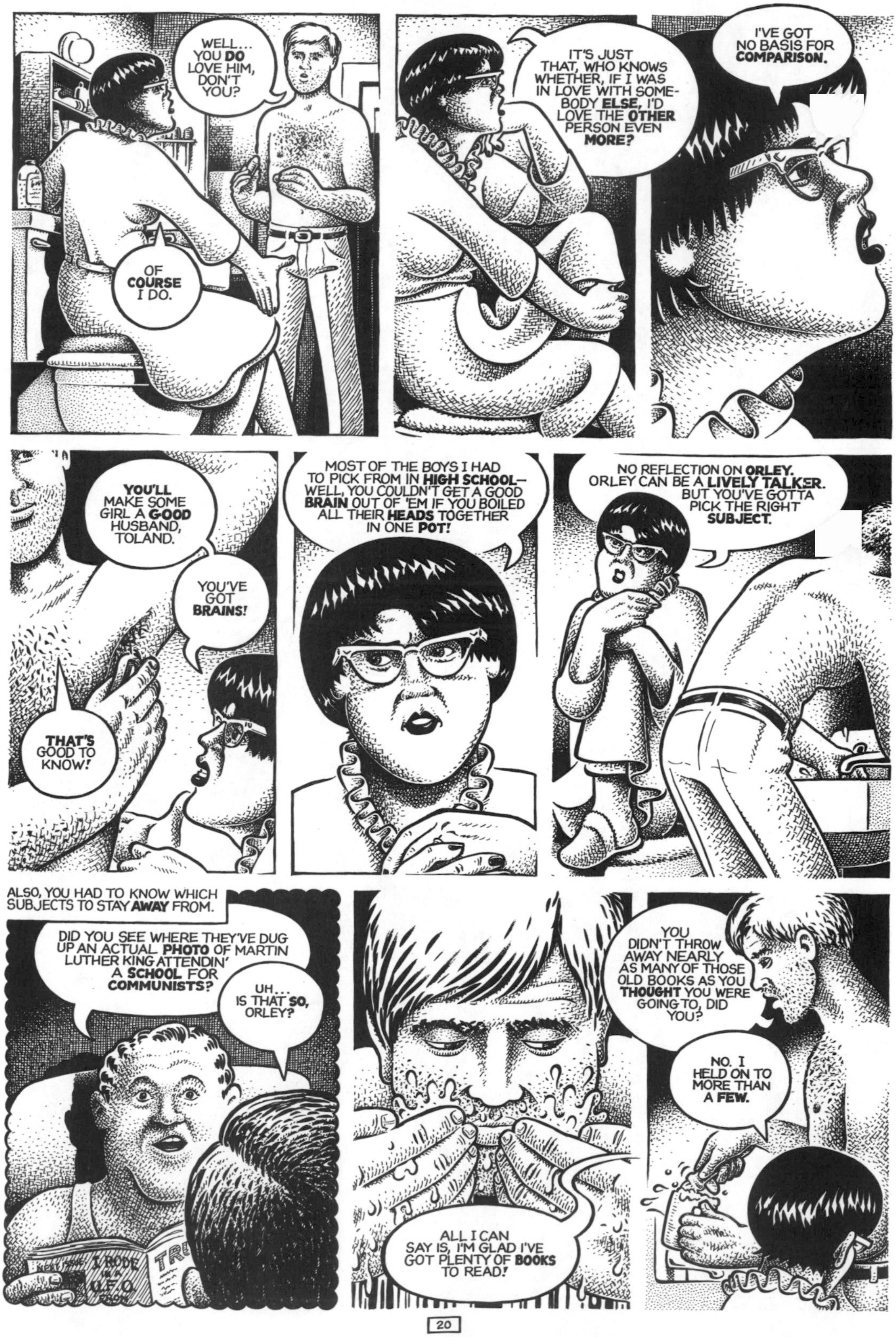
WELL... YOU DO LOVE HIM, DON'T YOU?
OF COURSE I DO.
IT'S JUST THAT, WHO KNOWS WHETHER, IF I WAS IN LOVE WITH SOMEBODY ELSE, I'D LOVE THE OTHER PERSON EVEN MORE?
I'VE GOT NO BASIS FOR COMPARISON.
YOU'LL MAKE SOME GIRL A GOOD HUSBAND, TOLAND.
YOU'VE GOT BRAINS!
THAT'S GOOD TO KNOW!
MOST OF THE BOYS I HAD TO PICK FROM IN HIGH SCHOOL— WELL, YOU COULDN'T GET A GOOD BRAIN OUT OF 'EM IF YOU BOILED ALL THEIR HEADS TOGETHER IN ONE POT!
NO REFLECTION ON ORLEY. ORLEY CAN BE A LIVELY TALKER. BUT YOU'VE GOTTA PICK THE RIGHT SUBJECT.
ALSO, YOU HAD TO KNOW WHICH SUBJECTS TO STAY AWAY FROM.
DID YOU SEE WHERE THEY'VE DUG UP AN ACTUAL PHOTO OF MARTIN LUTHER KING ATTENDIN' A SCHOOL FOR COMMUNISTS?
UH... IS THAT SO, ORLEY?
I RODE IN A U.F.O.
ALL I CAN SAY IS, I'M GLAD I'VE GOT PLENTY OF BOOKS TO READ!
YOU DIDN'T THROW AWAY NEARLY AS MANY OF THOSE OLD BOOKS AS YOU THOUGHT YOU WERE GOING TO, DID YOU?
NO. I HELD ON TO MORE THAN A FEW.

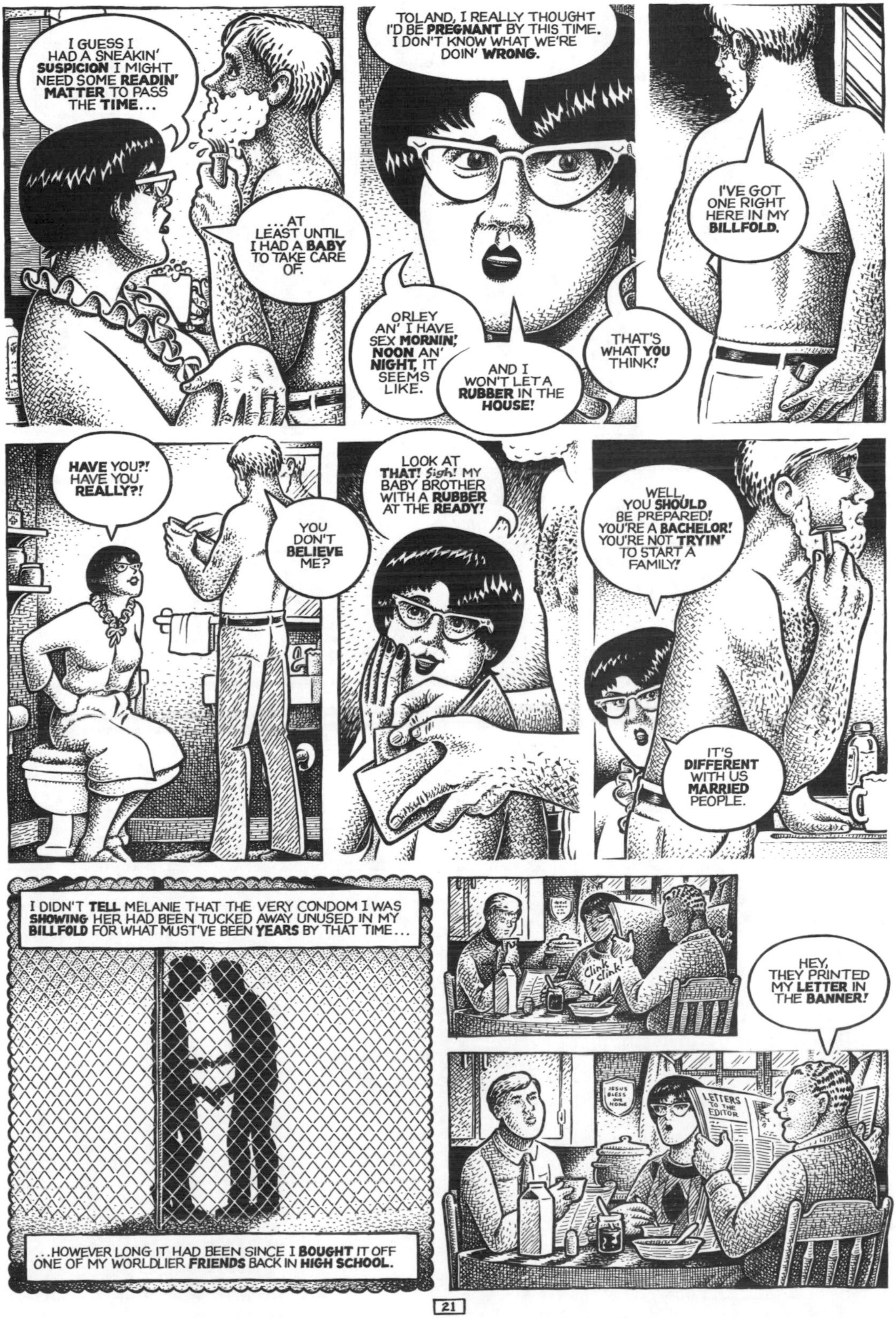

I GUESS I HAD A SNEAKIN' SUSPICION I MIGHT NEED SOME READIN' MATTER TO PASS THE TIME...
...AT LEAST UNTIL I HAD A BABY TO TAKE CARE OF.
TOLAND, I REALLY THOUGHT I'D BE PREGNANT BY THIS TIME. I DON'T KNOW WHAT WE'RE DOIN' WRONG.
ORLEY AN' I HAVE SEX MORNIN', NOON AN' NIGHT, IT SEEMS LIKE.
AND I WON'T LET A RUBBER IN THE HOUSE!
THAT'S WHAT YOU THINK!
I'VE GOT ONE RIGHT HERE IN MY BILLFOLD.
HAVE YOU?! HAVE YOU REALLY?!
YOU DON'T BELIEVE ME?
LOOK AT THAT! Sigh! MY BABY BROTHER WITH A RUBBER AT THE READY!
WELL, YOU SHOULD BE PREPARED! YOU'RE A BACHELOR! YOU'RE NOT TRYIN' TO START A FAMILY!
IT'S DIFFERENT WITH US MARRIED PEOPLE.
I DIDN'T TELL MELANIE THAT THE VERY CONDOM I WAS SHOWING HER HAD BEEN TUCKED AWAY UNUSED IN MY BILLFOLD FOR WHAT MUST'VE BEEN YEARS BY THAT TIME...
...HOWEVER LONG IT HAD BEEN SINCE I BOUGHT IT OFF ONE OF MY WORLDLIER FRIENDS BACK IN HIGH SCHOOL.
Clink clink!
HEY, THEY PRINTED MY LETTER IN THE BANNER!
JESUS BLESS OUR HOME
LETTERS TO THE EDITOR

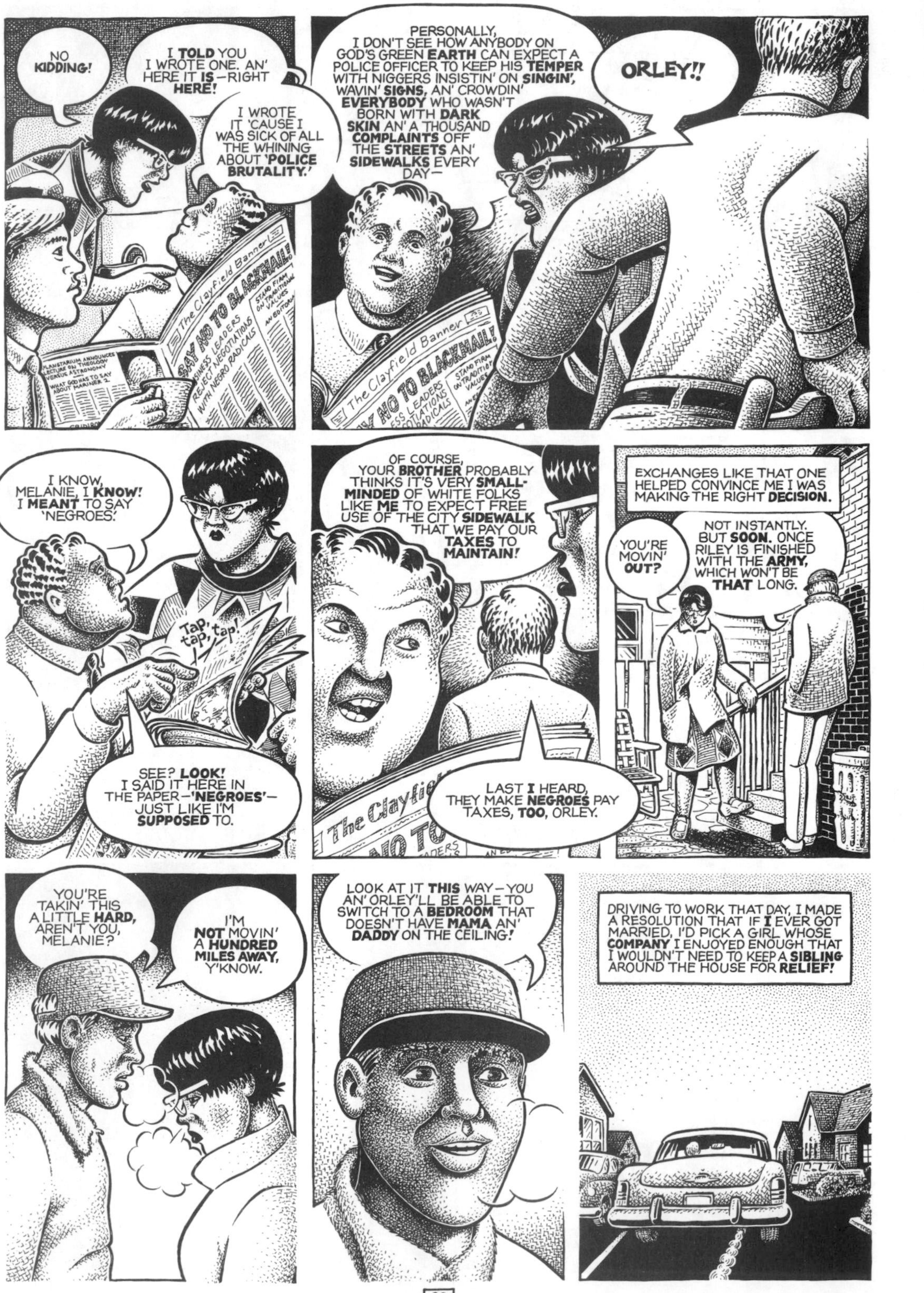
NO KIDDING!
I TOLD YOU I WROTE ONE. AN' HERE IT IS—RIGHT HERE!
I WROTE IT 'CAUSE I WAS SICK OF ALL THE WHINING ABOUT 'POLICE BRUTALITY.'
The Clayfield Banner
SAY NO TO BLACKMAIL!
PERSONALLY, I DON'T SEE HOW ANYBODY ON GOD'S GREEN EARTH CAN EXPECT A POLICE OFFICER TO KEEP HIS TEMPER WITH NIGGERS INSISTIN' ON SINGIN', WAVIN' SIGNS, AN' CROWDIN' EVERYBODY WHO WASN'T BORN WITH DARK SKIN AN' A THOUSAND COMPLAINTS OFF THE STREETS AN' SIDEWALKS EVERY DAY—
ORLEY!!
I KNOW, MELANIE, I KNOW! I MEANT TO SAY 'NEGROES.'
Tap, tap, tap!
SEE? LOOK! I SAID IT HERE IN THE PAPER—'NEGROES'—JUST LIKE I'M SUPPOSED TO.
OF COURSE, YOUR BROTHER PROBABLY THINKS IT'S VERY SMALL-MINDED OF WHITE FOLKS LIKE ME TO EXPECT FREE USE OF THE CITY SIDEWALK THAT WE PAY OUR TAXES TO MAINTAIN!
LAST I HEARD, THEY MAKE NEGROES PAY TAXES, TOO, ORLEY.
EXCHANGES LIKE THAT ONE HELPED CONVINCE ME I WAS MAKING THE RIGHT DECISION.
YOU'RE MOVIN' OUT?
NOT INSTANTLY. BUT SOON. ONCE RILEY IS FINISHED WITH THE ARMY, WHICH WON'T BE THAT LONG.
YOU'RE TAKIN' THIS A LITTLE HARD, AREN'T YOU, MELANIE?
I'M NOT MOVIN' A HUNDRED MILES AWAY, Y'KNOW.
LOOK AT IT THIS WAY—YOU AN' ORLEY'LL BE ABLE TO SWITCH TO A BEDROOM THAT DOESN'T HAVE MAMA AN' DADDY ON THE CEILING!
DRIVING TO WORK THAT DAY, I MADE A RESOLUTION THAT IF I EVER GOT MARRIED, I'D PICK A GIRL WHOSE COMPANY I ENJOYED ENOUGH THAT I WOULDN'T NEED TO KEEP A SIBLING AROUND THE HOUSE FOR RELIEF!

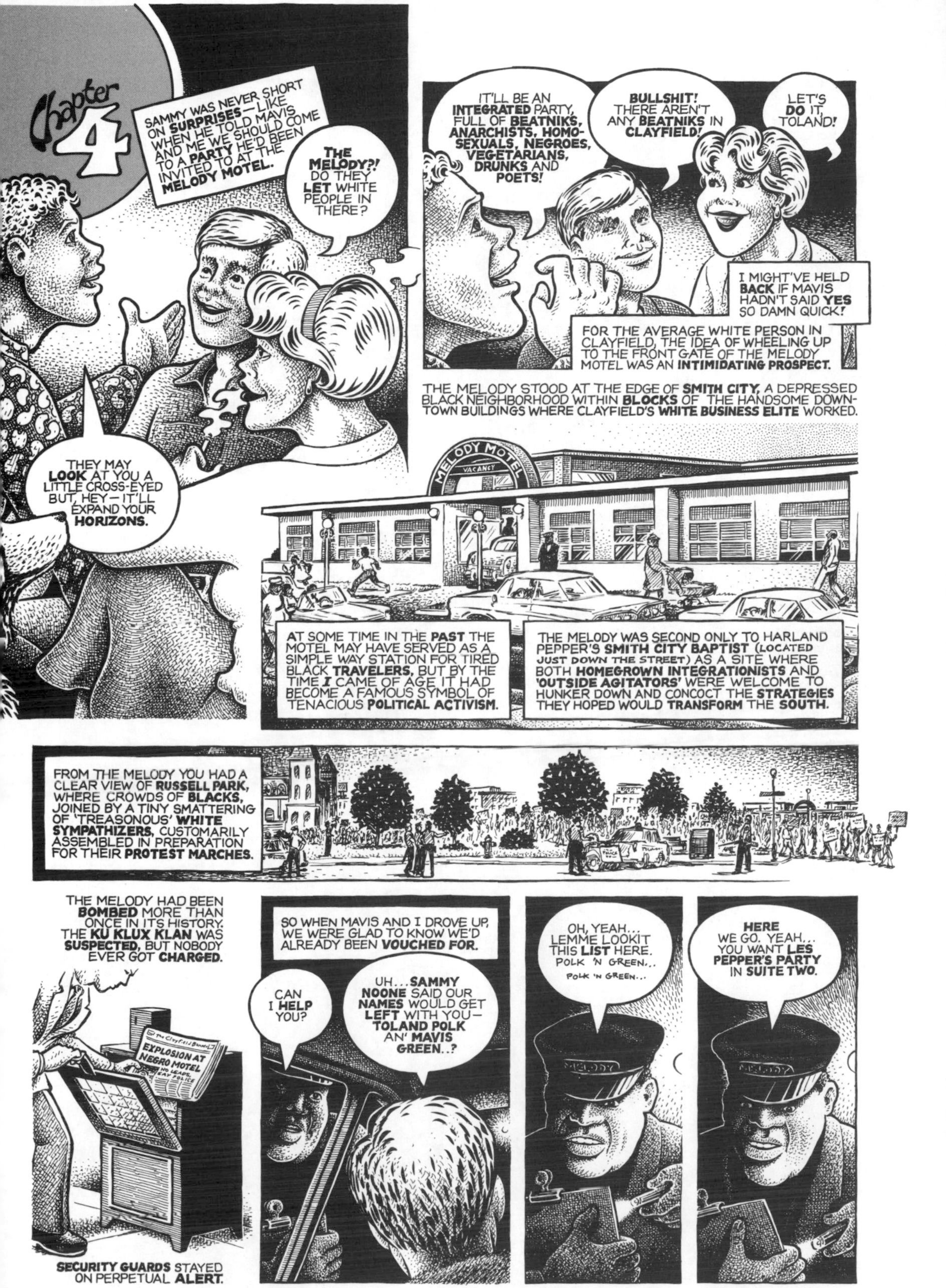
Chapter 4
SAMMY WAS NEVER SHORT ON SURPRISES—LIKE WHEN HE TOLD MAVIS AND ME WE SHOULD COME TO A PARTY HE'D BEEN INVITED TO AT THE MELODY MOTEL.
THE MELODY?! DO THEY LET WHITE PEOPLE IN THERE?
THEY MAY LOOK AT YOU A LITTLE CROSS-EYED BUT, HEY—IT'LL EXPAND YOUR HORIZONS.
IT'LL BE AN INTEGRATED PARTY, FULL OF BEATNIKS, ANARCHISTS, HOMOSEXUALS, NEGROES, VEGETARIANS, DRUNKS AND POETS!
BULLSHIT! THERE AREN'T ANY BEATNIKS IN CLAYFIELD!
LET'S DO IT, TOLAND!
I MIGHT'VE HELD BACK IF MAVIS HADN'T SAID YES SO DAMN QUICK!
FOR THE AVERAGE WHITE PERSON IN CLAYFIELD, THE IDEA OF WHEELING UP TO THE FRONT GATE OF THE MELODY MOTEL WAS AN INTIMIDATING PROSPECT.
THE MELODY STOOD AT THE EDGE OF SMITH CITY, A DEPRESSED BLACK NEIGHBORHOOD WITHIN BLOCKS OF THE HANDSOME DOWNTOWN BUILDINGS WHERE CLAYFIELD'S WHITE BUSINESS ELITE WORKED.
MELODY MOTEL
VACANCY
AT SOME TIME IN THE PAST THE MOTEL MAY HAVE SERVED AS A SIMPLE WAY STATION FOR TIRED BLACK TRAVELERS, BUT BY THE TIME I CAME OF AGE IT HAD BECOME A FAMOUS SYMBOL OF TENACIOUS POLITICAL ACTIVISM.
THE MELODY WAS SECOND ONLY TO HARLAND PEPPER'S SMITH CITY BAPTIST (LOCATED JUST DOWN THE STREET) AS A SITE WHERE BOTH HOMEGROWN INTEGRATIONISTS AND 'OUTSIDE AGITATORS' WERE WELCOME TO HUNKER DOWN AND CONCOCT THE STRATEGIES THEY HOPED WOULD TRANSFORM THE SOUTH.
FROM THE MELODY YOU HAD A CLEAR VIEW OF RUSSELL PARK, WHERE CROWDS OF BLACKS, JOINED BY A TINY SMATTERING OF 'TREASONOUS' WHITE SYMPATHIZERS, CUSTOMARILY ASSEMBLED IN PREPARATION FOR THEIR PROTEST MARCHES.
POLICE
THE MELODY HAD BEEN BOMBED MORE THAN ONCE IN ITS HISTORY. THE KU KLUX KLAN WAS SUSPECTED, BUT NOBODY EVER GOT CHARGED.
EXPLOSION AT NEGRO MOTEL
SECURITY GUARDS STAYED ON PERPETUAL ALERT.
SO WHEN MAVIS AND I DROVE UP, WE WERE GLAD TO KNOW WE'D ALREADY BEEN VOUCHED FOR.
CAN I HELP YOU?
UH... SAMMY NOONE SAID OUR NAMES WOULD GET LEFT WITH YOU—TOLAND POLK AN' MAVIS GREEN..?
OH, YEAH... LEMME LOOKIT THIS LIST HERE. POLK 'N GREEN... POLK 'N GREEN...
MELODY
HERE WE GO. YEAH... YOU WANT LES PEPPER'S PARTY IN SUITE TWO.
MELODY

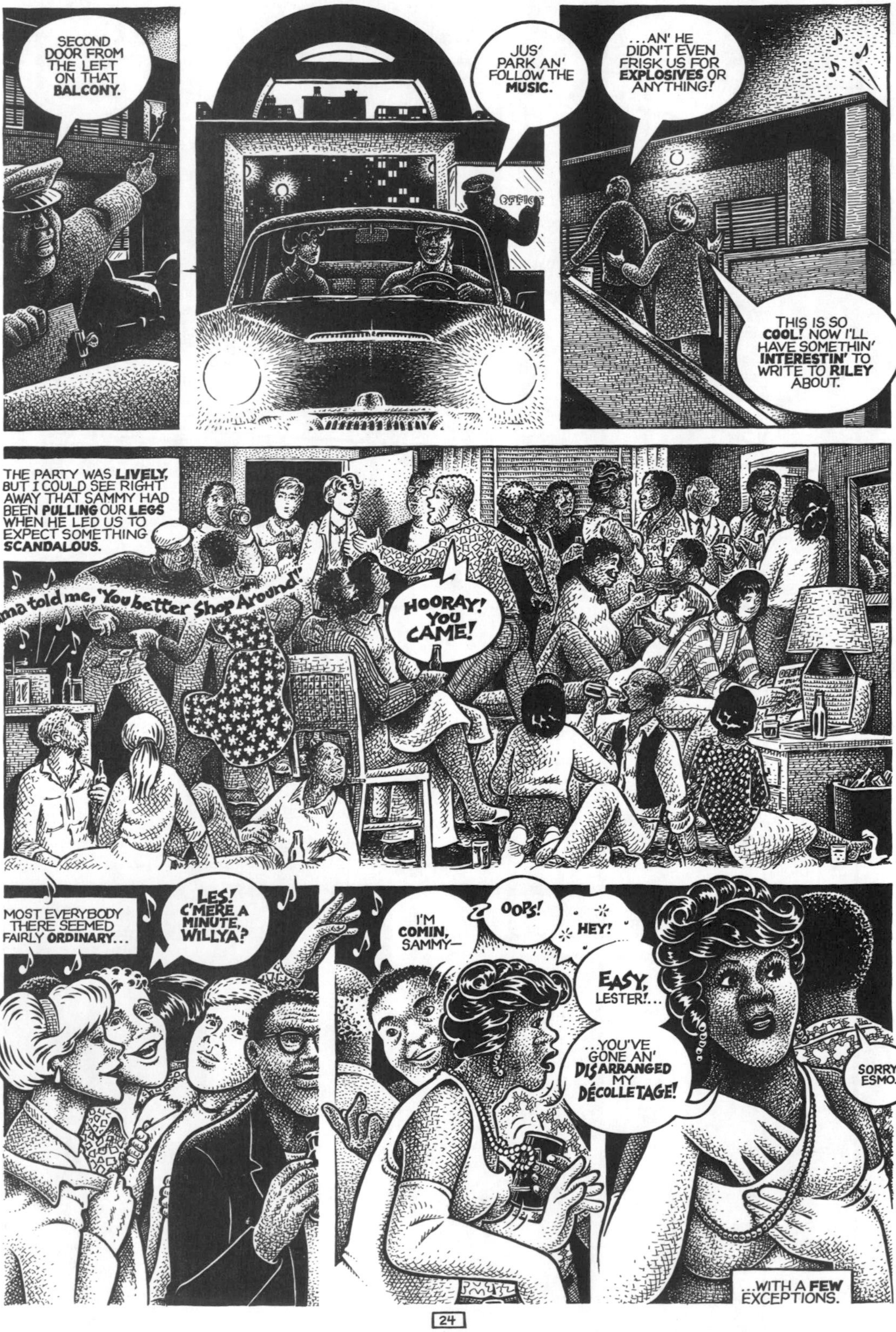
SECOND DOOR FROM THE LEFT ON THAT BALCONY.
JUS' PARK AN' FOLLOW THE MUSIC.
OFFICE
...AN' HE DIDN'T EVEN FRISK US FOR EXPLOSIVES OR ANYTHING!
THIS IS SO COOL! NOW I'LL HAVE SOMETHIN' INTERESTIN' TO WRITE TO RILEY ABOUT.
THE PARTY WAS LIVELY, BUT I COULD SEE RIGHT AWAY THAT SAMMY HAD BEEN PULLING OUR LEGS WHEN HE LED US TO EXPECT SOMETHING SCANDALOUS.
My mama told me, "You better Shop Around!"
HOORAY! YOU CAME!
MOST EVERYBODY THERE SEEMED FAIRLY ORDINARY...
LES! C'MERE A MINUTE, WILLYA?
I'M COMIN, SAMMY—
OOPS!
HEY!
EASY, LESTER!...
...YOU'VE GONE AN' DISARRANGED MY DÉCOLLETAGE!
SORRY, ESMO.
...WITH A FEW EXCEPTIONS.

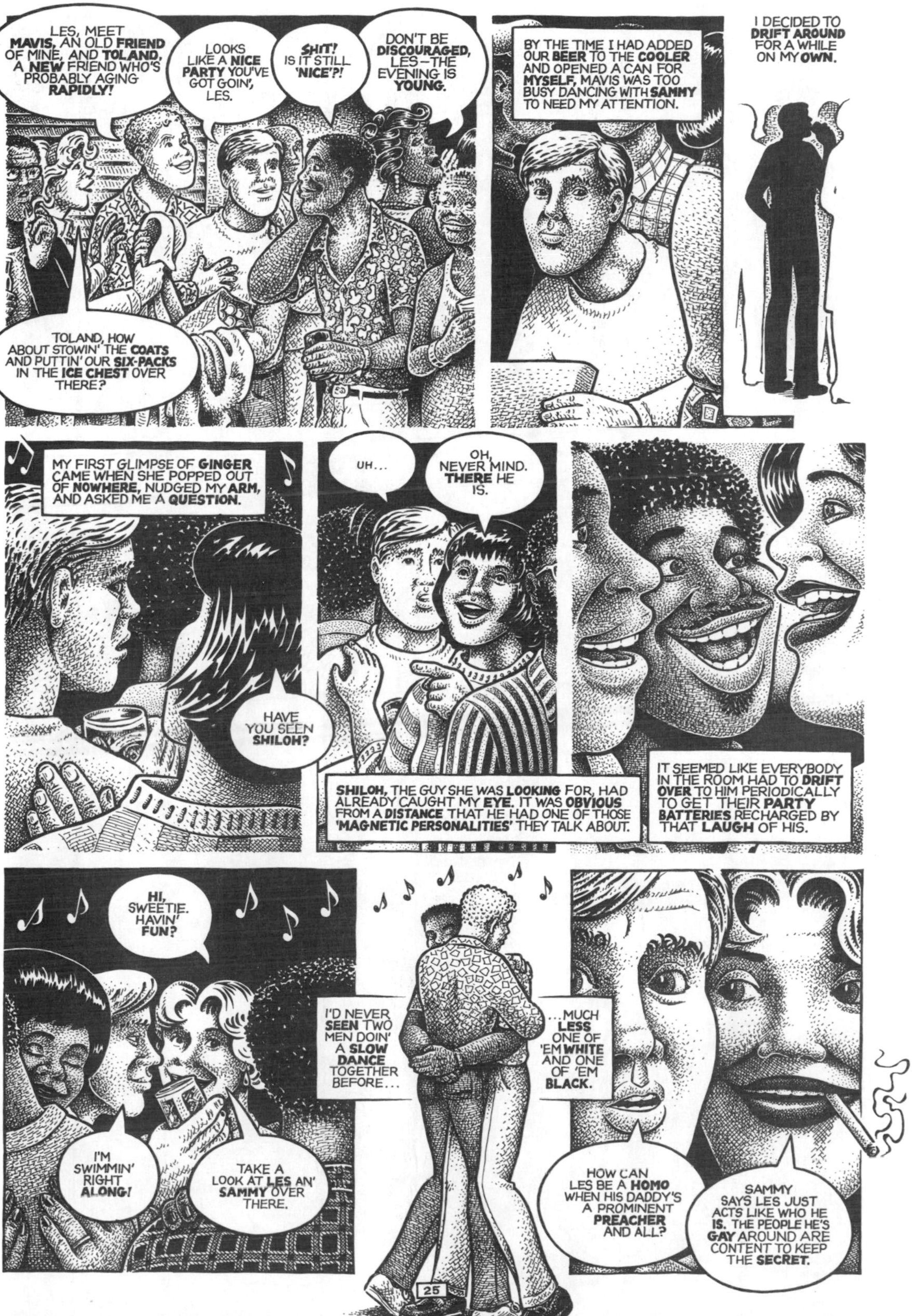
LES, MEET MAVIS, AN OLD FRIEND OF MINE, AND TOLAND, A NEW FRIEND WHO'S PROBABLY AGING RAPIDLY!
LOOKS LIKE A NICE PARTY YOU'VE GOT GOIN', LES.
SHIT! IS IT STILL 'NICE'?!
DON'T BE DISCOURAGED, LES—THE EVENING IS YOUNG.
TOLAND, HOW ABOUT STOWIN' THE COATS AND PUTTIN' OUR SIX-PACKS IN THE ICE CHEST OVER THERE?
BY THE TIME I HAD ADDED OUR BEER TO THE COOLER AND OPENED A CAN FOR MYSELF, MAVIS WAS TOO BUSY DANCING WITH SAMMY TO NEED MY ATTENTION.
I DECIDED TO DRIFT AROUND FOR A WHILE ON MY OWN.
MY FIRST GLIMPSE OF GINGER CAME WHEN SHE POPPED OUT OF NOWHERE, NUDGED MY ARM, AND ASKED ME A QUESTION.
HAVE YOU SEEN SHILOH?
UH...
OH, NEVER MIND. THERE HE IS.
SHILOH, THE GUY SHE WAS LOOKING FOR, HAD ALREADY CAUGHT MY EYE. IT WAS OBVIOUS FROM A DISTANCE THAT HE HAD ONE OF THOSE 'MAGNETIC PERSONALITIES' THEY TALK ABOUT.
IT SEEMED LIKE EVERYBODY IN THE ROOM HAD TO DRIFT OVER TO HIM PERIODICALLY TO GET THEIR PARTY BATTERIES RECHARGED BY THAT LAUGH OF HIS.
HI, SWEETIE. HAVIN' FUN?
I'M SWIMMIN' RIGHT ALONG!
TAKE A LOOK AT LES AN' SAMMY OVER THERE.
I'D NEVER SEEN TWO MEN DOIN' A SLOW DANCE TOGETHER BEFORE...
...MUCH LESS ONE OF 'EM WHITE AND ONE OF 'EM BLACK.
HOW CAN LES BE A HOMO WHEN HIS DADDY'S A PROMINENT PREACHER AND ALL?
SAMMY SAYS LES JUST ACTS LIKE WHO HE IS. THE PEOPLE HE'S GAY AROUND ARE CONTENT TO KEEP THE SECRET.

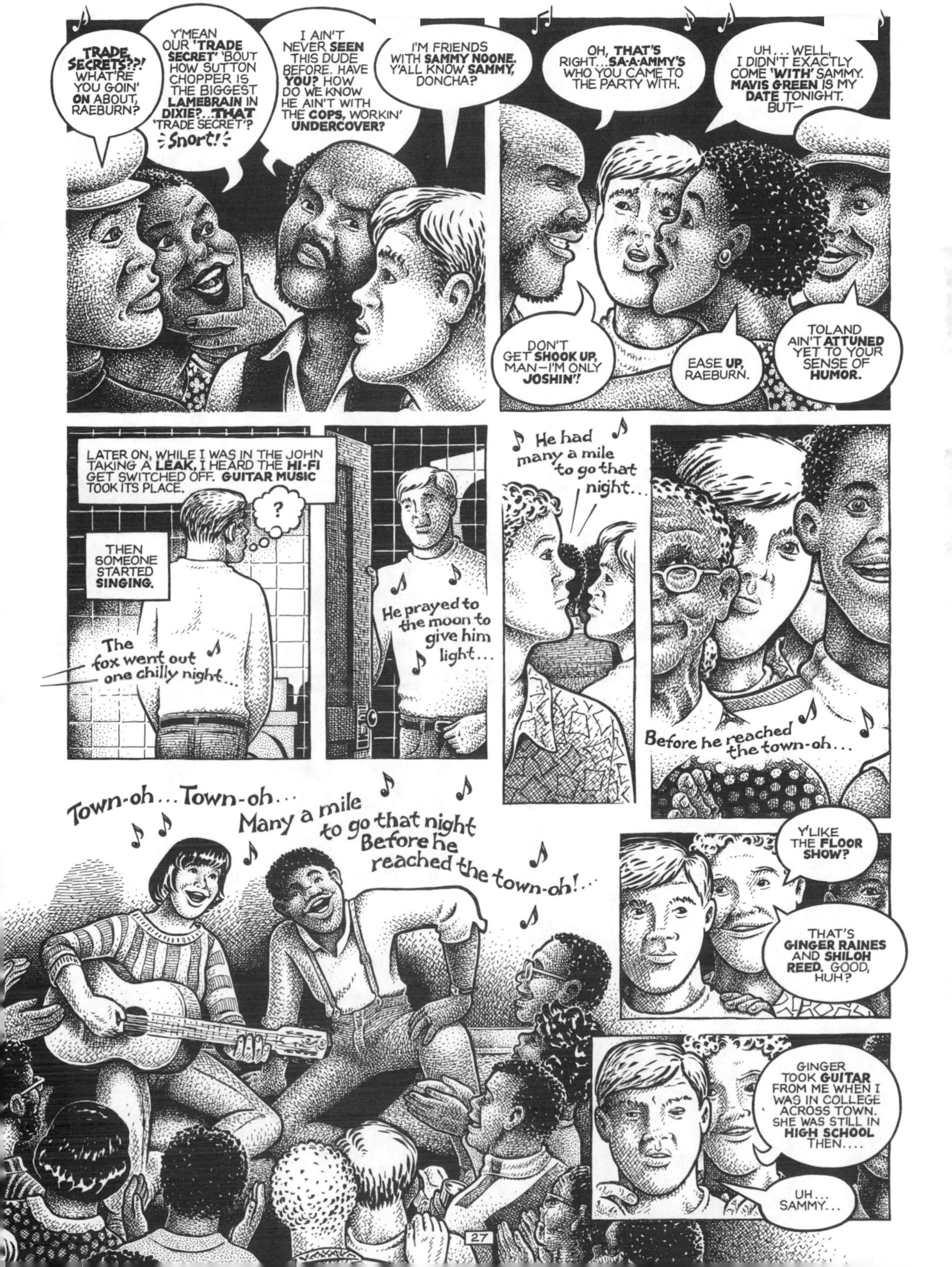

TRADE SECRETS??! WHAT'RE YOU GOIN' ON ABOUT, RAEBURN?
Y'MEAN OUR 'TRADE SECRET' 'BOUT HOW SUTTON CHOPPER IS THE BIGGEST LAMEBRAIN IN DIXIE?...THAT 'TRADE SECRET'?
Snort!
I AIN'T NEVER SEEN THIS DUDE BEFORE. HAVE YOU? HOW DO WE KNOW HE AIN'T WITH THE COPS, WORKIN' UNDERCOVER?
I'M FRIENDS WITH SAMMY NOONE. Y'ALL KNOW SAMMY, DONCHA?
OH, THAT'S RIGHT...SA-A-AMMY'S WHO YOU CAME TO THE PARTY WITH.
UH... WELL, I DIDN'T EXACTLY COME 'WITH' SAMMY. MAVIS GREEN IS MY DATE TONIGHT. BUT—
DON'T GET SHOOK UP, MAN—I'M ONLY JOSHIN'!
EASE UP, RAEBURN.
TOLAND AIN'T ATTUNED YET TO YOUR SENSE OF HUMOR.
LATER ON, WHILE I WAS IN THE JOHN TAKING A LEAK, I HEARD THE HI-FI GET SWITCHED OFF. GUITAR MUSIC TOOK ITS PLACE.
?
THEN SOMEONE STARTED SINGING.
The fox went out one chilly night...
He prayed to the moon to give him light...
He had many a mile to go that night...
Before he reached the town-oh...
Town-oh... Town-oh... Many a mile to go that night Before he reached the town-oh!...
Y'LIKE THE FLOOR SHOW?
THAT'S GINGER RAINES AND SHILOH REED. GOOD, HUH?
GINGER TOOK GUITAR FROM ME WHEN I WAS IN COLLEGE ACROSS TOWN. SHE WAS STILL IN HIGH SCHOOL THEN....
UH... SAMMY...

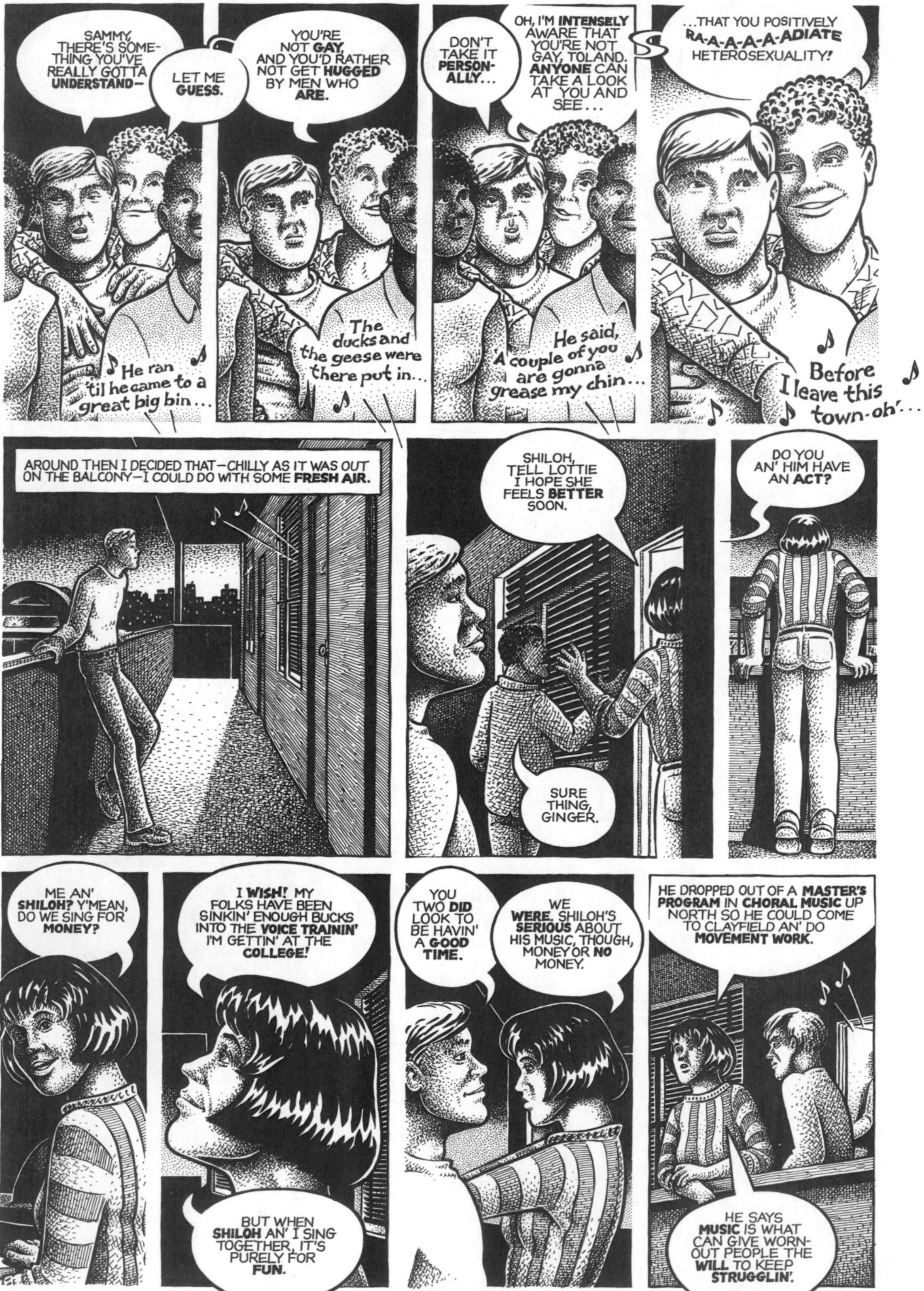
SAMMY, THERE'S SOMETHING YOU'VE REALLY GOTTA UNDERSTAND—
LET ME GUESS.
He ran 'til he came to a great big bin...
YOU'RE NOT GAY, AND YOU'D RATHER NOT GET HUGGED BY MEN WHO ARE.
The ducks and the geese were there put in...
DON'T TAKE IT PERSONALLY...
OH, I'M INTENSELY AWARE THAT YOU'RE NOT GAY, TOLAND. ANYONE CAN TAKE A LOOK AT YOU AND SEE...
He said, 'A couple of you are gonna grease my chin...
...THAT YOU POSITIVELY RA-A-A-A-A-ADIATE HETEROSEXUALITY!
Before I leave this town-oh'...
AROUND THEN I DECIDED THAT—CHILLY AS IT WAS OUT ON THE BALCONY—I COULD DO WITH SOME FRESH AIR.
SHILOH, TELL LOTTIE I HOPE SHE FEELS BETTER SOON.
SURE THING, GINGER.
DO YOU AN' HIM HAVE AN ACT?
ME AN' SHILOH? Y'MEAN, DO WE SING FOR MONEY?
I WISH! MY FOLKS HAVE BEEN SINKIN' ENOUGH BUCKS INTO THE VOICE TRAININ' I'M GETTIN' AT THE COLLEGE!
BUT WHEN SHILOH AN' I SING TOGETHER, IT'S PURELY FOR FUN.
YOU TWO DID LOOK TO BE HAVIN' A GOOD TIME.
WE WERE. SHILOH'S SERIOUS ABOUT HIS MUSIC, THOUGH, MONEY OR NO MONEY.
HE DROPPED OUT OF A MASTER'S PROGRAM IN CHORAL MUSIC UP NORTH SO HE COULD COME TO CLAYFIELD AN' DO MOVEMENT WORK.
HE SAYS MUSIC IS WHAT CAN GIVE WORN-OUT PEOPLE THE WILL TO KEEP STRUGGLIN'.

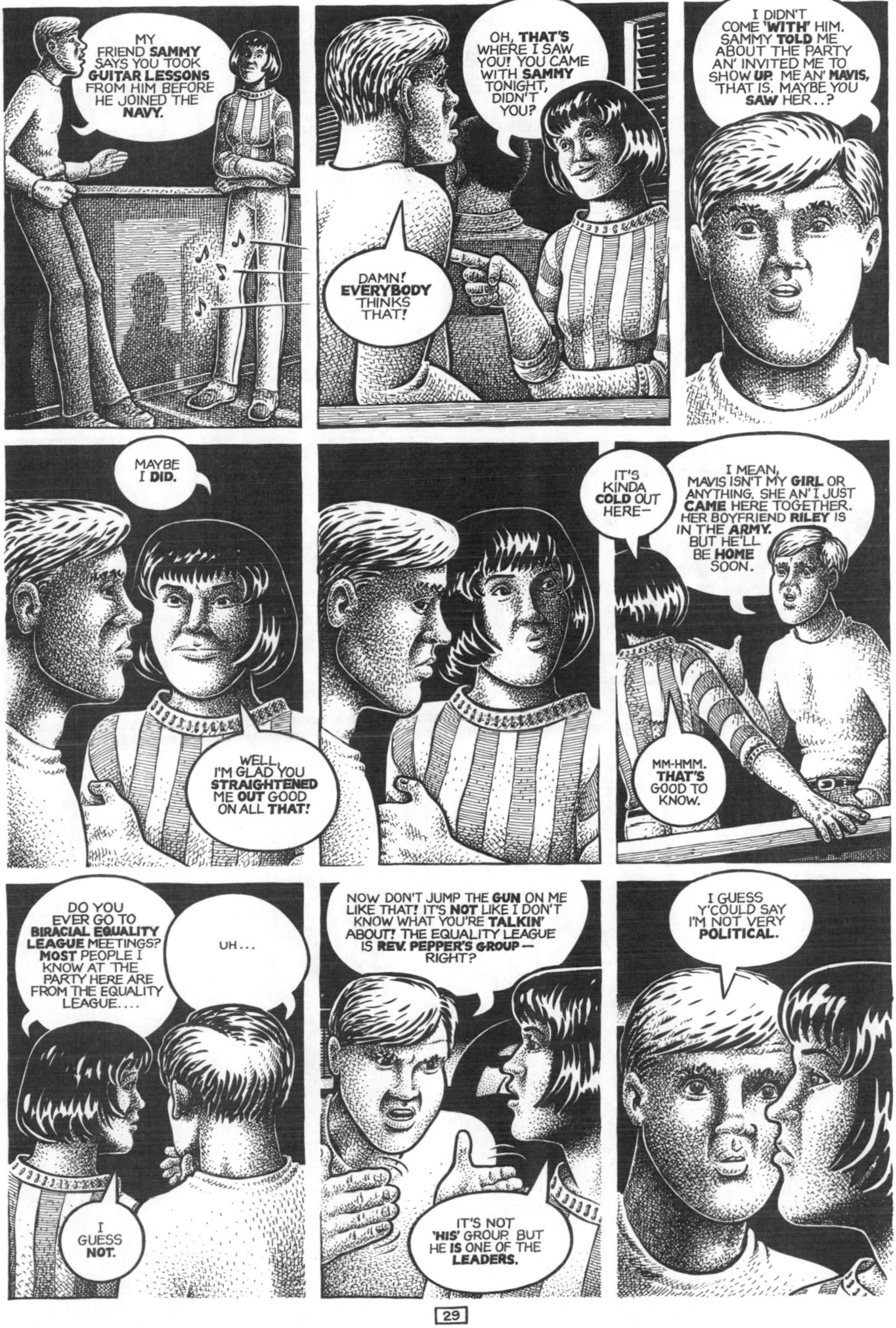
MY FRIEND **SAMMY** SAYS YOU TOOK **GUITAR LESSONS** FROM HIM BEFORE HE JOINED THE **NAVY.**
OH, **THAT'S** WHERE I SAW YOU! YOU CAME WITH **SAMMY** TONIGHT, DIDN'T YOU?
DAMN! **EVERYBODY** THINKS THAT!
I DIDN'T COME **'WITH'** HIM. SAMMY **TOLD** ME ABOUT THE PARTY AN' INVITED ME TO SHOW **UP.** ME AN' **MAVIS,** THAT IS. MAYBE YOU **SAW** HER..?
MAYBE I **DID.**
WELL, I'M GLAD YOU **STRAIGHTENED** ME **OUT** GOOD ON ALL **THAT!**
IT'S KINDA **COLD** OUT HERE–
I MEAN, MAVIS ISN'T MY **GIRL** OR ANYTHING. SHE AN' I JUST **CAME** HERE TOGETHER. HER BOYFRIEND **RILEY** IS IN THE **ARMY.** BUT HE'LL BE **HOME** SOON.
MM-HMM. **THAT'S** GOOD TO KNOW.
DO YOU EVER GO TO **BIRACIAL EQUALITY LEAGUE** MEETINGS? **MOST** PEOPLE I KNOW AT THE PARTY HERE ARE FROM THE EQUALITY LEAGUE....
UH...
I GUESS **NOT.**
NOW DON'T JUMP THE **GUN** ON ME LIKE THAT! IT'S **NOT** LIKE I DON'T KNOW WHAT YOU'RE **TALKIN'** ABOUT! THE EQUALITY LEAGUE IS **REV. PEPPER'S GROUP** — RIGHT?
IT'S NOT **'HIS'** GROUP. BUT HE **IS** ONE OF THE **LEADERS.**
I GUESS Y'COULD SAY I'M NOT VERY **POLITICAL.**

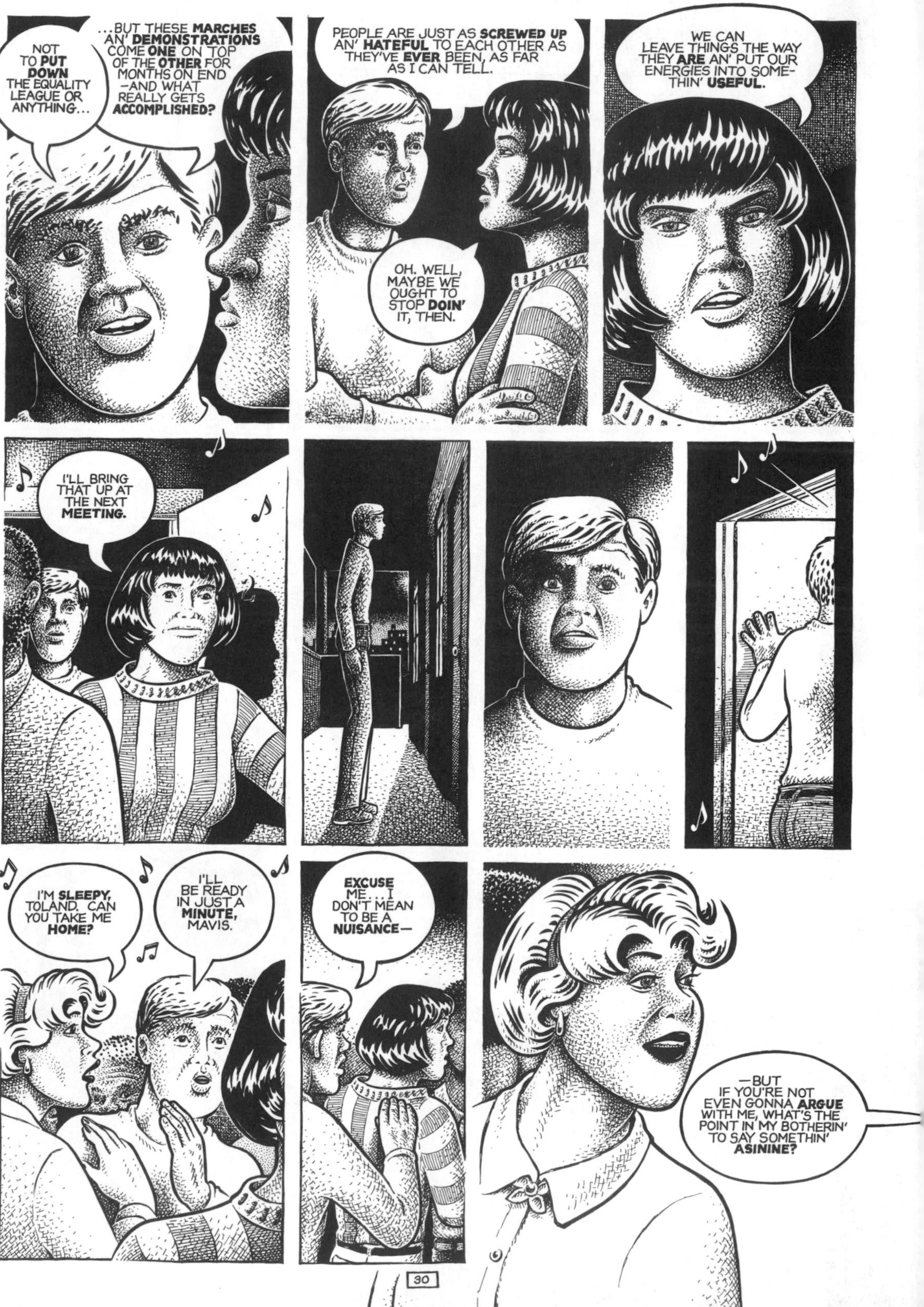

NOT TO PUT DOWN THE EQUALITY LEAGUE OR ANYTHING...
...BUT THESE MARCHES AN' DEMONSTRATIONS COME ONE ON TOP OF THE OTHER FOR MONTHS ON END —AND WHAT REALLY GETS ACCOMPLISHED?
PEOPLE ARE JUST AS SCREWED UP AN' HATEFUL TO EACH OTHER AS THEY'VE EVER BEEN, AS FAR AS I CAN TELL.
OH. WELL, MAYBE WE OUGHT TO STOP DOIN' IT, THEN.
WE CAN LEAVE THINGS THE WAY THEY ARE AN' PUT OUR ENERGIES INTO SOME-THIN' USEFUL.
I'LL BRING THAT UP AT THE NEXT MEETING.
I'M SLEEPY, TOLAND. CAN YOU TAKE ME HOME?
I'LL BE READY IN JUST A MINUTE, MAVIS.
EXCUSE ME... I DON'T MEAN TO BE A NUISANCE—
—BUT IF YOU'RE NOT EVEN GONNA ARGUE WITH ME, WHAT'S THE POINT IN MY BOTHERIN' TO SAY SOMETHIN' ASININE?

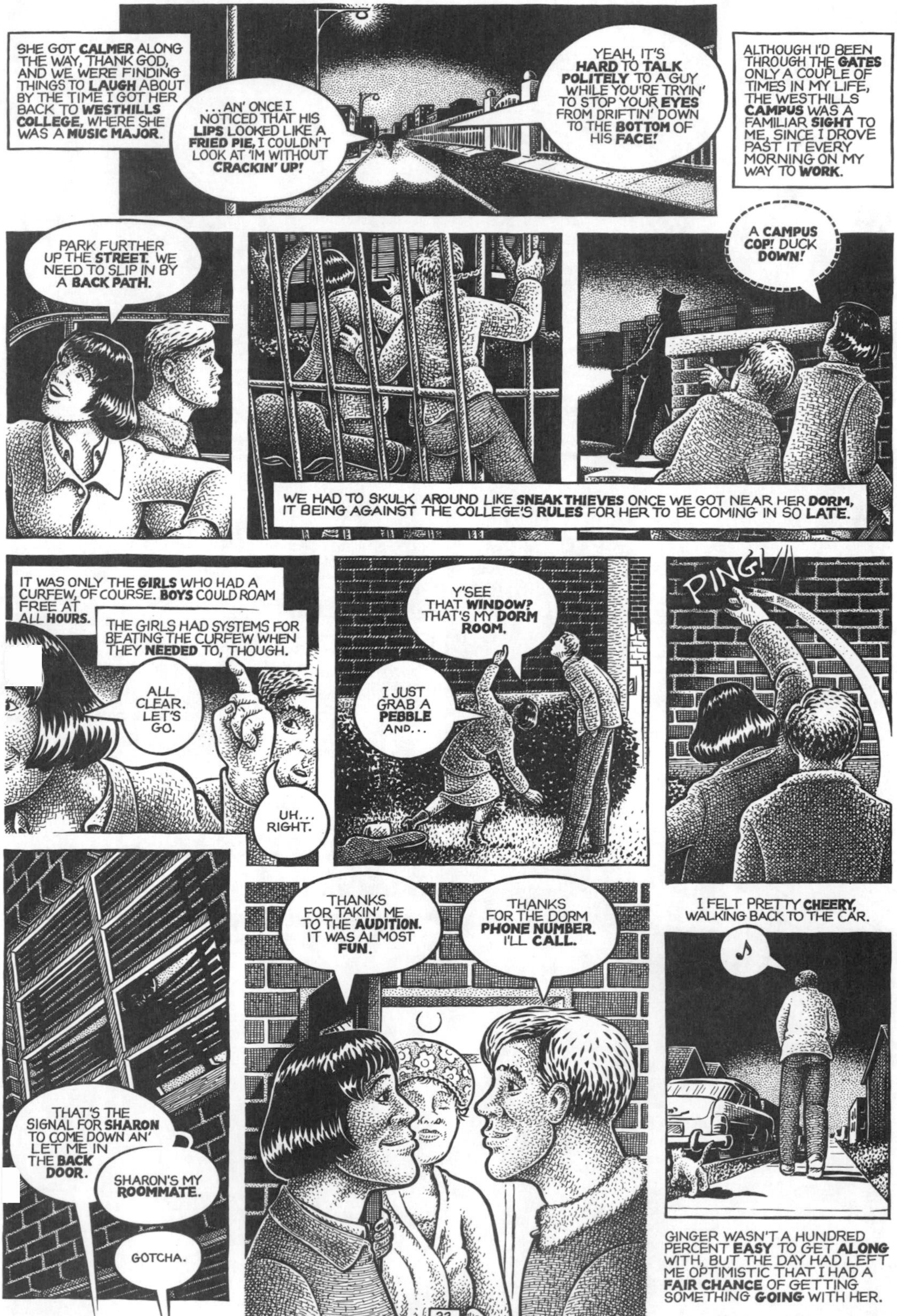

SHE GOT CALMER ALONG THE WAY, THANK GOD, AND WE WERE FINDING THINGS TO LAUGH ABOUT BY THE TIME I GOT HER BACK TO WESTHILLS COLLEGE, WHERE SHE WAS A MUSIC MAJOR.
...AN' ONCE I NOTICED THAT HIS LIPS LOOKED LIKE A FRIED PIE, I COULDN'T LOOK AT 'IM WITHOUT CRACKIN' UP!
YEAH, IT'S HARD TO TALK POLITELY TO A GUY WHILE YOU'RE TRYIN' TO STOP YOUR EYES FROM DRIFTIN' DOWN TO THE BOTTOM OF HIS FACE!
ALTHOUGH I'D BEEN THROUGH THE GATES ONLY A COUPLE OF TIMES IN MY LIFE, THE WESTHILLS CAMPUS WAS A FAMILIAR SIGHT TO ME, SINCE I DROVE PAST IT EVERY MORNING ON MY WAY TO WORK.
PARK FURTHER UP THE STREET. WE NEED TO SLIP IN BY A BACK PATH.
A CAMPUS COP! DUCK DOWN!
WE HAD TO SKULK AROUND LIKE SNEAK THIEVES ONCE WE GOT NEAR HER DORM, IT BEING AGAINST THE COLLEGE'S RULES FOR HER TO BE COMING IN SO LATE.
IT WAS ONLY THE GIRLS WHO HAD A CURFEW, OF COURSE. BOYS COULD ROAM FREE AT ALL HOURS.
THE GIRLS HAD SYSTEMS FOR BEATING THE CURFEW WHEN THEY NEEDED TO, THOUGH.
ALL CLEAR. LET'S GO.
UH... RIGHT.
Y'SEE THAT WINDOW? THAT'S MY DORM ROOM.
I JUST GRAB A PEBBLE AND...
PING!
THAT'S THE SIGNAL FOR SHARON TO COME DOWN AN' LET ME IN THE BACK DOOR.
SHARON'S MY ROOMMATE.
GOTCHA.
THANKS FOR TAKIN' ME TO THE AUDITION. IT WAS ALMOST FUN.
THANKS FOR THE DORM PHONE NUMBER. I'LL CALL.
I FELT PRETTY CHEERY, WALKING BACK TO THE CAR.
♪
GINGER WASN'T A HUNDRED PERCENT EASY TO GET ALONG WITH, BUT THE DAY HAD LEFT ME OPTIMISTIC THAT I HAD A FAIR CHANCE OF GETTING SOMETHING GOING WITH HER.

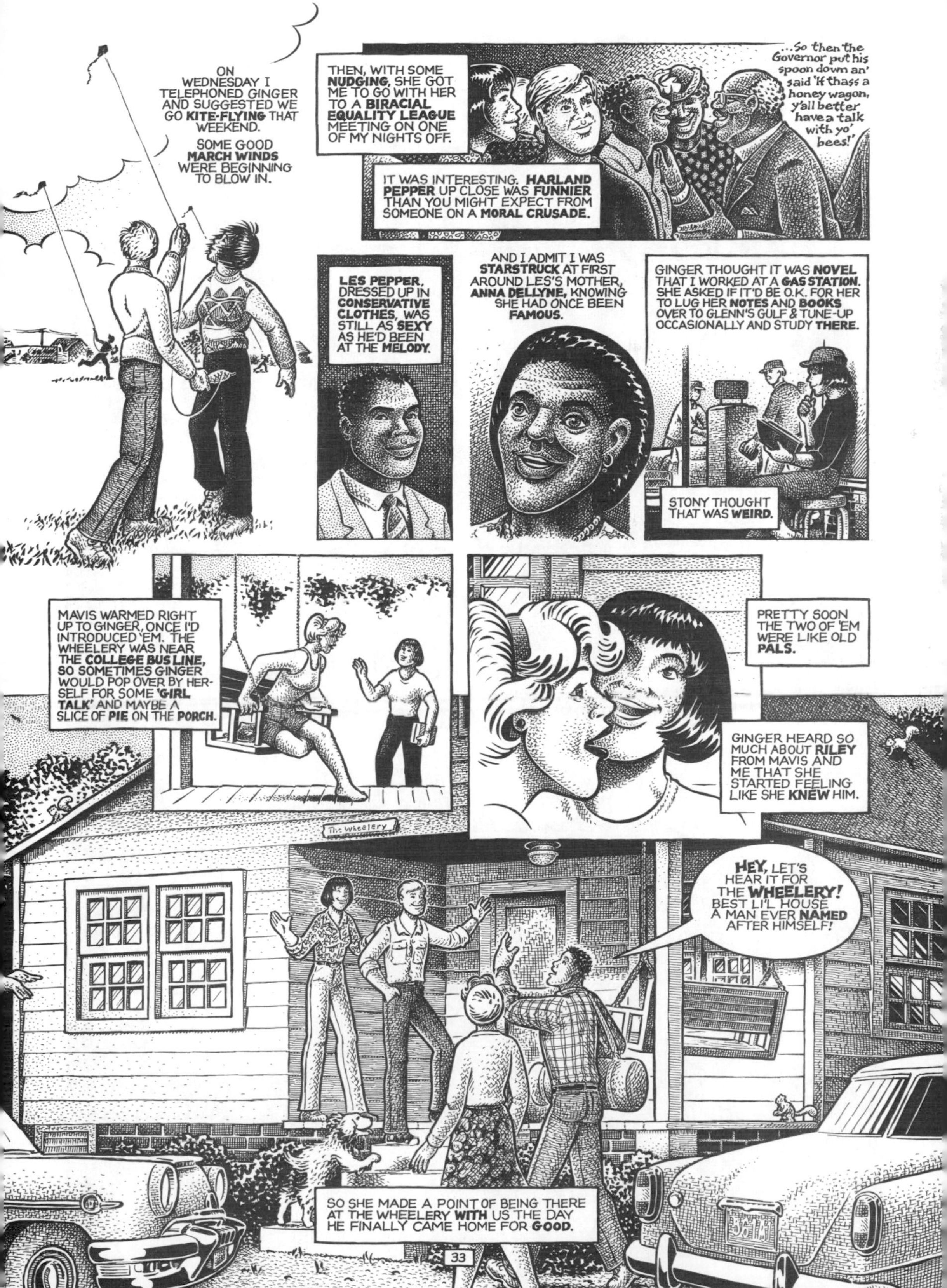
ON WEDNESDAY I TELEPHONED GINGER AND SUGGESTED WE GO KITE-FLYING THAT WEEKEND.
SOME GOOD MARCH WINDS WERE BEGINNING TO BLOW IN.
THEN, WITH SOME NUDGING, SHE GOT ME TO GO WITH HER TO A BIRACIAL EQUALITY LEAGUE MEETING ON ONE OF MY NIGHTS OFF.
...So then the Governor put his spoon down an' said 'If thass a honey wagon, y'all better have a talk with yo' bees!'
IT WAS INTERESTING. HARLAND PEPPER UP CLOSE WAS FUNNIER THAN YOU MIGHT EXPECT FROM SOMEONE ON A MORAL CRUSADE.
LES PEPPER, DRESSED UP IN CONSERVATIVE CLOTHES, WAS STILL AS SEXY AS HE'D BEEN AT THE MELODY.
AND I ADMIT I WAS STARSTRUCK AT FIRST AROUND LES'S MOTHER, ANNA DELLYNE, KNOWING SHE HAD ONCE BEEN FAMOUS.
GINGER THOUGHT IT WAS NOVEL THAT I WORKED AT A GAS STATION. SHE ASKED IF IT'D BE O.K. FOR HER TO LUG HER NOTES AND BOOKS OVER TO GLENN'S GULF & TUNE-UP OCCASIONALLY AND STUDY THERE.
STONY THOUGHT THAT WAS WEIRD.
MAVIS WARMED RIGHT UP TO GINGER, ONCE I'D INTRODUCED 'EM. THE WHEELERY WAS NEAR THE COLLEGE BUS LINE, SO SOMETIMES GINGER WOULD POP OVER BY HER-SELF FOR SOME 'GIRL TALK' AND MAYBE A SLICE OF PIE ON THE PORCH.
PRETTY SOON THE TWO OF 'EM WERE LIKE OLD PALS.
GINGER HEARD SO MUCH ABOUT RILEY FROM MAVIS AND ME THAT SHE STARTED FEELING LIKE SHE KNEW HIM.
The Wheelery
HEY, LET'S HEAR IT FOR THE WHEELERY! BEST LI'L HOUSE A MAN EVER NAMED AFTER HIMSELF!
SO SHE MADE A POINT OF BEING THERE AT THE WHEELERY WITH US THE DAY HE FINALLY CAME HOME FOR GOOD.

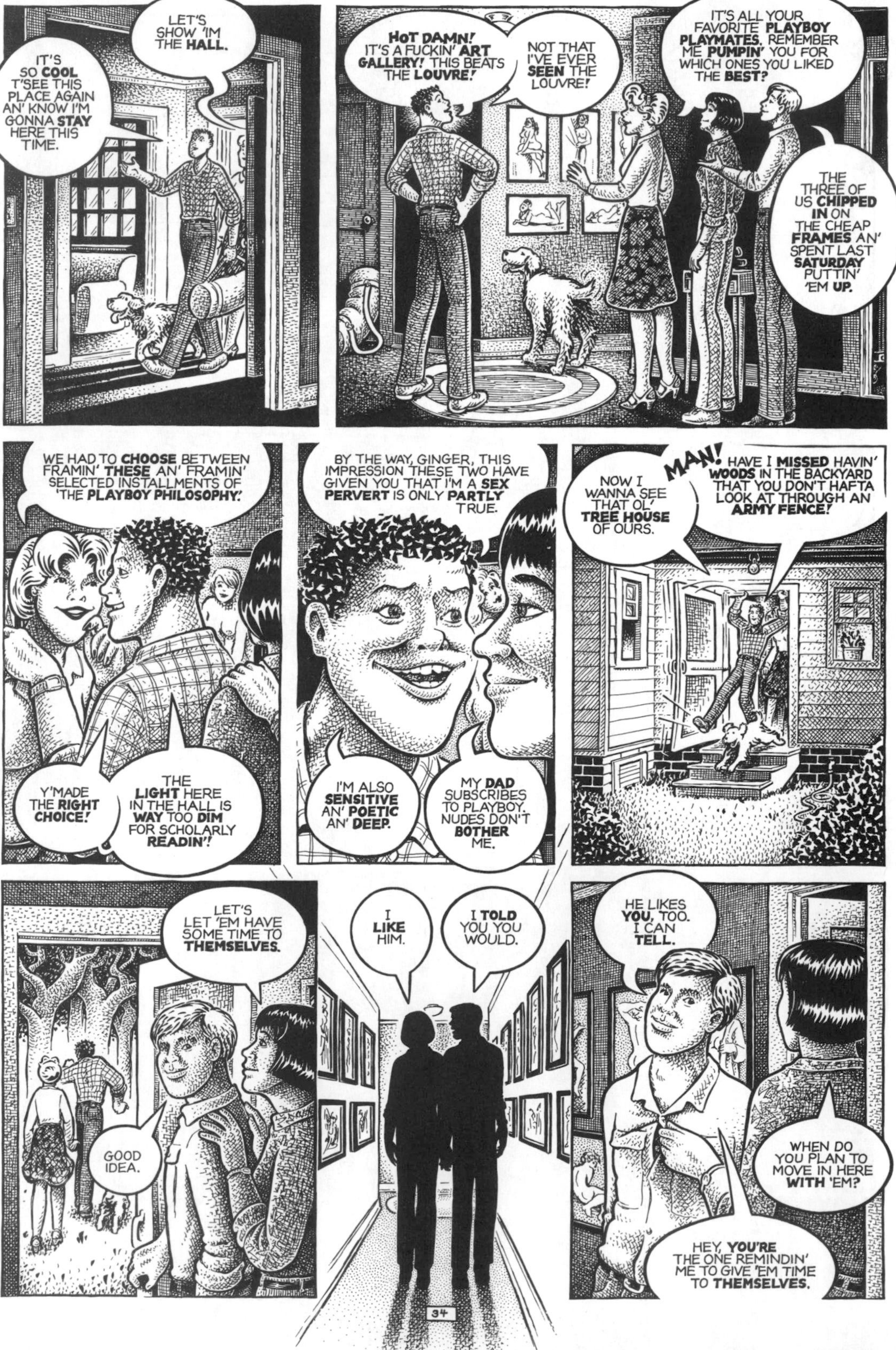
LET'S SHOW 'IM THE HALL.
IT'S SO COOL T'SEE THIS PLACE AGAIN AN' KNOW I'M GONNA STAY HERE THIS TIME.
HOT DAMN! IT'S A FUCKIN' ART GALLERY! THIS BEATS THE LOUVRE!
NOT THAT I'VE EVER SEEN THE LOUVRE!
IT'S ALL YOUR FAVORITE PLAYBOY PLAYMATES. REMEMBER ME PUMPIN' YOU FOR WHICH ONES YOU LIKED THE BEST?
THE THREE OF US CHIPPED IN ON THE CHEAP FRAMES AN' SPENT LAST SATURDAY PUTTIN' 'EM UP.
WE HAD TO CHOOSE BETWEEN FRAMIN' THESE AN' FRAMIN' SELECTED INSTALLMENTS OF 'THE PLAYBOY PHILOSOPHY.'
Y'MADE THE RIGHT CHOICE!
THE LIGHT HERE IN THE HALL IS WAY TOO DIM FOR SCHOLARLY READIN'!
BY THE WAY, GINGER, THIS IMPRESSION THESE TWO HAVE GIVEN YOU THAT I'M A SEX PERVERT IS ONLY PARTLY TRUE.
I'M ALSO SENSITIVE AN' POETIC AN' DEEP.
MY DAD SUBSCRIBES TO PLAYBOY. NUDES DON'T BOTHER ME.
NOW I WANNA SEE THAT OL' TREE HOUSE OF OURS.
MAN!
HAVE I MISSED HAVIN' WOODS IN THE BACKYARD THAT YOU DON'T HAFTA LOOK AT THROUGH AN ARMY FENCE!
LET'S LET 'EM HAVE SOME TIME TO THEMSELVES.
GOOD IDEA.
I LIKE HIM.
I TOLD YOU YOU WOULD.
HE LIKES YOU, TOO. I CAN TELL.
WHEN DO YOU PLAN TO MOVE IN HERE WITH 'EM?
HEY, YOU'RE THE ONE REMINDIN' ME TO GIVE 'EM TIME TO THEMSELVES.

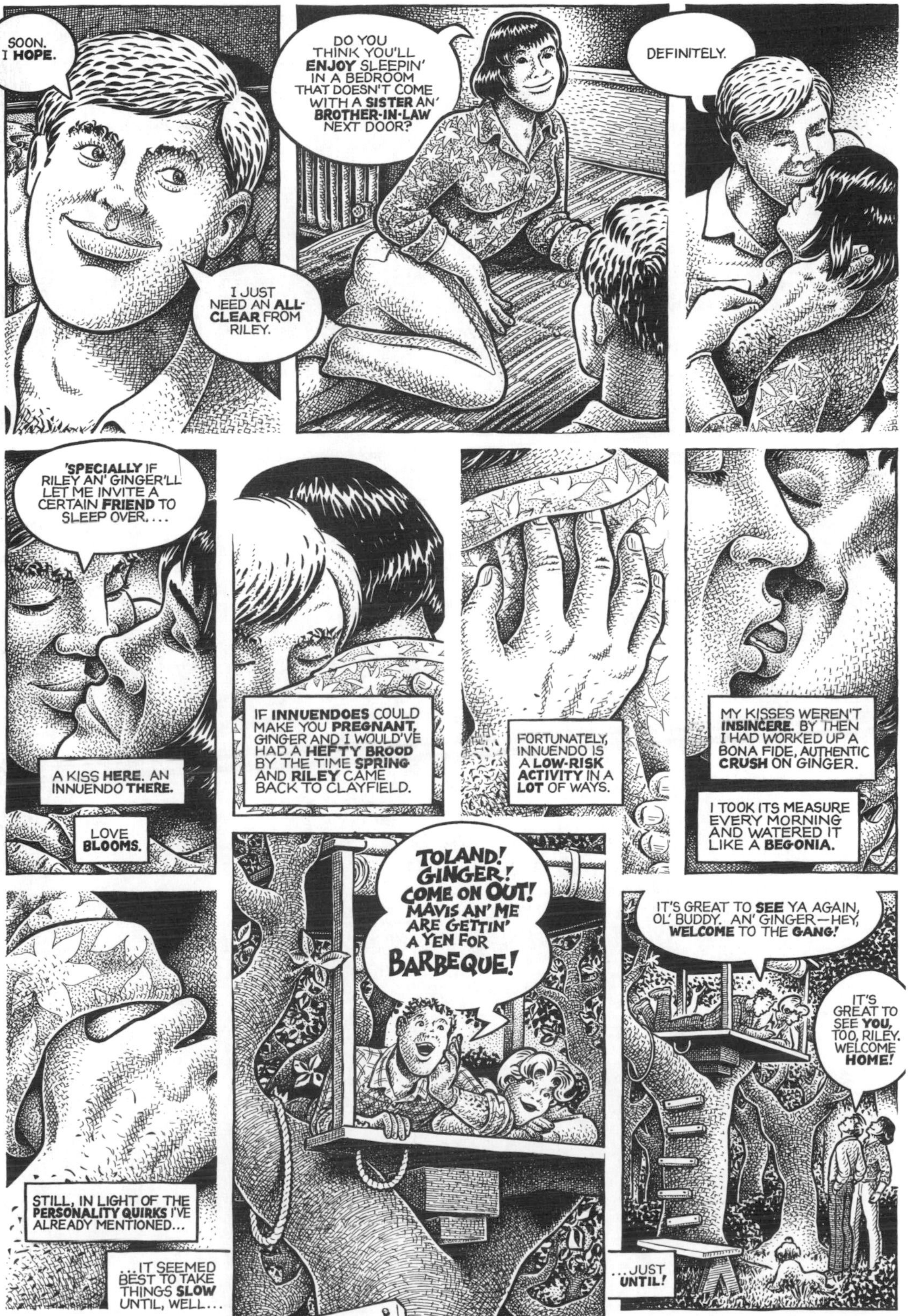
SOON. I HOPE.
I JUST NEED AN ALL-CLEAR FROM RILEY.
DO YOU THINK YOU'LL ENJOY SLEEPIN' IN A BEDROOM THAT DOESN'T COME WITH A SISTER AN' BROTHER-IN-LAW NEXT DOOR?
DEFINITELY.
'SPECIALLY IF RILEY AN' GINGER'LL LET ME INVITE A CERTAIN FRIEND TO SLEEP OVER....
A KISS HERE. AN INNUENDO THERE.
LOVE BLOOMS.
IF INNUENDOES COULD MAKE YOU PREGNANT, GINGER AND I WOULD'VE HAD A HEFTY BROOD BY THE TIME SPRING AND RILEY CAME BACK TO CLAYFIELD.
FORTUNATELY, INNUENDO IS A LOW-RISK ACTIVITY IN A LOT OF WAYS.
MY KISSES WEREN'T INSINCERE. BY THEN I HAD WORKED UP A BONA FIDE, AUTHENTIC CRUSH ON GINGER.
I TOOK ITS MEASURE EVERY MORNING AND WATERED IT LIKE A BEGONIA.
STILL, IN LIGHT OF THE PERSONALITY QUIRKS I'VE ALREADY MENTIONED...
...IT SEEMED BEST TO TAKE THINGS SLOW UNTIL, WELL...
TOLAND! GINGER! COME ON OUT! MAVIS AN' ME ARE GETTIN' A YEN FOR BARBEQUE!
IT'S GREAT TO SEE YA AGAIN, OL' BUDDY. AN' GINGER—HEY, WELCOME TO THE GANG!
IT'S GREAT TO SEE YOU, TOO, RILEY. WELCOME HOME!
...JUST UNTIL!

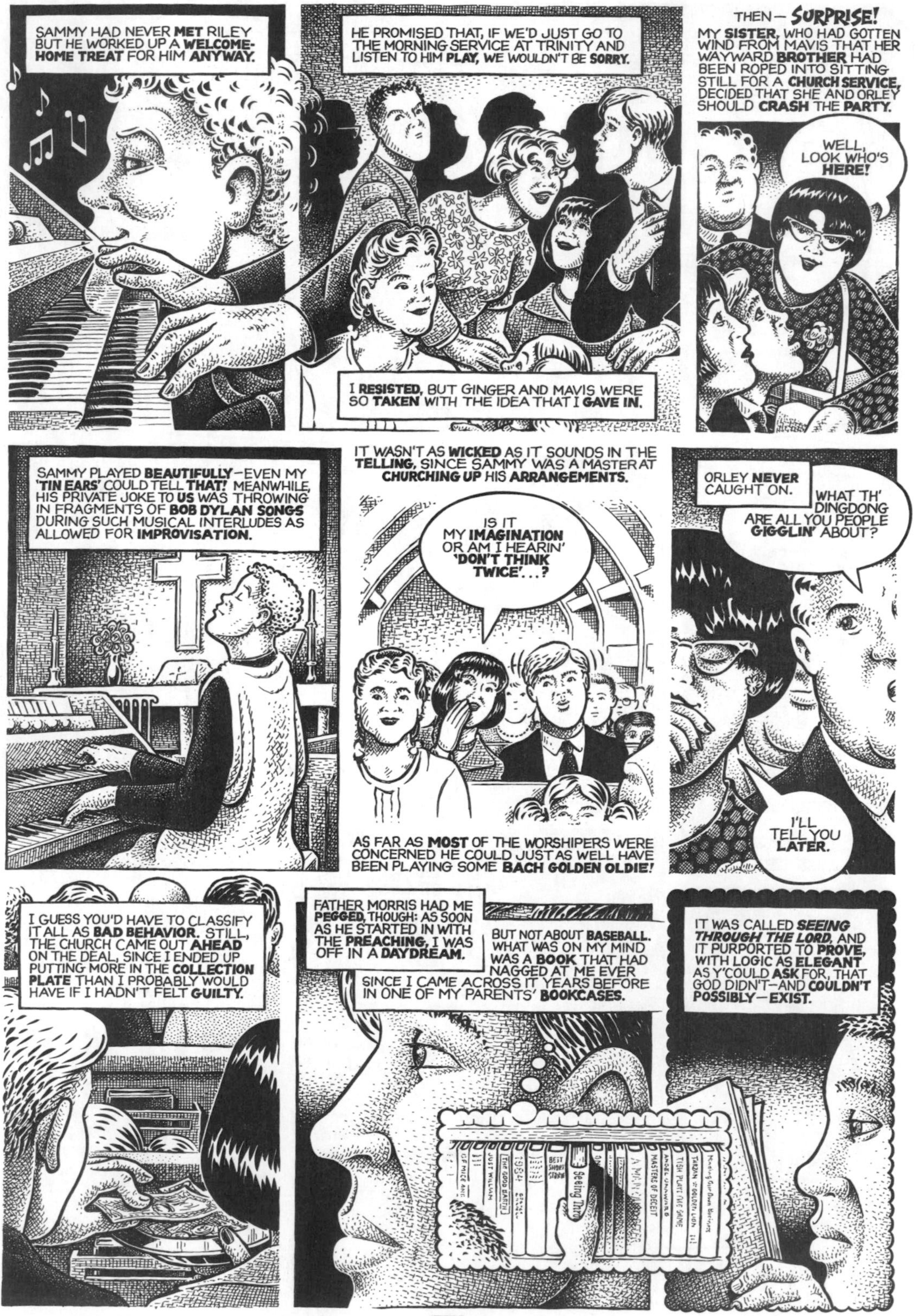
SAMMY HAD NEVER **MET** RILEY BUT HE WORKED UP A **WELCOME-HOME TREAT** FOR HIM **ANYWAY.**
HE PROMISED THAT, IF WE'D JUST GO TO THE MORNING SERVICE AT TRINITY AND LISTEN TO HIM **PLAY, WE** WOULDN'T BE **SORRY.**
I **RESISTED**, BUT GINGER AND MAVIS WERE SO **TAKEN** WITH THE IDEA THAT I **GAVE IN.**
THEN— **SURPRISE!**
MY **SISTER**, WHO HAD GOTTEN WIND FROM MAVIS THAT HER WAYWARD **BROTHER** HAD BEEN ROPED INTO SITTING STILL FOR A **CHURCH SERVICE**, DECIDED THAT SHE AND ORLEY SHOULD **CRASH** THE **PARTY.**
WELL, LOOK WHO'S **HERE!**
SAMMY PLAYED **BEAUTIFULLY**—EVEN MY **'TIN EARS'** COULD TELL **THAT!** MEANWHILE, HIS PRIVATE JOKE TO **US** WAS THROWING IN FRAGMENTS OF **BOB DYLAN SONGS** DURING SUCH MUSICAL INTERLUDES AS ALLOWED FOR **IMPROVISATION.**
IT WASN'T AS **WICKED** AS IT SOUNDS IN THE **TELLING**, SINCE SAMMY WAS A MASTER AT **CHURCHING UP** HIS **ARRANGEMENTS.**
IS IT MY **IMAGINATION** OR AM I HEARIN' **'DON'T THINK TWICE'**. . .?
AS FAR AS **MOST** OF THE WORSHIPERS WERE CONCERNED HE COULD JUST AS WELL HAVE BEEN PLAYING SOME **BACH GOLDEN OLDIE!**
ORLEY **NEVER** CAUGHT ON.
WHAT TH' DINGDONG ARE ALL YOU PEOPLE **GIGGLIN'** ABOUT?
I'LL TELL YOU **LATER.**
I GUESS YOU'D HAVE TO CLASSIFY IT ALL AS **BAD BEHAVIOR.** STILL, THE CHURCH CAME OUT **AHEAD** ON THE DEAL, SINCE I ENDED UP PUTTING MORE IN THE **COLLECTION PLATE** THAN I PROBABLY WOULD HAVE IF I HADN'T FELT **GUILTY.**
FATHER MORRIS HAD ME **PEGGED**, THOUGH: AS SOON AS HE STARTED IN WITH THE **PREACHING**, I WAS OFF IN A **DAYDREAM.**
BUT NOT ABOUT **BASEBALL.** WHAT WAS ON MY MIND WAS A **BOOK** THAT HAD NAGGED AT ME EVER
SINCE I CAME ACROSS IT YEARS BEFORE IN ONE OF MY PARENTS' **BOOKCASES.**
IT WAS CALLED ***SEEING THROUGH THE LORD***, AND IT PURPORTED TO **PROVE**, WITH LOGIC AS **ELEGANT** AS Y'COULD **ASK** FOR, THAT GOD DIDN'T—AND **COULDN'T** POSSIBLY—**EXIST.**

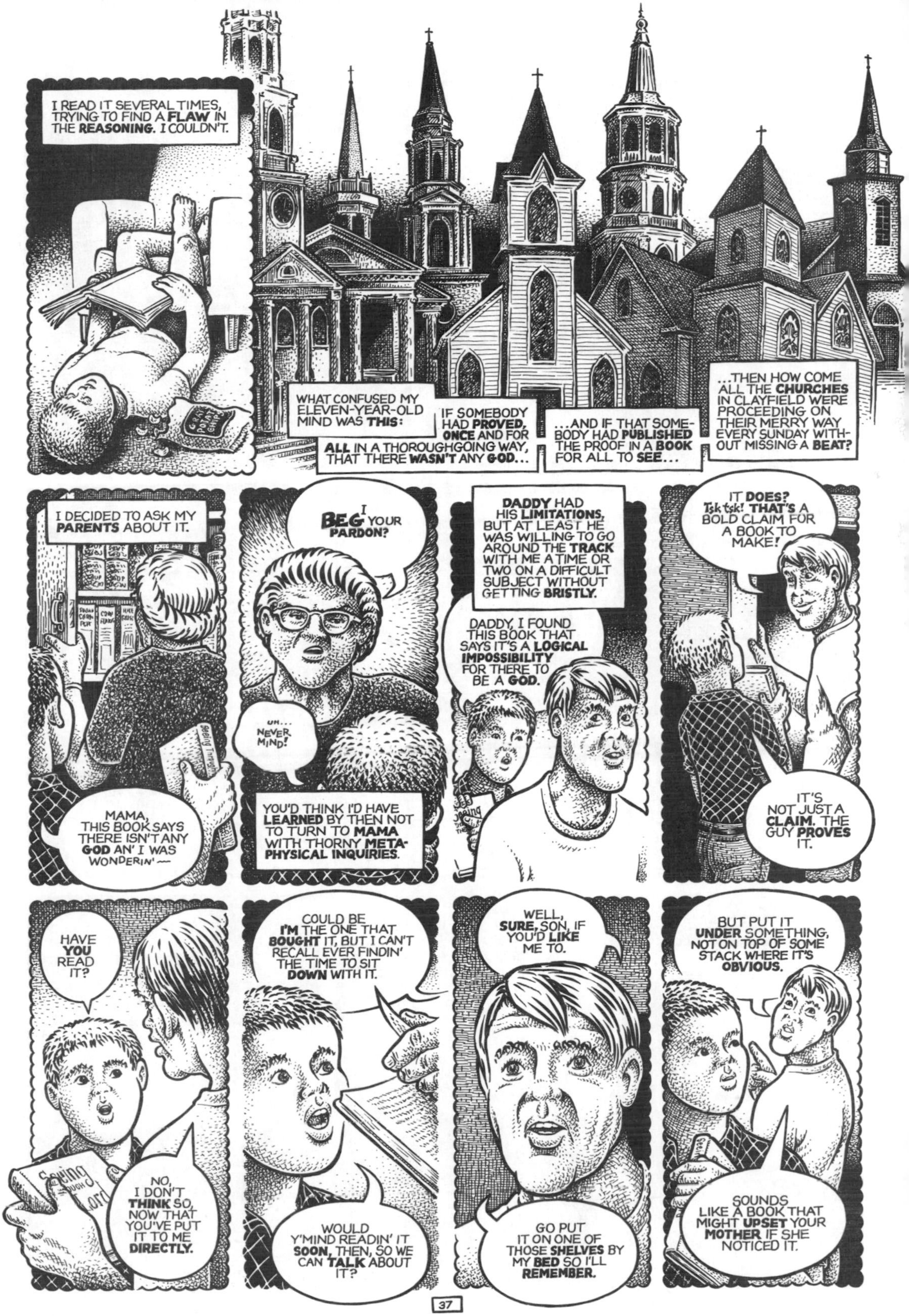
I READ IT SEVERAL TIMES, TRYING TO FIND A **FLAW** IN THE **REASONING**. I COULDN'T.
WHAT CONFUSED MY ELEVEN-YEAR-OLD MIND WAS **THIS**:
IF SOMEBODY HAD **PROVED**, **ONCE** AND FOR **ALL** IN A THOROUGHGOING WAY, THAT THERE **WASN'T** ANY **GOD**...
...AND IF THAT SOMEBODY HAD **PUBLISHED** THE PROOF IN A **BOOK** FOR ALL TO **SEE**...
...THEN HOW COME ALL THE **CHURCHES** IN CLAYFIELD WERE PROCEEDING ON THEIR MERRY WAY EVERY SUNDAY WITHOUT MISSING A **BEAT**?
I DECIDED TO ASK MY **PARENTS** ABOUT IT.
MAMA, THIS BOOK SAYS THERE ISN'T ANY **GOD** AN' I WAS WONDERIN'—
BEG YOUR **PARDON**?
UH... NEVER MIND!
YOU'D THINK I'D HAVE **LEARNED** BY THEN NOT TO TURN TO **MAMA** WITH THORNY **META-PHYSICAL INQUIRIES**.
DADDY HAD HIS **LIMITATIONS**, BUT AT LEAST HE WAS WILLING TO GO AROUND THE **TRACK** WITH ME A TIME OR TWO ON A DIFFICULT SUBJECT WITHOUT GETTING **BRISTLY**.
DADDY, I FOUND THIS BOOK THAT SAYS IT'S A **LOGICAL IMPOSSIBILITY** FOR THERE TO BE A **GOD**.
IT **DOES**? Tsk tsk! **THAT'S** A BOLD CLAIM FOR A BOOK TO MAKE!
IT'S NOT JUST A **CLAIM**. THE GUY **PROVES** IT.
HAVE **YOU** READ IT?
NO, I DON'T **THINK** SO, NOW THAT YOU'VE PUT IT TO ME **DIRECTLY**.
COULD BE **I'M** THE ONE THAT **BOUGHT** IT, BUT I CAN'T RECALL EVER FINDIN' THE TIME TO SIT **DOWN** WITH IT.
WOULD Y'MIND READIN' IT **SOON**, THEN, SO WE CAN **TALK** ABOUT IT?
WELL, **SURE**, SON, IF YOU'D **LIKE** ME TO.
GO PUT IT ON ONE OF THOSE **SHELVES** BY MY **BED** SO I'LL **REMEMBER**.
BUT PUT IT **UNDER** SOMETHING, NOT ON TOP OF SOME STACK WHERE IT'S **OBVIOUS**.
SOUNDS LIKE A BOOK THAT MIGHT **UPSET** YOUR **MOTHER** IF SHE NOTICED IT.

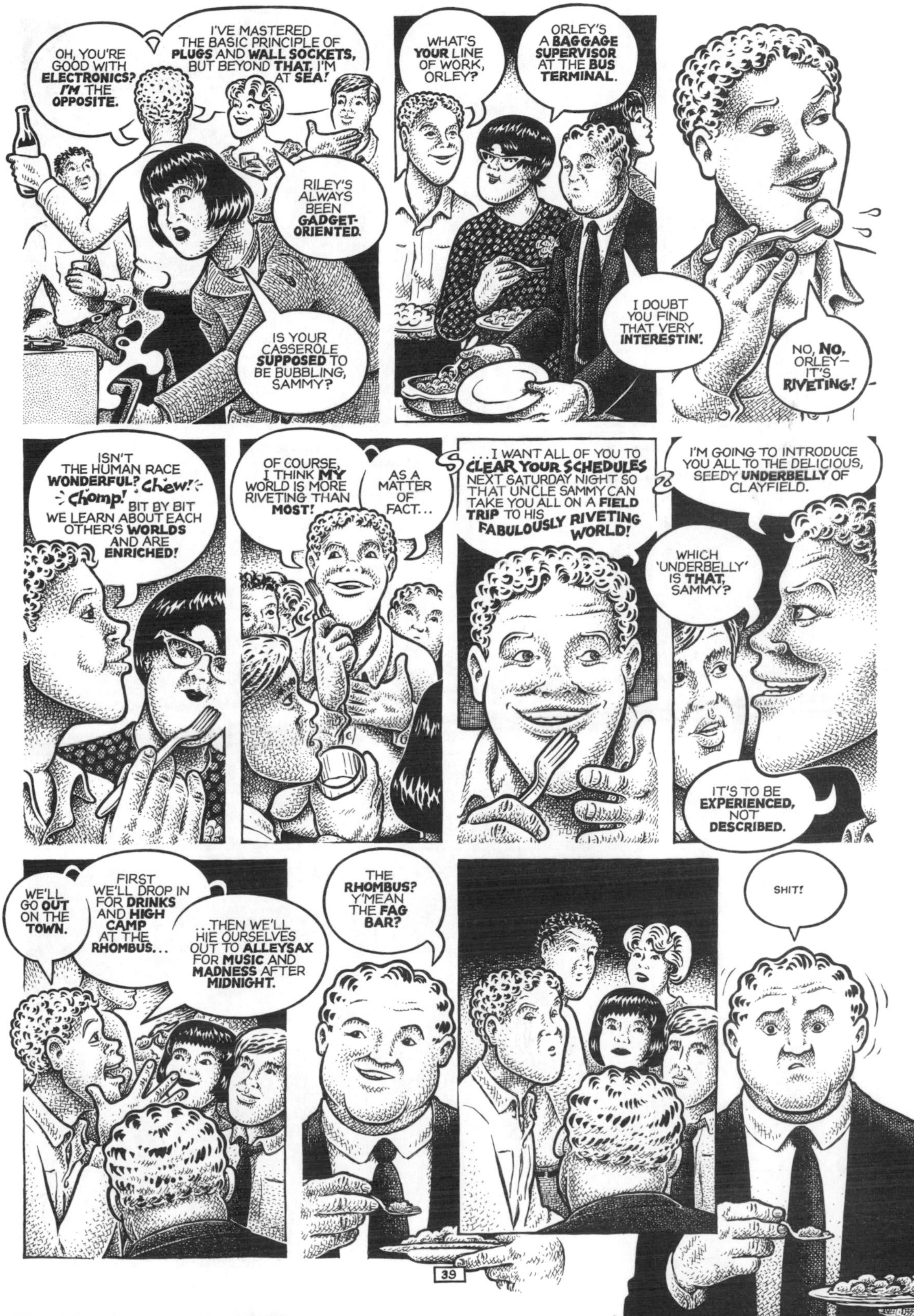
OH, YOU'RE GOOD WITH ELECTRONICS? I'M THE OPPOSITE.
I'VE MASTERED THE BASIC PRINCIPLE OF PLUGS AND WALL SOCKETS, BUT BEYOND THAT, I'M AT SEA!
RILEY'S ALWAYS BEEN GADGET-ORIENTED.
IS YOUR CASSEROLE SUPPOSED TO BE BUBBLING, SAMMY?
WHAT'S YOUR LINE OF WORK, ORLEY?
ORLEY'S A BAGGAGE SUPERVISOR AT THE BUS TERMINAL.
I DOUBT YOU FIND THAT VERY INTERESTIN'.
NO, NO, ORLEY— IT'S RIVETING!
ISN'T THE HUMAN RACE WONDERFUL? Chomp! Chew! BIT BY BIT WE LEARN ABOUT EACH OTHER'S WORLDS AND ARE ENRICHED!
OF COURSE, I THINK MY WORLD IS MORE RIVETING THAN MOST!
AS A MATTER OF FACT...
...I WANT ALL OF YOU TO CLEAR YOUR SCHEDULES NEXT SATURDAY NIGHT SO THAT UNCLE SAMMY CAN TAKE YOU ALL ON A FIELD TRIP TO HIS FABULOUSLY RIVETING WORLD!
I'M GOING TO INTRODUCE YOU ALL TO THE DELICIOUS, SEEDY UNDERBELLY OF CLAYFIELD.
WHICH 'UNDERBELLY' IS THAT, SAMMY?
IT'S TO BE EXPERIENCED, NOT DESCRIBED.
WE'LL GO OUT ON THE TOWN.
FIRST WE'LL DROP IN FOR DRINKS AND HIGH CAMP AT THE RHOMBUS...
...THEN WE'LL HIE OURSELVES OUT TO ALLEYSAX FOR MUSIC AND MADNESS AFTER MIDNIGHT.
THE RHOMBUS? Y'MEAN THE FAG BAR?
SHIT!

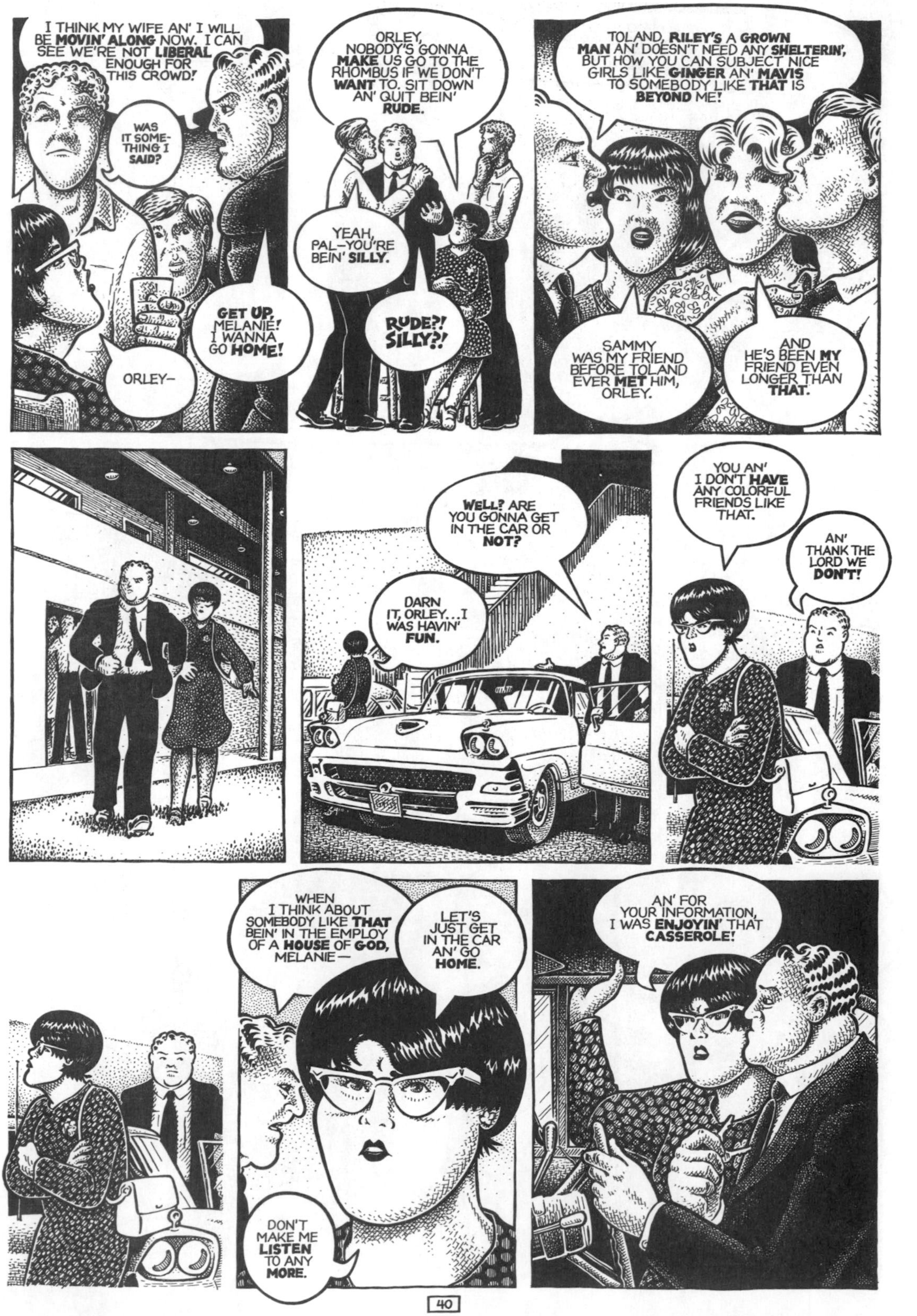
I THINK MY WIFE AN' I WILL BE MOVIN' ALONG NOW. I CAN SEE WE'RE NOT LIBERAL ENOUGH FOR THIS CROWD!
WAS IT SOMETHING I SAID?
GET UP, MELANIE! I WANNA GO HOME!
ORLEY—
ORLEY, NOBODY'S GONNA MAKE US GO TO THE RHOMBUS IF WE DON'T WANT TO. SIT DOWN AN' QUIT BEIN' RUDE.
YEAH, PAL—YOU'RE BEIN' SILLY.
RUDE?! SILLY?!
TOLAND, RILEY'S A GROWN MAN AN' DOESN'T NEED ANY SHELTERIN', BUT HOW YOU CAN SUBJECT NICE GIRLS LIKE GINGER AN' MAVIS TO SOMEBODY LIKE THAT IS BEYOND ME!
SAMMY WAS MY FRIEND BEFORE TOLAND EVER MET HIM, ORLEY.
AND HE'S BEEN MY FRIEND EVEN LONGER THAN THAT.
WELL? ARE YOU GONNA GET IN THE CAR OR NOT?
DARN IT, ORLEY... I WAS HAVIN' FUN.
YOU AN' I DON'T HAVE ANY COLORFUL FRIENDS LIKE THAT.
AN' THANK THE LORD WE DON'T!
WHEN I THINK ABOUT SOMEBODY LIKE THAT BEIN' IN THE EMPLOY OF A HOUSE OF GOD, MELANIE—
LET'S JUST GET IN THE CAR AN' GO HOME.
DON'T MAKE ME LISTEN TO ANY MORE.
AN' FOR YOUR INFORMATION, I WAS ENJOYIN' THAT CASSEROLE!

Chapter 6

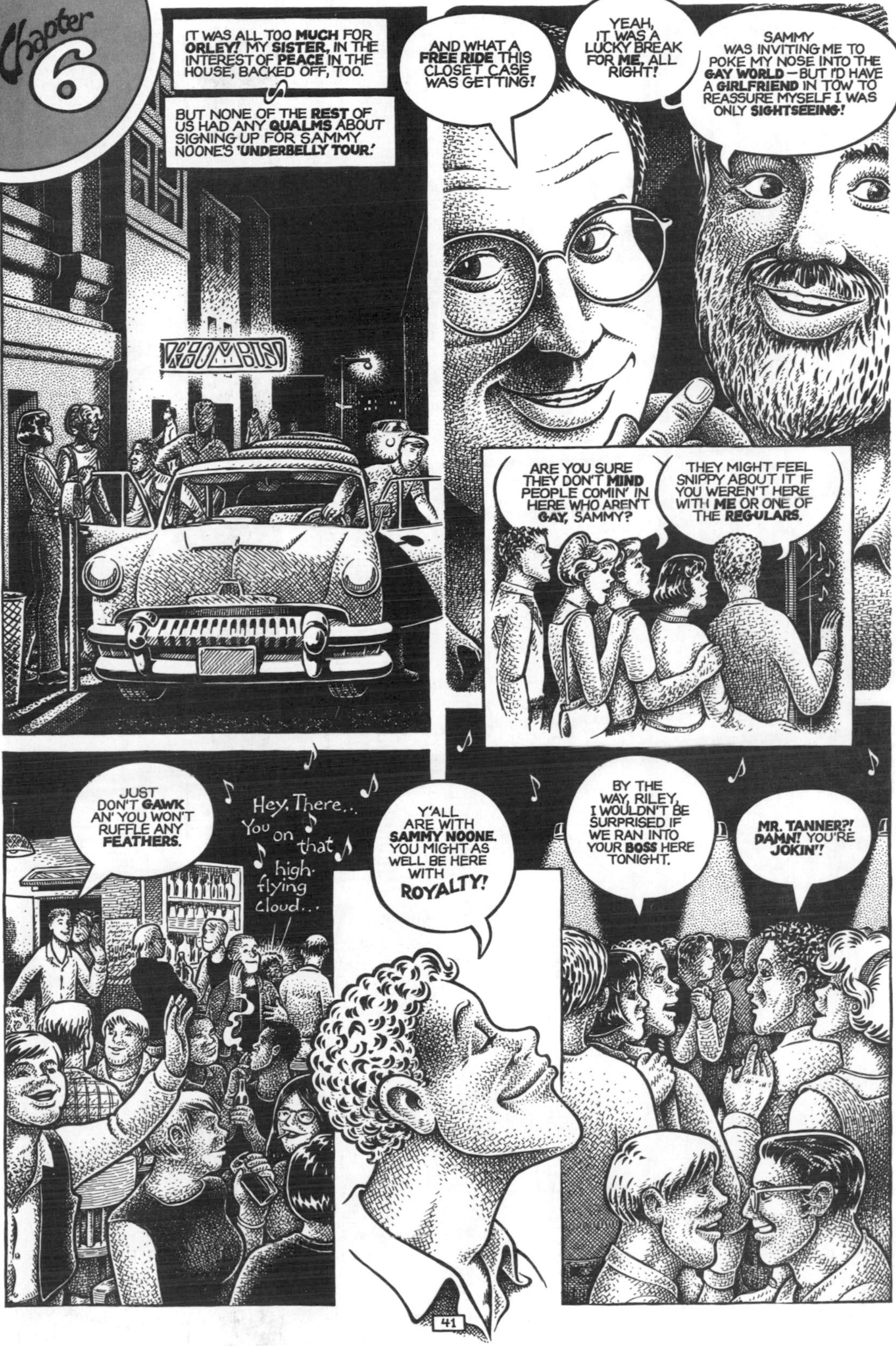

IT WAS ALL TOO MUCH FOR ORLEY! MY SISTER, IN THE INTEREST OF PEACE IN THE HOUSE, BACKED OFF, TOO.
BUT NONE OF THE REST OF US HAD ANY QUALMS ABOUT SIGNING UP FOR SAMMY NOONE'S 'UNDERBELLY TOUR.'
AND WHAT A FREE RIDE THIS CLOSET CASE WAS GETTING!
YEAH, IT WAS A LUCKY BREAK FOR ME, ALL RIGHT!
SAMMY WAS INVITING ME TO POKE MY NOSE INTO THE GAY WORLD — BUT I'D HAVE A GIRLFRIEND IN TOW TO REASSURE MYSELF I WAS ONLY SIGHTSEEING!
ARE YOU SURE THEY DON'T MIND PEOPLE COMIN' IN HERE WHO AREN'T GAY, SAMMY?
THEY MIGHT FEEL SNIPPY ABOUT IT IF YOU WEREN'T HERE WITH ME OR ONE OF THE REGULARS.
JUST DON'T GAWK AN' YOU WON'T RUFFLE ANY FEATHERS.
Hey, There.. You on that high-flying cloud...
Y'ALL ARE WITH SAMMY NOONE. YOU MIGHT AS WELL BE HERE WITH ROYALTY!
BY THE WAY, RILEY, I WOULDN'T BE SURPRISED IF WE RAN INTO YOUR BOSS HERE TONIGHT.
MR. TANNER?! DAMN! YOU'RE JOKIN'!

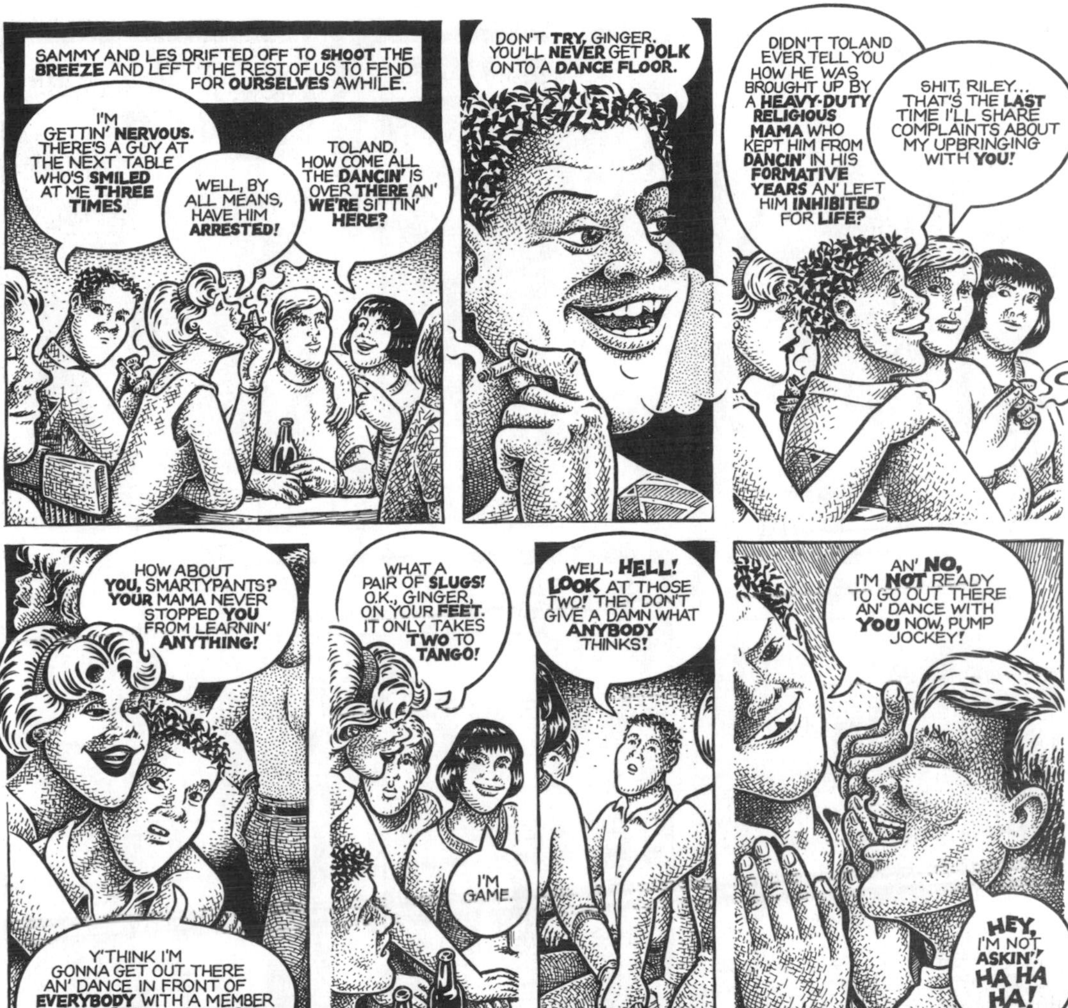
SAMMY AND LES DRIFTED OFF TO SHOOT THE BREEZE AND LEFT THE REST OF US TO FEND FOR OURSELVES AWHILE.
I'M GETTIN' NERVOUS. THERE'S A GUY AT THE NEXT TABLE WHO'S SMILED AT ME THREE TIMES.
WELL, BY ALL MEANS, HAVE HIM ARRESTED!
TOLAND, HOW COME ALL THE DANCIN' IS OVER THERE AN' WE'RE SITTIN' HERE?
DON'T TRY, GINGER. YOU'LL NEVER GET POLK ONTO A DANCE FLOOR.
DIDN'T TOLAND EVER TELL YOU HOW HE WAS BROUGHT UP BY A HEAVY-DUTY RELIGIOUS MAMA WHO KEPT HIM FROM DANCIN' IN HIS FORMATIVE YEARS AN' LEFT HIM INHIBITED FOR LIFE?
SHIT, RILEY... THAT'S THE LAST TIME I'LL SHARE COMPLAINTS ABOUT MY UPBRINGING WITH YOU!
HOW ABOUT YOU, SMARTYPANTS? YOUR MAMA NEVER STOPPED YOU FROM LEARNIN' ANYTHING!
Y'THINK I'M GONNA GET OUT THERE AN' DANCE IN FRONT OF EVERYBODY WITH A MEMBER OF THE OPPOSITE SEX?! I'D FEEL CONSPICUOUS!
WHAT A PAIR OF SLUGS! O.K., GINGER, ON YOUR FEET. IT ONLY TAKES TWO TO TANGO!
I'M GAME.
WELL, HELL! LOOK AT THOSE TWO! THEY DON'T GIVE A DAMN WHAT ANYBODY THINKS!
AN' NO, I'M NOT READY TO GO OUT THERE AN' DANCE WITH YOU NOW, PUMP JOCKEY!
HEY, I'M NOT ASKIN'! HA HA HA!
Grumble... WELL, I THINK THE GUY AT THE NEXT TABLE MAY BE ABOUT TO.
I'M GOIN' TO THE BAR FOR ANOTHER DRINK.
tap tap! tap...
THIS PLACE HAS SURE GONE DOWN-HILL SINCE THEY STARTED LETTIN' SO MANY NIGGERS IN.

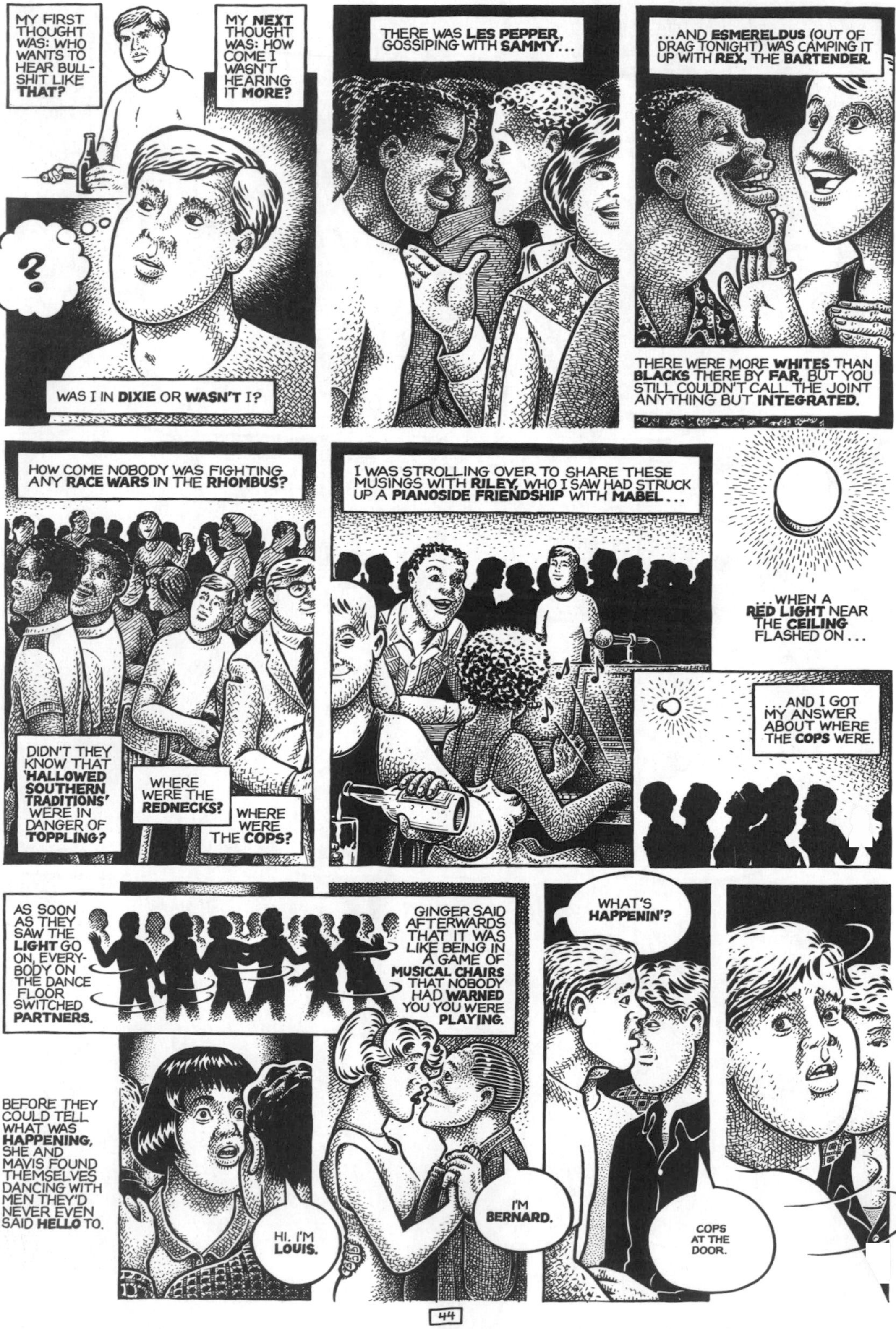

MY FIRST THOUGHT WAS: WHO WANTS TO HEAR BULL-SHIT LIKE THAT?
MY NEXT THOUGHT WAS: HOW COME I WASN'T HEARING IT MORE?
WAS I IN DIXIE OR WASN'T I?
THERE WAS LES PEPPER, GOSSIPING WITH SAMMY...
...AND ESMERELDUS (OUT OF DRAG TONIGHT) WAS CAMPING IT UP WITH REX, THE BARTENDER.
THERE WERE MORE WHITES THAN BLACKS THERE BY FAR, BUT YOU STILL COULDN'T CALL THE JOINT ANYTHING BUT INTEGRATED.
HOW COME NOBODY WAS FIGHTING ANY RACE WARS IN THE RHOMBUS?
DIDN'T THEY KNOW THAT 'HALLOWED SOUTHERN TRADITIONS' WERE IN DANGER OF TOPPLING?
WHERE WERE THE REDNECKS?
WHERE WERE THE COPS?
I WAS STROLLING OVER TO SHARE THESE MUSINGS WITH RILEY, WHO I SAW HAD STRUCK UP A PIANOSIDE FRIENDSHIP WITH MABEL...
...WHEN A RED LIGHT NEAR THE CEILING FLASHED ON...
...AND I GOT MY ANSWER ABOUT WHERE THE COPS WERE.
AS SOON AS THEY SAW THE LIGHT GO ON, EVERY-BODY ON THE DANCE FLOOR SWITCHED PARTNERS.
GINGER SAID AFTERWARDS THAT IT WAS LIKE BEING IN A GAME OF MUSICAL CHAIRS THAT NOBODY HAD WARNED YOU YOU WERE PLAYING.
BEFORE THEY COULD TELL WHAT WAS HAPPENING, SHE AND MAVIS FOUND THEMSELVES DANCING WITH MEN THEY'D NEVER EVEN SAID HELLO TO.
HI. I'M LOUIS.
I'M BERNARD.
WHAT'S HAPPENIN'?
COPS AT THE DOOR.

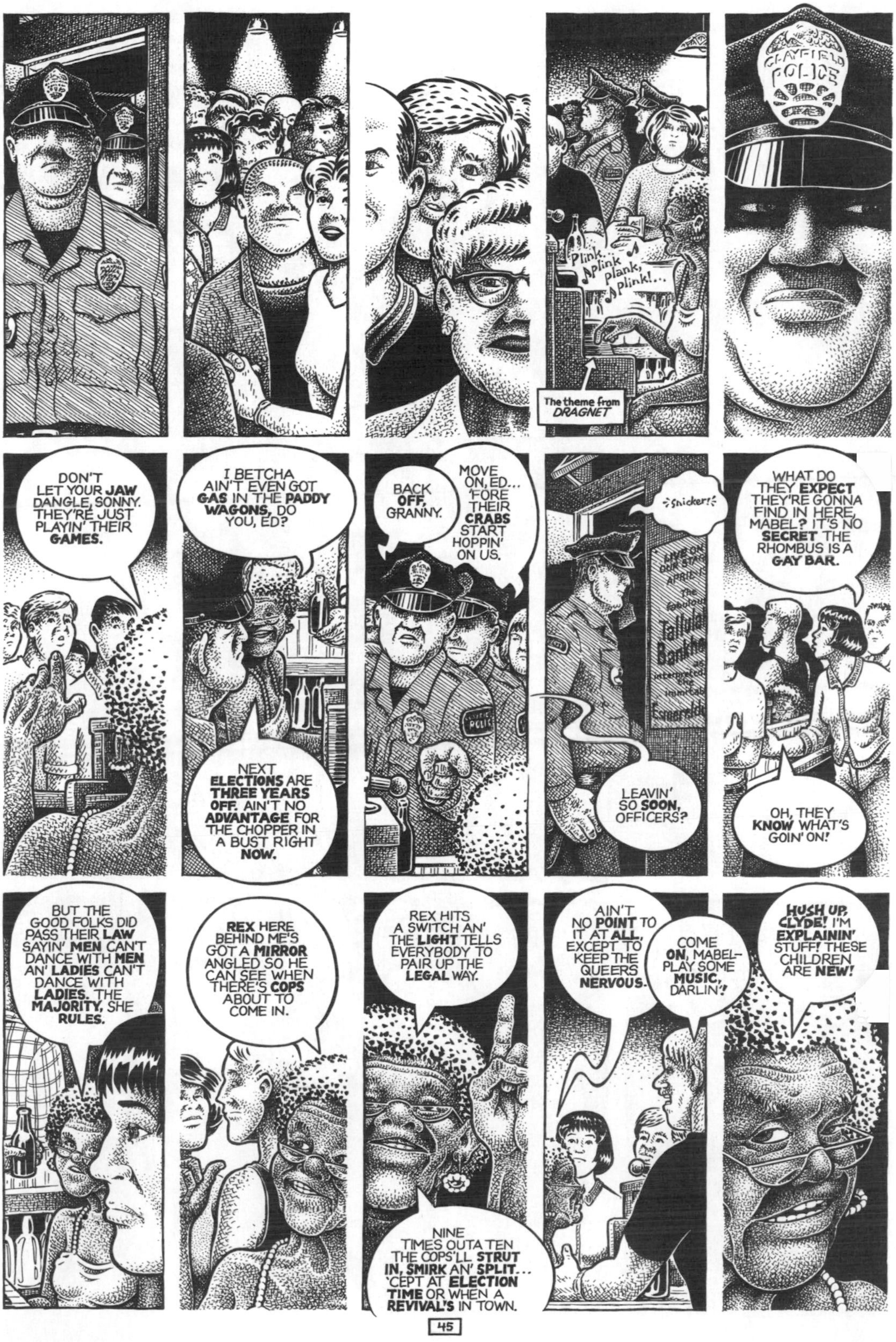
Plink, Aplink plank, Aplink!...
The theme from DRAGNET
DON'T LET YOUR JAW DANGLE, SONNY. THEY'RE JUST PLAYIN' THEIR GAMES.
I BETCHA AIN'T EVEN GOT GAS IN THE PADDY WAGONS, DO YOU, ED?
NEXT ELECTIONS ARE THREE YEARS OFF. AIN'T NO ADVANTAGE FOR THE CHOPPER IN A BUST RIGHT NOW.
BACK OFF, GRANNY.
MOVE ON, ED... 'FORE THEIR CRABS START HOPPIN' ON US.
Snicker!
LEAVIN' SO SOON, OFFICERS?
WHAT DO THEY EXPECT THEY'RE GONNA FIND IN HERE, MABEL? IT'S NO SECRET THE RHOMBUS IS A GAY BAR.
OH, THEY KNOW WHAT'S GOIN' ON!
BUT THE GOOD FOLKS DID PASS THEIR LAW SAYIN' MEN CAN'T DANCE WITH MEN AN' LADIES CAN'T DANCE WITH LADIES. THE MAJORITY, SHE RULES.
REX HERE BEHIND ME'S GOT A MIRROR ANGLED SO HE CAN SEE WHEN THERE'S COPS ABOUT TO COME IN.
REX HITS A SWITCH AN' THE LIGHT TELLS EVERYBODY TO PAIR UP THE LEGAL WAY.
NINE TIMES OUTA TEN THE COPS'LL STRUT IN, SMIRK AN' SPLIT... 'CEPT AT ELECTION TIME OR WHEN A REVIVAL'S IN TOWN.
AIN'T NO POINT TO IT AT ALL, EXCEPT TO KEEP THE QUEERS NERVOUS.
COME ON, MABEL-PLAY SOME MUSIC, DARLIN'!
HUSH UP, CLYDE! I'M EXPLAININ' STUFF! THESE CHILDREN ARE NEW!

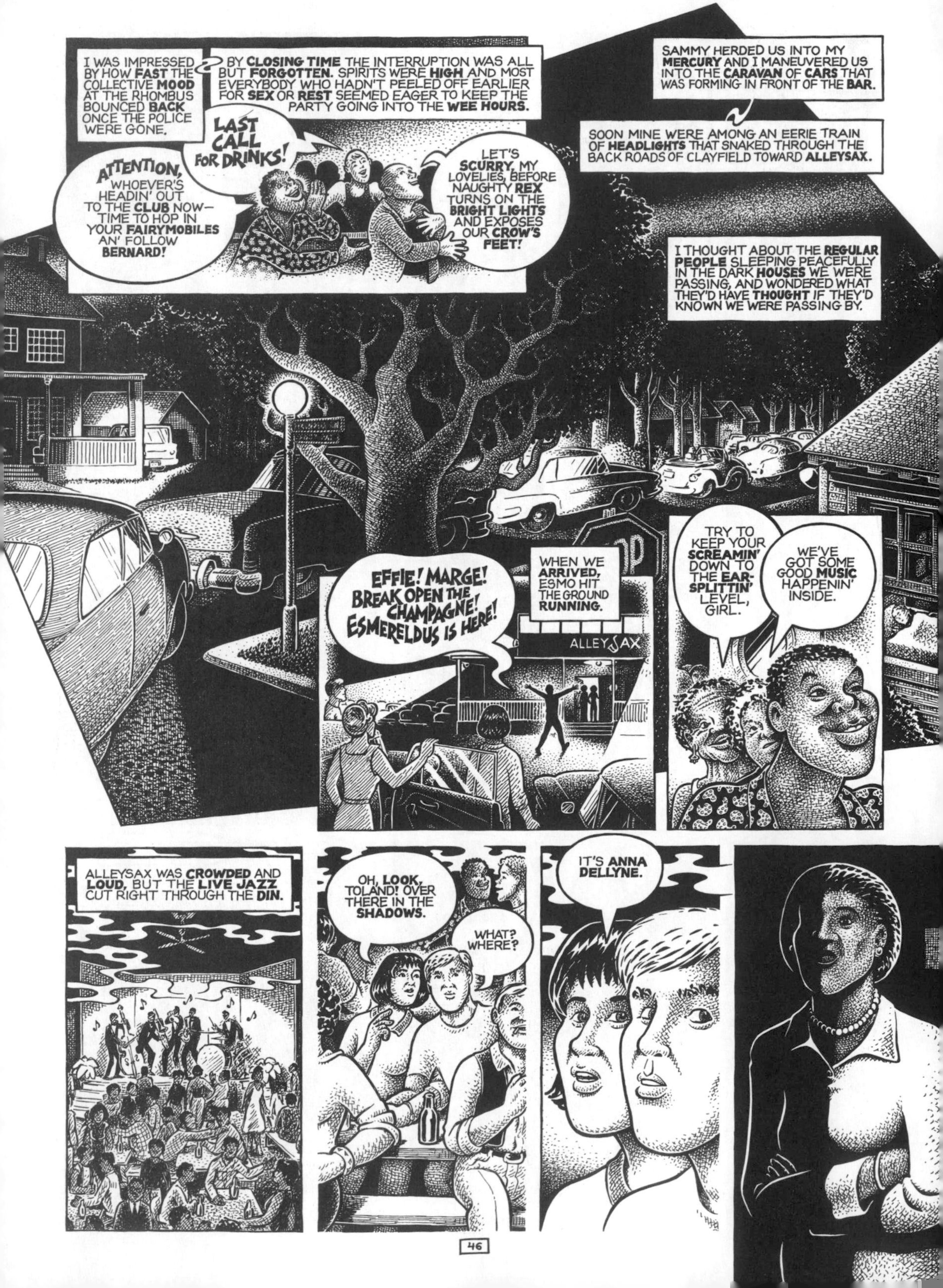
I WAS IMPRESSED BY HOW FAST THE COLLECTIVE MOOD AT THE RHOMBUS BOUNCED BACK ONCE THE POLICE WERE GONE.
BY CLOSING TIME THE INTERRUPTION WAS ALL BUT FORGOTTEN. SPIRITS WERE HIGH AND MOST EVERYBODY WHO HADN'T PEELED OFF EARLIER FOR SEX OR REST SEEMED EAGER TO KEEP THE PARTY GOING INTO THE WEE HOURS.
LAST CALL FOR DRINKS!
ATTENTION, WHOEVER'S HEADIN' OUT TO THE CLUB NOW— TIME TO HOP IN YOUR FAIRYMOBILES AN' FOLLOW BERNARD!
LET'S SCURRY, MY LOVELIES, BEFORE NAUGHTY REX TURNS ON THE BRIGHT LIGHTS AND EXPOSES OUR CROW'S FEET!
SAMMY HERDED US INTO MY MERCURY AND I MANEUVERED US INTO THE CARAVAN OF CARS THAT WAS FORMING IN FRONT OF THE BAR.
SOON MINE WERE AMONG AN EERIE TRAIN OF HEADLIGHTS THAT SNAKED THROUGH THE BACK ROADS OF CLAYFIELD TOWARD ALLEYSAX.
I THOUGHT ABOUT THE REGULAR PEOPLE SLEEPING PEACEFULLY IN THE DARK HOUSES WE WERE PASSING, AND WONDERED WHAT THEY'D HAVE THOUGHT IF THEY'D KNOWN WE WERE PASSING BY.
WHEN WE ARRIVED, ESMO HIT THE GROUND RUNNING.
EFFIE! MARGE! BREAK OPEN THE CHAMPAGNE! ESMERELDUS IS HERE!
ALLEY SAX
TRY TO KEEP YOUR SCREAMIN' DOWN TO THE EAR-SPLITTIN' LEVEL, GIRL.
WE'VE GOT SOME GOOD MUSIC HAPPENIN' INSIDE.
ALLEYSAX WAS CROWDED AND LOUD, BUT THE LIVE JAZZ CUT RIGHT THROUGH THE DIN.
OH, LOOK, TOLAND! OVER THERE IN THE SHADOWS.
WHAT? WHERE?
IT'S ANNA DELLYNE.

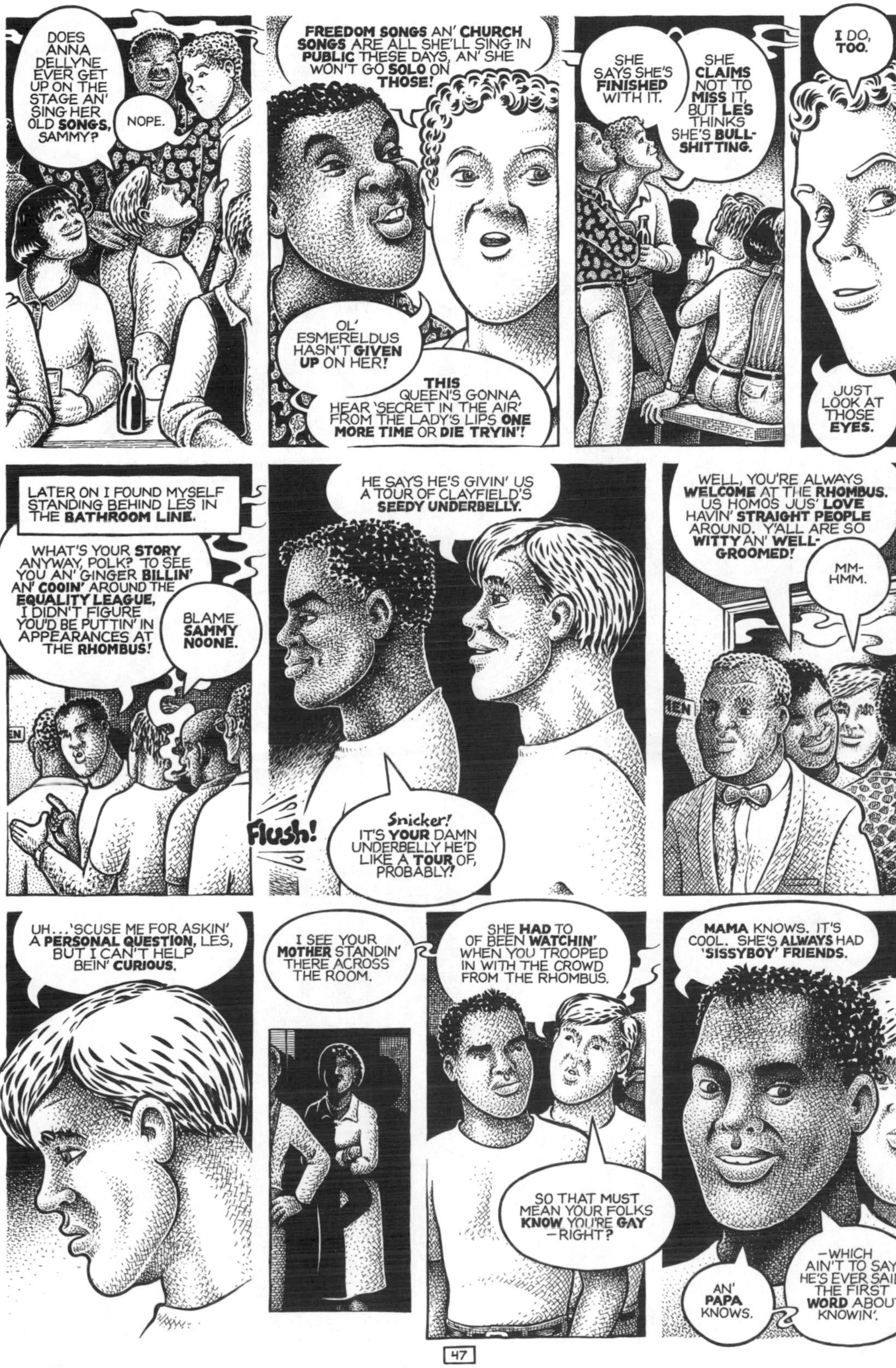
DOES ANNA DELLYNE EVER GET UP ON THE STAGE AN' SING HER OLD SONGS, SAMMY?
NOPE.
FREEDOM SONGS AN' CHURCH SONGS ARE ALL SHE'LL SING IN PUBLIC THESE DAYS, AN' SHE WON'T GO SOLO ON THOSE!
OL' ESMERELDUS HASN'T GIVEN UP ON HER!
THIS QUEEN'S GONNA HEAR 'SECRET IN THE AIR' FROM THE LADY'S LIPS ONE MORE TIME OR DIE TRYIN'!
SHE SAYS SHE'S FINISHED WITH IT.
SHE CLAIMS NOT TO MISS IT, BUT LES THINKS SHE'S BULL-SHITTING.
I DO, TOO.
JUST LOOK AT THOSE EYES.
LATER ON I FOUND MYSELF STANDING BEHIND LES IN THE BATHROOM LINE.
WHAT'S YOUR STORY ANYWAY, POLK? TO SEE YOU AN' GINGER BILLIN' AN' COOIN' AROUND THE EQUALITY LEAGUE, I DIDN'T FIGURE YOU'D BE PUTTIN' IN APPEARANCES AT THE RHOMBUS!
BLAME SAMMY NOONE.
HE SAYS HE'S GIVIN' US A TOUR OF CLAYFIELD'S SEEDY UNDERBELLY.
FLUSH!
Snicker! IT'S YOUR DAMN UNDERBELLY HE'D LIKE A TOUR OF, PROBABLY!
WELL, YOU'RE ALWAYS WELCOME AT THE RHOMBUS. US HOMOS JUS' LOVE HAVIN' STRAIGHT PEOPLE AROUND. Y'ALL ARE SO WITTY AN' WELL-GROOMED!
MM-HMM.
UH... 'SCUSE ME FOR ASKIN' A PERSONAL QUESTION, LES, BUT I CAN'T HELP BEIN' CURIOUS.
I SEE YOUR MOTHER STANDIN' THERE ACROSS THE ROOM.
SHE HAD TO OF BEEN WATCHIN' WHEN YOU TROOPED IN WITH THE CROWD FROM THE RHOMBUS.
SO THAT MUST MEAN YOUR FOLKS KNOW YOU'RE GAY —RIGHT?
MAMA KNOWS. IT'S COOL. SHE'S ALWAYS HAD 'SISSYBOY' FRIENDS.
AN' PAPA KNOWS.
—WHICH AIN'T TO SAY HE'S EVER SAID THE FIRST WORD ABOUT KNOWIN'.

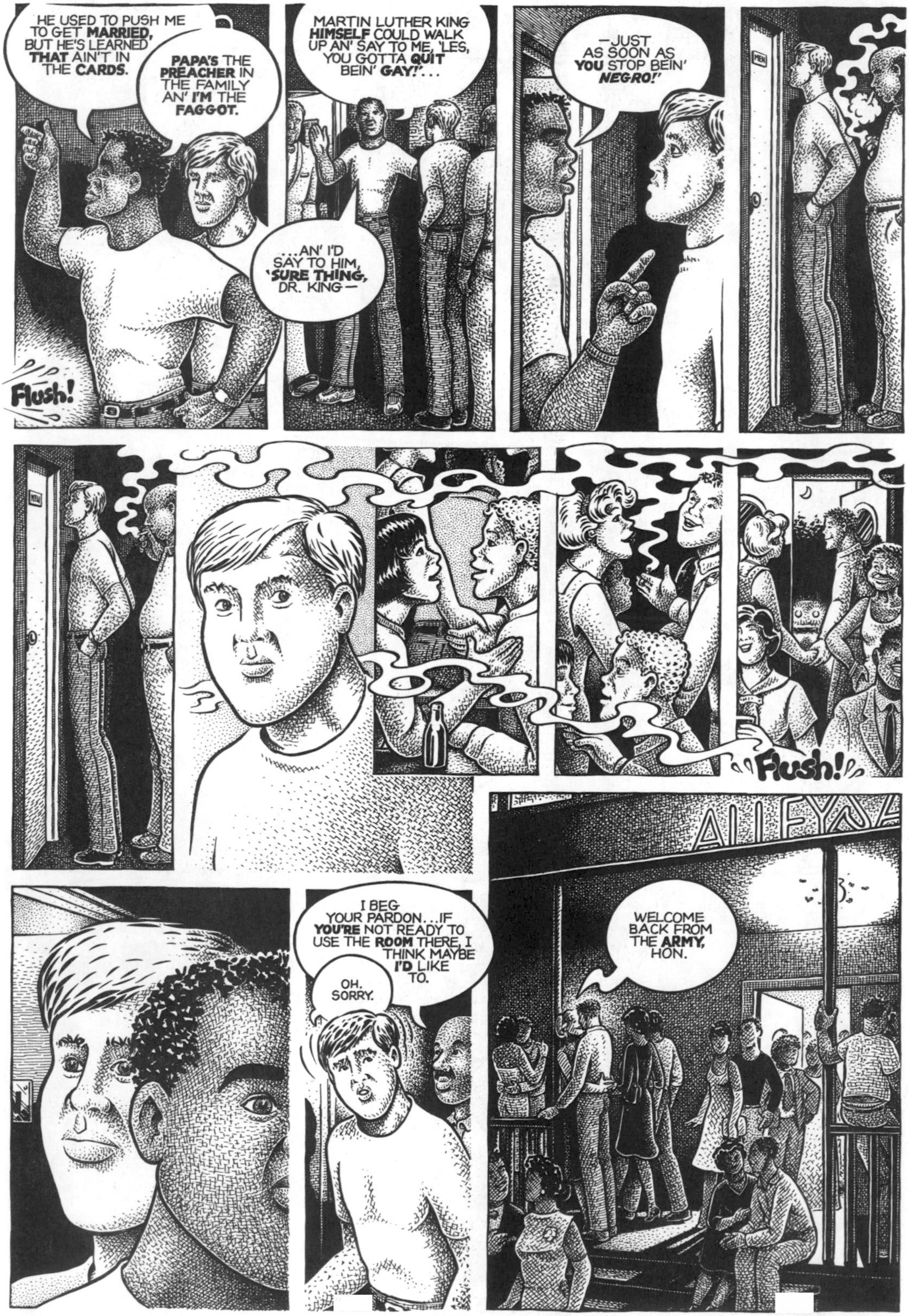
HE USED TO PUSH ME TO GET **MARRIED**, BUT HE'S LEARNED **THAT** AIN'T IN THE **CARDS**.
PAPA'S THE **PREACHER** IN THE FAMILY AN' **I'M** THE **FAGGOT**.
Flush!
MARTIN LUTHER KING **HIMSELF** COULD WALK UP AN' SAY TO ME, 'LES, YOU GOTTA **QUIT** BEIN' **GAY**!'...
...AN' I'D SAY TO HIM, **'SURE THING**, DR. KING—
—JUST AS SOON AS **YOU** STOP BEIN' ***NEGRO!'***
MEN
Flush!
WELCOME BACK FROM THE **ARMY**, HON.
I BEG YOUR PARDON...IF **YOU'RE** NOT READY TO USE THE **ROOM** THERE, I THINK MAYBE **I'D** LIKE TO.
OH. SORRY.

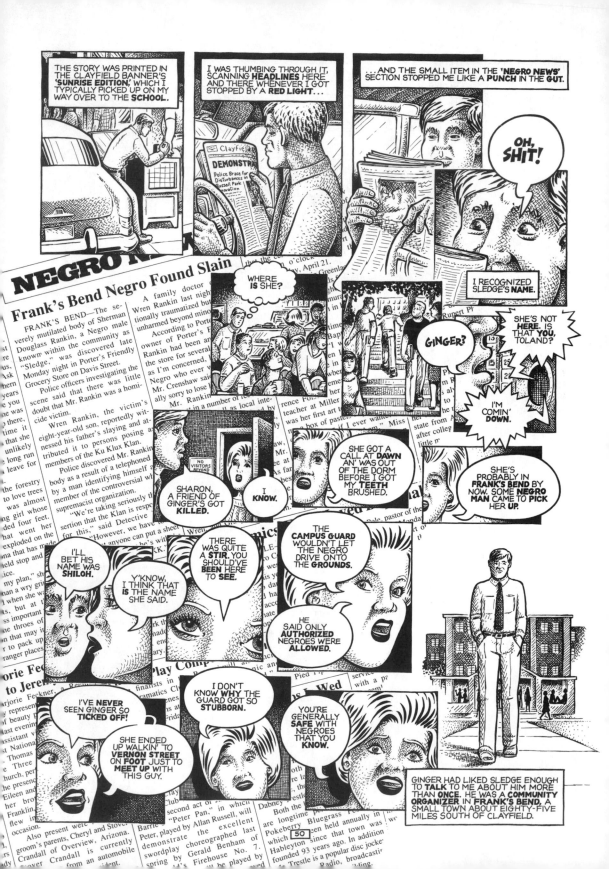

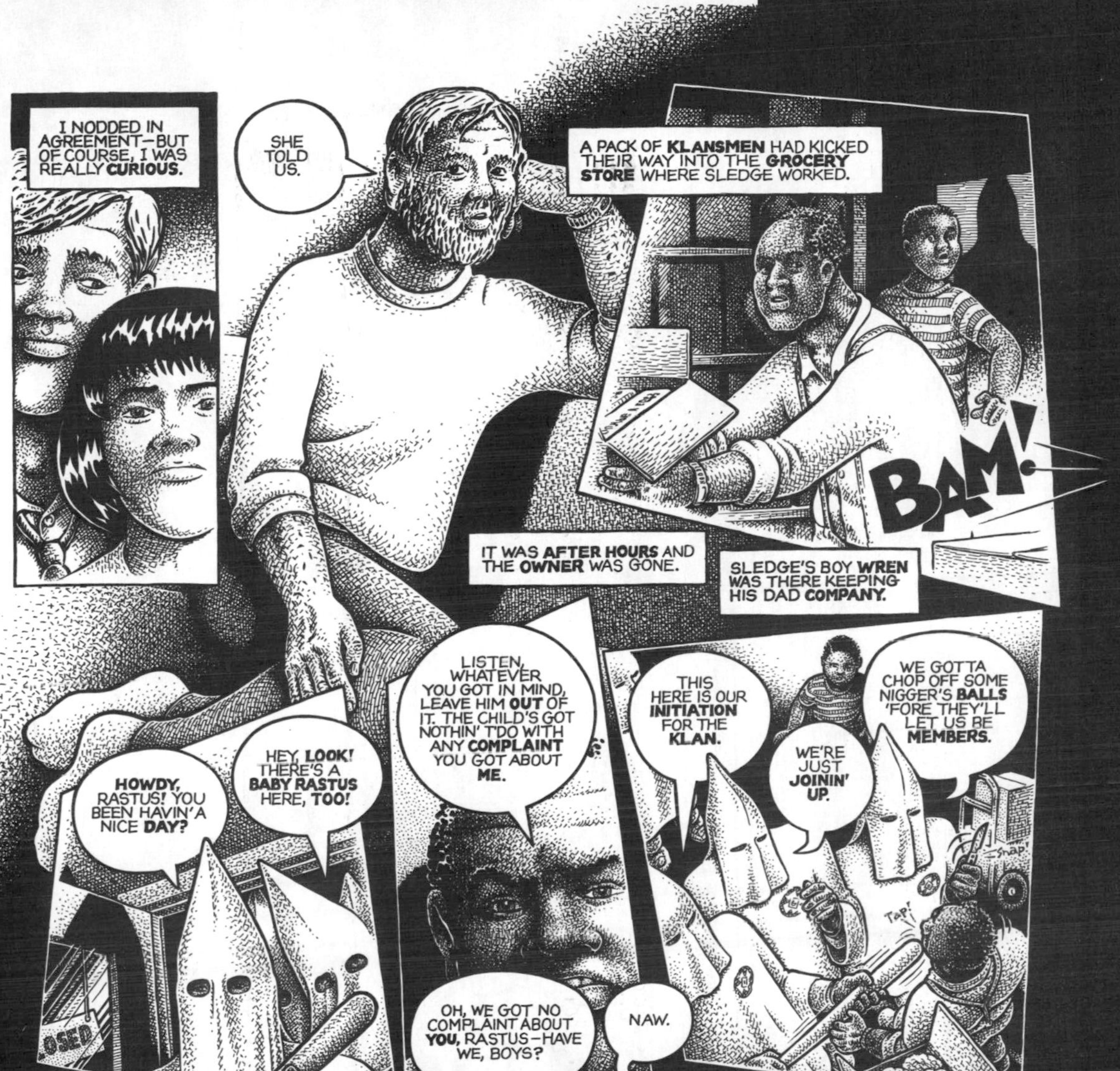
I NODDED IN AGREEMENT—BUT OF COURSE, I WAS REALLY CURIOUS.
SHE TOLD US.
A PACK OF KLANSMEN HAD KICKED THEIR WAY INTO THE GROCERY STORE WHERE SLEDGE WORKED.
BAM!
IT WAS AFTER HOURS AND THE OWNER WAS GONE.
SLEDGE'S BOY WREN WAS THERE KEEPING HIS DAD COMPANY.
HOWDY, RASTUS! YOU BEEN HAVIN' A NICE DAY?
HEY, LOOK! THERE'S A BABY RASTUS HERE, TOO!
LISTEN, WHATEVER YOU GOT IN MIND, LEAVE HIM OUT OF IT. THE CHILD'S GOT NOTHIN' T'DO WITH ANY COMPLAINT YOU GOT ABOUT ME.
OH, WE GOT NO COMPLAINT ABOUT YOU, RASTUS—HAVE WE, BOYS?
NAW.
THIS HERE IS OUR INITIATION FOR THE KLAN.
WE'RE JUST JOININ' UP.
WE GOTTA CHOP OFF SOME NIGGER'S BALLS 'FORE THEY'LL LET US BE MEMBERS.
SNAP
TAP!
YOU WERE HANDY TO THE NEIGHBORHOOD, RASTUS, SO YOU GOT ELECTED.
DADDY—
OW!
BE STILL, BOY!
TELL 'IM WHAT TO DO, RASTUS.
WREN TOLD SHILOH LATER ON THAT THE KILLERS NEVER ONCE CALLED SLEDGE BY HIS NAME. THEY KEPT SAYING 'RASTUS.'
SHILOH DOUBTED THEY EVEN KNEW WHO SLEDGE WAS. HE WAS JUST BLACK AND HANDY.

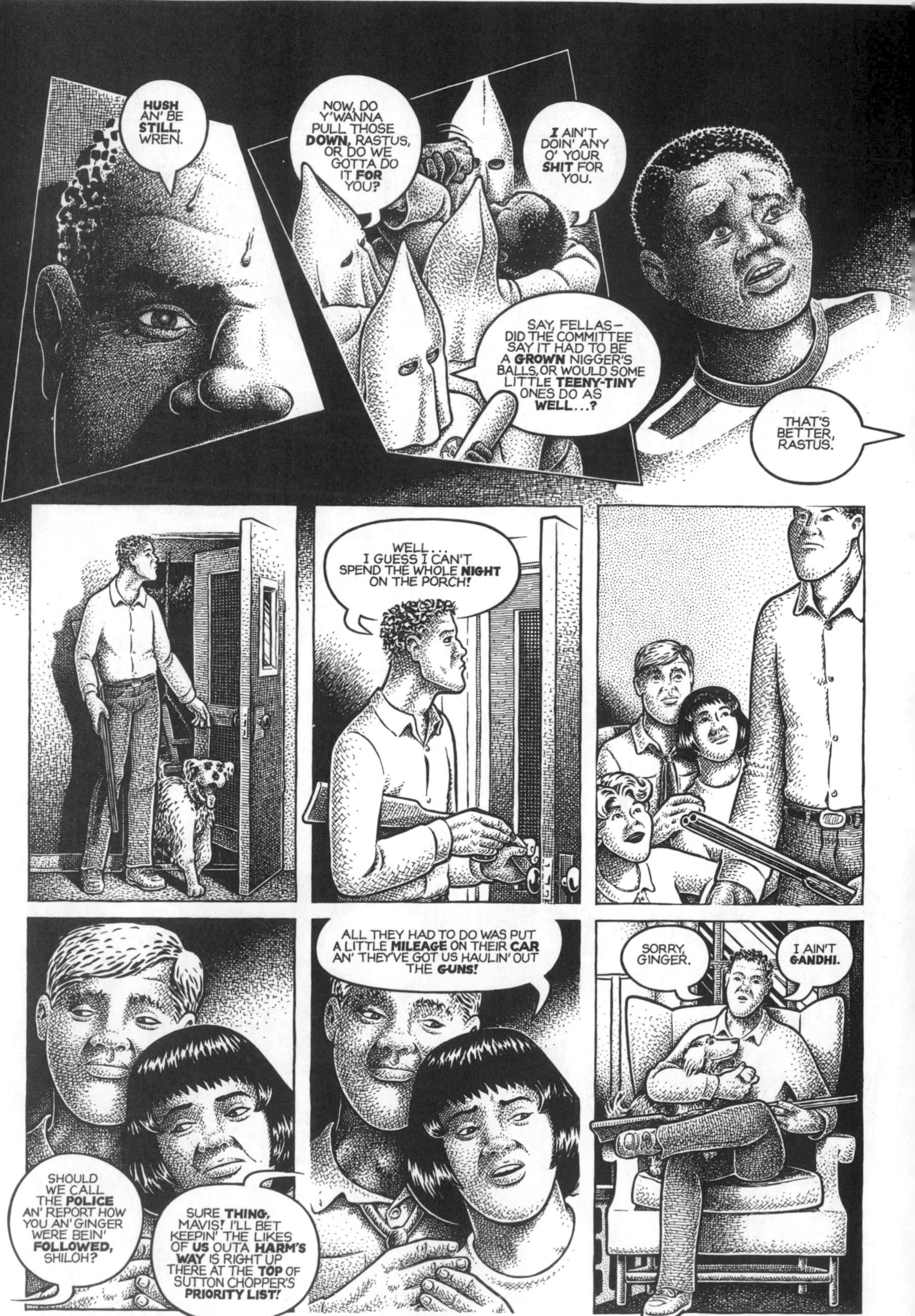
HUSH AN' BE STILL, WREN.
NOW, DO Y'WANNA PULL THOSE DOWN, RASTUS, OR DO WE GOTTA DO IT FOR YOU?
I AIN'T DOIN' ANY O' YOUR SHIT FOR YOU.
SAY, FELLAS— DID THE COMMITTEE SAY IT HAD TO BE A GROWN NIGGER'S BALLS, OR WOULD SOME LITTLE TEENY-TINY ONES DO AS WELL...?
THAT'S BETTER, RASTUS.
WELL... I GUESS I CAN'T SPEND THE WHOLE NIGHT ON THE PORCH!
SHOULD WE CALL THE POLICE AN' REPORT HOW YOU AN' GINGER WERE BEIN' FOLLOWED, SHILOH?
SURE THING, MAVIS! I'LL BET KEEPIN' THE LIKES OF US OUTA HARM'S WAY IS RIGHT UP THERE AT THE TOP OF SUTTON CHOPPER'S PRIORITY LIST!
ALL THEY HAD TO DO WAS PUT A LITTLE MILEAGE ON THEIR CAR AN' THEY'VE GOT US HAULIN' OUT THE GUNS!
SORRY, GINGER.
I AIN'T GANDHI.

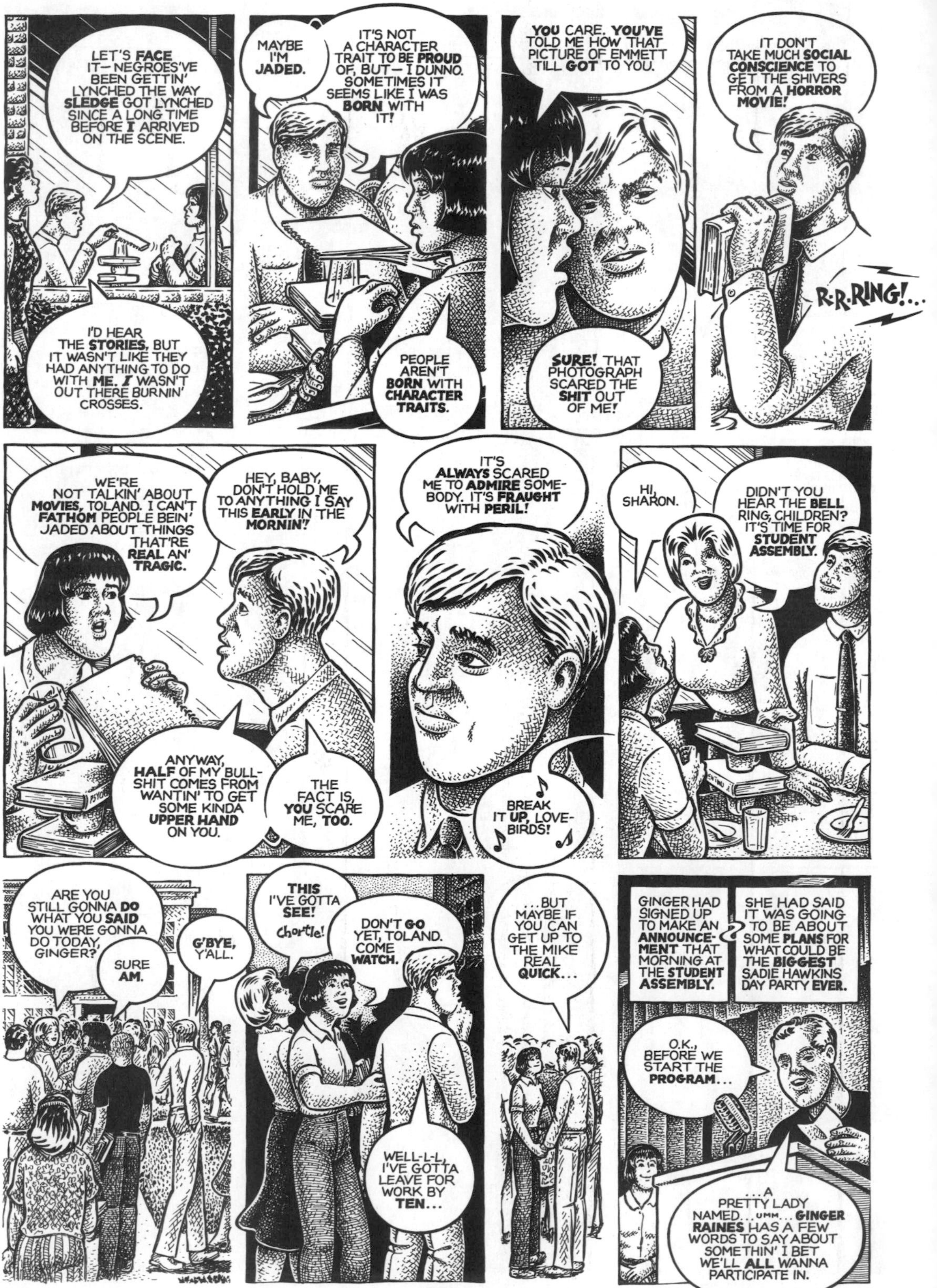
LET'S FACE IT— NEGROES'VE BEEN GETTIN' LYNCHED THE WAY SLEDGE GOT LYNCHED SINCE A LONG TIME BEFORE I ARRIVED ON THE SCENE.
I'D HEAR THE STORIES, BUT IT WASN'T LIKE THEY HAD ANYTHING TO DO WITH ME. I WASN'T OUT THERE BURNIN' CROSSES.
MAYBE I'M JADED.
IT'S NOT A CHARACTER TRAIT TO BE PROUD OF, BUT— I DUNNO. SOMETIMES IT SEEMS LIKE I WAS BORN WITH IT!
PEOPLE AREN'T BORN WITH CHARACTER TRAITS.
YOU CARE. YOU'VE TOLD ME HOW THAT PICTURE OF EMMETT TILL GOT TO YOU.
SURE! THAT PHOTOGRAPH SCARED THE SHIT OUT OF ME!
IT DON'T TAKE MUCH SOCIAL CONSCIENCE TO GET THE SHIVERS FROM A HORROR MOVIE!
R-R-RING!...
WE'RE NOT TALKIN' ABOUT MOVIES, TOLAND. I CAN'T FATHOM PEOPLE BEIN' JADED ABOUT THINGS THAT'RE REAL AN' TRAGIC.
HEY, BABY, DON'T HOLD ME TO ANYTHING I SAY THIS EARLY IN THE MORNIN'!
ANYWAY, HALF OF MY BULL-SHIT COMES FROM WANTIN' TO GET SOME KINDA UPPER HAND ON YOU.
THE FACT IS, YOU SCARE ME, TOO.
IT'S ALWAYS SCARED ME TO ADMIRE SOME-BODY. IT'S FRAUGHT WITH PERIL!
BREAK IT UP, LOVE-BIRDS!
HI, SHARON.
DIDN'T YOU HEAR THE BELL RING, CHILDREN? IT'S TIME FOR STUDENT ASSEMBLY.
ARE YOU STILL GONNA DO WHAT YOU SAID YOU WERE GONNA DO TODAY, GINGER?
SURE AM.
G'BYE, Y'ALL.
THIS I'VE GOTTA SEE!
Chortle!
DON'T GO YET, TOLAND. COME WATCH.
WELL-L-L, I'VE GOTTA LEAVE FOR WORK BY TEN...
...BUT MAYBE IF YOU CAN GET UP TO THE MIKE REAL QUICK...
GINGER HAD SIGNED UP TO MAKE AN ANNOUNCE-MENT THAT MORNING AT THE STUDENT ASSEMBLY.
SHE HAD SAID IT WAS GOING TO BE ABOUT SOME PLANS FOR WHAT COULD BE THE BIGGEST SADIE HAWKINS DAY PARTY EVER.
O.K., BEFORE WE START THE PROGRAM...
...A PRETTY LADY NAMED...UMM...GINGER RAINES HAS A FEW WORDS TO SAY ABOUT SOMETHIN' I BET WE'LL ALL WANNA PARTICIPATE IN.

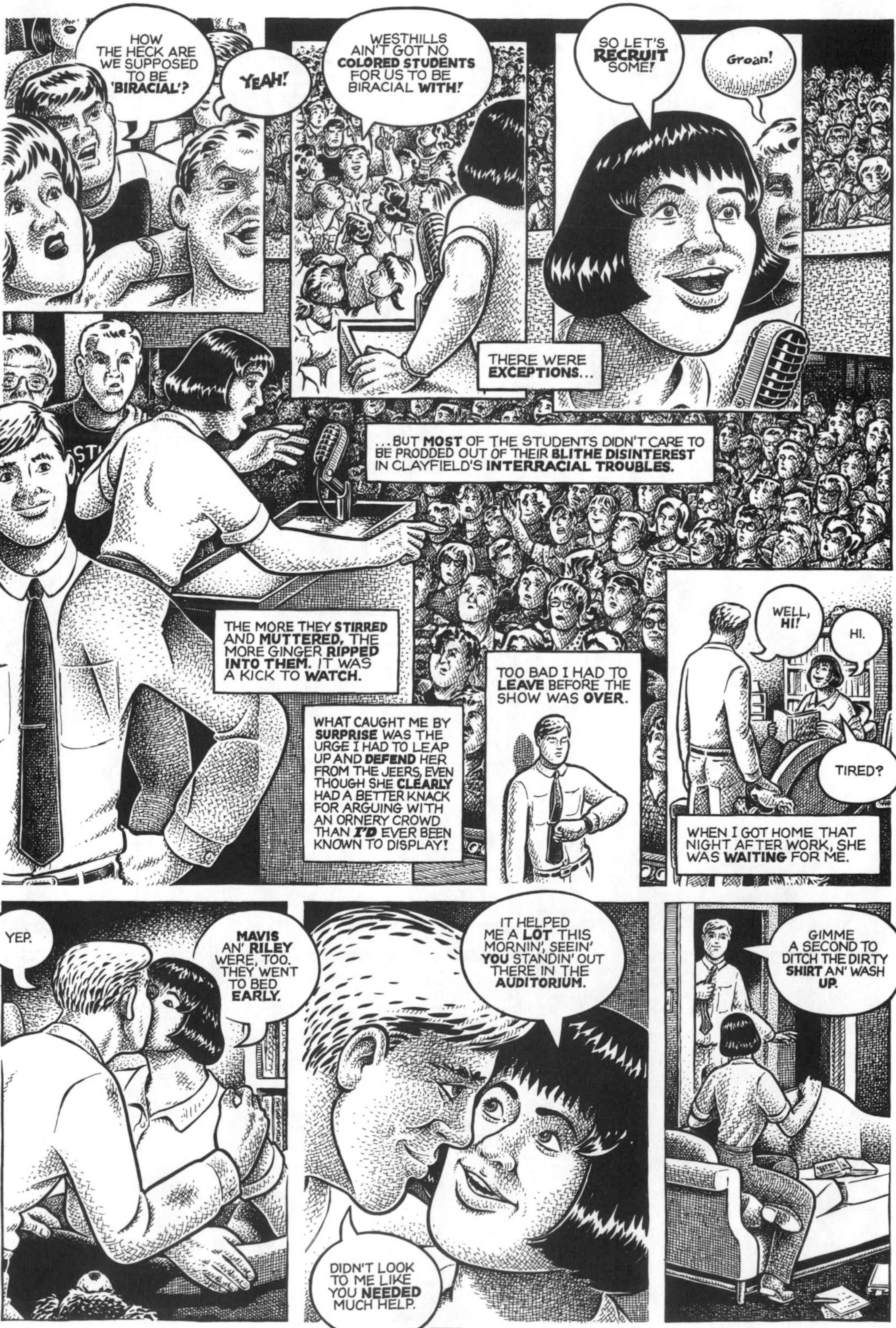

HOW THE HECK ARE WE SUPPOSED TO BE 'BIRACIAL'?
YEAH!
WESTHILLS AIN'T GOT NO COLORED STUDENTS FOR US TO BE BIRACIAL WITH!
SO LET'S RECRUIT SOME!
Groan!
THERE WERE EXCEPTIONS...
...BUT MOST OF THE STUDENTS DIDN'T CARE TO BE PRODDED OUT OF THEIR BLITHE DISINTEREST IN CLAYFIELD'S INTERRACIAL TROUBLES.
THE MORE THEY STIRRED AND MUTTERED, THE MORE GINGER RIPPED INTO THEM. IT WAS A KICK TO WATCH.
WHAT CAUGHT ME BY SURPRISE WAS THE URGE I HAD TO LEAP UP AND DEFEND HER FROM THE JEERS, EVEN THOUGH SHE CLEARLY HAD A BETTER KNACK FOR ARGUING WITH AN ORNERY CROWD THAN I'D EVER BEEN KNOWN TO DISPLAY!
TOO BAD I HAD TO LEAVE BEFORE THE SHOW WAS OVER.
WELL, HI!
HI.
TIRED?
WHEN I GOT HOME THAT NIGHT AFTER WORK, SHE WAS WAITING FOR ME.
YEP.
MAVIS AN' RILEY WERE, TOO. THEY WENT TO BED EARLY.
IT HELPED ME A LOT THIS MORNIN', SEEIN' YOU STANDIN' OUT THERE IN THE AUDITORIUM.
DIDN'T LOOK TO ME LIKE YOU NEEDED MUCH HELP.
GIMME A SECOND TO DITCH THE DIRTY SHIRT AN' WASH UP.

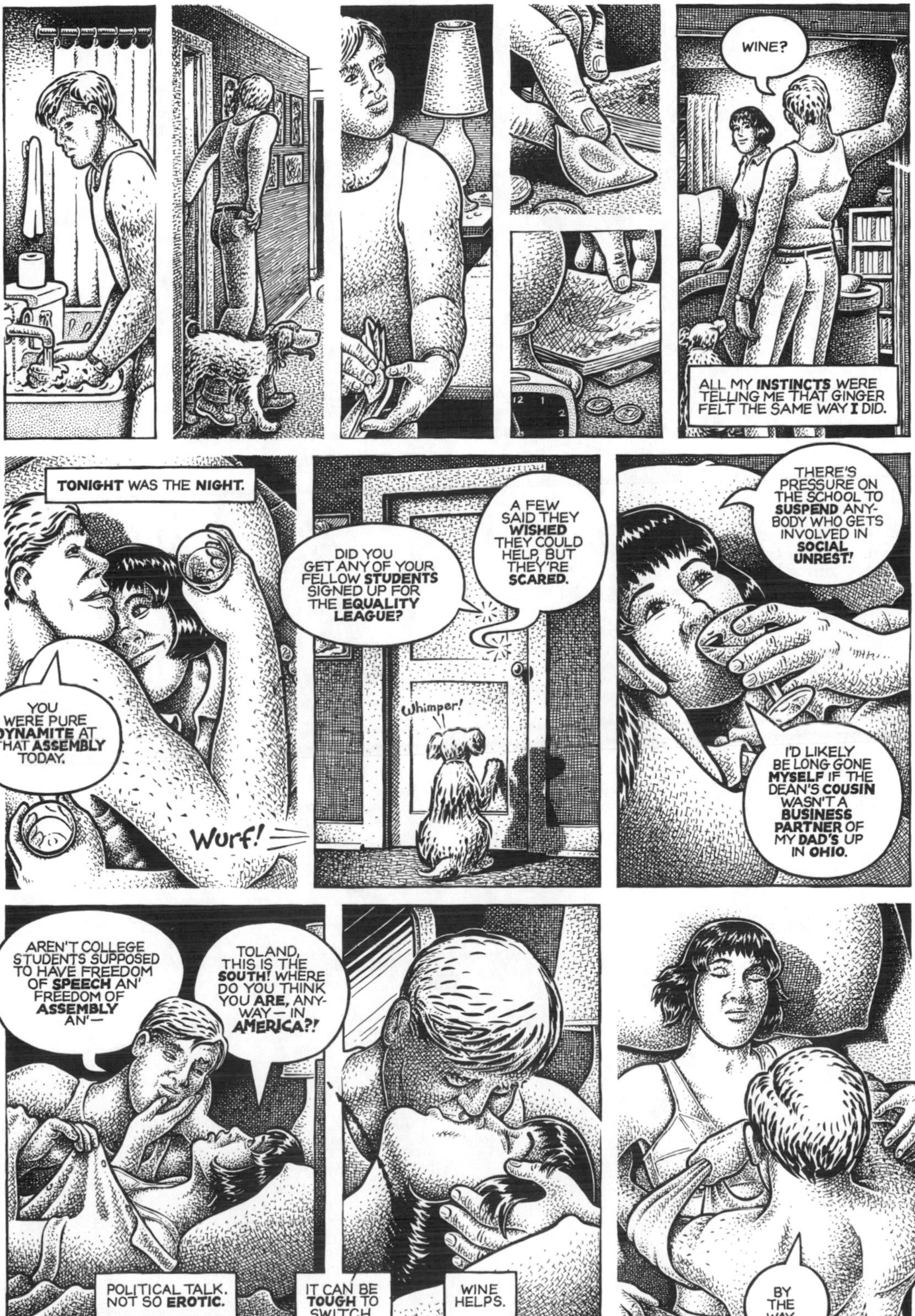
WINE?
ALL MY INSTINCTS WERE TELLING ME THAT GINGER FELT THE SAME WAY I DID.
TONIGHT WAS THE NIGHT.
YOU WERE PURE DYNAMITE AT THAT ASSEMBLY TODAY.
Wurf!
DID YOU GET ANY OF YOUR FELLOW STUDENTS SIGNED UP FOR THE EQUALITY LEAGUE?
A FEW SAID THEY WISHED THEY COULD HELP, BUT THEY'RE SCARED.
Whimper!
THERE'S PRESSURE ON THE SCHOOL TO SUSPEND ANYBODY WHO GETS INVOLVED IN SOCIAL UNREST!
I'D LIKELY BE LONG GONE MYSELF IF THE DEAN'S COUSIN WASN'T A BUSINESS PARTNER OF MY DAD'S UP IN OHIO.
AREN'T COLLEGE STUDENTS SUPPOSED TO HAVE FREEDOM OF SPEECH AN' FREEDOM OF ASSEMBLY AN'—
TOLAND, THIS IS THE SOUTH! WHERE DO YOU THINK YOU ARE, ANYWAY— IN AMERICA?!
POLITICAL TALK. NOT SO EROTIC.
IT CAN BE TOUGH TO SWITCH GEARS.
WINE HELPS.
BY THE WAY...

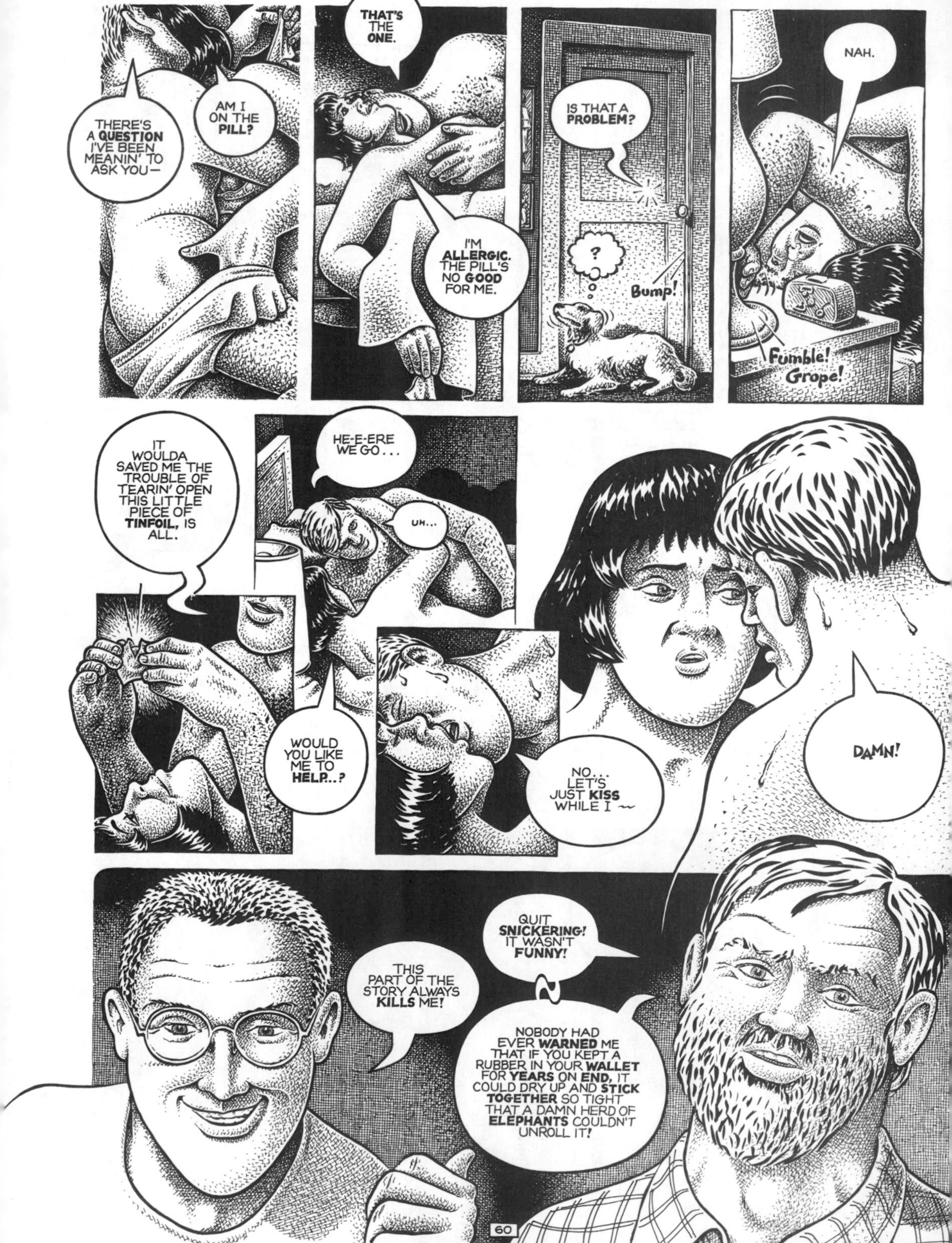
THERE'S A **QUESTION** I'VE BEEN MEANIN' TO ASK YOU—
AM I ON THE **PILL?**
THAT'S THE **ONE.**
I'M **ALLERGIC.** THE PILL'S NO **GOOD** FOR ME.
IS THAT A **PROBLEM?**
?
Bump!
NAH.
Fumble! Grope!
IT WOULDA SAVED ME THE TROUBLE OF TEARIN' OPEN THIS LITTLE PIECE OF **TINFOIL,** IS ALL.
HE-E-ERE WE GO . . .
UH...
WOULD YOU LIKE ME TO **HELP...?**
NO... LET'S JUST **KISS** WHILE I ~
DAMN!
THIS PART OF THE STORY ALWAYS **KILLS** ME!
QUIT **SNICKERING!** IT WASN'T **FUNNY!**
NOBODY HAD EVER **WARNED** ME THAT IF YOU KEPT A RUBBER IN YOUR **WALLET** FOR **YEARS ON END,** IT COULD DRY UP AND **STICK TOGETHER** SO TIGHT THAT A DAMN HERD OF **ELEPHANTS** COULDN'T UNROLL IT!

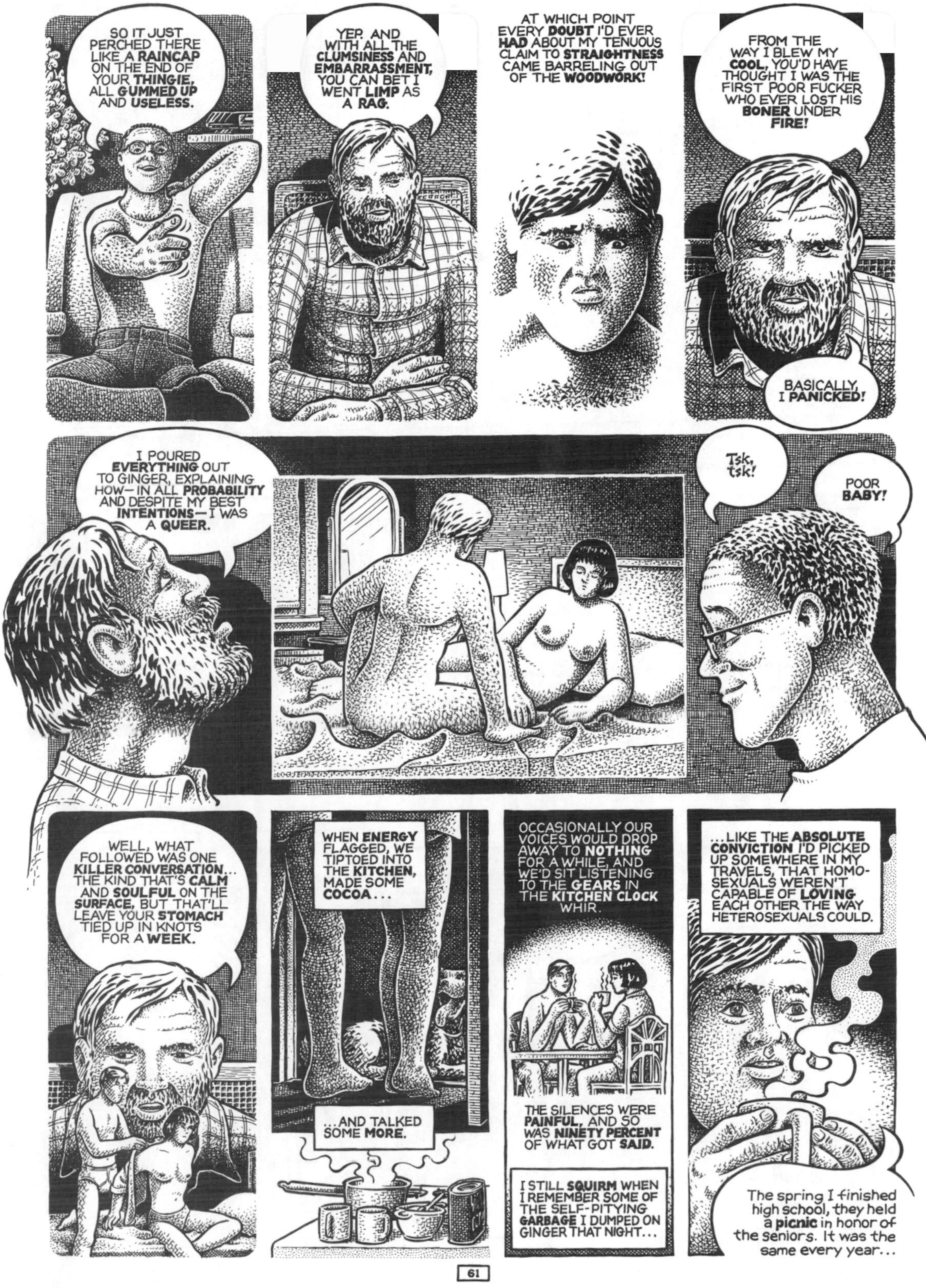
SO IT JUST PERCHED THERE LIKE A RAINCAP ON THE END OF YOUR THINGIE, ALL GUMMED UP AND USELESS.
YEP. AND WITH ALL THE CLUMSINESS AND EMBARRASSMENT, YOU CAN BET I WENT LIMP AS A RAG.
AT WHICH POINT EVERY DOUBT I'D EVER HAD ABOUT MY TENUOUS CLAIM TO STRAIGHTNESS CAME BARRELING OUT OF THE WOODWORK!
FROM THE WAY I BLEW MY COOL, YOU'D HAVE THOUGHT I WAS THE FIRST POOR FUCKER WHO EVER LOST HIS BONER UNDER FIRE!
BASICALLY, I PANICKED!
I POURED EVERYTHING OUT TO GINGER, EXPLAINING HOW—IN ALL PROBABILITY AND DESPITE MY BEST INTENTIONS—I WAS A QUEER.
Tsk, tsk!
POOR BABY!
WELL, WHAT FOLLOWED WAS ONE KILLER CONVERSATION... THE KIND THAT'S CALM AND SOULFUL ON THE SURFACE, BUT THAT'LL LEAVE YOUR STOMACH TIED UP IN KNOTS FOR A WEEK.
WHEN ENERGY FLAGGED, WE TIPTOED INTO THE KITCHEN, MADE SOME COCOA...
...AND TALKED SOME MORE.
OCCASIONALLY OUR VOICES WOULD DROP AWAY TO NOTHING FOR A WHILE, AND WE'D SIT LISTENING TO THE GEARS IN THE KITCHEN CLOCK WHIR.
THE SILENCES WERE PAINFUL, AND SO WAS NINETY PERCENT OF WHAT GOT SAID.
I STILL SQUIRM WHEN I REMEMBER SOME OF THE SELF-PITYING GARBAGE I DUMPED ON GINGER THAT NIGHT...
...LIKE THE ABSOLUTE CONVICTION I'D PICKED UP SOMEWHERE IN MY TRAVELS, THAT HOMO-SEXUALS WEREN'T CAPABLE OF LOVING EACH OTHER THE WAY HETEROSEXUALS COULD.
The spring I finished high school, they held a picnic in honor of the seniors. It was the same every year...

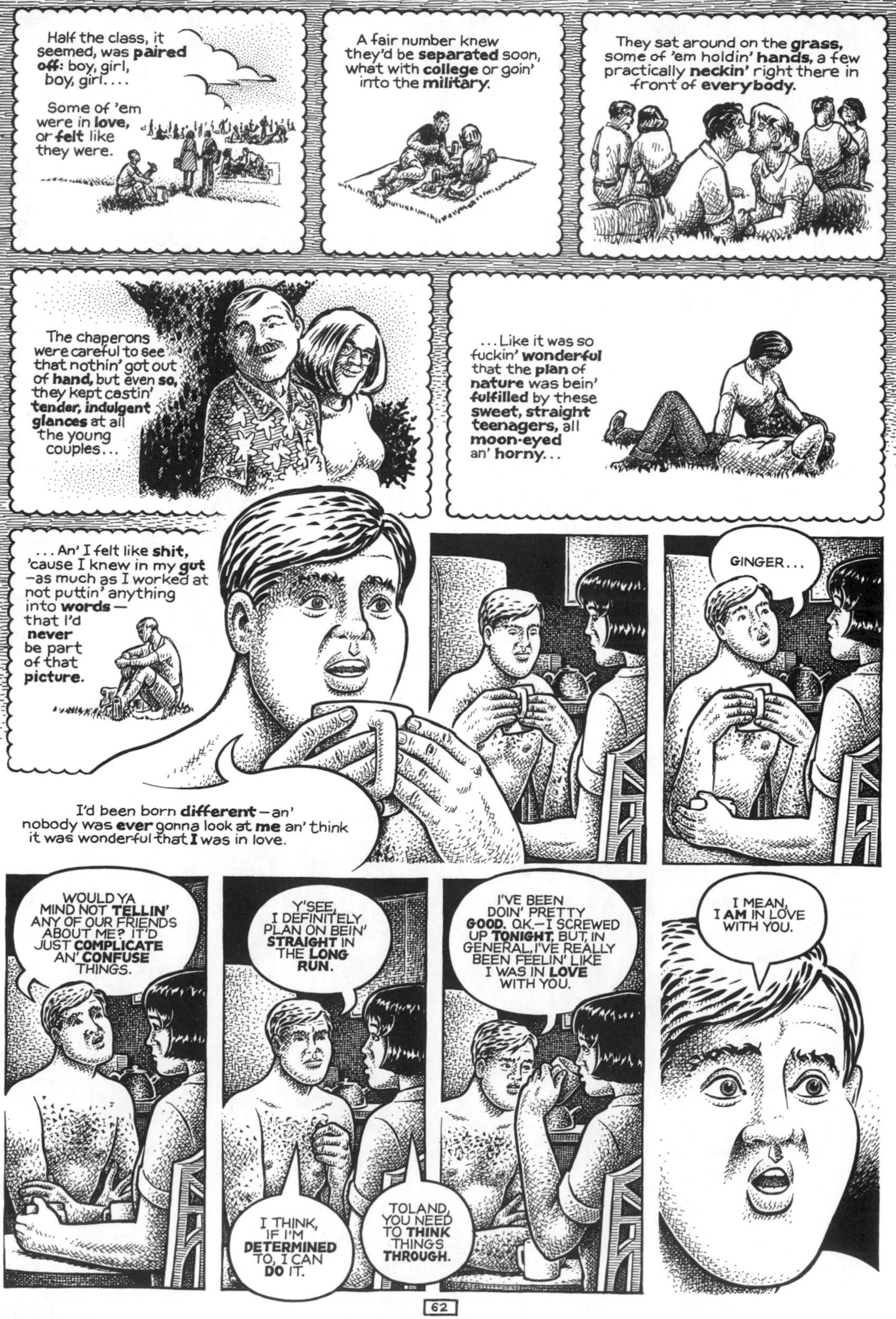

Half the class, it seemed, was **paired off**: boy, girl, boy, girl....
Some of 'em were in **love**, or **felt** like they were.
A fair number knew they'd be **separated** soon, what with **college** or goin' into the **military**.
They sat around on the **grass**, some of 'em holdin' **hands**, a few practically **neckin'** right there in front of **everybody**.
The chaperons were careful to see that nothin' got out of **hand**, but even **so**, they kept castin' **tender, indulgent glances** at all the young couples...
...Like it was so fuckin' **wonderful** that the **plan** of **nature** was bein' **fulfilled** by these **sweet, straight teenagers**, all **moon-eyed** an' **horny**...
...An' I felt like **shit**, 'cause I knew in my **gut** —as much as I worked at not puttin' anything into **words**— that I'd **never** be part of that **picture**.
I'd been born **different** —an' nobody was **ever** gonna look at **me** an' think it was wonderful that **I** was in love.
GINGER...
WOULD YA MIND NOT **TELLIN'** ANY OF OUR FRIENDS ABOUT ME? IT'D JUST **COMPLICATE** AN' **CONFUSE** THINGS.
Y'SEE, I DEFINITELY PLAN ON BEIN' **STRAIGHT** IN THE **LONG RUN**.
I THINK, IF I'M **DETERMINED** TO, I CAN **DO** IT.
TOLAND, YOU NEED TO **THINK** THINGS **THROUGH**.
I'VE BEEN DOIN' PRETTY **GOOD**. O.K.—I SCREWED UP **TONIGHT**, BUT, IN GENERAL, I'VE REALLY BEEN FEELIN' LIKE I WAS IN **LOVE** WITH YOU.
I MEAN, I **AM** IN LOVE WITH YOU.

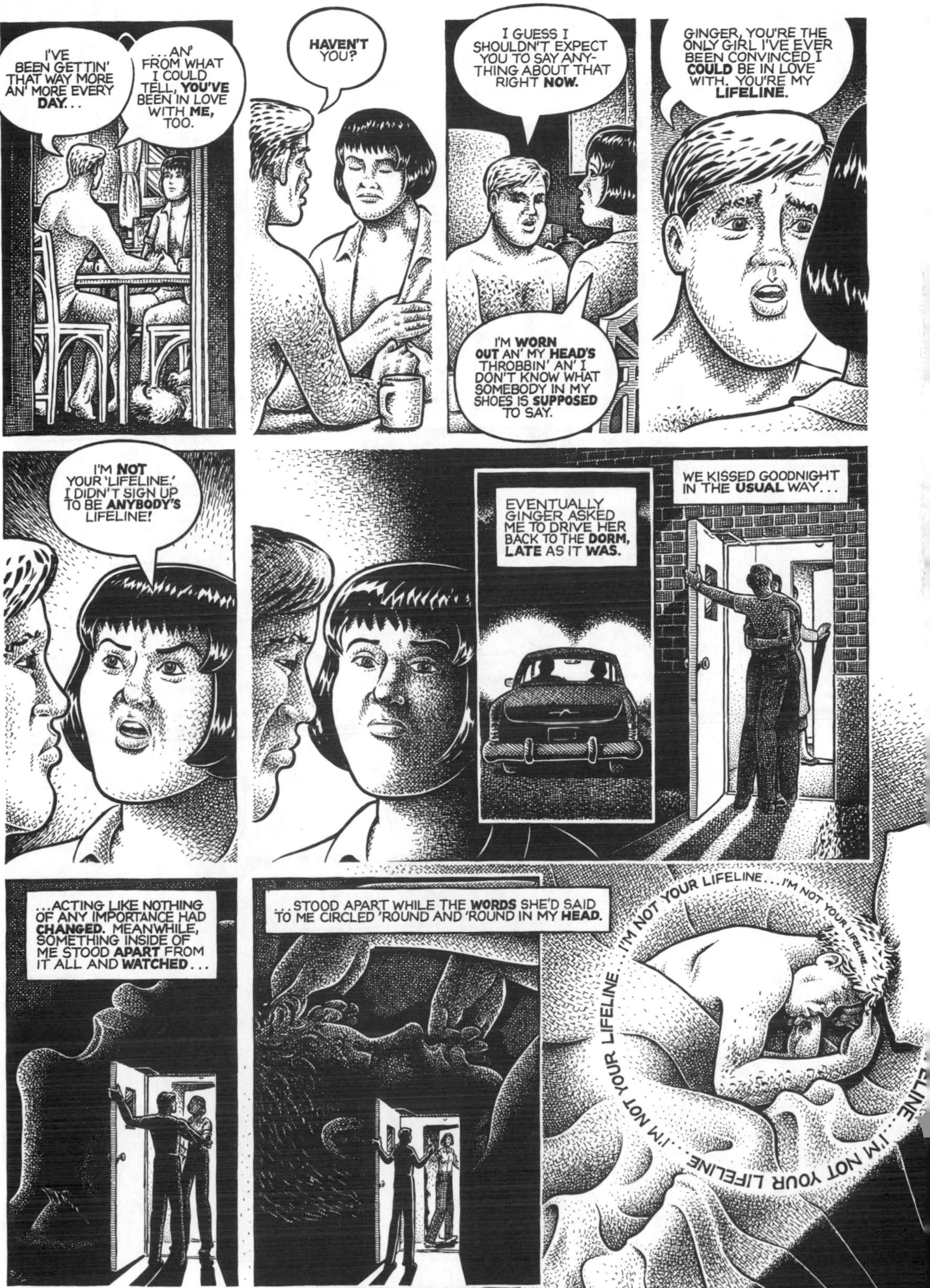
I'VE BEEN GETTIN' THAT WAY MORE AN' MORE EVERY DAY...
...AN' FROM WHAT I COULD TELL, YOU'VE BEEN IN LOVE WITH ME, TOO.
HAVEN'T YOU?
I GUESS I SHOULDN'T EXPECT YOU TO SAY ANY-THING ABOUT THAT RIGHT NOW.
I'M WORN OUT AN' MY HEAD'S THROBBIN' AN' I DON'T KNOW WHAT SOMEBODY IN MY SHOES IS SUPPOSED TO SAY.
GINGER, YOU'RE THE ONLY GIRL I'VE EVER BEEN CONVINCED I COULD BE IN LOVE WITH. YOU'RE MY LIFELINE.
I'M NOT YOUR 'LIFELINE.' I DIDN'T SIGN UP TO BE ANYBODY'S LIFELINE!
EVENTUALLY GINGER ASKED ME TO DRIVE HER BACK TO THE DORM, LATE AS IT WAS.
WE KISSED GOODNIGHT IN THE USUAL WAY...
...ACTING LIKE NOTHING OF ANY IMPORTANCE HAD CHANGED. MEANWHILE, SOMETHING INSIDE OF ME STOOD APART FROM IT ALL AND WATCHED...
...STOOD APART WHILE THE WORDS SHE'D SAID TO ME CIRCLED 'ROUND AND 'ROUND IN MY HEAD.
I'M NOT YOUR LIFELINE...I'M NOT YOUR LIFELINE...I'M NOT YOUR LIFELINE...I'M NOT YOUR LIFELINE...I'M NOT YOUR LIFELINE

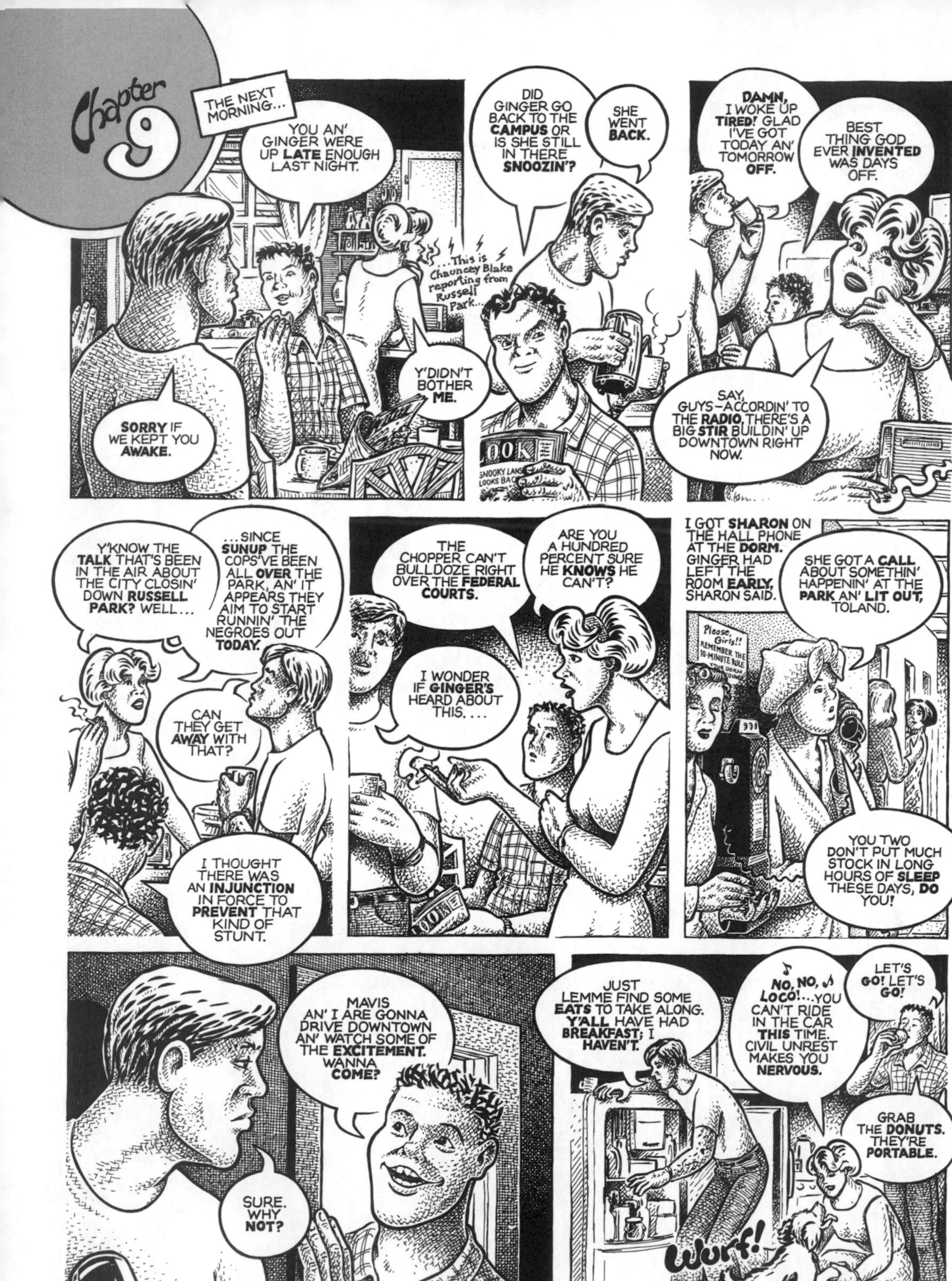
Chapter 9
THE NEXT MORNING...
YOU AN' GINGER WERE UP LATE ENOUGH LAST NIGHT.
SORRY IF WE KEPT YOU AWAKE.
...This is Chauncey Blake reporting from Russell Park...
Y'DIDN'T BOTHER ME.
DID GINGER GO BACK TO THE CAMPUS OR IS SHE STILL IN THERE SNOOZIN'?
SHE WENT BACK.
LOOK
SNOOKY LANS LOOKS BAC
DAMN, I WOKE UP TIRED! GLAD I'VE GOT TODAY AN' TOMORROW OFF.
BEST THING GOD EVER INVENTED WAS DAYS OFF.
SAY, GUYS—ACCORDIN' TO THE RADIO, THERE'S A BIG STIR BUILDIN' UP DOWNTOWN RIGHT NOW.
Y'KNOW THE TALK THAT'S BEEN IN THE AIR ABOUT THE CITY CLOSIN' DOWN RUSSELL PARK? WELL...
...SINCE SUNUP THE COPS'VE BEEN ALL OVER THE PARK, AN' IT APPEARS THEY AIM TO START RUNNIN' THE NEGROES OUT TODAY.
CAN THEY GET AWAY WITH THAT?
I THOUGHT THERE WAS AN INJUNCTION IN FORCE TO PREVENT THAT KIND OF STUNT.
THE CHOPPER CAN'T BULLDOZE RIGHT OVER THE FEDERAL COURTS.
ARE YOU A HUNDRED PERCENT SURE HE KNOWS HE CAN'T?
I WONDER IF GINGER'S HEARD ABOUT THIS....
I GOT SHARON ON THE HALL PHONE AT THE DORM. GINGER HAD LEFT THE ROOM EARLY, SHARON SAID.
SHE GOT A CALL ABOUT SOMETHIN' HAPPENIN' AT THE PARK AN' LIT OUT, TOLAND.
Please, Girls!! REMEMBER THE 10-MINUTE RULE
YOU TWO DON'T PUT MUCH STOCK IN LONG HOURS OF SLEEP THESE DAYS, DO YOU!
MAVIS AN' I ARE GONNA DRIVE DOWNTOWN AN' WATCH SOME OF THE EXCITEMENT. WANNA COME?
SURE. WHY NOT?
JUST LEMME FIND SOME EATS TO TAKE ALONG. Y'ALL HAVE HAD BREAKFAST; I HAVEN'T.
NO, NO, LOCO!...YOU CAN'T RIDE IN THE CAR THIS TIME. CIVIL UNREST MAKES YOU NERVOUS.
LET'S GO! LET'S GO!
GRAB THE DONUTS. THEY'RE PORTABLE.
Wurf!
WE PILED INTO RILEY'S CAR AND HEADED DOWNTOWN.

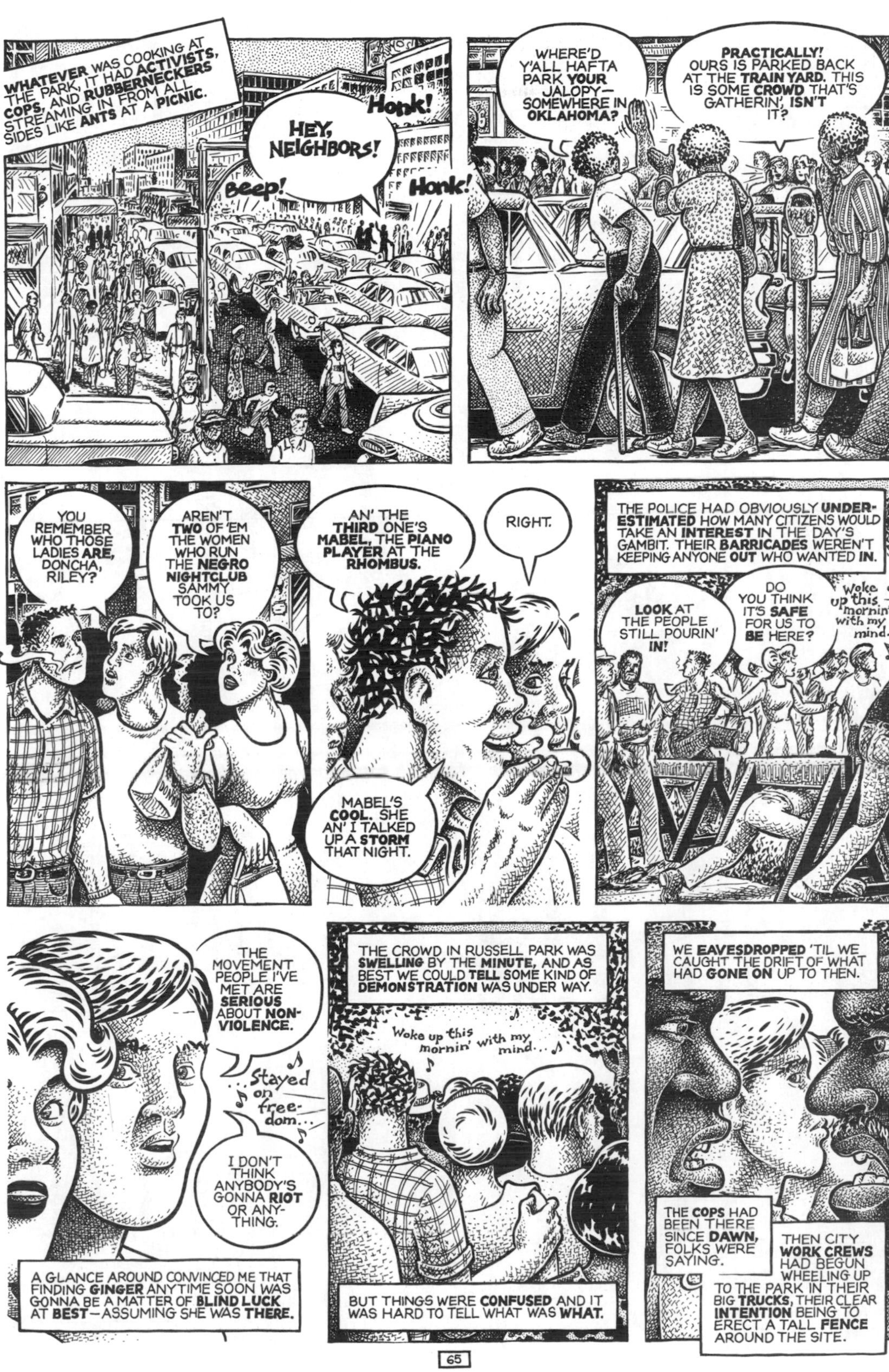
WHATEVER WAS COOKING AT THE PARK, IT HAD ACTIVISTS, COPS, AND RUBBERNECKERS STREAMING IN FROM ALL SIDES LIKE ANTS AT A PICNIC.
Honk!
HEY, NEIGHBORS!
Beep!
Honk!
WHERE'D Y'ALL HAFTA PARK YOUR JALOPY— SOMEWHERE IN OKLAHOMA?
PRACTICALLY! OURS IS PARKED BACK AT THE TRAIN YARD. THIS IS SOME CROWD THAT'S GATHERIN', ISN'T IT?
YOU REMEMBER WHO THOSE LADIES ARE, DONCHA, RILEY?
AREN'T TWO OF 'EM THE WOMEN WHO RUN THE NEGRO NIGHTCLUB SAMMY TOOK US TO?
AN' THE THIRD ONE'S MABEL, THE PIANO PLAYER AT THE RHOMBUS.
RIGHT.
MABEL'S COOL. SHE AN' I TALKED UP A STORM THAT NIGHT.
THE POLICE HAD OBVIOUSLY UNDER-ESTIMATED HOW MANY CITIZENS WOULD TAKE AN INTEREST IN THE DAY'S GAMBIT. THEIR BARRICADES WEREN'T KEEPING ANYONE OUT WHO WANTED IN.
LOOK AT THE PEOPLE STILL POURIN' IN!
DO YOU THINK IT'S SAFE FOR US TO BE HERE?
Woke up this mornin' with my mind...
POLICE LINE
THE MOVEMENT PEOPLE I'VE MET ARE SERIOUS ABOUT NON-VIOLENCE.
...Stayed on free-dom...
I DON'T THINK ANYBODY'S GONNA RIOT OR ANY-THING.
A GLANCE AROUND CONVINCED ME THAT FINDING GINGER ANYTIME SOON WAS GONNA BE A MATTER OF BLIND LUCK AT BEST—ASSUMING SHE WAS THERE.
THE CROWD IN RUSSELL PARK WAS SWELLING BY THE MINUTE, AND AS BEST WE COULD TELL SOME KIND OF DEMONSTRATION WAS UNDER WAY.
Woke up this mornin' with my mind...
BUT THINGS WERE CONFUSED AND IT WAS HARD TO TELL WHAT WAS WHAT.
WE EAVESDROPPED 'TIL WE CAUGHT THE DRIFT OF WHAT HAD GONE ON UP TO THEN.
THE COPS HAD BEEN THERE SINCE DAWN, FOLKS WERE SAYING.
THEN CITY WORK CREWS HAD BEGUN WHEELING UP TO THE PARK IN THEIR BIG TRUCKS, THEIR CLEAR INTENTION BEING TO ERECT A TALL FENCE AROUND THE SITE.

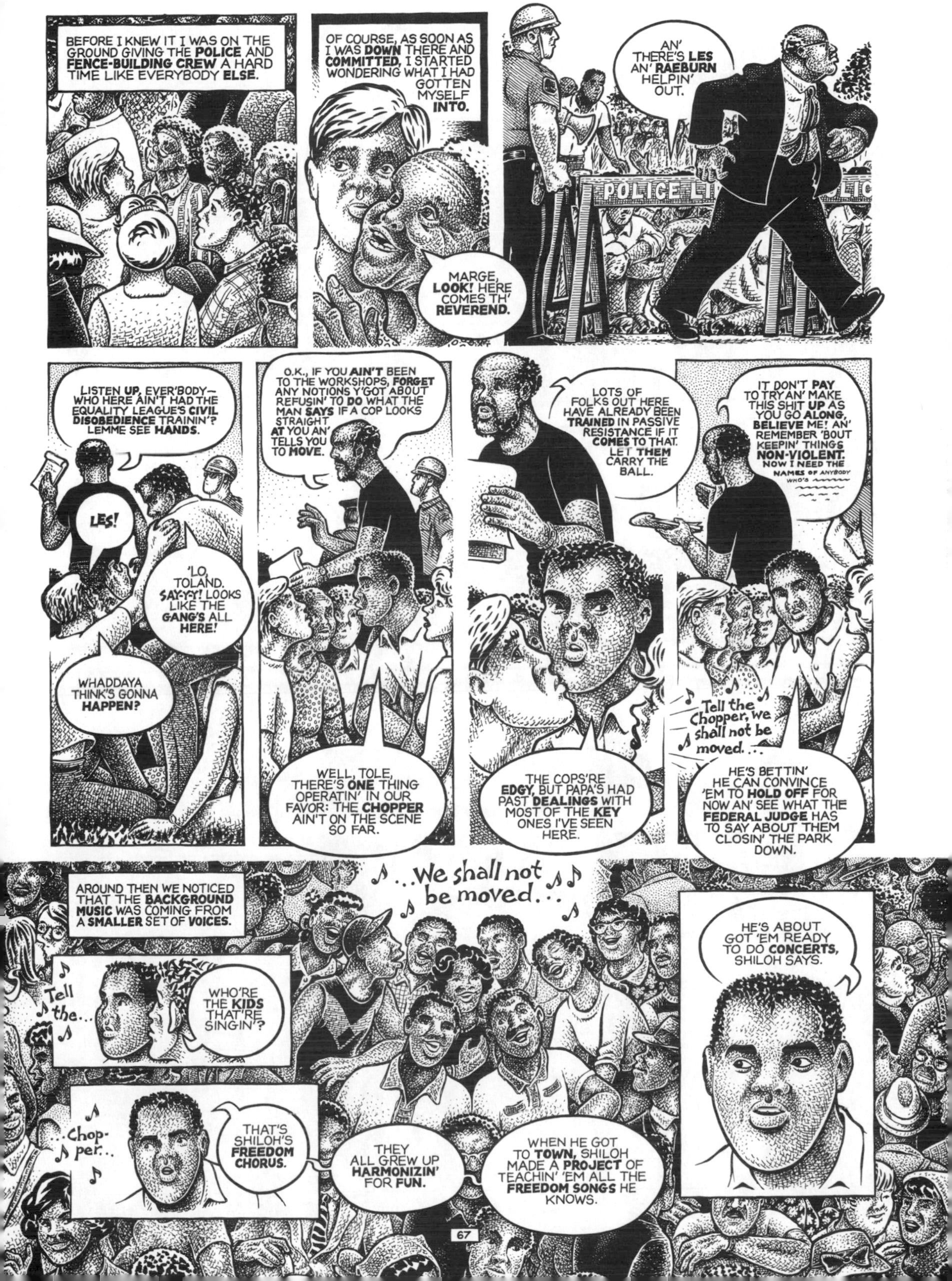
BEFORE I KNEW IT I WAS ON THE GROUND GIVING THE POLICE AND FENCE-BUILDING CREW A HARD TIME LIKE EVERYBODY ELSE.
OF COURSE, AS SOON AS I WAS DOWN THERE AND COMMITTED, I STARTED WONDERING WHAT I HAD GOTTEN MYSELF INTO.
MARGE, LOOK! HERE COMES TH' REVEREND.
AN' THERE'S LES AN' RAEBURN HELPIN' OUT.
POLICE LI
LIC
LISTEN UP, EVER'BODY— WHO HERE AIN'T HAD THE EQUALITY LEAGUE'S CIVIL DISOBEDIENCE TRAININ'? LEMME SEE HANDS.
LES!
'LO, TOLAND. SAY-Y-Y! LOOKS LIKE THE GANG'S ALL HERE!
WHADDAYA THINK'S GONNA HAPPEN?
O.K., IF YOU AIN'T BEEN TO THE WORKSHOPS, FORGET ANY NOTIONS Y'GOT ABOUT REFUSIN' TO DO WHAT THE MAN SAYS IF A COP LOOKS STRAIGHT AT YOU AN' TELLS YOU TO MOVE.
WELL, TOLE, THERE'S ONE THING OPERATIN' IN OUR FAVOR: THE CHOPPER AIN'T ON THE SCENE SO FAR.
LOTS OF FOLKS OUT HERE HAVE ALREADY BEEN TRAINED IN PASSIVE RESISTANCE IF IT COMES TO THAT. LET THEM CARRY THE BALL.
THE COPS'RE EDGY, BUT PAPA'S HAD PAST DEALINGS WITH MOST OF THE KEY ONES I'VE SEEN HERE.
IT DON'T PAY TO TRY AN' MAKE THIS SHIT UP AS YOU GO ALONG, BELIEVE ME! AN' REMEMBER 'BOUT KEEPIN' THINGS NON-VIOLENT. NOW I NEED THE NAMES OF ANYBODY WHO'S
Tell the Chopper, we shall not be moved...
HE'S BETTIN' HE CAN CONVINCE 'EM TO HOLD OFF FOR NOW AN' SEE WHAT THE FEDERAL JUDGE HAS TO SAY ABOUT THEM CLOSIN' THE PARK DOWN.
AROUND THEN WE NOTICED THAT THE BACKGROUND MUSIC WAS COMING FROM A SMALLER SET OF VOICES.
...We shall not be moved...
Tell the...
WHO'RE THE KIDS THAT'RE SINGIN'?
...Chop-per...
THAT'S SHILOH'S FREEDOM CHORUS.
THEY ALL GREW UP HARMONIZIN' FOR FUN.
WHEN HE GOT TO TOWN, SHILOH MADE A PROJECT OF TEACHIN' 'EM ALL THE FREEDOM SONGS HE KNOWS.
HE'S ABOUT GOT 'EM READY TO DO CONCERTS, SHILOH SAYS.

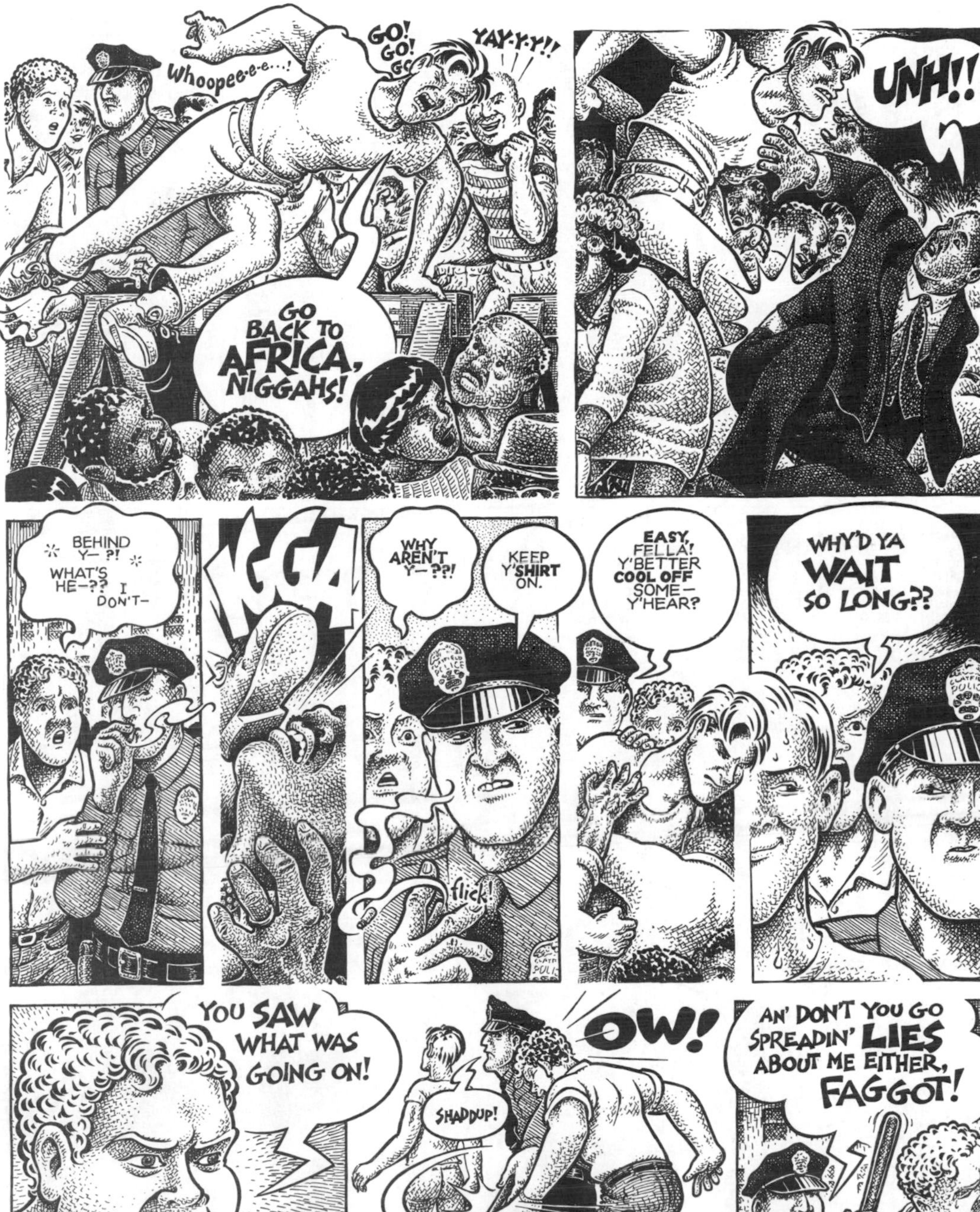
Whoopee-e-e...!
GO! GO!
YAY-Y-Y!!
GO BACK TO AFRICA, NIGGAHS!
UNH!!
BEHIND Y— ?! WHAT'S HE—?? I DON'T-
WHY AREN'T Y— ??!
KEEP Y'SHIRT ON.
flick!
EASY, FELLA! Y'BETTER COOL OFF SOME— Y'HEAR?
WHY'D YA WAIT SO LONG??
YOU SAW WHAT WAS GOING ON!
YOU JUST STOOD THERE WHILE HE GOT IN A FEW MORE KICKS!
OW!
SHADDUP!
WHACK!
AN' DON'T YOU GO SPREADIN' LIES ABOUT ME EITHER, FAGGOT!

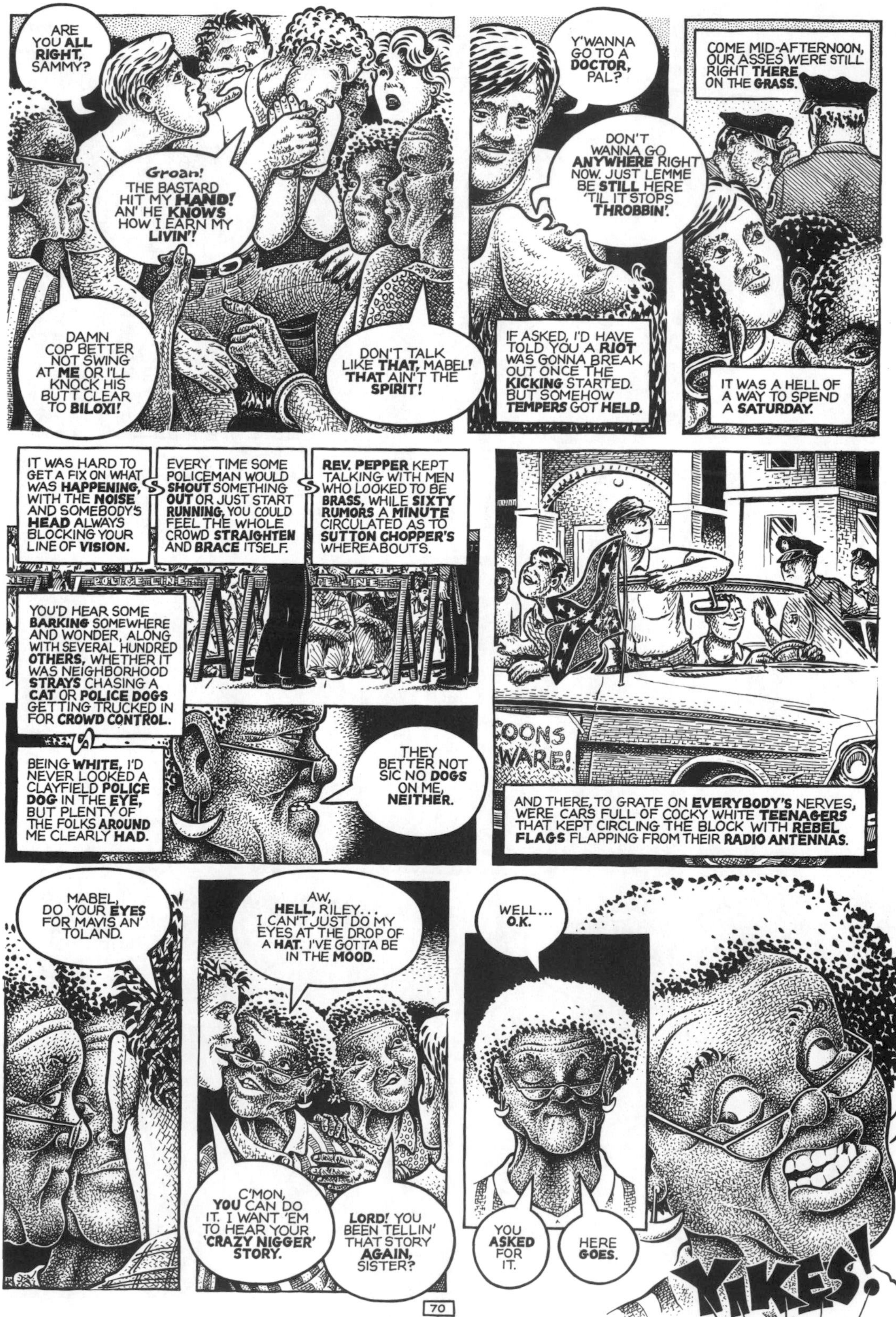
ARE YOU ALL RIGHT, SAMMY?
Groan! THE BASTARD HIT MY HAND! AN' HE KNOWS HOW I EARN MY LIVIN'!
DAMN COP BETTER NOT SWING AT ME OR I'LL KNOCK HIS BUTT CLEAR TO BILOXI!
DON'T TALK LIKE THAT, MABEL! THAT AIN'T THE SPIRIT!
Y'WANNA GO TO A DOCTOR, PAL?
DON'T WANNA GO ANYWHERE RIGHT NOW. JUST LEMME BE STILL HERE 'TIL IT STOPS THROBBIN'.
IF ASKED, I'D HAVE TOLD YOU A RIOT WAS GONNA BREAK OUT ONCE THE KICKING STARTED. BUT SOMEHOW TEMPERS GOT HELD.
COME MID-AFTERNOON, OUR ASSES WERE STILL RIGHT THERE ON THE GRASS.
IT WAS A HELL OF A WAY TO SPEND A SATURDAY.
IT WAS HARD TO GET A FIX ON WHAT WAS HAPPENING, WITH THE NOISE AND SOMEBODY'S HEAD ALWAYS BLOCKING YOUR LINE OF VISION.
EVERY TIME SOME POLICEMAN WOULD SHOUT SOMETHING OUT OR JUST START RUNNING, YOU COULD FEEL THE WHOLE CROWD STRAIGHTEN AND BRACE ITSELF.
REV. PEPPER KEPT TALKING WITH MEN WHO LOOKED TO BE BRASS, WHILE SIXTY RUMORS A MINUTE CIRCULATED AS TO SUTTON CHOPPER'S WHEREABOUTS.
YOU'D HEAR SOME BARKING SOMEWHERE AND WONDER, ALONG WITH SEVERAL HUNDRED OTHERS, WHETHER IT WAS NEIGHBORHOOD STRAYS CHASING A CAT OR POLICE DOGS GETTING TRUCKED IN FOR CROWD CONTROL.
BEING WHITE, I'D NEVER LOOKED A CLAYFIELD POLICE DOG IN THE EYE, BUT PLENTY OF THE FOLKS AROUND ME CLEARLY HAD.
THEY BETTER NOT SIC NO DOGS ON ME, NEITHER.
COONS WARE!
AND THERE, TO GRATE ON EVERYBODY'S NERVES, WERE CARS FULL OF COCKY WHITE TEENAGERS THAT KEPT CIRCLING THE BLOCK WITH REBEL FLAGS FLAPPING FROM THEIR RADIO ANTENNAS.
MABEL, DO YOUR EYES FOR MAVIS AN' TOLAND.
AW, HELL, RILEY... I CAN'T JUST DO MY EYES AT THE DROP OF A HAT. I'VE GOTTA BE IN THE MOOD.
C'MON, YOU CAN DO IT. I WANT 'EM TO HEAR YOUR 'CRAZY NIGGER' STORY.
LORD! YOU BEEN TELLIN' THAT STORY AGAIN, SISTER?
WELL... O.K.
YOU ASKED FOR IT.
HERE GOES.
YIKES!

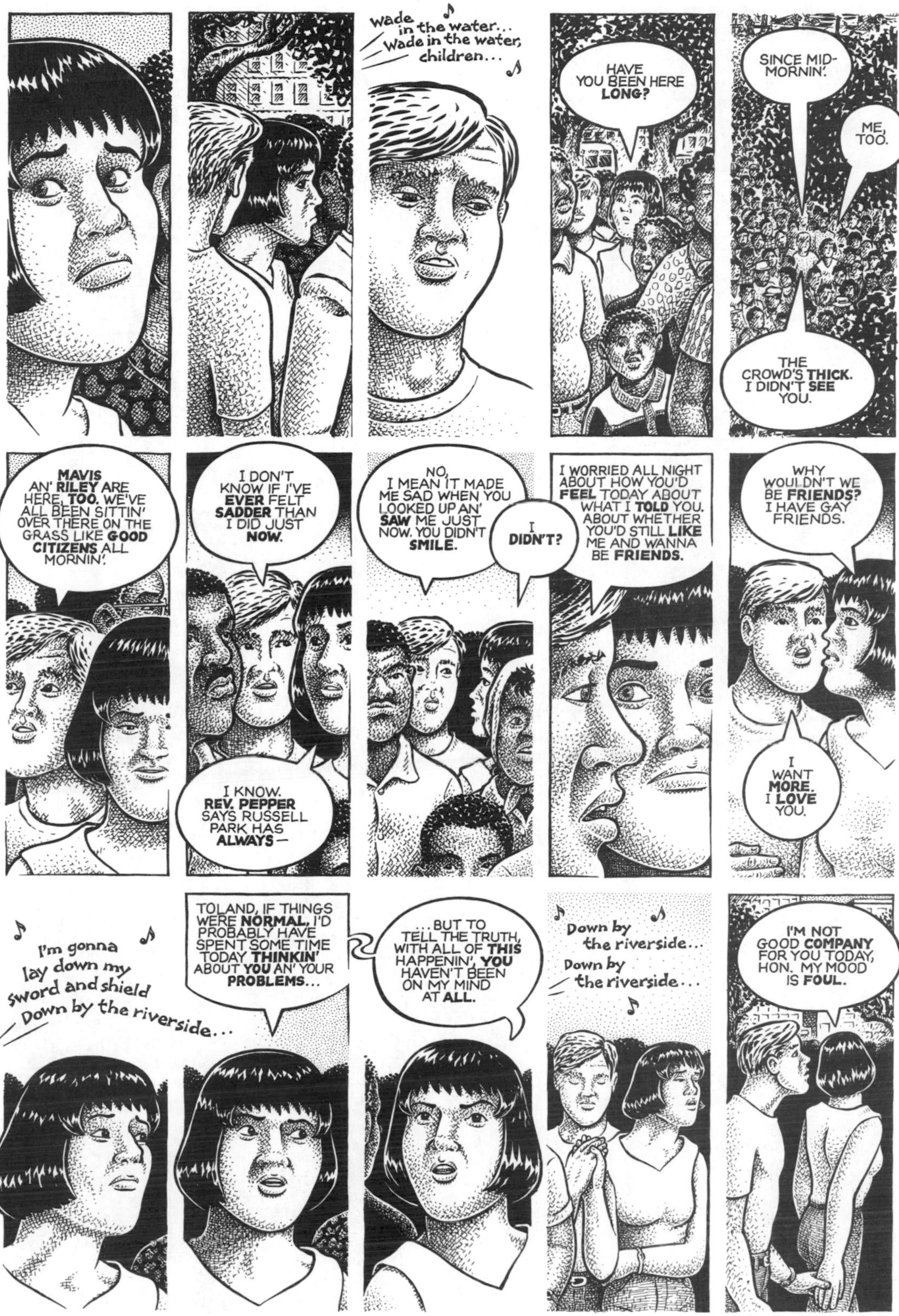
Wade in the water... Wade in the water, children...
HAVE YOU BEEN HERE LONG?
SINCE MID-MORNIN'.
ME, TOO.
THE CROWD'S THICK. I DIDN'T SEE YOU.
MAVIS AN' RILEY ARE HERE, TOO. WE'VE ALL BEEN SITTIN' OVER THERE ON THE GRASS LIKE GOOD CITIZENS ALL MORNIN'.
I DON'T KNOW IF I'VE EVER FELT SADDER THAN I DID JUST NOW.
I KNOW. REV. PEPPER SAYS RUSSELL PARK HAS ALWAYS—
NO, I MEAN IT MADE ME SAD WHEN YOU LOOKED UP AN' SAW ME JUST NOW. YOU DIDN'T SMILE.
I DIDN'T?
I WORRIED ALL NIGHT ABOUT HOW YOU'D FEEL TODAY ABOUT WHAT I TOLD YOU. ABOUT WHETHER YOU'D STILL LIKE ME AND WANNA BE FRIENDS.
WHY WOULDN'T WE BE FRIENDS? I HAVE GAY FRIENDS.
I WANT MORE. I LOVE YOU.
I'm gonna lay down my sword and shield Down by the riverside...
TOLAND, IF THINGS WERE NORMAL, I'D PROBABLY HAVE SPENT SOME TIME TODAY THINKIN' ABOUT YOU AN' YOUR PROBLEMS...
...BUT TO TELL THE TRUTH, WITH ALL OF THIS HAPPENIN', YOU HAVEN'T BEEN ON MY MIND AT ALL.
Down by the riverside... Down by the riverside...
I'M NOT GOOD COMPANY FOR YOU TODAY, HON. MY MOOD IS FOUL.

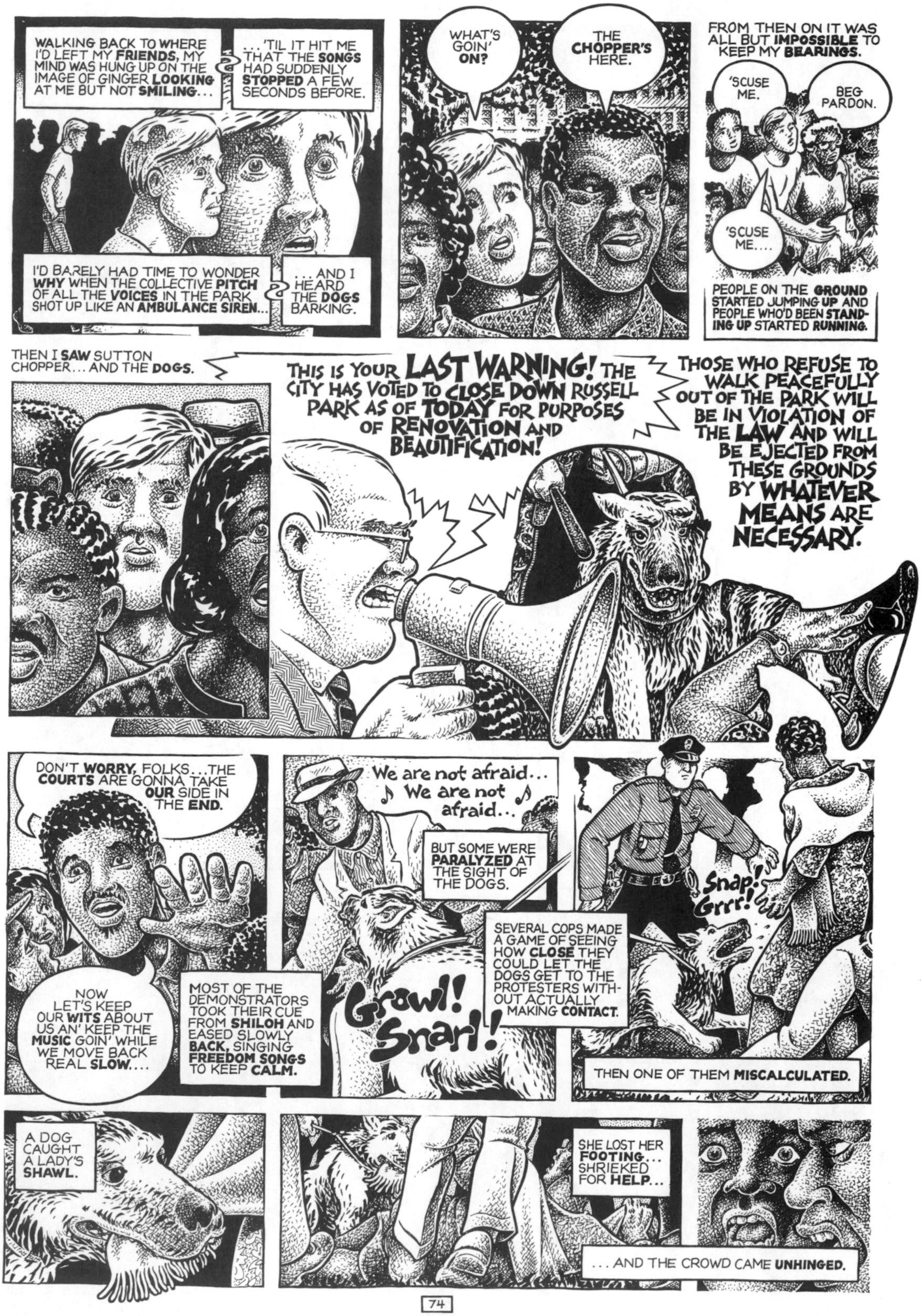

WALKING BACK TO WHERE I'D LEFT MY FRIENDS, MY MIND WAS HUNG UP ON THE IMAGE OF GINGER LOOKING AT ME BUT NOT SMILING...
...'TIL IT HIT ME THAT THE SONGS HAD SUDDENLY STOPPED A FEW SECONDS BEFORE.
I'D BARELY HAD TIME TO WONDER WHY WHEN THE COLLECTIVE PITCH OF ALL THE VOICES IN THE PARK SHOT UP LIKE AN AMBULANCE SIREN...
...AND I HEARD THE DOGS BARKING.
WHAT'S GOIN' ON?
THE CHOPPER'S HERE.
FROM THEN ON IT WAS ALL BUT IMPOSSIBLE TO KEEP MY BEARINGS.
'SCUSE ME.
BEG PARDON.
'SCUSE ME....
PEOPLE ON THE GROUND STARTED JUMPING UP AND PEOPLE WHO'D BEEN STANDING UP STARTED RUNNING.
THEN I SAW SUTTON CHOPPER... AND THE DOGS.
THIS IS YOUR LAST WARNING! THE CITY HAS VOTED TO CLOSE DOWN RUSSELL PARK AS OF TODAY FOR PURPOSES OF RENOVATION AND BEAUTIFICATION!
THOSE WHO REFUSE TO WALK PEACEFULLY OUT OF THE PARK WILL BE IN VIOLATION OF THE LAW AND WILL BE EJECTED FROM THESE GROUNDS BY WHATEVER MEANS ARE NECESSARY.
DON'T WORRY, FOLKS...THE COURTS ARE GONNA TAKE OUR SIDE IN THE END.
NOW LET'S KEEP OUR WITS ABOUT US AN' KEEP THE MUSIC GOIN' WHILE WE MOVE BACK REAL SLOW....
MOST OF THE DEMONSTRATORS TOOK THEIR CUE FROM SHILOH AND EASED SLOWLY BACK, SINGING FREEDOM SONGS TO KEEP CALM.
We are not afraid... ♪ We are not afraid... ♪
BUT SOME WERE PARALYZED AT THE SIGHT OF THE DOGS.
Growl! Snarl!
SEVERAL COPS MADE A GAME OF SEEING HOW CLOSE THEY COULD LET THE DOGS GET TO THE PROTESTERS WITHOUT ACTUALLY MAKING CONTACT.
Snap! Grrr!
THEN ONE OF THEM MISCALCULATED.
A DOG CAUGHT A LADY'S SHAWL.
SHE LOST HER FOOTING... SHRIEKED FOR HELP...
...AND THE CROWD CAME UNHINGED.

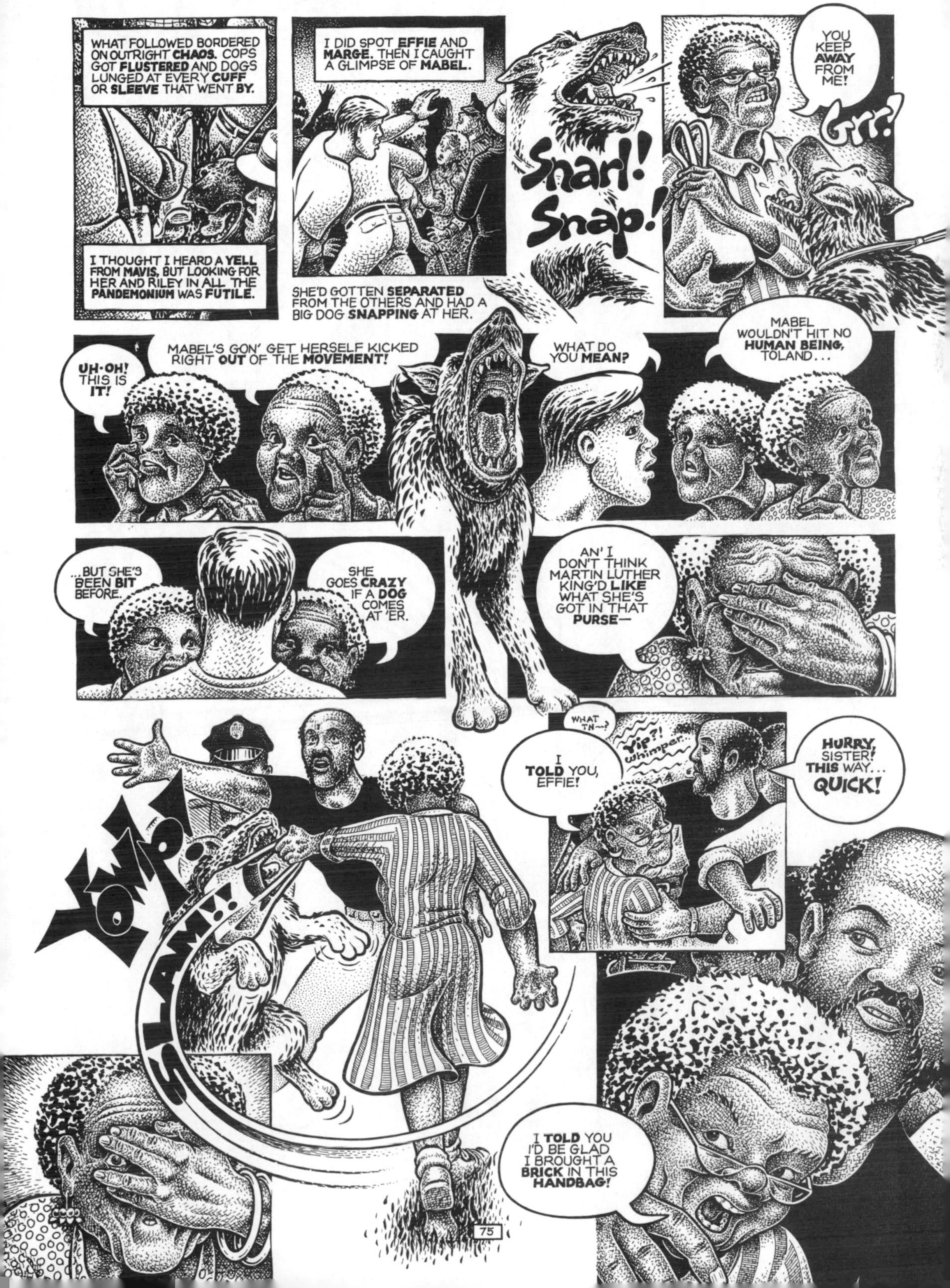
WHAT FOLLOWED BORDERED ON OUTRIGHT CHAOS. COPS GOT FLUSTERED AND DOGS LUNGED AT EVERY CUFF OR SLEEVE THAT WENT BY.
I THOUGHT I HEARD A YELL FROM MAVIS, BUT LOOKING FOR HER AND RILEY IN ALL THE PANDEMONIUM WAS FUTILE.
I DID SPOT EFFIE AND MARGE. THEN I CAUGHT A GLIMPSE OF MABEL.
SHE'D GOTTEN SEPARATED FROM THE OTHERS AND HAD A BIG DOG SNAPPING AT HER.
Snarl!
Snap!
YOU KEEP AWAY FROM ME!
Grr!
UH-OH! THIS IS IT!
MABEL'S GON' GET HERSELF KICKED RIGHT OUT OF THE MOVEMENT!
WHAT DO YOU MEAN?
MABEL WOULDN'T HIT NO HUMAN BEING, TOLAND...
...BUT SHE'S BEEN BIT BEFORE.
SHE GOES CRAZY IF A DOG COMES AT 'ER.
AN' I DON'T THINK MARTIN LUTHER KING'D LIKE WHAT SHE'S GOT IN THAT PURSE—
YOWP!
SLAM!!
WHAT TH—?
Yip?! whimper.
I TOLD YOU, EFFIE!
HURRY, SISTER! THIS WAY... QUICK!
I TOLD YOU I'D BE GLAD I BROUGHT A BRICK IN THIS HANDBAG!

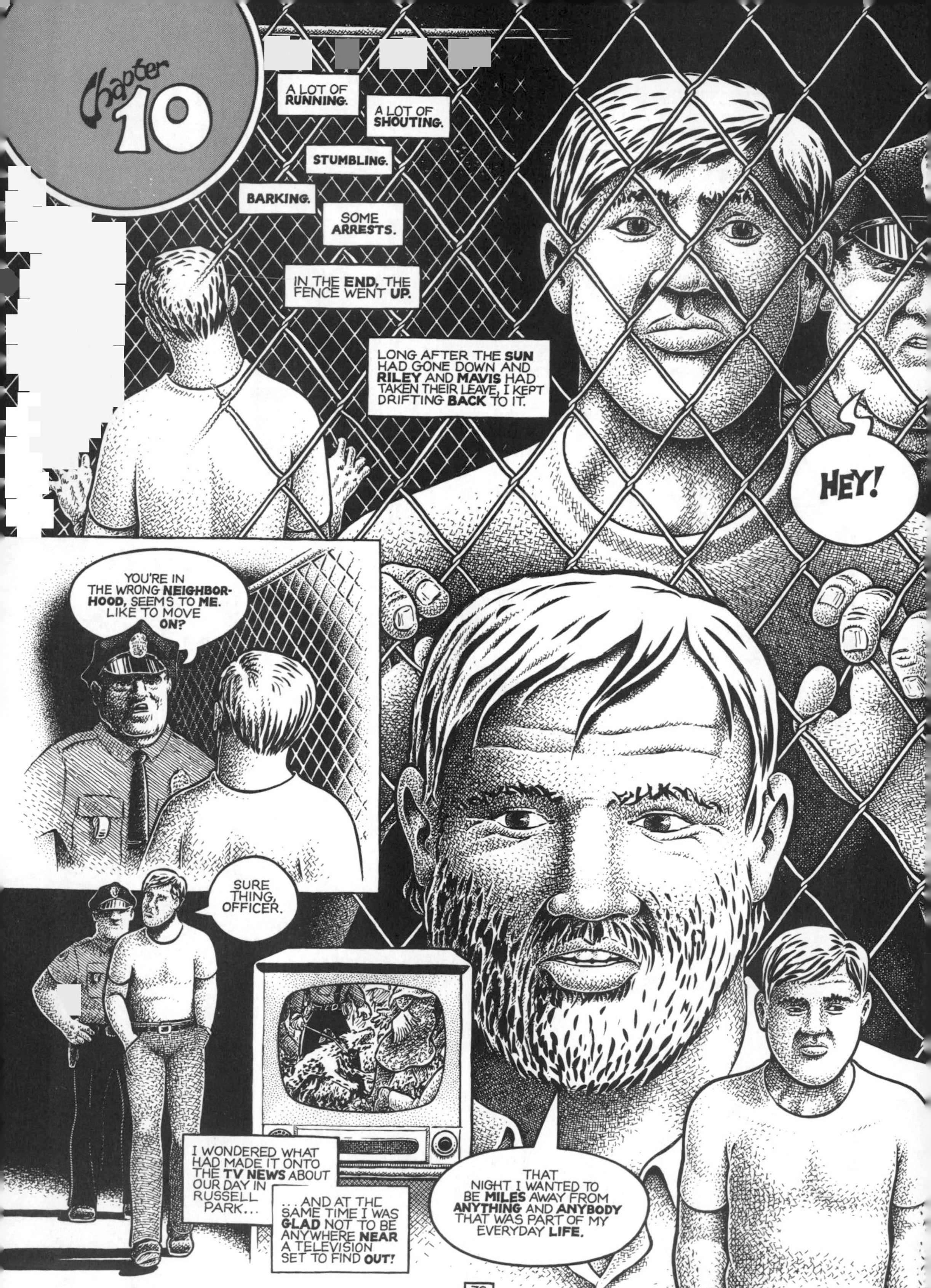
Chapter 10
A LOT OF RUNNING.
A LOT OF SHOUTING.
STUMBLING.
BARKING.
SOME ARRESTS.
IN THE END, THE FENCE WENT UP.
LONG AFTER THE SUN HAD GONE DOWN AND RILEY AND MAVIS HAD TAKEN THEIR LEAVE, I KEPT DRIFTING BACK TO IT.
HEY!
YOU'RE IN THE WRONG NEIGHBORHOOD, SEEMS TO ME. LIKE TO MOVE ON?
SURE THING, OFFICER.
I WONDERED WHAT HAD MADE IT ONTO THE TV NEWS ABOUT OUR DAY IN RUSSELL PARK...
...AND AT THE SAME TIME I WAS GLAD NOT TO BE ANYWHERE NEAR A TELEVISION SET TO FIND OUT!
THAT NIGHT I WANTED TO BE MILES AWAY FROM ANYTHING AND ANYBODY THAT WAS PART OF MY EVERYDAY LIFE.

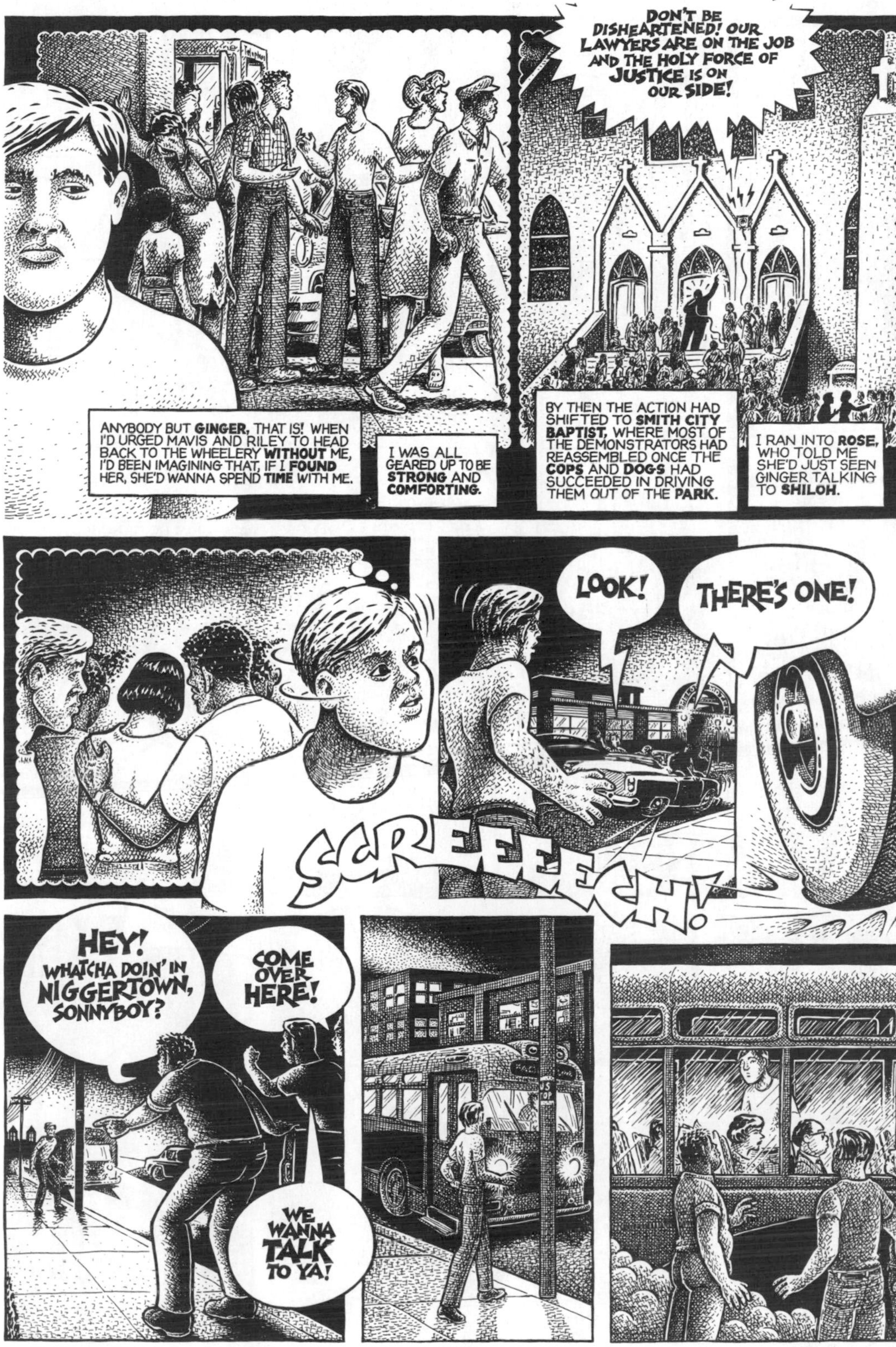
ANYBODY BUT GINGER, THAT IS! WHEN I'D URGED MAVIS AND RILEY TO HEAD BACK TO THE WHEELERY WITHOUT ME, I'D BEEN IMAGINING THAT, IF I FOUND HER, SHE'D WANNA SPEND TIME WITH ME.
I WAS ALL GEARED UP TO BE STRONG AND COMFORTING.
DON'T BE DISHEARTENED! OUR LAWYERS ARE ON THE JOB AND THE HOLY FORCE OF JUSTICE IS ON OUR SIDE!
BY THEN THE ACTION HAD SHIFTED TO SMITH CITY BAPTIST, WHERE MOST OF THE DEMONSTRATORS HAD REASSEMBLED ONCE THE COPS AND DOGS HAD SUCCEEDED IN DRIVING THEM OUT OF THE PARK.
I RAN INTO ROSE, WHO TOLD ME SHE'D JUST SEEN GINGER TALKING TO SHILOH.
LOOK!
THERE'S ONE!
SCREEEEECH!
HEY! WHATCHA DOIN' IN NIGGERTOWN, SONNYBOY?
COME OVER HERE!
WE WANNA TALK TO YA!

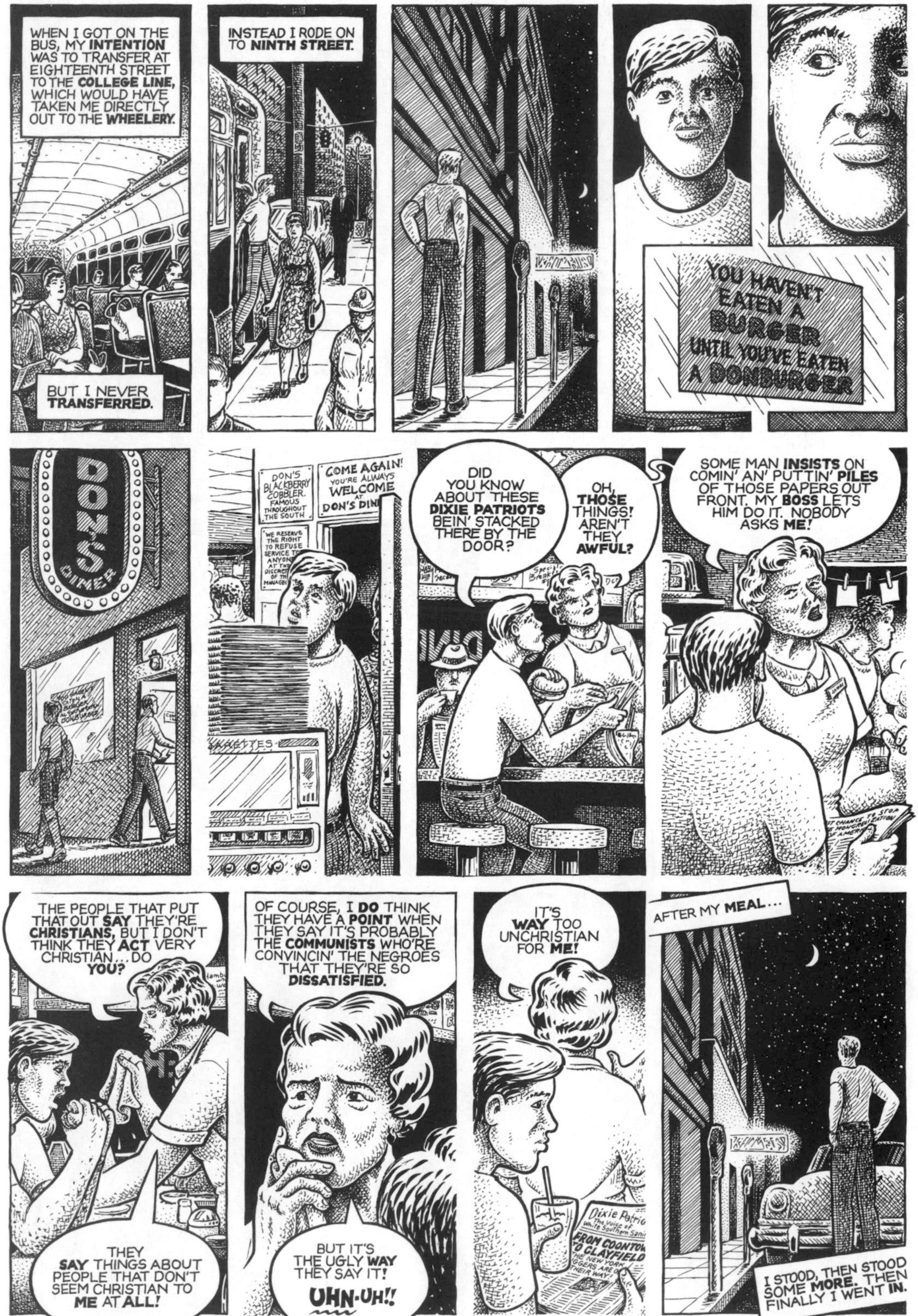

WHEN I GOT ON THE BUS, MY **INTENTION** WAS TO TRANSFER AT EIGHTEENTH STREET TO THE **COLLEGE LINE**, WHICH WOULD HAVE TAKEN ME DIRECTLY OUT TO THE **WHEELERY**.
BUT I NEVER **TRANSFERRED**.
INSTEAD I RODE ON TO **NINTH STREET**.
YOU HAVEN'T EATEN A BURGER UNTIL YOU'VE EATEN A DONBURGER
DON'S DINER
DON'S BLACKBERRY COBBLER. FAMOUS THROUGHOUT THE SOUTH
COME AGAIN! YOU'RE ALWAYS WELCOME AT DON'S DIN
DID YOU KNOW ABOUT THESE **DIXIE PATRIOTS** BEIN' STACKED THERE BY THE DOOR?
OH, **THOSE** THINGS! AREN'T THEY **AWFUL?**
SOME MAN **INSISTS** ON COMIN' AN' PUTTIN' **PILES** OF THOSE PAPERS OUT FRONT. MY **BOSS** LETS HIM DO IT. NOBODY ASKS **ME!**
THE PEOPLE THAT PUT THAT OUT **SAY** THEY'RE **CHRISTIANS**, BUT I DON'T THINK THEY **ACT** VERY CHRISTIAN... DO **YOU?**
THEY **SAY** THINGS ABOUT PEOPLE THAT DON'T SEEM CHRISTIAN TO **ME** AT **ALL!**
OF COURSE, **I DO** THINK THEY HAVE A **POINT** WHEN THEY SAY IT'S PROBABLY THE **COMMUNISTS** WHO'RE CONVINCIN' THE NEGROES THAT THEY'RE SO **DISSATISFIED**.
BUT IT'S THE UGLY **WAY** THEY SAY IT!
UHN-UH!!
IT'S **WAY** TOO UNCHRISTIAN FOR **ME!**
AFTER MY **MEAL**...
I STOOD, THEN STOOD SOME **MORE**. THEN FINALLY I WENT **IN**.

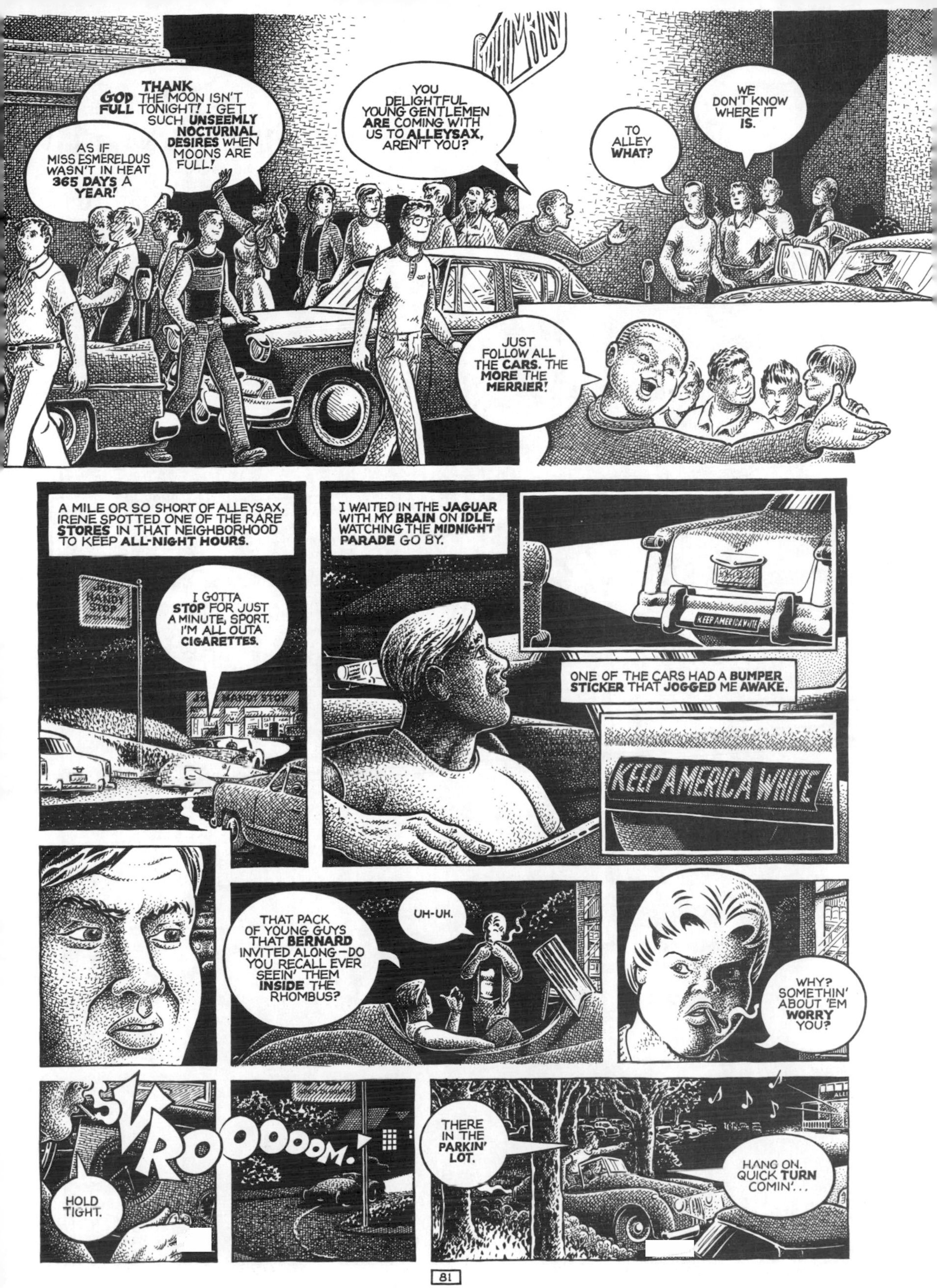
THANK GOD THE MOON ISN'T FULL TONIGHT! I GET SUCH UNSEEMLY NOCTURNAL DESIRES WHEN MOONS ARE FULL!
AS IF MISS ESMERELDUS WASN'T IN HEAT 365 DAYS A YEAR!
YOU DELIGHTFUL YOUNG GENTLEMEN ARE COMING WITH US TO ALLEYSAX, AREN'T YOU?
TO ALLEY WHAT?
WE DON'T KNOW WHERE IT IS.
JUST FOLLOW ALL THE CARS. THE MORE THE MERRIER!
A MILE OR SO SHORT OF ALLEYSAX, IRENE SPOTTED ONE OF THE RARE STORES IN THAT NEIGHBORHOOD TO KEEP ALL-NIGHT HOURS.
JOE'S HANDY STOP
I GOTTA STOP FOR JUST A MINUTE, SPORT. I'M ALL OUTA CIGARETTES.
I WAITED IN THE JAGUAR WITH MY BRAIN ON IDLE, WATCHING THE MIDNIGHT PARADE GO BY.
KEEP AMERICA WHITE
ONE OF THE CARS HAD A BUMPER STICKER THAT JOGGED ME AWAKE.
KEEP AMERICA WHITE
THAT PACK OF YOUNG GUYS THAT BERNARD INVITED ALONG—DO YOU RECALL EVER SEEIN' THEM INSIDE THE RHOMBUS?
UH-UH.
WHY? SOMETHIN' ABOUT 'EM WORRY YOU?
SVROOOOOOM!
HOLD TIGHT.
THERE IN THE PARKIN' LOT.
HANG ON. QUICK TURN COMIN'...

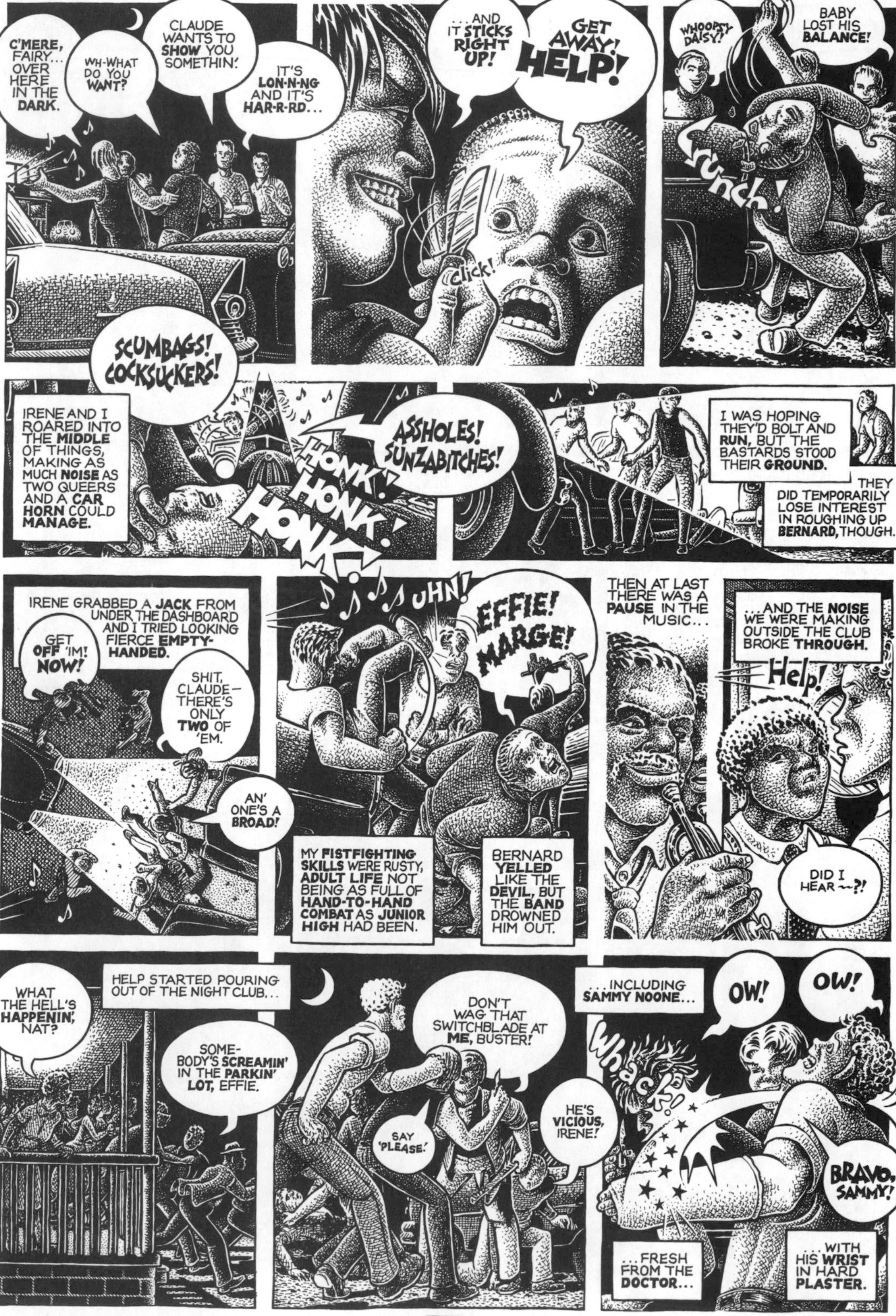
C'MERE, FAIRY... OVER HERE IN THE DARK.
WH-WHAT DO YOU WANT?
CLAUDE WANTS TO SHOW YOU SOMETHIN'.
IT'S LON-N-NG AND IT'S HAR-R-RD...
...AND IT STICKS RIGHT UP!
Click!
GET AWAY! HELP!
WHOOPSY DAISY!
BABY LOST HIS BALANCE!
Crunch!
SCUMBAGS! COCKSUCKERS!
IRENE AND I ROARED INTO THE MIDDLE OF THINGS, MAKING AS MUCH NOISE AS TWO QUEERS AND A CAR HORN COULD MANAGE.
ASSHOLES! SUNZABITCHES!
HONK! HONK! HONK!
I WAS HOPING THEY'D BOLT AND RUN, BUT THE BASTARDS STOOD THEIR GROUND.
THEY DID TEMPORARILY LOSE INTEREST IN ROUGHING UP BERNARD, THOUGH.
IRENE GRABBED A JACK FROM UNDER THE DASHBOARD AND I TRIED LOOKING FIERCE EMPTY-HANDED.
GET OFF 'IM! NOW!
SHIT, CLAUDE— THERE'S ONLY TWO OF 'EM.
AN' ONE'S A BROAD!
UHN!
EFFIE! MARGE!
MY FISTFIGHTING SKILLS WERE RUSTY, ADULT LIFE NOT BEING AS FULL OF HAND-TO-HAND COMBAT AS JUNIOR HIGH HAD BEEN.
BERNARD YELLED LIKE THE DEVIL, BUT THE BAND DROWNED HIM OUT.
THEN AT LAST THERE WAS A PAUSE IN THE MUSIC...
...AND THE NOISE WE WERE MAKING OUTSIDE THE CLUB BROKE THROUGH.
Help!
DID I HEAR ~?!
WHAT THE HELL'S HAPPENIN', NAT?
HELP STARTED POURING OUT OF THE NIGHT CLUB...
SOME-BODY'S SCREAMIN' IN THE PARKIN' LOT, EFFIE.
DON'T WAG THAT SWITCHBLADE AT ME, BUSTER!
SAY 'PLEASE.'
HE'S VICIOUS, IRENE!
...INCLUDING SAMMY NOONE...
OW!
OW!
Whack!
BRAVO, SAMMY!
...FRESH FROM THE DOCTOR...
...WITH HIS WRIST IN HARD PLASTER.

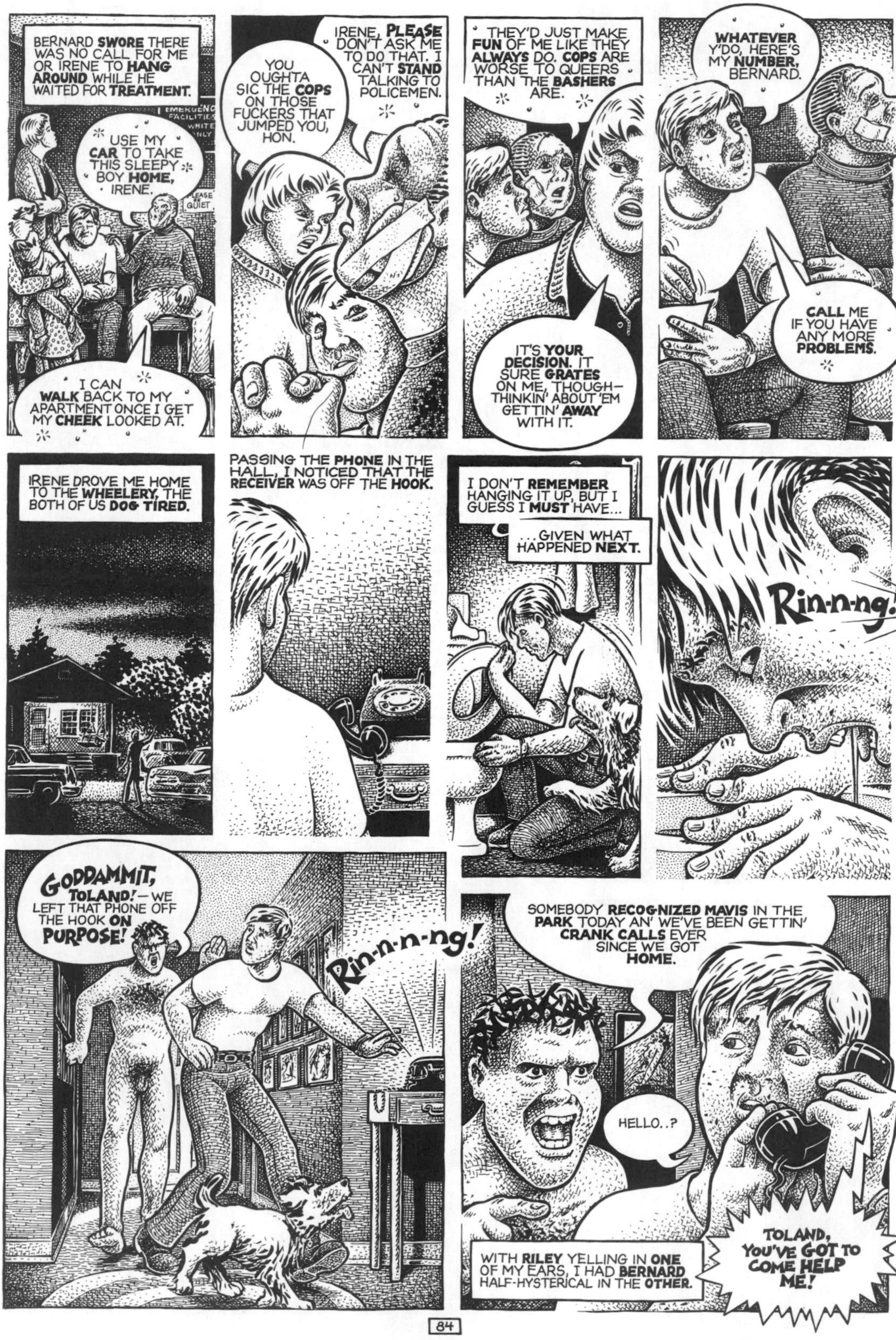

BERNARD SWORE THERE WAS NO CALL FOR ME OR IRENE TO HANG AROUND WHILE HE WAITED FOR TREATMENT.
USE MY CAR TO TAKE THIS SLEEPY BOY HOME, IRENE.
I CAN WALK BACK TO MY APARTMENT ONCE I GET MY CHEEK LOOKED AT.
YOU OUGHTA SIC THE COPS ON THOSE FUCKERS THAT JUMPED YOU, HON.
IRENE, PLEASE DON'T ASK ME TO DO THAT. I CAN'T STAND TALKING TO POLICEMEN.
THEY'D JUST MAKE FUN OF ME LIKE THEY ALWAYS DO. COPS ARE WORSE TO QUEERS THAN THE BASHERS ARE.
IT'S YOUR DECISION. IT SURE GRATES ON ME, THOUGH— THINKIN' ABOUT 'EM GETTIN' AWAY WITH IT.
WHATEVER Y'DO, HERE'S MY NUMBER, BERNARD.
CALL ME IF YOU HAVE ANY MORE PROBLEMS.
IRENE DROVE ME HOME TO THE WHEELERY, THE BOTH OF US DOG TIRED.
PASSING THE PHONE IN THE HALL, I NOTICED THAT THE RECEIVER WAS OFF THE HOOK.
I DON'T REMEMBER HANGING IT UP, BUT I GUESS I MUST HAVE...
...GIVEN WHAT HAPPENED NEXT.
Rin-n-ng!
GODDAMMIT, TOLAND!— WE LEFT THAT PHONE OFF THE HOOK ON PURPOSE!
Rin-n-n-ng!
SOMEBODY RECOGNIZED MAVIS IN THE PARK TODAY AN' WE'VE BEEN GETTIN' CRANK CALLS EVER SINCE WE GOT HOME.
HELLO..?
WITH RILEY YELLING IN ONE OF MY EARS, I HAD BERNARD HALF-HYSTERICAL IN THE OTHER.
TOLAND, YOU'VE GOT TO COME HELP ME!

Chapter 11

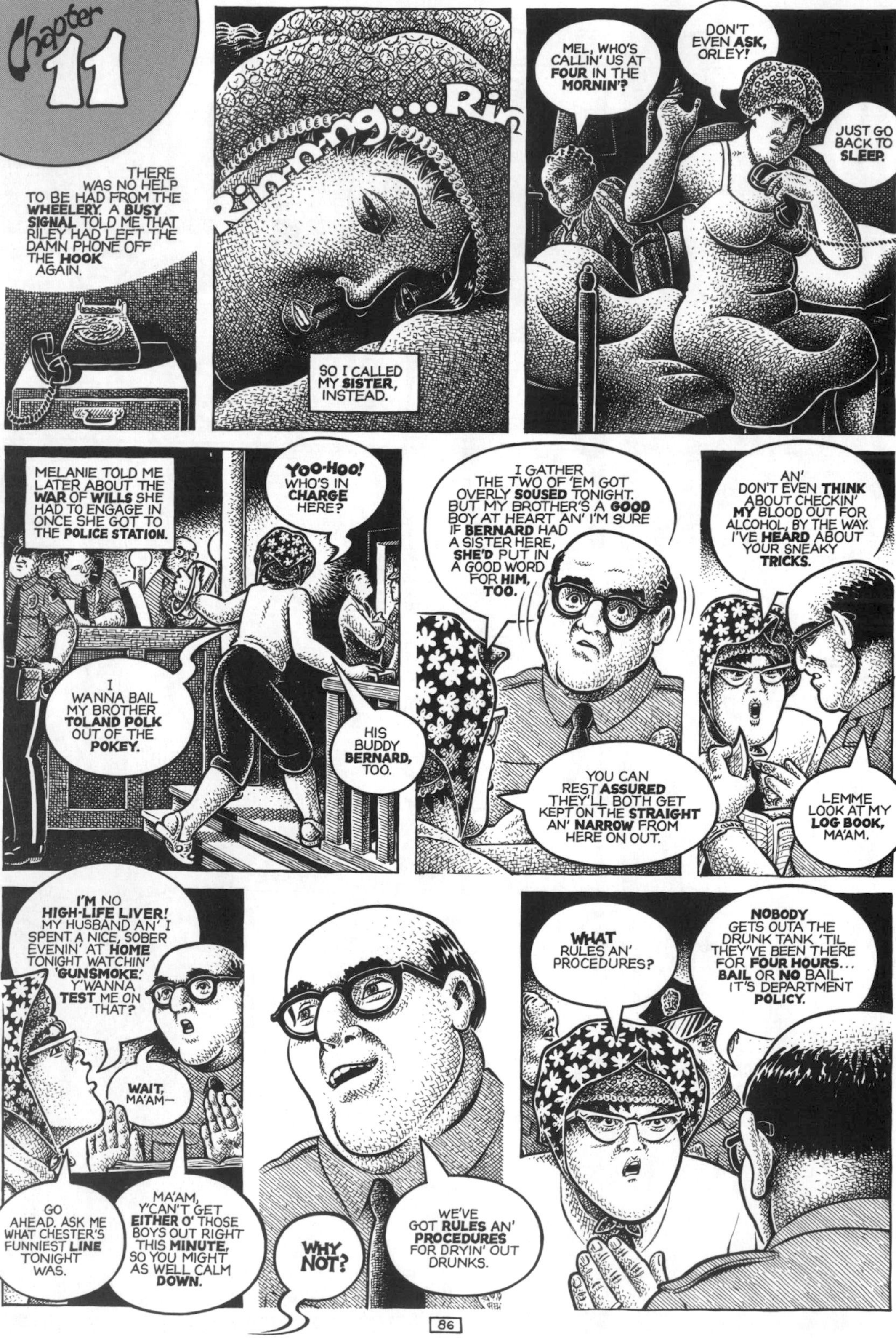

THERE WAS NO HELP TO BE HAD FROM THE WHEELERY. A BUSY SIGNAL TOLD ME THAT RILEY HAD LEFT THE DAMN PHONE OFF THE HOOK AGAIN.
RI-N-N-NG...RIN
SO I CALLED MY SISTER, INSTEAD.
MEL, WHO'S CALLIN' US AT FOUR IN THE MORNIN'?
DON'T EVEN ASK, ORLEY!
JUST GO BACK TO SLEEP.
MELANIE TOLD ME LATER ABOUT THE WAR OF WILLS SHE HAD TO ENGAGE IN ONCE SHE GOT TO THE POLICE STATION.
YOO-HOO! WHO'S IN CHARGE HERE?
I WANNA BAIL MY BROTHER TOLAND POLK OUT OF THE POKEY.
HIS BUDDY BERNARD, TOO.
I GATHER THE TWO OF 'EM GOT OVERLY SOUSED TONIGHT. BUT MY BROTHER'S A GOOD BOY AT HEART AN' I'M SURE IF BERNARD HAD A SISTER HERE, SHE'D PUT IN A GOOD WORD FOR HIM, TOO.
YOU CAN REST ASSURED THEY'LL BOTH GET KEPT ON THE STRAIGHT AN' NARROW FROM HERE ON OUT.
AN' DON'T EVEN THINK ABOUT CHECKIN' MY BLOOD OUT FOR ALCOHOL, BY THE WAY. I'VE HEARD ABOUT YOUR SNEAKY TRICKS.
LEMME LOOK AT MY LOG BOOK, MA'AM.
I'M NO HIGH-LIFE LIVER! MY HUSBAND AN' I SPENT A NICE, SOBER EVENIN' AT HOME TONIGHT WATCHIN' 'GUNSMOKE.' Y'WANNA TEST ME ON THAT?
WAIT, MA'AM—
GO AHEAD, ASK ME WHAT CHESTER'S FUNNIEST LINE TONIGHT WAS.
MA'AM, Y'CAN'T GET EITHER O' THOSE BOYS OUT RIGHT THIS MINUTE, SO YOU MIGHT AS WELL CALM DOWN.
WHY NOT?
WE'VE GOT RULES AN' PROCEDURES FOR DRYIN' OUT DRUNKS.
WHAT RULES AN' PROCEDURES?
NOBODY GETS OUTA THE DRUNK TANK 'TIL THEY'VE BEEN THERE FOR FOUR HOURS... BAIL OR NO BAIL... IT'S DEPARTMENT POLICY.

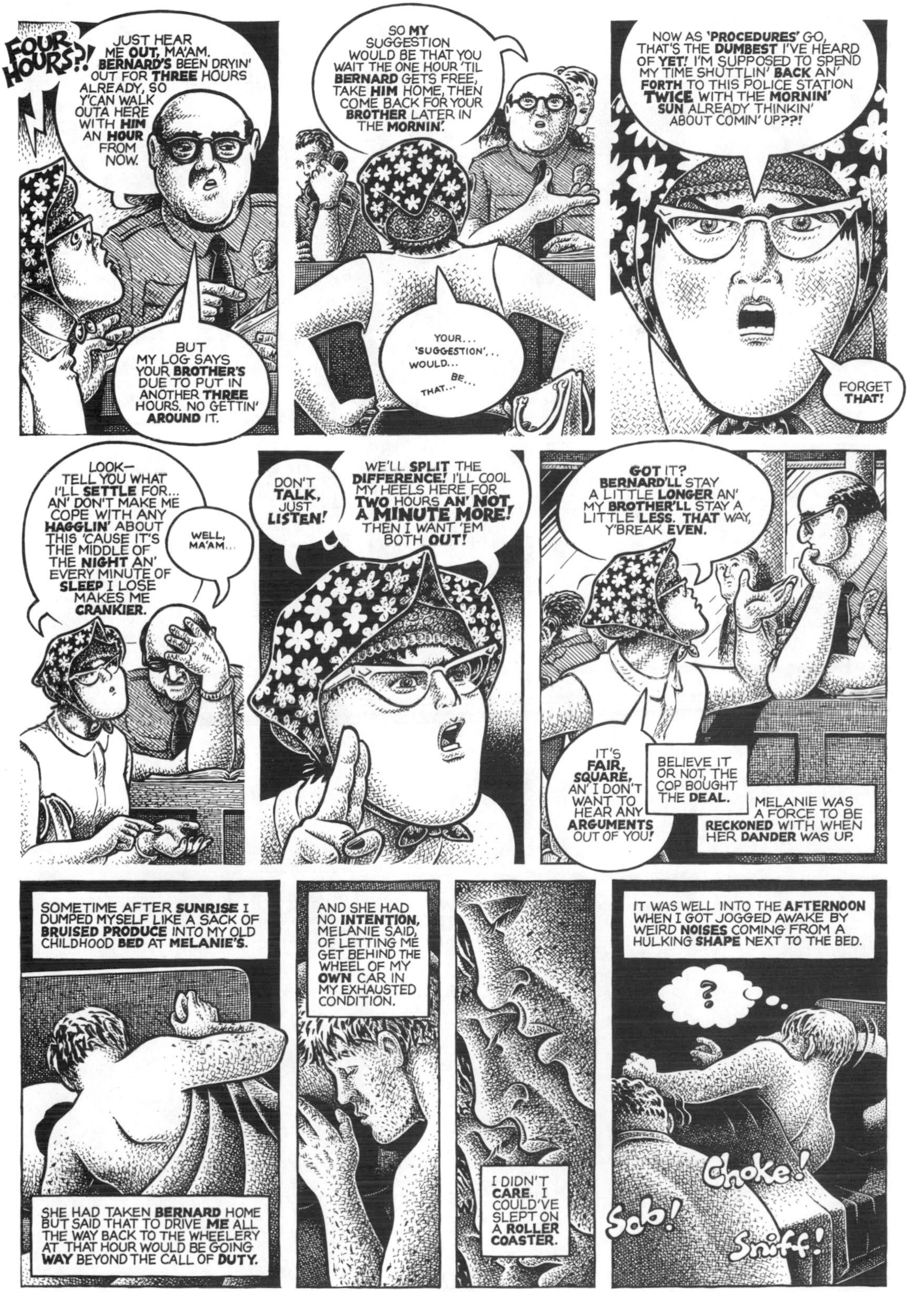
FOUR HOURS?!
JUST HEAR ME OUT, MA'AM. BERNARD'S BEEN DRYIN' OUT FOR THREE HOURS ALREADY, SO Y'CAN WALK OUTA HERE WITH HIM AN HOUR FROM NOW.
BUT MY LOG SAYS YOUR BROTHER'S DUE TO PUT IN ANOTHER THREE HOURS. NO GETTIN' AROUND IT.
SO MY SUGGESTION WOULD BE THAT YOU WAIT THE ONE HOUR 'TIL BERNARD GETS FREE, TAKE HIM HOME, THEN COME BACK FOR YOUR BROTHER LATER IN THE MORNIN'.
YOUR... 'SUGGESTION'... WOULD... BE... THAT...
NOW AS 'PROCEDURES' GO, THAT'S THE DUMBEST I'VE HEARD OF YET! I'M SUPPOSED TO SPEND MY TIME SHUTTLIN' BACK AN' FORTH TO THIS POLICE STATION TWICE WITH THE MORNIN' SUN ALREADY THINKIN' ABOUT COMIN' UP??!
FORGET THAT!
LOOK— TELL YOU WHAT I'LL SETTLE FOR... AN' DON'T MAKE ME COPE WITH ANY HAGGLIN' ABOUT THIS 'CAUSE IT'S THE MIDDLE OF THE NIGHT AN' EVERY MINUTE OF SLEEP I LOSE MAKES ME CRANKIER.
WELL, MA'AM...
DON'T TALK, JUST LISTEN!
WE'LL SPLIT THE DIFFERENCE! I'LL COOL MY HEELS HERE FOR TWO HOURS AN' NOT A MINUTE MORE! THEN I WANT 'EM BOTH OUT!
GOT IT? BERNARD'LL STAY A LITTLE LONGER AN' MY BROTHER'LL STAY A LITTLE LESS. THAT WAY, Y'BREAK EVEN.
IT'S FAIR, SQUARE, AN' I DON'T WANT TO HEAR ANY ARGUMENTS OUT OF YOU!
BELIEVE IT OR NOT, THE COP BOUGHT THE DEAL.
MELANIE WAS A FORCE TO BE RECKONED WITH WHEN HER DANDER WAS UP.
SOMETIME AFTER SUNRISE I DUMPED MYSELF LIKE A SACK OF BRUISED PRODUCE INTO MY OLD CHILDHOOD BED AT MELANIE'S.
SHE HAD TAKEN BERNARD HOME BUT SAID THAT TO DRIVE ME ALL THE WAY BACK TO THE WHEELERY AT THAT HOUR WOULD BE GOING WAY BEYOND THE CALL OF DUTY.
AND SHE HAD NO INTENTION, MELANIE SAID, OF LETTING ME GET BEHIND THE WHEEL OF MY OWN CAR IN MY EXHAUSTED CONDITION.
I DIDN'T CARE. I COULD'VE SLEPT ON A ROLLER COASTER.
IT WAS WELL INTO THE AFTERNOON WHEN I GOT JOGGED AWAKE BY WEIRD NOISES COMING FROM A HULKING SHAPE NEXT TO THE BED.
?
Choke!
Sob!
Sniff!

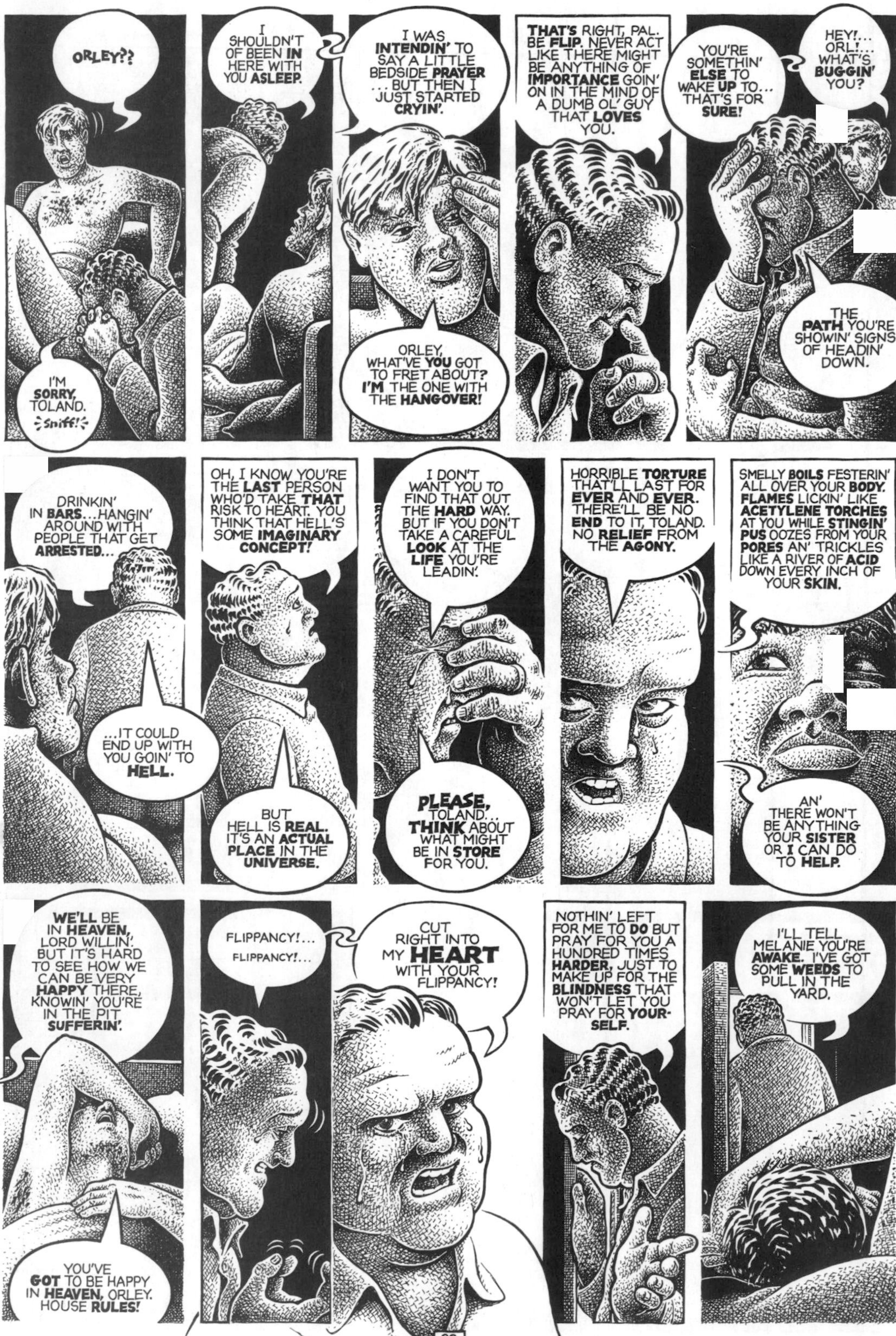

ORLEY??
I'M SORRY, TOLAND.
SNIFF!
I SHOULDN'T OF BEEN IN HERE WITH YOU ASLEEP.
I WAS INTENDIN' TO SAY A LITTLE BEDSIDE PRAYER ... BUT THEN I JUST STARTED CRYIN'.
ORLEY, WHAT'VE YOU GOT TO FRET ABOUT? I'M THE ONE WITH THE HANGOVER!
THAT'S RIGHT, PAL. BE FLIP. NEVER ACT LIKE THERE MIGHT BE ANYTHING OF IMPORTANCE GOIN' ON IN THE MIND OF A DUMB OL' GUY THAT LOVES YOU.
YOU'RE SOMETHIN' ELSE TO WAKE UP TO... THAT'S FOR SURE!
HEY!... ORL!... WHAT'S BUGGIN' YOU?
THE PATH YOU'RE SHOWIN' SIGNS OF HEADIN' DOWN.
DRINKIN' IN BARS...HANGIN' AROUND WITH PEOPLE THAT GET ARRESTED...
...IT COULD END UP WITH YOU GOIN' TO HELL.
OH, I KNOW YOU'RE THE LAST PERSON WHO'D TAKE THAT RISK TO HEART. YOU THINK THAT HELL'S SOME IMAGINARY CONCEPT!
BUT HELL IS REAL. IT'S AN ACTUAL PLACE IN THE UNIVERSE.
I DON'T WANT YOU TO FIND THAT OUT THE HARD WAY. BUT IF YOU DON'T TAKE A CAREFUL LOOK AT THE LIFE YOU'RE LEADIN'.
PLEASE, TOLAND... THINK ABOUT WHAT MIGHT BE IN STORE FOR YOU.
HORRIBLE TORTURE THAT'LL LAST FOR EVER AND EVER. THERE'LL BE NO END TO IT, TOLAND. NO RELIEF FROM THE AGONY.
SMELLY BOILS FESTERIN' ALL OVER YOUR BODY. FLAMES LICKIN' LIKE ACETYLENE TORCHES AT YOU WHILE STINGIN' PUS OOZES FROM YOUR PORES AN' TRICKLES LIKE A RIVER OF ACID DOWN EVERY INCH OF YOUR SKIN.
AN' THERE WON'T BE ANYTHING YOUR SISTER OR I CAN DO TO HELP.
WE'LL BE IN HEAVEN, LORD WILLIN'. BUT IT'S HARD TO SEE HOW WE CAN BE VERY HAPPY THERE, KNOWIN' YOU'RE IN THE PIT SUFFERIN'.
YOU'VE GOT TO BE HAPPY IN HEAVEN, ORLEY. HOUSE RULES!
FLIPPANCY!... FLIPPANCY!...
CUT RIGHT INTO MY HEART WITH YOUR FLIPPANCY!
NOTHIN' LEFT FOR ME TO DO BUT PRAY FOR YOU A HUNDRED TIMES HARDER, JUST TO MAKE UP FOR THE BLINDNESS THAT WON'T LET YOU PRAY FOR YOUR-SELF.
I'LL TELL MELANIE YOU'RE AWAKE. I'VE GOT SOME WEEDS TO PULL IN THE YARD.

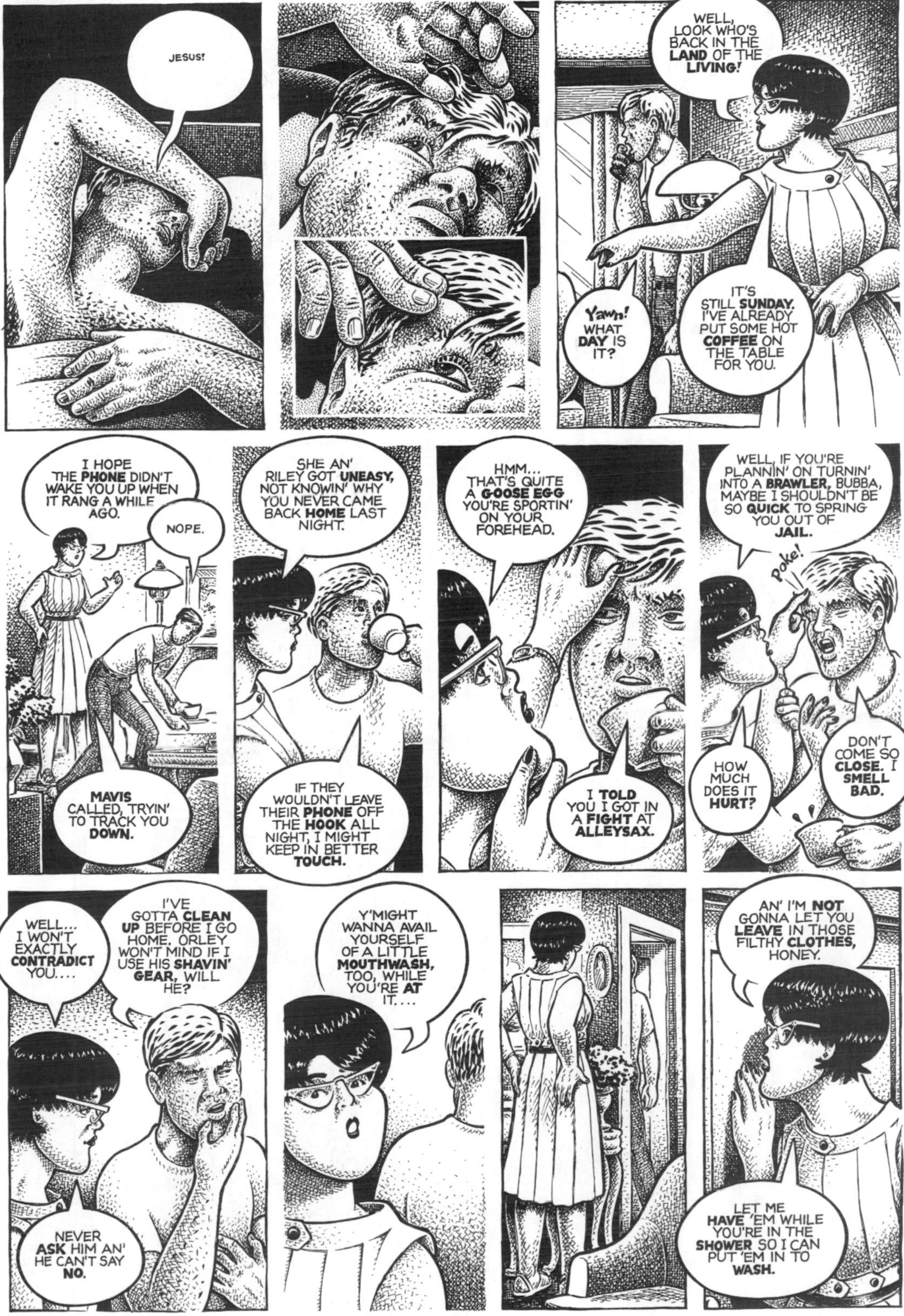
JESUS!
WELL, LOOK WHO'S BACK IN THE LAND OF THE LIVING!
Yawn! WHAT DAY IS IT?
IT'S STILL SUNDAY. I'VE ALREADY PUT SOME HOT COFFEE ON THE TABLE FOR YOU.
I HOPE THE PHONE DIDN'T WAKE YOU UP WHEN IT RANG A WHILE AGO.
NOPE.
MAVIS CALLED, TRYIN' TO TRACK YOU DOWN.
SHE AN' RILEY GOT UNEASY, NOT KNOWIN' WHY YOU NEVER CAME BACK HOME LAST NIGHT.
IF THEY WOULDN'T LEAVE THEIR PHONE OFF THE HOOK ALL NIGHT, I MIGHT KEEP IN BETTER TOUCH.
HMM... THAT'S QUITE A GOOSE EGG YOU'RE SPORTIN' ON YOUR FOREHEAD.
I TOLD YOU I GOT IN A FIGHT AT ALLEYSAX.
WELL, IF YOU'RE PLANNIN' ON TURNIN' INTO A BRAWLER, BUBBA, MAYBE I SHOULDN'T BE SO QUICK TO SPRING YOU OUT OF JAIL.
Poke!
HOW MUCH DOES IT HURT?
DON'T COME SO CLOSE. I SMELL BAD.
WELL... I WON'T EXACTLY CONTRADICT YOU....
I'VE GOTTA CLEAN UP BEFORE I GO HOME. ORLEY WON'T MIND IF I USE HIS SHAVIN' GEAR, WILL HE?
NEVER ASK HIM AN' HE CAN'T SAY NO.
Y'MIGHT WANNA AVAIL YOURSELF OF A LITTLE MOUTHWASH, TOO, WHILE YOU'RE AT IT....
AN' I'M NOT GONNA LET YOU LEAVE IN THOSE FILTHY CLOTHES, HONEY.
LET ME HAVE 'EM WHILE YOU'RE IN THE SHOWER SO I CAN PUT 'EM IN TO WASH.

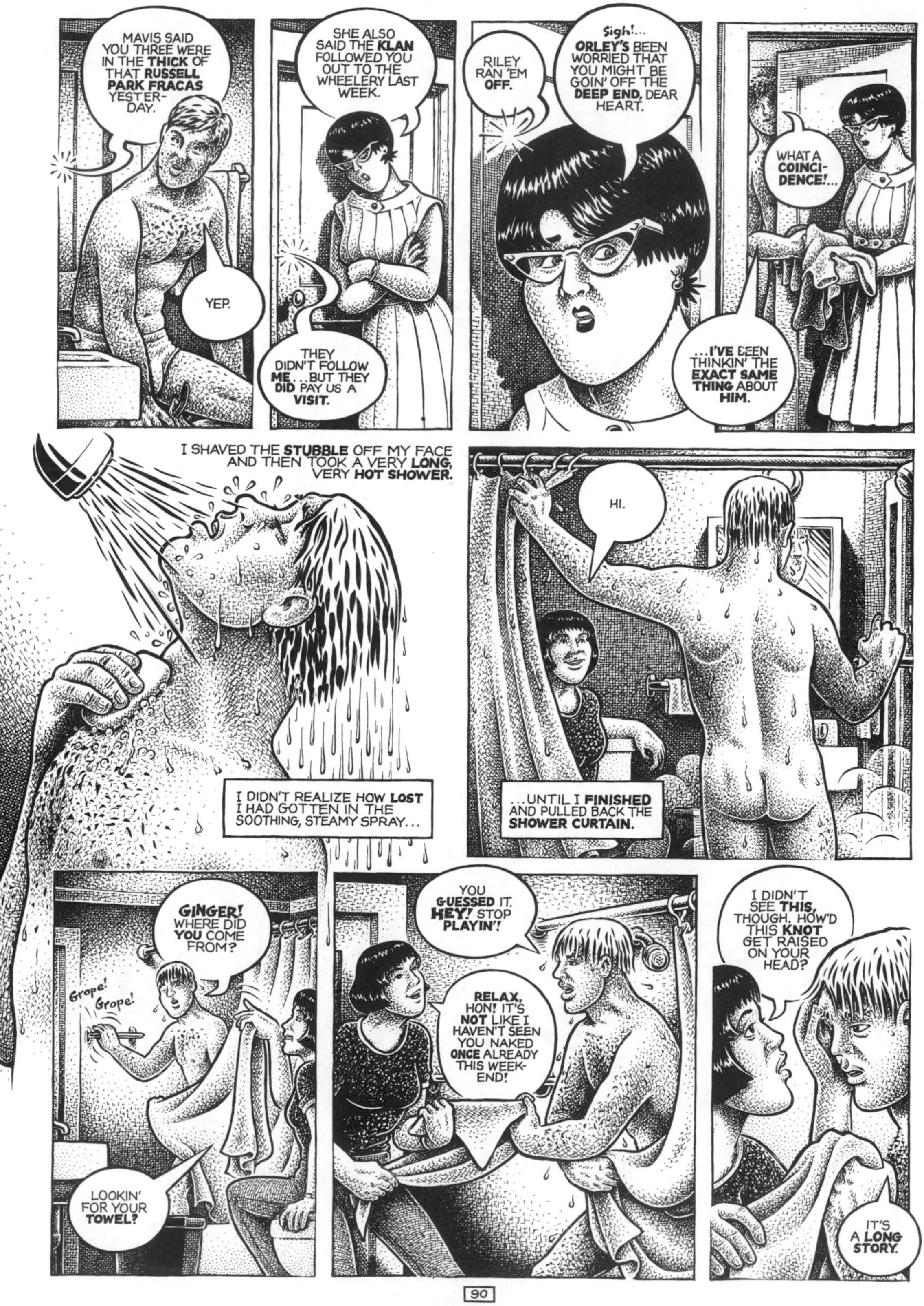

MAVIS SAID YOU THREE WERE IN THE THICK OF THAT RUSSELL PARK FRACAS YESTER-DAY.
YEP.
SHE ALSO SAID THE KLAN FOLLOWED YOU OUT TO THE WHEELERY LAST WEEK.
THEY DIDN'T FOLLOW ME. . .BUT THEY DID PAY US A VISIT.
RILEY RAN 'EM OFF.
Sigh!... ORLEY'S BEEN WORRIED THAT YOU MIGHT BE GOIN' OFF THE DEEP END, DEAR HEART.
WHAT A COINCI-DENCE!...
...I'VE BEEN THINKIN' THE EXACT SAME THING ABOUT HIM.
I SHAVED THE STUBBLE OFF MY FACE AND THEN TOOK A VERY LONG, VERY HOT SHOWER.
I DIDN'T REALIZE HOW LOST I HAD GOTTEN IN THE SOOTHING, STEAMY SPRAY. . .
HI.
...UNTIL I FINISHED AND PULLED BACK THE SHOWER CURTAIN.
GINGER! WHERE DID YOU COME FROM?
Grope! Grope!
LOOKIN' FOR YOUR TOWEL?
YOU GUESSED IT. HEY! STOP PLAYIN'!
RELAX, HON! IT'S NOT LIKE I HAVEN'T SEEN YOU NAKED ONCE ALREADY THIS WEEK-END!
I DIDN'T SEE THIS, THOUGH. HOW'D THIS KNOT GET RAISED ON YOUR HEAD?
IT'S A LONG STORY.

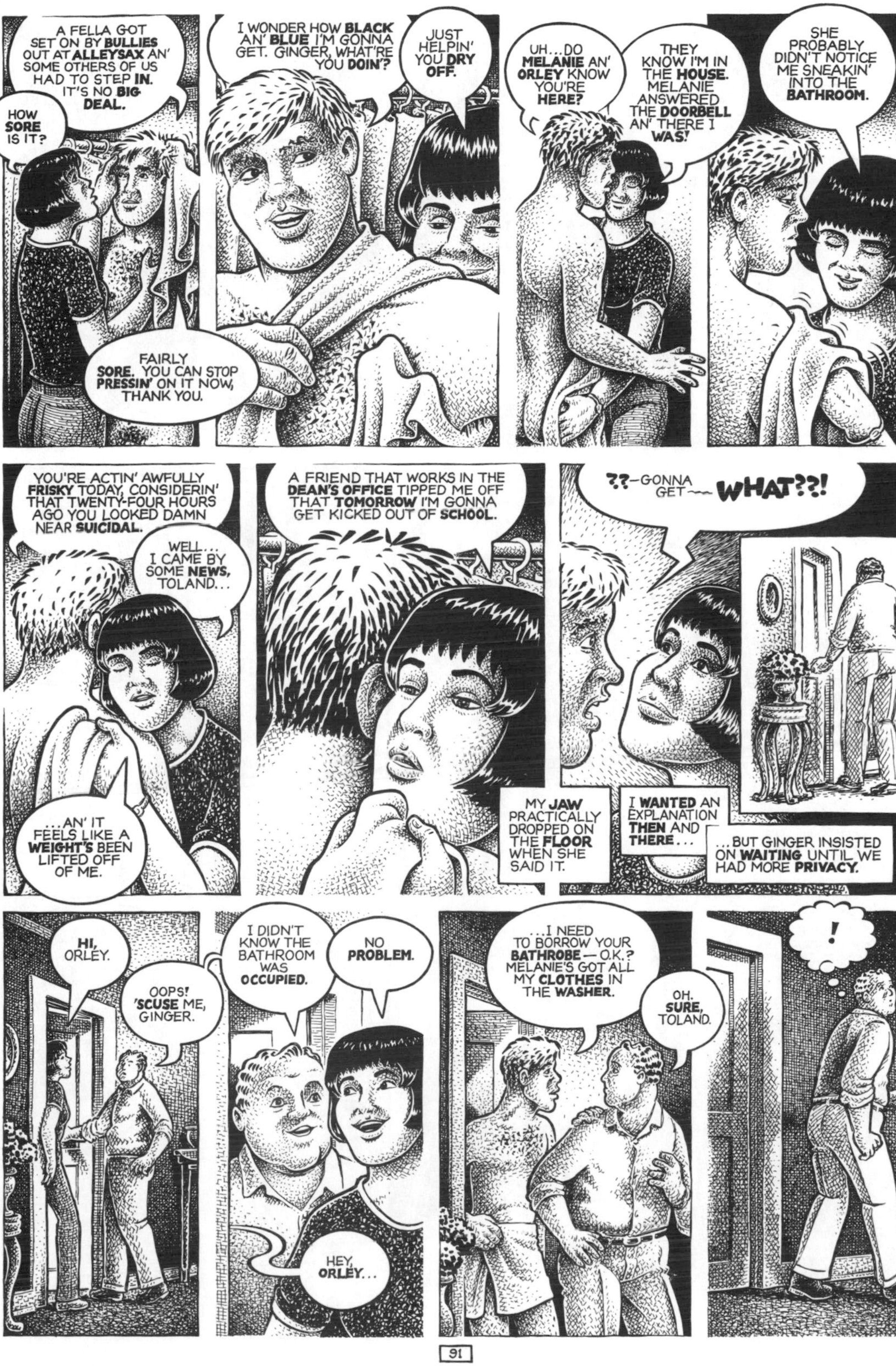
A FELLA GOT SET ON BY BULLIES OUT AT ALLEYSAX AN' SOME OTHERS OF US HAD TO STEP IN. IT'S NO BIG DEAL.
HOW SORE IS IT?
FAIRLY SORE. YOU CAN STOP PRESSIN' ON IT NOW, THANK YOU.
I WONDER HOW BLACK AN' BLUE I'M GONNA GET. GINGER, WHAT'RE YOU DOIN'?
JUST HELPIN' YOU DRY OFF.
UH...DO MELANIE AN' ORLEY KNOW YOU'RE HERE?
THEY KNOW I'M IN THE HOUSE. MELANIE ANSWERED THE DOORBELL AN' THERE I WAS!
SHE PROBABLY DIDN'T NOTICE ME SNEAKIN' INTO THE BATHROOM.
YOU'RE ACTIN' AWFULLY FRISKY TODAY, CONSIDERIN' THAT TWENTY-FOUR HOURS AGO YOU LOOKED DAMN NEAR SUICIDAL.
WELL... I CAME BY SOME NEWS, TOLAND...
...AN' IT FEELS LIKE A WEIGHT'S BEEN LIFTED OFF OF ME.
A FRIEND THAT WORKS IN THE DEAN'S OFFICE TIPPED ME OFF THAT TOMORROW I'M GONNA GET KICKED OUT OF SCHOOL.
??-GONNA GET— WHAT??!
MY JAW PRACTICALLY DROPPED ON THE FLOOR WHEN SHE SAID IT.
I WANTED AN EXPLANATION THEN AND THERE...
...BUT GINGER INSISTED ON WAITING UNTIL WE HAD MORE PRIVACY.
HI, ORLEY.
OOPS! 'SCUSE ME, GINGER.
I DIDN'T KNOW THE BATHROOM WAS OCCUPIED.
NO PROBLEM.
HEY, ORLEY...
...I NEED TO BORROW YOUR BATHROBE — O.K.? MELANIE'S GOT ALL MY CLOTHES IN THE WASHER.
OH. SURE, TOLAND.
!

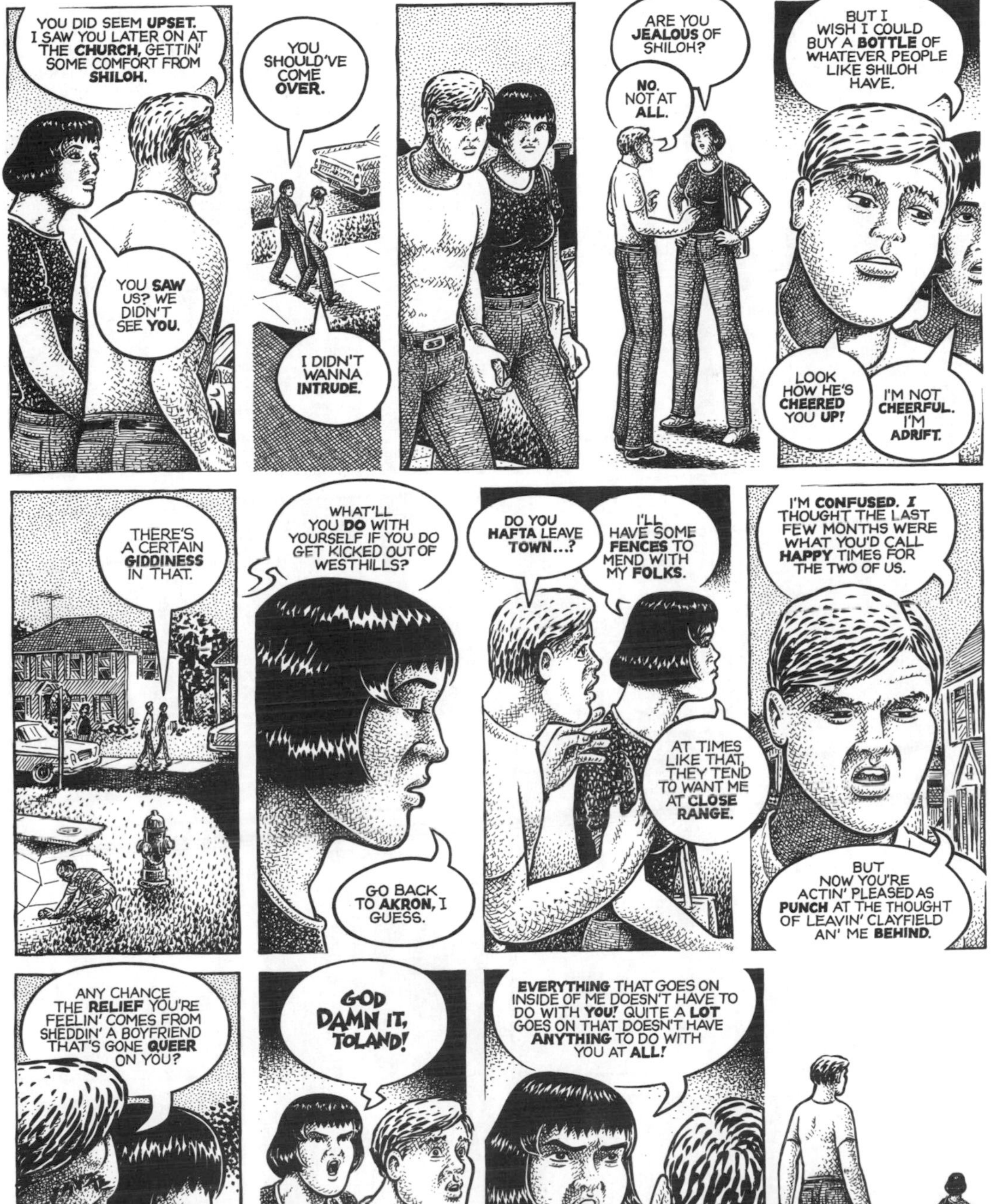
YOU DID SEEM UPSET. I SAW YOU LATER ON AT THE CHURCH, GETTIN' SOME COMFORT FROM SHILOH.
YOU SAW US? WE DIDN'T SEE YOU.
YOU SHOULD'VE COME OVER.
I DIDN'T WANNA INTRUDE.
ARE YOU JEALOUS OF SHILOH?
NO. NOT AT ALL.
BUT I WISH I COULD BUY A BOTTLE OF WHATEVER PEOPLE LIKE SHILOH HAVE.
LOOK HOW HE'S CHEERED YOU UP!
I'M NOT CHEERFUL. I'M ADRIFT.
THERE'S A CERTAIN GIDDINESS IN THAT.
WHAT'LL YOU DO WITH YOURSELF IF YOU DO GET KICKED OUT OF WESTHILLS?
GO BACK TO AKRON, I GUESS.
DO YOU HAFTA LEAVE TOWN...?
I'LL HAVE SOME FENCES TO MEND WITH MY FOLKS.
AT TIMES LIKE THAT, THEY TEND TO WANT ME AT CLOSE RANGE.
I'M CONFUSED. I THOUGHT THE LAST FEW MONTHS WERE WHAT YOU'D CALL HAPPY TIMES FOR THE TWO OF US.
BUT NOW YOU'RE ACTIN' PLEASED AS PUNCH AT THE THOUGHT OF LEAVIN' CLAYFIELD AN' ME BEHIND.
ANY CHANCE THE RELIEF YOU'RE FEELIN' COMES FROM SHEDDIN' A BOYFRIEND THAT'S GONE QUEER ON YOU?
GOD DAMN IT, TOLAND!
EVERYTHING THAT GOES ON INSIDE OF ME DOESN'T HAVE TO DO WITH YOU! QUITE A LOT GOES ON THAT DOESN'T HAVE ANYTHING TO DO WITH YOU AT ALL!

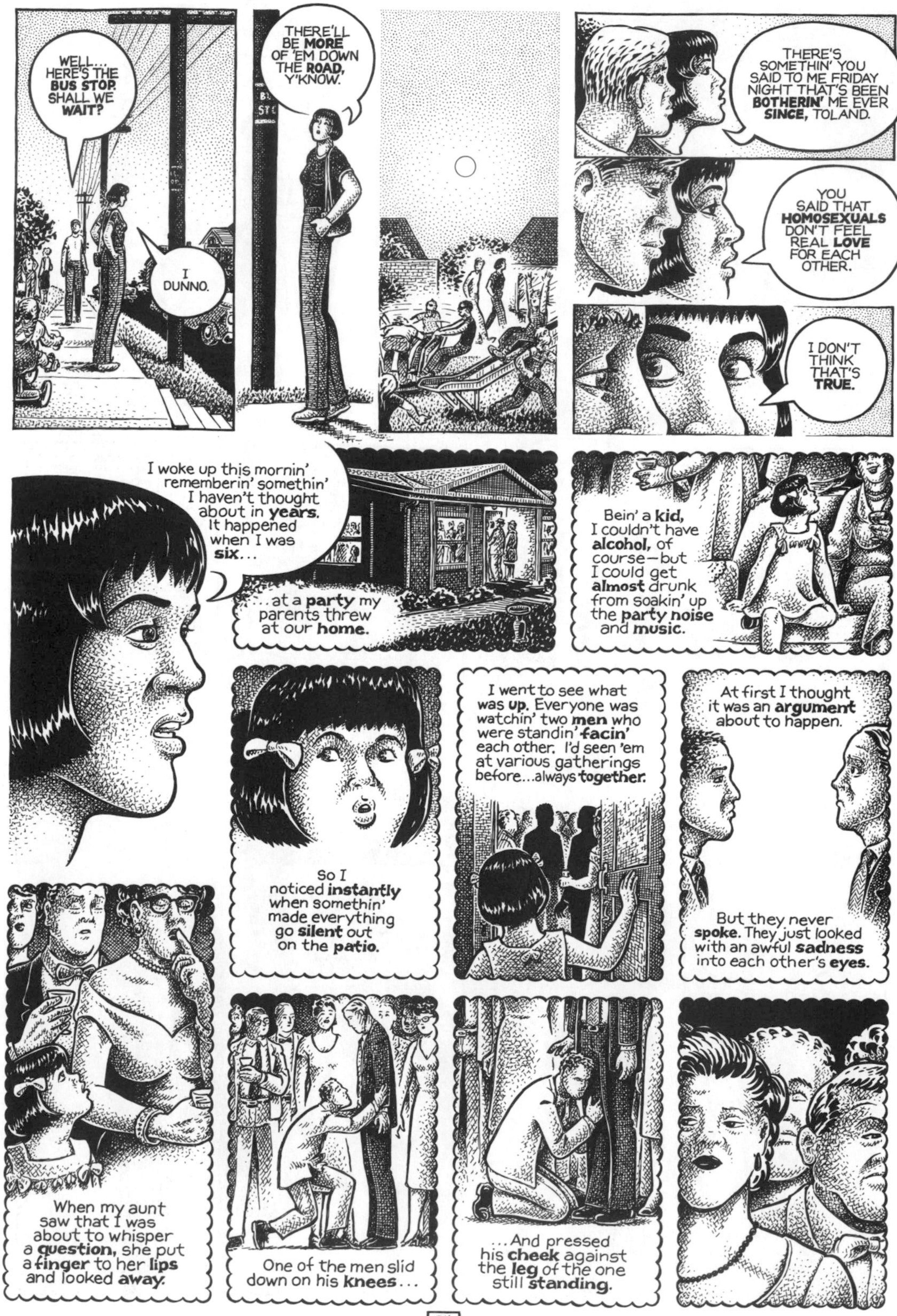
WELL... HERE'S THE BUS STOP. SHALL WE WAIT?
I DUNNO.
THERE'LL BE MORE OF 'EM DOWN THE ROAD, Y'KNOW.
THERE'S SOMETHIN' YOU SAID TO ME FRIDAY NIGHT THAT'S BEEN BOTHERIN' ME EVER SINCE, TOLAND.
YOU SAID THAT HOMOSEXUALS DON'T FEEL REAL LOVE FOR EACH OTHER.
I DON'T THINK THAT'S TRUE.
I woke up this mornin' rememberin' somethin' I haven't thought about in years. It happened when I was six...
...at a party my parents threw at our home.
Bein' a kid, I couldn't have alcohol, of course—but I could get almost drunk from soakin' up the party noise and music.
So I noticed instantly when somethin' made everything go silent out on the patio.
I went to see what was up. Everyone was watchin' two men who were standin' facin' each other. I'd seen 'em at various gatherings before...always together.
At first I thought it was an argument about to happen.
But they never spoke. They just looked with an awful sadness into each other's eyes.
When my aunt saw that I was about to whisper a question, she put a finger to her lips and looked away.
One of the men slid down on his knees...
...And pressed his cheek against the leg of the one still standing.

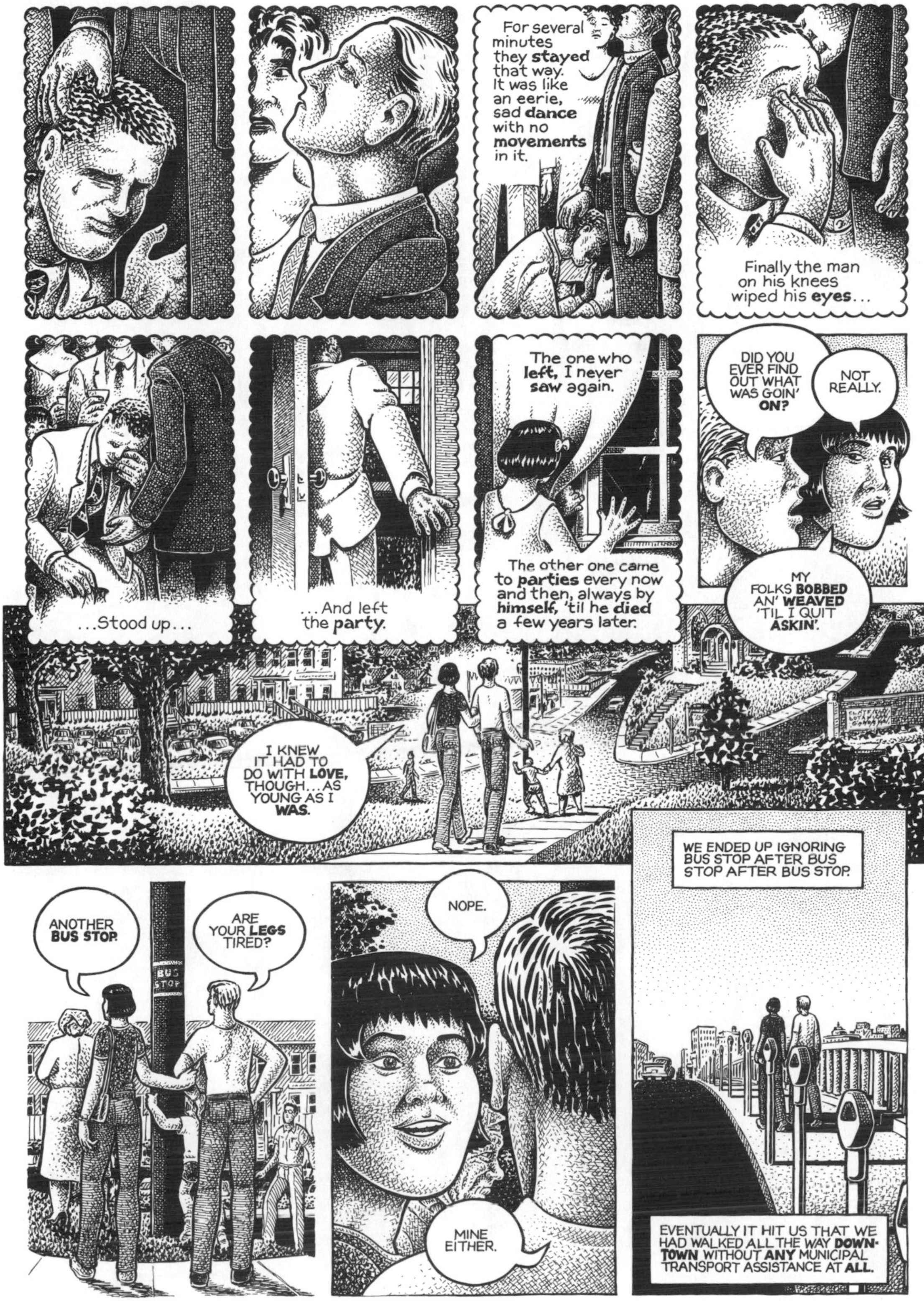
For several minutes they stayed that way. It was like an eerie, sad dance with no movements in it.
Finally the man on his knees wiped his eyes...
...Stood up...
...And left the party.
The one who left, I never saw again.
The other one came to parties every now and then, always by himself, 'til he died a few years later.
DID YOU EVER FIND OUT WHAT WAS GOIN' ON?
NOT REALLY.
MY FOLKS BOBBED AN' WEAVED 'TIL I QUIT ASKIN'.
I KNEW IT HAD TO DO WITH LOVE, THOUGH... AS YOUNG AS I WAS.
ANOTHER BUS STOP.
ARE YOUR LEGS TIRED?
BUS STOP
NOPE.
MINE EITHER.
WE ENDED UP IGNORING BUS STOP AFTER BUS STOP AFTER BUS STOP.
EVENTUALLY IT HIT US THAT WE HAD WALKED ALL THE WAY DOWNTOWN WITHOUT ANY MUNICIPAL TRANSPORT ASSISTANCE AT ALL.

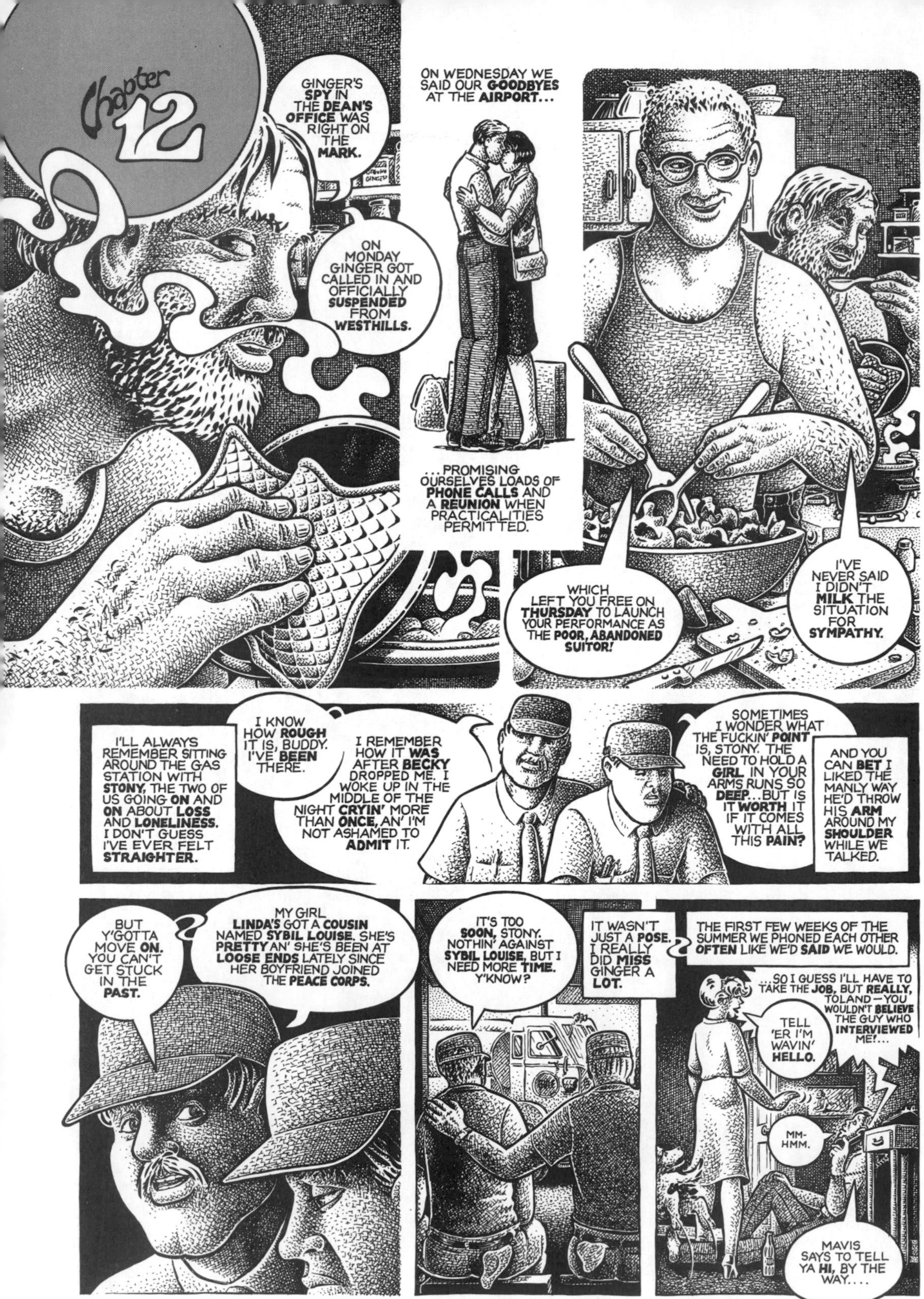
Chapter 12
GINGER'S SPY IN THE DEAN'S OFFICE WAS RIGHT ON THE MARK.
ON MONDAY GINGER GOT CALLED IN AND OFFICIALLY SUSPENDED FROM WESTHILLS.
ON WEDNESDAY WE SAID OUR GOODBYES AT THE AIRPORT...
...PROMISING OURSELVES LOADS OF PHONE CALLS AND A REUNION WHEN PRACTICALITIES PERMITTED.
WHICH LEFT YOU FREE ON THURSDAY TO LAUNCH YOUR PERFORMANCE AS THE POOR, ABANDONED SUITOR!
I'VE NEVER SAID I DIDN'T MILK THE SITUATION FOR SYMPATHY.
I'LL ALWAYS REMEMBER SITTING AROUND THE GAS STATION WITH STONY, THE TWO OF US GOING ON AND ON ABOUT LOSS AND LONELINESS. I DON'T GUESS I'VE EVER FELT STRAIGHTER.
I KNOW HOW ROUGH IT IS, BUDDY. I'VE BEEN THERE.
I REMEMBER HOW IT WAS AFTER BECKY DROPPED ME. I WOKE UP IN THE MIDDLE OF THE NIGHT CRYIN' MORE THAN ONCE, AN' I'M NOT ASHAMED TO ADMIT IT.
SOMETIMES I WONDER WHAT THE FUCKIN' POINT IS, STONY. THE NEED TO HOLD A GIRL IN YOUR ARMS RUNS SO DEEP...BUT IS IT WORTH IT IF IT COMES WITH ALL THIS PAIN?
AND YOU CAN BET I LIKED THE MANLY WAY HE'D THROW HIS ARM AROUND MY SHOULDER WHILE WE TALKED.
BUT Y'GOTTA MOVE ON. YOU CAN'T GET STUCK IN THE PAST.
MY GIRL LINDA'S GOT A COUSIN NAMED SYBIL LOUISE. SHE'S PRETTY AN' SHE'S BEEN AT LOOSE ENDS LATELY SINCE HER BOYFRIEND JOINED THE PEACE CORPS.
IT'S TOO SOON, STONY. NOTHIN' AGAINST SYBIL LOUISE, BUT I NEED MORE TIME. Y'KNOW?
IT WASN'T JUST A POSE. I REALLY DID MISS GINGER A LOT.
THE FIRST FEW WEEKS OF THE SUMMER WE PHONED EACH OTHER OFTEN LIKE WE'D SAID WE WOULD.
...SO I GUESS I'LL HAVE TO TAKE THE JOB, BUT REALLY, TOLAND—YOU WOULDN'T BELIEVE THE GUY WHO INTERVIEWED ME!...
TELL 'ER I'M WAVIN' HELLO.
MM-HMM.
MAVIS SAYS TO TELL YA HI, BY THE WAY....

BUT THEN I FELT MYSELF GETTING MORE AND MORE **WITHDRAWN** AND CALLING HER **LESS** AND **LESS**.

IT WASN'T ONLY **GINGER** I WAS PULLING BACK FROM.

The Clayfield Banner
BIRCH SOCIETY CONDEMNS TEST-BAN TREATY TALKS

I STOPPED SHOWING UP AT **EQUALITY LEAGUE** MEETINGS OR EVEN KEEPING UP WITH HOW REV. PEPPER'S **SKIRMISHES** WITH THE **CITY** WERE FARING.

I EVEN STARTED FEELING PUT **OFF** BY SAMMY NOONE.

LOOK, TOLAND! SAMMY'S **CAST** IS OFF.

HEY, THAT'S **GREAT**.

LIKE OUR **LORD** ON **EASTER MORN**, MY HAND IS **RISEN** FROM THE DEAD!

FATHER MORRIS — BEING A GOOD **LIBERAL** WHO **APPROVED** OF PROTESTS LIKE THE ONE AT RUSSELL PARK — HAD AVERTED **ONE** POTENTIAL CRISIS BY KEEPING SAMMY ON THE CHURCH **PAYROLL** DURING THE PERIOD WHEN HE COULDN'T **PLAY**.

YOU'D THINK I'D HAVE SIMPLY FELT **PLEASED** FOR HIM, BUT FOR SOME REASON SAMMY'S PERPETUAL DEVIL-MAY-CARE **ATTITUDE** HAD BEGUN GETTING ON MY **NERVES**.

! ? **TOLAND!**

HOW SOON ARE YA GONNA BE READY TO **PERFORM** AGAIN?

WITH PROPER **PRACTICE** I EXPECT MY TALENTED **DIGITS** TO BE FULLY REHABILITATED IN **RECORD TIME!**

SOON I'LL BE *TANTALIZING HER TITTIES WITH SHIMMERING TRILL-L-L-LS!...*

...VISITING VENTURESOME GLISSANDOS ON HER QUAKING NETHER-REGIONS!...

I'M SURE **MAVIS** WILL FREELY OFFER UP HER SEMI-VIRGINAL **BODY** FOR MY FIVE-FINGER **EXERCISES!**

NATCH! WHAT'RE FRIENDS FOR?

...AHH, MAVEEZ, ZEE MACHO PASSION, SHE EEZ RIZEENG...

nibble!

SAMMY, THAT **TICKLES!**

SPARE US YOUR **STRAIGHT** ACT, SAMMY. IT JUST AIN'T **CONVINCIN'!**

BABY, WE'VE BEEN CUTTIN' LOTS OF **SLACK** FOR YOU AN' YOUR **MOODS** LATELY, BUT IF YOU'RE EVER **RUDE** LIKE THAT TO SAMMY **AGAIN**, YOU CAN START LOOKIN' FOR OTHER **QUARTERS!**

MAVIS HAD **NEVER** BLOWN HER **TOP** AT ME LIKE THAT BEFORE. MY STOMACH STILL GETS **WOBBLY** THINKING **BACK** ON IT.

MY SISTER COULD **TELL** I WAS **DEPRESSED**.

TOLAND, IF YOU DON'T AT LEAST MAKE A **STAB** AT SHAKIN' OFF THESE **BLUES**, YOU'RE GONNA DRIVE THE **REST** OF US OUT OF OUR **GOURDS**.

NOW, ORLEY AN' I WANT **YOU** AN' MAVIS AN' RILEY TO COME OVER SUNDAY AFTERNOON FOR A **BARBEQUE**.

AN' IF YOU DON'T BRING A BETTER **DISPOSITION** WITH YOU, IT'S GONNA BE **YOU** THAT GETS **BARBE-QUED!**

AN' FOR GOD'S SAKE, BRING A **DATE**.

I KNOW YOU'D RATHER **GINGER** WAS HERE, BUT YOU **CAN'T** STOP HAVIN' A SOCIAL LIFE **ENTIRELY!**

I TOOK HER **ADVICE**.

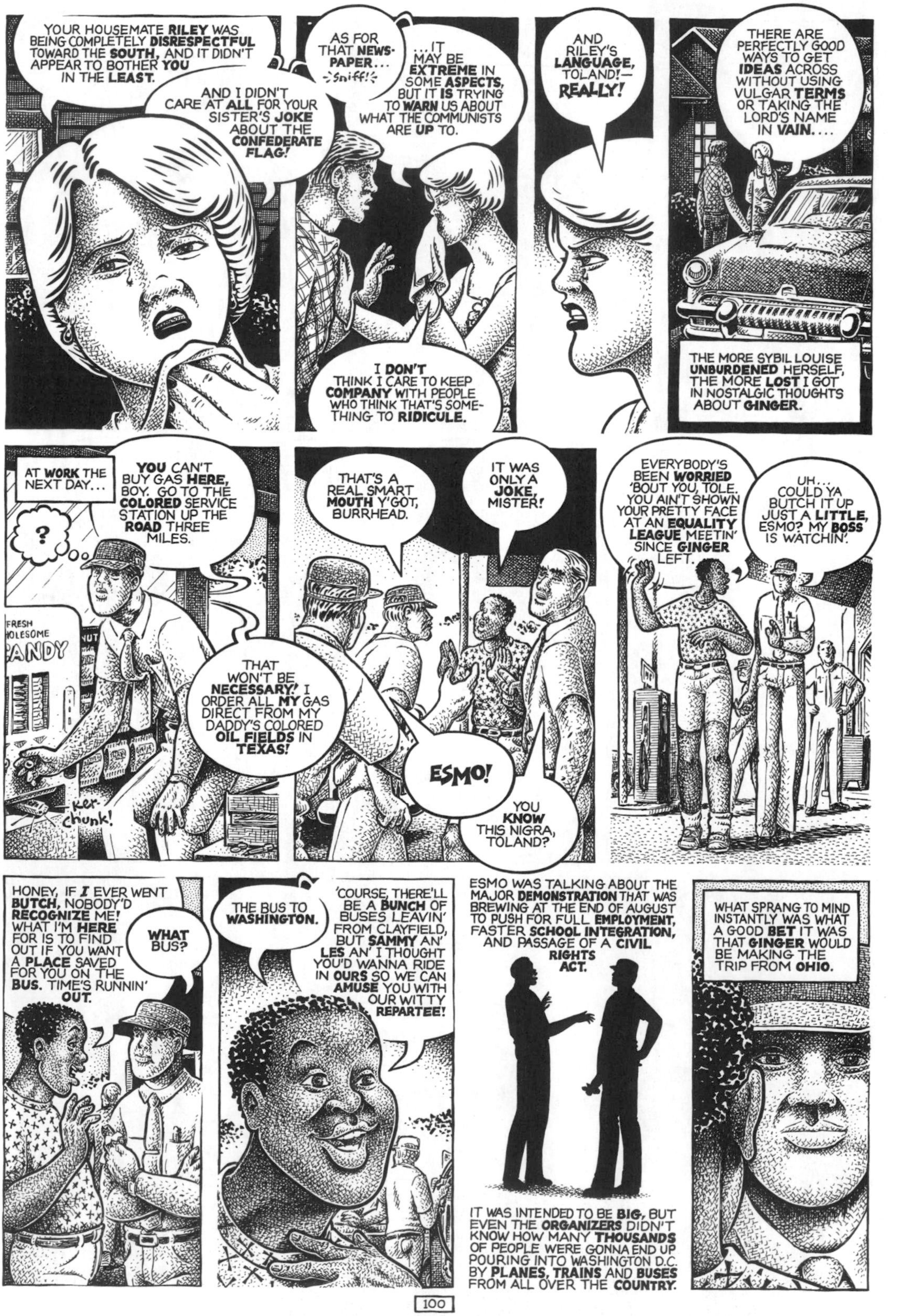
YOUR HOUSEMATE RILEY WAS BEING COMPLETELY DISRESPECTFUL TOWARD THE SOUTH, AND IT DIDN'T APPEAR TO BOTHER YOU IN THE LEAST.
AND I DIDN'T CARE AT ALL FOR YOUR SISTER'S JOKE ABOUT THE CONFEDERATE FLAG!
AS FOR THAT NEWS-PAPER... -sniff!-
...IT MAY BE EXTREME IN SOME ASPECTS, BUT IT IS TRYING TO WARN US ABOUT WHAT THE COMMUNISTS ARE UP TO.
I DON'T THINK I CARE TO KEEP COMPANY WITH PEOPLE WHO THINK THAT'S SOME-THING TO RIDICULE.
AND RILEY'S LANGUAGE, TOLAND!— REALLY!
THERE ARE PERFECTLY GOOD WAYS TO GET IDEAS ACROSS WITHOUT USING VULGAR TERMS OR TAKING THE LORD'S NAME IN VAIN....
THE MORE SYBIL LOUISE UNBURDENED HERSELF, THE MORE LOST I GOT IN NOSTALGIC THOUGHTS ABOUT GINGER.
AT WORK THE NEXT DAY...
YOU CAN'T BUY GAS HERE, BOY. GO TO THE COLORED SERVICE STATION UP THE ROAD THREE MILES.
?
FRESH WHOLESOME CANDY
ker-chunk!
THAT WON'T BE NECESSARY! I ORDER ALL MY GAS DIRECT FROM MY DADDY'S COLORED OIL FIELDS IN TEXAS!
THAT'S A REAL SMART MOUTH Y'GOT, BURRHEAD.
IT WAS ONLY A JOKE, MISTER!
ESMO!
YOU KNOW THIS NIGRA, TOLAND?
EVERYBODY'S BEEN WORRIED 'BOUT YOU, TOLE. YOU AIN'T SHOWN YOUR PRETTY FACE AT AN EQUALITY LEAGUE MEETIN' SINCE GINGER LEFT.
UH... COULD YA BUTCH IT UP JUST A LITTLE, ESMO? MY BOSS IS WATCHIN'.
HONEY, IF I EVER WENT BUTCH, NOBODY'D RECOGNIZE ME! WHAT I'M HERE FOR IS TO FIND OUT IF YOU WANT A PLACE SAVED FOR YOU ON THE BUS. TIME'S RUNNIN' OUT.
WHAT BUS?
THE BUS TO WASHINGTON.
'COURSE, THERE'LL BE A BUNCH OF BUSES LEAVIN' FROM CLAYFIELD, BUT SAMMY AN' LES AN' I THOUGHT YOU'D WANNA RIDE IN OURS SO WE CAN AMUSE YOU WITH OUR WITTY REPARTEE!
ESMO WAS TALKING ABOUT THE MAJOR DEMONSTRATION THAT WAS BREWING AT THE END OF AUGUST TO PUSH FOR FULL EMPLOYMENT, FASTER SCHOOL INTEGRATION, AND PASSAGE OF A CIVIL RIGHTS ACT.
IT WAS INTENDED TO BE BIG, BUT EVEN THE ORGANIZERS DIDN'T KNOW HOW MANY THOUSANDS OF PEOPLE WERE GONNA END UP POURING INTO WASHINGTON D.C. BY PLANES, TRAINS AND BUSES FROM ALL OVER THE COUNTRY.
WHAT SPRANG TO MIND INSTANTLY WAS WHAT A GOOD BET IT WAS THAT GINGER WOULD BE MAKING THE TRIP FROM OHIO.

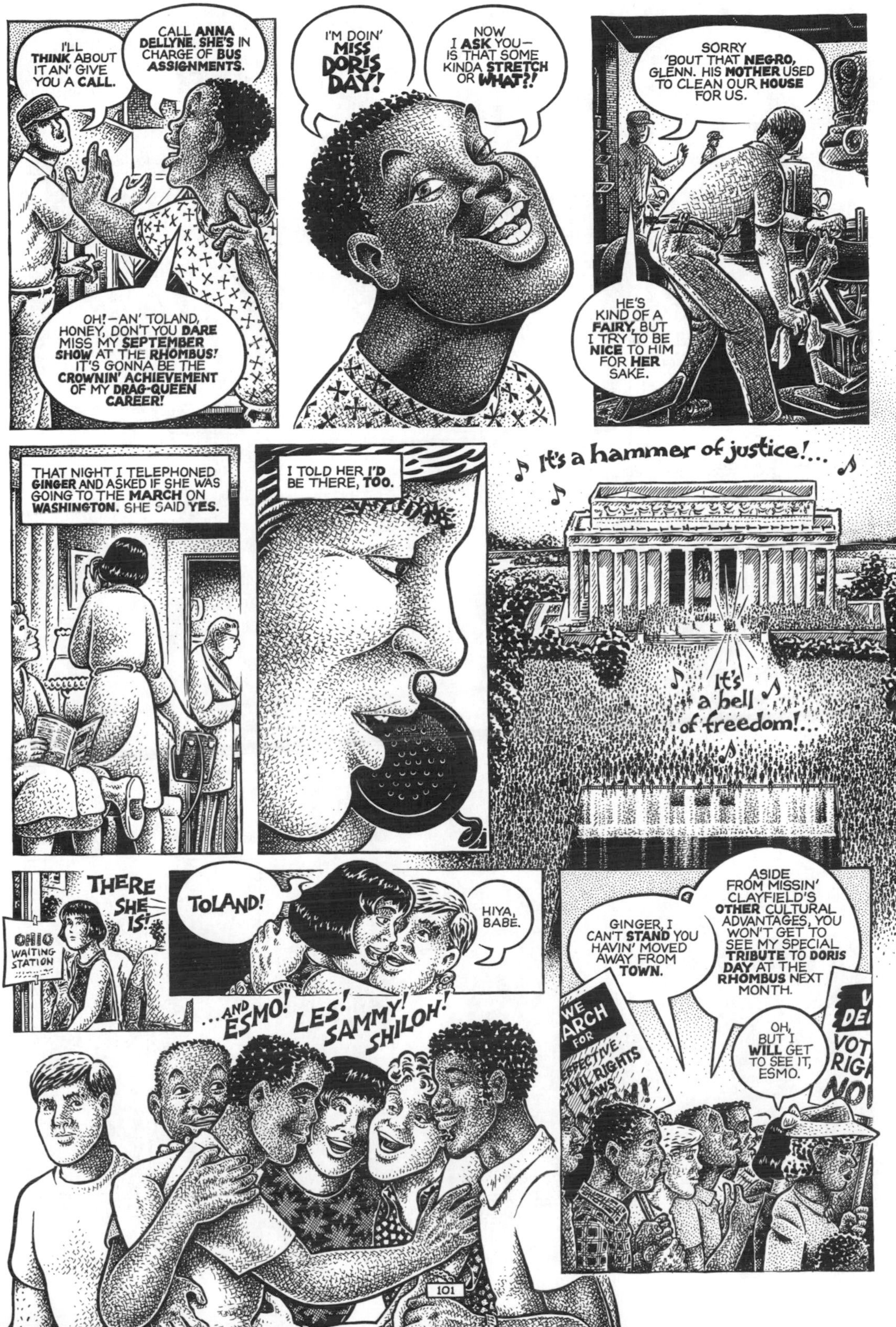

I'LL THINK ABOUT IT AN' GIVE YOU A CALL.
CALL ANNA DELLYNE. SHE'S IN CHARGE OF BUS ASSIGNMENTS.
OH!—AN' TOLAND, HONEY, DON'T YOU DARE MISS MY SEPTEMBER SHOW AT THE RHOMBUS! IT'S GONNA BE THE CROWNIN' ACHIEVEMENT OF MY DRAG-QUEEN CAREER!
I'M DOIN' MISS DORIS DAY!
NOW I ASK YOU—IS THAT SOME KINDA STRETCH OR WHAT?!
SORRY 'BOUT THAT NEGRO, GLENN. HIS MOTHER USED TO CLEAN OUR HOUSE FOR US.
HE'S KIND OF A FAIRY, BUT I TRY TO BE NICE TO HIM FOR HER SAKE.
THAT NIGHT I TELEPHONED GINGER AND ASKED IF SHE WAS GOING TO THE MARCH ON WASHINGTON. SHE SAID YES.
I TOLD HER I'D BE THERE, TOO.
It's a hammer of justice!...
It's a bell of freedom!...
OHIO WAITING STATION
THERE SHE IS!
TOLAND!
HIYA, BABE.
...AND ESMO! LES! SAMMY! SHILOH!
GINGER, I CAN'T STAND YOU HAVIN' MOVED AWAY FROM TOWN.
ASIDE FROM MISSIN' CLAYFIELD'S OTHER CULTURAL ADVANTAGES, YOU WON'T GET TO SEE MY SPECIAL TRIBUTE TO DORIS DAY AT THE RHOMBUS NEXT MONTH.
OH, BUT I WILL GET TO SEE IT, ESMO.

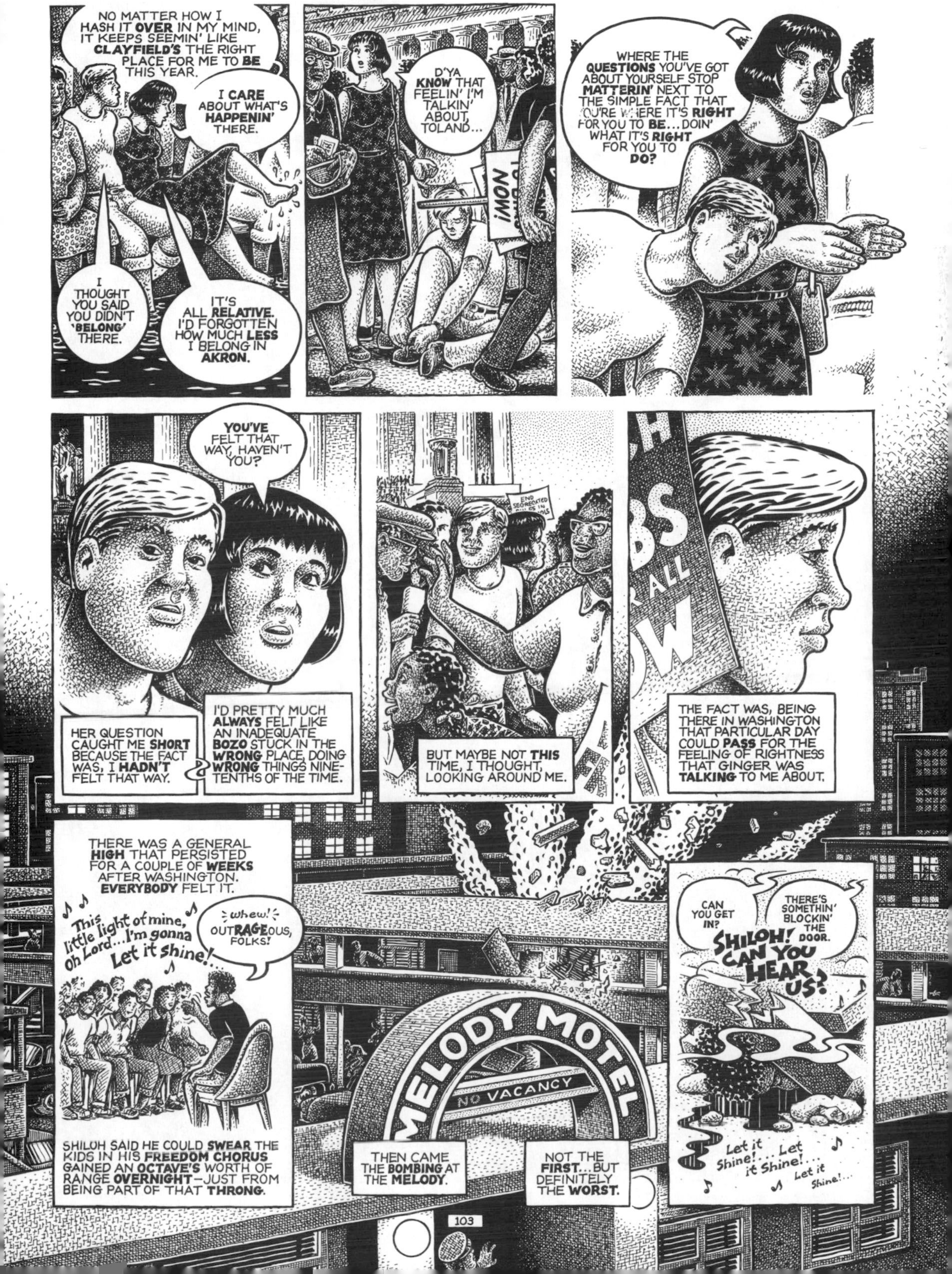

NO MATTER HOW I HASH IT OVER IN MY MIND, IT KEEPS SEEMIN' LIKE CLAYFIELD'S THE RIGHT PLACE FOR ME TO BE THIS YEAR.
I CARE ABOUT WHAT'S HAPPENIN' THERE.
I THOUGHT YOU SAID YOU DIDN'T 'BELONG' THERE.
IT'S ALL RELATIVE. I'D FORGOTTEN HOW MUCH LESS I BELONG IN AKRON.
D'YA KNOW THAT FEELIN' I'M TALKIN' ABOUT, TOLAND...
NOW!
WHERE THE QUESTIONS YOU'VE GOT ABOUT YOURSELF STOP MATTERIN' NEXT TO THE SIMPLE FACT THAT YOU'RE WHERE IT'S RIGHT FOR YOU TO BE... DOIN' WHAT IT'S RIGHT FOR YOU TO DO?
YOU'VE FELT THAT WAY, HAVEN'T YOU?
HER QUESTION CAUGHT ME SHORT BECAUSE THE FACT WAS, I HADN'T FELT THAT WAY.
I'D PRETTY MUCH ALWAYS FELT LIKE AN INADEQUATE BOZO STUCK IN THE WRONG PLACE, DOING WRONG THINGS NINE-TENTHS OF THE TIME.
END SEGREGATED
BUT MAYBE NOT THIS TIME, I THOUGHT, LOOKING AROUND ME.
THE FACT WAS, BEING THERE IN WASHINGTON THAT PARTICULAR DAY COULD PASS FOR THE FEELING OF RIGHTNESS THAT GINGER WAS TALKING TO ME ABOUT.
THERE WAS A GENERAL HIGH THAT PERSISTED FOR A COUPLE OF WEEKS AFTER WASHINGTON. EVERYBODY FELT IT.
This little light of mine, Oh Lord... I'm gonna Let it Shine!...
whew! OUTRAGEOUS, FOLKS!
SHILOH SAID HE COULD SWEAR THE KIDS IN HIS FREEDOM CHORUS GAINED AN OCTAVE'S WORTH OF RANGE OVERNIGHT—JUST FROM BEING PART OF THAT THRONG.
MELODY MOTEL
NO VACANCY
THEN CAME THE BOMBING AT THE MELODY.
NOT THE FIRST... BUT DEFINITELY THE WORST.
CAN YOU GET IN?
THERE'S SOMETHIN' BLOCKIN' THE DOOR.
SHILOH! CAN YOU HEAR US?
Let it Shine!... Let it Shine!... Let it Shine!...

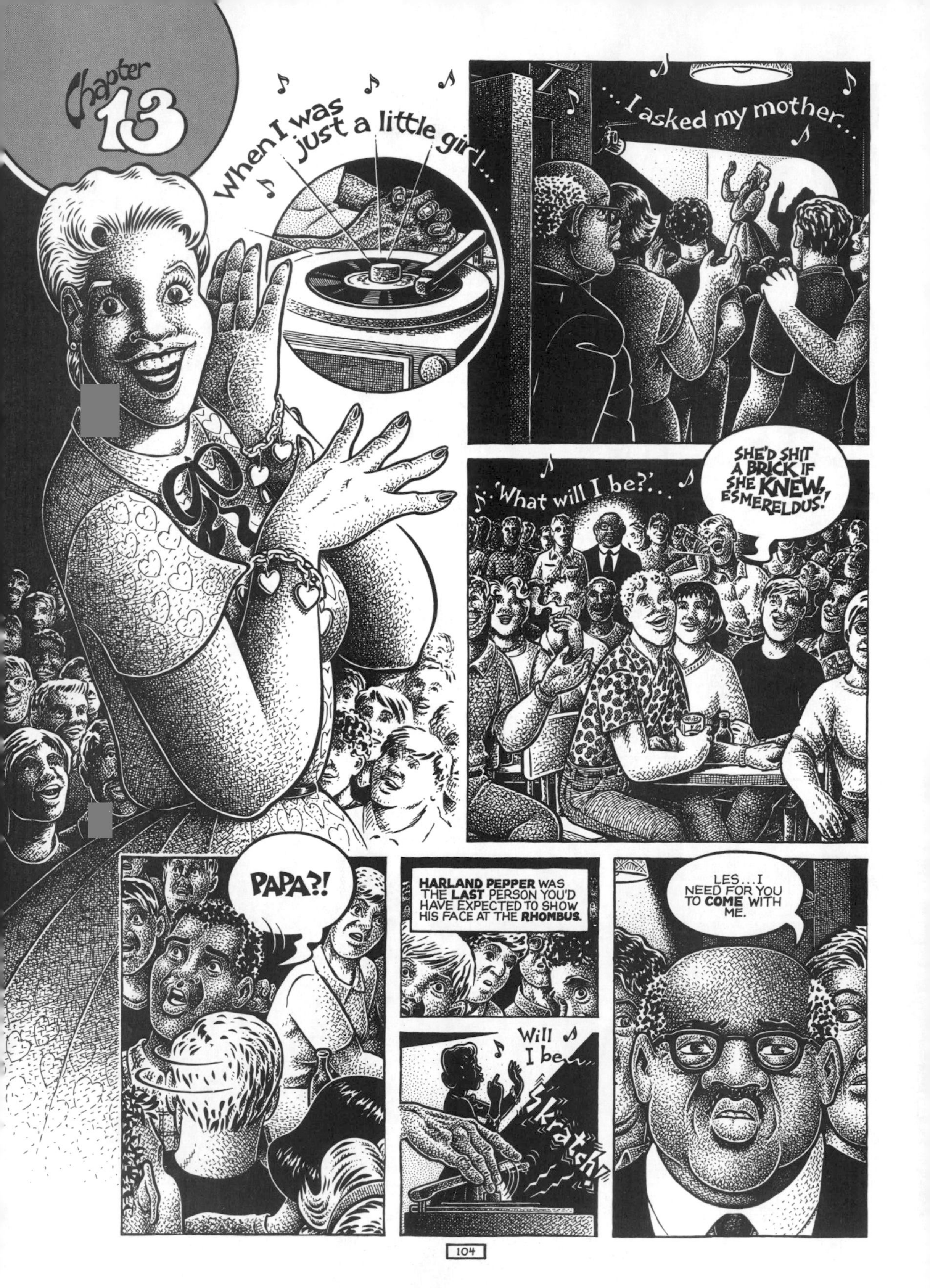
Chapter 13
When I was just a little girl...
...I asked my mother...
'What will I be?'...
SHE'D SHIT A BRICK IF SHE KNEW, ESMERELDUS!
PAPA?!
HARLAND PEPPER WAS THE LAST PERSON YOU'D HAVE EXPECTED TO SHOW HIS FACE AT THE RHOMBUS.
Will I be...
Skratch!
LES...I NEED FOR YOU TO COME WITH ME.

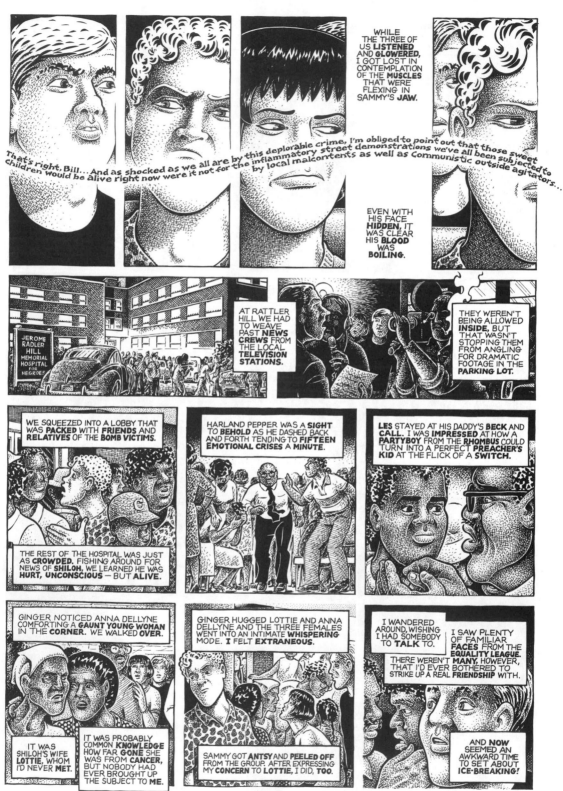

WHILE THE THREE OF US **LISTENED** AND **GLOWERED**, I GOT LOST IN CONTEMPLATION OF THE **MUSCLES** THAT WERE FLEXING IN SAMMY'S **JAW**.

That's right, Bill... And as shocked as we all are by this deplorable crime, I'm obliged to point out that those sweet children would be alive right now were it not for the inflammatory street demonstrations we've all been subjected to by local malcontents as well as Communistic outside agitators...

EVEN WITH HIS FACE **HIDDEN**, IT WAS CLEAR HIS **BLOOD** WAS **BOILING**.

JEROME RADLER HILL MEMORIAL HOSPITAL FOR NEGROES

AT RATTLER HILL WE HAD TO WEAVE PAST **NEWS CREWS** FROM THE LOCAL **TELEVISION STATIONS**.

THEY WEREN'T BEING ALLOWED **INSIDE**, BUT THAT WASN'T STOPPING THEM FROM ANGLING FOR DRAMATIC FOOTAGE IN THE **PARKING LOT**.

WE SQUEEZED INTO A LOBBY THAT WAS **PACKED** WITH **FRIENDS** AND **RELATIVES** OF THE **BOMB VICTIMS**.

THE REST OF THE HOSPITAL WAS JUST AS **CROWDED**. FISHING AROUND FOR NEWS OF **SHILOH**, WE LEARNED HE WAS **HURT, UNCONSCIOUS** — BUT **ALIVE**.

HARLAND PEPPER WAS A **SIGHT** TO **BEHOLD** AS HE DASHED BACK AND FORTH TENDING TO **FIFTEEN EMOTIONAL CRISES** A MINUTE.

LES STAYED AT HIS DADDY'S **BECK** AND **CALL**. I WAS **IMPRESSED** AT HOW A **PARTYBOY** FROM THE **RHOMBUS** COULD TURN INTO A PERFECT **PREACHER'S KID** AT THE FLICK OF A **SWITCH**.

GINGER NOTICED ANNA DELLYNE COMFORTING A **GAUNT YOUNG WOMAN** IN THE **CORNER**. WE WALKED **OVER**.

IT WAS SHILOH'S WIFE **LOTTIE**, WHOM I'D NEVER **MET**.

IT WAS PROBABLY COMMON **KNOWLEDGE** HOW FAR **GONE** SHE WAS FROM **CANCER**, BUT NOBODY HAD EVER BROUGHT UP THE SUBJECT TO **ME**.

GINGER HUGGED LOTTIE AND ANNA DELLYNE AND THE THREE FEMALES WENT INTO AN INTIMATE **WHISPERING** MODE. I FELT **EXTRANEOUS**.

SAMMY GOT **ANTSY** AND **PEELED OFF** FROM THE GROUP. AFTER EXPRESSING MY **CONCERN** TO **LOTTIE**, I DID, **TOO**.

I WANDERED AROUND, WISHING I HAD SOMEBODY TO **TALK** TO.

I SAW PLENTY OF FAMILIAR **FACES** FROM THE **EQUALITY LEAGUE**. THERE WEREN'T **MANY**, HOWEVER, THAT I'D EVER BOTHERED TO STRIKE UP A REAL **FRIENDSHIP** WITH.

AND **NOW** SEEMED AN AWKWARD TIME TO SET ABOUT **ICE-BREAKING!**

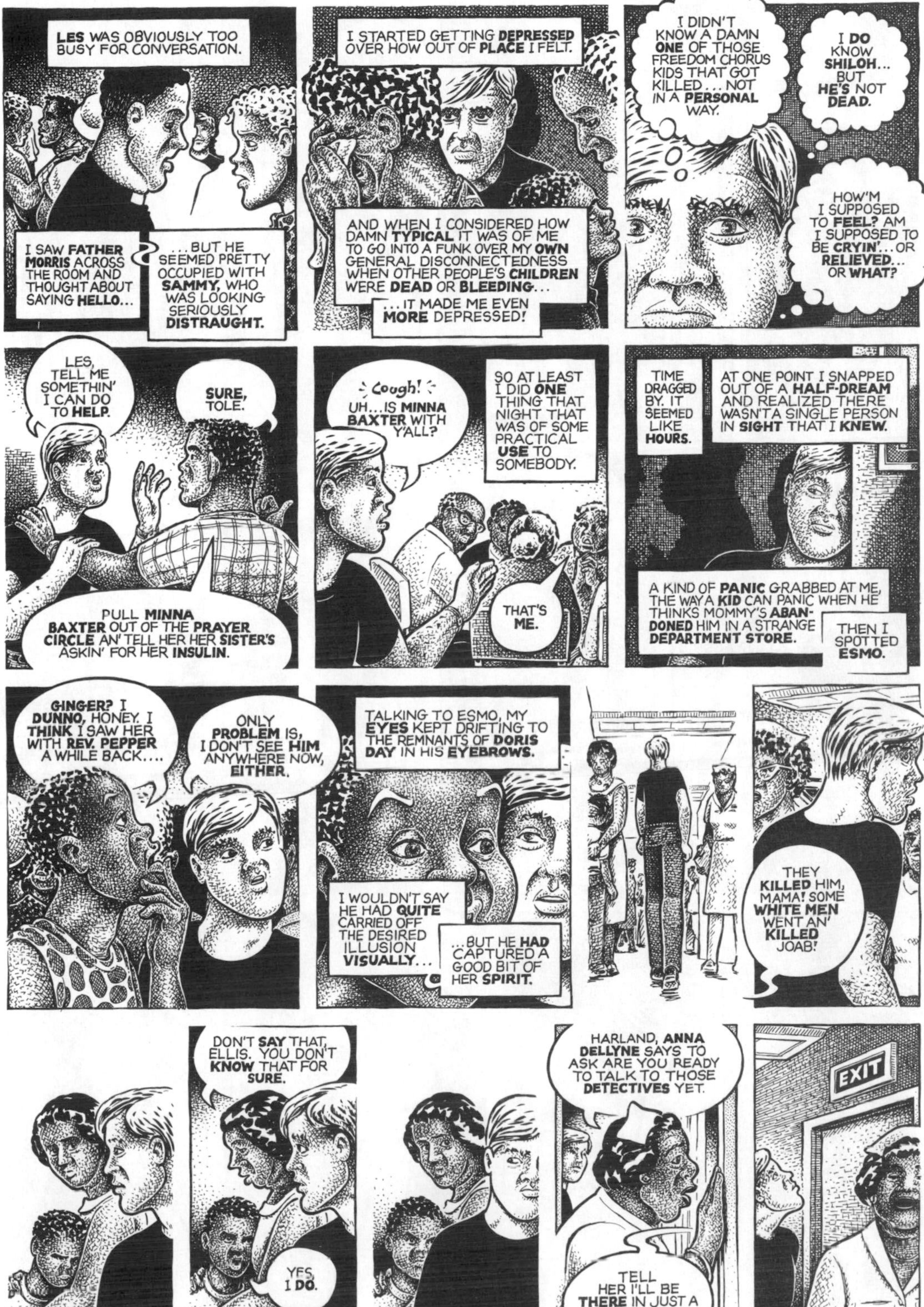
LES WAS OBVIOUSLY TOO BUSY FOR CONVERSATION.
I SAW FATHER MORRIS ACROSS THE ROOM AND THOUGHT ABOUT SAYING HELLO...
...BUT HE SEEMED PRETTY OCCUPIED WITH SAMMY, WHO WAS LOOKING SERIOUSLY DISTRAUGHT.
I STARTED GETTING DEPRESSED OVER HOW OUT OF PLACE I FELT.
AND WHEN I CONSIDERED HOW DAMN TYPICAL IT WAS OF ME TO GO INTO A FUNK OVER MY OWN GENERAL DISCONNECTEDNESS WHEN OTHER PEOPLE'S CHILDREN WERE DEAD OR BLEEDING...
...IT MADE ME EVEN MORE DEPRESSED!
I DIDN'T KNOW A DAMN ONE OF THOSE FREEDOM CHORUS KIDS THAT GOT KILLED... NOT IN A PERSONAL WAY.
I DO KNOW SHILOH... BUT HE'S NOT DEAD.
HOW'M I SUPPOSED TO FEEL? AM I SUPPOSED TO BE CRYIN'... OR RELIEVED... OR WHAT?
LES, TELL ME SOMETHIN' I CAN DO TO HELP.
SURE, TOLE.
PULL MINNA BAXTER OUT OF THE PRAYER CIRCLE AN' TELL HER HER SISTER'S ASKIN' FOR HER INSULIN.
Cough!
UH...IS MINNA BAXTER WITH Y'ALL?
SO AT LEAST I DID ONE THING THAT NIGHT THAT WAS OF SOME PRACTICAL USE TO SOMEBODY.
THAT'S ME.
TIME DRAGGED BY. IT SEEMED LIKE HOURS.
AT ONE POINT I SNAPPED OUT OF A HALF-DREAM AND REALIZED THERE WASN'T A SINGLE PERSON IN SIGHT THAT I KNEW.
A KIND OF PANIC GRABBED AT ME, THE WAY A KID CAN PANIC WHEN HE THINKS MOMMY'S ABANDONED HIM IN A STRANGE DEPARTMENT STORE.
THEN I SPOTTED ESMO.
GINGER? I DUNNO, HONEY. I THINK I SAW HER WITH REV. PEPPER A WHILE BACK....
ONLY PROBLEM IS, I DON'T SEE HIM ANYWHERE NOW, EITHER.
TALKING TO ESMO, MY EYES KEPT DRIFTING TO THE REMNANTS OF DORIS DAY IN HIS EYEBROWS.
I WOULDN'T SAY HE HAD QUITE CARRIED OFF THE DESIRED ILLUSION VISUALLY...
...BUT HE HAD CAPTURED A GOOD BIT OF HER SPIRIT.
THEY KILLED HIM, MAMA! SOME WHITE MEN WENT AN' KILLED JOAB!
DON'T SAY THAT, ELLIS. YOU DON'T KNOW THAT FOR SURE.
YES, I DO.
HARLAND, ANNA DELLYNE SAYS TO ASK ARE YOU READY TO TALK TO THOSE DETECTIVES YET.
TELL HER I'LL BE THERE IN JUST A FEW MINUTES, PAULINE.
EXIT

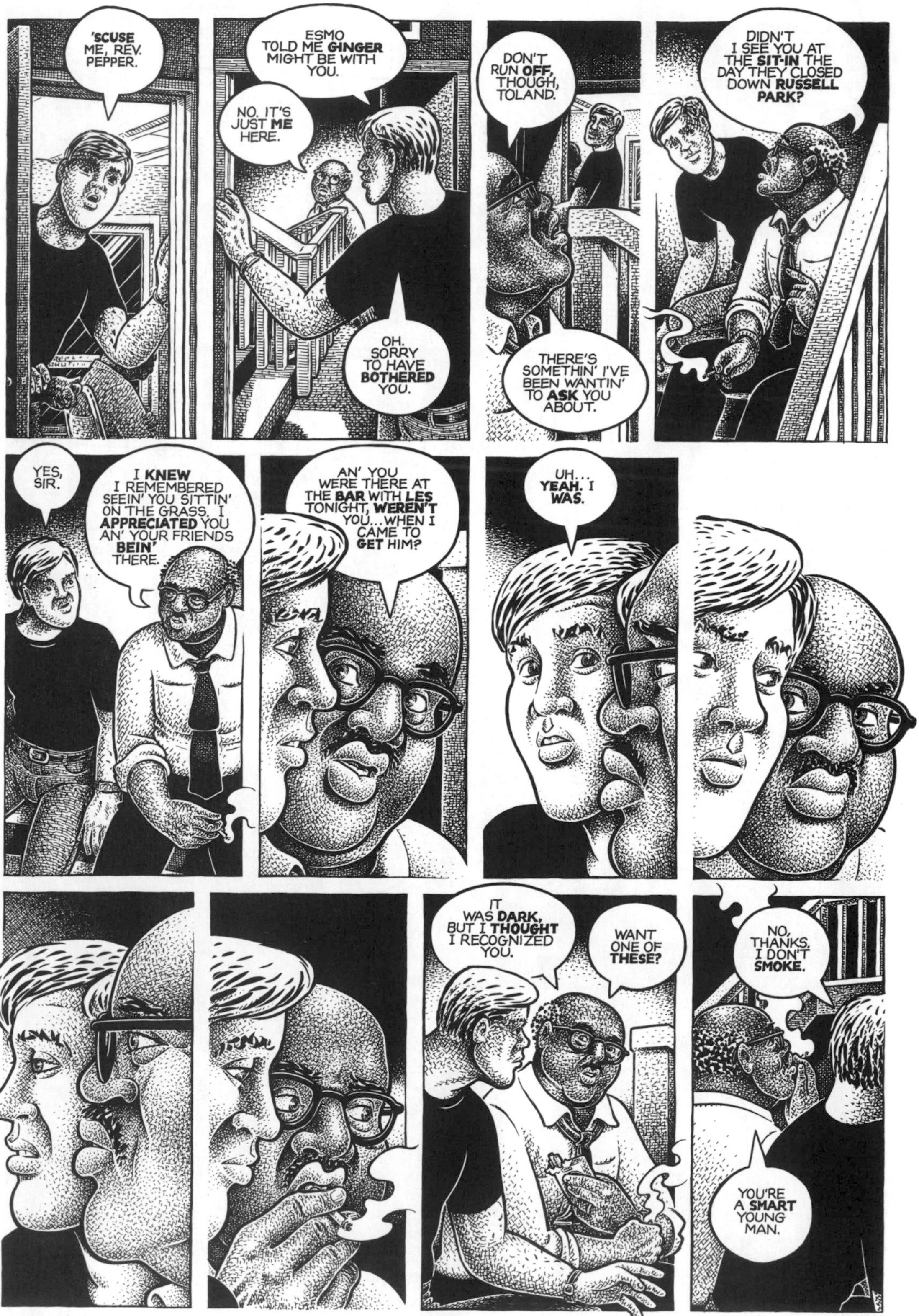
'SCUSE ME, REV. PEPPER.
ESMO TOLD ME GINGER MIGHT BE WITH YOU.
NO, IT'S JUST ME HERE.
OH. SORRY TO HAVE BOTHERED YOU.
DON'T RUN OFF, THOUGH, TOLAND.
THERE'S SOMETHIN' I'VE BEEN WANTIN' TO ASK YOU ABOUT.
DIDN'T I SEE YOU AT THE SIT-IN THE DAY THEY CLOSED DOWN RUSSELL PARK?
YES, SIR.
I KNEW I REMEMBERED SEEIN' YOU SITTIN' ON THE GRASS. I APPRECIATED YOU AN' YOUR FRIENDS BEIN' THERE.
AN' YOU WERE THERE AT THE BAR WITH LES TONIGHT, WEREN'T YOU...WHEN I CAME TO GET HIM?
UH... YEAH. I WAS.
IT WAS DARK, BUT I THOUGHT I RECOGNIZED YOU.
WANT ONE OF THESE?
NO, THANKS. I DON'T SMOKE.
YOU'RE A SMART YOUNG MAN.

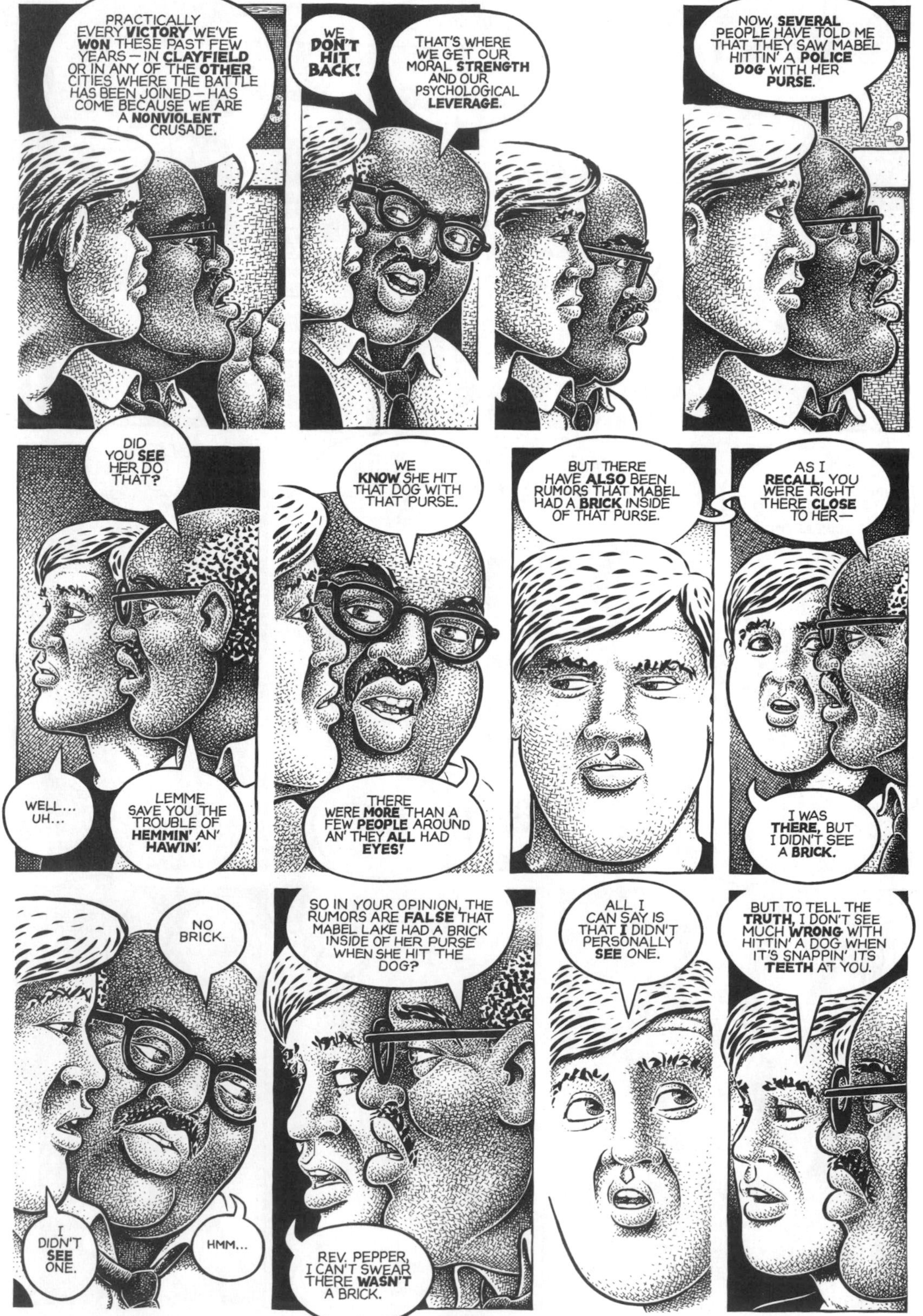

PRACTICALLY EVERY VICTORY WE'VE WON THESE PAST FEW YEARS — IN CLAYFIELD OR IN ANY OF THE OTHER CITIES WHERE THE BATTLE HAS BEEN JOINED — HAS COME BECAUSE WE ARE A NONVIOLENT CRUSADE.
WE DON'T HIT BACK!
THAT'S WHERE WE GET OUR MORAL STRENGTH AND OUR PSYCHOLOGICAL LEVERAGE.
NOW, SEVERAL PEOPLE HAVE TOLD ME THAT THEY SAW MABEL HITTIN' A POLICE DOG WITH HER PURSE.
DID YOU SEE HER DO THAT?
WELL... UH...
LEMME SAVE YOU THE TROUBLE OF HEMMIN' AN' HAWIN'.
WE KNOW SHE HIT THAT DOG WITH THAT PURSE.
THERE WERE MORE THAN A FEW PEOPLE AROUND AN' THEY ALL HAD EYES!
BUT THERE HAVE ALSO BEEN RUMORS THAT MABEL HAD A BRICK INSIDE OF THAT PURSE.
AS I RECALL, YOU WERE RIGHT THERE CLOSE TO HER—
I WAS THERE, BUT I DIDN'T SEE A BRICK.
NO BRICK.
I DIDN'T SEE ONE.
HMM...
SO IN YOUR OPINION, THE RUMORS ARE FALSE THAT MABEL LAKE HAD A BRICK INSIDE OF HER PURSE WHEN SHE HIT THE DOG?
REV. PEPPER, I CAN'T SWEAR THERE WASN'T A BRICK.
ALL I CAN SAY IS THAT I DIDN'T PERSONALLY SEE ONE.
BUT TO TELL THE TRUTH, I DON'T SEE MUCH WRONG WITH HITTIN' A DOG WHEN IT'S SNAPPIN' ITS TEETH AT YOU.

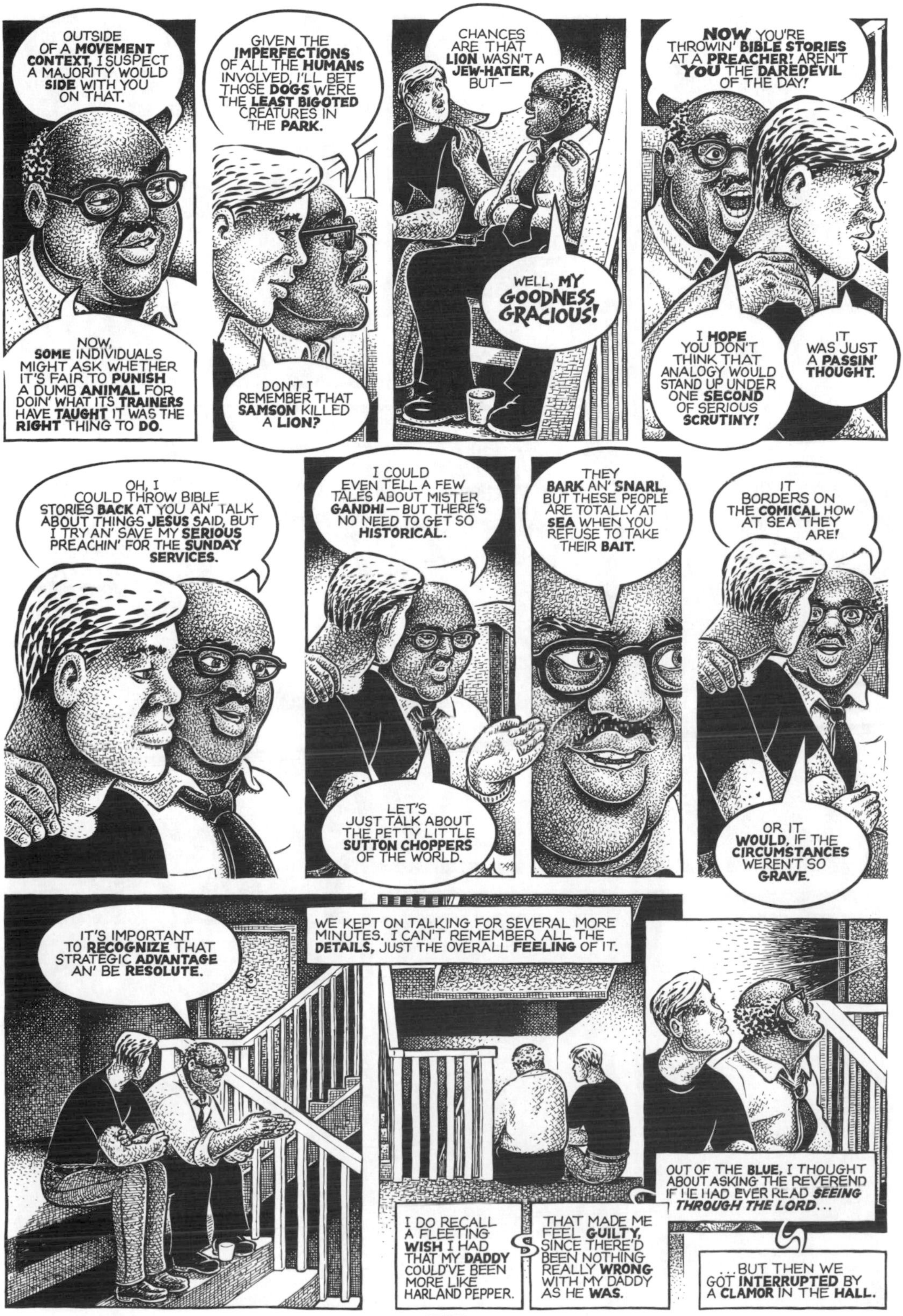

OUTSIDE OF A MOVEMENT CONTEXT, I SUSPECT A MAJORITY WOULD SIDE WITH YOU ON THAT.
NOW, SOME INDIVIDUALS MIGHT ASK WHETHER IT'S FAIR TO PUNISH A DUMB ANIMAL FOR DOIN' WHAT ITS TRAINERS HAVE TAUGHT IT WAS THE RIGHT THING TO DO.
GIVEN THE IMPERFECTIONS OF ALL THE HUMANS INVOLVED, I'LL BET THOSE DOGS WERE THE LEAST BIGOTED CREATURES IN THE PARK.
DON'T I REMEMBER THAT SAMSON KILLED A LION?
CHANCES ARE THAT LION WASN'T A JEW-HATER, BUT—
WELL, MY GOODNESS GRACIOUS!
NOW YOU'RE THROWIN' BIBLE STORIES AT A PREACHER! AREN'T YOU THE DAREDEVIL OF THE DAY!
I HOPE YOU DON'T THINK THAT ANALOGY WOULD STAND UP UNDER ONE SECOND OF SERIOUS SCRUTINY!
IT WAS JUST A PASSIN' THOUGHT.
OH, I COULD THROW BIBLE STORIES BACK AT YOU AN' TALK ABOUT THINGS JESUS SAID, BUT I TRY AN' SAVE MY SERIOUS PREACHIN' FOR THE SUNDAY SERVICES.
I COULD EVEN TELL A FEW TALES ABOUT MISTER GANDHI — BUT THERE'S NO NEED TO GET SO HISTORICAL.
LET'S JUST TALK ABOUT THE PETTY LITTLE SUTTON CHOPPERS OF THE WORLD.
THEY BARK AN' SNARL, BUT THESE PEOPLE ARE TOTALLY AT SEA WHEN YOU REFUSE TO TAKE THEIR BAIT.
IT BORDERS ON THE COMICAL HOW AT SEA THEY ARE!
OR IT WOULD, IF THE CIRCUMSTANCES WEREN'T SO GRAVE.
IT'S IMPORTANT TO RECOGNIZE THAT STRATEGIC ADVANTAGE AN' BE RESOLUTE.
WE KEPT ON TALKING FOR SEVERAL MORE MINUTES. I CAN'T REMEMBER ALL THE DETAILS, JUST THE OVERALL FEELING OF IT.
I DO RECALL A FLEETING WISH I HAD THAT MY DADDY COULD'VE BEEN MORE LIKE HARLAND PEPPER.
THAT MADE ME FEEL GUILTY, SINCE THERE'D BEEN NOTHING REALLY WRONG WITH MY DADDY AS HE WAS.
OUT OF THE BLUE, I THOUGHT ABOUT ASKING THE REVEREND IF HE HAD EVER READ SEEING THROUGH THE LORD...
...BUT THEN WE GOT INTERRUPTED BY A CLAMOR IN THE HALL.

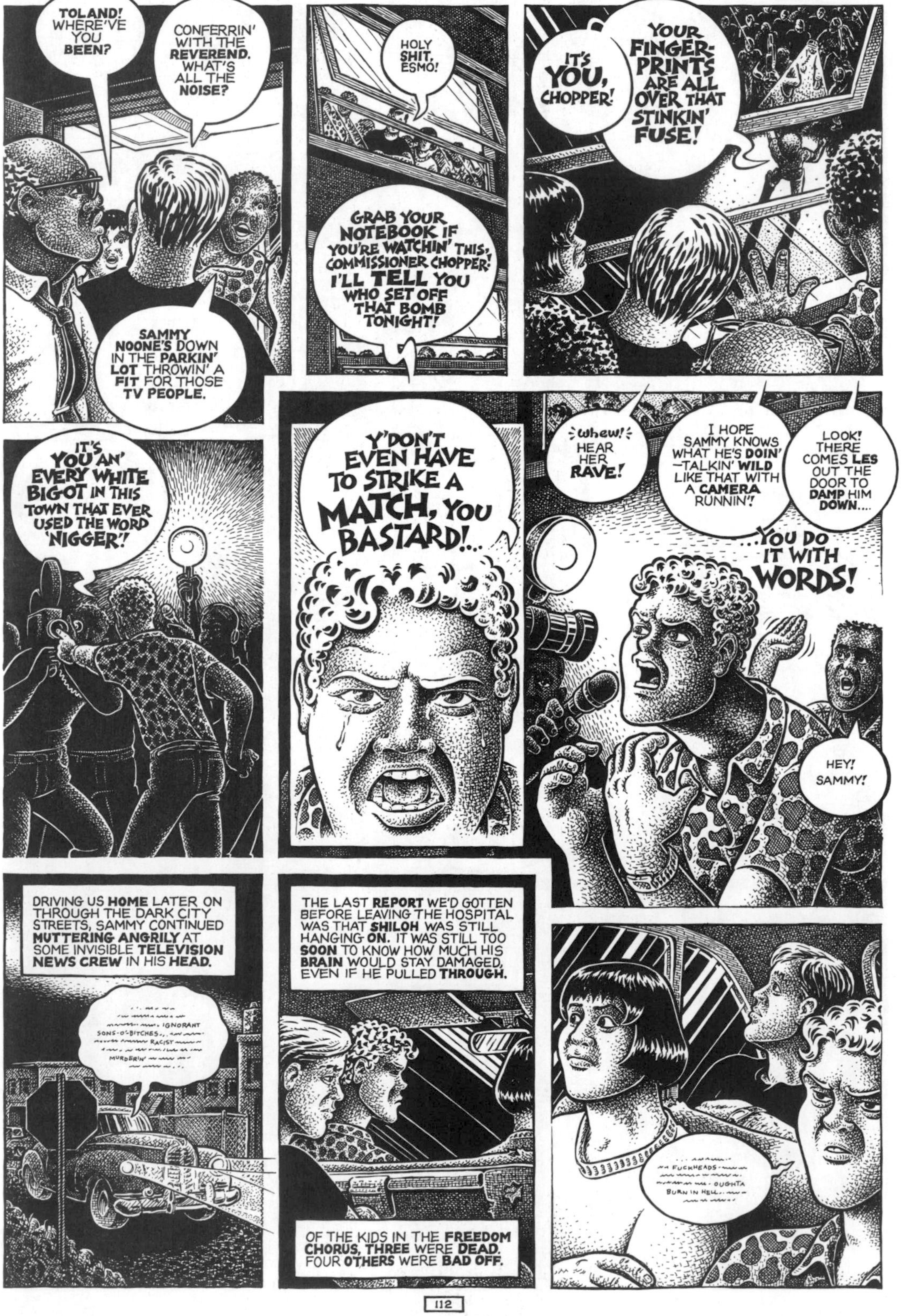
TOLAND! WHERE'VE YOU BEEN?
CONFERRIN' WITH THE REVEREND. WHAT'S ALL THE NOISE?
SAMMY NOONE'S DOWN IN THE PARKIN' LOT THROWIN' A FIT FOR THOSE TV PEOPLE.
HOLY SHIT, ESMO!
GRAB YOUR NOTEBOOK IF YOU'RE WATCHIN' THIS, COMMISSIONER CHOPPER! I'LL TELL YOU WHO SET OFF THAT BOMB TONIGHT!
IT'S YOU, CHOPPER!
YOUR FINGER-PRINTS ARE ALL OVER THAT STINKIN' FUSE!
IT'S YOU AN' EVERY WHITE BIGOT IN THIS TOWN THAT EVER USED THE WORD 'NIGGER'!
Y'DON'T EVEN HAVE TO STRIKE A MATCH, YOU BASTARD!...
whew! HEAR HER RAVE!
I HOPE SAMMY KNOWS WHAT HE'S DOIN' —TALKIN' WILD LIKE THAT WITH A CAMERA RUNNIN'!
LOOK! THERE COMES LES OUT THE DOOR TO DAMP HIM DOWN....
...YOU DO IT WITH WORDS!
HEY! SAMMY!
DRIVING US HOME LATER ON THROUGH THE DARK CITY STREETS, SAMMY CONTINUED MUTTERING ANGRILY AT SOME INVISIBLE TELEVISION NEWS CREW IN HIS HEAD.
IGNORANT SONS-O'-BITCHES... RACIST MURDERIN'
THE LAST REPORT WE'D GOTTEN BEFORE LEAVING THE HOSPITAL WAS THAT SHILOH WAS STILL HANGING ON. IT WAS STILL TOO SOON TO KNOW HOW MUCH HIS BRAIN WOULD STAY DAMAGED, EVEN IF HE PULLED THROUGH.
OF THE KIDS IN THE FREEDOM CHORUS, THREE WERE DEAD. FOUR OTHERS WERE BAD OFF.
FUCKHEADS OUGHTA BURN IN HELL..

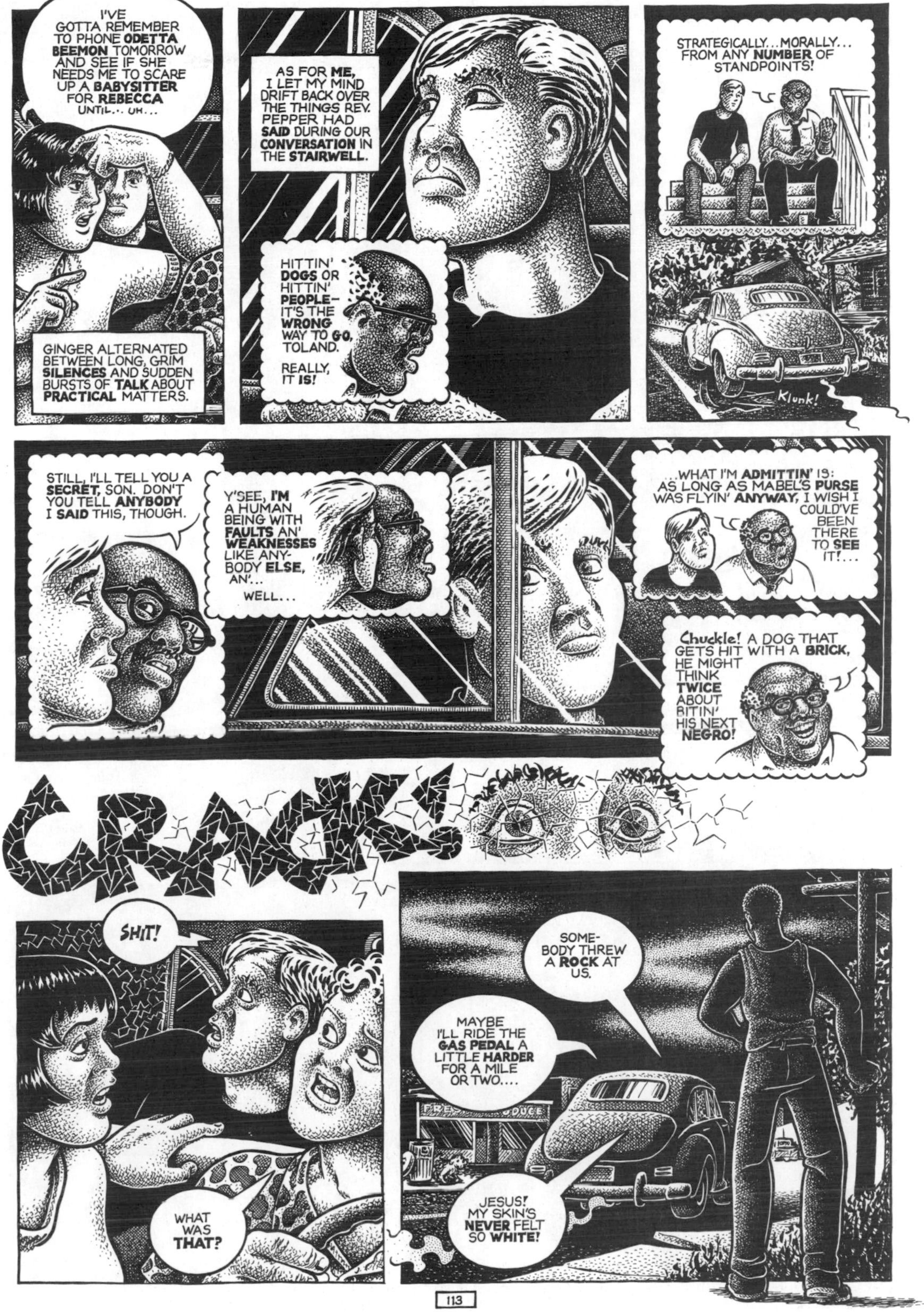
I'VE GOTTA REMEMBER TO PHONE ODETTA BEEMON TOMORROW AND SEE IF SHE NEEDS ME TO SCARE UP A BABYSITTER FOR REBECCA UNTIL... UH...
GINGER ALTERNATED BETWEEN LONG, GRIM SILENCES AND SUDDEN BURSTS OF TALK ABOUT PRACTICAL MATTERS.
AS FOR ME, I LET MY MIND DRIFT BACK OVER THE THINGS REV. PEPPER HAD SAID DURING OUR CONVERSATION IN THE STAIRWELL.
HITTIN' DOGS OR HITTIN' PEOPLE– IT'S THE WRONG WAY TO GO, TOLAND.
REALLY, IT IS!
STRATEGICALLY...MORALLY... FROM ANY NUMBER OF STANDPOINTS!
Klunk!
STILL, I'LL TELL YOU A SECRET, SON. DON'T YOU TELL ANYBODY I SAID THIS, THOUGH.
Y'SEE, I'M A HUMAN BEING WITH FAULTS AN' WEAKNESSES LIKE ANY-BODY ELSE, AN'...
WELL...
...WHAT I'M ADMITTIN' IS: AS LONG AS MABEL'S PURSE WAS FLYIN' ANYWAY, I WISH I COULD'VE BEEN THERE TO SEE IT!...
Chuckle! A DOG THAT GETS HIT WITH A BRICK, HE MIGHT THINK TWICE ABOUT BITIN' HIS NEXT NEGRO!
CRACK!
SHIT!
WHAT WAS THAT?
SOME-BODY THREW A ROCK AT US.
MAYBE I'LL RIDE THE GAS PEDAL A LITTLE HARDER FOR A MILE OR TWO....
JESUS! MY SKIN'S NEVER FELT SO WHITE!

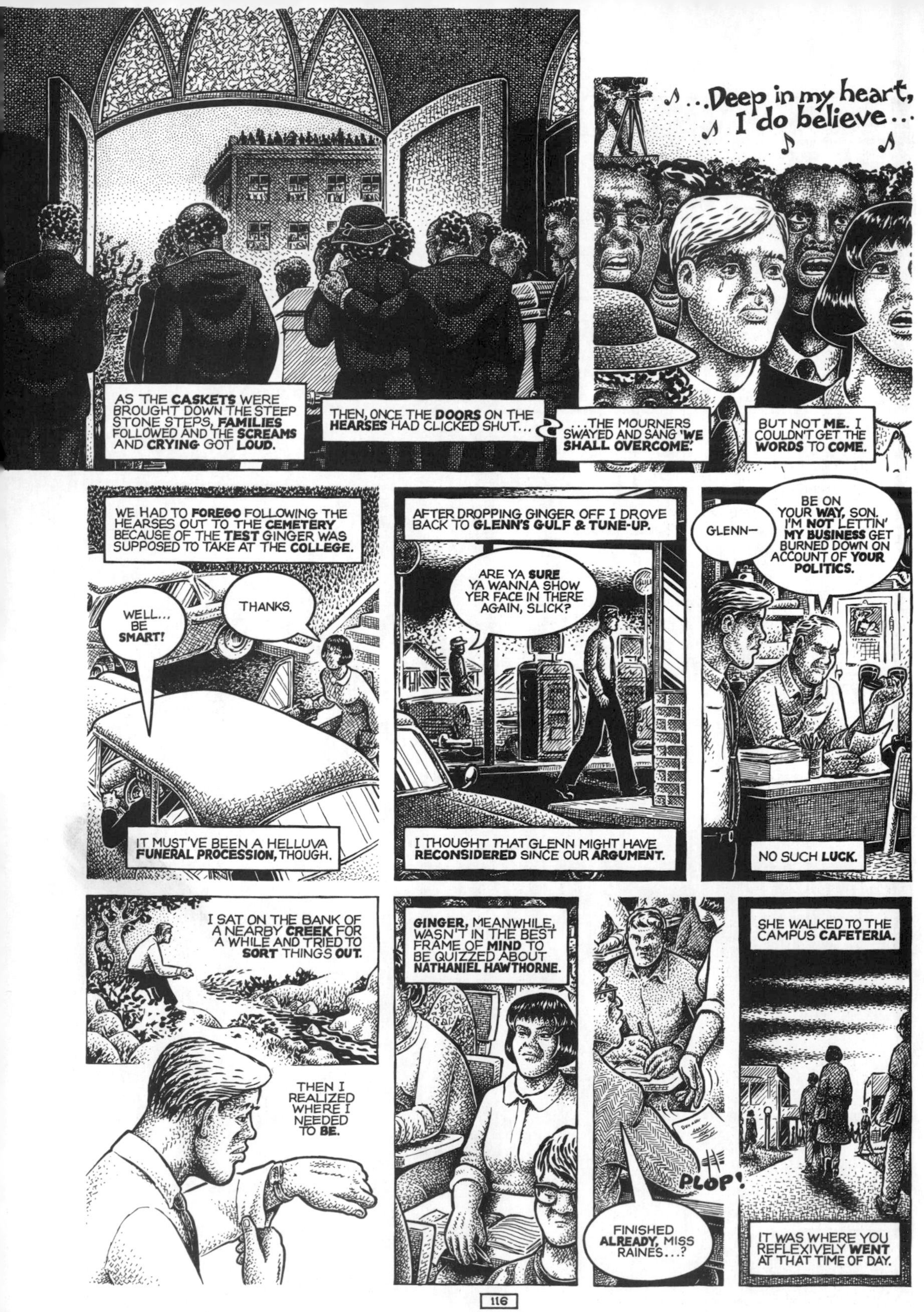
AS THE CASKETS WERE BROUGHT DOWN THE STEEP STONE STEPS, FAMILIES FOLLOWED AND THE SCREAMS AND CRYING GOT LOUD.
THEN, ONCE THE DOORS ON THE HEARSES HAD CLICKED SHUT...
...Deep in my heart, I do believe...
...THE MOURNERS SWAYED AND SANG 'WE SHALL OVERCOME.'
BUT NOT ME. I COULDN'T GET THE WORDS TO COME.
WE HAD TO FOREGO FOLLOWING THE HEARSES OUT TO THE CEMETERY BECAUSE OF THE TEST GINGER WAS SUPPOSED TO TAKE AT THE COLLEGE.
WELL... BE SMART!
THANKS.
IT MUST'VE BEEN A HELLUVA FUNERAL PROCESSION, THOUGH.
AFTER DROPPING GINGER OFF I DROVE BACK TO GLENN'S GULF & TUNE-UP.
ARE YA SURE YA WANNA SHOW YER FACE IN THERE AGAIN, SLICK?
I THOUGHT THAT GLENN MIGHT HAVE RECONSIDERED SINCE OUR ARGUMENT.
GLENN—
BE ON YOUR WAY, SON. I'M NOT LETTIN' MY BUSINESS GET BURNED DOWN ON ACCOUNT OF YOUR POLITICS.
NO SUCH LUCK.
I SAT ON THE BANK OF A NEARBY CREEK FOR A WHILE AND TRIED TO SORT THINGS OUT.
THEN I REALIZED WHERE I NEEDED TO BE.
GINGER, MEANWHILE, WASN'T IN THE BEST FRAME OF MIND TO BE QUIZZED ABOUT NATHANIEL HAWTHORNE.
PLOP!
FINISHED ALREADY, MISS RAINES...?
SHE WALKED TO THE CAMPUS CAFETERIA.
IT WAS WHERE YOU REFLEXIVELY WENT AT THAT TIME OF DAY.

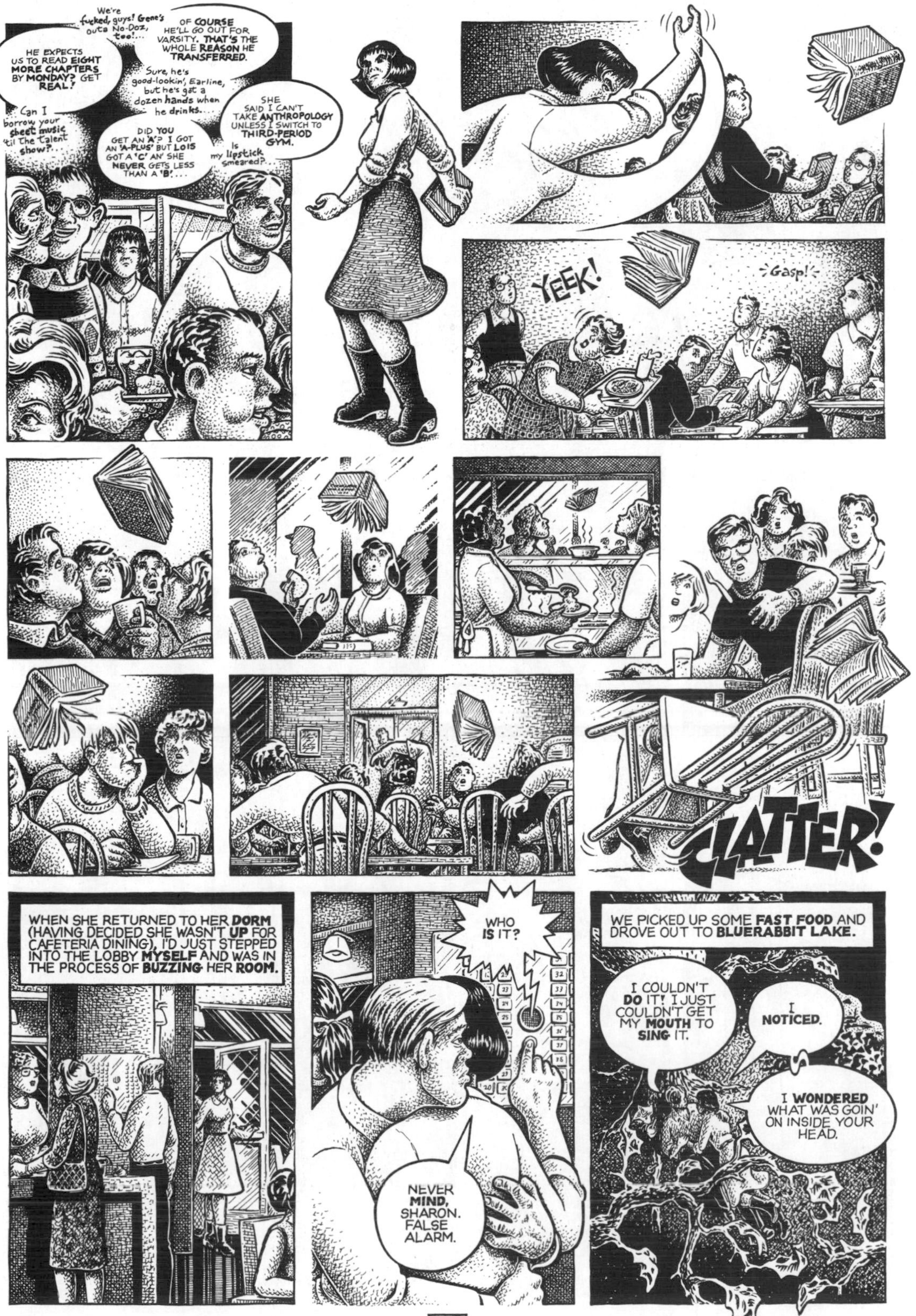
HE EXPECTS US TO READ EIGHT MORE CHAPTERS BY MONDAY? GET REAL!
We're fucked, guys! Gene's outa No-Doz, too!...
OF COURSE HE'LL GO OUT FOR VARSITY. THAT'S THE WHOLE REASON HE TRANSFERRED.
Sure, he's good-lookin', Earline, but he's got a dozen hands when he drinks...
Can I borrow your sheet music 'til the talent show?...
DID YOU GET AN 'A'? I GOT AN 'A-PLUS' BUT LOIS GOT A 'C' AN' SHE NEVER GETS LESS THAN A 'B'...
SHE SAID I CAN'T TAKE ANTHROPOLOGY UNLESS I SWITCH TO THIRD-PERIOD GYM.
Is my lipstick smeared?...
YEEK!
Gasp!
CLATTER!
WHEN SHE RETURNED TO HER DORM (HAVING DECIDED SHE WASN'T UP FOR CAFETERIA DINING), I'D JUST STEPPED INTO THE LOBBY MYSELF AND WAS IN THE PROCESS OF BUZZING HER ROOM.
WHO IS IT?
NEVER MIND, SHARON. FALSE ALARM.
WE PICKED UP SOME FAST FOOD AND DROVE OUT TO BLUERABBIT LAKE.
I COULDN'T DO IT! I JUST COULDN'T GET MY MOUTH TO SING IT.
I NOTICED.
I WONDERED WHAT WAS GOIN' ON INSIDE YOUR HEAD.

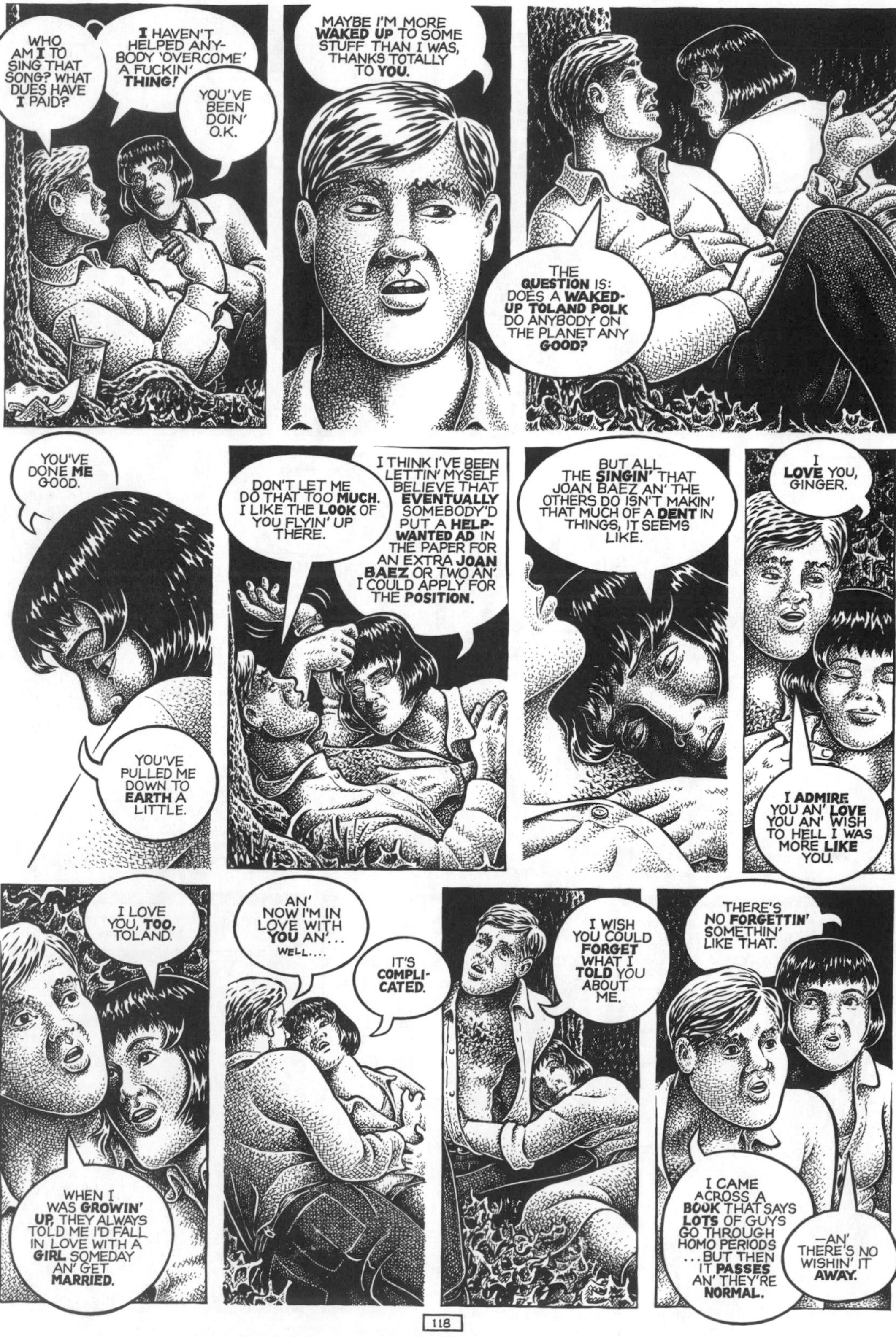
WHO AM **I** TO SING THAT SONG? WHAT DUES HAVE **I** PAID?
I HAVEN'T HELPED ANYBODY 'OVERCOME' A FUCKIN' **THING!**
YOU'VE BEEN DOIN' O.K.
MAYBE I'M MORE **WAKED UP** TO SOME STUFF THAN I WAS, THANKS TOTALLY TO **YOU**.
THE **QUESTION** IS: DOES A **WAKED-UP TOLAND POLK** DO ANYBODY ON THE PLANET ANY **GOOD?**
YOU'VE DONE **ME** GOOD.
YOU'VE PULLED ME DOWN TO **EARTH** A LITTLE.
DON'T LET ME DO THAT TOO **MUCH**. I LIKE THE **LOOK** OF YOU FLYIN' UP THERE.
I THINK I'VE BEEN LETTIN' MYSELF BELIEVE THAT **EVENTUALLY** SOMEBODY'D PUT A **HELP-WANTED AD** IN THE PAPER FOR AN EXTRA **JOAN BAEZ** OR TWO AN' I COULD APPLY FOR THE **POSITION**.
BUT ALL THE **SINGIN'** THAT JOAN BAEZ AN' THE OTHERS DO ISN'T MAKIN' THAT MUCH OF A **DENT** IN THINGS, IT SEEMS LIKE.
I **LOVE** YOU, GINGER.
I ADMIRE YOU AN' **LOVE** YOU AN' WISH TO HELL I WAS MORE **LIKE** YOU.
I LOVE YOU, **TOO**, TOLAND.
WHEN I WAS **GROWIN' UP**, THEY ALWAYS TOLD ME I'D FALL IN LOVE WITH A **GIRL** SOMEDAY AN' GET **MARRIED**.
AN' NOW I'M IN LOVE WITH **YOU** AN'... WELL....
IT'S **COMPLICATED**.
I WISH YOU COULD **FORGET** WHAT I **TOLD** YOU ABOUT ME.
THERE'S **NO FORGETTIN'** SOMETHIN' LIKE THAT.
I CAME ACROSS A **BOOK** THAT SAYS **LOTS** OF GUYS GO THROUGH HOMO PERIODS ...BUT THEN IT **PASSES** AN' THEY'RE **NORMAL**.
—AN' THERE'S NO WISHIN' IT **AWAY**.

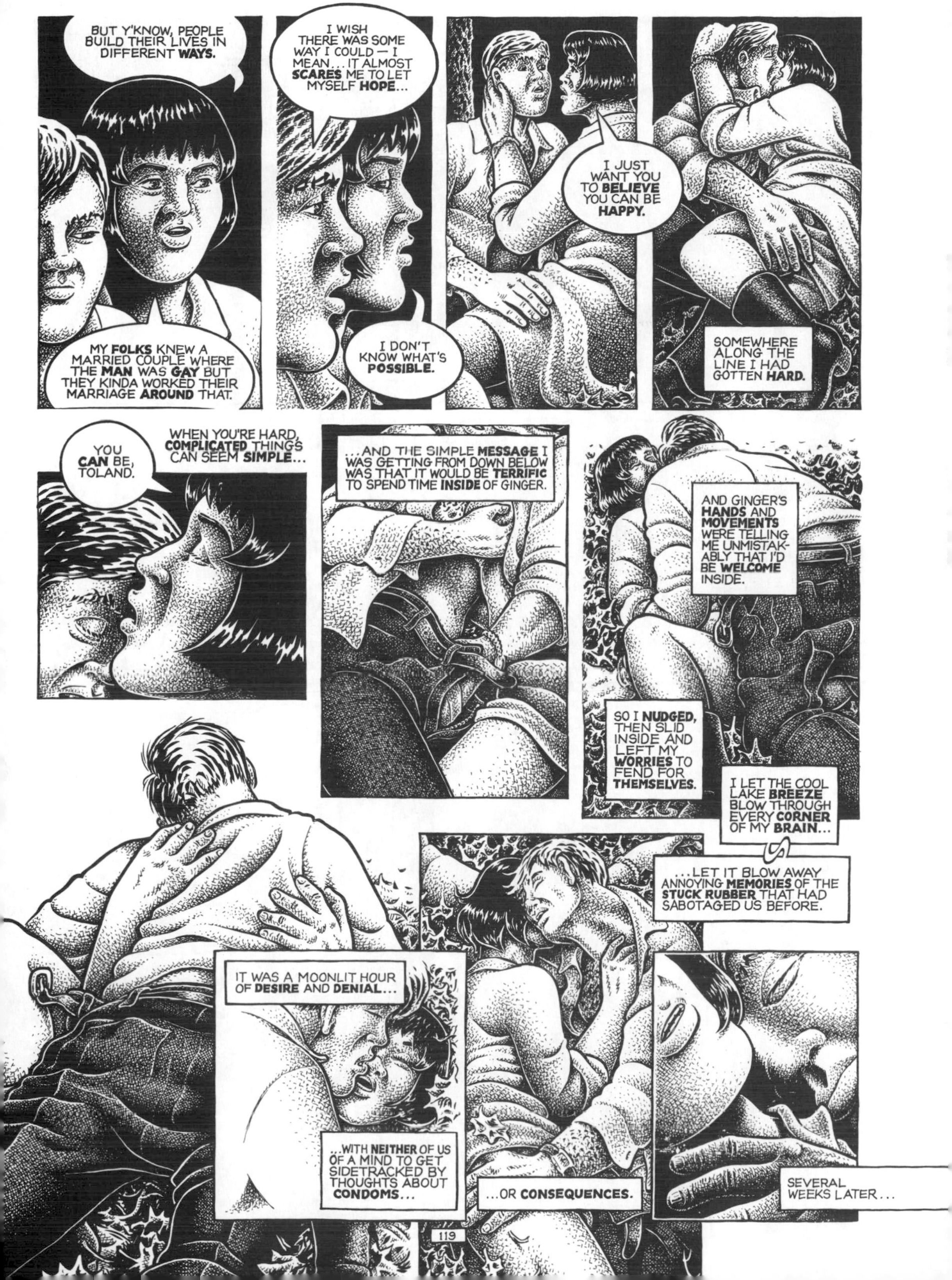
BUT Y'KNOW, PEOPLE BUILD THEIR LIVES IN DIFFERENT **WAYS.**
MY **FOLKS** KNEW A MARRIED COUPLE WHERE THE **MAN** WAS **GAY** BUT THEY KINDA WORKED THEIR MARRIAGE **AROUND** THAT.
I WISH THERE WAS SOME WAY I COULD — I MEAN... IT ALMOST **SCARES** ME TO LET MYSELF **HOPE**...
I DON'T KNOW WHAT'S **POSSIBLE.**
I JUST WANT YOU TO **BELIEVE** YOU CAN BE **HAPPY.**
SOMEWHERE ALONG THE LINE I HAD GOTTEN **HARD.**
YOU **CAN** BE, TOLAND.
WHEN YOU'RE HARD, **COMPLICATED** THINGS CAN SEEM **SIMPLE**...
...AND THE SIMPLE **MESSAGE** I WAS GETTING FROM DOWN BELOW WAS THAT IT WOULD BE **TERRIFIC** TO SPEND TIME **INSIDE** OF GINGER.
AND GINGER'S **HANDS** AND **MOVEMENTS** WERE TELLING ME UNMISTAKABLY THAT I'D BE **WELCOME** INSIDE.
SO I **NUDGED,** THEN SLID INSIDE AND LEFT MY **WORRIES** TO FEND FOR **THEMSELVES.**
I LET THE COOL LAKE **BREEZE** BLOW THROUGH EVERY **CORNER** OF MY **BRAIN**...
...LET IT BLOW AWAY ANNOYING **MEMORIES** OF THE **STUCK RUBBER** THAT HAD SABOTAGED US BEFORE.
IT WAS A MOONLIT HOUR OF **DESIRE** AND **DENIAL**...
...WITH **NEITHER** OF US OF A MIND TO GET SIDETRACKED BY THOUGHTS ABOUT **CONDOMS**...
...OR **CONSEQUENCES.**
SEVERAL WEEKS LATER...

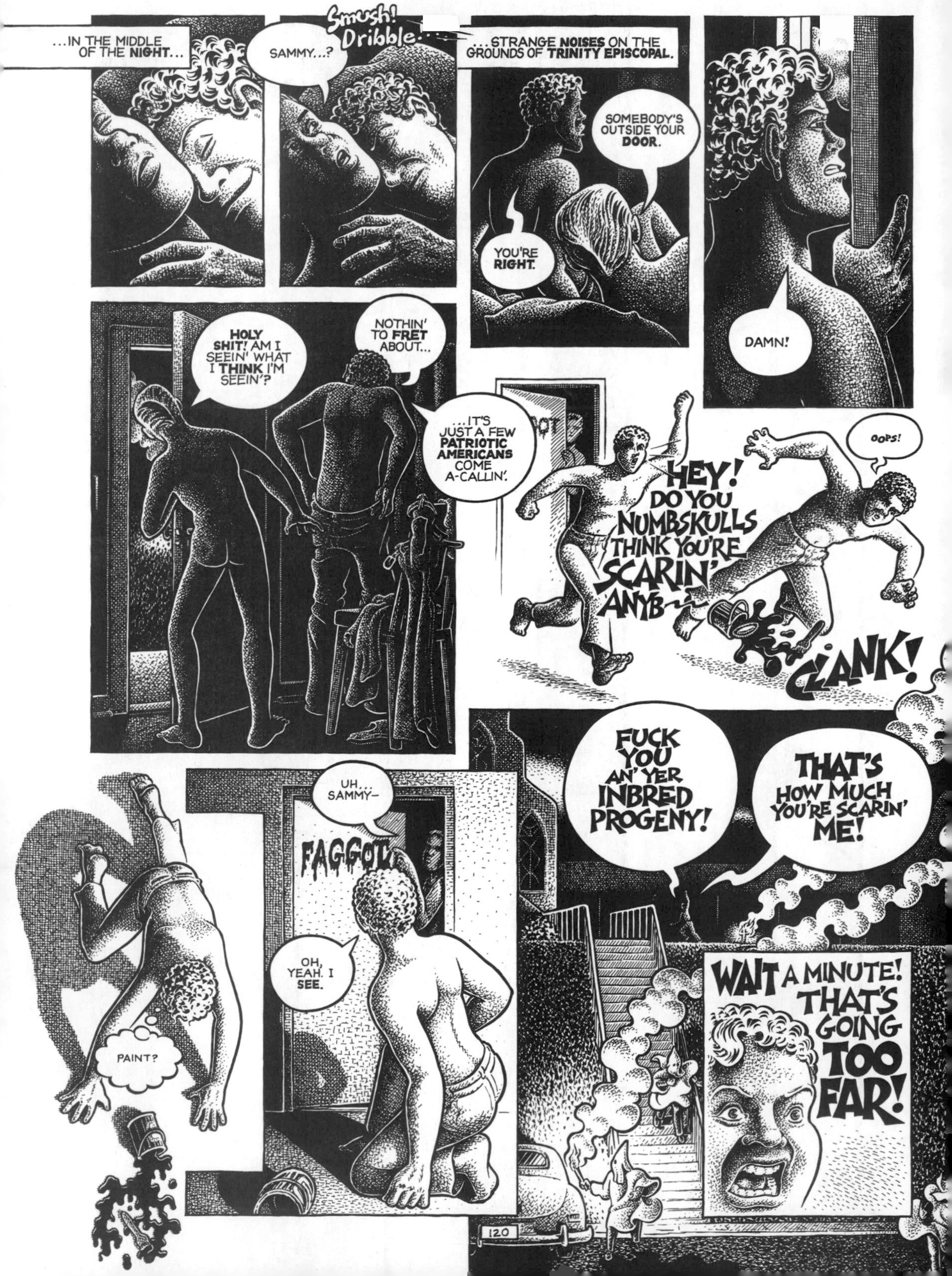
...IN THE MIDDLE OF THE NIGHT...
SAMMY...?
Smush! Dribble!
...STRANGE NOISES ON THE GROUNDS OF TRINITY EPISCOPAL.
SOMEBODY'S OUTSIDE YOUR DOOR.
YOU'RE RIGHT.
DAMN!
HOLY SHIT! AM I SEEIN' WHAT I THINK I'M SEEIN'?
NOTHIN' TO FRET ABOUT...
...IT'S JUST A FEW PATRIOTIC AMERICANS COME A-CALLIN'.
HEY! DO YOU NUMBSKULLS THINK YOU'RE SCARIN' ANYB—
OOPS!
CLANK!
PAINT?
UH... SAMMY—
FAGGOT
OH, YEAH. I SEE.
FUCK YOU AN' YER INBRED PROGENY!
THAT'S HOW MUCH YOU'RE SCARIN' ME!
WAIT A MINUTE! THAT'S GOING TOO FAR!
120

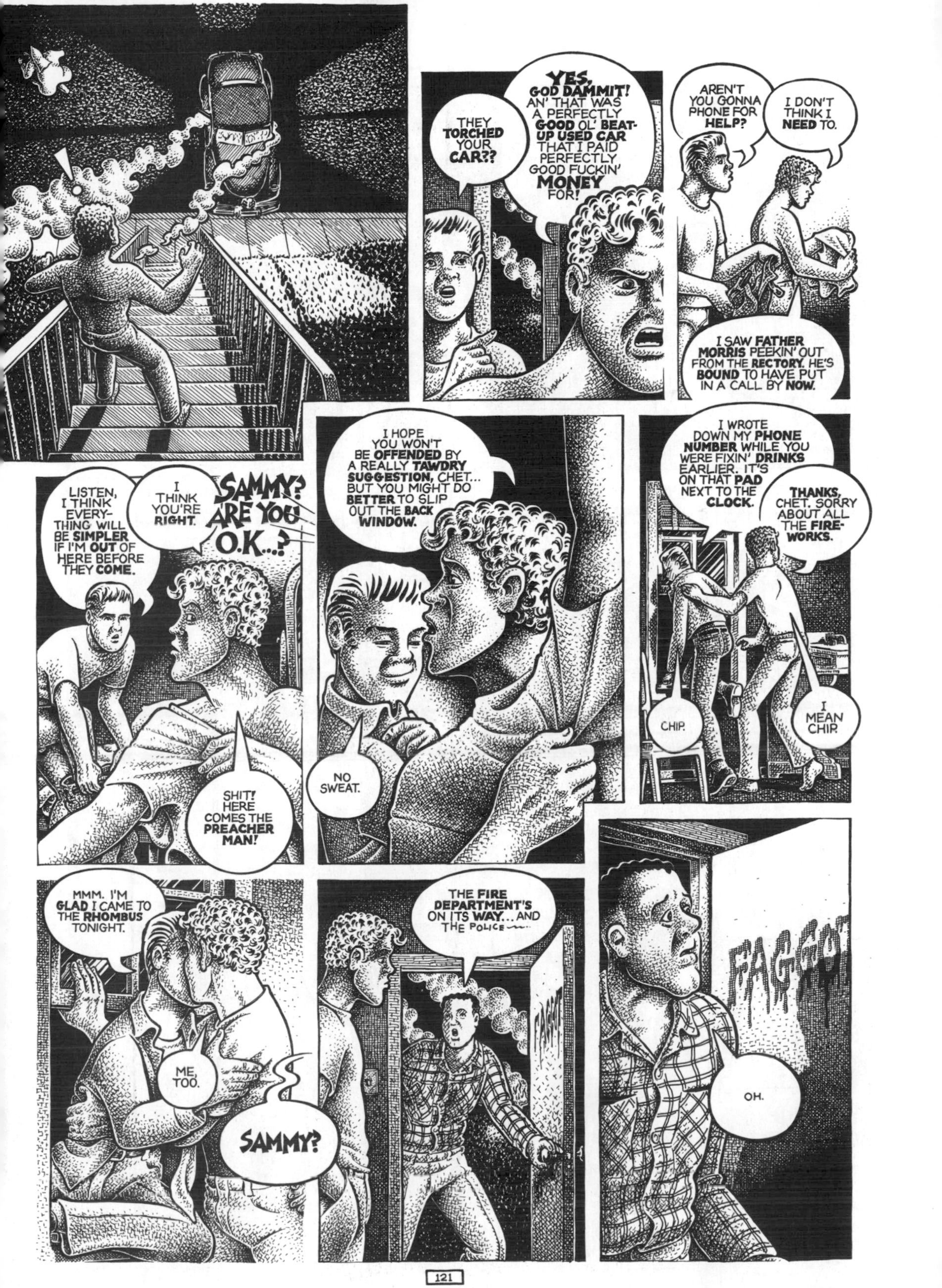
!
THEY TORCHED YOUR CAR??
YES, GOD DAMMIT! AN' THAT WAS A PERFECTLY GOOD OL' BEAT-UP USED CAR THAT I PAID PERFECTLY GOOD FUCKIN' MONEY FOR!
AREN'T YOU GONNA PHONE FOR HELP?
I DON'T THINK I NEED TO.
I SAW FATHER MORRIS PEEKIN' OUT FROM THE RECTORY. HE'S BOUND TO HAVE PUT IN A CALL BY NOW.
LISTEN, I THINK EVERY-THING WILL BE SIMPLER IF I'M OUT OF HERE BEFORE THEY COME.
I THINK YOU'RE RIGHT.
SAMMY? ARE YOU O.K...?
SHIT! HERE COMES THE PREACHER MAN!
I HOPE YOU WON'T BE OFFENDED BY A REALLY TAWDRY SUGGESTION, CHET... BUT YOU MIGHT DO BETTER TO SLIP OUT THE BACK WINDOW.
NO SWEAT.
I WROTE DOWN MY PHONE NUMBER WHILE YOU WERE FIXIN' DRINKS EARLIER. IT'S ON THAT PAD NEXT TO THE CLOCK.
THANKS, CHET. SORRY ABOUT ALL THE FIRE-WORKS.
CHIP.
I MEAN CHIP.
MMM. I'M GLAD I CAME TO THE RHOMBUS TONIGHT.
ME, TOO.
SAMMY?
THE FIRE DEPARTMENT'S ON ITS WAY... AND THE POLICE
FAGGOT
OH.
FAGGOT

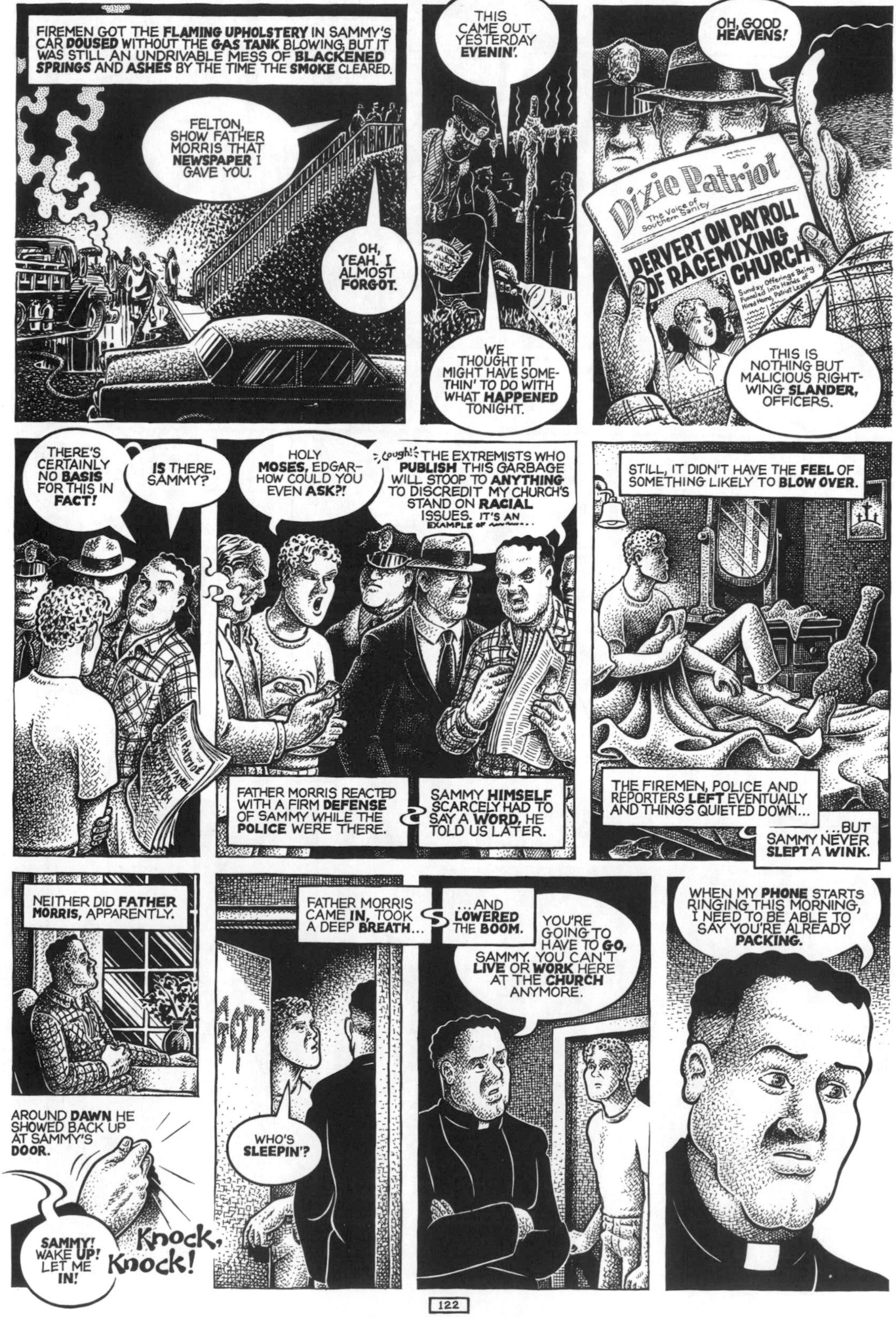
FIREMEN GOT THE FLAMING UPHOLSTERY IN SAMMY'S CAR DOUSED WITHOUT THE GAS TANK BLOWING; BUT IT WAS STILL AN UNDRIVABLE MESS OF BLACKENED SPRINGS AND ASHES BY THE TIME THE SMOKE CLEARED.
FELTON, SHOW FATHER MORRIS THAT NEWSPAPER I GAVE YOU.
OH, YEAH. I ALMOST FORGOT.
THIS CAME OUT YESTERDAY EVENIN'.
WE THOUGHT IT MIGHT HAVE SOMETHIN' TO DO WITH WHAT HAPPENED TONIGHT.
OH, GOOD HEAVENS!
Dixie Patriot
The Voice of Southern Sanity
PERVERT ON PAYROLL OF RACEMIXING CHURCH
Sunday Offerings Being Funneled Into Hands of Hired Homo, Patriot Learns
THIS IS NOTHING BUT MALICIOUS RIGHT-WING SLANDER, OFFICERS.
THERE'S CERTAINLY NO BASIS FOR THIS IN FACT!
IS THERE, SAMMY?
HOLY MOSES, EDGAR-- HOW COULD YOU EVEN ASK?!
cough!
THE EXTREMISTS WHO PUBLISH THIS GARBAGE WILL STOOP TO ANYTHING TO DISCREDIT MY CHURCH'S STAND ON RACIAL ISSUES. IT'S AN EXAMPLE OF ...
FATHER MORRIS REACTED WITH A FIRM DEFENSE OF SAMMY WHILE THE POLICE WERE THERE.
SAMMY HIMSELF SCARCELY HAD TO SAY A WORD, HE TOLD US LATER.
STILL, IT DIDN'T HAVE THE FEEL OF SOMETHING LIKELY TO BLOW OVER.
THE FIREMEN, POLICE AND REPORTERS LEFT EVENTUALLY AND THINGS QUIETED DOWN...
...BUT SAMMY NEVER SLEPT A WINK.
NEITHER DID FATHER MORRIS, APPARENTLY.
AROUND DAWN HE SHOWED BACK UP AT SAMMY'S DOOR.
SAMMY! WAKE UP! LET ME IN!
Knock, Knock!
WHO'S SLEEPIN'?
FATHER MORRIS CAME IN, TOOK A DEEP BREATH...
...AND LOWERED THE BOOM.
YOU'RE GOING TO HAVE TO GO, SAMMY. YOU CAN'T LIVE OR WORK HERE AT THE CHURCH ANYMORE.
WHEN MY PHONE STARTS RINGING THIS MORNING, I NEED TO BE ABLE TO SAY YOU'RE ALREADY PACKING.

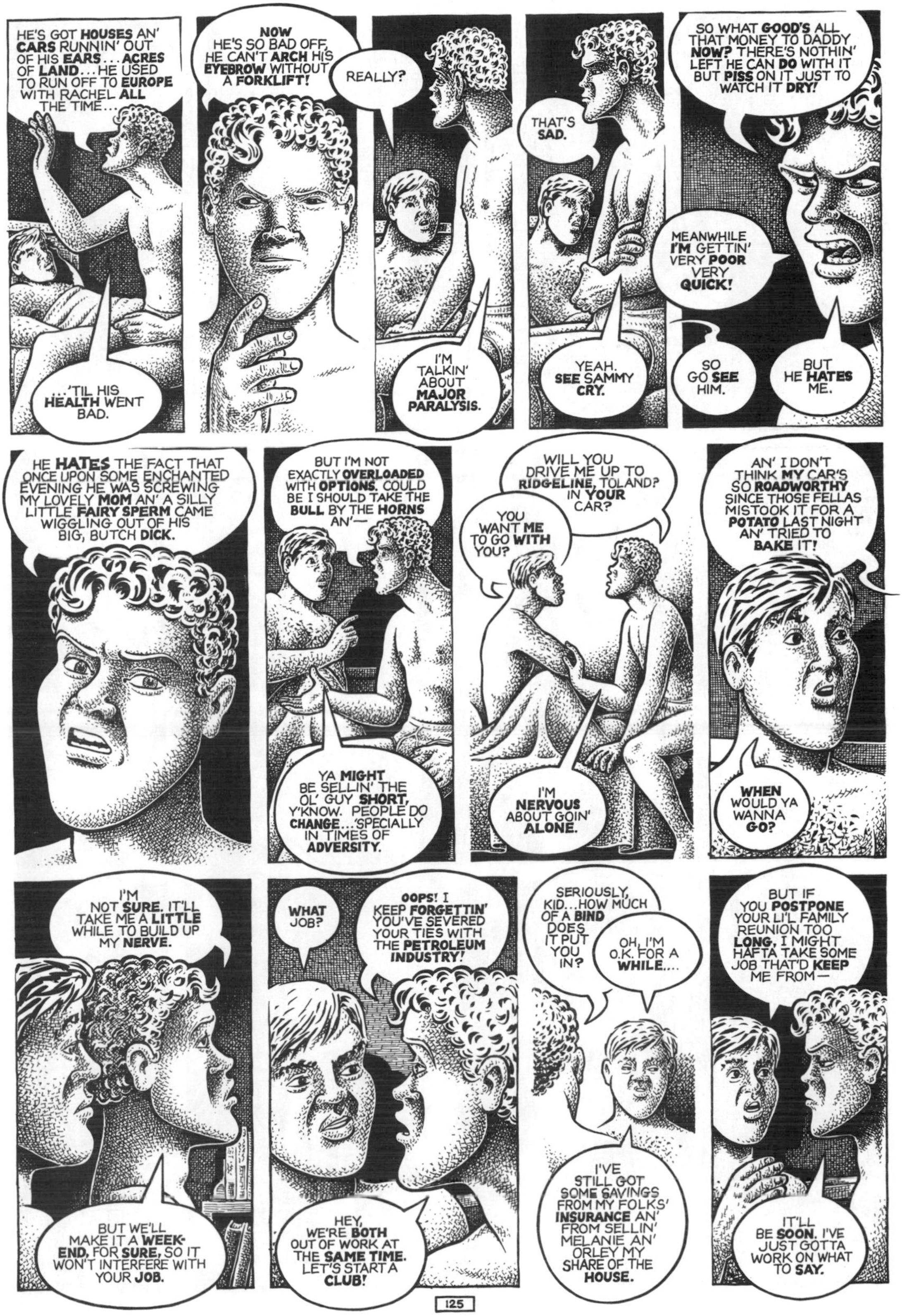
HE'S GOT HOUSES AN' CARS RUNNIN' OUT OF HIS EARS... ACRES OF LAND... HE USED TO RUN OFF TO EUROPE WITH RACHEL ALL THE TIME...
...'TIL HIS HEALTH WENT BAD.
NOW HE'S SO BAD OFF, HE CAN'T ARCH HIS EYEBROW WITHOUT A FORKLIFT!
REALLY?
I'M TALKIN' ABOUT MAJOR PARALYSIS.
THAT'S SAD.
YEAH. SEE SAMMY CRY.
SO WHAT GOOD'S ALL THAT MONEY TO DADDY NOW? THERE'S NOTHIN' LEFT HE CAN DO WITH IT BUT PISS ON IT JUST TO WATCH IT DRY!
MEANWHILE I'M GETTIN' VERY POOR VERY QUICK!
SO GO SEE HIM.
BUT HE HATES ME.
HE HATES THE FACT THAT ONCE UPON SOME ENCHANTED EVENING HE WAS SCREWING MY LOVELY MOM AN' A SILLY LITTLE FAIRY SPERM CAME WIGGLING OUT OF HIS BIG, BUTCH DICK.
BUT I'M NOT EXACTLY OVERLOADED WITH OPTIONS. COULD BE I SHOULD TAKE THE BULL BY THE HORNS AN'—
YA MIGHT BE SELLIN' THE OL' GUY SHORT, Y'KNOW. PEOPLE DO CHANGE... 'SPECIALLY IN TIMES OF ADVERSITY.
WILL YOU DRIVE ME UP TO RIDGELINE, TOLAND? IN YOUR CAR?
YOU WANT ME TO GO WITH YOU?
I'M NERVOUS ABOUT GOIN' ALONE.
AN' I DON'T THINK MY CAR'S SO ROADWORTHY SINCE THOSE FELLAS MISTOOK IT FOR A POTATO LAST NIGHT AN' TRIED TO BAKE IT!
WHEN WOULD YA WANNA GO?
I'M NOT SURE. IT'LL TAKE ME A LITTLE WHILE TO BUILD UP MY NERVE.
BUT WE'LL MAKE IT A WEEK-END, FOR SURE, SO IT WON'T INTERFERE WITH YOUR JOB.
WHAT JOB?
OOPS! I KEEP FORGETTIN' YOU'VE SEVERED YOUR TIES WITH THE PETROLEUM INDUSTRY!
HEY, WE'RE BOTH OUT OF WORK AT THE SAME TIME. LET'S START A CLUB!
SERIOUSLY, KID... HOW MUCH OF A BIND DOES IT PUT YOU IN?
OH, I'M O.K. FOR A WHILE....
I'VE STILL GOT SOME SAVINGS FROM MY FOLKS' INSURANCE AN' FROM SELLIN' MELANIE AN' ORLEY MY SHARE OF THE HOUSE.
BUT IF YOU POSTPONE YOUR LI'L FAMILY REUNION TOO LONG, I MIGHT HAFTA TAKE SOME JOB THAT'D KEEP ME FROM—
IT'LL BE SOON. I'VE JUST GOTTA WORK ON WHAT TO SAY.

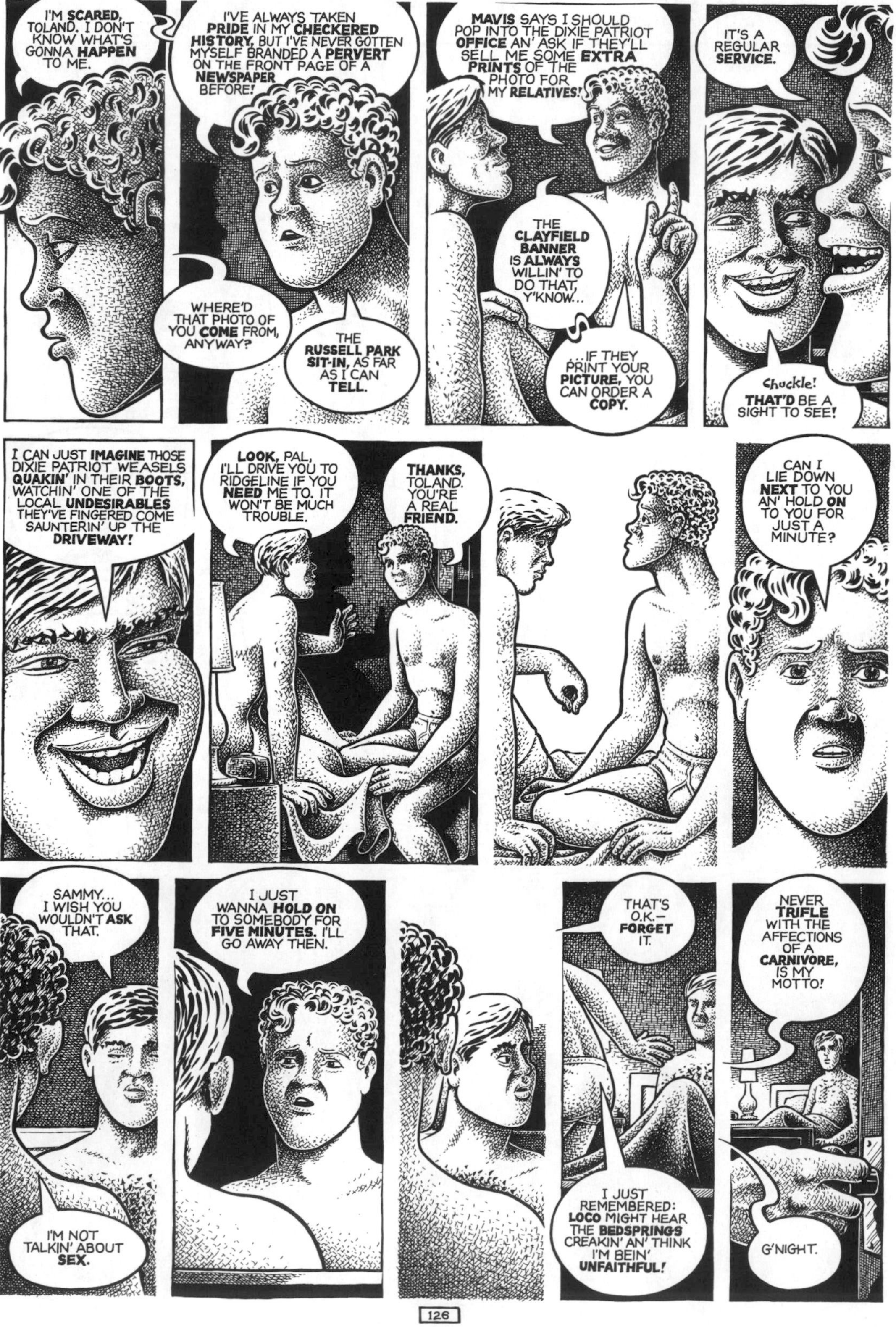
I'M SCARED, TOLAND. I DON'T KNOW WHAT'S GONNA HAPPEN TO ME.
I'VE ALWAYS TAKEN PRIDE IN MY CHECKERED HISTORY, BUT I'VE NEVER GOTTEN MYSELF BRANDED A PERVERT ON THE FRONT PAGE OF A NEWSPAPER BEFORE!
WHERE'D THAT PHOTO OF YOU COME FROM, ANYWAY?
THE RUSSELL PARK SIT-IN, AS FAR AS I CAN TELL.
MAVIS SAYS I SHOULD POP INTO THE DIXIE PATRIOT OFFICE AN' ASK IF THEY'LL SELL ME SOME EXTRA PRINTS OF THE PHOTO FOR MY RELATIVES!
THE CLAYFIELD BANNER IS ALWAYS WILLIN' TO DO THAT, Y'KNOW...
...IF THEY PRINT YOUR PICTURE, YOU CAN ORDER A COPY.
IT'S A REGULAR SERVICE.
Chuckle! THAT'D BE A SIGHT TO SEE!
I CAN JUST IMAGINE THOSE DIXIE PATRIOT WEASELS QUAKIN' IN THEIR BOOTS, WATCHIN' ONE OF THE LOCAL UNDESIRABLES THEY'VE FINGERED COME SAUNTERIN' UP THE DRIVEWAY!
LOOK, PAL, I'LL DRIVE YOU TO RIDGELINE IF YOU NEED ME TO. IT WON'T BE MUCH TROUBLE.
THANKS, TOLAND. YOU'RE A REAL FRIEND.
CAN I LIE DOWN NEXT TO YOU AN' HOLD ON TO YOU FOR JUST A MINUTE?
SAMMY... I WISH YOU WOULDN'T ASK THAT.
I'M NOT TALKIN' ABOUT SEX.
I JUST WANNA HOLD ON TO SOMEBODY FOR FIVE MINUTES. I'LL GO AWAY THEN.
THAT'S O.K.— FORGET IT.
I JUST REMEMBERED: LOCO MIGHT HEAR THE BEDSPRINGS CREAKIN' AN' THINK I'M BEIN' UNFAITHFUL!
NEVER TRIFLE WITH THE AFFECTIONS OF A CARNIVORE, IS MY MOTTO!
G'NIGHT.

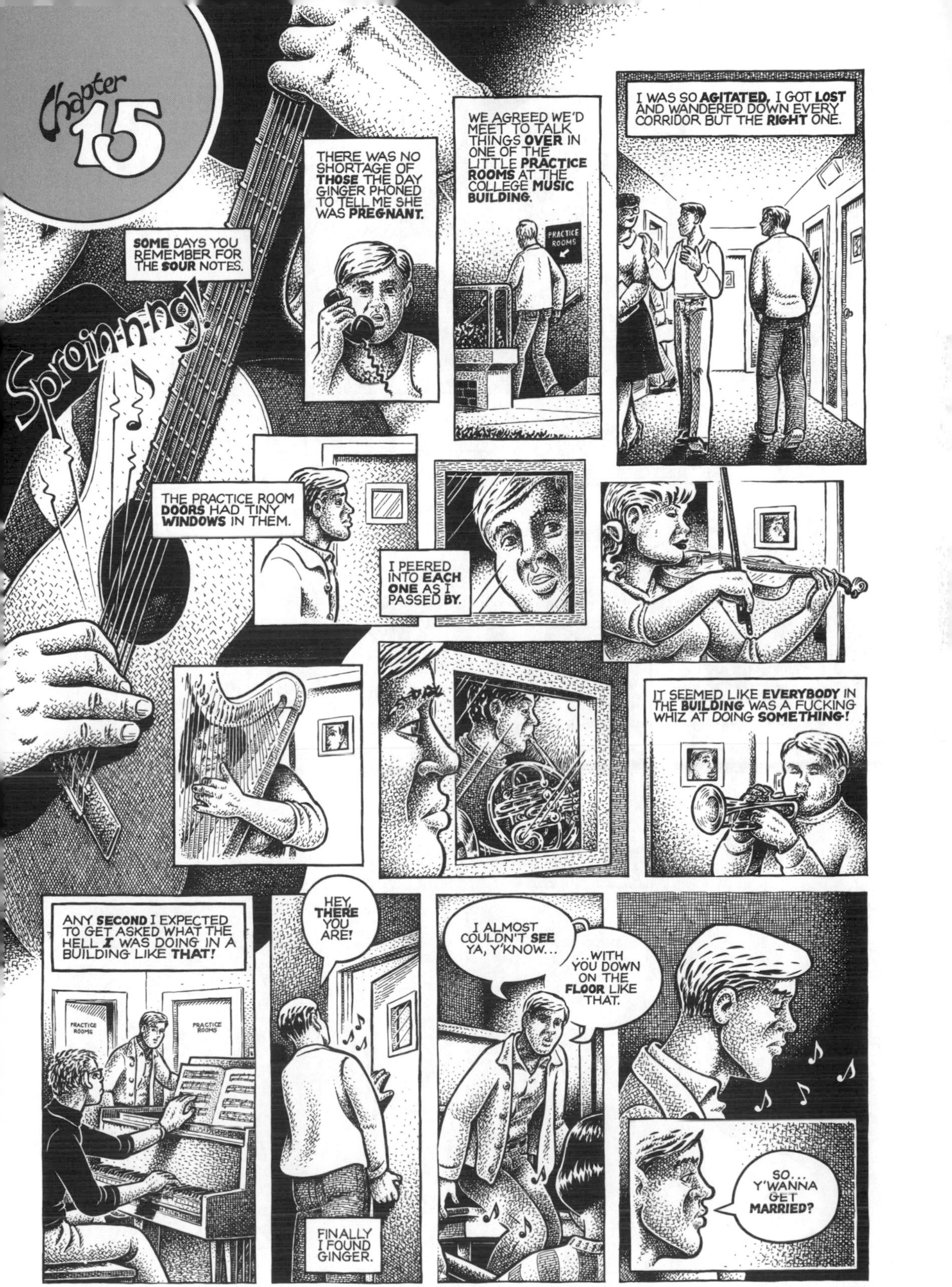
Chapter 15
SOME DAYS YOU REMEMBER FOR THE SOUR NOTES.
Sproin-n-ng!
THERE WAS NO SHORTAGE OF THOSE THE DAY GINGER PHONED TO TELL ME SHE WAS PREGNANT.
WE AGREED WE'D MEET TO TALK THINGS OVER IN ONE OF THE LITTLE PRACTICE ROOMS AT THE COLLEGE MUSIC BUILDING.
PRACTICE ROOMS
I WAS SO AGITATED, I GOT LOST AND WANDERED DOWN EVERY CORRIDOR BUT THE RIGHT ONE.
THE PRACTICE ROOM DOORS HAD TINY WINDOWS IN THEM.
I PEERED INTO EACH ONE AS I PASSED BY.
IT SEEMED LIKE EVERYBODY IN THE BUILDING WAS A FUCKING WHIZ AT DOING SOMETHING!
ANY SECOND I EXPECTED TO GET ASKED WHAT THE HELL I WAS DOING IN A BUILDING LIKE THAT!
PRACTICE ROOMS
PRACTICE ROOMS
HEY, THERE YOU ARE!
FINALLY I FOUND GINGER.
I ALMOST COULDN'T SEE YA, Y'KNOW...
...WITH YOU DOWN ON THE FLOOR LIKE THAT.
SO... Y'WANNA GET MARRIED?

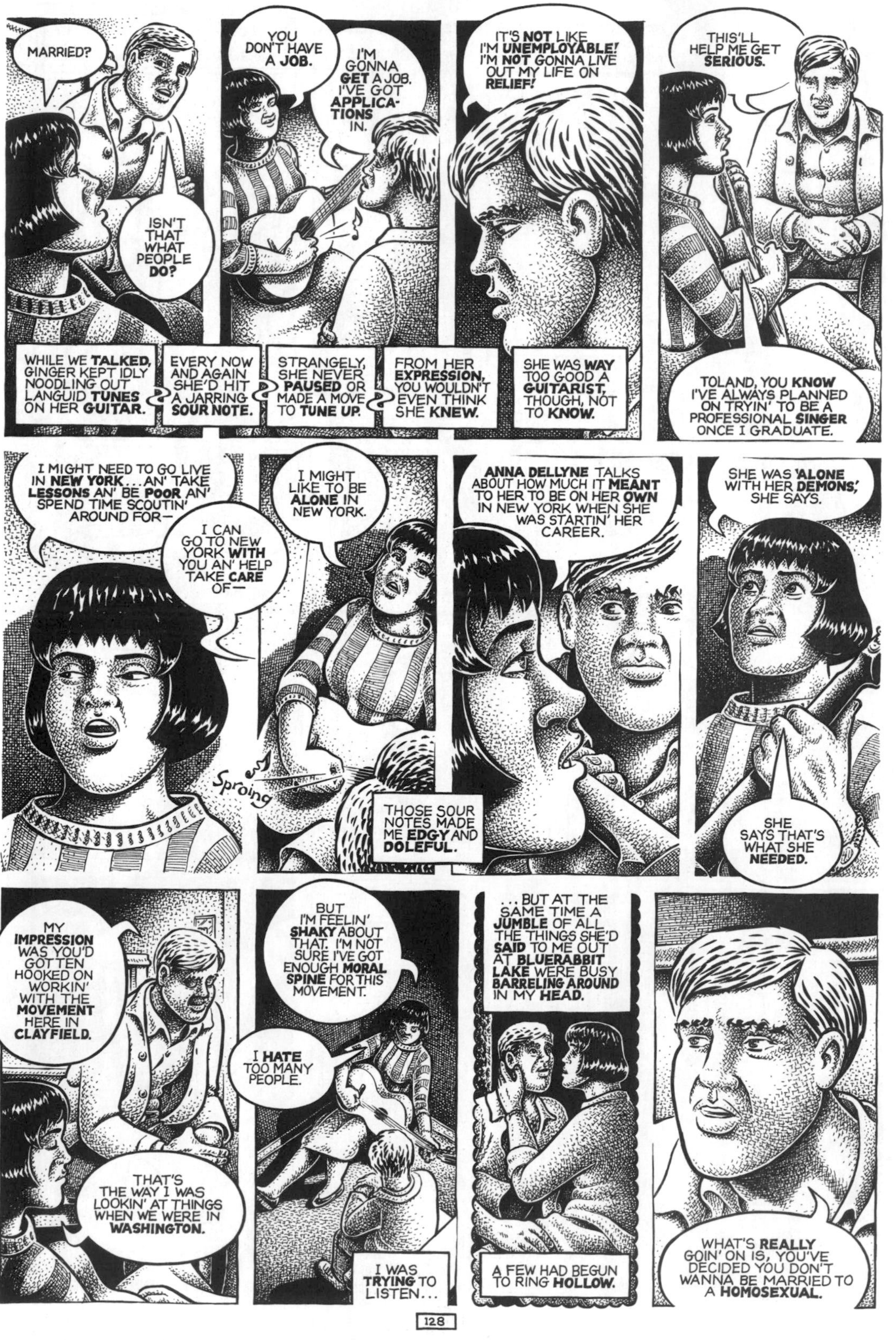
MARRIED?
ISN'T THAT WHAT PEOPLE DO?
YOU DON'T HAVE A JOB.
I'M GONNA GET A JOB. I'VE GOT APPLICATIONS IN.
IT'S NOT LIKE I'M UNEMPLOYABLE! I'M NOT GONNA LIVE OUT MY LIFE ON RELIEF!
THIS'LL HELP ME GET SERIOUS.
WHILE WE TALKED, GINGER KEPT IDLY NOODLING OUT LANGUID TUNES ON HER GUITAR.
EVERY NOW AND AGAIN SHE'D HIT A JARRING SOUR NOTE.
STRANGELY, SHE NEVER PAUSED OR MADE A MOVE TO TUNE UP.
FROM HER EXPRESSION, YOU WOULDN'T EVEN THINK SHE KNEW.
SHE WAS WAY TOO GOOD A GUITARIST, THOUGH, NOT TO KNOW.
TOLAND, YOU KNOW I'VE ALWAYS PLANNED ON TRYIN' TO BE A PROFESSIONAL SINGER ONCE I GRADUATE.
I MIGHT NEED TO GO LIVE IN NEW YORK... AN' TAKE LESSONS AN' BE POOR AN' SPEND TIME SCOUTIN' AROUND FOR—
I CAN GO TO NEW YORK WITH YOU AN' HELP TAKE CARE OF—
I MIGHT LIKE TO BE ALONE IN NEW YORK.
Sproing
THOSE SOUR NOTES MADE ME EDGY AND DOLEFUL.
ANNA DELLYNE TALKS ABOUT HOW MUCH IT MEANT TO HER TO BE ON HER OWN IN NEW YORK WHEN SHE WAS STARTIN' HER CAREER.
SHE WAS 'ALONE WITH HER DEMONS,' SHE SAYS.
SHE SAYS THAT'S WHAT SHE NEEDED.
MY IMPRESSION WAS YOU'D GOTTEN HOOKED ON WORKIN' WITH THE MOVEMENT HERE IN CLAYFIELD.
THAT'S THE WAY I WAS LOOKIN' AT THINGS WHEN WE WERE IN WASHINGTON.
BUT I'M FEELIN' SHAKY ABOUT THAT. I'M NOT SURE I'VE GOT ENOUGH MORAL SPINE FOR THIS MOVEMENT.
I HATE TOO MANY PEOPLE.
I WAS TRYING TO LISTEN...
... BUT AT THE SAME TIME A JUMBLE OF ALL THE THINGS SHE'D SAID TO ME OUT AT BLUERABBIT LAKE WERE BUSY BARRELING AROUND IN MY HEAD.
A FEW HAD BEGUN TO RING HOLLOW.
WHAT'S REALLY GOIN' ON IS, YOU'VE DECIDED YOU DON'T WANNA BE MARRIED TO A HOMOSEXUAL.

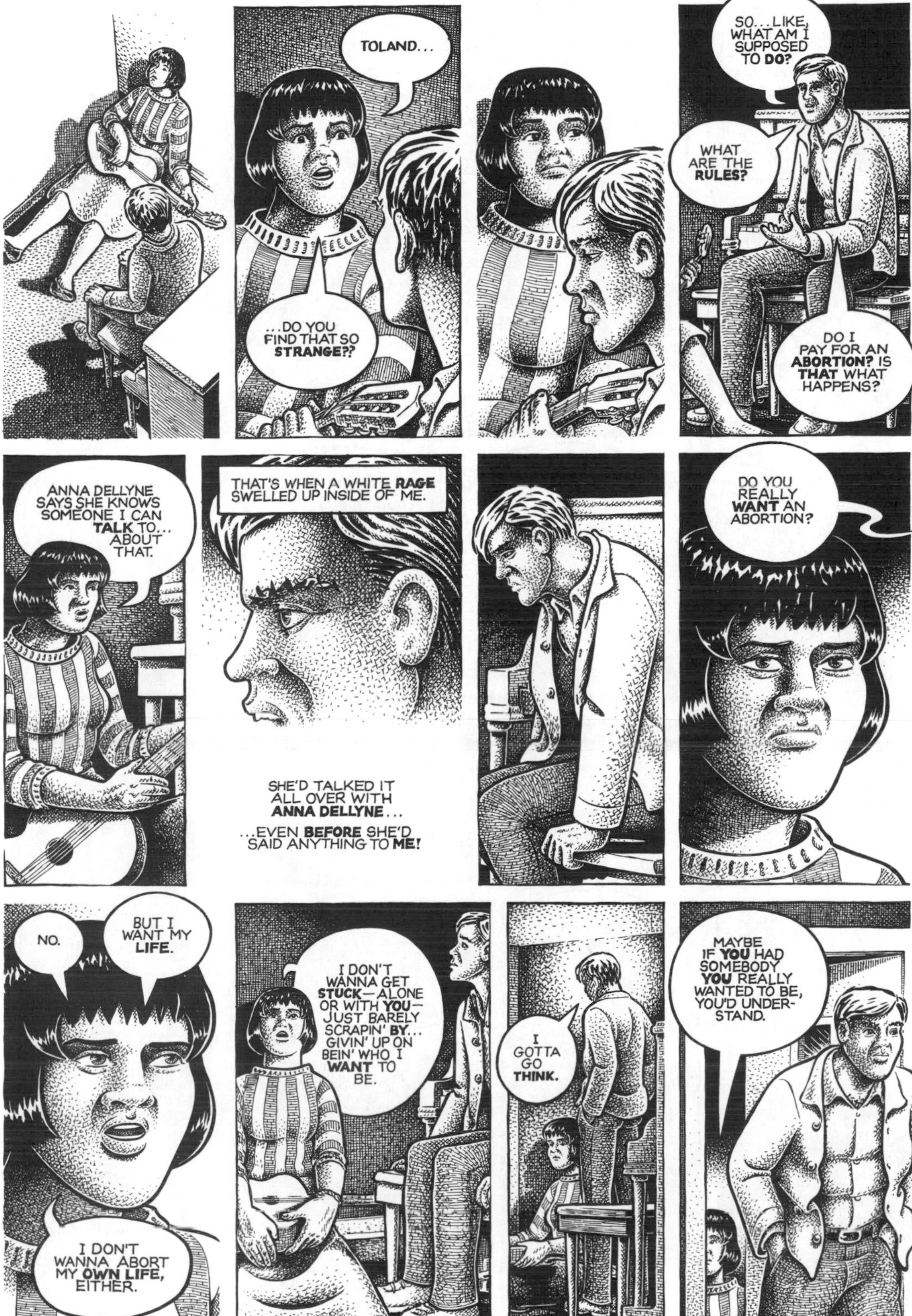
TOLAND...
...DO YOU FIND THAT SO STRANGE?
SO...LIKE, WHAT AM I SUPPOSED TO DO?
WHAT ARE THE RULES?
DO I PAY FOR AN ABORTION? IS THAT WHAT HAPPENS?
ANNA DELLYNE SAYS SHE KNOWS SOMEONE I CAN TALK TO... ABOUT THAT.
THAT'S WHEN A WHITE RAGE SWELLED UP INSIDE OF ME.
SHE'D TALKED IT ALL OVER WITH ANNA DELLYNE...
...EVEN BEFORE SHE'D SAID ANYTHING TO ME!
DO YOU REALLY WANT AN ABORTION?
NO.
BUT I WANT MY LIFE.
I DON'T WANNA ABORT MY OWN LIFE, EITHER.
I DON'T WANNA GET STUCK—ALONE OR WITH YOU—JUST BARELY SCRAPIN' BY... GIVIN' UP ON BEIN' WHO I WANT TO BE.
I GOTTA GO THINK.
MAYBE IF YOU HAD SOMEBODY YOU REALLY WANTED TO BE, YOU'D UNDERSTAND.

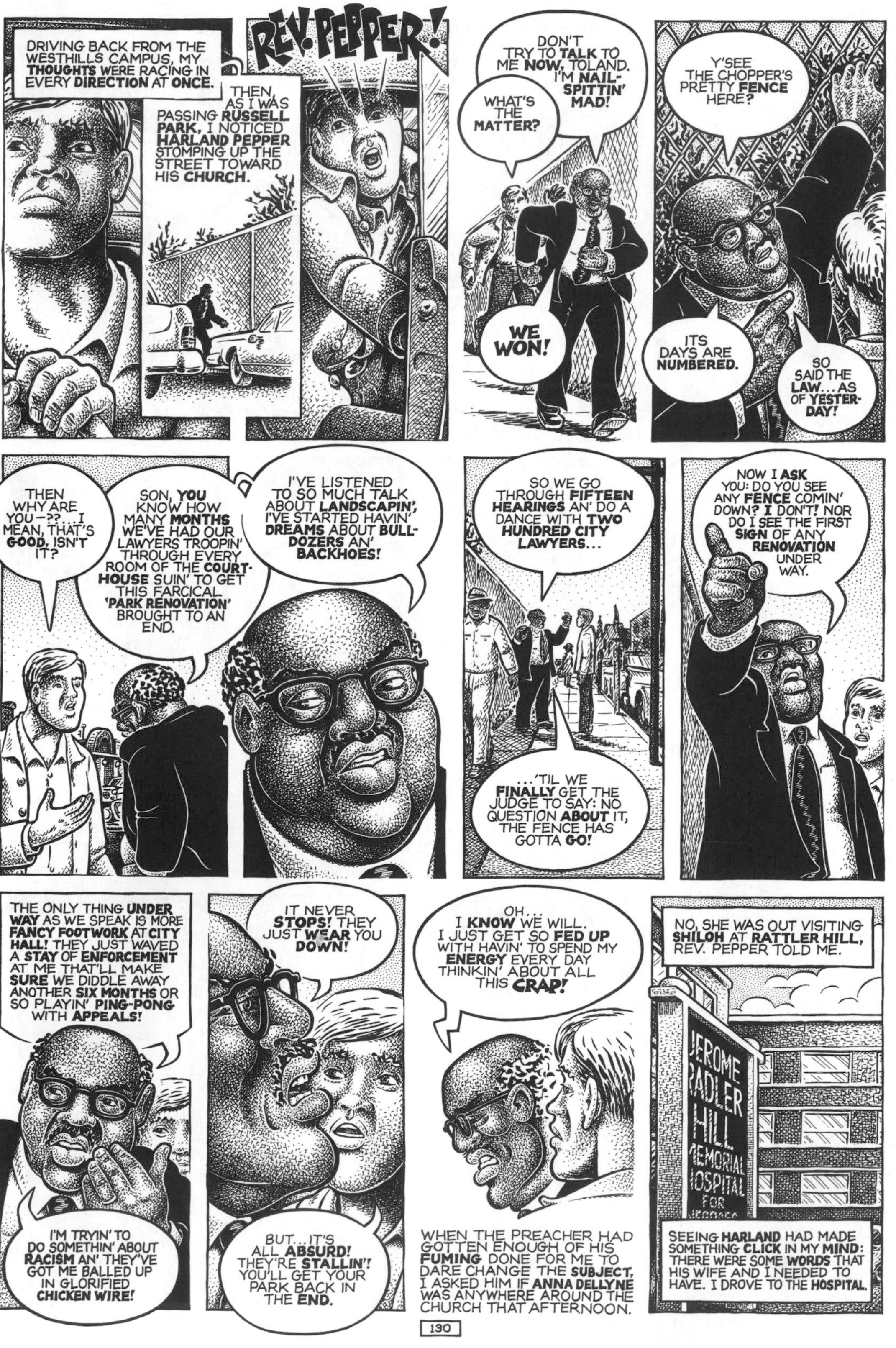
DRIVING BACK FROM THE WESTHILLS CAMPUS, MY THOUGHTS WERE RACING IN EVERY DIRECTION AT ONCE.
THEN, AS I WAS PASSING RUSSELL PARK, I NOTICED HARLAND PEPPER STOMPING UP THE STREET TOWARD HIS CHURCH.
REV. PEPPER!
WHAT'S THE MATTER?
DON'T TRY TO TALK TO ME NOW, TOLAND. I'M NAIL-SPITTIN' MAD!
WE WON!
Y'SEE THE CHOPPER'S PRETTY FENCE HERE?
ITS DAYS ARE NUMBERED.
SO SAID THE LAW... AS OF YESTER-DAY!
THEN WHY ARE YOU—??... I MEAN, THAT'S GOOD, ISN'T IT?
SON, YOU KNOW HOW MANY MONTHS WE'VE HAD OUR LAWYERS TROOPIN' THROUGH EVERY ROOM OF THE COURT-HOUSE SUIN' TO GET THIS FARCICAL 'PARK RENOVATION' BROUGHT TO AN END.
I'VE LISTENED TO SO MUCH TALK ABOUT LANDSCAPIN', I'VE STARTED HAVIN' DREAMS ABOUT BULL-DOZERS AN' BACKHOES!
SO WE GO THROUGH FIFTEEN HEARINGS AN' DO A DANCE WITH TWO HUNDRED CITY LAWYERS...
...'TIL WE FINALLY GET THE JUDGE TO SAY: NO QUESTION ABOUT IT, THE FENCE HAS GOTTA GO!
NOW I ASK YOU: DO YOU SEE ANY FENCE COMIN' DOWN? I DON'T! NOR DO I SEE THE FIRST SIGN OF ANY RENOVATION UNDER WAY.
THE ONLY THING UNDER WAY AS WE SPEAK IS MORE FANCY FOOTWORK AT CITY HALL! THEY JUST WAVED A STAY OF ENFORCEMENT AT ME THAT'LL MAKE SURE WE DIDDLE AWAY ANOTHER SIX MONTHS OR SO PLAYIN' PING-PONG WITH APPEALS!
I'M TRYIN' TO DO SOMETHIN' ABOUT RACISM AN' THEY'VE GOT ME BALLED UP IN GLORIFIED CHICKEN WIRE!
IT NEVER STOPS! THEY JUST WEAR YOU DOWN!
BUT... IT'S ALL ABSURD! THEY'RE STALLIN'! YOU'LL GET YOUR PARK BACK IN THE END.
OH... I KNOW WE WILL. I JUST GET SO FED UP WITH HAVIN' TO SPEND MY ENERGY EVERY DAY THINKIN' ABOUT ALL THIS CRAP!
WHEN THE PREACHER HAD GOTTEN ENOUGH OF HIS FUMING DONE FOR ME TO DARE CHANGE THE SUBJECT, I ASKED HIM IF ANNA DELLYNE WAS ANYWHERE AROUND THE CHURCH THAT AFTERNOON.
NO, SHE WAS OUT VISITING SHILOH AT RATTLER HILL, REV. PEPPER TOLD ME.
MEMORIAL
HOSPITAL
FOR
SEEING HARLAND HAD MADE SOMETHING CLICK IN MY MIND: THERE WERE SOME WORDS THAT HIS WIFE AND I NEEDED TO HAVE. I DROVE TO THE HOSPITAL.

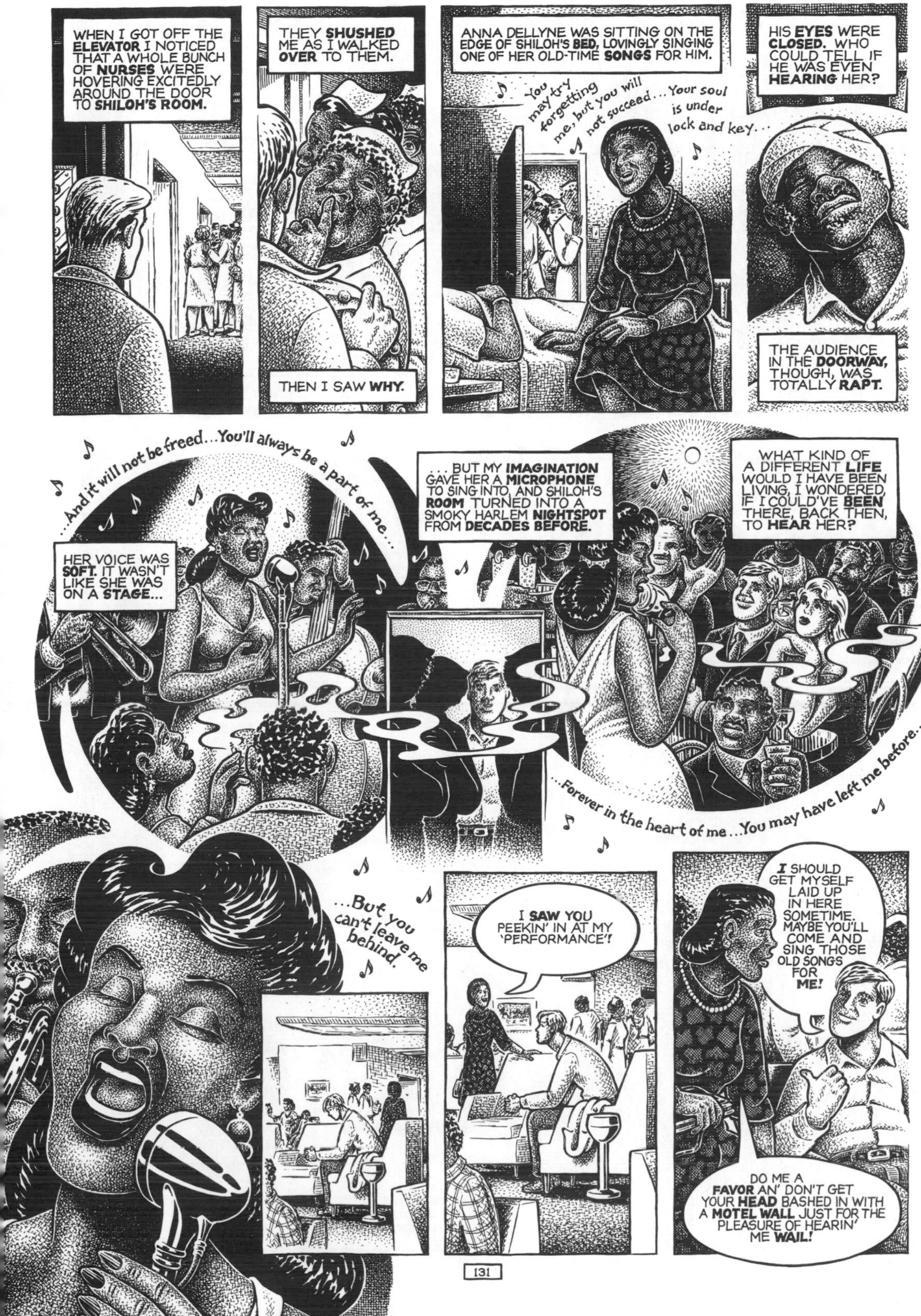
WHEN I GOT OFF THE ELEVATOR I NOTICED THAT A WHOLE BUNCH OF NURSES WERE HOVERING EXCITEDLY AROUND THE DOOR TO SHILOH'S ROOM.
THEY SHUSHED ME AS I WALKED OVER TO THEM.
THEN I SAW WHY.
ANNA DELLYNE WAS SITTING ON THE EDGE OF SHILOH'S BED, LOVINGLY SINGING ONE OF HER OLD-TIME SONGS FOR HIM.
You may try forgetting me, but you will not succeed... Your soul is under lock and key...
HIS EYES WERE CLOSED. WHO COULD TELL IF HE WAS EVEN HEARING HER?
THE AUDIENCE IN THE DOORWAY, THOUGH, WAS TOTALLY RAPT.
...And it will not be freed... You'll always be a part of me...
HER VOICE WAS SOFT. IT WASN'T LIKE SHE WAS ON A STAGE...
...BUT MY IMAGINATION GAVE HER A MICROPHONE TO SING INTO, AND SHILOH'S ROOM TURNED INTO A SMOKY HARLEM NIGHTSPOT FROM DECADES BEFORE.
WHAT KIND OF A DIFFERENT LIFE WOULD I HAVE BEEN LIVING, I WONDERED, IF I COULD'VE BEEN THERE, BACK THEN, TO HEAR HER?
...Forever in the heart of me... You may have left me before...
...But you can't leave me behind.
I SAW YOU PEEKIN' IN AT MY 'PERFORMANCE'!
I SHOULD GET MYSELF LAID UP IN HERE SOMETIME. MAYBE YOU'LL COME AND SING THOSE OLD SONGS FOR ME!
DO ME A FAVOR AN' DON'T GET YOUR HEAD BASHED IN WITH A MOTEL WALL JUST FOR THE PLEASURE OF HEARIN' ME WAIL!

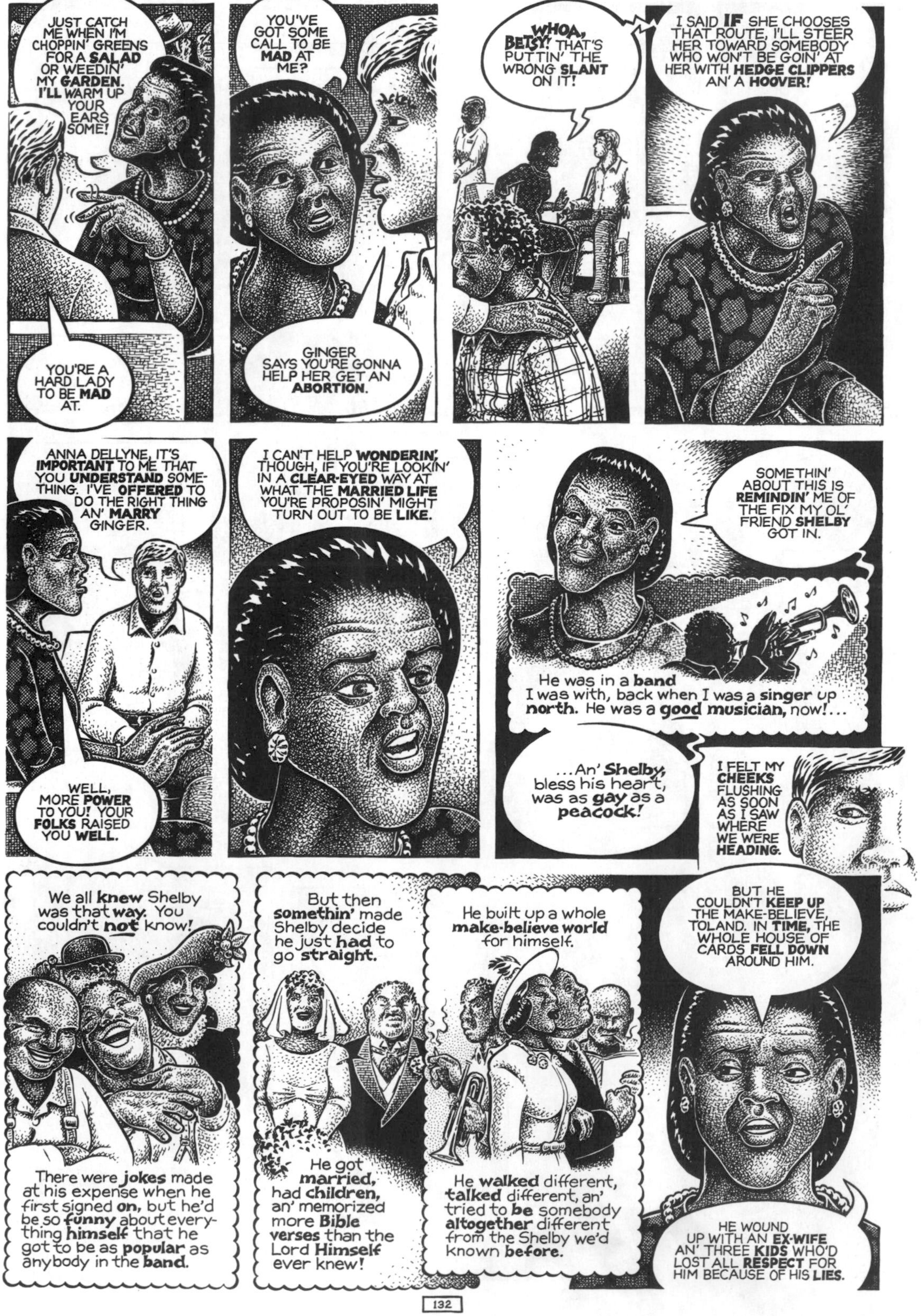

JUST CATCH ME WHEN I'M CHOPPIN' GREENS FOR A SALAD OR WEEDIN' MY GARDEN. I'LL WARM UP YOUR EARS SOME!
YOU'RE A HARD LADY TO BE MAD AT.
YOU'VE GOT SOME CALL TO BE MAD AT ME?
GINGER SAYS YOU'RE GONNA HELP HER GET AN ABORTION.
WHOA, BETSY! THAT'S PUTTIN' THE WRONG SLANT ON IT!
I SAID IF SHE CHOOSES THAT ROUTE, I'LL STEER HER TOWARD SOMEBODY WHO WON'T BE GOIN' AT HER WITH HEDGE CLIPPERS AN' A HOOVER!
ANNA DELLYNE, IT'S IMPORTANT TO ME THAT YOU UNDERSTAND SOMETHING. I'VE OFFERED TO DO THE RIGHT THING AN' MARRY GINGER.
WELL, MORE POWER TO YOU! YOUR FOLKS RAISED YOU WELL.
I CAN'T HELP WONDERIN', THOUGH, IF YOU'RE LOOKIN' IN A CLEAR-EYED WAY AT WHAT THE MARRIED LIFE YOU'RE PROPOSIN' MIGHT TURN OUT TO BE LIKE.
SOMETHIN' ABOUT THIS IS REMINDIN' ME OF THE FIX MY OL' FRIEND SHELBY GOT IN.
He was in a band I was with, back when I was a singer up north. He was a good musician, now!...
...An' Shelby, bless his heart, was as gay as a peacock!
I FELT MY CHEEKS FLUSHING AS SOON AS I SAW WHERE WE WERE HEADING.
We all knew Shelby was that way. You couldn't not know!
There were jokes made at his expense when he first signed on, but he'd be so funny about everything himself that he got to be as popular as anybody in the band.
But then somethin' made Shelby decide he just had to go straight.
He got married, had children, an' memorized more Bible verses than the Lord Himself ever knew!
He built up a whole make-believe world for himself.
He walked different, talked different, an' tried to be somebody altogether different from the Shelby we'd known before.
BUT HE COULDN'T KEEP UP THE MAKE-BELIEVE, TOLAND. IN TIME, THE WHOLE HOUSE OF CARDS FELL DOWN AROUND HIM.
HE WOUND UP WITH AN EX-WIFE AN' THREE KIDS WHO'D LOST ALL RESPECT FOR HIM BECAUSE OF HIS LIES.

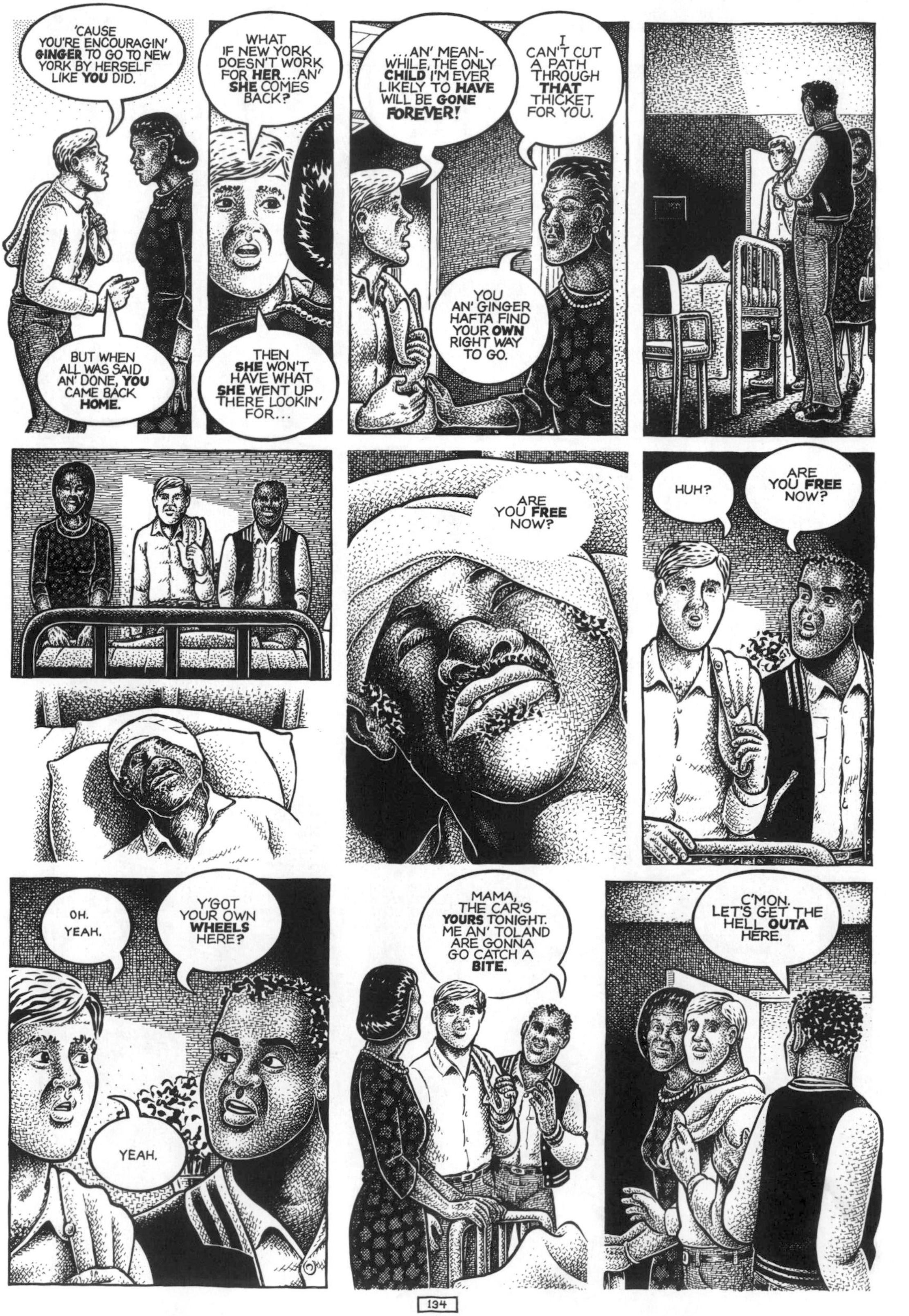
'CAUSE YOU'RE ENCOURAGIN' GINGER TO GO TO NEW YORK BY HERSELF LIKE YOU DID.
BUT WHEN ALL WAS SAID AN' DONE, YOU CAME BACK HOME.
WHAT IF NEW YORK DOESN'T WORK FOR HER...AN' SHE COMES BACK?
THEN SHE WON'T HAVE WHAT SHE WENT UP THERE LOOKIN' FOR...
...AN' MEAN-WHILE, THE ONLY CHILD I'M EVER LIKELY TO HAVE WILL BE GONE FOREVER!
I CAN'T CUT A PATH THROUGH THAT THICKET FOR YOU.
YOU AN' GINGER HAFTA FIND YOUR OWN RIGHT WAY TO GO.
ARE YOU FREE NOW?
HUH?
ARE YOU FREE NOW?
OH. YEAH.
Y'GOT YOUR OWN WHEELS HERE?
YEAH.
MAMA, THE CAR'S YOURS TONIGHT. ME AN' TOLAND ARE GONNA GO CATCH A BITE.
C'MON. LET'S GET THE HELL OUTA HERE.

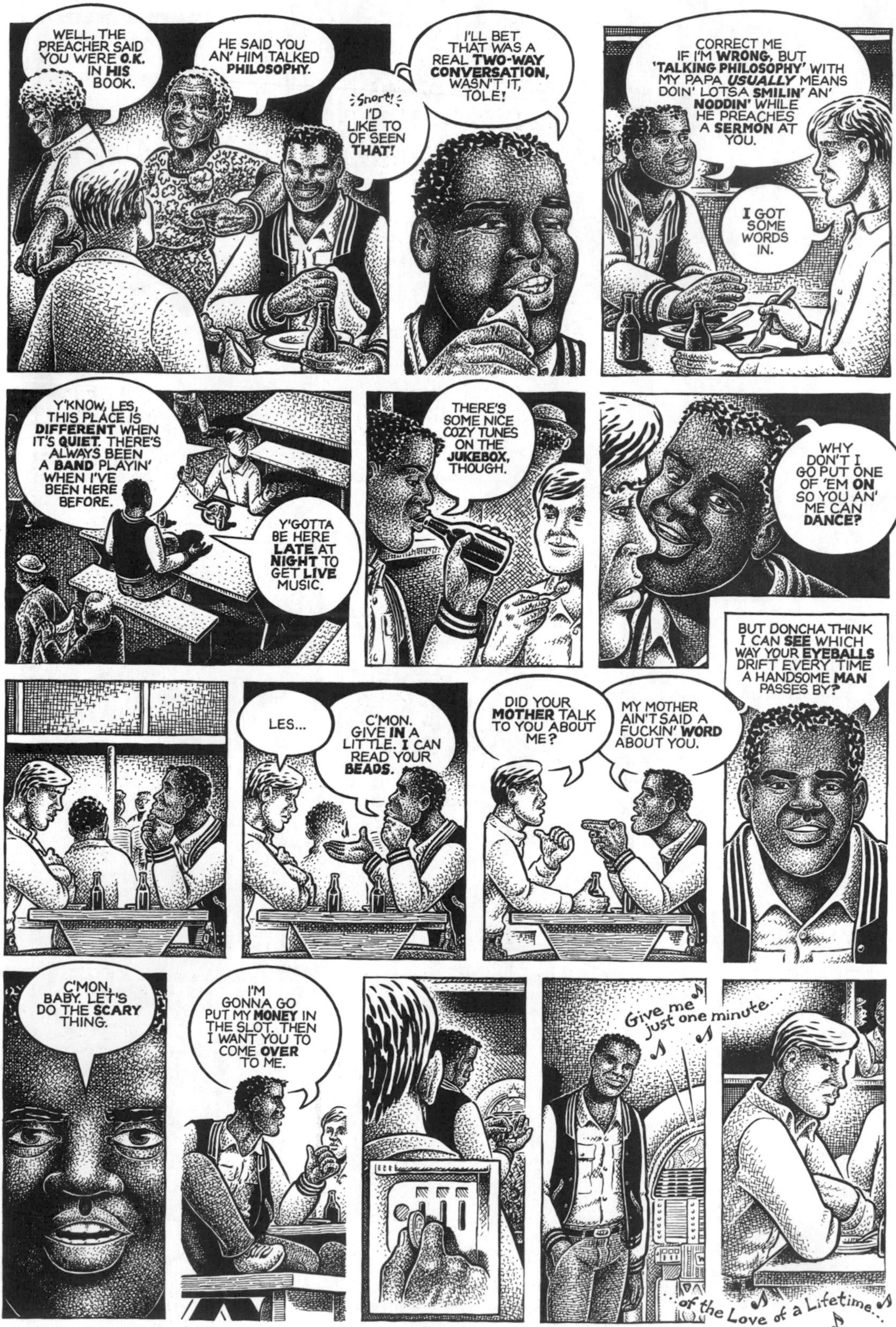
WELL, THE PREACHER SAID YOU WERE O.K. IN HIS BOOK.
HE SAID YOU AN' HIM TALKED PHILOSOPHY.
Snort!
I'D LIKE TO OF SEEN THAT!
I'LL BET THAT WAS A REAL TWO-WAY CONVERSATION, WASN'T IT, TOLE!
CORRECT ME IF I'M WRONG, BUT 'TALKING PHILOSOPHY' WITH MY PAPA USUALLY MEANS DOIN' LOTSA SMILIN' AN' NODDIN' WHILE HE PREACHES A SERMON AT YOU.
I GOT SOME WORDS IN.
Y'KNOW, LES, THIS PLACE IS DIFFERENT WHEN IT'S QUIET. THERE'S ALWAYS BEEN A BAND PLAYIN' WHEN I'VE BEEN HERE BEFORE.
Y'GOTTA BE HERE LATE AT NIGHT TO GET LIVE MUSIC.
THERE'S SOME NICE COZY TUNES ON THE JUKEBOX, THOUGH.
WHY DON'T I GO PUT ONE OF 'EM ON SO YOU AN' ME CAN DANCE?
LES...
C'MON. GIVE IN A LITTLE. I CAN READ YOUR BEADS.
DID YOUR MOTHER TALK TO YOU ABOUT ME?
MY MOTHER AIN'T SAID A FUCKIN' WORD ABOUT YOU.
BUT DONCHA THINK I CAN SEE WHICH WAY YOUR EYEBALLS DRIFT EVERY TIME A HANDSOME MAN PASSES BY?
C'MON, BABY. LET'S DO THE SCARY THING.
I'M GONNA GO PUT MY MONEY IN THE SLOT. THEN I WANT YOU TO COME OVER TO ME.
Give me just one minute...
...of the Love of a Lifetime...

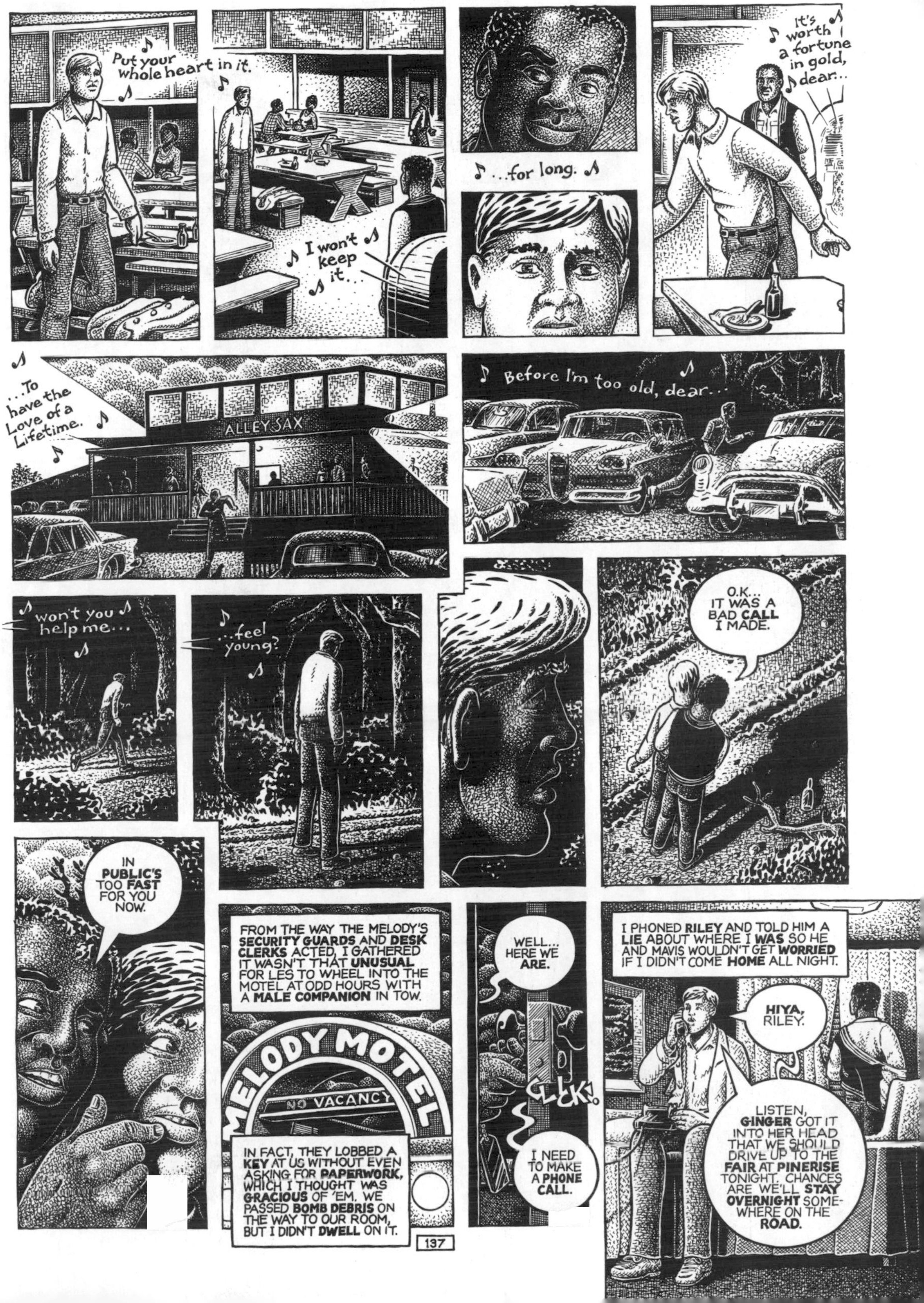
Put your whole heart in it.
I won't keep it...
...for long.
It's worth a fortune in gold, dear...
...To have the Love of a Lifetime.
ALLEY SAX
Before I'm too old, dear...
won't you help me...
...feel young?
O.K... IT WAS A BAD CALL I MADE.
IN PUBLIC'S TOO FAST FOR YOU NOW.
FROM THE WAY THE MELODY'S SECURITY GUARDS AND DESK CLERKS ACTED, I GATHERED IT WASN'T THAT UNUSUAL FOR LES TO WHEEL INTO THE MOTEL AT ODD HOURS WITH A MALE COMPANION IN TOW.
MELODY MOTEL
NO VACANCY
IN FACT, THEY LOBBED A KEY AT US WITHOUT EVEN ASKING FOR PAPERWORK, WHICH I THOUGHT WAS GRACIOUS OF 'EM. WE PASSED BOMB DEBRIS ON THE WAY TO OUR ROOM, BUT I DIDN'T DWELL ON IT.
WELL... HERE WE ARE.
CLICK!
I NEED TO MAKE A PHONE CALL.
I PHONED RILEY AND TOLD HIM A LIE ABOUT WHERE I WAS SO HE AND MAVIS WOULDN'T GET WORRIED IF I DIDN'T COME HOME ALL NIGHT.
HIYA, RILEY.
LISTEN, GINGER GOT IT INTO HER HEAD THAT WE SHOULD DRIVE UP TO THE FAIR AT PINERISE TONIGHT. CHANCES ARE WE'LL STAY OVERNIGHT SOMEWHERE ON THE ROAD.

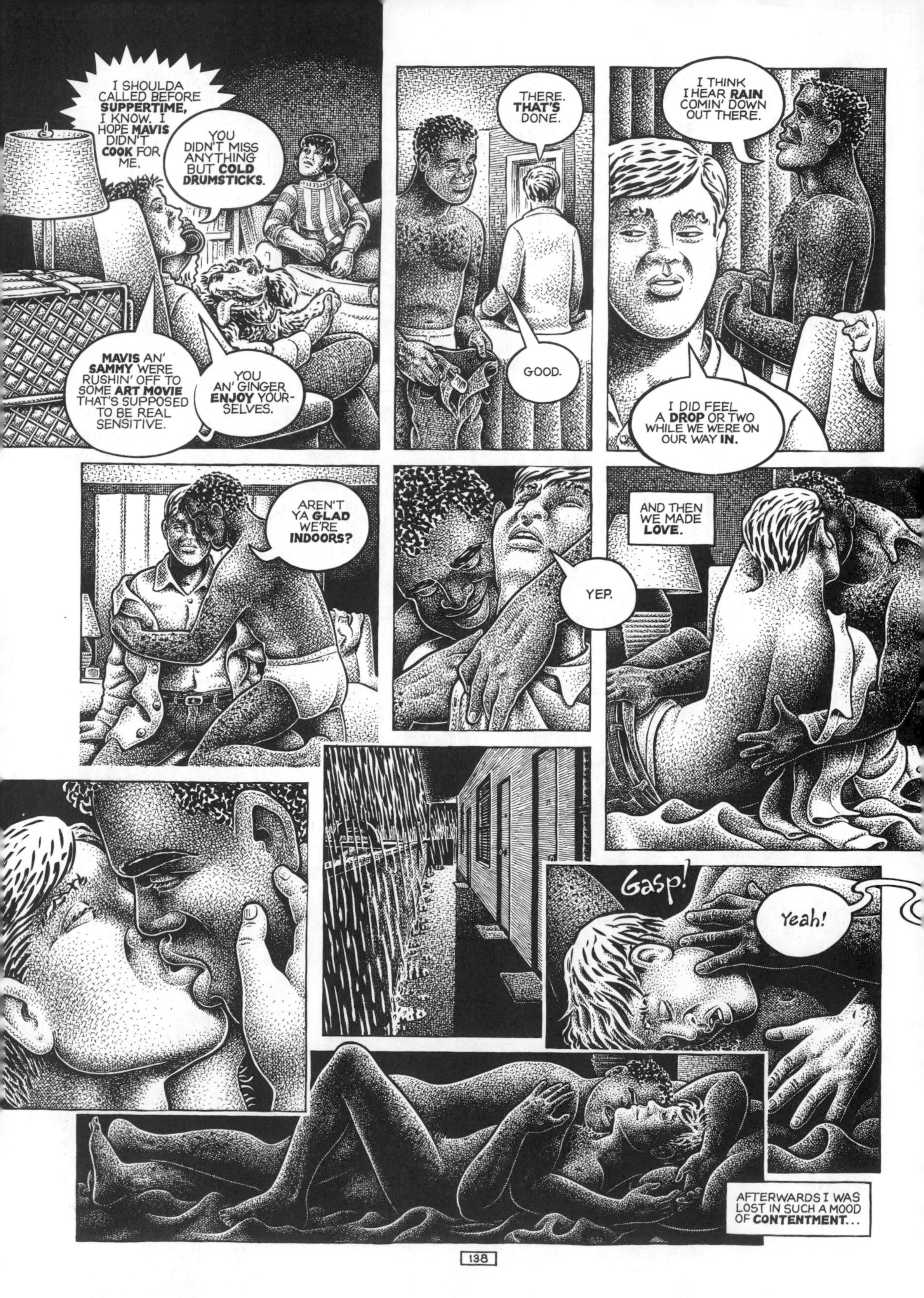
I SHOULDA CALLED BEFORE SUPPERTIME, I KNOW. I HOPE MAVIS DIDN'T COOK FOR ME.
YOU DIDN'T MISS ANYTHING BUT COLD DRUMSTICKS.
MAVIS AN' SAMMY WERE RUSHIN' OFF TO SOME ART MOVIE THAT'S SUPPOSED TO BE REAL SENSITIVE.
YOU AN' GINGER ENJOY YOURSELVES.
THERE. THAT'S DONE.
GOOD.
I THINK I HEAR RAIN COMIN' DOWN OUT THERE.
I DID FEEL A DROP OR TWO WHILE WE WERE ON OUR WAY IN.
AREN'T YA GLAD WE'RE INDOORS?
YEP.
AND THEN WE MADE LOVE.
Gasp!
Yeah!
AFTERWARDS I WAS LOST IN SUCH A MOOD OF CONTENTMENT...

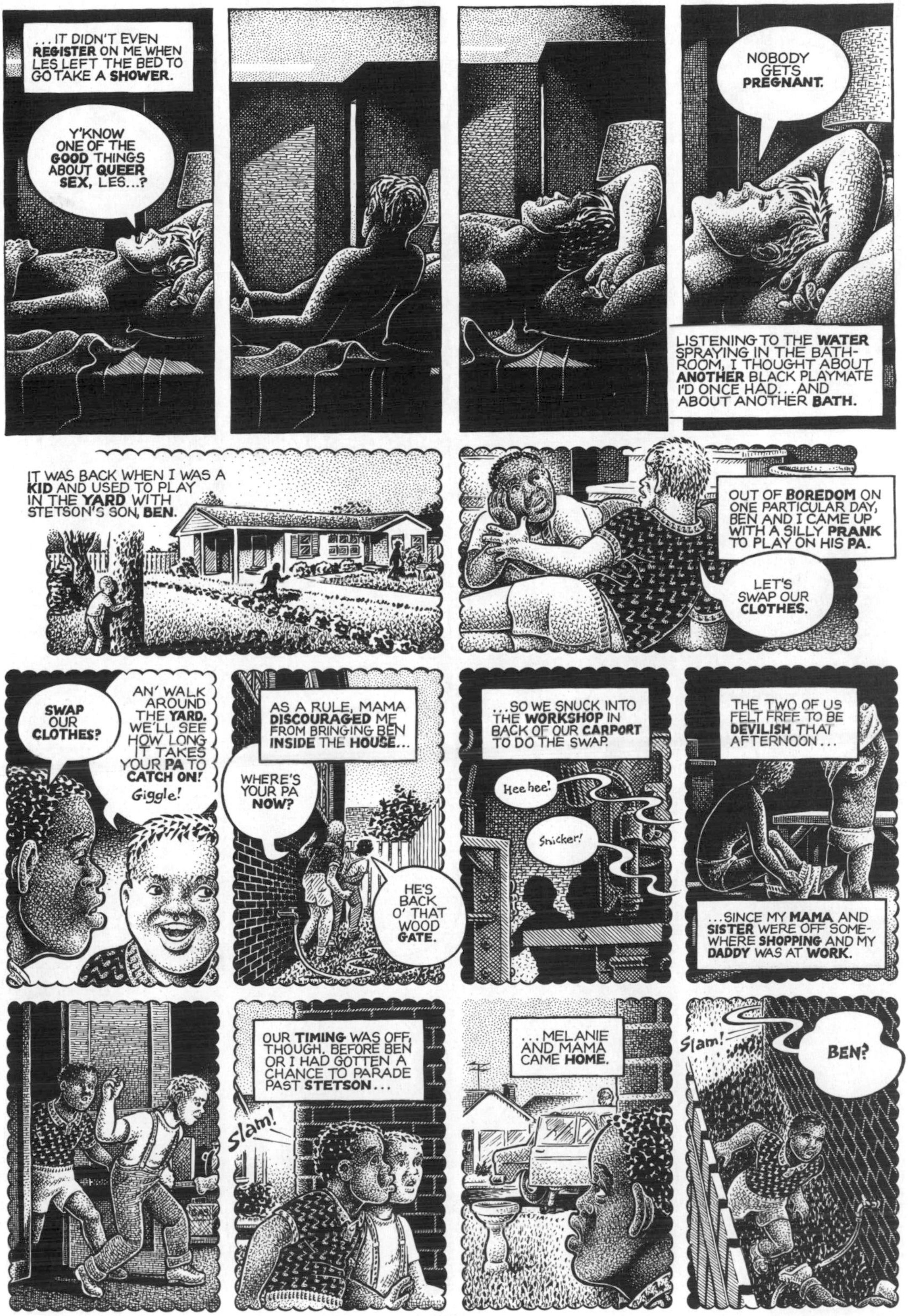
...IT DIDN'T EVEN REGISTER ON ME WHEN LES LEFT THE BED TO GO TAKE A SHOWER.
Y'KNOW ONE OF THE GOOD THINGS ABOUT QUEER SEX, LES...?
NOBODY GETS PREGNANT.
LISTENING TO THE WATER SPRAYING IN THE BATHROOM, I THOUGHT ABOUT ANOTHER BLACK PLAYMATE I'D ONCE HAD... AND ABOUT ANOTHER BATH.
IT WAS BACK WHEN I WAS A KID AND USED TO PLAY IN THE YARD WITH STETSON'S SON, BEN.
OUT OF BOREDOM ON ONE PARTICULAR DAY, BEN AND I CAME UP WITH A SILLY PRANK TO PLAY ON HIS PA.
LET'S SWAP OUR CLOTHES.
SWAP OUR CLOTHES?
AN' WALK AROUND THE YARD. WE'LL SEE HOW LONG IT TAKES YOUR PA TO CATCH ON! Giggle!
AS A RULE, MAMA DISCOURAGED ME FROM BRINGING BEN INSIDE THE HOUSE...
WHERE'S YOUR PA NOW?
HE'S BACK O' THAT WOOD GATE.
...SO WE SNUCK INTO THE WORKSHOP IN BACK OF OUR CARPORT TO DO THE SWAP.
Hee hee!
Snicker!
THE TWO OF US FELT FREE TO BE DEVILISH THAT AFTERNOON...
...SINCE MY MAMA AND SISTER WERE OFF SOMEWHERE SHOPPING AND MY DADDY WAS AT WORK.
OUR TIMING WAS OFF, THOUGH. BEFORE BEN OR I HAD GOTTEN A CHANCE TO PARADE PAST STETSON...
Slam!
...MELANIE AND MAMA CAME HOME.
Slam!
BEN?

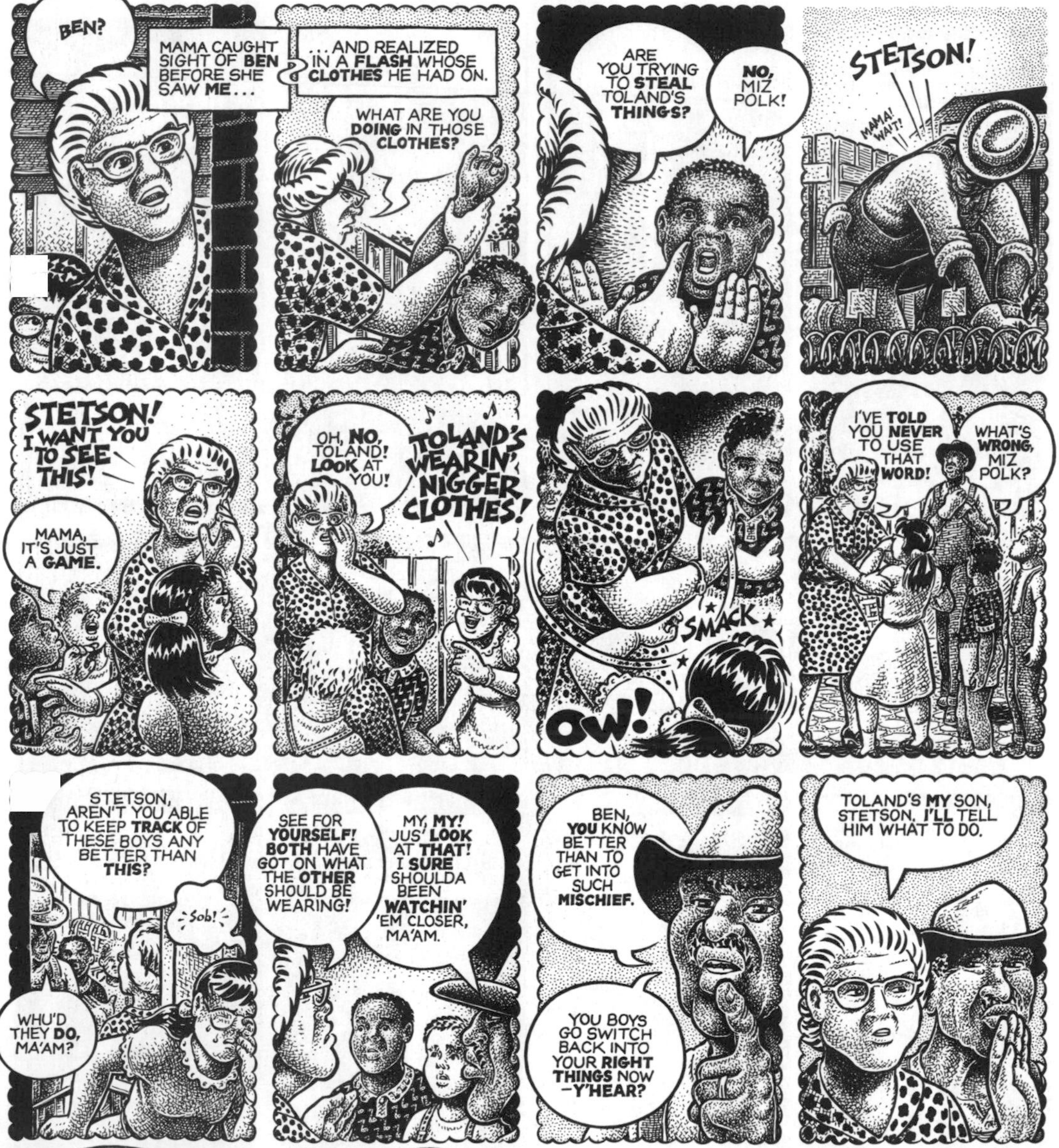
BEN?
MAMA CAUGHT SIGHT OF BEN BEFORE SHE SAW ME...
& ...AND REALIZED IN A FLASH WHOSE CLOTHES HE HAD ON.
WHAT ARE YOU DOING IN THOSE CLOTHES?
ARE YOU TRYING TO STEAL TOLAND'S THINGS?
NO, MIZ POLK!
STETSON!
MAMA! WAIT!
STETSON! I WANT YOU TO SEE THIS!
MAMA, IT'S JUST A GAME.
OH, NO, TOLAND! LOOK AT YOU!
TOLAND'S WEARIN' NIGGER CLOTHES!
SMACK
OW!
I'VE TOLD YOU NEVER TO USE THAT WORD!
WHAT'S WRONG, MIZ POLK?
STETSON, AREN'T YOU ABLE TO KEEP TRACK OF THESE BOYS ANY BETTER THAN THIS?
Sob!
WHU'D THEY DO, MA'AM?
SEE FOR YOURSELF! BOTH HAVE GOT ON WHAT THE OTHER SHOULD BE WEARING!
MY, MY! JUS' LOOK AT THAT! I SURE SHOULDA BEEN WATCHIN' 'EM CLOSER, MA'AM.
BEN, YOU KNOW BETTER THAN TO GET INTO SUCH MISCHIEF.
YOU BOYS GO SWITCH BACK INTO YOUR RIGHT THINGS NOW —Y'HEAR?
TOLAND'S MY SON, STETSON, I'LL TELL HIM WHAT TO DO.
TOLAND, YOU GO INSIDE AND TAKE A BATH RIGHT NOW!
A BATH?!
AND CHANGE INTO FRESH CLOTHES WHEN YOU'RE DONE.
A BATH, MAMA?? NOW??
MAKE QUICK BUSINESS OF IT AND IT WON'T TAKE LONG.
BEN, AS SOON AS TOLAND IS OUT OF YOUR CLOTHES, I'LL BRING THEM TO YOU.
YES'M.
YOU CAN CHANGE IN THE CARPORT.
BUT THERE'S LOTS MORE PLAYIN' TIME LEFT THIS AFTERNOON, MAMA—
TOLAND POLK, ARE YOU ARGUING WITH ME...?
NO, MA'AM.
GOOD.

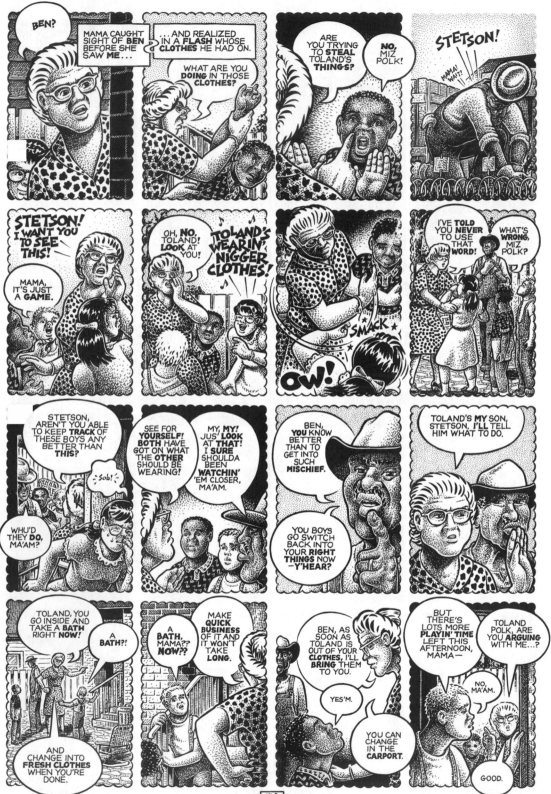

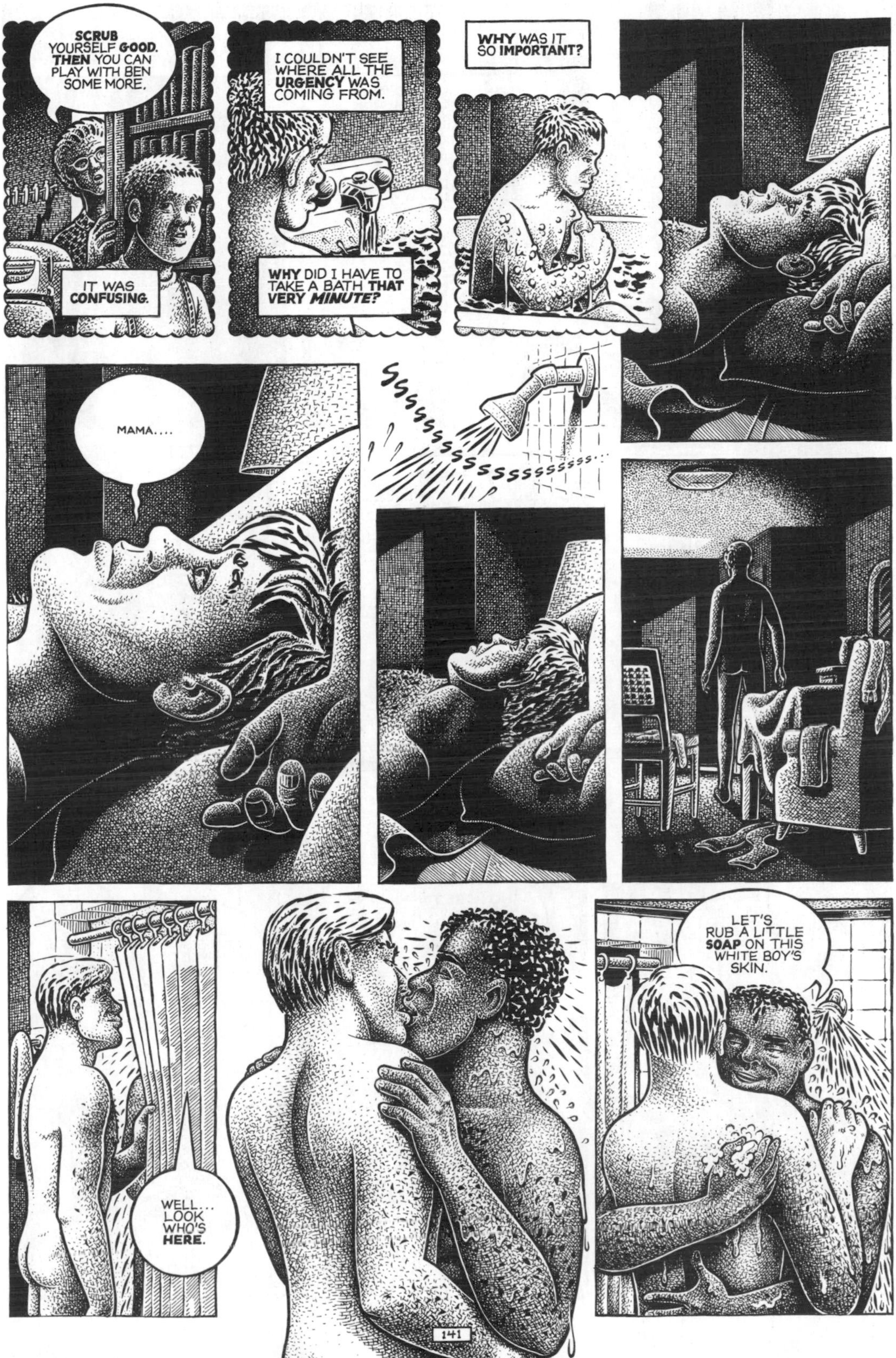
SCRUB YOURSELF GOOD. THEN YOU CAN PLAY WITH BEN SOME MORE.
IT WAS CONFUSING.
I COULDN'T SEE WHERE ALL THE URGENCY WAS COMING FROM.
WHY DID I HAVE TO TAKE A BATH THAT VERY MINUTE?
WHY WAS IT SO IMPORTANT?
MAMA....
SSSSSSSSSSSSSSSSSSSSSSSS...
WELL... LOOK WHO'S HERE.
LET'S RUB A LITTLE SOAP ON THIS WHITE BOY'S SKIN.

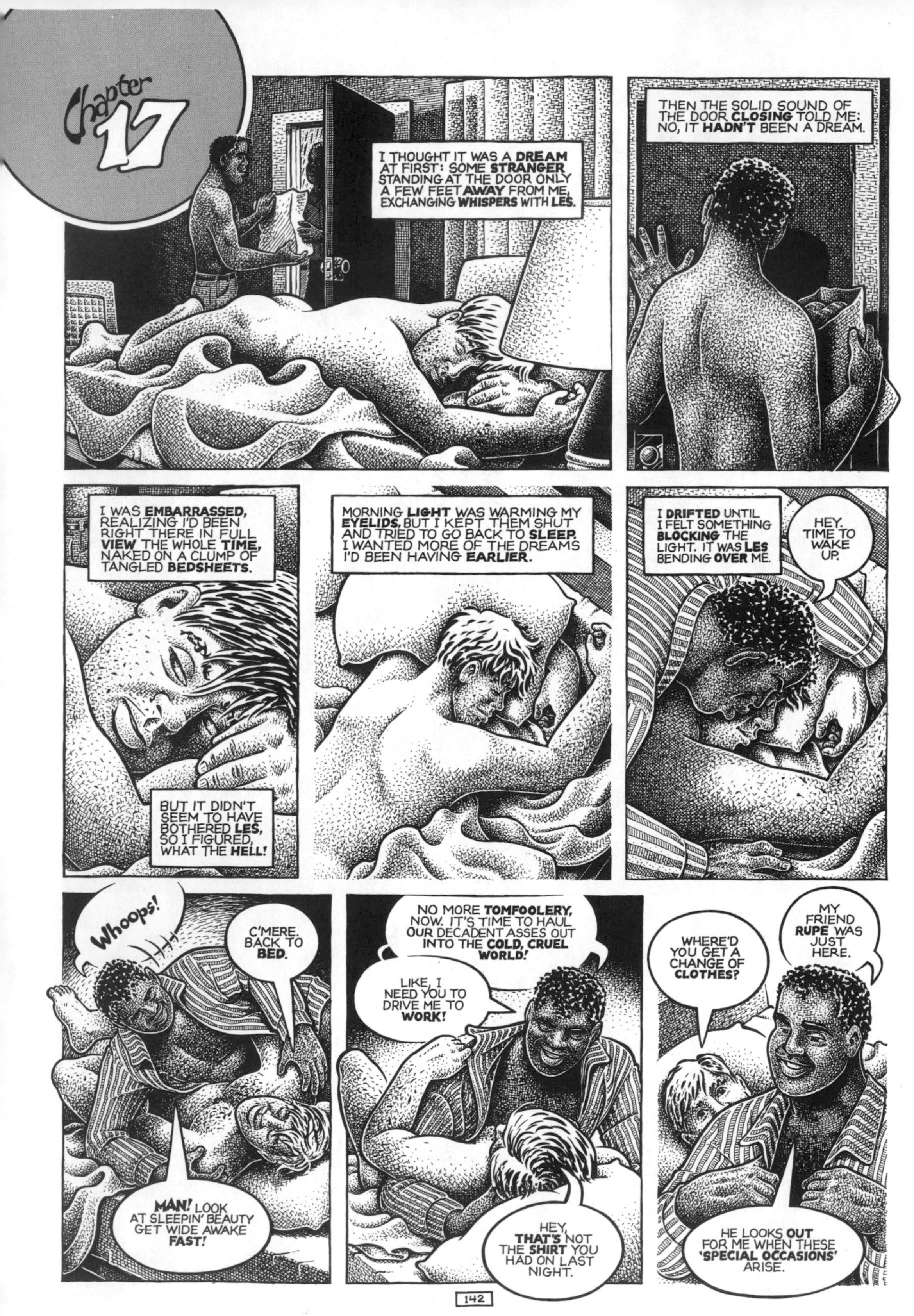
Chapter 17
I THOUGHT IT WAS A DREAM AT FIRST: SOME STRANGER STANDING AT THE DOOR ONLY A FEW FEET AWAY FROM ME, EXCHANGING WHISPERS WITH LES.
THEN THE SOLID SOUND OF THE DOOR CLOSING TOLD ME: NO, IT HADN'T BEEN A DREAM.
I WAS EMBARRASSED, REALIZING I'D BEEN RIGHT THERE IN FULL VIEW THE WHOLE TIME, NAKED ON A CLUMP OF TANGLED BEDSHEETS.
BUT IT DIDN'T SEEM TO HAVE BOTHERED LES, SO I FIGURED, WHAT THE HELL!
MORNING LIGHT WAS WARMING MY EYELIDS, BUT I KEPT THEM SHUT AND TRIED TO GO BACK TO SLEEP. I WANTED MORE OF THE DREAMS I'D BEEN HAVING EARLIER.
I DRIFTED UNTIL I FELT SOMETHING BLOCKING THE LIGHT. IT WAS LES BENDING OVER ME.
HEY. TIME TO WAKE UP.
Whoops!
C'MERE. BACK TO BED.
MAN! LOOK AT SLEEPIN' BEAUTY GET WIDE AWAKE FAST!
NO MORE TOMFOOLERY, NOW. IT'S TIME TO HAUL OUR DECADENT ASSES OUT INTO THE COLD, CRUEL WORLD!
LIKE, I NEED YOU TO DRIVE ME TO WORK!
HEY, THAT'S NOT THE SHIRT YOU HAD ON LAST NIGHT.
WHERE'D YOU GET A CHANGE OF CLOTHES?
MY FRIEND RUPE WAS JUST HERE.
HE LOOKS OUT FOR ME WHEN THESE 'SPECIAL OCCASIONS' ARISE.

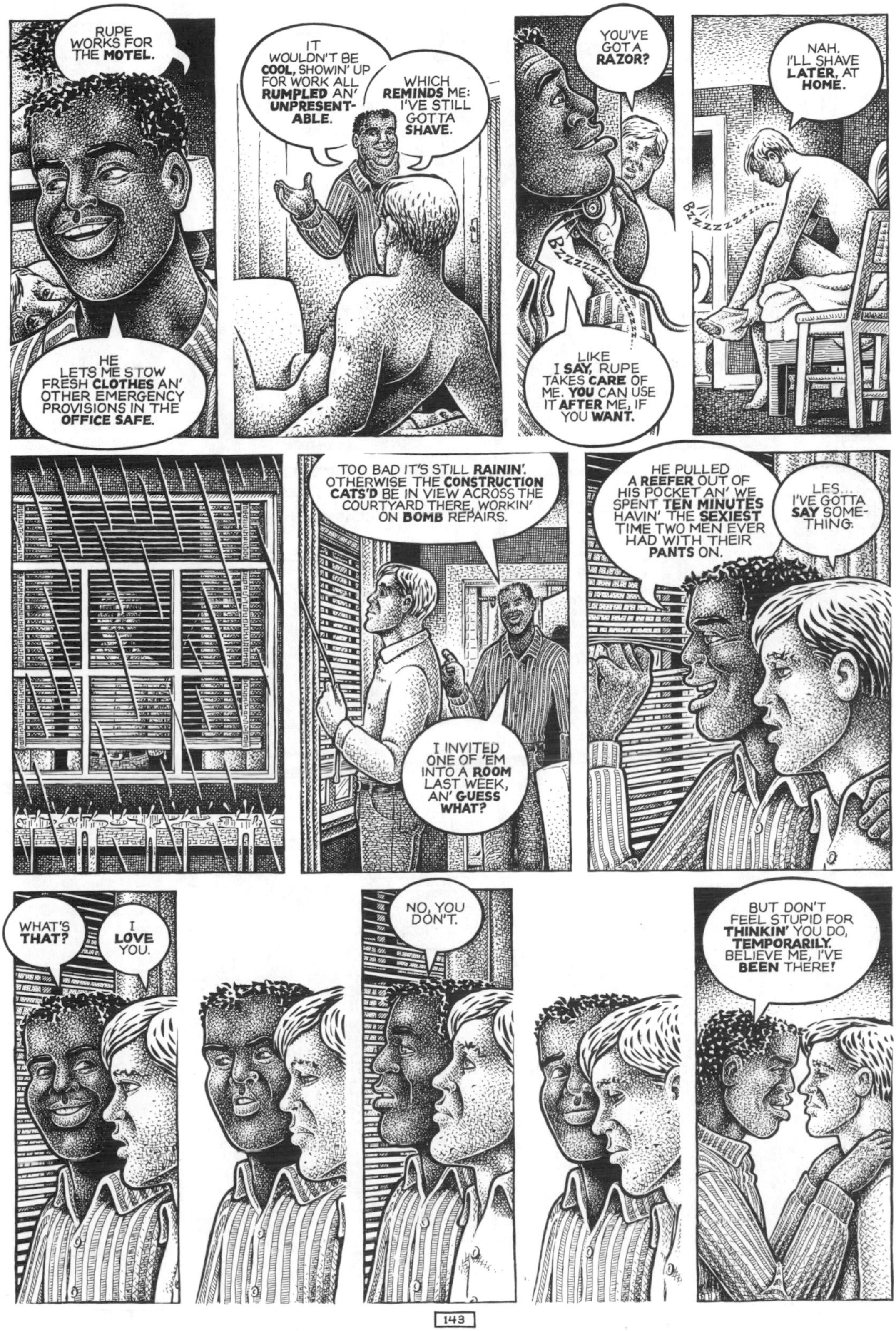
RUPE WORKS FOR THE **MOTEL**.
HE LETS ME STOW FRESH **CLOTHES** AN' OTHER EMERGENCY PROVISIONS IN THE **OFFICE SAFE**.
IT WOULDN'T BE **COOL**, SHOWIN' UP FOR WORK ALL **RUMPLED** AN' **UNPRESENT-ABLE**.
WHICH **REMINDS** ME: I'VE STILL GOTTA **SHAVE**.
YOU'VE GOT A **RAZOR?**
BZZZZZZZZZZZZZZ
LIKE I **SAY**, RUPE TAKES **CARE** OF ME. **YOU** CAN USE IT **AFTER** ME, IF YOU **WANT**.
NAH. I'LL SHAVE **LATER**, AT **HOME**.
BZZZZZZZZZ
TOO BAD IT'S STILL **RAININ'**. OTHERWISE THE **CONSTRUCTION CATS'D** BE IN VIEW ACROSS THE COURTYARD THERE, WORKIN' ON **BOMB** REPAIRS.
I INVITED ONE OF 'EM INTO A **ROOM** LAST WEEK, AN' **GUESS WHAT?**
HE PULLED A **REEFER** OUT OF HIS POCKET AN' WE SPENT **TEN MINUTES** HAVIN' THE **SEXIEST** TIME TWO MEN EVER HAD WITH THEIR **PANTS** ON.
LES... I'VE GOTTA **SAY** SOME-THING.
WHAT'S **THAT?**
I **LOVE** YOU.
NO, YOU DON'T.
BUT DON'T FEEL STUPID FOR **THINKIN'** YOU DO, **TEMPORARILY**. BELIEVE ME, I'VE **BEEN** THERE!

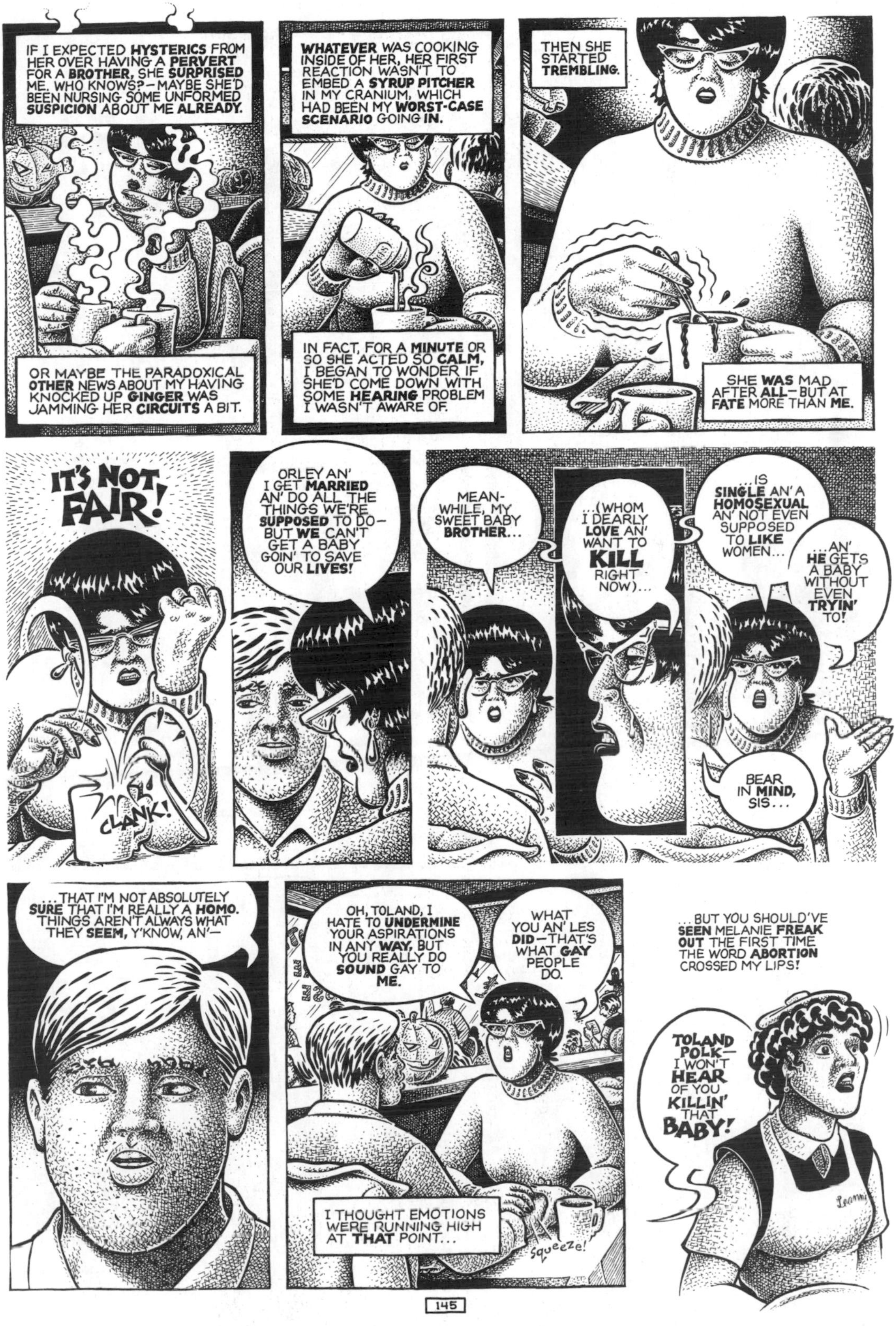

IF I EXPECTED HYSTERICS FROM HER OVER HAVING A PERVERT FOR A BROTHER, SHE SURPRISED ME. WHO KNOWS?—MAYBE SHE'D BEEN NURSING SOME UNFORMED SUSPICION ABOUT ME ALREADY.
OR MAYBE THE PARADOXICAL OTHER NEWS ABOUT MY HAVING KNOCKED UP GINGER WAS JAMMING HER CIRCUITS A BIT.
WHATEVER WAS COOKING INSIDE OF HER, HER FIRST REACTION WASN'T TO EMBED A SYRUP PITCHER IN MY CRANIUM, WHICH HAD BEEN MY WORST-CASE SCENARIO GOING IN.
IN FACT, FOR A MINUTE OR SO SHE ACTED SO CALM, I BEGAN TO WONDER IF SHE'D COME DOWN WITH SOME HEARING PROBLEM I WASN'T AWARE OF.
THEN SHE STARTED TREMBLING.
SHE WAS MAD AFTER ALL—BUT AT FATE MORE THAN ME.
IT'S NOT FAIR!
CLANK!
ORLEY AN' I GET MARRIED AN' DO ALL THE THINGS WE'RE SUPPOSED TO DO—BUT WE CAN'T GET A BABY GOIN' TO SAVE OUR LIVES!
MEAN-WHILE, MY SWEET BABY BROTHER...
...(WHOM I DEARLY LOVE AN' WANT TO KILL RIGHT NOW)...
...IS SINGLE AN' A HOMOSEXUAL AN' NOT EVEN SUPPOSED TO LIKE WOMEN...
...AN' HE GETS A BABY WITHOUT EVEN TRYIN' TO!
BEAR IN MIND, SIS...
...THAT I'M NOT ABSOLUTELY SURE THAT I'M REALLY A HOMO. THINGS AREN'T ALWAYS WHAT THEY SEEM, Y'KNOW, AN'—
OH, TOLAND, I HATE TO UNDERMINE YOUR ASPIRATIONS IN ANY WAY, BUT YOU REALLY DO SOUND GAY TO ME.
WHAT YOU AN' LES DID—THAT'S WHAT GAY PEOPLE DO.
I THOUGHT EMOTIONS WERE RUNNING HIGH AT THAT POINT...
SQUEEZE!
...BUT YOU SHOULD'VE SEEN MELANIE FREAK OUT THE FIRST TIME THE WORD ABORTION CROSSED MY LIPS!
TOLAND POLK—I WON'T HEAR OF YOU KILLIN' THAT BABY!

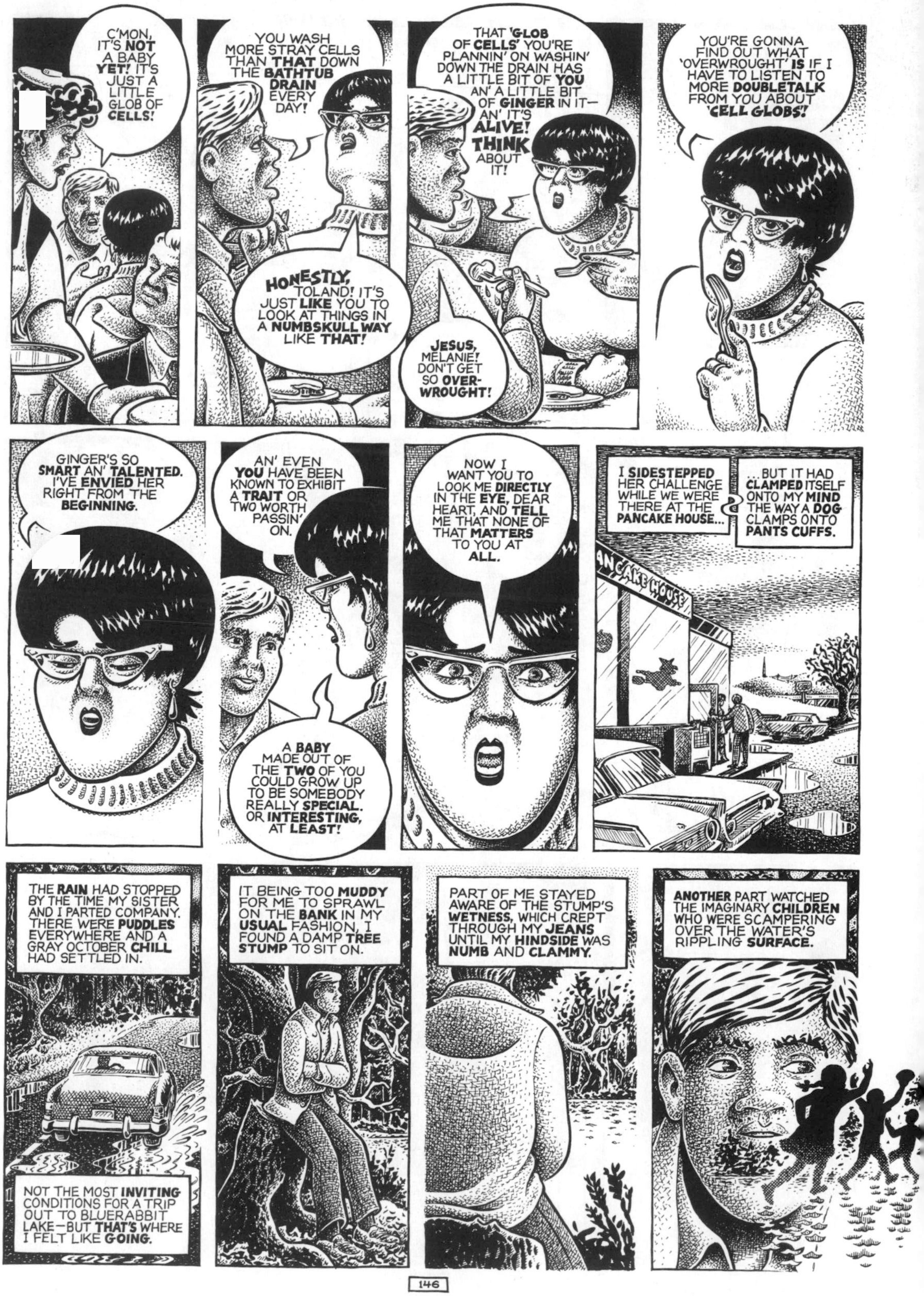
C'MON, IT'S NOT A BABY YET! IT'S JUST A LITTLE GLOB OF CELLS!
YOU WASH MORE STRAY CELLS THAN THAT DOWN THE BATHTUB DRAIN EVERY DAY!
HONESTLY, TOLAND! IT'S JUST LIKE YOU TO LOOK AT THINGS IN A NUMBSKULL WAY LIKE THAT!
THAT 'GLOB OF CELLS' YOU'RE PLANNIN' ON WASHIN' DOWN THE DRAIN HAS A LITTLE BIT OF YOU AN' A LITTLE BIT OF GINGER IN IT— AN' IT'S ALIVE! THINK ABOUT IT!
JESUS, MELANIE! DON'T GET SO OVER-WROUGHT!
YOU'RE GONNA FIND OUT WHAT 'OVERWROUGHT' IS IF I HAVE TO LISTEN TO MORE DOUBLETALK FROM YOU ABOUT 'CELL GLOBS!'
GINGER'S SO SMART AN' TALENTED. I'VE ENVIED HER RIGHT FROM THE BEGINNING.
AN' EVEN YOU HAVE BEEN KNOWN TO EXHIBIT A TRAIT OR TWO WORTH PASSIN' ON.
A BABY MADE OUT OF THE TWO OF YOU COULD GROW UP TO BE SOMEBODY REALLY SPECIAL. OR INTERESTING, AT LEAST!
NOW I WANT YOU TO LOOK ME DIRECTLY IN THE EYE, DEAR HEART, AND TELL ME THAT NONE OF THAT MATTERS TO YOU AT ALL.
I SIDESTEPPED HER CHALLENGE WHILE WE WERE THERE AT THE PANCAKE HOUSE...
& ...BUT IT HAD CLAMPED ITSELF ONTO MY MIND THE WAY A DOG CLAMPS ONTO PANTS CUFFS.
PANCAKE HOUSE
THE RAIN HAD STOPPED BY THE TIME MY SISTER AND I PARTED COMPANY. THERE WERE PUDDLES EVERYWHERE AND A GRAY OCTOBER CHILL HAD SETTLED IN.
NOT THE MOST INVITING CONDITIONS FOR A TRIP OUT TO BLUERABBIT LAKE—BUT THAT'S WHERE I FELT LIKE GOING.
IT BEING TOO MUDDY FOR ME TO SPRAWL ON THE BANK IN MY USUAL FASHION, I FOUND A DAMP TREE STUMP TO SIT ON.
PART OF ME STAYED AWARE OF THE STUMP'S WETNESS, WHICH CREPT THROUGH MY JEANS UNTIL MY HINDSIDE WAS NUMB AND CLAMMY.
ANOTHER PART WATCHED THE IMAGINARY CHILDREN WHO WERE SCAMPERING OVER THE WATER'S RIPPLING SURFACE.

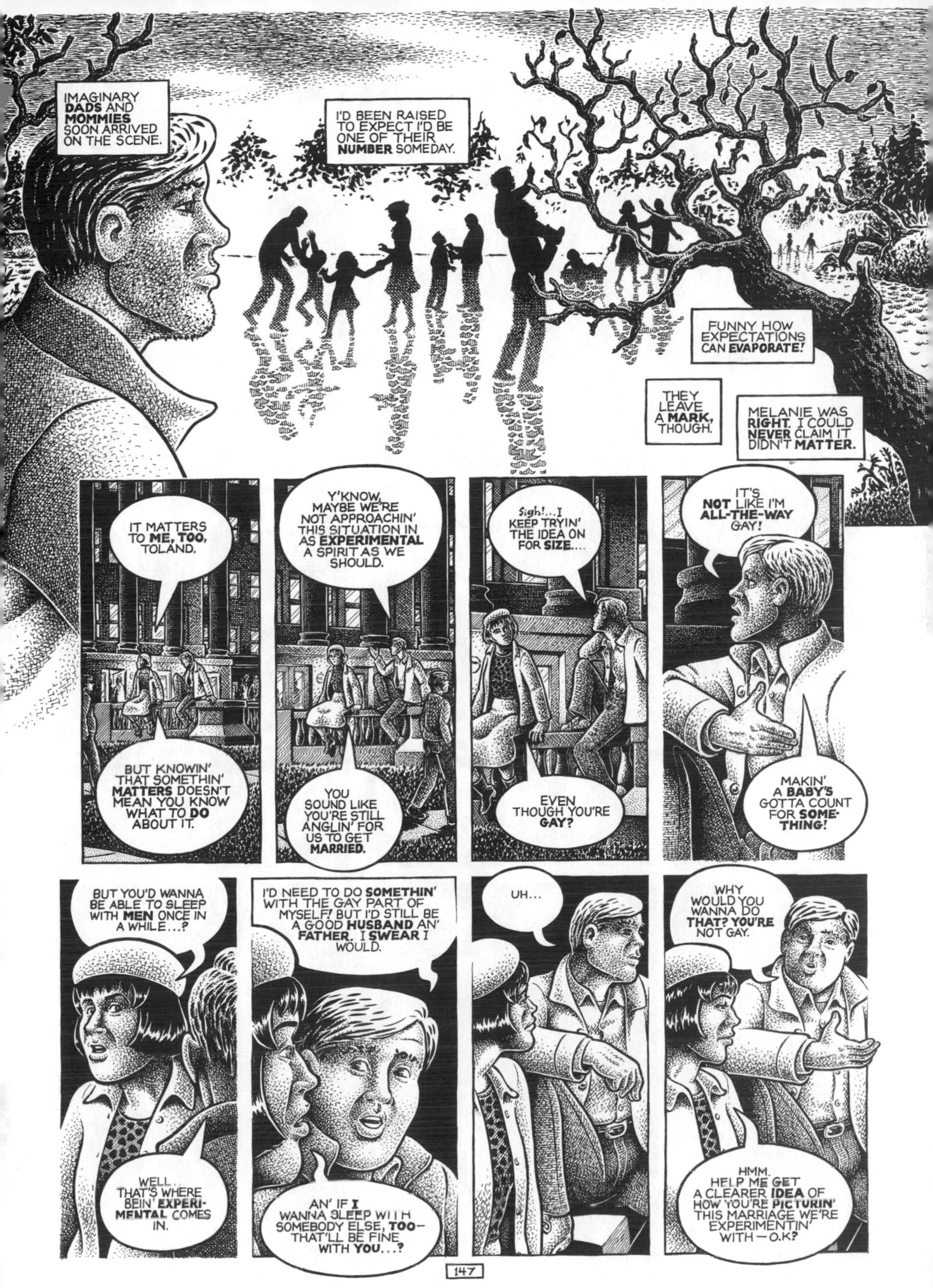

IMAGINARY DADS AND MOMMIES SOON ARRIVED ON THE SCENE.
I'D BEEN RAISED TO EXPECT I'D BE ONE OF THEIR NUMBER SOMEDAY.
FUNNY HOW EXPECTATIONS CAN EVAPORATE!
THEY LEAVE A MARK, THOUGH.
MELANIE WAS RIGHT. I COULD NEVER CLAIM IT DIDN'T MATTER.
IT MATTERS TO ME, TOO, TOLAND.
BUT KNOWIN' THAT SOMETHIN' MATTERS DOESN'T MEAN YOU KNOW WHAT TO DO ABOUT IT.
Y'KNOW, MAYBE WE'RE NOT APPROACHIN' THIS SITUATION IN AS EXPERIMENTAL A SPIRIT AS WE SHOULD.
YOU SOUND LIKE YOU'RE STILL ANGLIN' FOR US TO GET MARRIED.
Sigh!... I KEEP TRYIN' THE IDEA ON FOR SIZE....
EVEN THOUGH YOU'RE GAY?
IT'S NOT LIKE I'M ALL-THE-WAY GAY!
MAKIN' A BABY'S GOTTA COUNT FOR SOME-THING!
BUT YOU'D WANNA BE ABLE TO SLEEP WITH MEN ONCE IN A WHILE...?
WELL... THAT'S WHERE BEIN' EXPERI-MENTAL COMES IN.
I'D NEED TO DO SOMETHIN' WITH THE GAY PART OF MYSELF! BUT I'D STILL BE A GOOD HUSBAND AN' FATHER. I SWEAR I WOULD.
AN' IF I WANNA SLEEP WITH SOMEBODY ELSE, TOO— THAT'LL BE FINE WITH YOU...?
UH...
WHY WOULD YOU WANNA DO THAT? YOU'RE NOT GAY.
HMM. HELP ME GET A CLEARER IDEA OF HOW YOU'RE PICTURIN' THIS MARRIAGE WE'RE EXPERIMENTIN' WITH — O.K.?

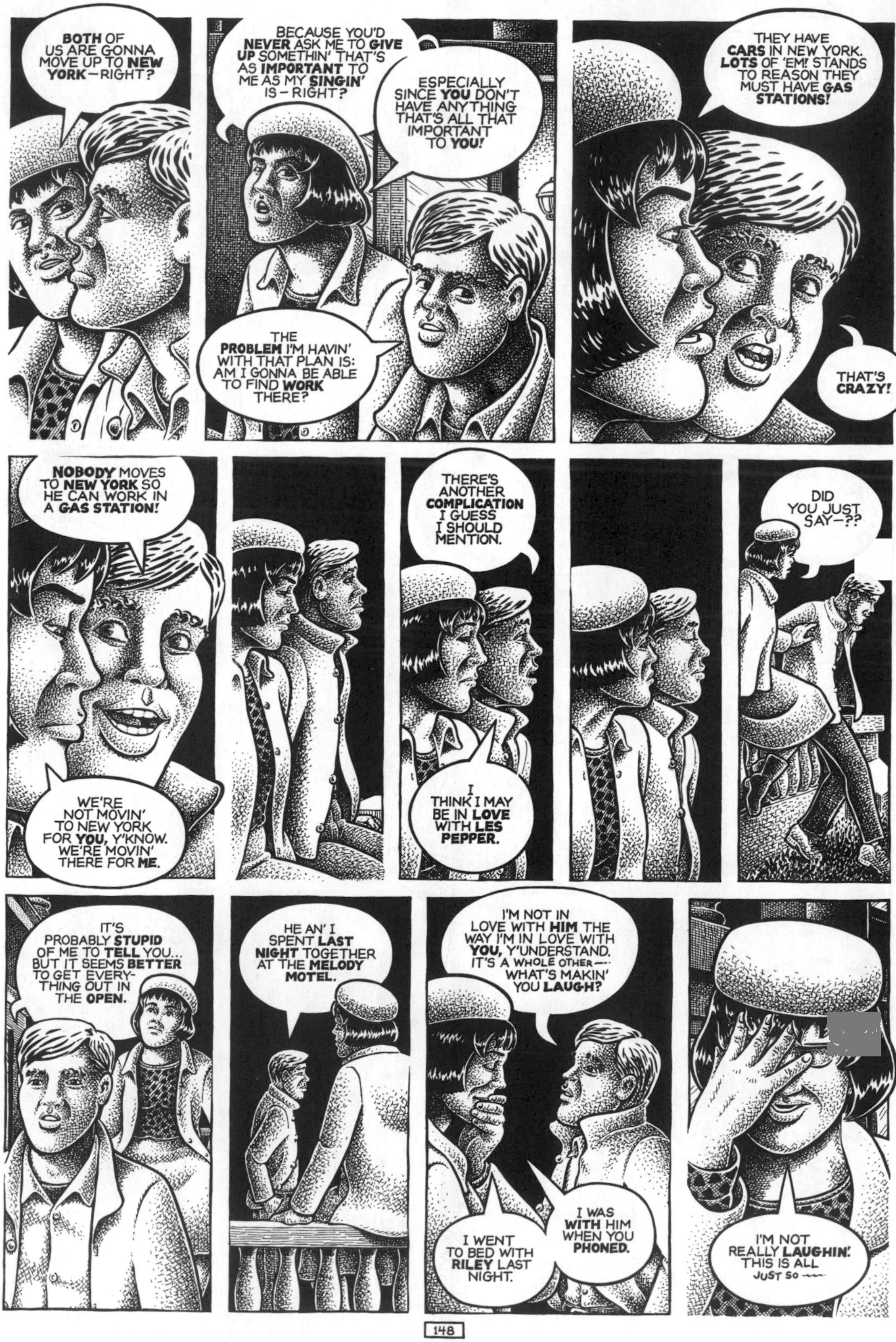
BOTH OF US ARE GONNA MOVE UP TO NEW YORK—RIGHT?
BECAUSE YOU'D NEVER ASK ME TO GIVE UP SOMETHIN' THAT'S AS IMPORTANT TO ME AS MY SINGIN' IS—RIGHT?
ESPECIALLY SINCE YOU DON'T HAVE ANYTHING THAT'S ALL THAT IMPORTANT TO YOU!
THE PROBLEM I'M HAVIN' WITH THAT PLAN IS: AM I GONNA BE ABLE TO FIND WORK THERE?
THEY HAVE CARS IN NEW YORK. LOTS OF 'EM! STANDS TO REASON THEY MUST HAVE GAS STATIONS!
THAT'S CRAZY!
NOBODY MOVES TO NEW YORK SO HE CAN WORK IN A GAS STATION!
WE'RE NOT MOVIN' TO NEW YORK FOR YOU, Y'KNOW. WE'RE MOVIN' THERE FOR ME.
THERE'S ANOTHER COMPLICATION I GUESS I SHOULD MENTION.
I THINK I MAY BE IN LOVE WITH LES PEPPER.
DID YOU JUST SAY—??
IT'S PROBABLY STUPID OF ME TO TELL YOU... BUT IT SEEMS BETTER TO GET EVERYTHING OUT IN THE OPEN.
HE AN' I SPENT LAST NIGHT TOGETHER AT THE MELODY MOTEL.
I'M NOT IN LOVE WITH HIM THE WAY I'M IN LOVE WITH YOU, Y'UNDERSTAND. IT'S A WHOLE OTHER— WHAT'S MAKIN' YOU LAUGH?
I WENT TO BED WITH RILEY LAST NIGHT.
I WAS WITH HIM WHEN YOU PHONED.
I'M NOT REALLY LAUGHIN'. THIS IS ALL JUST SO—

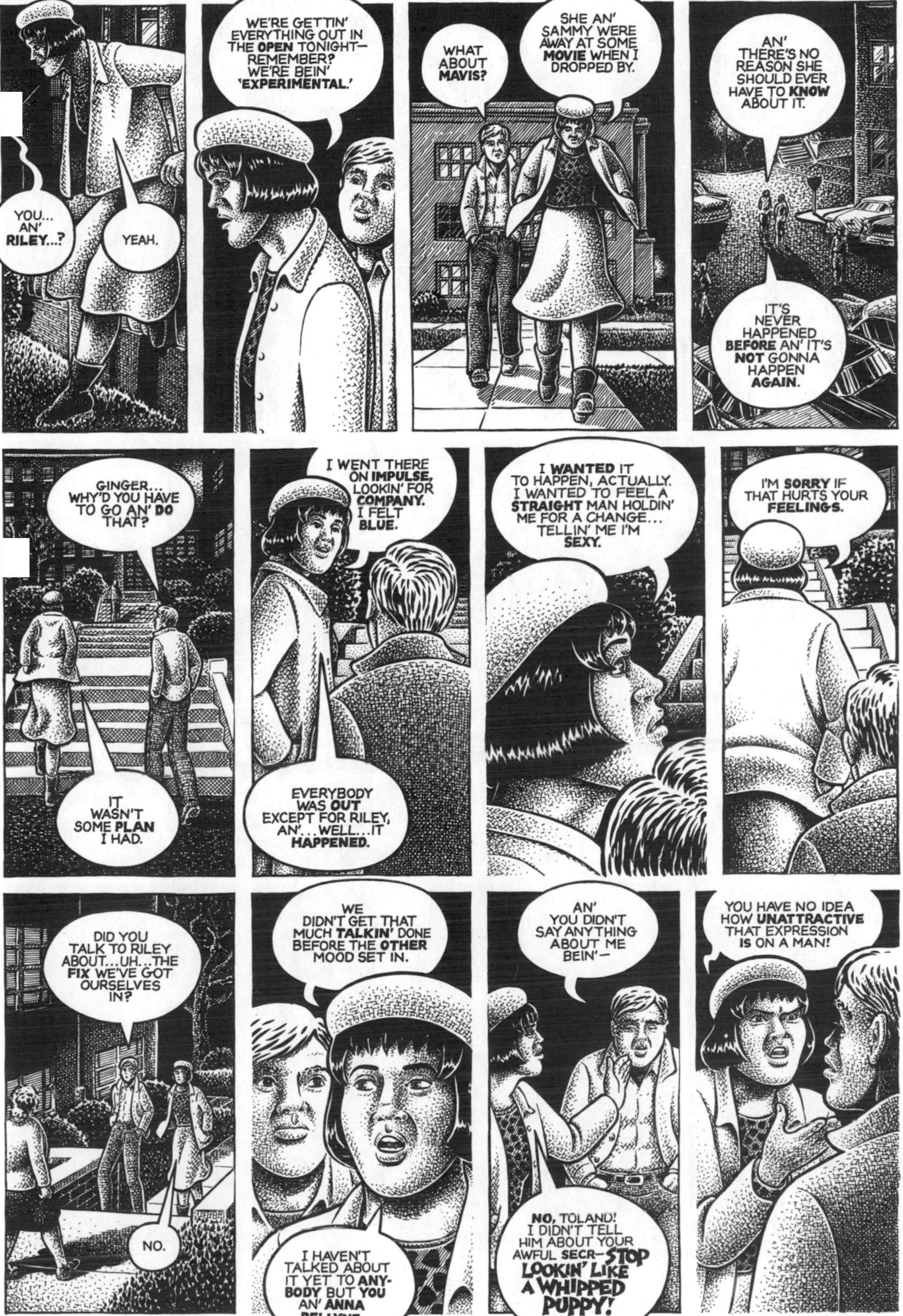
YOU... AN' RILEY...?
YEAH.
WE'RE GETTIN' EVERYTHING OUT IN THE OPEN TONIGHT— REMEMBER? WE'RE BEIN' 'EXPERIMENTAL.'
WHAT ABOUT MAVIS?
SHE AN' SAMMY WERE AWAY AT SOME MOVIE WHEN I DROPPED BY.
AN' THERE'S NO REASON SHE SHOULD EVER HAVE TO KNOW ABOUT IT.
IT'S NEVER HAPPENED BEFORE AN' IT'S NOT GONNA HAPPEN AGAIN.
GINGER... WHY'D YOU HAVE TO GO AN' DO THAT?
IT WASN'T SOME PLAN I HAD.
I WENT THERE ON IMPULSE, LOOKIN' FOR COMPANY. I FELT BLUE.
EVERYBODY WAS OUT EXCEPT FOR RILEY, AN'... WELL... IT HAPPENED.
I WANTED IT TO HAPPEN, ACTUALLY. I WANTED TO FEEL A STRAIGHT MAN HOLDIN' ME FOR A CHANGE... TELLIN' ME I'M SEXY.
I'M SORRY IF THAT HURTS YOUR FEELINGS.
DID YOU TALK TO RILEY ABOUT... UH... THE FIX WE'VE GOT OURSELVES IN?
NO.
WE DIDN'T GET THAT MUCH TALKIN' DONE BEFORE THE OTHER MOOD SET IN.
I HAVEN'T TALKED ABOUT IT YET TO ANY-BODY BUT YOU AN' ANNA DELLYNE.
AN' YOU DIDN'T SAY ANYTHING ABOUT ME BEIN'—
NO, TOLAND! I DIDN'T TELL HIM ABOUT YOUR AWFUL SECR—STOP LOOKIN' LIKE A WHIPPED PUPPY!
YOU HAVE NO IDEA HOW UNATTRACTIVE THAT EXPRESSION IS ON A MAN!

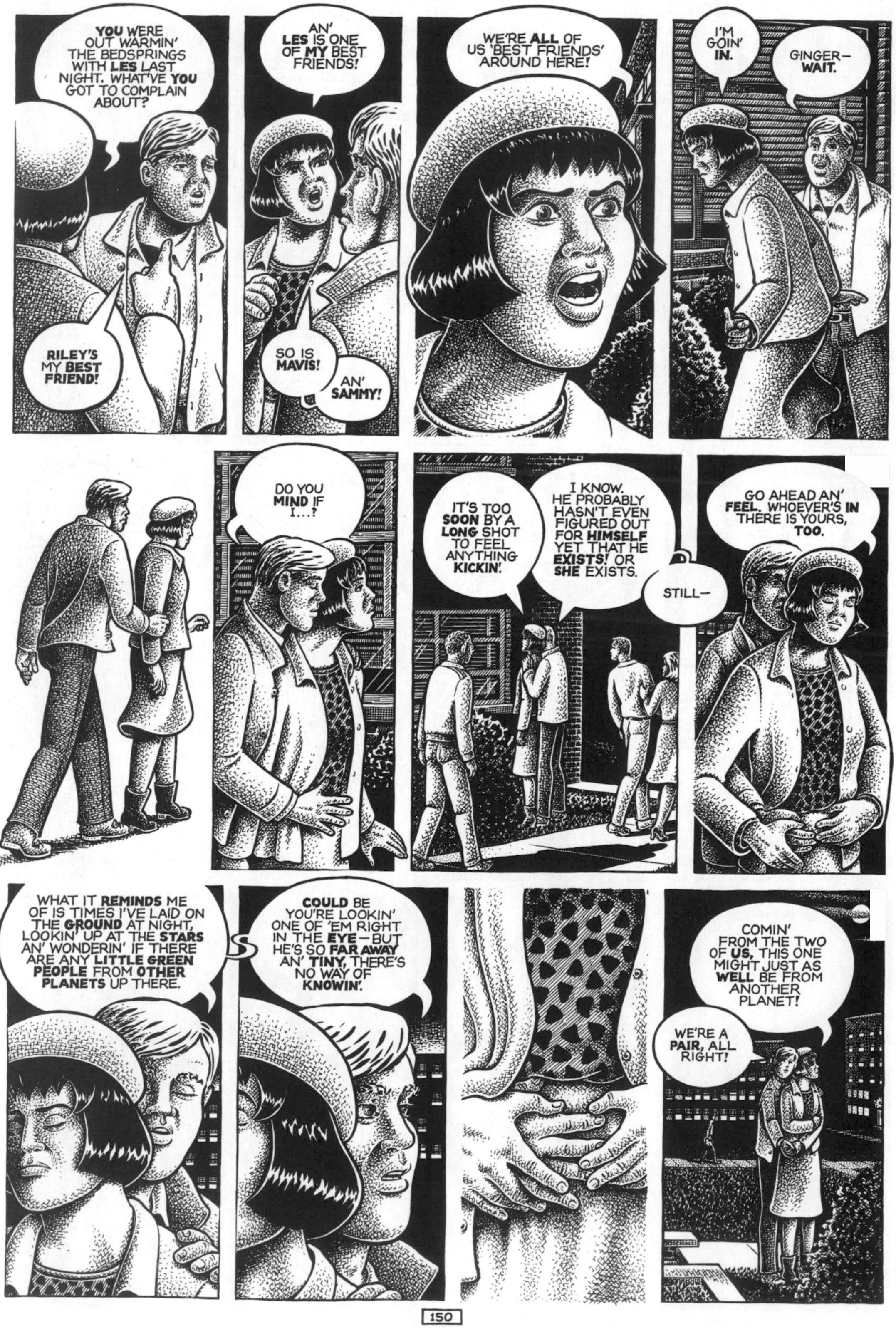
YOU WERE OUT WARMIN' THE BEDSPRINGS WITH LES LAST NIGHT. WHAT'VE YOU GOT TO COMPLAIN ABOUT?
RILEY'S MY BEST FRIEND!
AN' LES IS ONE OF MY BEST FRIENDS!
SO IS MAVIS!
AN' SAMMY!
WE'RE ALL OF US 'BEST FRIENDS' AROUND HERE!
I'M GOIN' IN.
GINGER— WAIT.
DO YOU MIND IF I...?
IT'S TOO SOON BY A LONG SHOT TO FEEL ANYTHING KICKIN'.
I KNOW. HE PROBABLY HASN'T EVEN FIGURED OUT FOR HIMSELF YET THAT HE EXISTS! OR SHE EXISTS.
STILL—
GO AHEAD AN' FEEL. WHOEVER'S IN THERE IS YOURS, TOO.
WHAT IT REMINDS ME OF IS TIMES I'VE LAID ON THE GROUND AT NIGHT, LOOKIN' UP AT THE STARS AN' WONDERIN' IF THERE ARE ANY LITTLE GREEN PEOPLE FROM OTHER PLANETS UP THERE.
COULD BE YOU'RE LOOKIN' ONE OF 'EM RIGHT IN THE EYE—BUT HE'S SO FAR AWAY AN' TINY, THERE'S NO WAY OF KNOWIN'.
COMIN' FROM THE TWO OF US, THIS ONE MIGHT JUST AS WELL BE FROM ANOTHER PLANET!
WE'RE A PAIR, ALL RIGHT!

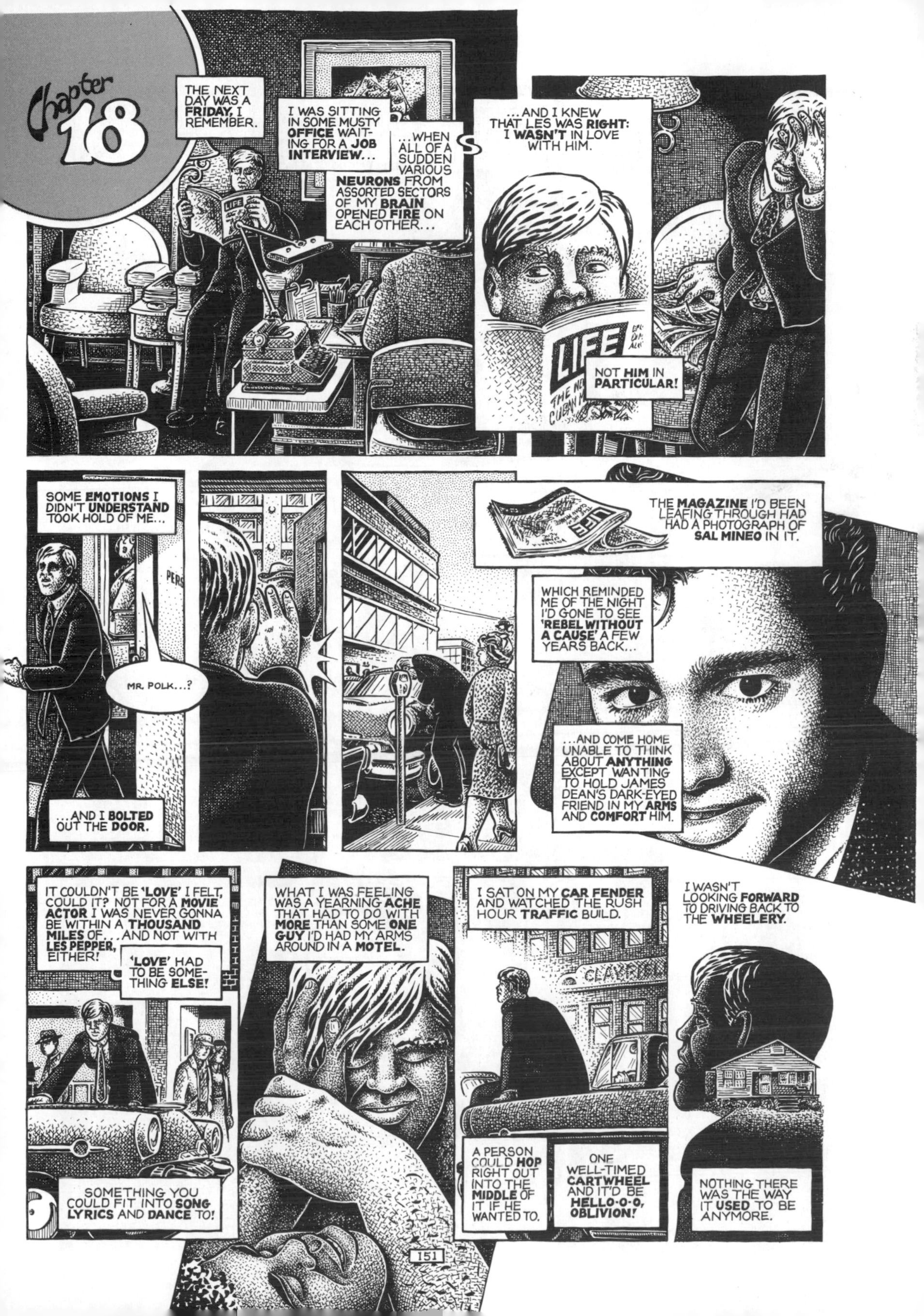
Chapter 18
THE NEXT DAY WAS A FRIDAY, I REMEMBER.
I WAS SITTING IN SOME MUSTY OFFICE WAITING FOR A JOB INTERVIEW...
...WHEN ALL OF A SUDDEN VARIOUS NEURONS FROM ASSORTED SECTORS OF MY BRAIN OPENED FIRE ON EACH OTHER...
...AND I KNEW THAT LES WAS RIGHT: I WASN'T IN LOVE WITH HIM.
LIFE
NOT HIM IN PARTICULAR!
SOME EMOTIONS I DIDN'T UNDERSTAND TOOK HOLD OF ME...
MR. POLK...?
...AND I BOLTED OUT THE DOOR.
THE MAGAZINE I'D BEEN LEAFING THROUGH HAD HAD A PHOTOGRAPH OF SAL MINEO IN IT.
WHICH REMINDED ME OF THE NIGHT I'D GONE TO SEE 'REBEL WITHOUT A CAUSE' A FEW YEARS BACK...
...AND COME HOME UNABLE TO THINK ABOUT ANYTHING EXCEPT WANTING TO HOLD JAMES DEAN'S DARK-EYED FRIEND IN MY ARMS AND COMFORT HIM.
IT COULDN'T BE 'LOVE' I FELT, COULD IT? NOT FOR A MOVIE ACTOR I WAS NEVER GONNA BE WITHIN A THOUSAND MILES OF... AND NOT WITH LES PEPPER, EITHER!
'LOVE' HAD TO BE SOMETHING ELSE!
SOMETHING YOU COULD FIT INTO SONG LYRICS AND DANCE TO!
WHAT I WAS FEELING WAS A YEARNING ACHE THAT HAD TO DO WITH MORE THAN SOME ONE GUY I'D HAD MY ARMS AROUND IN A MOTEL.
I SAT ON MY CAR FENDER AND WATCHED THE RUSH HOUR TRAFFIC BUILD.
A PERSON COULD HOP RIGHT OUT INTO THE MIDDLE OF IT IF HE WANTED TO.
ONE WELL-TIMED CARTWHEEL AND IT'D BE HELLO-O-O, OBLIVION!
I WASN'T LOOKING FORWARD TO DRIVING BACK TO THE WHEELERY.
NOTHING THERE WAS THE WAY IT USED TO BE ANYMORE.

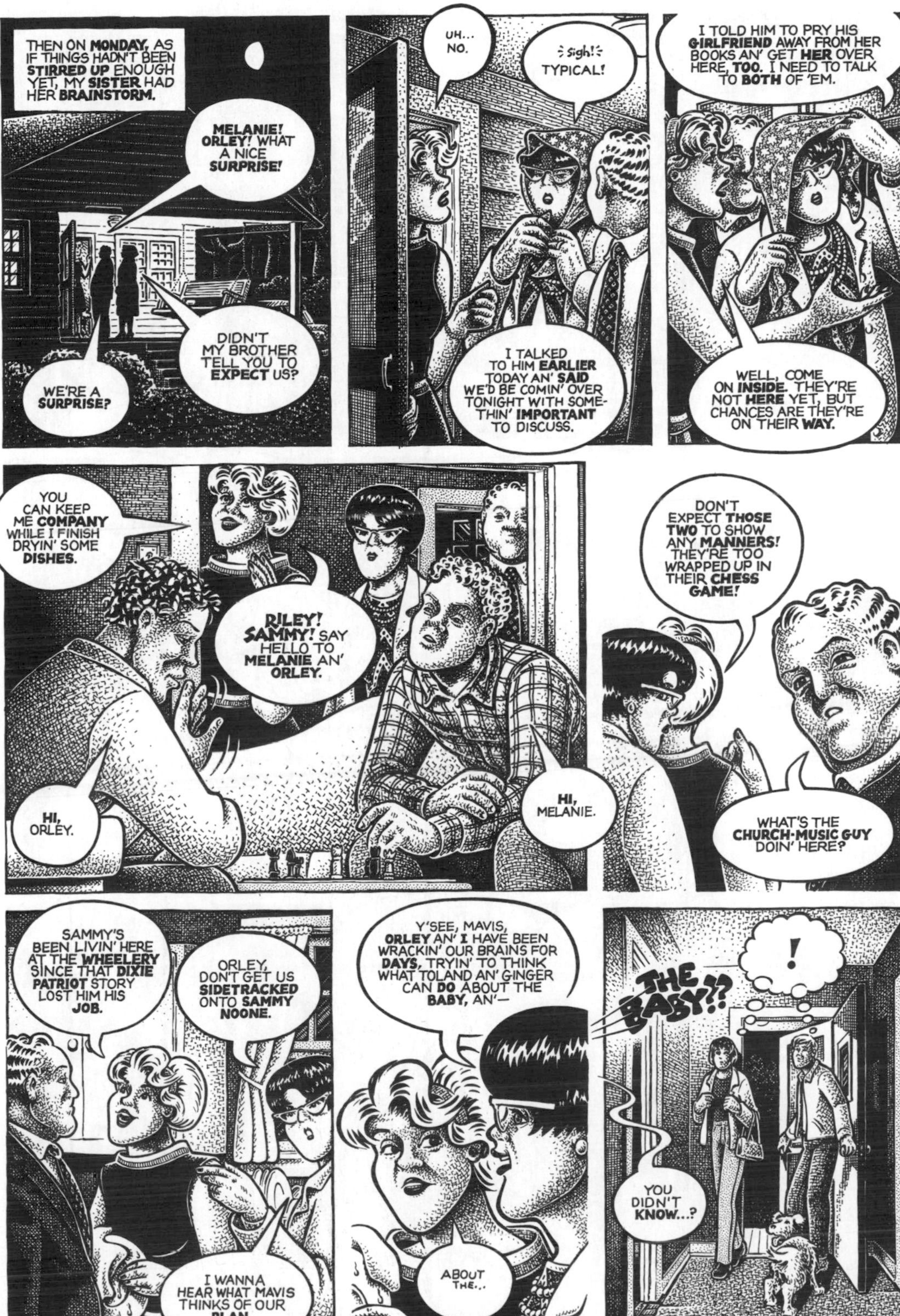

THEN ON MONDAY, AS IF THINGS HADN'T BEEN STIRRED UP ENOUGH YET, MY SISTER HAD HER BRAINSTORM.
MELANIE! ORLEY! WHAT A NICE SURPRISE!
WE'RE A SURPRISE?
DIDN'T MY BROTHER TELL YOU TO EXPECT US?
UH... NO.
Sigh! TYPICAL!
I TALKED TO HIM EARLIER TODAY AN' SAID WE'D BE COMIN' OVER TONIGHT WITH SOME-THIN' IMPORTANT TO DISCUSS.
I TOLD HIM TO PRY HIS GIRLFRIEND AWAY FROM HER BOOKS AN' GET HER OVER HERE, TOO. I NEED TO TALK TO BOTH OF 'EM.
WELL, COME ON INSIDE. THEY'RE NOT HERE YET, BUT CHANCES ARE THEY'RE ON THEIR WAY.
YOU CAN KEEP ME COMPANY WHILE I FINISH DRYIN' SOME DISHES.
RILEY! SAMMY! SAY HELLO TO MELANIE AN' ORLEY.
HI, ORLEY.
HI, MELANIE.
DON'T EXPECT THOSE TWO TO SHOW ANY MANNERS! THEY'RE TOO WRAPPED UP IN THEIR CHESS GAME!
WHAT'S THE CHURCH-MUSIC GUY DOIN' HERE?
SAMMY'S BEEN LIVIN' HERE AT THE WHEELERY SINCE THAT DIXIE PATRIOT STORY LOST HIM HIS JOB.
ORLEY, DON'T GET US SIDETRACKED ONTO SAMMY NOONE.
I WANNA HEAR WHAT MAVIS THINKS OF OUR PLAN.
Y'SEE, MAVIS, ORLEY AN' I HAVE BEEN WRACKIN' OUR BRAINS FOR DAYS, TRYIN' TO THINK WHAT TOLAND AN' GINGER CAN DO ABOUT THE BABY, AN'—
ABOUT THE...
THE BABY??
!
YOU DIDN'T KNOW...?

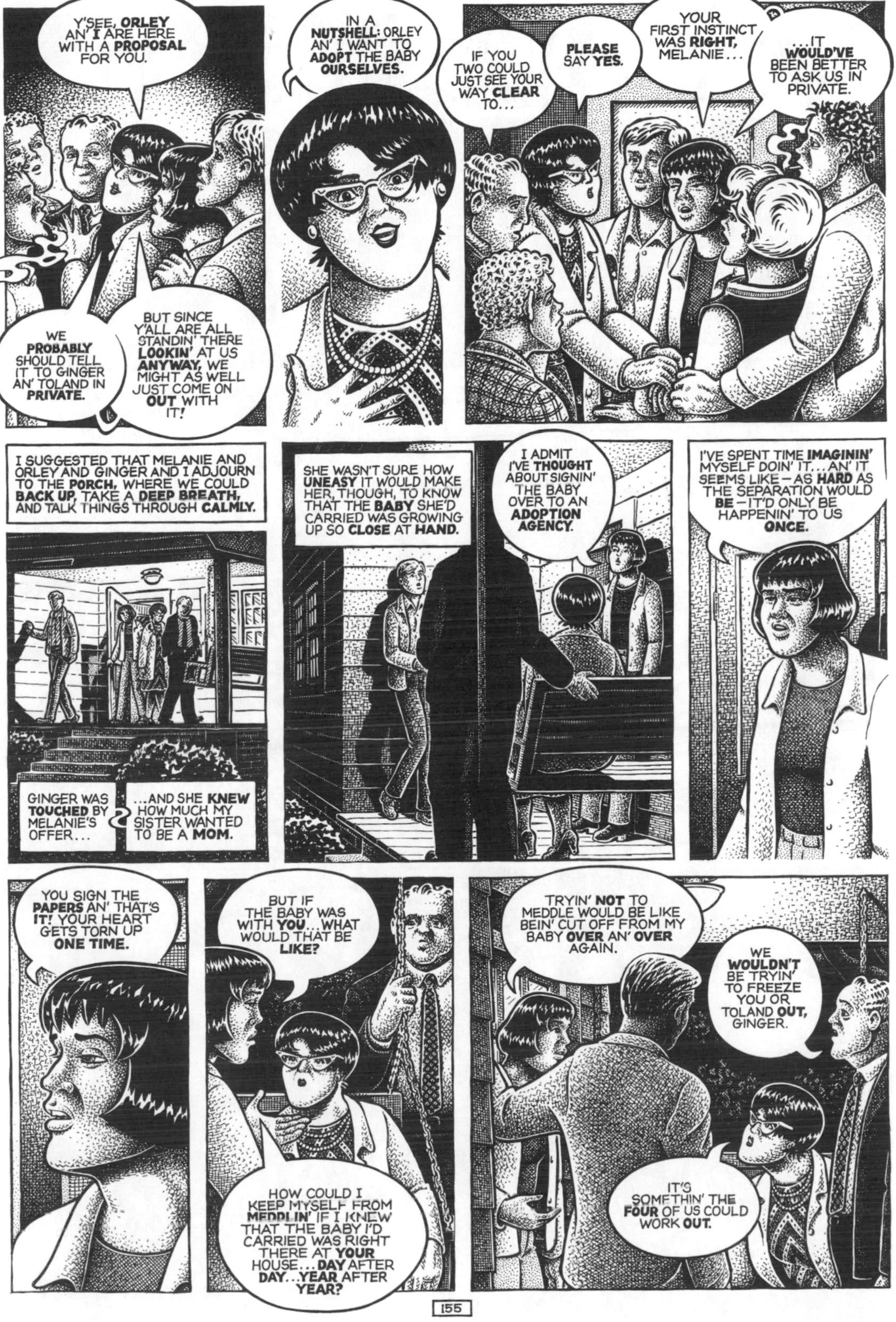
Y'SEE, ORLEY AN' I ARE HERE WITH A PROPOSAL FOR YOU.
WE PROBABLY SHOULD TELL IT TO GINGER AN' TOLAND IN PRIVATE.
BUT SINCE Y'ALL ARE ALL STANDIN' THERE LOOKIN' AT US ANYWAY, WE MIGHT AS WELL JUST COME ON OUT WITH IT!
IN A NUTSHELL: ORLEY AN' I WANT TO ADOPT THE BABY OURSELVES.
IF YOU TWO COULD JUST SEE YOUR WAY CLEAR TO...
PLEASE SAY YES.
YOUR FIRST INSTINCT WAS RIGHT, MELANIE...
...IT WOULD'VE BEEN BETTER TO ASK US IN PRIVATE.
I SUGGESTED THAT MELANIE AND ORLEY AND GINGER AND I ADJOURN TO THE PORCH, WHERE WE COULD BACK UP, TAKE A DEEP BREATH, AND TALK THINGS THROUGH CALMLY.
GINGER WAS TOUCHED BY MELANIE'S OFFER...
...AND SHE KNEW HOW MUCH MY SISTER WANTED TO BE A MOM.
SHE WASN'T SURE HOW UNEASY IT WOULD MAKE HER, THOUGH, TO KNOW THAT THE BABY SHE'D CARRIED WAS GROWING UP SO CLOSE AT HAND.
I ADMIT I'VE THOUGHT ABOUT SIGNIN' THE BABY OVER TO AN ADOPTION AGENCY.
I'VE SPENT TIME IMAGININ' MYSELF DOIN' IT... AN' IT SEEMS LIKE—AS HARD AS THE SEPARATION WOULD BE—IT'D ONLY BE HAPPENIN' TO US ONCE.
YOU SIGN THE PAPERS AN' THAT'S IT! YOUR HEART GETS TORN UP ONE TIME.
BUT IF THE BABY WAS WITH YOU...WHAT WOULD THAT BE LIKE?
HOW COULD I KEEP MYSELF FROM MEDDLIN' IF I KNEW THAT THE BABY I'D CARRIED WAS RIGHT THERE AT YOUR HOUSE...DAY AFTER DAY...YEAR AFTER YEAR?
TRYIN' NOT TO MEDDLE WOULD BE LIKE BEIN' CUT OFF FROM MY BABY OVER AN' OVER AGAIN.
WE WOULDN'T BE TRYIN' TO FREEZE YOU OR TOLAND OUT, GINGER.
IT'S SOMETHIN' THE FOUR OF US COULD WORK OUT.

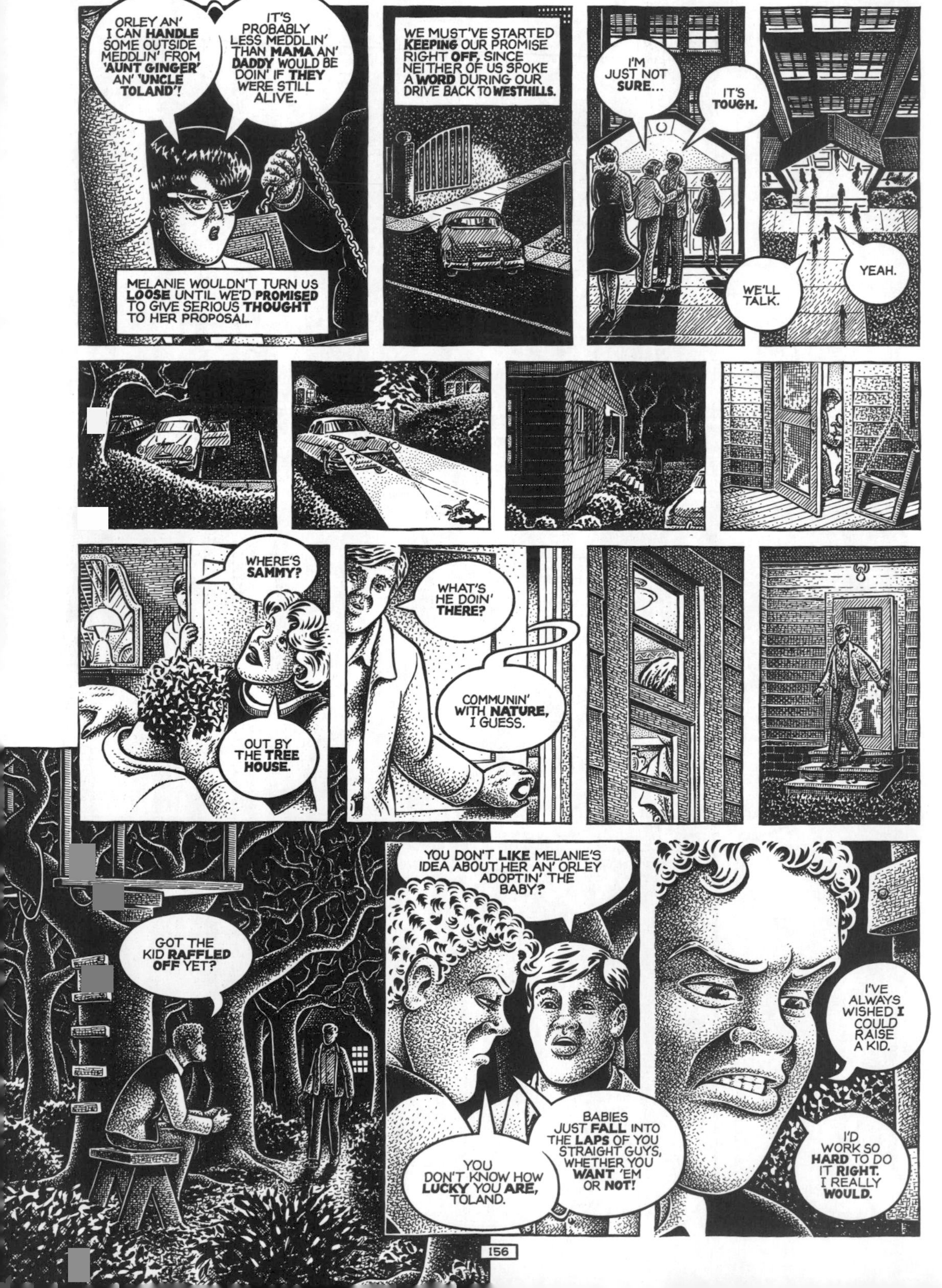
ORLEY AN' I CAN HANDLE SOME OUTSIDE MEDDLIN' FROM 'AUNT GINGER' AN' 'UNCLE TOLAND'!
IT'S PROBABLY LESS MEDDLIN' THAN MAMA AN' DADDY WOULD BE DOIN' IF THEY WERE STILL ALIVE.
MELANIE WOULDN'T TURN US LOOSE UNTIL WE'D PROMISED TO GIVE SERIOUS THOUGHT TO HER PROPOSAL.
WE MUST'VE STARTED KEEPING OUR PROMISE RIGHT OFF, SINCE NEITHER OF US SPOKE A WORD DURING OUR DRIVE BACK TO WESTHILLS.
I'M JUST NOT SURE...
IT'S TOUGH.
WE'LL TALK.
YEAH.
WHERE'S SAMMY?
OUT BY THE TREE HOUSE.
WHAT'S HE DOIN' THERE?
COMMUNIN' WITH NATURE, I GUESS.
GOT THE KID RAFFLED OFF YET?
YOU DON'T LIKE MELANIE'S IDEA ABOUT HER AN' ORLEY ADOPTIN' THE BABY?
YOU DON'T KNOW HOW LUCKY YOU ARE, TOLAND.
BABIES JUST FALL INTO THE LAPS OF YOU STRAIGHT GUYS, WHETHER YOU WANT 'EM OR NOT!
I'VE ALWAYS WISHED I COULD RAISE A KID.
I'D WORK SO HARD TO DO IT RIGHT. I REALLY WOULD.

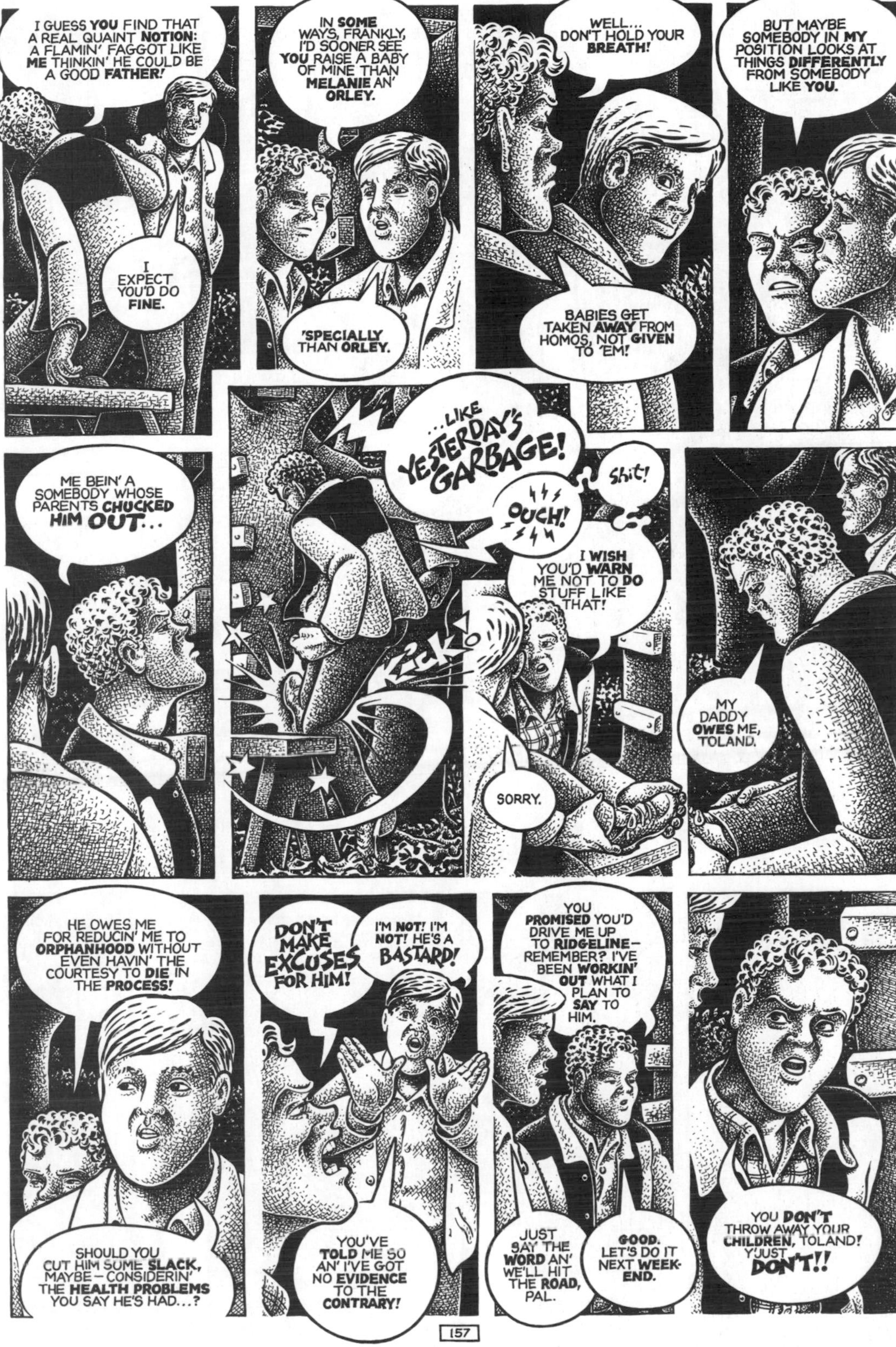
I GUESS YOU FIND THAT A REAL QUAINT NOTION: A FLAMIN' FAGGOT LIKE ME THINKIN' HE COULD BE A GOOD FATHER!
I EXPECT YOU'D DO FINE.
IN SOME WAYS, FRANKLY, I'D SOONER SEE YOU RAISE A BABY OF MINE THAN MELANIE AN' ORLEY.
'SPECIALLY THAN ORLEY.
WELL... DON'T HOLD YOUR BREATH!
BABIES GET TAKEN AWAY FROM HOMOS, NOT GIVEN TO 'EM!
BUT MAYBE SOMEBODY IN MY POSITION LOOKS AT THINGS DIFFERENTLY FROM SOMEBODY LIKE YOU.
ME BEIN' A SOMEBODY WHOSE PARENTS CHUCKED HIM OUT...
...LIKE YESTERDAY'S GARBAGE!
KICK
OUCH!
Shit!
I WISH YOU'D WARN ME NOT TO DO STUFF LIKE THAT!
SORRY.
MY DADDY OWES ME, TOLAND.
HE OWES ME FOR REDUCIN' ME TO ORPHANHOOD WITHOUT EVEN HAVIN' THE COURTESY TO DIE IN THE PROCESS!
SHOULD YOU CUT HIM SOME SLACK, MAYBE — CONSIDERIN' THE HEALTH PROBLEMS YOU SAY HE'S HAD...?
DON'T MAKE EXCUSES FOR HIM!
I'M NOT! I'M NOT! HE'S A BASTARD!
YOU'VE TOLD ME SO AN' I'VE GOT NO EVIDENCE TO THE CONTRARY!
YOU PROMISED YOU'D DRIVE ME UP TO RIDGELINE — REMEMBER? I'VE BEEN WORKIN' OUT WHAT I PLAN TO SAY TO HIM.
JUST SAY THE WORD AN' WE'LL HIT THE ROAD, PAL.
GOOD. LET'S DO IT NEXT WEEK-END.
YOU DON'T THROW AWAY YOUR CHILDREN, TOLAND! Y'JUST DON'T!!

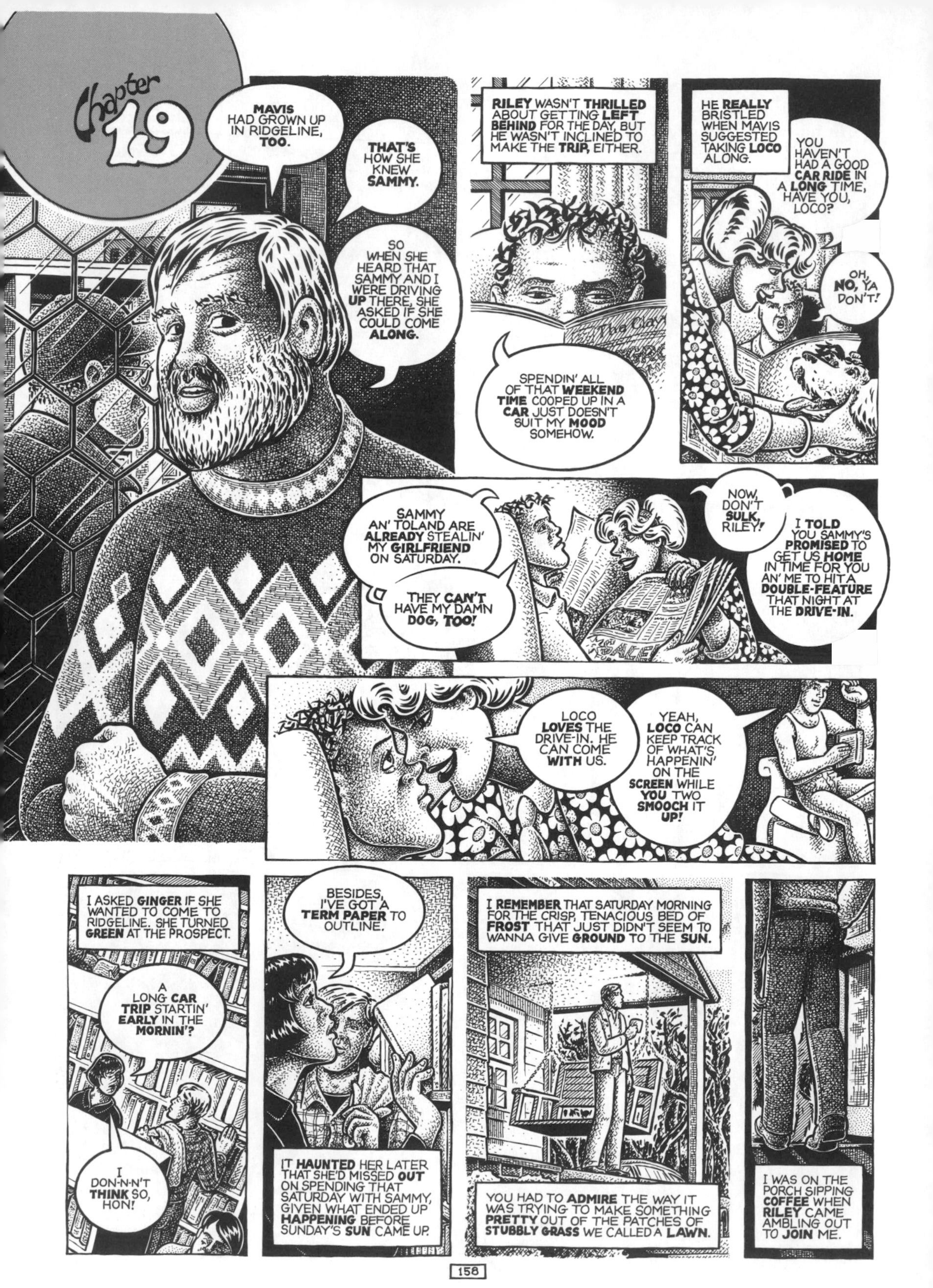
Chapter 19
MAVIS HAD GROWN UP IN RIDGELINE, TOO.
THAT'S HOW SHE KNEW SAMMY.
SO WHEN SHE HEARD THAT SAMMY AND I WERE DRIVING UP THERE, SHE ASKED IF SHE COULD COME ALONG.
RILEY WASN'T THRILLED ABOUT GETTING LEFT BEHIND FOR THE DAY, BUT HE WASN'T INCLINED TO MAKE THE TRIP, EITHER.
SPENDIN' ALL OF THAT WEEKEND TIME COOPED UP IN A CAR JUST DOESN'T SUIT MY MOOD SOMEHOW.
HE REALLY BRISTLED WHEN MAVIS SUGGESTED TAKING LOCO ALONG.
YOU HAVEN'T HAD A GOOD CAR RIDE IN A LONG TIME, HAVE YOU, LOCO?
OH, NO, YA DON'T!
SAMMY AN' TOLAND ARE ALREADY STEALIN' MY GIRLFRIEND ON SATURDAY.
THEY CAN'T HAVE MY DAMN DOG, TOO!
NOW, DON'T SULK, RILEY!
I TOLD YOU SAMMY'S PROMISED TO GET US HOME IN TIME FOR YOU AN' ME TO HIT A DOUBLE-FEATURE THAT NIGHT AT THE DRIVE-IN.
LOCO LOVES THE DRIVE-IN. HE CAN COME WITH US.
YEAH, LOCO CAN KEEP TRACK OF WHAT'S HAPPENIN' ON THE SCREEN WHILE YOU TWO SMOOCH IT UP!
I ASKED GINGER IF SHE WANTED TO COME TO RIDGELINE. SHE TURNED GREEN AT THE PROSPECT.
A LONG CAR TRIP STARTIN' EARLY IN THE MORNIN'?
I DON-N-N'T THINK SO, HON!
BESIDES, I'VE GOT A TERM PAPER TO OUTLINE.
IT HAUNTED HER LATER THAT SHE'D MISSED OUT ON SPENDING THAT SATURDAY WITH SAMMY, GIVEN WHAT ENDED UP HAPPENING BEFORE SUNDAY'S SUN CAME UP.
I REMEMBER THAT SATURDAY MORNING FOR THE CRISP, TENACIOUS BED OF FROST THAT JUST DIDN'T SEEM TO WANNA GIVE GROUND TO THE SUN.
YOU HAD TO ADMIRE THE WAY IT WAS TRYING TO MAKE SOMETHING PRETTY OUT OF THE PATCHES OF STUBBLY GRASS WE CALLED A LAWN.
I WAS ON THE PORCH SIPPING COFFEE WHEN RILEY CAME AMBLING OUT TO JOIN ME.

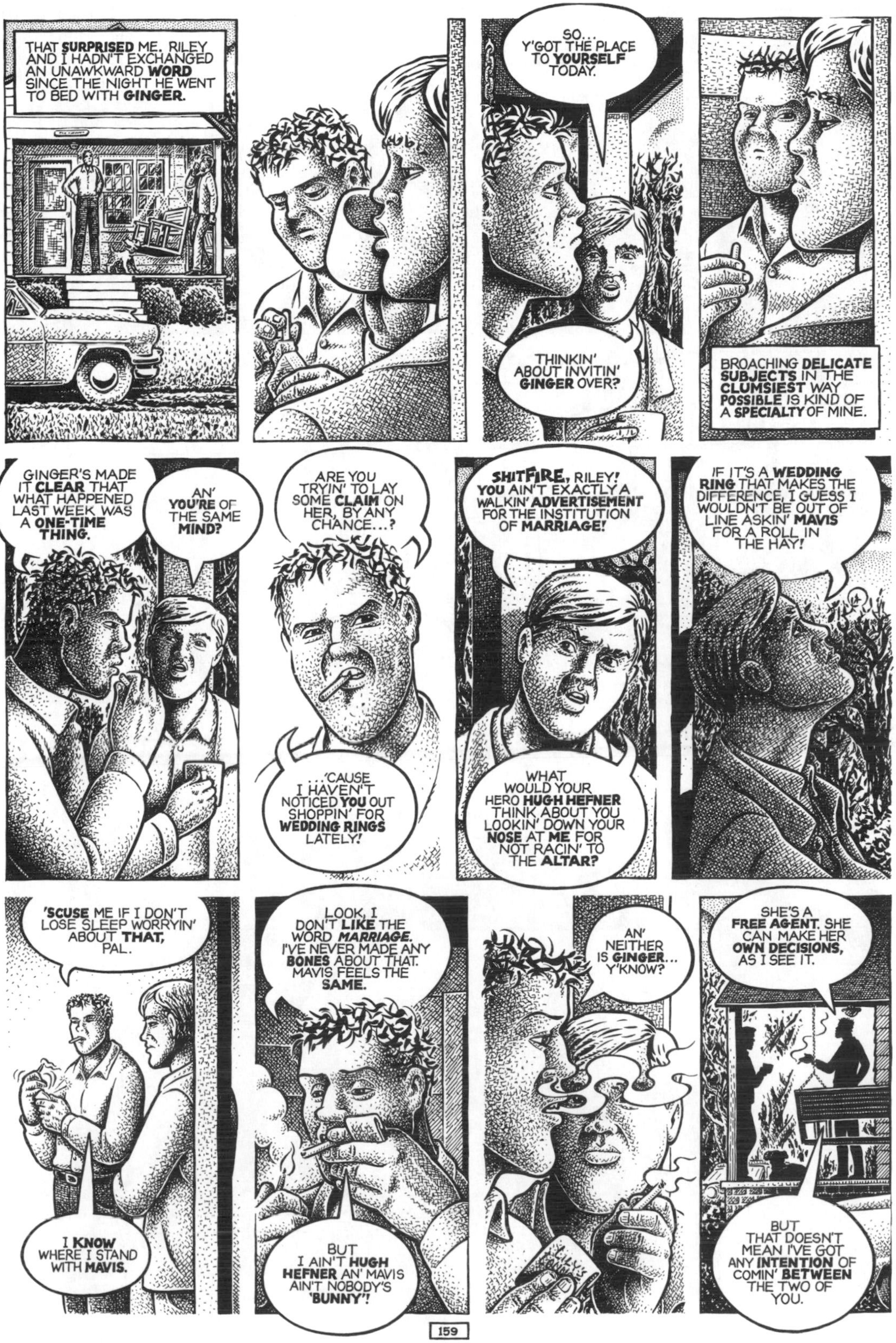
THAT **SURPRISED** ME. RILEY AND I HADN'T EXCHANGED AN UNAWKWARD **WORD** SINCE THE NIGHT HE WENT TO BED WITH **GINGER**.
SO... Y'GOT THE PLACE TO **YOURSELF** TODAY.
THINKIN' ABOUT INVITIN' **GINGER** OVER?
BROACHING **DELICATE SUBJECTS** IN THE **CLUMSIEST** WAY **POSSIBLE** IS KIND OF A **SPECIALTY** OF MINE.
GINGER'S MADE IT **CLEAR** THAT WHAT HAPPENED LAST WEEK WAS A **ONE-TIME THING**.
AN' **YOU'RE** OF THE SAME **MIND?**
ARE YOU TRYIN' TO LAY SOME **CLAIM** ON HER, BY ANY CHANCE...?
...'CAUSE I HAVEN'T NOTICED **YOU** OUT SHOPPIN' FOR **WEDDING RINGS** LATELY!
SHITFIRE, RILEY! **YOU** AIN'T EXACTLY A WALKIN' **ADVERTISEMENT** FOR THE INSTITUTION OF **MARRIAGE!**
WHAT WOULD YOUR HERO **HUGH HEFNER** THINK ABOUT YOU LOOKIN' DOWN YOUR **NOSE** AT **ME** FOR NOT RACIN' TO THE **ALTAR?**
IF IT'S A **WEDDING RING** THAT MAKES THE DIFFERENCE, I GUESS I WOULDN'T BE OUT OF LINE ASKIN' **MAVIS** FOR A ROLL IN THE HAY!
'SCUSE ME IF I DON'T LOSE SLEEP WORRYIN' ABOUT **THAT,** PAL.
I **KNOW** WHERE I STAND WITH **MAVIS.**
LOOK, I DON'T **LIKE** THE WORD ***MARRIAGE***. I'VE NEVER MADE ANY **BONES** ABOUT THAT. MAVIS FEELS THE **SAME**.
BUT I AIN'T **HUGH HEFNER** AN' MAVIS AIN'T NOBODY'S **'BUNNY'!**
AN' NEITHER IS **GINGER**... Y'KNOW?
SHE'S A **FREE AGENT**. SHE CAN MAKE HER **OWN DECISIONS,** AS I SEE IT.
BUT THAT DOESN'T MEAN I'VE GOT ANY **INTENTION** OF COMIN' **BETWEEN** THE TWO OF YOU.

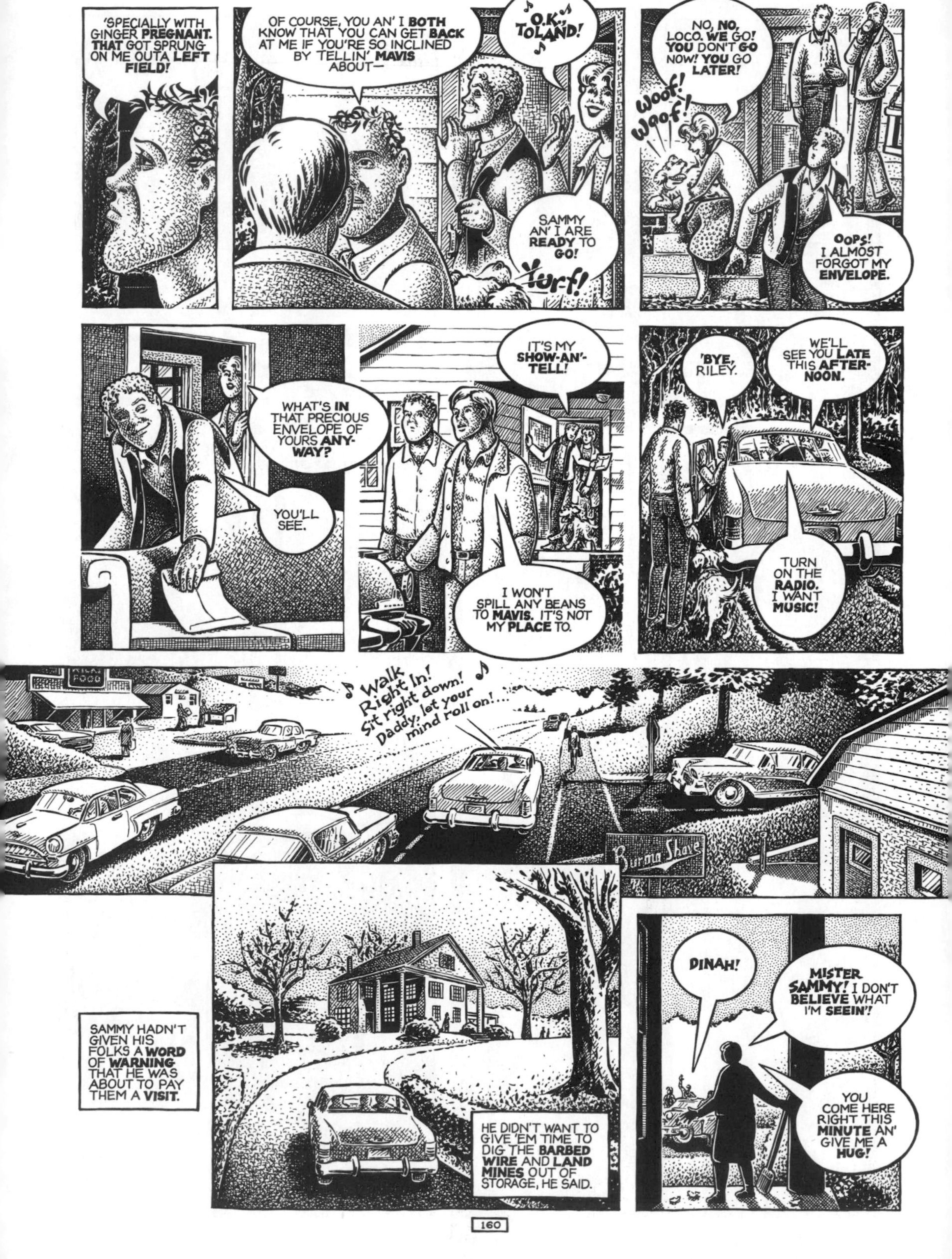

'SPECIALLY WITH GINGER PREGNANT. THAT GOT SPRUNG ON ME OUTA LEFT FIELD!
OF COURSE, YOU AN' I BOTH KNOW THAT YOU CAN GET BACK AT ME IF YOU'RE SO INCLINED BY TELLIN' MAVIS ABOUT—
O.K., TOLAND!
SAMMY AN' I ARE READY TO GO!
Yurf!
NO, NO, LOCO. WE GO! YOU DON'T GO NOW! YOU GO LATER!
Woof! Woof!
OOPS! I ALMOST FORGOT MY ENVELOPE.
WHAT'S IN THAT PRECIOUS ENVELOPE OF YOURS ANY-WAY?
YOU'LL SEE.
IT'S MY SHOW-AN'-TELL!
I WON'T SPILL ANY BEANS TO MAVIS. IT'S NOT MY PLACE TO.
'BYE, RILEY.
WE'LL SEE YOU LATE THIS AFTER-NOON.
TURN ON THE RADIO. I WANT MUSIC!
Walk Right In! Sit right down! Daddy, let your mind roll on!...
Burma Shave
SAMMY HADN'T GIVEN HIS FOLKS A WORD OF WARNING THAT HE WAS ABOUT TO PAY THEM A VISIT.
HE DIDN'T WANT TO GIVE 'EM TIME TO DIG THE BARBED WIRE AND LAND MINES OUT OF STORAGE, HE SAID.
DINAH!
MISTER SAMMY! I DON'T BELIEVE WHAT I'M SEEIN'!
YOU COME HERE RIGHT THIS MINUTE AN' GIVE ME A HUG!

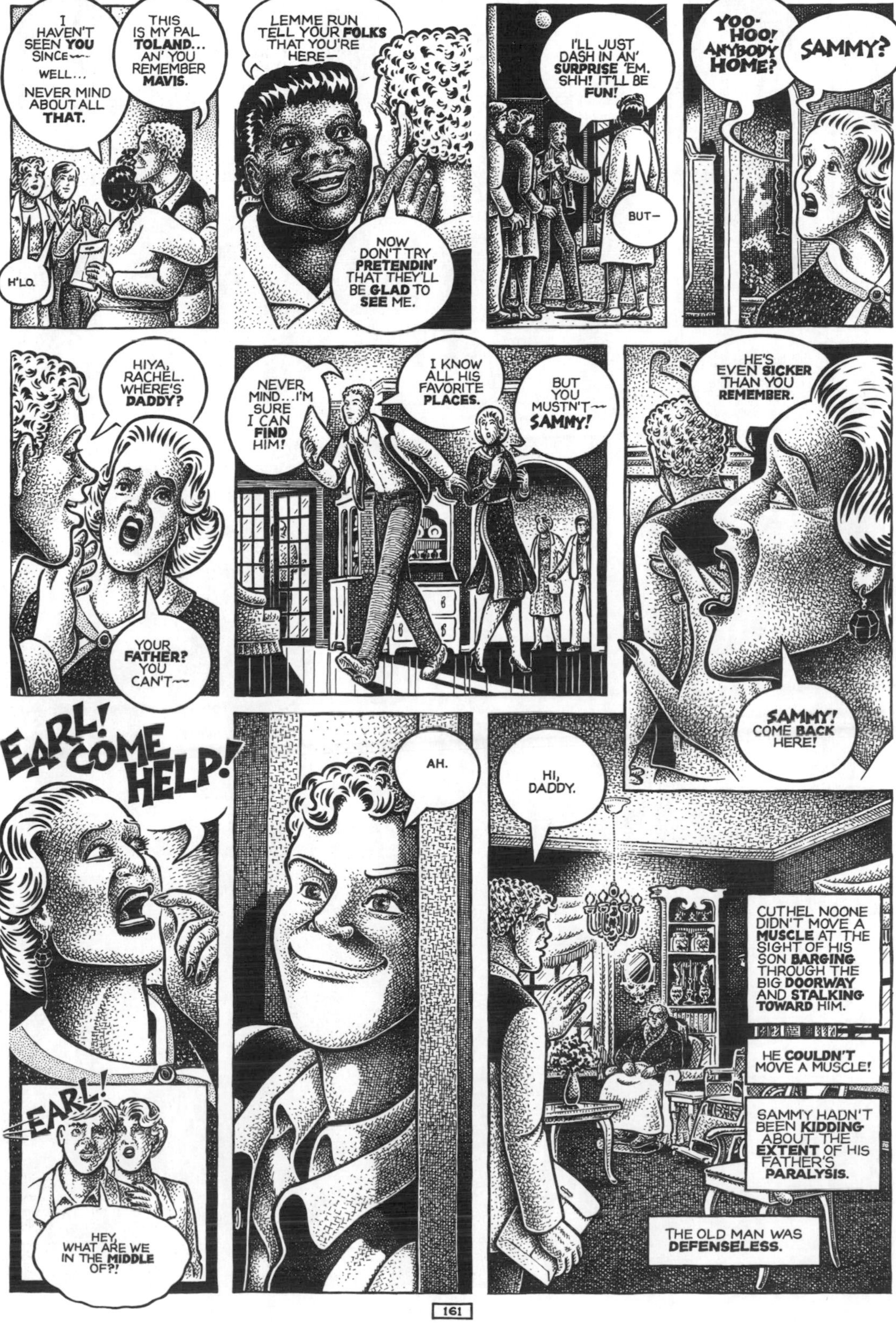

I HAVEN'T SEEN YOU SINCE~~ WELL... NEVER MIND ABOUT ALL THAT.
THIS IS MY PAL TOLAND... AN' YOU REMEMBER MAVIS.
H'LO.
LEMME RUN TELL YOUR FOLKS THAT YOU'RE HERE—
NOW DON'T TRY PRETENDIN' THAT THEY'LL BE GLAD TO SEE ME.
I'LL JUST DASH IN AN' SURPRISE 'EM. SHH! IT'LL BE FUN!
BUT—
YOO-HOO! ANYBODY HOME?
SAMMY?
HIYA, RACHEL. WHERE'S DADDY?
YOUR FATHER? YOU CAN'T~~
NEVER MIND...I'M SURE I CAN FIND HIM!
I KNOW ALL HIS FAVORITE PLACES.
BUT YOU MUSTN'T~~ SAMMY!
HE'S EVEN SICKER THAN YOU REMEMBER.
SAMMY! COME BACK HERE!
EARL! COME HELP!
EARL!
HEY, WHAT ARE WE IN THE MIDDLE OF?!
AH.
HI, DADDY.
CUTHEL NOONE DIDN'T MOVE A MUSCLE AT THE SIGHT OF HIS SON BARGING THROUGH THE BIG DOORWAY AND STALKING TOWARD HIM.
HE COULDN'T MOVE A MUSCLE!
SAMMY HADN'T BEEN KIDDING ABOUT THE EXTENT OF HIS FATHER'S PARALYSIS.
THE OLD MAN WAS DEFENSELESS.

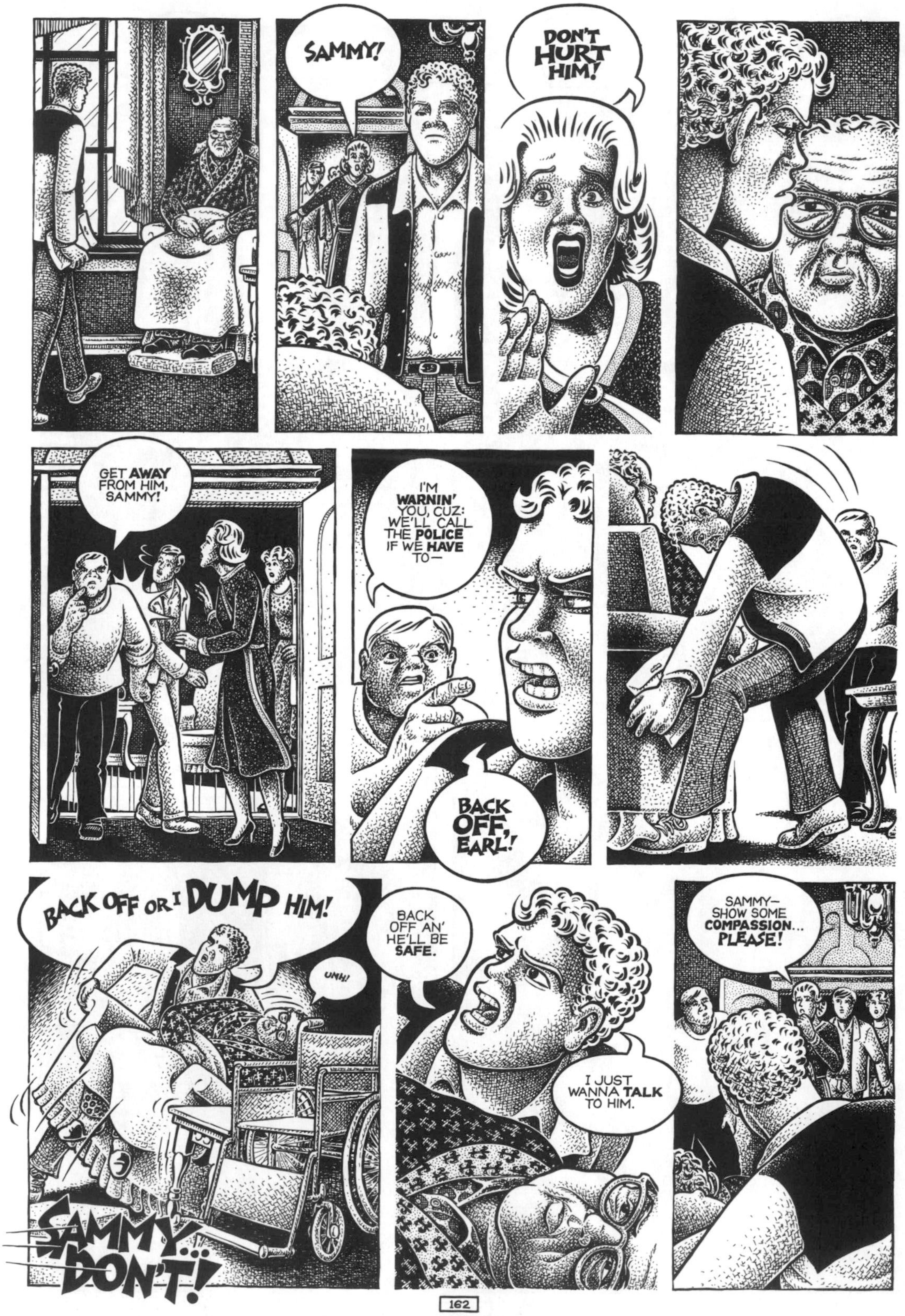
SAMMY!
DON'T HURT HIM!
GET AWAY FROM HIM, SAMMY!
I'M WARNIN' YOU, CUZ: WE'LL CALL THE POLICE IF WE HAVE TO—
BACK OFF, EARL!
BACK OFF OR I DUMP HIM!
UNH!
SAMMY... DON'T!
BACK OFF AN' HE'LL BE SAFE.
I JUST WANNA TALK TO HIM.
SAMMY— SHOW SOME COMPASSION... PLEASE!

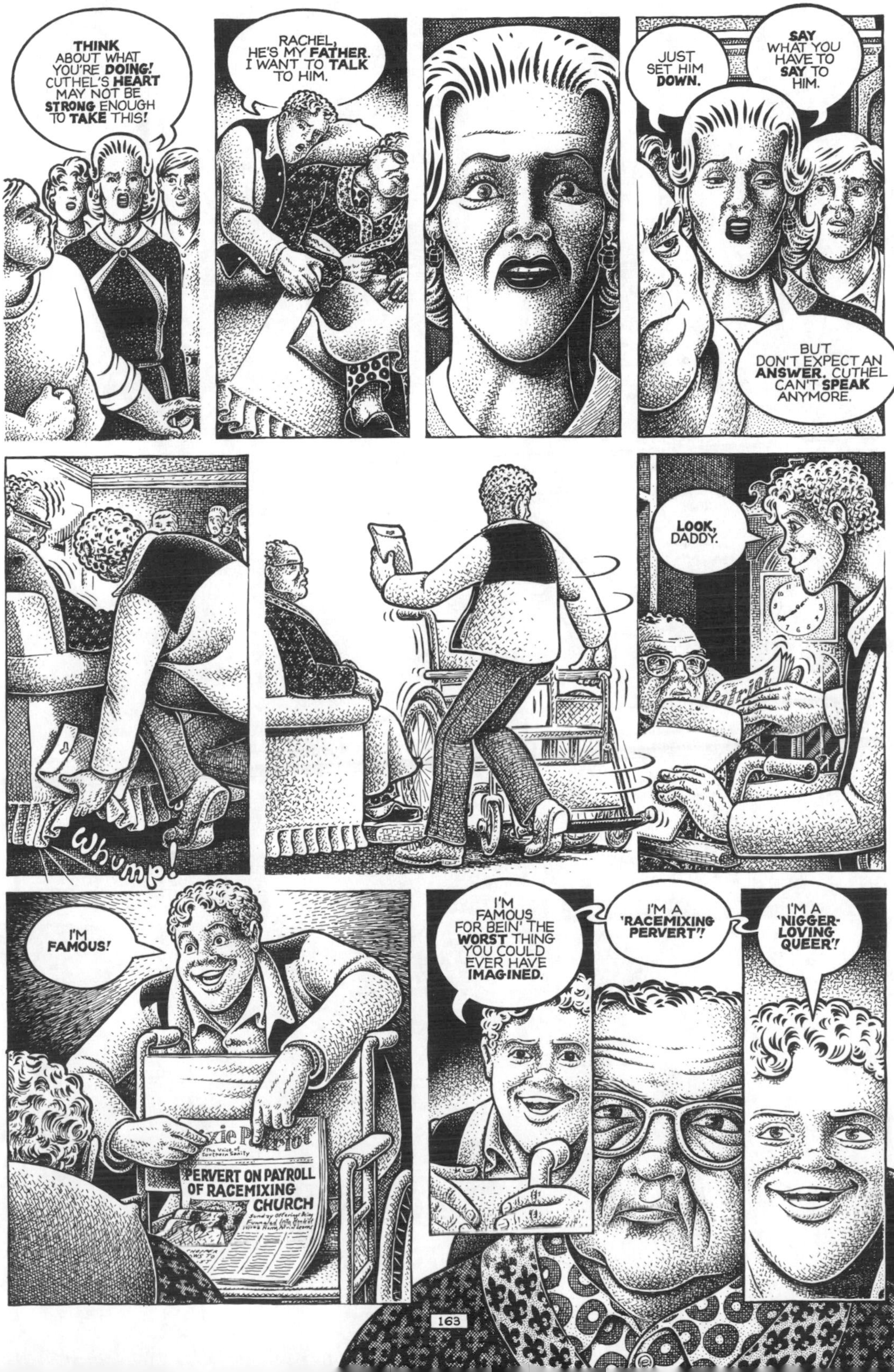
THINK ABOUT WHAT YOU'RE DOING! CUTHEL'S HEART MAY NOT BE STRONG ENOUGH TO TAKE THIS!
RACHEL, HE'S MY FATHER. I WANT TO TALK TO HIM.
JUST SET HIM DOWN.
SAY WHAT YOU HAVE TO SAY TO HIM.
BUT DON'T EXPECT AN ANSWER. CUTHEL CAN'T SPEAK ANYMORE.
Whump!
LOOK, DADDY.
I'M FAMOUS!
The Voice of Southern Sanity
PERVERT ON PAYROLL OF RACEMIXING CHURCH
I'M FAMOUS FOR BEIN' THE WORST THING YOU COULD EVER HAVE IMAGINED.
I'M A 'RACEMIXING PERVERT'!
I'M A 'NIGGER-LOVING QUEER'!

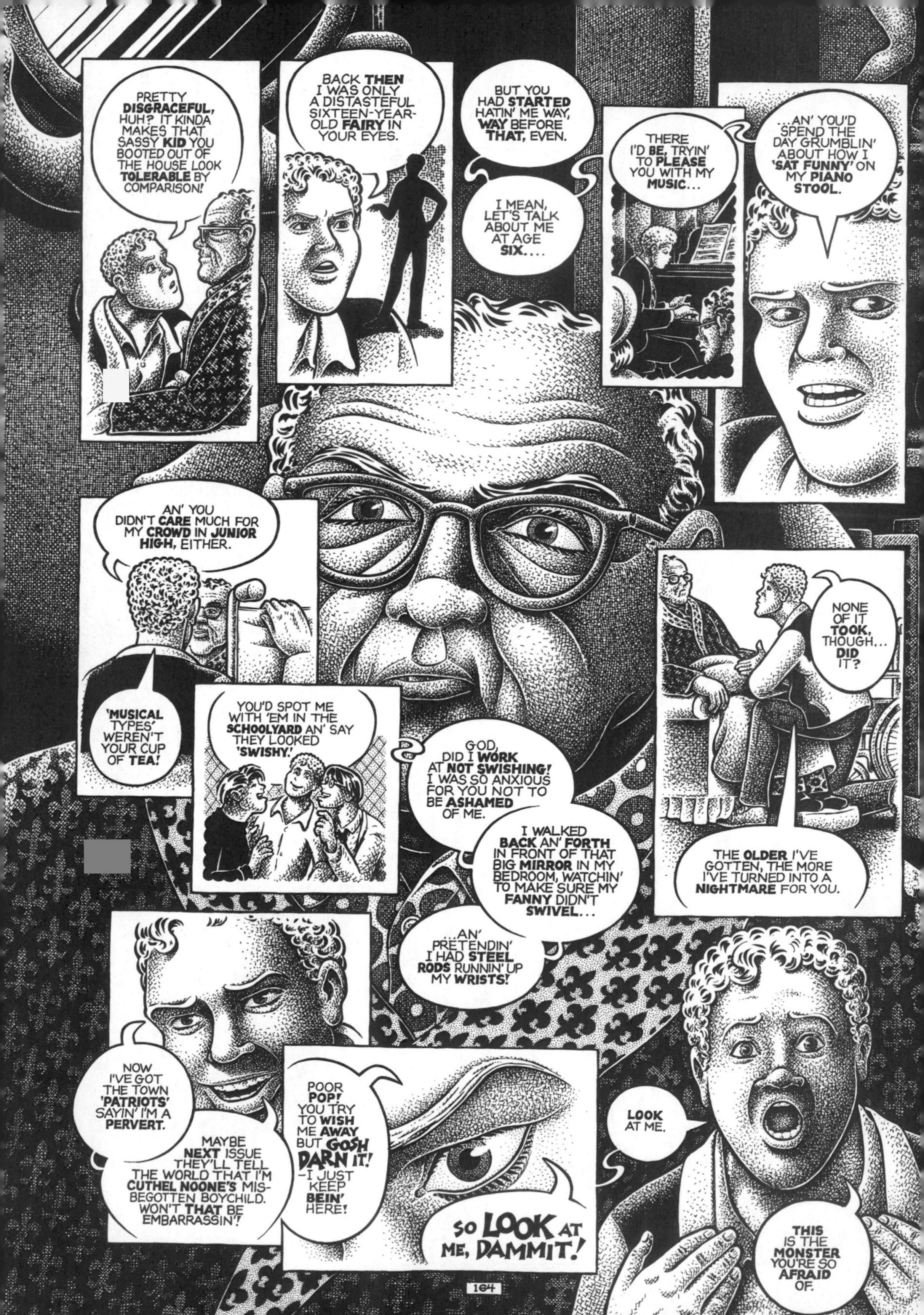
PRETTY DISGRACEFUL, HUH? IT KINDA MAKES THAT SASSY KID YOU BOOTED OUT OF THE HOUSE LOOK TOLERABLE BY COMPARISON!
BACK THEN I WAS ONLY A DISTASTEFUL SIXTEEN-YEAR-OLD FAIRY IN YOUR EYES.
BUT YOU HAD STARTED HATIN' ME WAY, WAY BEFORE THAT, EVEN.
I MEAN, LET'S TALK ABOUT ME AT AGE SIX....
THERE I'D BE, TRYIN' TO PLEASE YOU WITH MY MUSIC...
...AN' YOU'D SPEND THE DAY GRUMBLIN' ABOUT HOW I 'SAT FUNNY' ON MY PIANO STOOL.
AN' YOU DIDN'T CARE MUCH FOR MY CROWD IN JUNIOR HIGH, EITHER.
'MUSICAL TYPES' WEREN'T YOUR CUP OF TEA!
YOU'D SPOT ME WITH 'EM IN THE SCHOOLYARD AN' SAY THEY LOOKED 'SWISHY.'
GOD, DID I WORK AT NOT SWISHING! I WAS SO ANXIOUS FOR YOU NOT TO BE ASHAMED OF ME.
I WALKED BACK AN' FORTH IN FRONT OF THAT BIG MIRROR IN MY BEDROOM, WATCHIN' TO MAKE SURE MY FANNY DIDN'T SWIVEL...
...AN' PRETENDIN' I HAD STEEL RODS RUNNIN' UP MY WRISTS!
NONE OF IT TOOK, THOUGH,... DID IT?
THE OLDER I'VE GOTTEN, THE MORE I'VE TURNED INTO A NIGHTMARE FOR YOU.
NOW I'VE GOT THE TOWN 'PATRIOTS' SAYIN' I'M A PERVERT.
MAYBE NEXT ISSUE THEY'LL TELL THE WORLD THAT I'M CUTHEL NOONE'S MIS-BEGOTTEN BOYCHILD. WON'T THAT BE EMBARRASSIN'!
POOR POP! YOU TRY TO WISH ME AWAY BUT GOSH DARN IT! —I JUST KEEP BEIN' HERE!
SO LOOK AT ME, DAMMIT!
LOOK AT ME.
THIS IS THE MONSTER YOU'RE SO AFRAID OF.

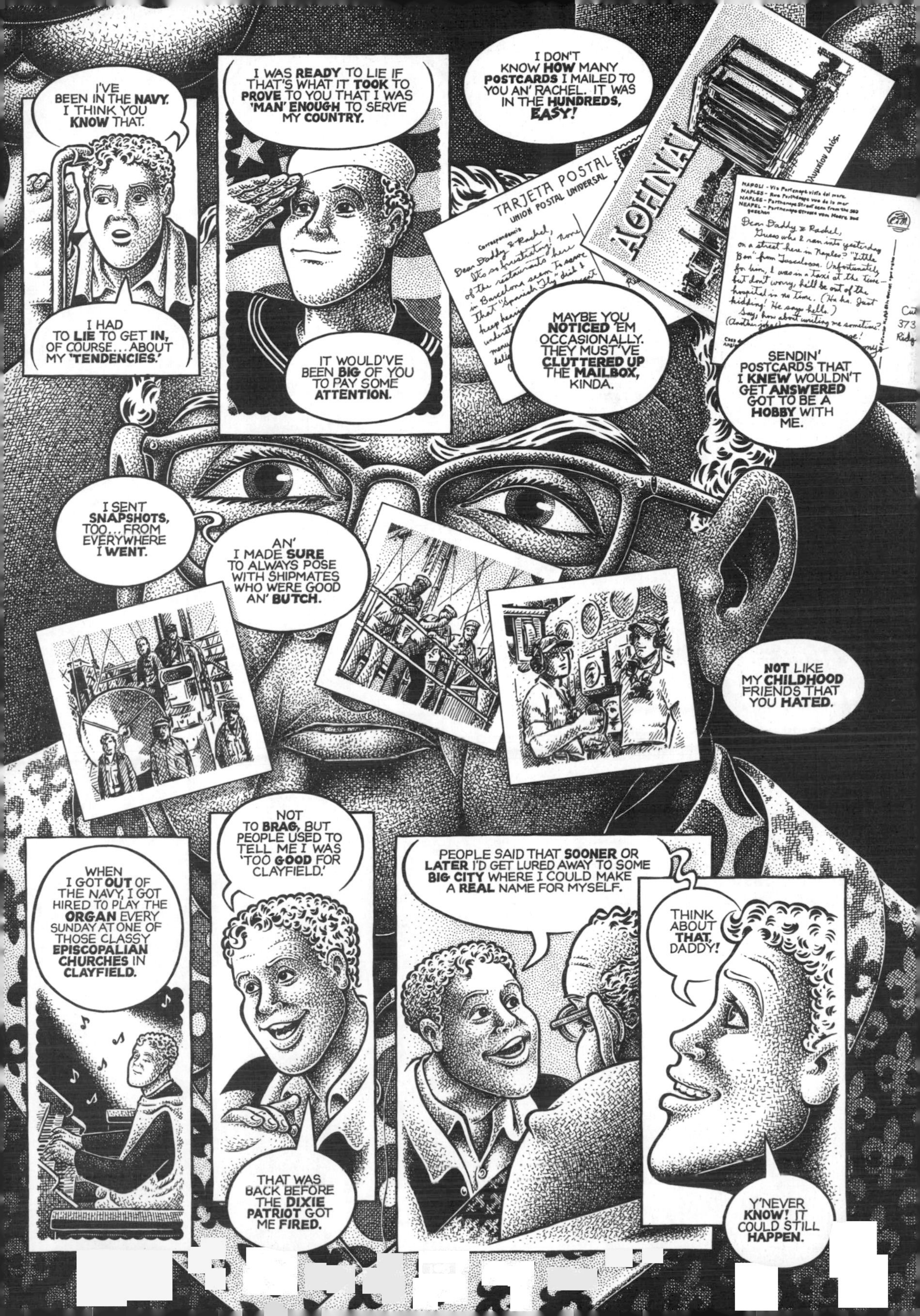
I'VE BEEN IN THE NAVY. I THINK YOU KNOW THAT.
I HAD TO LIE TO GET IN, OF COURSE... ABOUT MY 'TENDENCIES.'
I WAS READY TO LIE IF THAT'S WHAT IT TOOK TO PROVE TO YOU THAT I WAS 'MAN' ENOUGH TO SERVE MY COUNTRY.
IT WOULD'VE BEEN BIG OF YOU TO PAY SOME ATTENTION.
I DON'T KNOW HOW MANY POSTCARDS I MAILED TO YOU AN' RACHEL. IT WAS IN THE HUNDREDS, EASY!
TARJETA POSTAL
UNION POSTAL UNIVERSAL
Dear Daddy & Rachel,
MAYBE YOU NOTICED 'EM OCCASIONALLY. THEY MUST'VE CLUTTERED UP THE MAILBOX, KINDA.
NAPOLI - Via Partenope vista dal mare
Dear Daddy & Rachel,
Guess who I ran into yesterday on a street here in Naples? "Little Bon" from Tuscaloosa. Unfortunately for him, I was in a taxi at the time — but don't worry, he'll be out of the hospital in no time. (Ha ha. Just kidding! He says hello.)
Say, how about writing me sometime?
SENDIN' POSTCARDS THAT I KNEW WOULDN'T GET ANSWERED GOT TO BE A HOBBY WITH ME.
I SENT SNAPSHOTS, TOO... FROM EVERYWHERE I WENT.
AN' I MADE SURE TO ALWAYS POSE WITH SHIPMATES WHO WERE GOOD AN' BUTCH.
NOT LIKE MY CHILDHOOD FRIENDS THAT YOU HATED.
WHEN I GOT OUT OF THE NAVY, I GOT HIRED TO PLAY THE ORGAN EVERY SUNDAY AT ONE OF THOSE CLASSY EPISCOPALIAN CHURCHES IN CLAYFIELD.
NOT TO BRAG, BUT PEOPLE USED TO TELL ME I WAS 'TOO GOOD FOR CLAYFIELD.'
THAT WAS BACK BEFORE THE DIXIE PATRIOT GOT ME FIRED.
PEOPLE SAID THAT SOONER OR LATER I'D GET LURED AWAY TO SOME BIG CITY WHERE I COULD MAKE A REAL NAME FOR MYSELF.
THINK ABOUT THAT, DADDY!
Y'NEVER KNOW! IT COULD STILL HAPPEN.

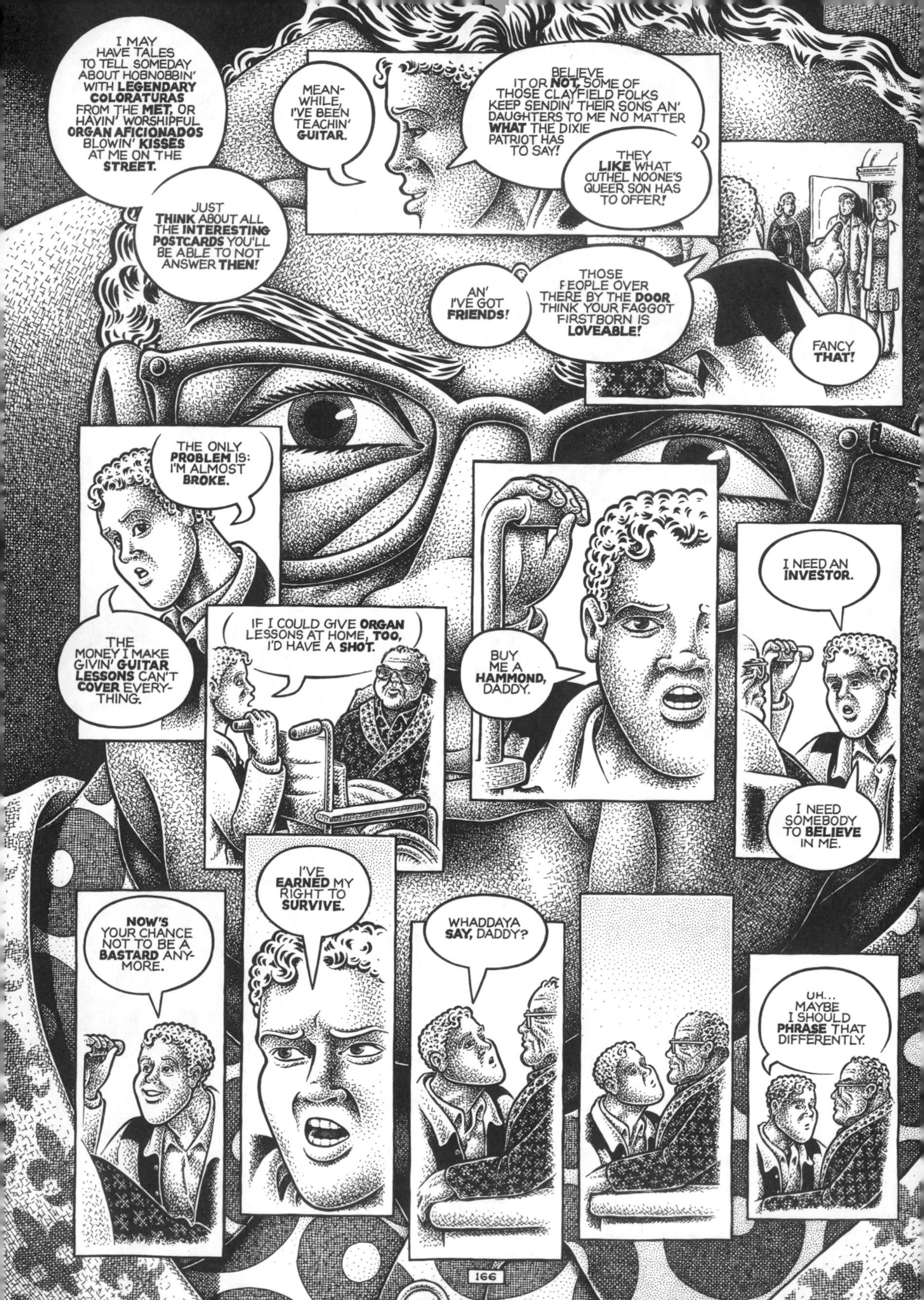

I MAY HAVE TALES TO TELL SOMEDAY ABOUT HOBNOBBIN' WITH **LEGENDARY COLORATURAS** FROM THE **MET**, OR HAVIN' WORSHIPFUL **ORGAN AFICIONADOS** BLOWIN' **KISSES** AT ME ON THE **STREET**.
JUST **THINK** ABOUT ALL THE **INTERESTING POSTCARDS** YOU'LL BE ABLE TO NOT ANSWER **THEN**!
MEAN-WHILE, I'VE BEEN TEACHIN' **GUITAR**.
BELIEVE IT OR **NOT**, SOME OF THOSE CLAYFIELD FOLKS KEEP SENDIN' THEIR SONS AN' DAUGHTERS TO ME NO MATTER **WHAT** THE DIXIE PATRIOT HAS TO SAY!
THEY **LIKE** WHAT CUTHEL NOONE'S QUEER SON HAS TO OFFER!
AN' I'VE GOT **FRIENDS**!
THOSE PEOPLE OVER THERE BY THE **DOOR** THINK YOUR FAGGOT FIRSTBORN IS **LOVEABLE**!
FANCY **THAT**!
THE ONLY **PROBLEM** IS: I'M ALMOST **BROKE**.
THE MONEY I MAKE GIVIN' **GUITAR LESSONS** CAN'T **COVER** EVERY-THING.
IF I COULD GIVE **ORGAN** LESSONS AT HOME, **TOO**, I'D HAVE A **SHOT**.
BUY ME A **HAMMOND**, DADDY.
I NEED AN **INVESTOR**.
I NEED SOMEBODY TO **BELIEVE** IN ME.
NOW'S YOUR CHANCE NOT TO BE A **BASTARD** ANY-MORE.
I'VE **EARNED** MY RIGHT TO **SURVIVE**.
WHADDAYA **SAY**, DADDY?
UH... MAYBE I SHOULD **PHRASE** THAT DIFFERENTLY.

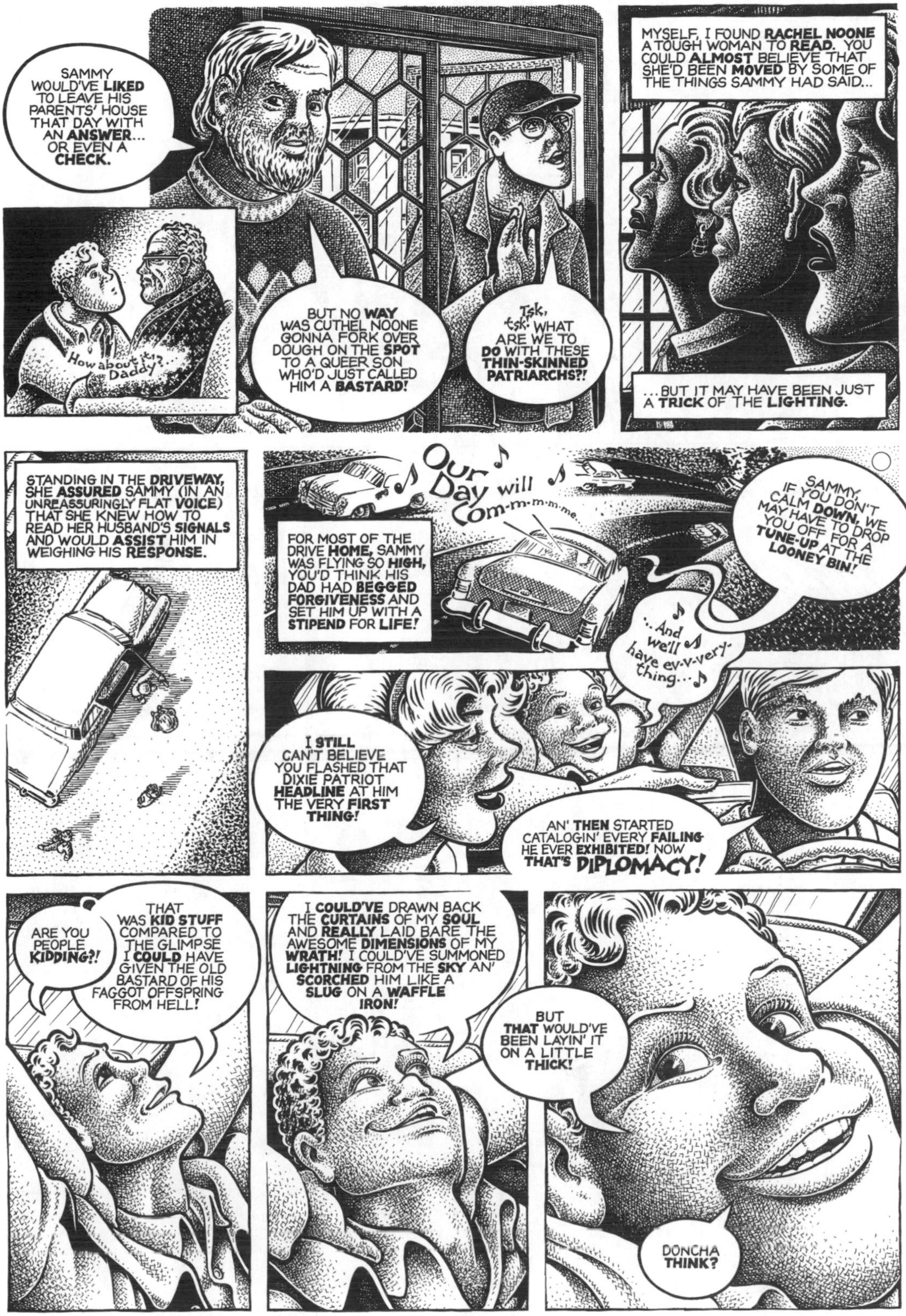
SAMMY WOULD'VE LIKED TO LEAVE HIS PARENTS' HOUSE THAT DAY WITH AN ANSWER... OR EVEN A CHECK.
How about it, Daddy?
BUT NO WAY WAS CUTHEL NOONE GONNA FORK OVER DOUGH ON THE SPOT TO A QUEER SON WHO'D JUST CALLED HIM A BASTARD!
Tsk, tsk. WHAT ARE WE TO DO WITH THESE THIN-SKINNED PATRIARCHS?!
MYSELF, I FOUND RACHEL NOONE A TOUGH WOMAN TO READ. YOU COULD ALMOST BELIEVE THAT SHE'D BEEN MOVED BY SOME OF THE THINGS SAMMY HAD SAID...
...BUT IT MAY HAVE BEEN JUST A TRICK OF THE LIGHTING.
STANDING IN THE DRIVEWAY, SHE ASSURED SAMMY (IN AN UNREASSURINGLY FLAT VOICE) THAT SHE KNEW HOW TO READ HER HUSBAND'S SIGNALS AND WOULD ASSIST HIM IN WEIGHING HIS RESPONSE.
Our Day will Com-m-m-m-me.
FOR MOST OF THE DRIVE HOME, SAMMY WAS FLYING SO HIGH, YOU'D THINK HIS DAD HAD BEGGED FORGIVENESS AND SET HIM UP WITH A STIPEND FOR LIFE!
SAMMY, IF YOU DON'T CALM DOWN, WE MAY HAVE TO DROP YOU OFF FOR A TUNE-UP AT THE LOONEY BIN!
...And we'll have ev-v-very-thing...
I STILL CAN'T BELIEVE YOU FLASHED THAT DIXIE PATRIOT HEADLINE AT HIM THE VERY FIRST THING!
AN' THEN STARTED CATALOGIN' EVERY FAILING HE EVER EXHIBITED! NOW THAT'S DIPLOMACY!
ARE YOU PEOPLE KIDDING?!
THAT WAS KID STUFF COMPARED TO THE GLIMPSE I COULD HAVE GIVEN THE OLD BASTARD OF HIS FAGGOT OFFSPRING FROM HELL!
I COULD'VE DRAWN BACK THE CURTAINS OF MY SOUL AND REALLY LAID BARE THE AWESOME DIMENSIONS OF MY WRATH! I COULD'VE SUMMONED LIGHTNING FROM THE SKY AN' SCORCHED HIM LIKE A SLUG ON A WAFFLE IRON!
BUT THAT WOULD'VE BEEN LAYIN' IT ON A LITTLE THICK!
DONCHA THINK?

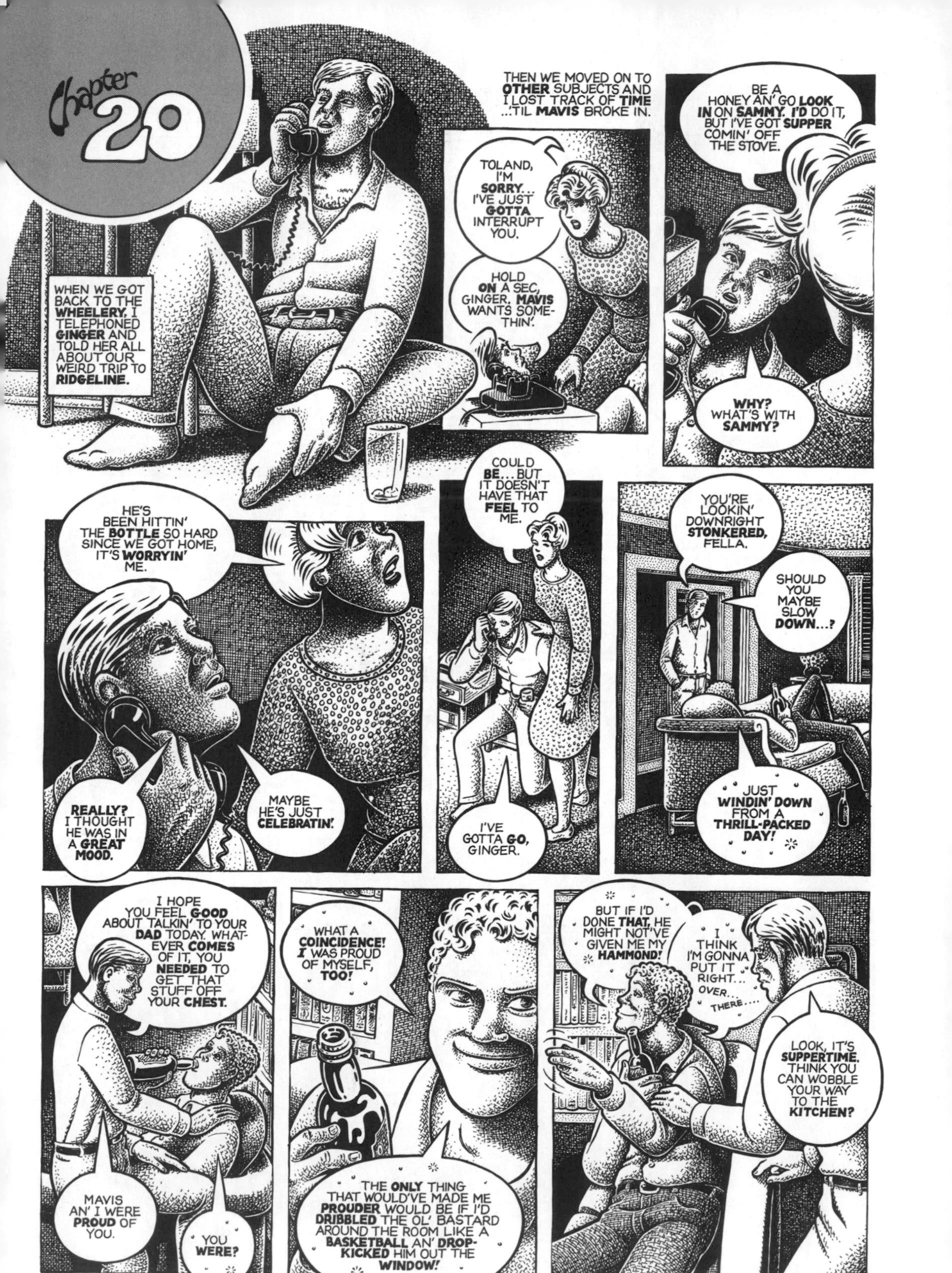
Chapter 20
WHEN WE GOT BACK TO THE WHEELERY, I TELEPHONED GINGER AND TOLD HER ALL ABOUT OUR WEIRD TRIP TO RIDGELINE.
THEN WE MOVED ON TO OTHER SUBJECTS AND I LOST TRACK OF TIME ...TIL MAVIS BROKE IN.
TOLAND, I'M SORRY... I'VE JUST GOTTA INTERRUPT YOU.
HOLD ON A SEC, GINGER. MAVIS WANTS SOME-THIN'.
BE A HONEY AN' GO LOOK IN ON SAMMY. I'D DO IT, BUT I'VE GOT SUPPER COMIN' OFF THE STOVE.
WHY? WHAT'S WITH SAMMY?
HE'S BEEN HITTIN' THE BOTTLE SO HARD SINCE WE GOT HOME, IT'S WORRYIN' ME.
REALLY? I THOUGHT HE WAS IN A GREAT MOOD.
MAYBE HE'S JUST CELEBRATIN'.
COULD BE... BUT IT DOESN'T HAVE THAT FEEL TO ME.
I'VE GOTTA GO, GINGER.
YOU'RE LOOKIN' DOWNRIGHT STONKERED, FELLA.
SHOULD YOU MAYBE SLOW DOWN...?
JUST WINDIN' DOWN FROM A THRILL-PACKED DAY!
I HOPE YOU FEEL GOOD ABOUT TALKIN' TO YOUR DAD TODAY. WHAT-EVER COMES OF IT, YOU NEEDED TO GET THAT STUFF OFF YOUR CHEST.
MAVIS AN' I WERE PROUD OF YOU.
YOU WERE?
WHAT A COINCIDENCE! I WAS PROUD OF MYSELF, TOO!
THE ONLY THING THAT WOULD'VE MADE ME PROUDER WOULD BE IF I'D DRIBBLED THE OL' BASTARD AROUND THE ROOM LIKE A BASKETBALL AN' DROP-KICKED HIM OUT THE WINDOW!
BUT IF I'D DONE THAT, HE MIGHT NOT'VE GIVEN ME MY HAMMOND!
I THINK I'M GONNA PUT IT RIGHT... OVER... THERE....
LOOK, IT'S SUPPERTIME. THINK YOU CAN WOBBLE YOUR WAY TO THE KITCHEN?

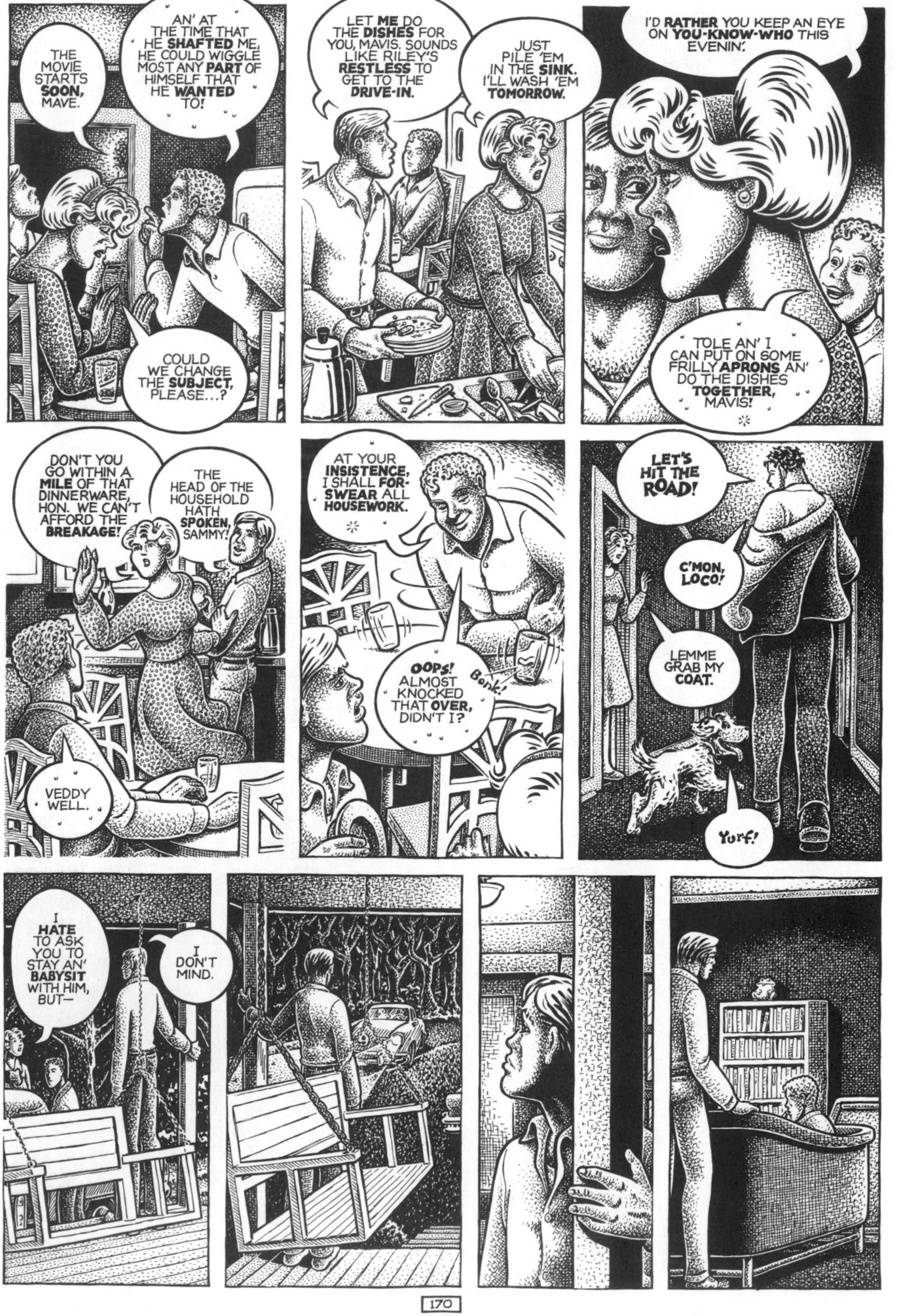
THE MOVIE STARTS SOON, MAVE.
AN' AT THE TIME THAT HE SHAFTED ME, HE COULD WIGGLE MOST ANY PART OF HIMSELF THAT HE WANTED TO!
COULD WE CHANGE THE SUBJECT, PLEASE...?
LET ME DO THE DISHES FOR YOU, MAVIS. SOUNDS LIKE RILEY'S RESTLESS TO GET TO THE DRIVE-IN.
JUST PILE 'EM IN THE SINK. I'LL WASH 'EM TOMORROW.
I'D RATHER YOU KEEP AN EYE ON YOU-KNOW-WHO THIS EVENIN'.
TOLE AN' I CAN PUT ON SOME FRILLY APRONS AN' DO THE DISHES TOGETHER, MAVIS!
DON'T YOU GO WITHIN A MILE OF THAT DINNERWARE, HON. WE CAN'T AFFORD THE BREAKAGE!
THE HEAD OF THE HOUSEHOLD HATH SPOKEN, SAMMY!
VEDDY WELL.
AT YOUR INSISTENCE, I SHALL FOR-SWEAR ALL HOUSEWORK.
Bonk!
OOPS! ALMOST KNOCKED THAT OVER, DIDN'T I?
LET'S HIT THE ROAD!
C'MON, LOCO!
LEMME GRAB MY COAT.
Yurf!
I HATE TO ASK YOU TO STAY AN' BABYSIT WITH HIM, BUT—
I DON'T MIND.

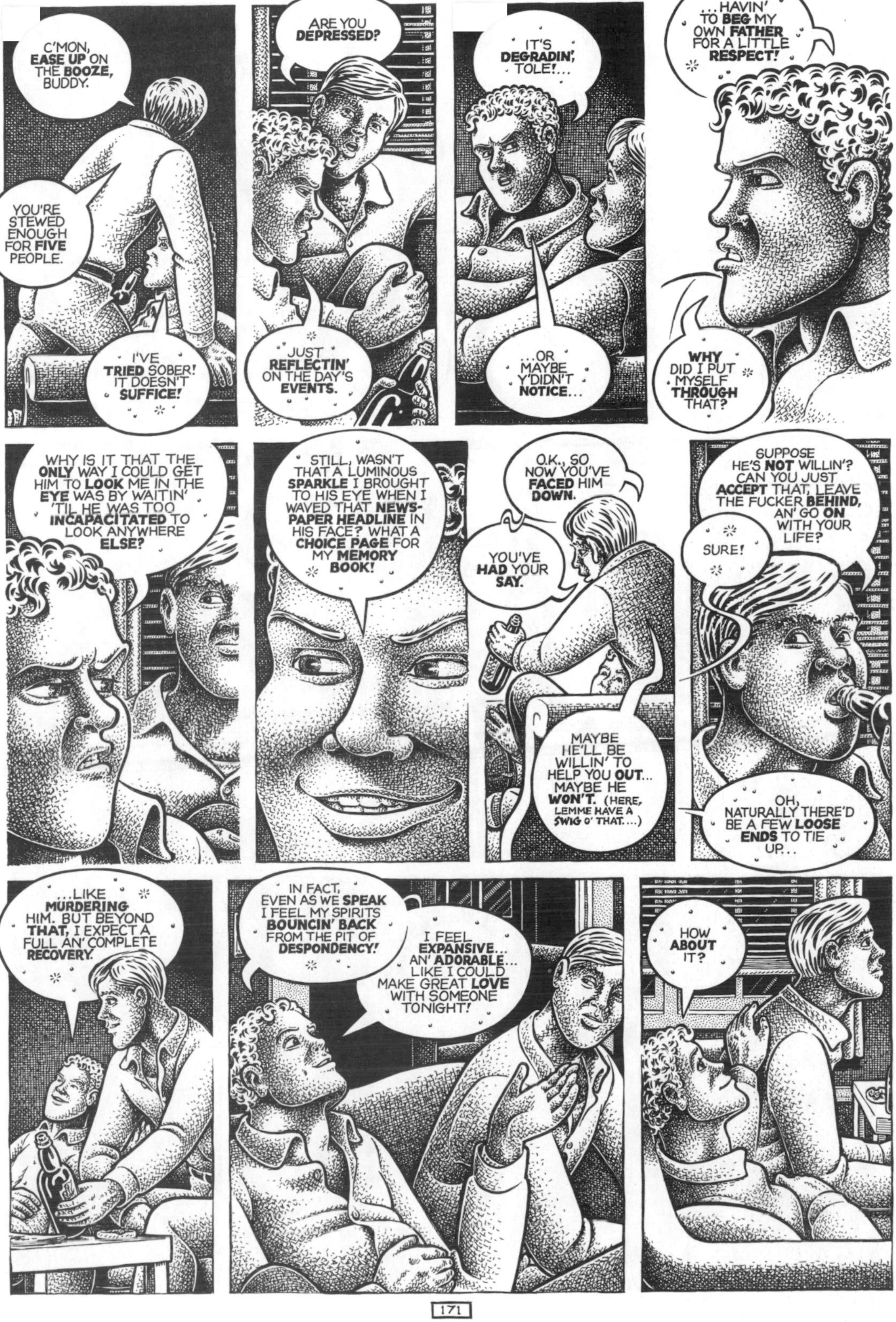
C'MON, EASE UP ON THE BOOZE, BUDDY.
YOU'RE STEWED ENOUGH FOR FIVE PEOPLE.
I'VE TRIED SOBER! IT DOESN'T SUFFICE!
ARE YOU DEPRESSED?
JUST REFLECTIN' ON THE DAY'S EVENTS.
IT'S DEGRADIN', TOLE!...
...OR MAYBE Y'DIDN'T NOTICE...
...HAVIN' TO BEG MY OWN FATHER FOR A LITTLE RESPECT!
WHY DID I PUT MYSELF THROUGH THAT?
WHY IS IT THAT THE ONLY WAY I COULD GET HIM TO LOOK ME IN THE EYE WAS BY WAITIN' 'TIL HE WAS TOO INCAPACITATED TO LOOK ANYWHERE ELSE?
STILL, WASN'T THAT A LUMINOUS SPARKLE I BROUGHT TO HIS EYE WHEN I WAVED THAT NEWS-PAPER HEADLINE IN HIS FACE? WHAT A CHOICE PAGE FOR MY MEMORY BOOK!
O.K., SO NOW YOU'VE FACED HIM DOWN.
YOU'VE HAD YOUR SAY.
MAYBE HE'LL BE WILLIN' TO HELP YOU OUT... MAYBE HE WON'T. (HERE, LEMME HAVE A SWIG O' THAT....)
SUPPOSE HE'S NOT WILLIN'? CAN YOU JUST ACCEPT THAT, LEAVE THE FUCKER BEHIND, AN' GO ON WITH YOUR LIFE?
SURE!
OH, NATURALLY THERE'D BE A FEW LOOSE ENDS TO TIE UP...
...LIKE MURDERING HIM. BUT BEYOND THAT, I EXPECT A FULL AN' COMPLETE RECOVERY.
IN FACT, EVEN AS WE SPEAK I FEEL MY SPIRITS BOUNCIN' BACK FROM THE PIT OF DESPONDENCY!
I FEEL EXPANSIVE... AN' ADORABLE... LIKE I COULD MAKE GREAT LOVE WITH SOMEONE TONIGHT!
HOW ABOUT IT?

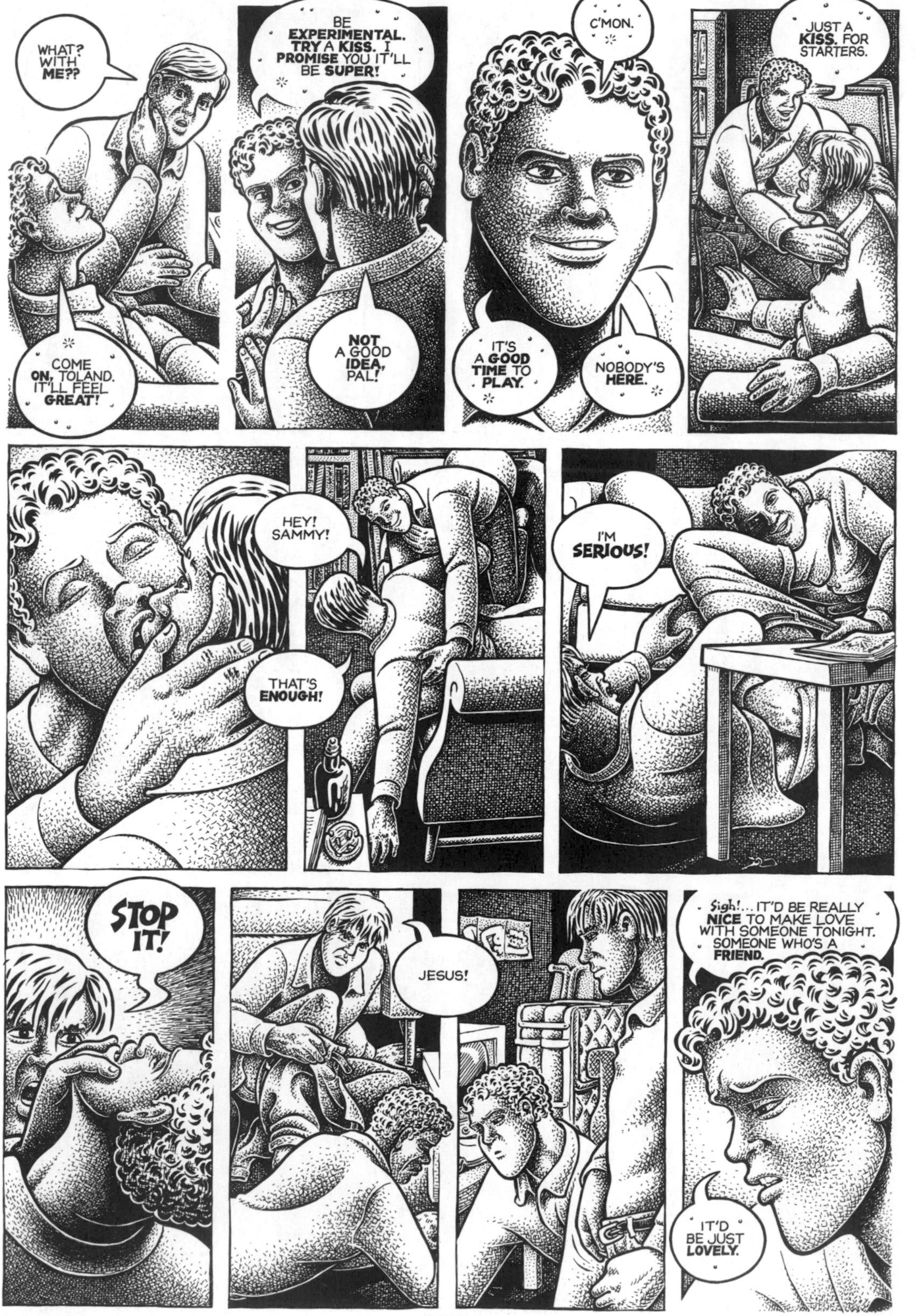
WHAT? WITH ME??
COME ON, TOLAND. IT'LL FEEL GREAT!
BE EXPERIMENTAL. TRY A KISS. I PROMISE YOU IT'LL BE SUPER!
NOT A GOOD IDEA, PAL!
C'MON.
IT'S A GOOD TIME TO PLAY.
NOBODY'S HERE.
JUST A KISS. FOR STARTERS.
HEY! SAMMY!
THAT'S ENOUGH!
I'M SERIOUS!
STOP IT!
JESUS!
Sigh!... IT'D BE REALLY NICE TO MAKE LOVE WITH SOMEONE TONIGHT. SOMEONE WHO'S A FRIEND.
IT'D BE JUST LOVELY.

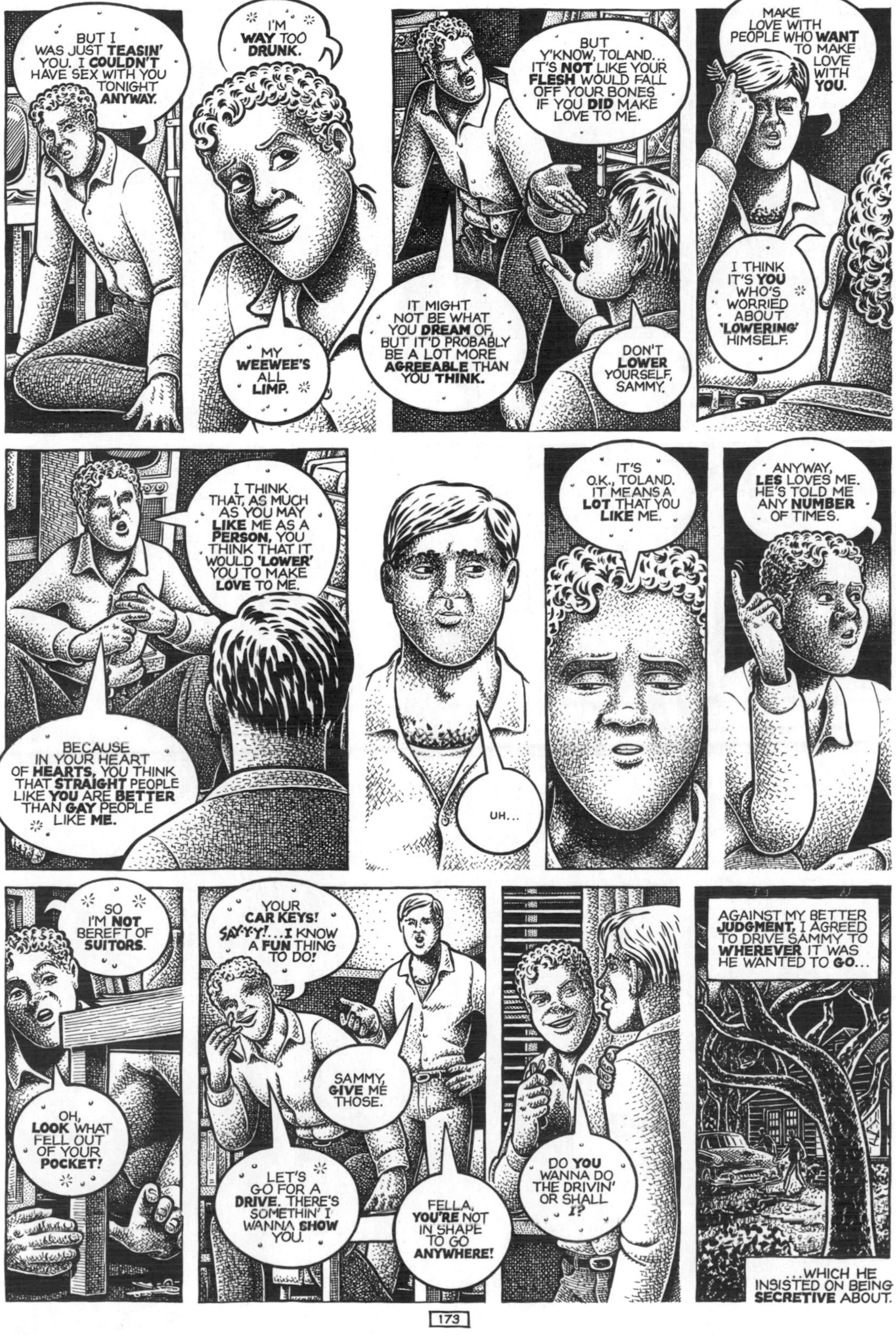
BUT I WAS JUST TEASIN' YOU. I COULDN'T HAVE SEX WITH YOU TONIGHT ANYWAY.
I'M WAY TOO DRUNK.
MY WEEWEE'S ALL LIMP.
BUT Y'KNOW, TOLAND... IT'S NOT LIKE YOUR FLESH WOULD FALL OFF YOUR BONES IF YOU DID MAKE LOVE TO ME.
IT MIGHT NOT BE WHAT YOU DREAM OF, BUT IT'D PROBABLY BE A LOT MORE AGREEABLE THAN YOU THINK.
DON'T LOWER YOURSELF, SAMMY.
MAKE LOVE WITH PEOPLE WHO WANT TO MAKE LOVE WITH YOU.
I THINK IT'S YOU WHO'S WORRIED ABOUT 'LOWERING' HIMSELF.
I THINK THAT, AS MUCH AS YOU MAY LIKE ME AS A PERSON, YOU THINK THAT IT WOULD 'LOWER' YOU TO MAKE LOVE TO ME.
BECAUSE IN YOUR HEART OF HEARTS, YOU THINK THAT STRAIGHT PEOPLE LIKE YOU ARE BETTER THAN GAY PEOPLE LIKE ME.
UH...
IT'S O.K., TOLAND. IT MEANS A LOT THAT YOU LIKE ME.
ANYWAY, LES LOVES ME. HE'S TOLD ME ANY NUMBER OF TIMES.
SO I'M NOT BEREFT OF SUITORS.
OH, LOOK WHAT FELL OUT OF YOUR POCKET!
YOUR CAR KEYS! SAY-Y-Y!... I KNOW A FUN THING TO DO!
SAMMY, GIVE ME THOSE.
LET'S GO FOR A DRIVE. THERE'S SOMETHIN' I WANNA SHOW YOU.
FELLA, YOU'RE NOT IN SHAPE TO GO ANYWHERE!
DO YOU WANNA DO THE DRIVIN' OR SHALL I?
AGAINST MY BETTER JUDGMENT, I AGREED TO DRIVE SAMMY TO WHEREVER IT WAS HE WANTED TO GO...
...WHICH HE INSISTED ON BEING SECRETIVE ABOUT.

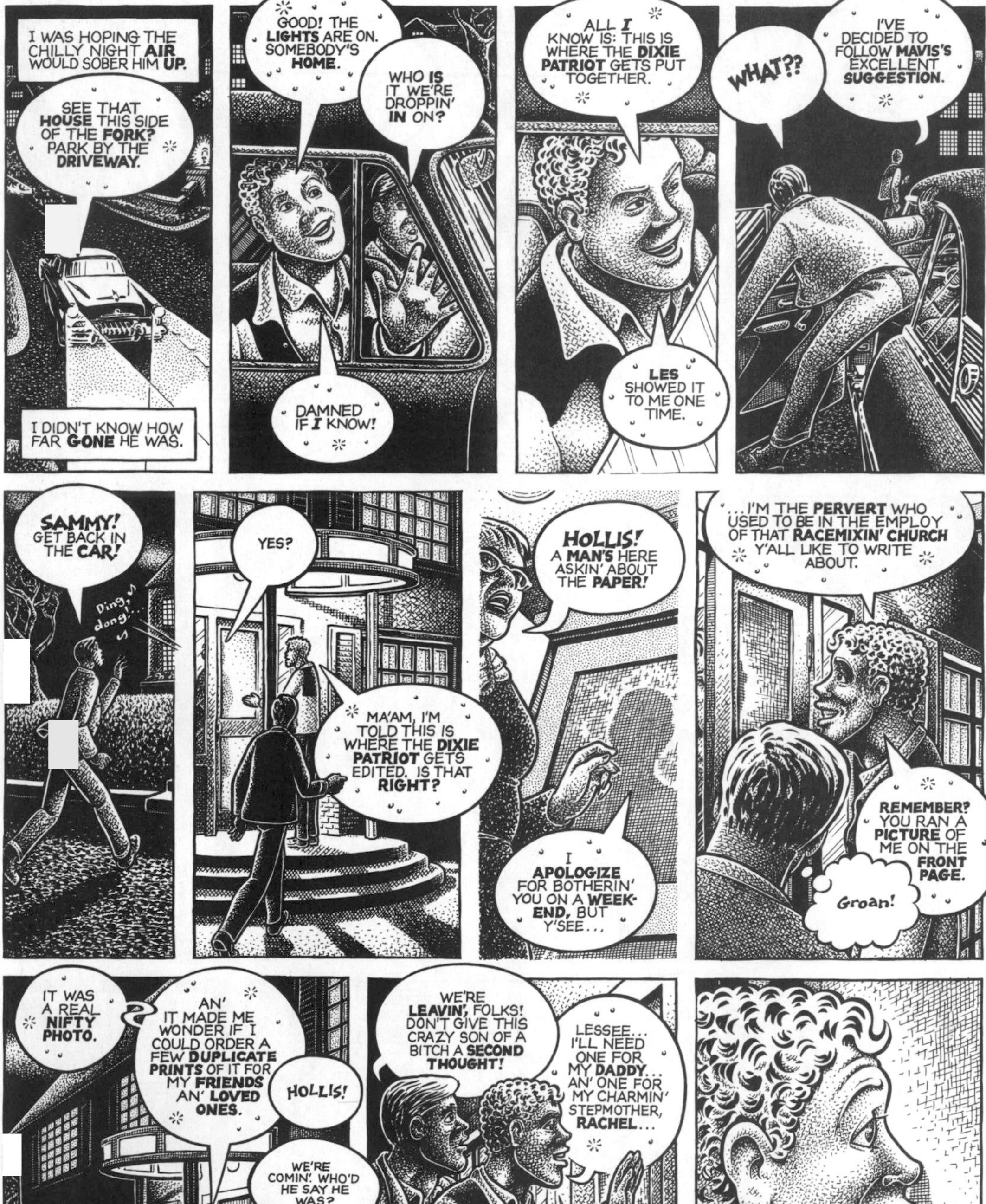
I WAS HOPING THE CHILLY NIGHT AIR WOULD SOBER HIM UP.
SEE THAT HOUSE THIS SIDE OF THE FORK? PARK BY THE DRIVEWAY.
I DIDN'T KNOW HOW FAR GONE HE WAS.
GOOD! THE LIGHTS ARE ON. SOMEBODY'S HOME.
WHO IS IT WE'RE DROPPIN' IN ON?
DAMNED IF I KNOW!
ALL I KNOW IS: THIS IS WHERE THE DIXIE PATRIOT GETS PUT TOGETHER.
LES SHOWED IT TO ME ONE TIME.
WHAT??
I'VE DECIDED TO FOLLOW MAVIS'S EXCELLENT SUGGESTION.
SAMMY! GET BACK IN THE CAR!
Ding, dong!
YES?
MA'AM, I'M TOLD THIS IS WHERE THE DIXIE PATRIOT GETS EDITED. IS THAT RIGHT?
HOLLIS! A MAN'S HERE ASKIN' ABOUT THE PAPER!
I APOLOGIZE FOR BOTHERIN' YOU ON A WEEK-END, BUT Y'SEE...
...I'M THE PERVERT WHO USED TO BE IN THE EMPLOY OF THAT RACEMIXIN' CHURCH Y'ALL LIKE TO WRITE ABOUT.
REMEMBER? YOU RAN A PICTURE OF ME ON THE FRONT PAGE.
Groan!
IT WAS A REAL NIFTY PHOTO.
AN' IT MADE ME WONDER IF I COULD ORDER A FEW DUPLICATE PRINTS OF IT FOR MY FRIENDS AN' LOVED ONES.
HOLLIS!
WE'RE COMIN'. WHO'D HE SAY HE WAS?
IT'S THE FAG FROM TRINITY.
YOU'RE KIDDIN'!
WE'RE LEAVIN', FOLKS! DON'T GIVE THIS CRAZY SON OF A BITCH A SECOND THOUGHT!
LESSEE... I'LL NEED ONE FOR MY DADDY... AN' ONE FOR MY CHARMIN' STEPMOTHER, RACHEL...
...AN' ONE FOR MY FAVORITE NEGRO, LESTER...
...AN' ONE FOR— OH, LOOK!
LOOK WHO'S IN THERE!
IT'S MY FAVORITE LAW ENFORCEMENT OFFICIAL!

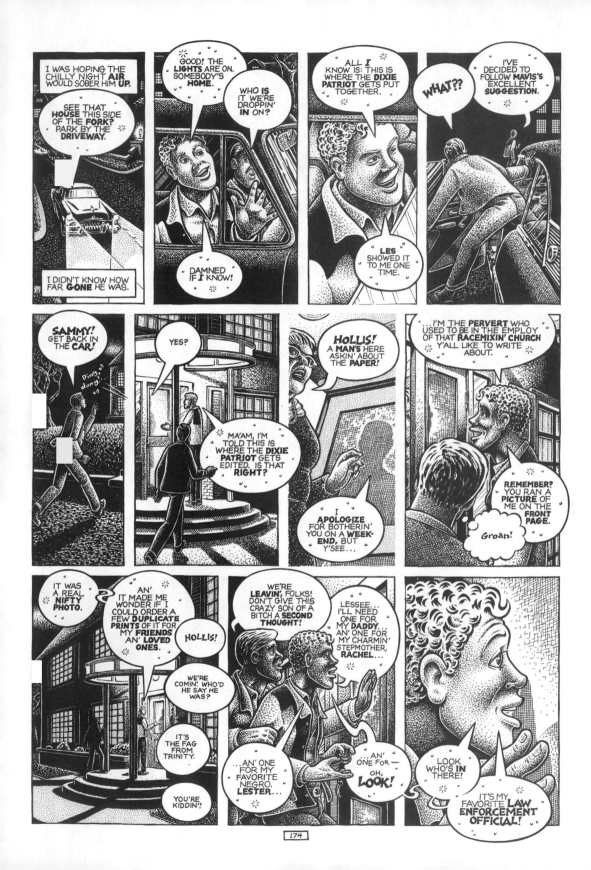

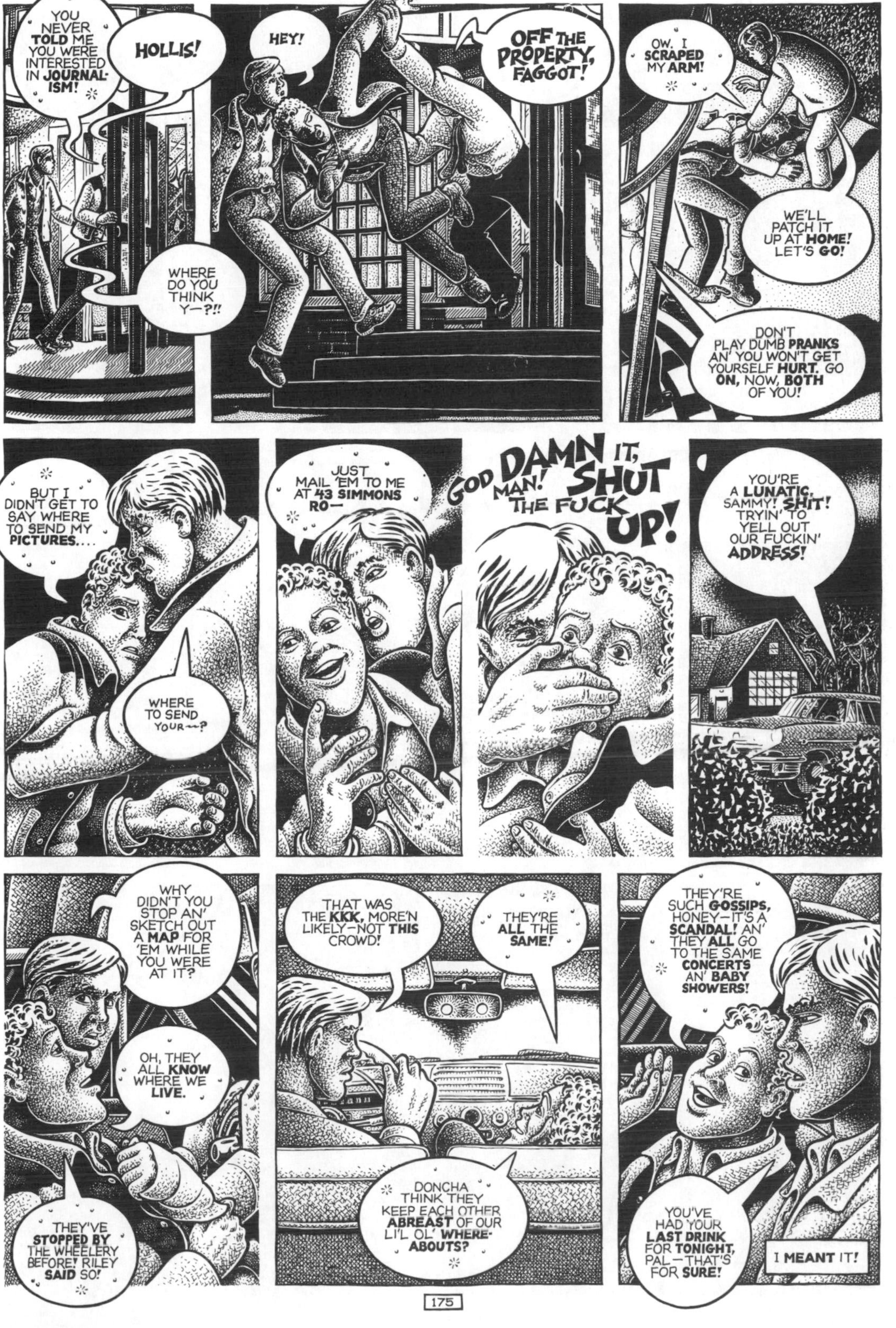
YOU NEVER TOLD ME YOU WERE INTERESTED IN JOURNALISM!
HOLLIS!
WHERE DO YOU THINK Y—?!!
HEY!
OFF THE PROPERTY, FAGGOT!
OW. I SCRAPED MY ARM!
WE'LL PATCH IT UP AT HOME! LET'S GO!
DON'T PLAY DUMB PRANKS AN' YOU WON'T GET YOURSELF HURT. GO ON, NOW, BOTH OF YOU!
BUT I DIDN'T GET TO SAY WHERE TO SEND MY PICTURES....
WHERE TO SEND YOUR—?
JUST MAIL 'EM TO ME AT 43 SIMMONS RO—
GOD DAMN IT, MAN! SHUT THE FUCK UP!
YOU'RE A LUNATIC, SAMMY! SHIT! TRYIN' TO YELL OUT OUR FUCKIN' ADDRESS!
WHY DIDN'T YOU STOP AN' SKETCH OUT A MAP FOR 'EM WHILE YOU WERE AT IT?
OH, THEY ALL KNOW WHERE WE LIVE.
THEY'VE STOPPED BY THE WHEELERY BEFORE! RILEY SAID SO!
THAT WAS THE KKK, MORE'N LIKELY—NOT THIS CROWD!
THEY'RE ALL THE SAME!
DONCHA THINK THEY KEEP EACH OTHER ABREAST OF OUR LI'L OL' WHEREABOUTS?
THEY'RE SUCH GOSSIPS, HONEY—IT'S A SCANDAL! AN' THEY ALL GO TO THE SAME CONCERTS AN' BABY SHOWERS!
YOU'VE HAD YOUR LAST DRINK FOR TONIGHT, PAL—THAT'S FOR SURE!
I MEANT IT!

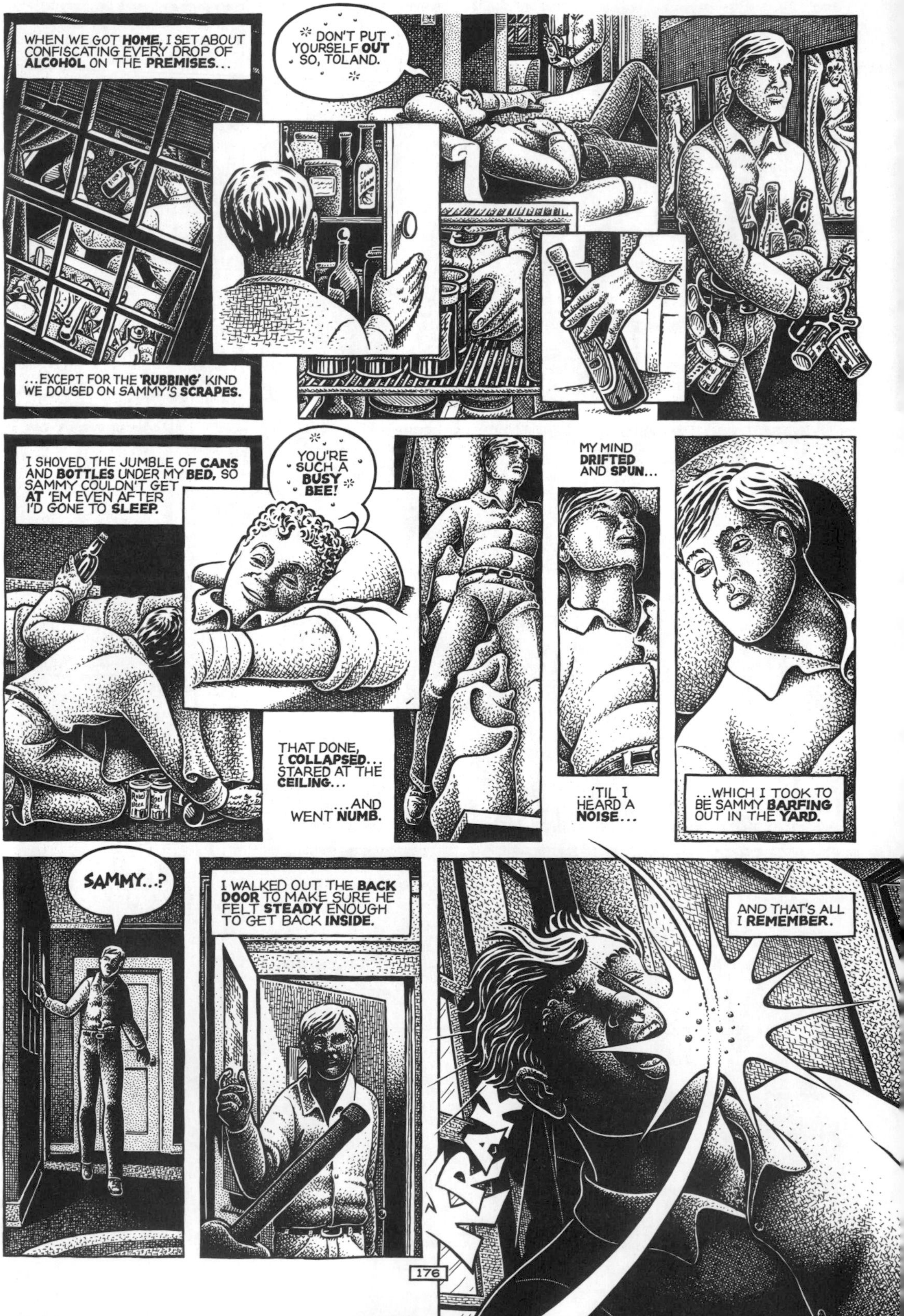

WHEN WE GOT HOME, I SET ABOUT CONFISCATING EVERY DROP OF ALCOHOL ON THE PREMISES...
DON'T PUT YOURSELF OUT SO, TOLAND.
...EXCEPT FOR THE 'RUBBING' KIND WE DOUSED ON SAMMY'S SCRAPES.
I SHOVED THE JUMBLE OF CANS AND BOTTLES UNDER MY BED, SO SAMMY COULDN'T GET AT 'EM EVEN AFTER I'D GONE TO SLEEP.
YOU'RE SUCH A BUSY BEE!
THAT DONE, I COLLAPSED... STARED AT THE CEILING...
...AND WENT NUMB.
MY MIND DRIFTED AND SPUN...
...'TIL I HEARD A NOISE...
...WHICH I TOOK TO BE SAMMY BARFING OUT IN THE YARD.
SAMMY...?
I WALKED OUT THE BACK DOOR TO MAKE SURE HE FELT STEADY ENOUGH TO GET BACK INSIDE.
AND THAT'S ALL I REMEMBER.
KRAK

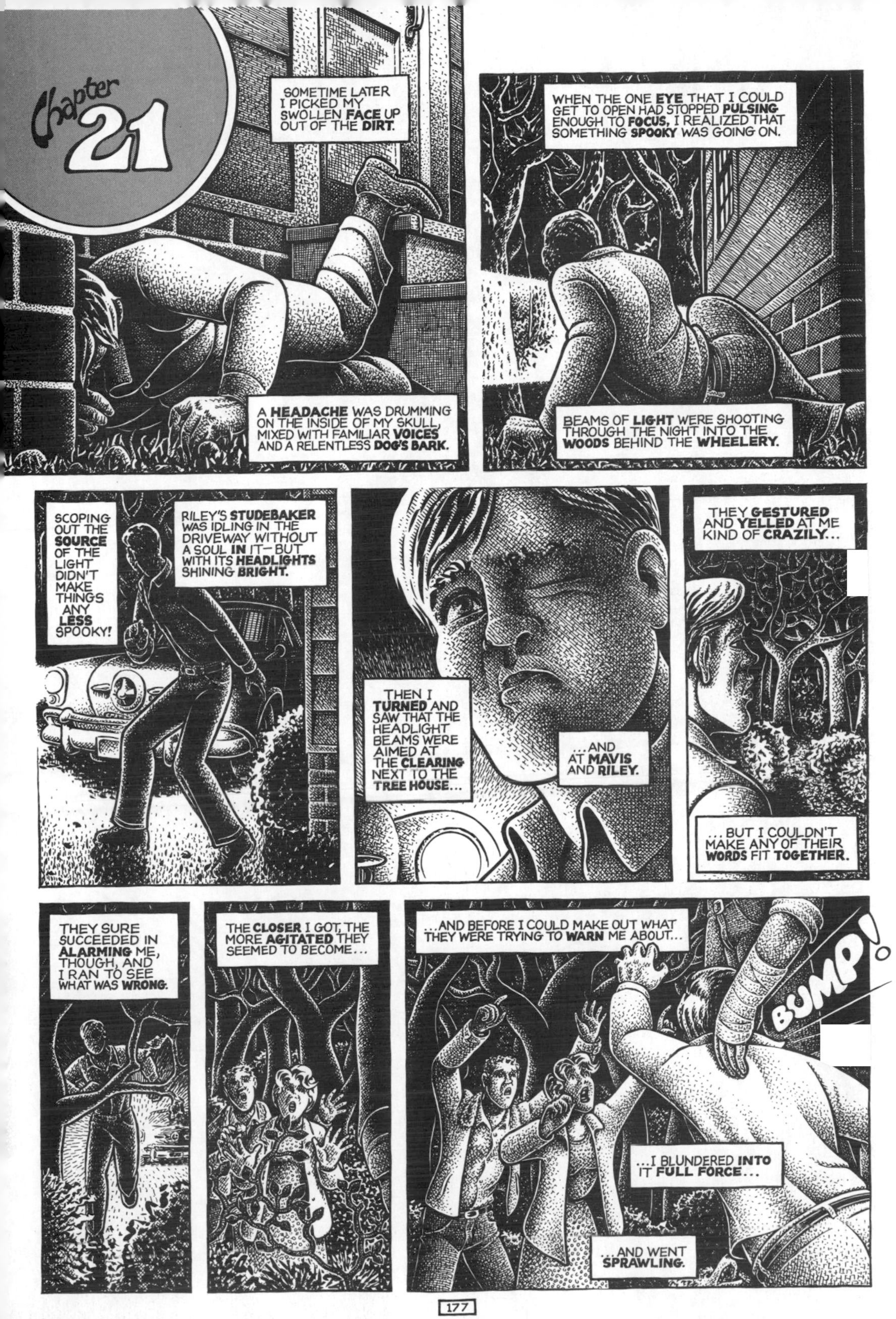
Chapter 21
SOMETIME LATER I PICKED MY SWOLLEN FACE UP OUT OF THE DIRT.
A HEADACHE WAS DRUMMING ON THE INSIDE OF MY SKULL, MIXED WITH FAMILIAR VOICES AND A RELENTLESS DOG'S BARK.
WHEN THE ONE EYE THAT I COULD GET TO OPEN HAD STOPPED PULSING ENOUGH TO FOCUS, I REALIZED THAT SOMETHING SPOOKY WAS GOING ON.
BEAMS OF LIGHT WERE SHOOTING THROUGH THE NIGHT INTO THE WOODS BEHIND THE WHEELERY.
SCOPING OUT THE SOURCE OF THE LIGHT DIDN'T MAKE THINGS ANY LESS SPOOKY!
RILEY'S STUDEBAKER WAS IDLING IN THE DRIVEWAY WITHOUT A SOUL IN IT— BUT WITH ITS HEADLIGHTS SHINING BRIGHT.
THEN I TURNED AND SAW THAT THE HEADLIGHT BEAMS WERE AIMED AT THE CLEARING NEXT TO THE TREE HOUSE...
...AND AT MAVIS AND RILEY.
THEY GESTURED AND YELLED AT ME KIND OF CRAZILY...
...BUT I COULDN'T MAKE ANY OF THEIR WORDS FIT TOGETHER.
THEY SURE SUCCEEDED IN ALARMING ME, THOUGH, AND I RAN TO SEE WHAT WAS WRONG.
THE CLOSER I GOT, THE MORE AGITATED THEY SEEMED TO BECOME...
...AND BEFORE I COULD MAKE OUT WHAT THEY WERE TRYING TO WARN ME ABOUT...
BUMP!
...I BLUNDERED INTO IT FULL FORCE...
...AND WENT SPRAWLING.

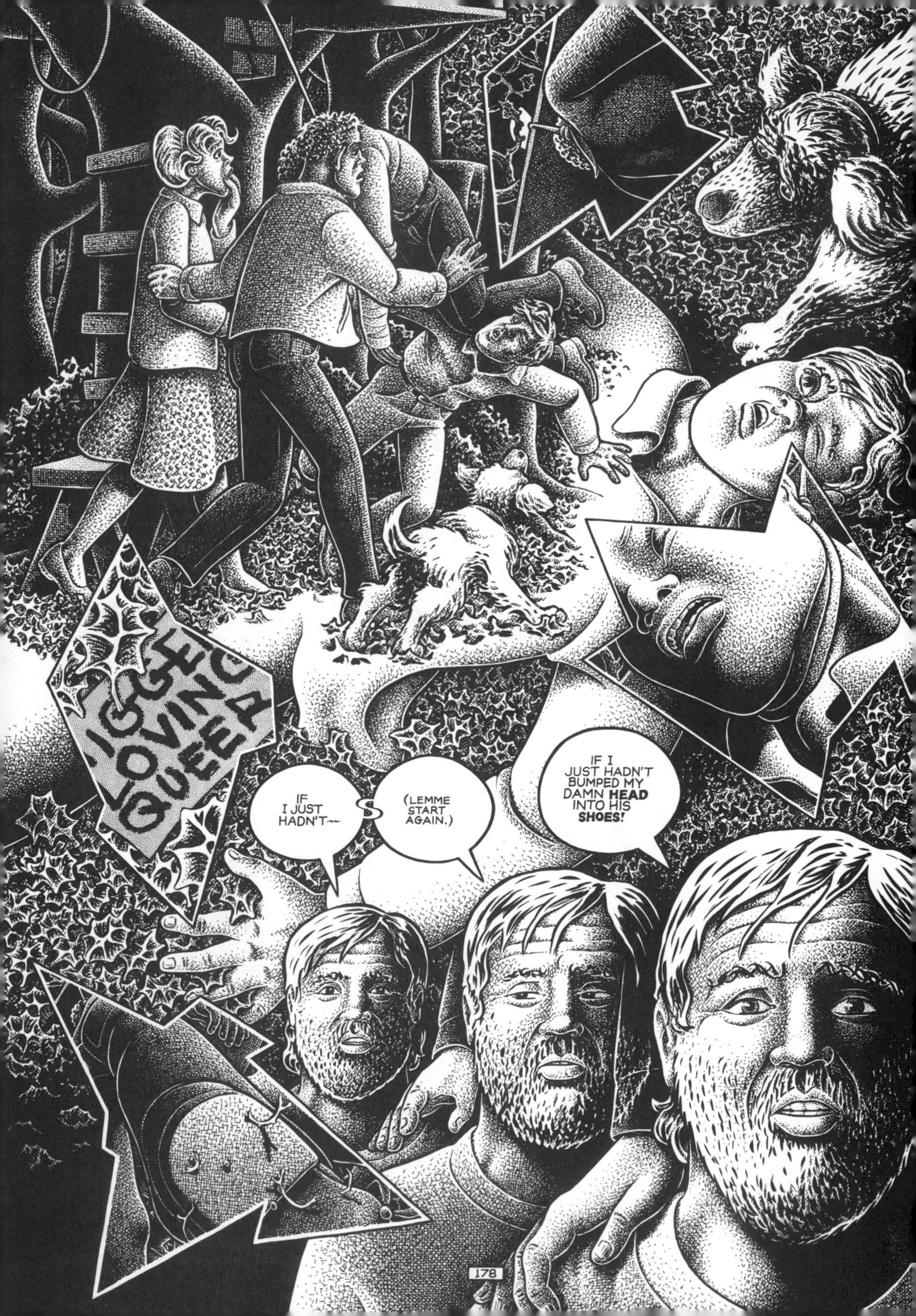
IF I JUST HADN'T--
(LEMME START AGAIN.)
IF I JUST HADN'T BUMPED MY DAMN **HEAD** INTO HIS **SHOES!**

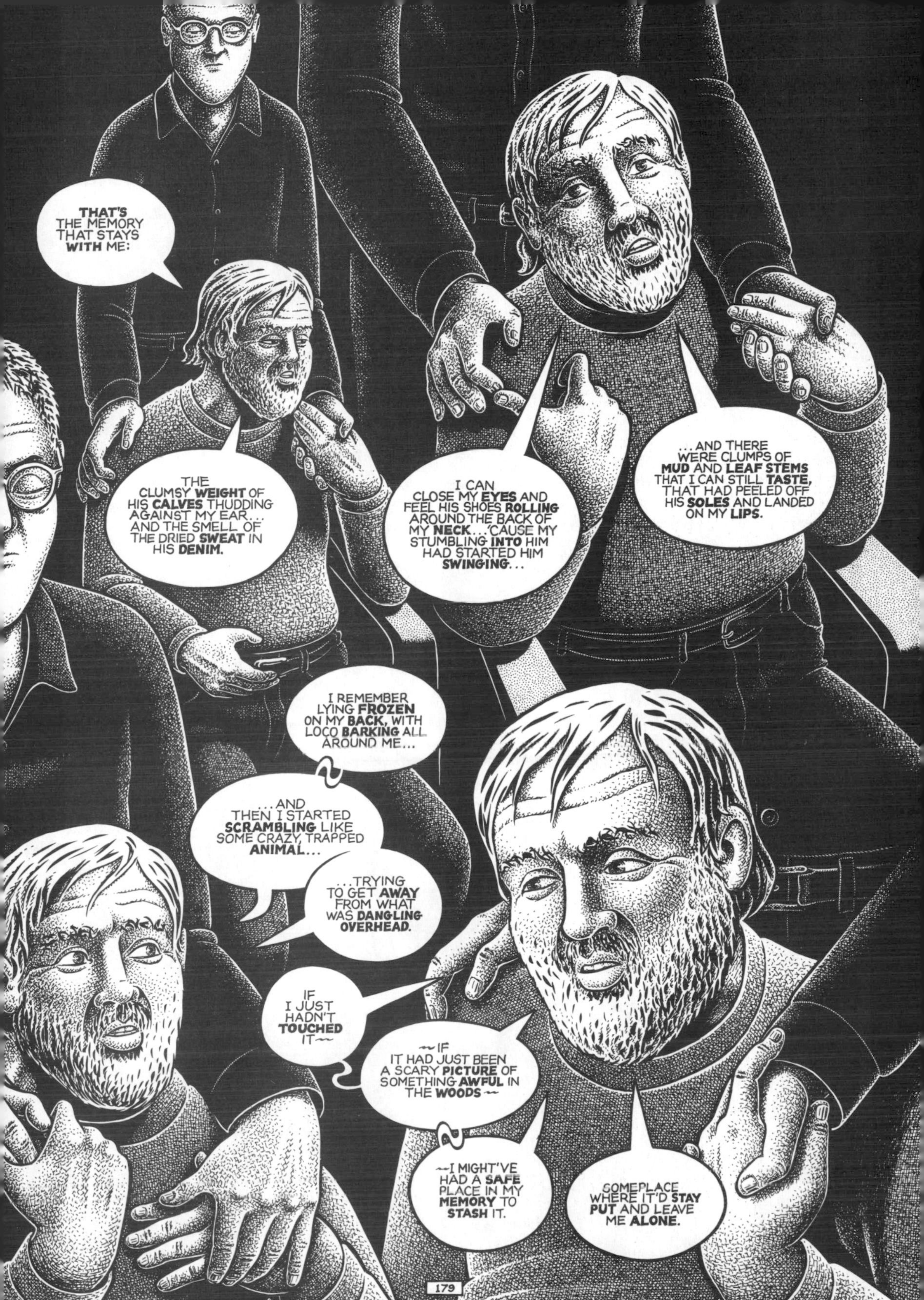
THAT'S THE MEMORY THAT STAYS WITH ME:
THE CLUMSY WEIGHT OF HIS CALVES THUDDING AGAINST MY EAR... AND THE SMELL OF THE DRIED SWEAT IN HIS DENIM.
I CAN CLOSE MY EYES AND FEEL HIS SHOES ROLLING AROUND THE BACK OF MY NECK... 'CAUSE MY STUMBLING INTO HIM HAD STARTED HIM SWINGING...
...AND THERE WERE CLUMPS OF MUD AND LEAF STEMS THAT I CAN STILL TASTE, THAT HAD PEELED OFF HIS SOLES AND LANDED ON MY LIPS.
I REMEMBER LYING FROZEN ON MY BACK, WITH LOCO BARKING ALL AROUND ME...
...AND THEN I STARTED SCRAMBLING LIKE SOME CRAZY, TRAPPED ANIMAL...
...TRYING TO GET AWAY FROM WHAT WAS DANGLING OVERHEAD.
IF I JUST HADN'T TOUCHED IT~
~IF IT HAD JUST BEEN A SCARY PICTURE OF SOMETHING AWFUL IN THE WOODS~
~I MIGHT'VE HAD A SAFE PLACE IN MY MEMORY TO STASH IT.
SOMEPLACE WHERE IT'D STAY PUT AND LEAVE ME ALONE.

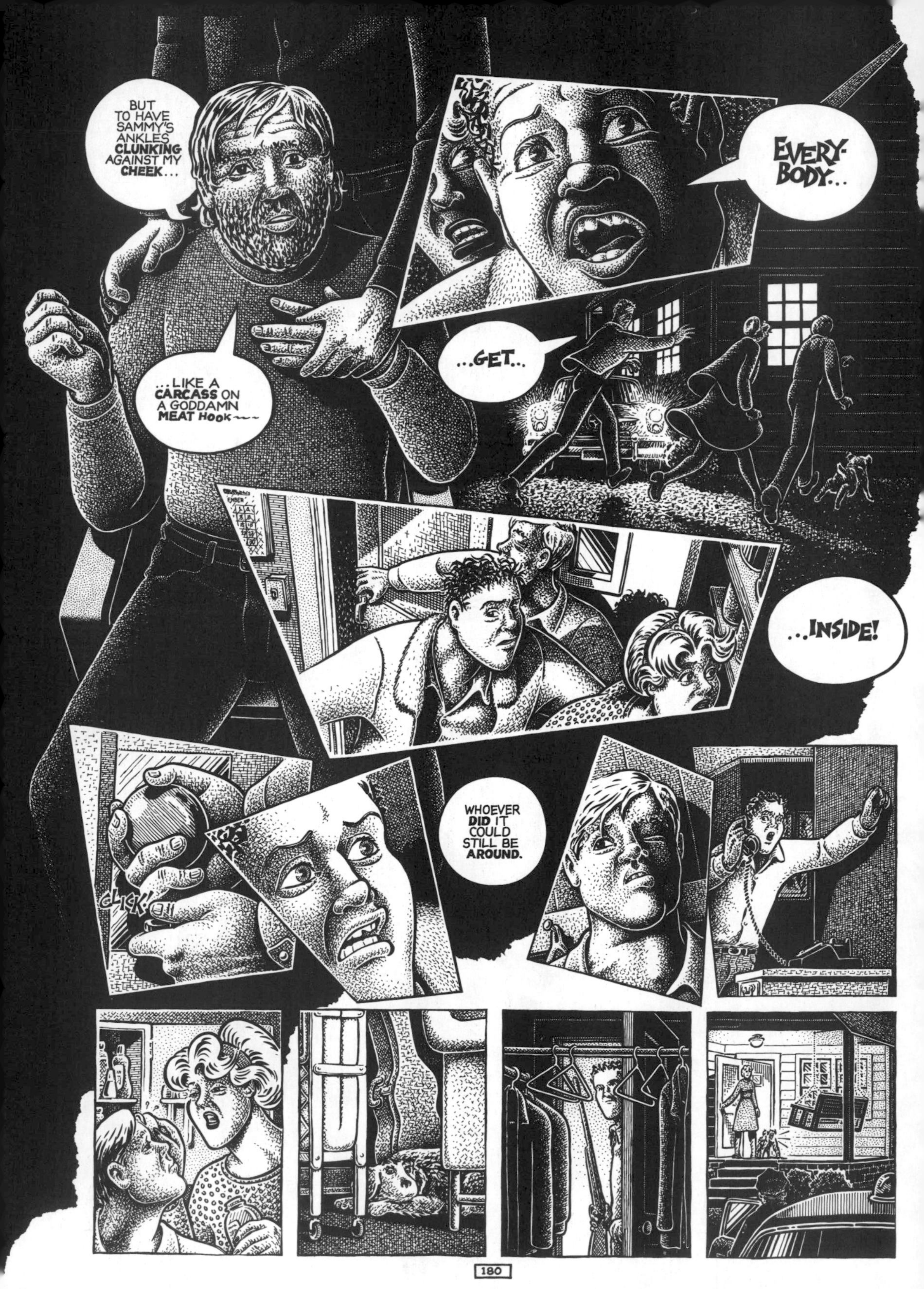
BUT TO HAVE SAMMY'S ANKLES CLUNKING AGAINST MY CHEEK...
EVERY-BODY...
...LIKE A CARCASS ON A GODDAMN MEAT HOOK~~~
...GET...
...INSIDE!
CLICK
WHOEVER DID IT COULD STILL BE AROUND.

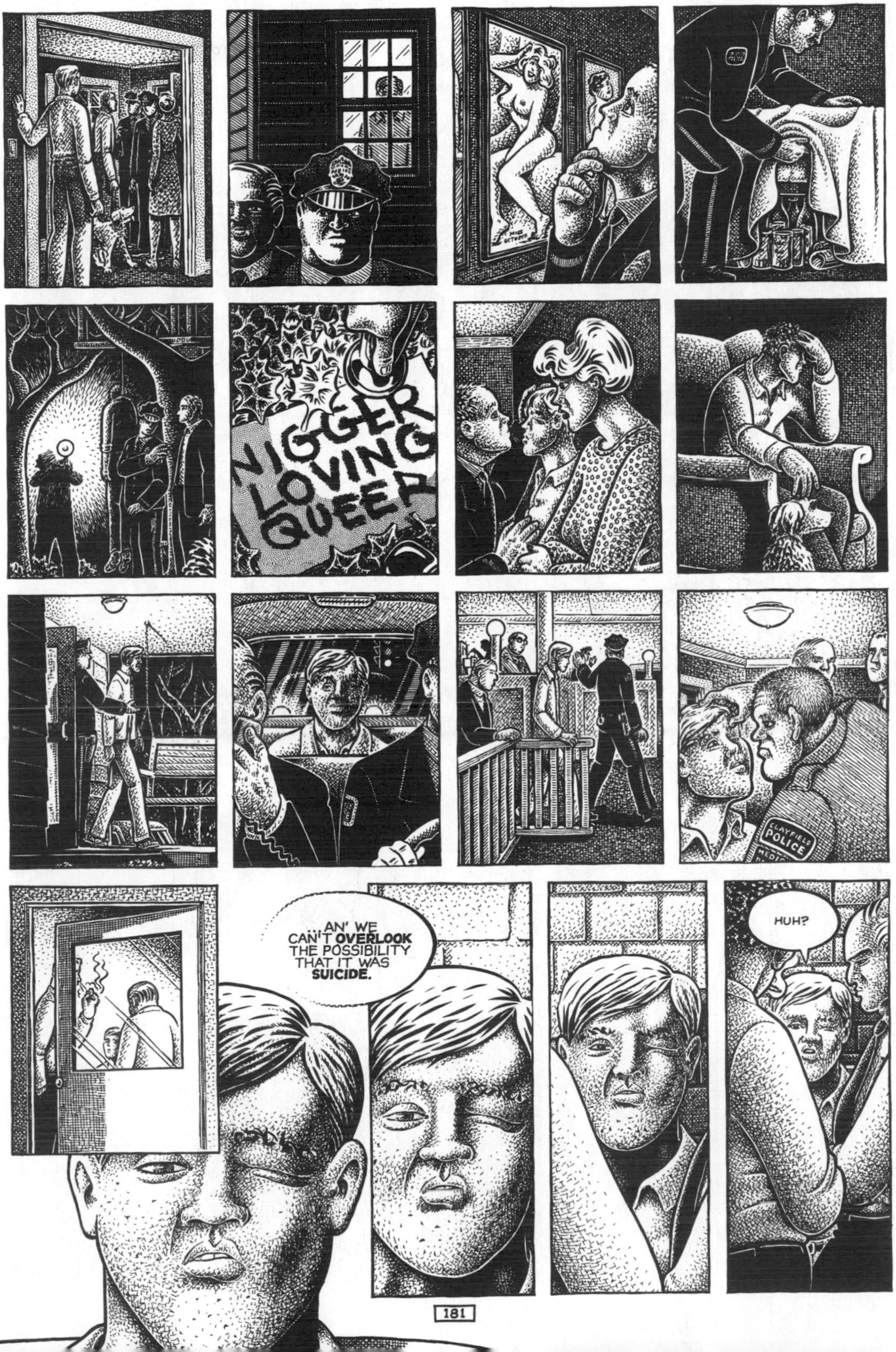
NIGGER
LOVING
QUEER
CLAYFIELD
POLICE
AN' WE CAN'T OVERLOOK THE POSSIBILITY THAT IT WAS SUICIDE.
HUH?

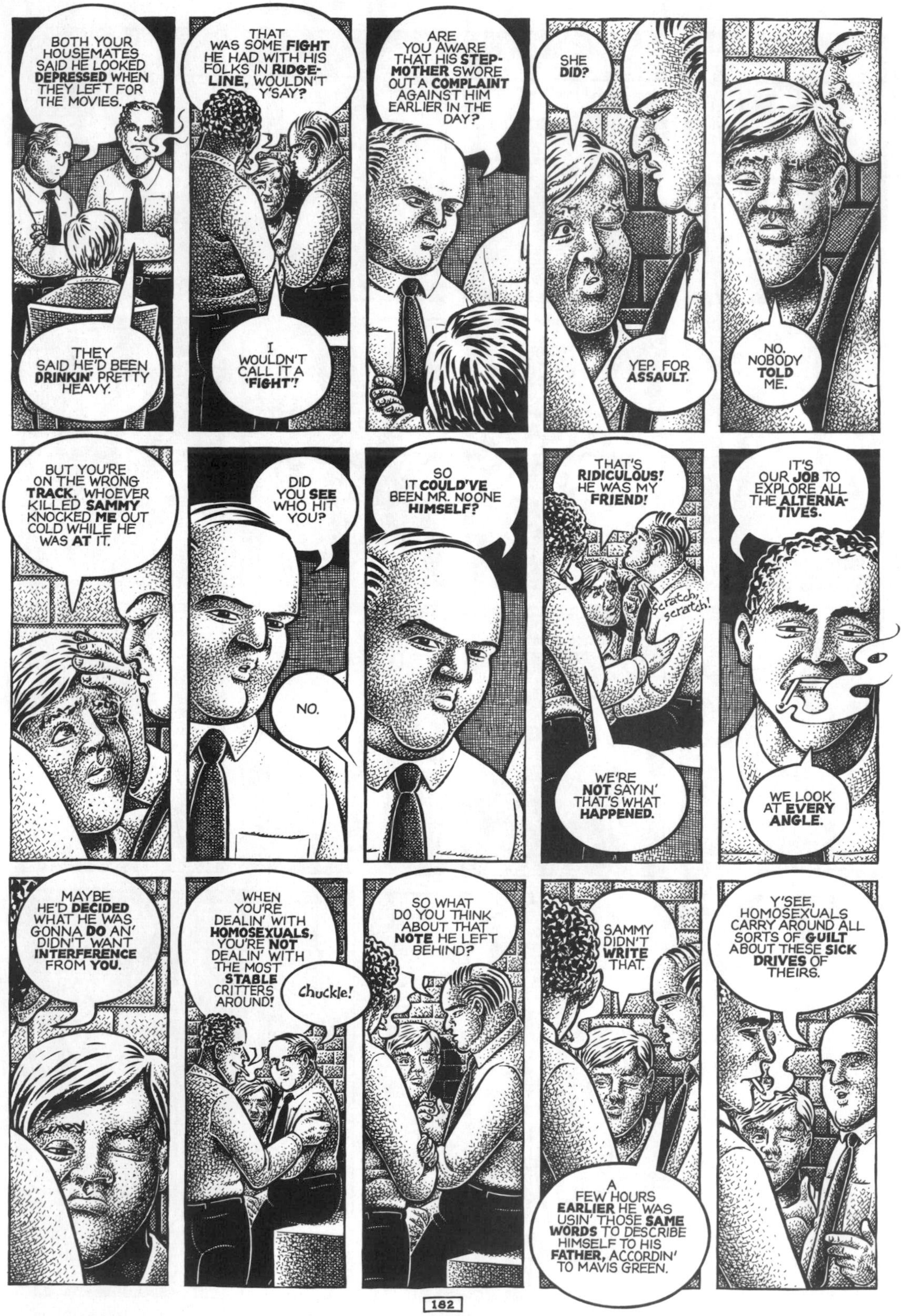
BOTH YOUR HOUSEMATES SAID HE LOOKED DEPRESSED WHEN THEY LEFT FOR THE MOVIES.
THEY SAID HE'D BEEN DRINKIN' PRETTY HEAVY.
THAT WAS SOME FIGHT HE HAD WITH HIS FOLKS IN RIDGE-LINE, WOULDN'T Y'SAY?
I WOULDN'T CALL IT A 'FIGHT'!
ARE YOU AWARE THAT HIS STEP-MOTHER SWORE OUT A COMPLAINT AGAINST HIM EARLIER IN THE DAY?
SHE DID?
YEP. FOR ASSAULT.
NO. NOBODY TOLD ME.
BUT YOU'RE ON THE WRONG TRACK. WHOEVER KILLED SAMMY KNOCKED ME OUT COLD WHILE HE WAS AT IT.
DID YOU SEE WHO HIT YOU?
NO.
SO IT COULD'VE BEEN MR. NOONE HIMSELF?
THAT'S RIDICULOUS! HE WAS MY FRIEND!
Scratch, scratch!
WE'RE NOT SAYIN' THAT'S WHAT HAPPENED.
IT'S OUR JOB TO EXPLORE ALL THE ALTERNA-TIVES.
WE LOOK AT EVERY ANGLE.
MAYBE HE'D DECIDED WHAT HE WAS GONNA DO AN' DIDN'T WANT INTERFERENCE FROM YOU.
WHEN YOU'RE DEALIN' WITH HOMOSEXUALS, YOU'RE NOT DEALIN' WITH THE MOST STABLE CRITTERS AROUND!
Chuckle!
SO WHAT DO YOU THINK ABOUT THAT NOTE HE LEFT BEHIND?
SAMMY DIDN'T WRITE THAT.
A FEW HOURS EARLIER HE WAS USIN' THOSE SAME WORDS TO DESCRIBE HIMSELF TO HIS FATHER, ACCORDIN' TO MAVIS GREEN.
Y'SEE, HOMOSEXUALS CARRY AROUND ALL SORTS OF GUILT ABOUT THESE SICK DRIVES OF THEIRS.

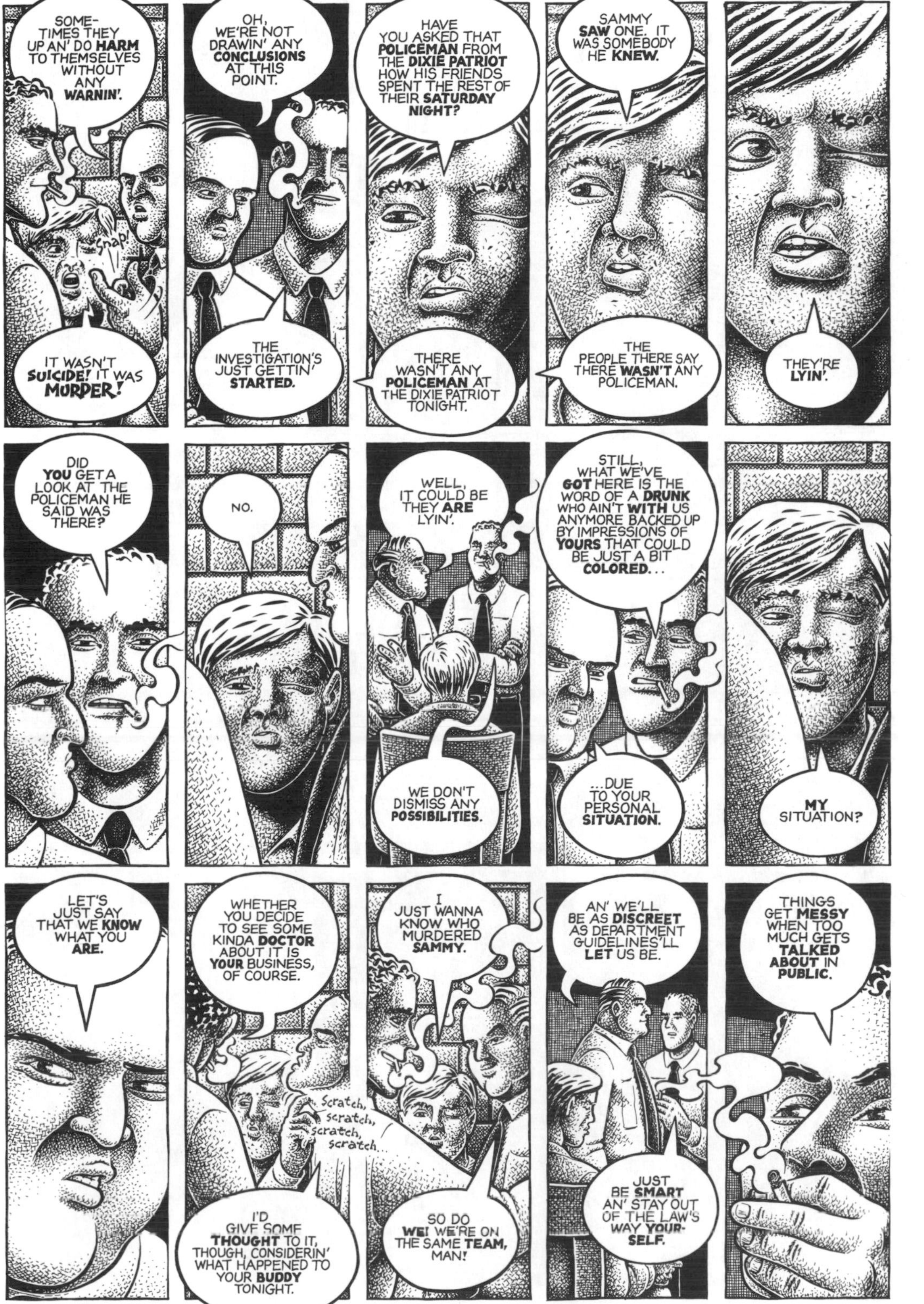
SOME-TIMES THEY UP AN' DO **HARM** TO THEMSELVES WITHOUT ANY **WARNIN'**.
Snap!
IT WASN'T **SUICIDE!** IT WAS **MURDER!**
OH, WE'RE NOT DRAWIN' ANY **CONCLUSIONS** AT THIS POINT.
THE INVESTIGATION'S JUST GETTIN' **STARTED.**
HAVE YOU ASKED THAT **POLICEMAN** FROM THE **DIXIE PATRIOT** HOW HIS FRIENDS SPENT THE REST OF THEIR **SATURDAY NIGHT?**
THERE WASN'T ANY **POLICEMAN** AT THE DIXIE PATRIOT TONIGHT.
SAMMY **SAW** ONE. IT WAS SOMEBODY HE **KNEW.**
THE PEOPLE THERE SAY THERE **WASN'T** ANY POLICEMAN.
THEY'RE **LYIN'**.
DID **YOU** GET A LOOK AT THE POLICEMAN HE SAID WAS THERE?
NO.
WELL, IT COULD BE THEY **ARE** LYIN'.
WE DON'T DISMISS ANY **POSSIBILITIES.**
STILL, WHAT WE'VE **GOT** HERE IS THE WORD OF A **DRUNK** WHO AIN'T **WITH** US ANYMORE BACKED UP BY IMPRESSIONS OF **YOURS** THAT COULD BE JUST A BIT **COLORED**...
...DUE TO YOUR PERSONAL **SITUATION.**
MY SITUATION?
LET'S JUST SAY THAT WE **KNOW** WHAT YOU **ARE.**
WHETHER YOU DECIDE TO SEE SOME KINDA **DOCTOR** ABOUT IT IS **YOUR** BUSINESS, OF COURSE.
Scratch, scratch, scratch, scratch...
I'D GIVE SOME **THOUGHT** TO IT, THOUGH, CONSIDERIN' WHAT HAPPENED TO YOUR **BUDDY** TONIGHT.
I JUST WANNA KNOW WHO MURDERED **SAMMY.**
SO DO **WE!** WE'RE ON THE SAME **TEAM,** MAN!
AN' WE'LL BE AS **DISCREET** AS DEPARTMENT GUIDELINES'LL **LET** US BE.
JUST BE **SMART** AN' STAY OUT OF THE LAW'S WAY **YOUR-SELF.**
THINGS GET **MESSY** WHEN TOO MUCH GETS **TALKED ABOUT** IN **PUBLIC.**

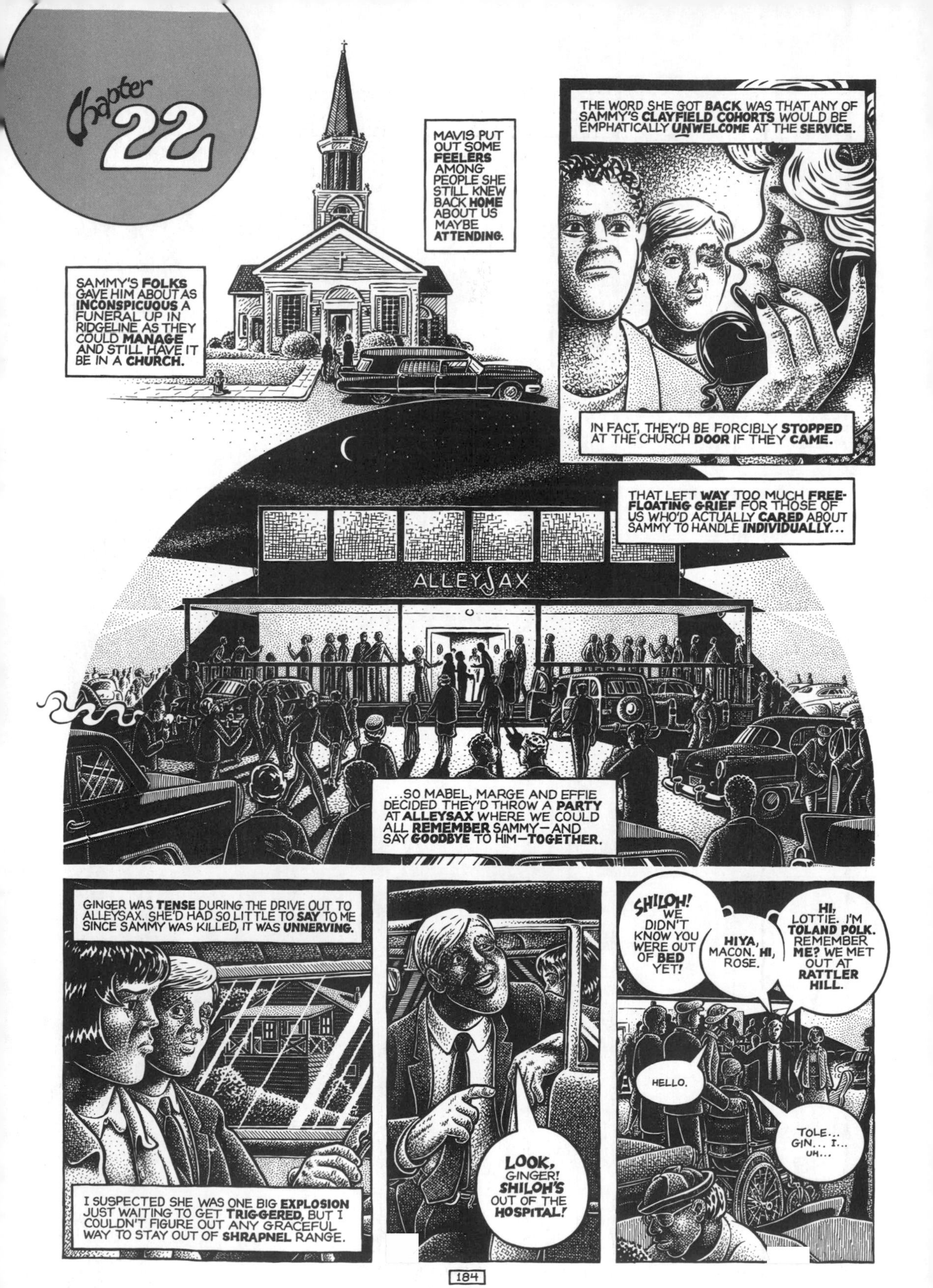
Chapter 22
SAMMY'S FOLKS GAVE HIM ABOUT AS INCONSPICUOUS A FUNERAL UP IN RIDGELINE AS THEY COULD MANAGE AND STILL HAVE IT BE IN A CHURCH.
MAVIS PUT OUT SOME FEELERS AMONG PEOPLE SHE STILL KNEW BACK HOME ABOUT US MAYBE ATTENDING.
THE WORD SHE GOT BACK WAS THAT ANY OF SAMMY'S CLAYFIELD COHORTS WOULD BE EMPHATICALLY UNWELCOME AT THE SERVICE.
IN FACT, THEY'D BE FORCIBLY STOPPED AT THE CHURCH DOOR IF THEY CAME.
THAT LEFT WAY TOO MUCH FREE-FLOATING GRIEF FOR THOSE OF US WHO'D ACTUALLY CARED ABOUT SAMMY TO HANDLE INDIVIDUALLY...
ALLEYSAX
...SO MABEL, MARGE AND EFFIE DECIDED THEY'D THROW A PARTY AT ALLEYSAX WHERE WE COULD ALL REMEMBER SAMMY—AND SAY GOODBYE TO HIM—TOGETHER.
GINGER WAS TENSE DURING THE DRIVE OUT TO ALLEYSAX. SHE'D HAD SO LITTLE TO SAY TO ME SINCE SAMMY WAS KILLED, IT WAS UNNERVING.
I SUSPECTED SHE WAS ONE BIG EXPLOSION JUST WAITING TO GET TRIGGERED, BUT I COULDN'T FIGURE OUT ANY GRACEFUL WAY TO STAY OUT OF SHRAPNEL RANGE.
LOOK, GINGER! SHILOH'S OUT OF THE HOSPITAL!
SHILOH! WE DIDN'T KNOW YOU WERE OUT OF BED YET!
HIYA, MACON. HI, ROSE.
HI, LOTTIE. I'M TOLAND POLK. REMEMBER ME? WE MET OUT AT RATTLER HILL.
HELLO.
TOLE... GIN... I... UH...

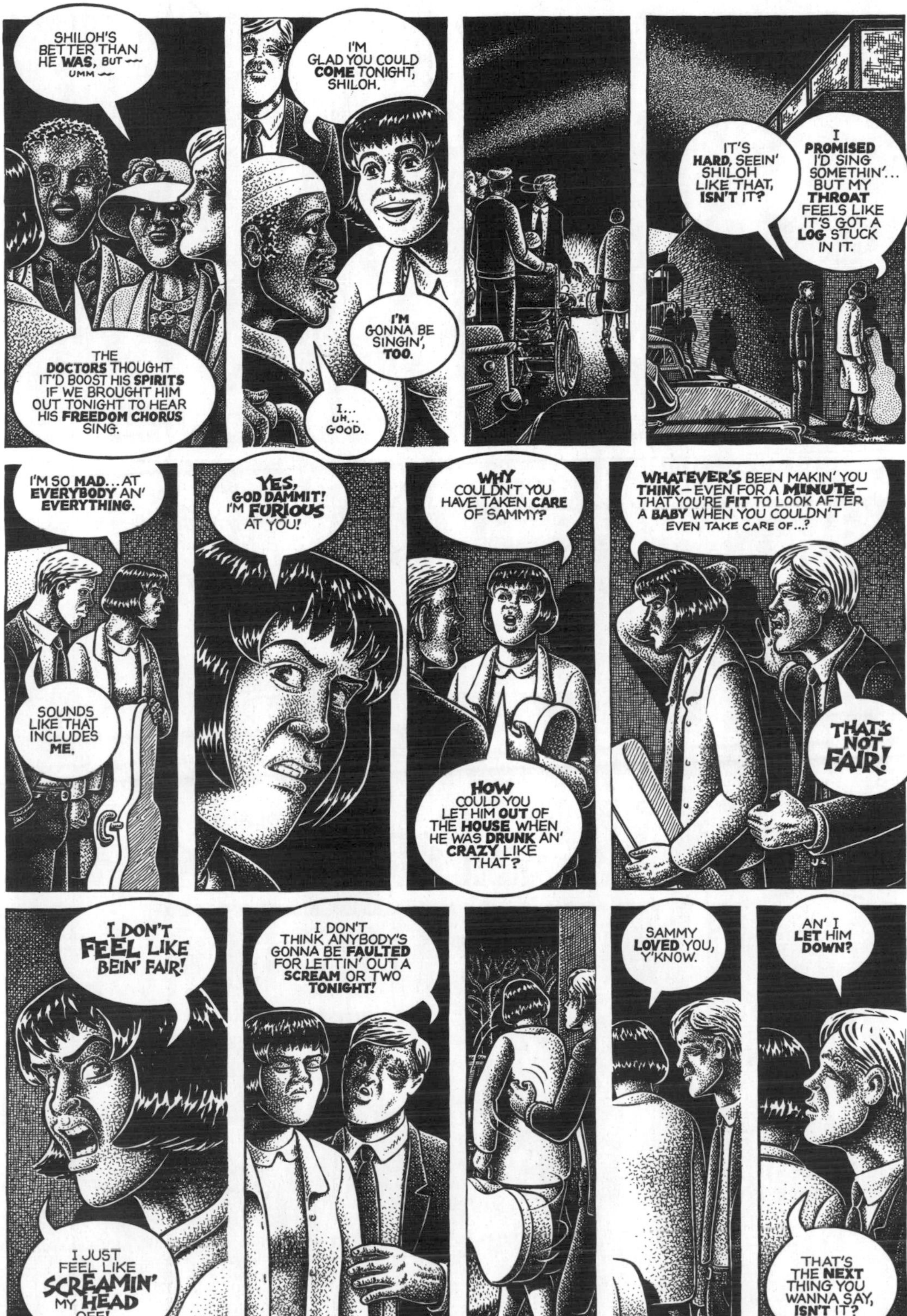
SHILOH'S BETTER THAN HE WAS, BUT — UMM —
THE DOCTORS THOUGHT IT'D BOOST HIS SPIRITS IF WE BROUGHT HIM OUT TONIGHT TO HEAR HIS FREEDOM CHORUS SING.
I'M GLAD YOU COULD COME TONIGHT, SHILOH.
I'M GONNA BE SINGIN', TOO.
I... UH... GOOD.
IT'S HARD, SEEIN' SHILOH LIKE THAT, ISN'T IT?
I PROMISED I'D SING SOMETHIN'... BUT MY THROAT FEELS LIKE IT'S GOT A LOG STUCK IN IT.
I'M SO MAD... AT EVERYBODY AN' EVERYTHING.
SOUNDS LIKE THAT INCLUDES ME.
YES, GOD DAMMIT! I'M FURIOUS AT YOU!
WHY COULDN'T YOU HAVE TAKEN CARE OF SAMMY?
HOW COULD YOU LET HIM OUT OF THE HOUSE WHEN HE WAS DRUNK AN' CRAZY LIKE THAT?
WHATEVER'S BEEN MAKIN' YOU THINK — EVEN FOR A MINUTE — THAT YOU'RE FIT TO LOOK AFTER A BABY WHEN YOU COULDN'T EVEN TAKE CARE OF...?
THAT'S NOT FAIR!
I DON'T FEEL LIKE BEIN' FAIR!
I JUST FEEL LIKE SCREAMIN' MY HEAD OFF!
I DON'T THINK ANYBODY'S GONNA BE FAULTED FOR LETTIN' OUT A SCREAM OR TWO TONIGHT!
SAMMY LOVED YOU, Y'KNOW.
AN' I LET HIM DOWN?
THAT'S THE NEXT THING YOU WANNA SAY, ISN'T IT?

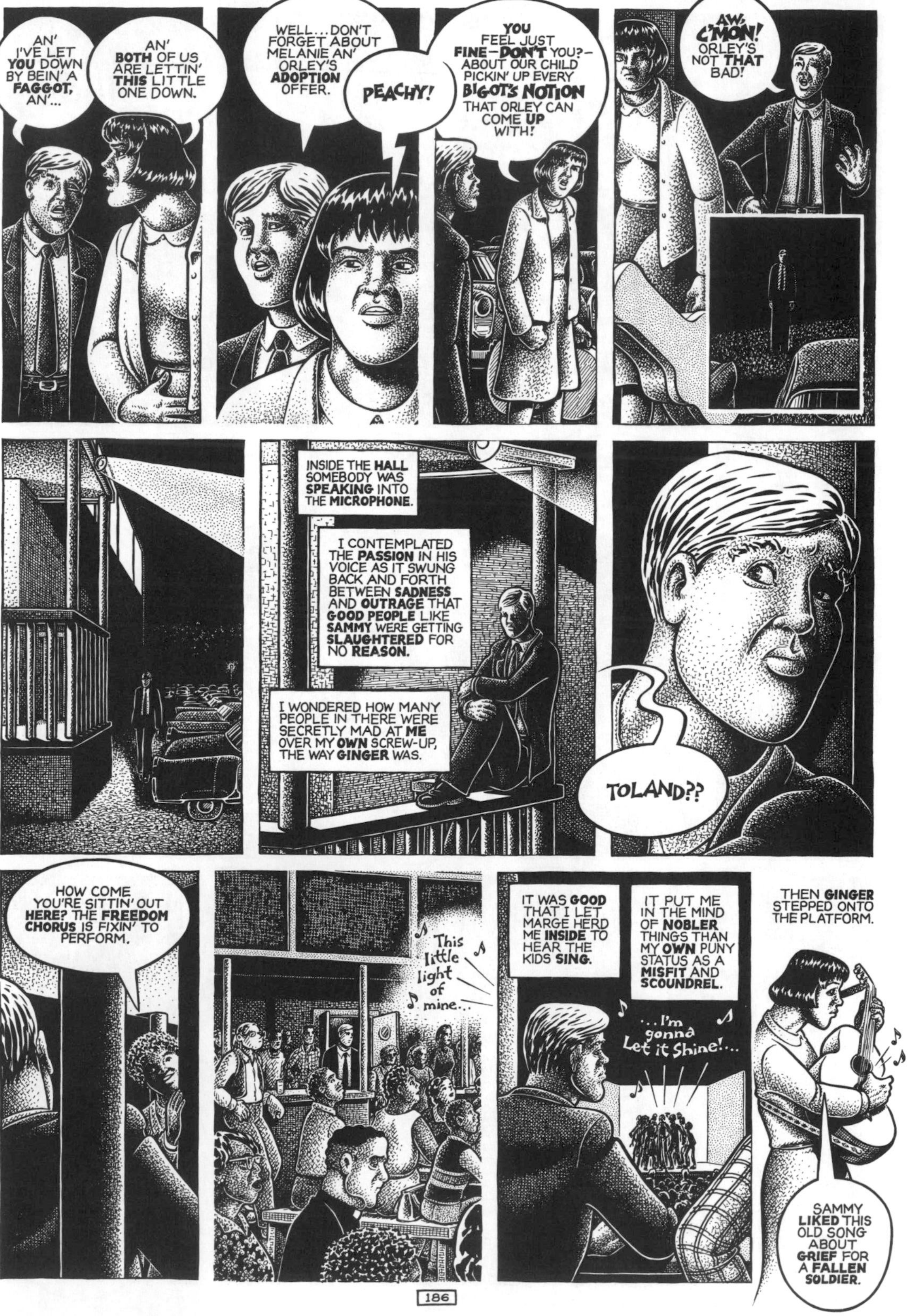

AN' I'VE LET YOU DOWN BY BEIN' A FAGGOT, AN'...
AN' BOTH OF US ARE LETTIN' THIS LITTLE ONE DOWN.
WELL... DON'T FORGET ABOUT MELANIE AN' ORLEY'S ADOPTION OFFER.
PEACHY!
YOU FEEL JUST FINE—DON'T YOU?— ABOUT OUR CHILD PICKIN' UP EVERY BIGOT'S NOTION THAT ORLEY CAN COME UP WITH!
AW, C'MON! ORLEY'S NOT THAT BAD!
INSIDE THE HALL SOMEBODY WAS SPEAKING INTO THE MICROPHONE.
I CONTEMPLATED THE PASSION IN HIS VOICE AS IT SWUNG BACK AND FORTH BETWEEN SADNESS AND OUTRAGE THAT GOOD PEOPLE LIKE SAMMY WERE GETTING SLAUGHTERED FOR NO REASON.
I WONDERED HOW MANY PEOPLE IN THERE WERE SECRETLY MAD AT ME OVER MY OWN SCREW-UP, THE WAY GINGER WAS.
TOLAND??
HOW COME YOU'RE SITTIN' OUT HERE? THE FREEDOM CHORUS IS FIXIN' TO PERFORM.
This little light of mine...
IT WAS GOOD THAT I LET MARGE HERD ME INSIDE TO HEAR THE KIDS SING.
IT PUT ME IN THE MIND OF NOBLER THINGS THAN MY OWN PUNY STATUS AS A MISFIT AND SCOUNDREL.
...I'm gonna Let it Shine!...
THEN GINGER STEPPED ONTO THE PLATFORM.
SAMMY LIKED THIS OLD SONG ABOUT GRIEF FOR A FALLEN SOLDIER.

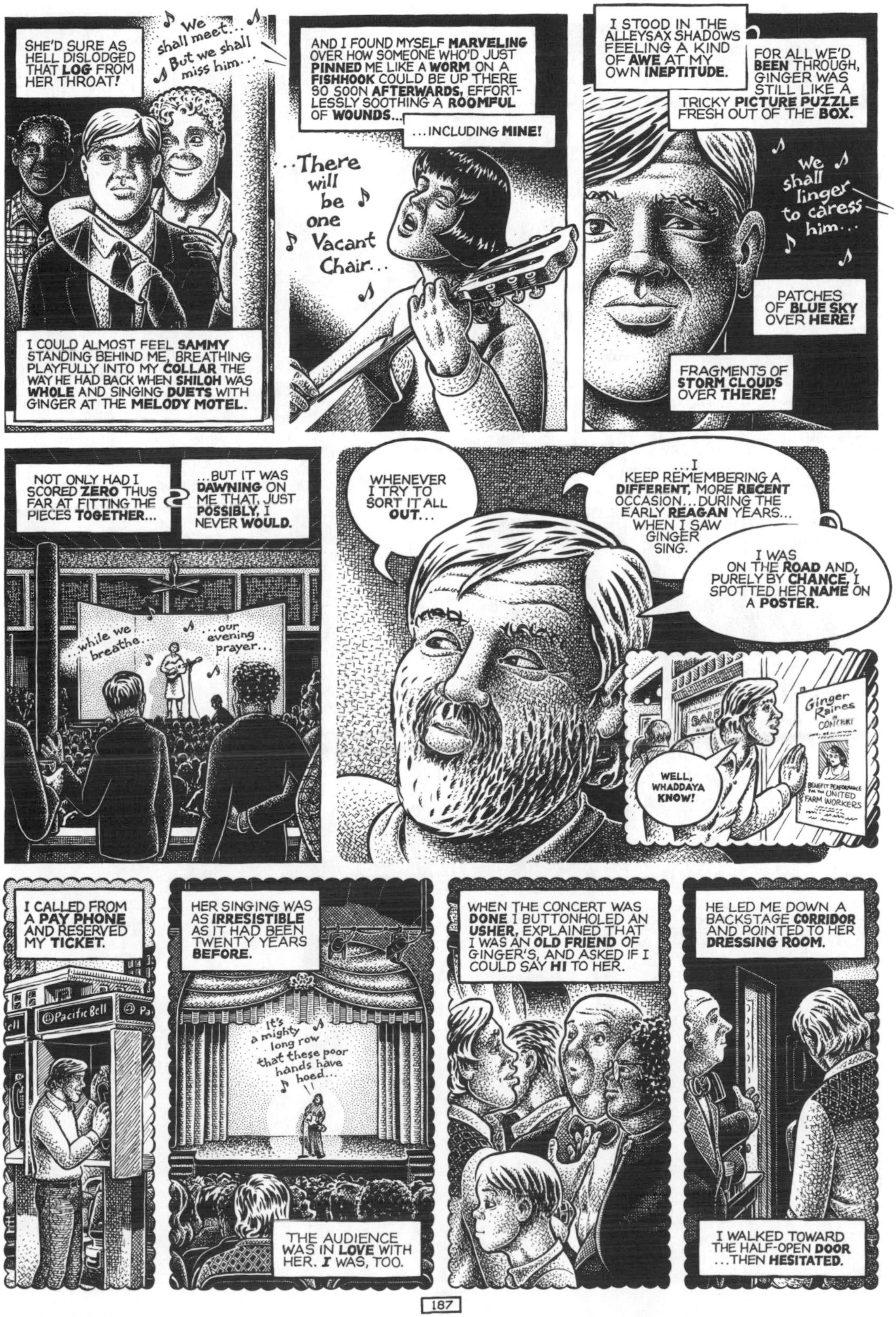

SHE'D SURE AS HELL DISLODGED THAT LOG FROM HER THROAT!
We shall meet... But we shall miss him...
I COULD ALMOST FEEL SAMMY STANDING BEHIND ME, BREATHING PLAYFULLY INTO MY COLLAR THE WAY HE HAD BACK WHEN SHILOH WAS WHOLE AND SINGING DUETS WITH GINGER AT THE MELODY MOTEL.
AND I FOUND MYSELF MARVELING OVER HOW SOMEONE WHO'D JUST PINNED ME LIKE A WORM ON A FISHHOOK COULD BE UP THERE SO SOON AFTERWARDS, EFFORTLESSLY SOOTHING A ROOMFUL OF WOUNDS...
...INCLUDING MINE!
...There will be one Vacant Chair...
I STOOD IN THE ALLEYSAX SHADOWS FEELING A KIND OF AWE AT MY OWN INEPTITUDE.
FOR ALL WE'D BEEN THROUGH, GINGER WAS STILL LIKE A TRICKY PICTURE PUZZLE FRESH OUT OF THE BOX.
We shall linger to caress him...
PATCHES OF BLUE SKY OVER HERE!
FRAGMENTS OF STORM CLOUDS OVER THERE!
NOT ONLY HAD I SCORED ZERO THUS FAR AT FITTING THE PIECES TOGETHER...
...BUT IT WAS DAWNING ON ME THAT, JUST POSSIBLY, I NEVER WOULD.
...while we breathe...
...our evening prayer...
WHENEVER I TRY TO SORT IT ALL OUT...
...I KEEP REMEMBERING A DIFFERENT, MORE RECENT OCCASION... DURING THE EARLY REAGAN YEARS... WHEN I SAW GINGER SING.
I WAS ON THE ROAD AND, PURELY BY CHANCE, I SPOTTED HER NAME ON A POSTER.
WELL, WHADDAYA KNOW!
Ginger Raines in CONCERT
BENEFIT PERFORMANCE FOR THE UNITED FARM WORKERS
I CALLED FROM A PAY PHONE AND RESERVED MY TICKET.
Pacific Bell
HER SINGING WAS AS IRRESISTIBLE AS IT HAD BEEN TWENTY YEARS BEFORE.
It's a mighty long row that these poor hands have hoed...
THE AUDIENCE WAS IN LOVE WITH HER. I WAS, TOO.
WHEN THE CONCERT WAS DONE I BUTTONHOLED AN USHER, EXPLAINED THAT I WAS AN OLD FRIEND OF GINGER'S, AND ASKED IF I COULD SAY HI TO HER.
HE LED ME DOWN A BACKSTAGE CORRIDOR AND POINTED TO HER DRESSING ROOM.
I WALKED TOWARD THE HALF-OPEN DOOR ...THEN HESITATED.

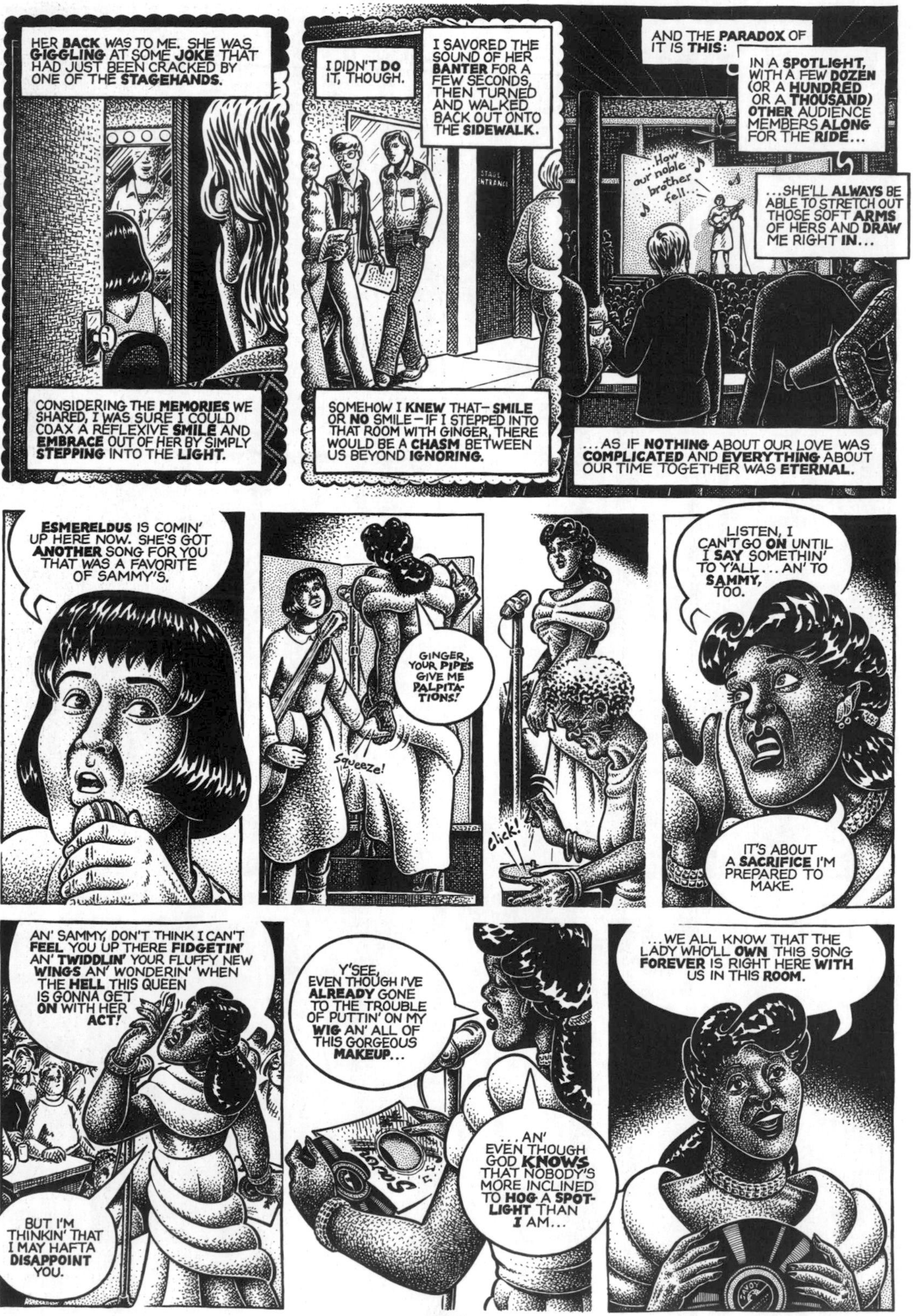

HER BACK WAS TO ME. SHE WAS GIGGLING AT SOME JOKE THAT HAD JUST BEEN CRACKED BY ONE OF THE STAGEHANDS.
CONSIDERING THE MEMORIES WE SHARED, I WAS SURE I COULD COAX A REFLEXIVE SMILE AND EMBRACE OUT OF HER BY SIMPLY STEPPING INTO THE LIGHT.
I DIDN'T DO IT, THOUGH.
I SAVORED THE SOUND OF HER BANTER FOR A FEW SECONDS, THEN TURNED AND WALKED BACK OUT ONTO THE SIDEWALK.
STAGE ENTRANCE
SOMEHOW I KNEW THAT– SMILE OR NO SMILE – IF I STEPPED INTO THAT ROOM WITH GINGER, THERE WOULD BE A CHASM BETWEEN US BEYOND IGNORING.
AND THE PARADOX OF IT IS THIS:
IN A SPOTLIGHT, WITH A FEW DOZEN (OR A HUNDRED OR A THOUSAND) OTHER AUDIENCE MEMBERS ALONG FOR THE RIDE...
...How our noble brother fell...
...SHE'LL ALWAYS BE ABLE TO STRETCH OUT THOSE SOFT ARMS OF HERS AND DRAW ME RIGHT IN...
...AS IF NOTHING ABOUT OUR LOVE WAS COMPLICATED AND EVERYTHING ABOUT OUR TIME TOGETHER WAS ETERNAL.
ESMERELDUS IS COMIN' UP HERE NOW. SHE'S GOT ANOTHER SONG FOR YOU THAT WAS A FAVORITE OF SAMMY'S.
GINGER, YOUR PIPES GIVE ME PALPITATIONS!
Squeeze!
Click!
LISTEN, I CAN'T GO ON UNTIL I SAY SOMETHIN' TO Y'ALL... AN' TO SAMMY, TOO.
IT'S ABOUT A SACRIFICE I'M PREPARED TO MAKE.
AN' SAMMY, DON'T THINK I CAN'T FEEL YOU UP THERE FIDGETIN' AN' TWIDDLIN' YOUR FLUFFY NEW WINGS AN' WONDERIN' WHEN THE HELL THIS QUEEN IS GONNA GET ON WITH HER ACT!
BUT I'M THINKIN' THAT I MAY HAFTA DISAPPOINT YOU.
Y'SEE, EVEN THOUGH I'VE ALREADY GONE TO THE TROUBLE OF PUTTIN' ON MY WIG AN' ALL OF THIS GORGEOUS MAKEUP...
...AN' EVEN THOUGH GOD KNOWS THAT NOBODY'S MORE INCLINED TO HOG A SPOTLIGHT THAN I AM...
...WE ALL KNOW THAT THE LADY WHO'LL OWN THIS SONG FOREVER IS RIGHT HERE WITH US IN THIS ROOM.
SAVOY

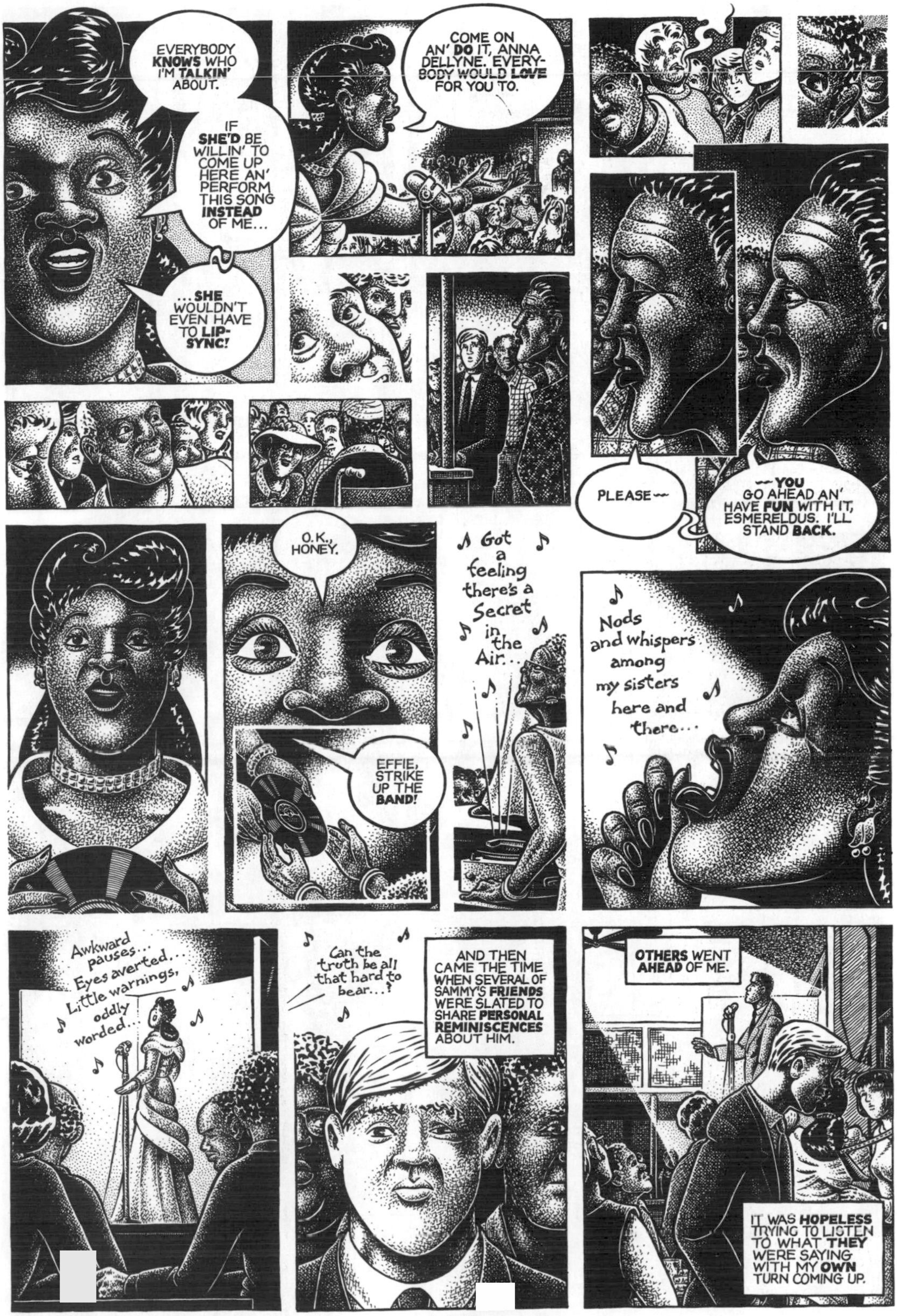
EVERYBODY KNOWS WHO I'M TALKIN' ABOUT.
IF SHE'D BE WILLIN' TO COME UP HERE AN' PERFORM THIS SONG INSTEAD OF ME...
...SHE WOULDN'T EVEN HAVE TO LIP-SYNC!
COME ON AN' DO IT, ANNA DELLYNE. EVERY-BODY WOULD LOVE FOR YOU TO.
PLEASE--
--YOU GO AHEAD AN' HAVE FUN WITH IT, ESMERELDUS. I'LL STAND BACK.
O.K., HONEY.
EFFIE, STRIKE UP THE BAND!
Got a feeling there's a Secret in the Air...
Nods and whispers among my sisters here and there...
Awkward pauses... Eyes averted... Little warnings, oddly worded...
Can the truth be all that hard to bear...?
AND THEN CAME THE TIME WHEN SEVERAL OF SAMMY'S FRIENDS WERE SLATED TO SHARE PERSONAL REMINISCENCES ABOUT HIM.
OTHERS WENT AHEAD OF ME.
IT WAS HOPELESS TRYING TO LISTEN TO WHAT THEY WERE SAYING WITH MY OWN TURN COMING UP.

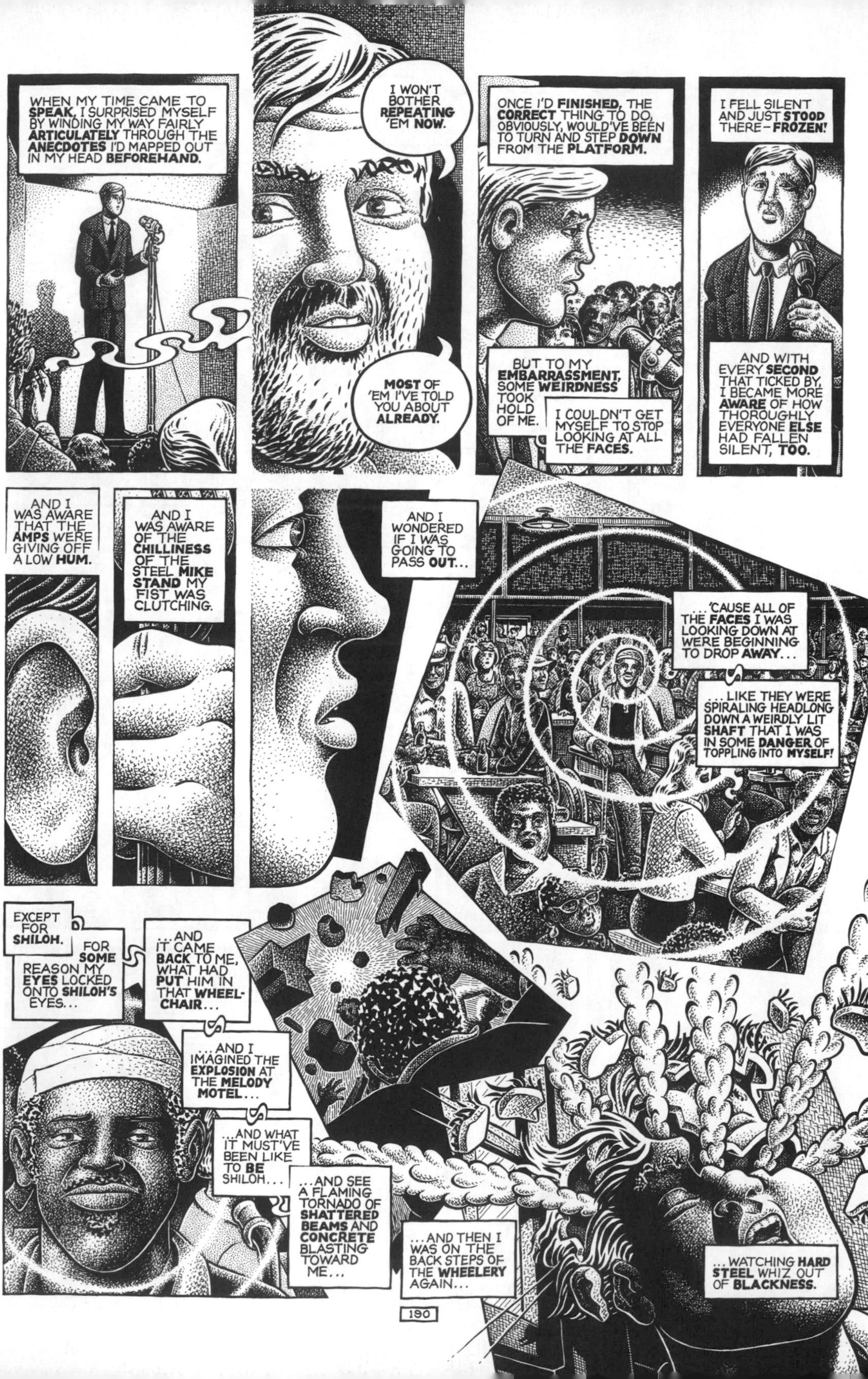

WHEN MY TIME CAME TO SPEAK, I SURPRISED MYSELF BY WINDING MY WAY FAIRLY ARTICULATELY THROUGH THE ANECDOTES I'D MAPPED OUT IN MY HEAD BEFOREHAND.
I WON'T BOTHER REPEATING 'EM NOW.
MOST OF 'EM I'VE TOLD YOU ABOUT ALREADY.
ONCE I'D FINISHED, THE CORRECT THING TO DO, OBVIOUSLY, WOULD'VE BEEN TO TURN AND STEP DOWN FROM THE PLATFORM.
BUT TO MY EMBARRASSMENT, SOME WEIRDNESS TOOK HOLD OF ME.
I COULDN'T GET MYSELF TO STOP LOOKING AT ALL THE FACES.
I FELL SILENT AND JUST STOOD THERE–FROZEN!
AND WITH EVERY SECOND THAT TICKED BY, I BECAME MORE AWARE OF HOW THOROUGHLY EVERYONE ELSE HAD FALLEN SILENT, TOO.
AND I WAS AWARE THAT THE AMPS WERE GIVING OFF A LOW HUM.
AND I WAS AWARE OF THE CHILLINESS OF THE STEEL MIKE STAND MY FIST WAS CLUTCHING.
AND I WONDERED IF I WAS GOING TO PASS OUT...
...'CAUSE ALL OF THE FACES I WAS LOOKING DOWN AT WERE BEGINNING TO DROP AWAY...
...LIKE THEY WERE SPIRALING HEADLONG DOWN A WEIRDLY LIT SHAFT THAT I WAS IN SOME DANGER OF TOPPLING INTO MYSELF!
EXCEPT FOR SHILOH.
FOR SOME REASON MY EYES LOCKED ONTO SHILOH'S EYES...
...AND IT CAME BACK TO ME, WHAT HAD PUT HIM IN THAT WHEEL-CHAIR...
...AND I IMAGINED THE EXPLOSION AT THE MELODY MOTEL...
...AND WHAT IT MUST'VE BEEN LIKE TO BE SHILOH...
...AND SEE A FLAMING TORNADO OF SHATTERED BEAMS AND CONCRETE BLASTING TOWARD ME...
...AND THEN I WAS ON THE BACK STEPS OF THE WHEELERY AGAIN...
...WATCHING HARD STEEL WHIZ OUT OF BLACKNESS.

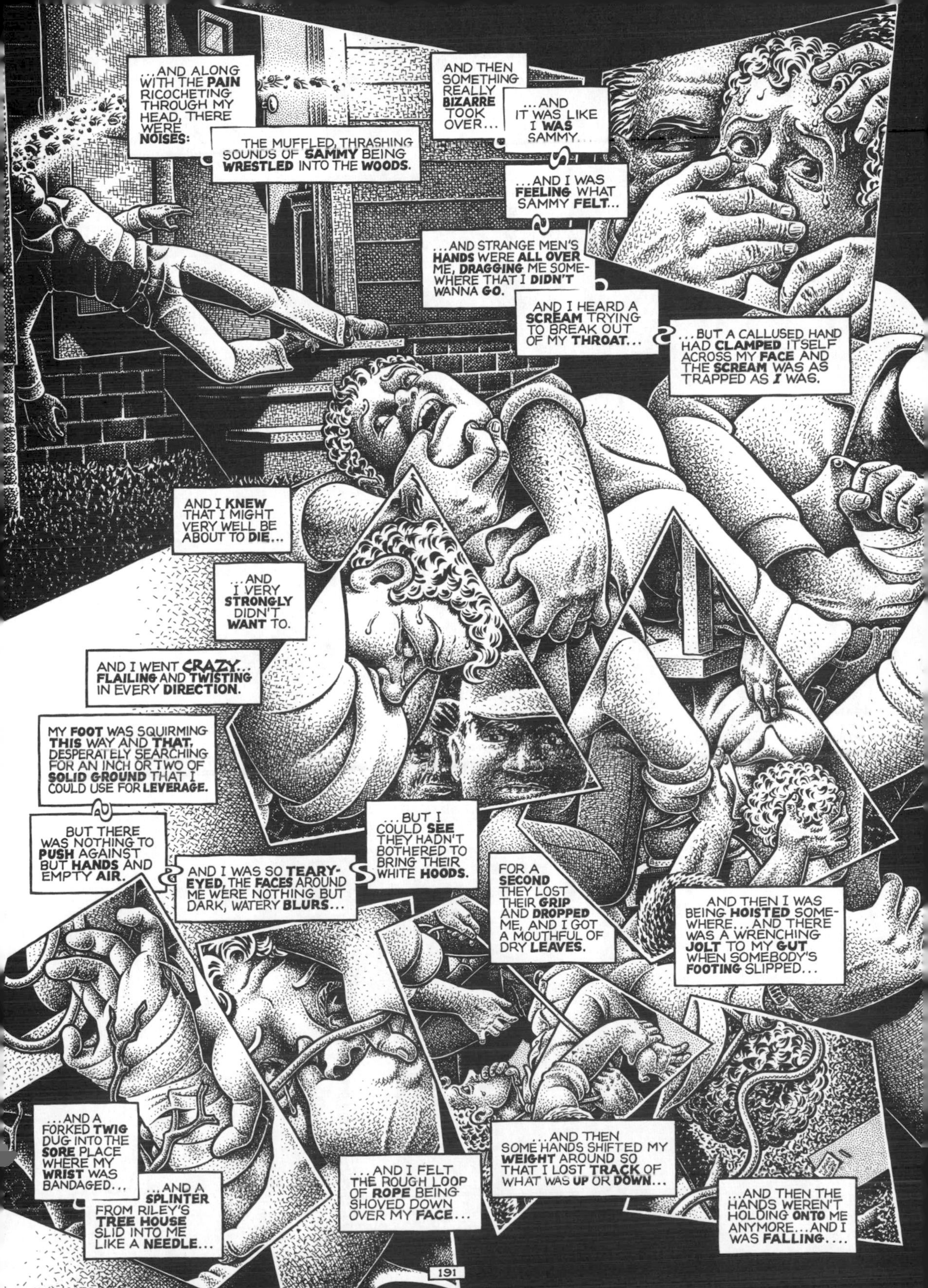
...AND ALONG WITH THE PAIN RICOCHETING THROUGH MY HEAD, THERE WERE NOISES:
THE MUFFLED, THRASHING SOUNDS OF SAMMY BEING WRESTLED INTO THE WOODS.
AND THEN SOMETHING REALLY BIZARRE TOOK OVER...
...AND IT WAS LIKE I WAS SAMMY...
...AND I WAS FEELING WHAT SAMMY FELT...
...AND STRANGE MEN'S HANDS WERE ALL OVER ME, DRAGGING ME SOMEWHERE THAT I DIDN'T WANNA GO.
AND I HEARD A SCREAM TRYING TO BREAK OUT OF MY THROAT...
...BUT A CALLUSED HAND HAD CLAMPED ITSELF ACROSS MY FACE AND THE SCREAM WAS AS TRAPPED AS I WAS.
AND I KNEW THAT I MIGHT VERY WELL BE ABOUT TO DIE...
...AND I VERY STRONGLY DIDN'T WANT TO.
AND I WENT CRAZY... FLAILING AND TWISTING IN EVERY DIRECTION.
MY FOOT WAS SQUIRMING THIS WAY AND THAT, DESPERATELY SEARCHING FOR AN INCH OR TWO OF SOLID GROUND THAT I COULD USE FOR LEVERAGE.
BUT THERE WAS NOTHING TO PUSH AGAINST BUT HANDS AND EMPTY AIR.
AND I WAS SO TEARY-EYED, THE FACES AROUND ME WERE NOTHING BUT DARK, WATERY BLURS...
...BUT I COULD SEE THEY HADN'T BOTHERED TO BRING THEIR WHITE HOODS.
FOR A SECOND THEY LOST THEIR GRIP AND DROPPED ME, AND I GOT A MOUTHFUL OF DRY LEAVES.
AND THEN I WAS BEING HOISTED SOMEWHERE... AND THERE WAS A WRENCHING JOLT TO MY GUT WHEN SOMEBODY'S FOOTING SLIPPED...
...AND A FORKED TWIG DUG INTO THE SORE PLACE WHERE MY WRIST WAS BANDAGED...
...AND A SPLINTER FROM RILEY'S TREE HOUSE SLID INTO ME LIKE A NEEDLE...
...AND I FELT THE ROUGH LOOP OF ROPE BEING SHOVED DOWN OVER MY FACE...
...AND THEN SOME HANDS SHIFTED MY WEIGHT AROUND SO THAT I LOST TRACK OF WHAT WAS UP OR DOWN...
...AND THEN THE HANDS WEREN'T HOLDING ONTO ME ANYMORE... AND I WAS FALLING....

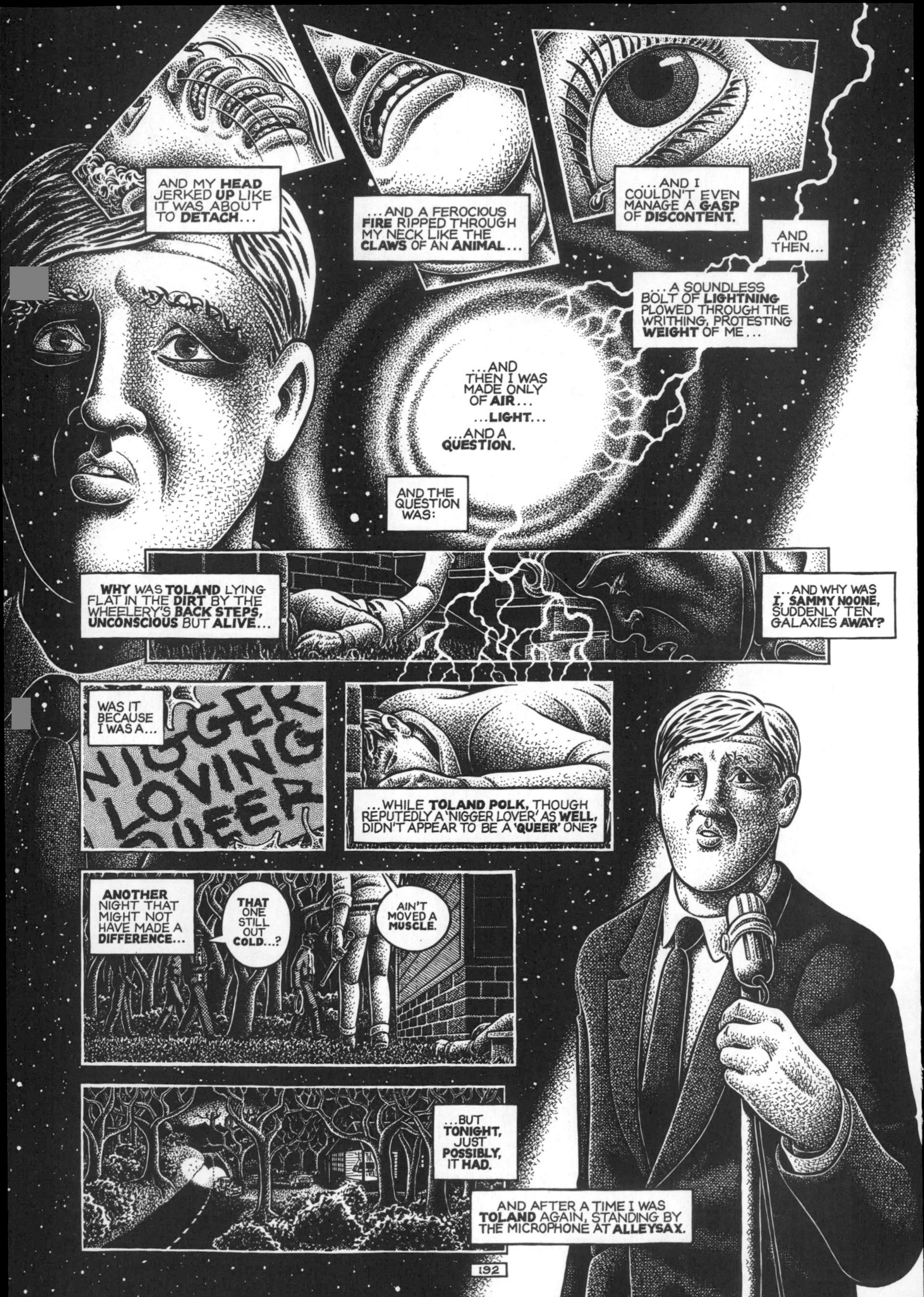
AND MY **HEAD** JERKED **UP** LIKE IT WAS ABOUT TO **DETACH**...
...AND A FEROCIOUS **FIRE** RIPPED THROUGH MY NECK LIKE THE **CLAWS** OF AN **ANIMAL**...
...AND I COULDN'T EVEN MANAGE A **GASP** OF **DISCONTENT**.
AND THEN...
...A SOUNDLESS BOLT OF **LIGHTNING** PLOWED THROUGH THE WRITHING, PROTESTING **WEIGHT** OF ME...
...AND THEN I WAS MADE ONLY OF **AIR**...
...**LIGHT**...
...AND A **QUESTION**.
AND THE QUESTION WAS:
WHY WAS **TOLAND** LYING FLAT IN THE **DIRT** BY THE WHEELERY'S **BACK STEPS**, **UNCONSCIOUS** BUT **ALIVE**...
...AND WHY WAS ***I*, SAMMY NOONE**, SUDDENLY TEN GALAXIES **AWAY**?
WAS IT BECAUSE I WAS A...
NIGGER
LOVING
...WHILE **TOLAND POLK**, THOUGH REPUTEDLY A 'NIGGER LOVER' AS **WELL**, DIDN'T APPEAR TO BE A '**QUEER**' ONE?
ANOTHER NIGHT THAT MIGHT NOT HAVE MADE A **DIFFERENCE**...
THAT ONE STILL OUT **COLD**...?
AIN'T MOVED A **MUSCLE**.
...BUT **TONIGHT**, JUST **POSSIBLY**, IT **HAD**.
AND AFTER A TIME I WAS **TOLAND** AGAIN, STANDING BY THE MICROPHONE AT **ALLEYSAX**.

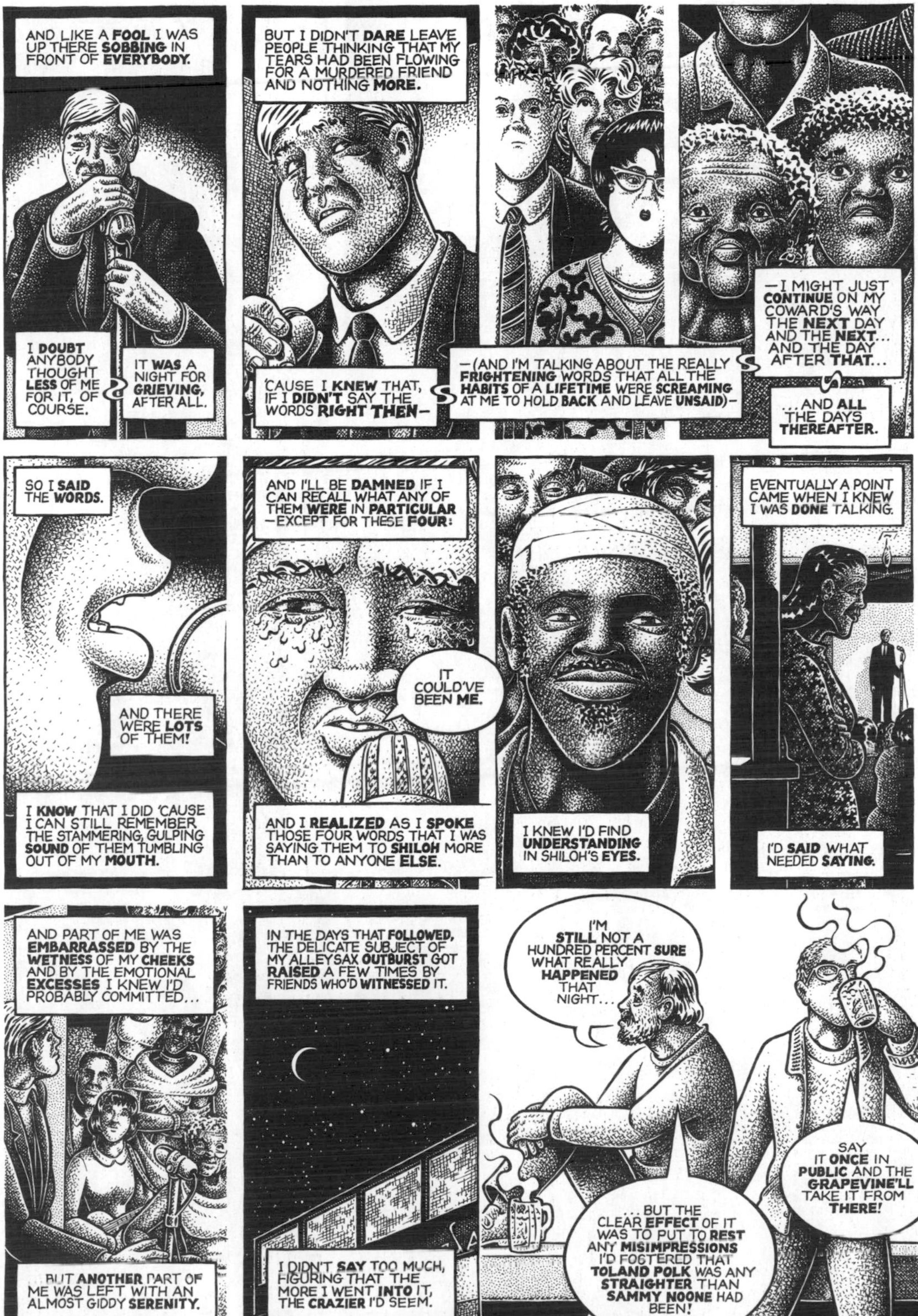

AND LIKE A FOOL I WAS UP THERE SOBBING IN FRONT OF EVERYBODY.
I DOUBT ANYBODY THOUGHT LESS OF ME FOR IT, OF COURSE.
IT WAS A NIGHT FOR GRIEVING, AFTER ALL.
BUT I DIDN'T DARE LEAVE PEOPLE THINKING THAT MY TEARS HAD BEEN FLOWING FOR A MURDERED FRIEND AND NOTHING MORE.
'CAUSE I KNEW THAT, IF I DIDN'T SAY THE WORDS RIGHT THEN—
—(AND I'M TALKING ABOUT THE REALLY FRIGHTENING WORDS THAT ALL THE HABITS OF A LIFETIME WERE SCREAMING AT ME TO HOLD BACK AND LEAVE UNSAID)—
—I MIGHT JUST CONTINUE ON MY COWARD'S WAY THE NEXT DAY AND THE NEXT... AND THE DAY AFTER THAT...
...AND ALL THE DAYS THEREAFTER.
SO I SAID THE WORDS.
AND THERE WERE LOTS OF THEM!
I KNOW THAT I DID 'CAUSE I CAN STILL REMEMBER THE STAMMERING, GULPING SOUND OF THEM TUMBLING OUT OF MY MOUTH.
AND I'LL BE DAMNED IF I CAN RECALL WHAT ANY OF THEM WERE IN PARTICULAR —EXCEPT FOR THESE FOUR:
IT COULD'VE BEEN ME.
AND I REALIZED AS I SPOKE THOSE FOUR WORDS THAT I WAS SAYING THEM TO SHILOH MORE THAN TO ANYONE ELSE.
I KNEW I'D FIND UNDERSTANDING IN SHILOH'S EYES.
EVENTUALLY A POINT CAME WHEN I KNEW I WAS DONE TALKING.
I'D SAID WHAT NEEDED SAYING.
AND PART OF ME WAS EMBARRASSED BY THE WETNESS OF MY CHEEKS AND BY THE EMOTIONAL EXCESSES I KNEW I'D PROBABLY COMMITTED...
...BUT ANOTHER PART OF ME WAS LEFT WITH AN ALMOST GIDDY SERENITY.
IN THE DAYS THAT FOLLOWED, THE DELICATE SUBJECT OF MY ALLEYSAX OUTBURST GOT RAISED A FEW TIMES BY FRIENDS WHO'D WITNESSED IT.
I DIDN'T SAY TOO MUCH, FIGURING THAT THE MORE I WENT INTO IT, THE CRAZIER I'D SEEM.
I'M STILL NOT A HUNDRED PERCENT SURE WHAT REALLY HAPPENED THAT NIGHT...
...BUT THE CLEAR EFFECT OF IT WAS TO PUT TO REST ANY MISIMPRESSIONS I'D FOSTERED THAT TOLAND POLK WAS ANY STRAIGHTER THAN SAMMY NOONE HAD BEEN!
SAY IT ONCE IN PUBLIC AND THE GRAPEVINE'LL TAKE IT FROM THERE!

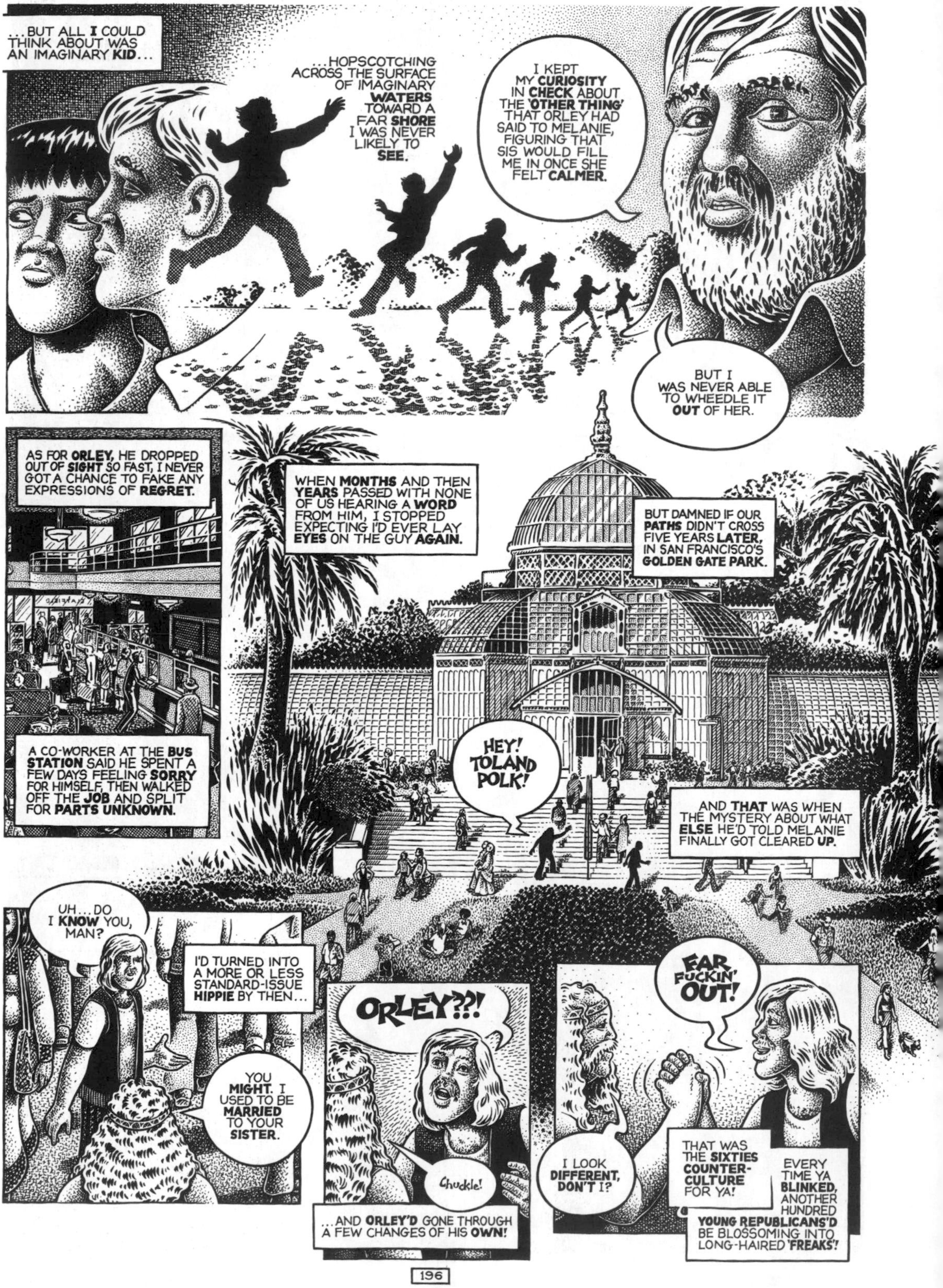

...BUT ALL I COULD THINK ABOUT WAS AN IMAGINARY KID...
...HOPSCOTCHING ACROSS THE SURFACE OF IMAGINARY WATERS TOWARD A FAR SHORE I WAS NEVER LIKELY TO SEE.
I KEPT MY CURIOSITY IN CHECK ABOUT THE 'OTHER THING' THAT ORLEY HAD SAID TO MELANIE, FIGURING THAT SIS WOULD FILL ME IN ONCE SHE FELT CALMER.
BUT I WAS NEVER ABLE TO WHEEDLE IT OUT OF HER.
AS FOR ORLEY, HE DROPPED OUT OF SIGHT SO FAST, I NEVER GOT A CHANCE TO FAKE ANY EXPRESSIONS OF REGRET.
A CO-WORKER AT THE BUS STATION SAID HE SPENT A FEW DAYS FEELING SORRY FOR HIMSELF, THEN WALKED OFF THE JOB AND SPLIT FOR PARTS UNKNOWN.
WHEN MONTHS AND THEN YEARS PASSED WITH NONE OF US HEARING A WORD FROM HIM, I STOPPED EXPECTING I'D EVER LAY EYES ON THE GUY AGAIN.
BUT DAMNED IF OUR PATHS DIDN'T CROSS FIVE YEARS LATER, IN SAN FRANCISCO'S GOLDEN GATE PARK.
HEY! TOLAND POLK!
AND THAT WAS WHEN THE MYSTERY ABOUT WHAT ELSE HE'D TOLD MELANIE FINALLY GOT CLEARED UP.
UH... DO I KNOW YOU, MAN?
I'D TURNED INTO A MORE OR LESS STANDARD-ISSUE HIPPIE BY THEN...
YOU MIGHT. I USED TO BE MARRIED TO YOUR SISTER.
ORLEY??!
Chuckle!
...AND ORLEY'D GONE THROUGH A FEW CHANGES OF HIS OWN!
FAR FUCKIN' OUT!
I LOOK DIFFERENT, DON'T I?
THAT WAS THE SIXTIES COUNTER-CULTURE FOR YA!
EVERY TIME YA BLINKED, ANOTHER HUNDRED YOUNG REPUBLICANS'D BE BLOSSOMING INTO LONG-HAIRED 'FREAKS'!

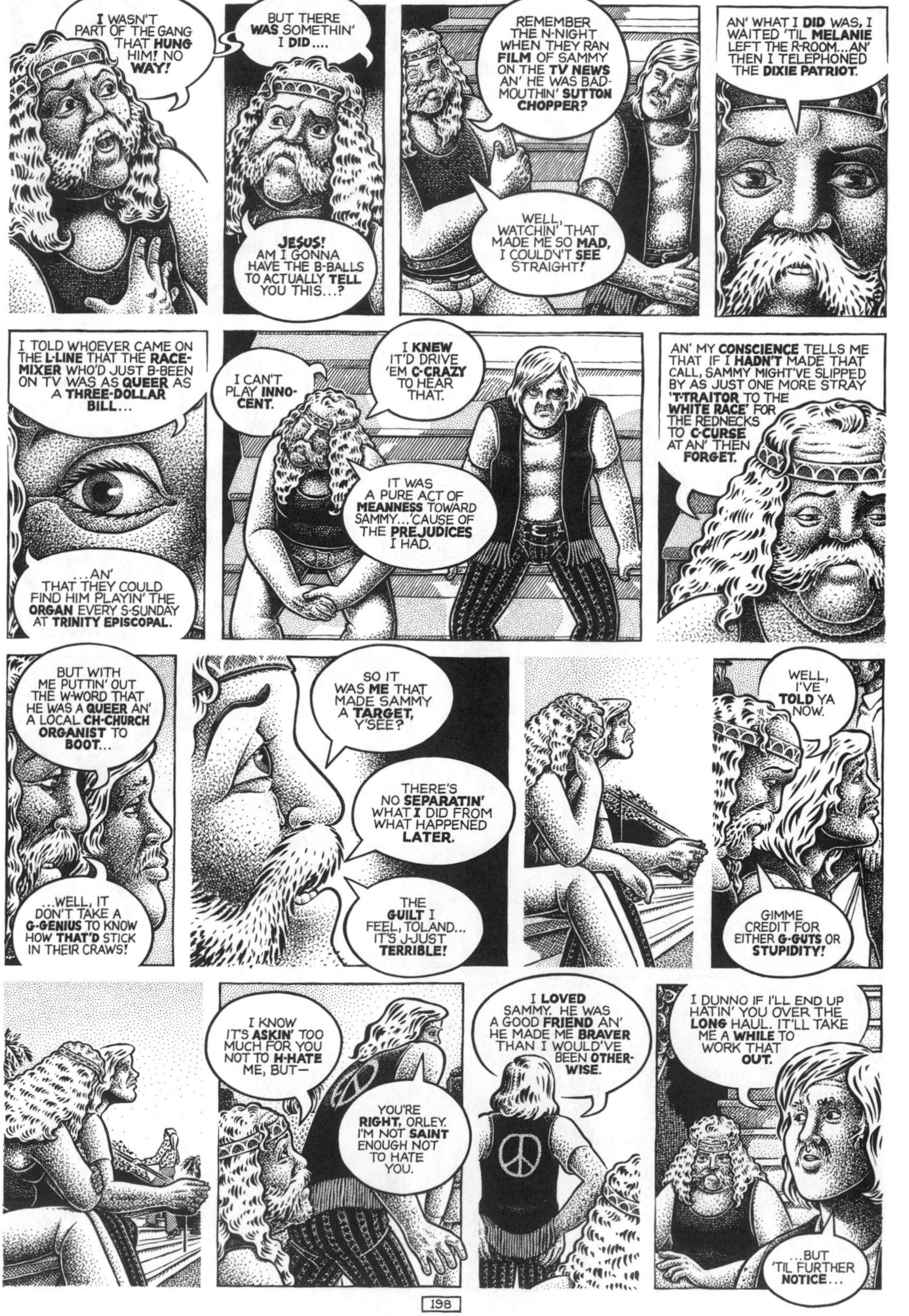

I WASN'T PART OF THE GANG THAT HUNG HIM! NO WAY!
BUT THERE WAS SOMETHIN' I DID....
JESUS! AM I GONNA HAVE THE B-BALLS TO ACTUALLY TELL YOU THIS...?
REMEMBER THE N-NIGHT WHEN THEY RAN FILM OF SAMMY ON THE TV NEWS AN' HE WAS BAD-MOUTHIN' SUTTON CHOPPER?
WELL, WATCHIN' THAT MADE ME SO MAD, I COULDN'T SEE STRAIGHT!
AN' WHAT I DID WAS, I WAITED 'TIL MELANIE LEFT THE R-ROOM...AN' THEN I TELEPHONED THE DIXIE PATRIOT.
I TOLD WHOEVER CAME ON THE L-LINE THAT THE RACE-MIXER WHO'D JUST B-BEEN ON TV WAS AS QUEER AS A THREE-DOLLAR BILL...
...AN' THAT THEY COULD FIND HIM PLAYIN' THE ORGAN EVERY S-SUNDAY AT TRINITY EPISCOPAL.
I CAN'T PLAY INNO-CENT.
I KNEW IT'D DRIVE 'EM C-CRAZY TO HEAR THAT.
IT WAS A PURE ACT OF MEANNESS TOWARD SAMMY...'CAUSE OF THE PREJUDICES I HAD.
AN' MY CONSCIENCE TELLS ME THAT IF I HADN'T MADE THAT CALL, SAMMY MIGHT'VE SLIPPED BY AS JUST ONE MORE STRAY 'T-TRAITOR TO THE WHITE RACE' FOR THE REDNECKS TO C-CURSE AT AN' THEN FORGET.
BUT WITH ME PUTTIN' OUT THE W-WORD THAT HE WAS A QUEER AN' A LOCAL CH-CHURCH ORGANIST TO BOOT...
...WELL, IT DON'T TAKE A G-GENIUS TO KNOW HOW THAT'D STICK IN THEIR CRAWS!
SO IT WAS ME THAT MADE SAMMY A TARGET, Y'SEE?
THERE'S NO SEPARATIN' WHAT I DID FROM WHAT HAPPENED LATER.
THE GUILT I FEEL, TOLAND... IT'S J-JUST TERRIBLE!
WELL, I'VE TOLD YA NOW.
GIMME CREDIT FOR EITHER G-GUTS OR STUPIDITY!
I KNOW IT'S ASKIN' TOO MUCH FOR YOU NOT TO H-HATE ME, BUT—
YOU'RE RIGHT, ORLEY. I'M NOT SAINT ENOUGH NOT TO HATE YOU.
I LOVED SAMMY. HE WAS A GOOD FRIEND AN' HE MADE ME BRAVER THAN I WOULD'VE BEEN OTHER-WISE.
I DUNNO IF I'LL END UP HATIN' YOU OVER THE LONG HAUL. IT'LL TAKE ME A WHILE TO WORK THAT OUT.
...BUT 'TIL FURTHER NOTICE...

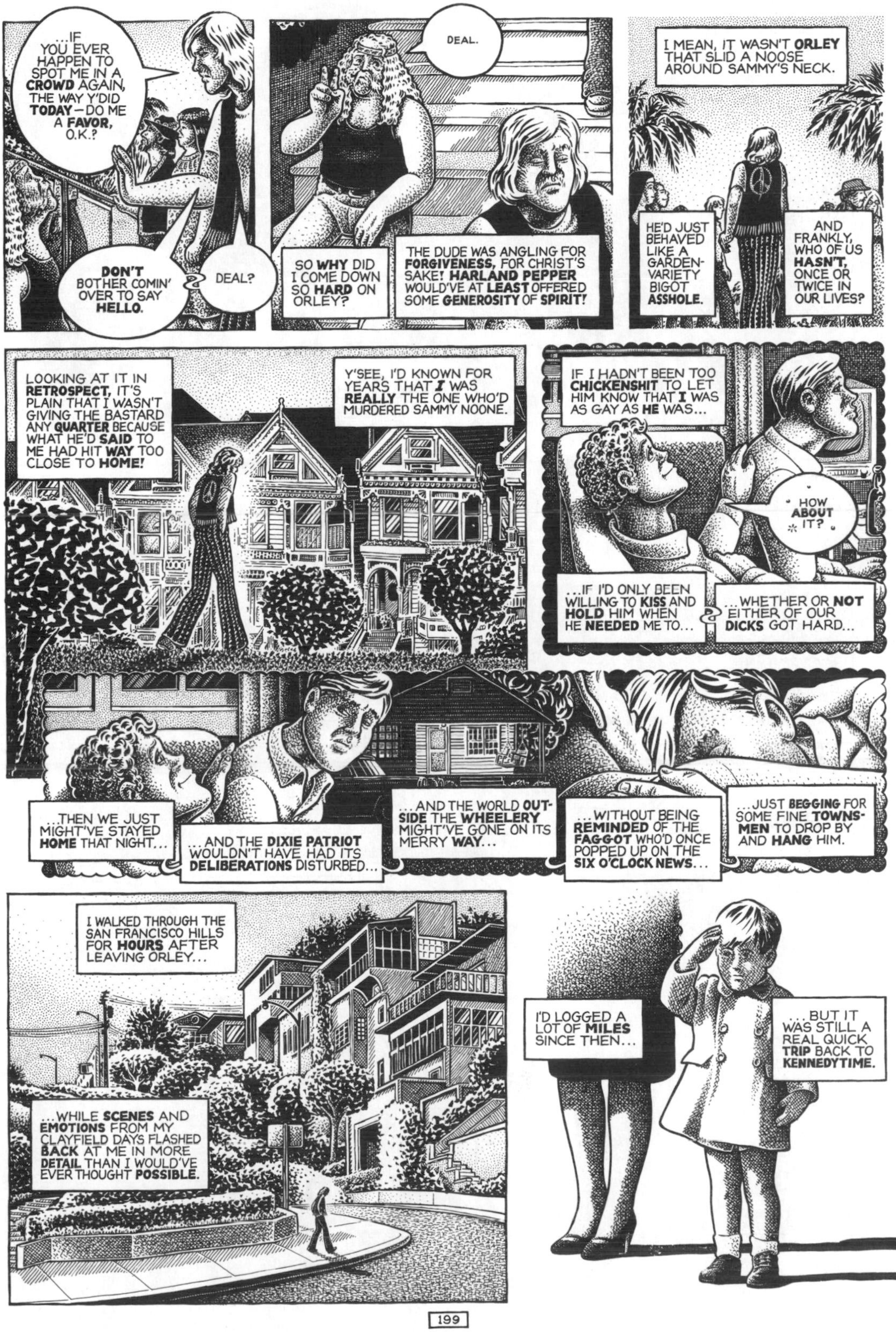
...IF YOU EVER HAPPEN TO SPOT ME IN A CROWD AGAIN, THE WAY Y'DID TODAY—DO ME A FAVOR, O.K.?
DON'T BOTHER COMIN' OVER TO SAY HELLO.
DEAL?
DEAL.
SO WHY DID I COME DOWN SO HARD ON ORLEY?
THE DUDE WAS ANGLING FOR FORGIVENESS, FOR CHRIST'S SAKE! HARLAND PEPPER WOULD'VE AT LEAST OFFERED SOME GENEROSITY OF SPIRIT!
I MEAN, IT WASN'T ORLEY THAT SLID A NOOSE AROUND SAMMY'S NECK.
HE'D JUST BEHAVED LIKE A GARDEN-VARIETY BIGOT ASSHOLE.
AND FRANKLY, WHO OF US HASN'T, ONCE OR TWICE IN OUR LIVES?
LOOKING AT IT IN RETROSPECT, IT'S PLAIN THAT I WASN'T GIVING THE BASTARD ANY QUARTER BECAUSE WHAT HE'D SAID TO ME HAD HIT WAY TOO CLOSE TO HOME!
Y'SEE, I'D KNOWN FOR YEARS THAT I WAS REALLY THE ONE WHO'D MURDERED SAMMY NOONE.
IF I HADN'T BEEN TOO CHICKENSHIT TO LET HIM KNOW THAT I WAS AS GAY AS HE WAS...
HOW ABOUT IT?
...IF I'D ONLY BEEN WILLING TO KISS AND HOLD HIM WHEN HE NEEDED ME TO...
...WHETHER OR NOT EITHER OF OUR DICKS GOT HARD...
...THEN WE JUST MIGHT'VE STAYED HOME THAT NIGHT...
...AND THE DIXIE PATRIOT WOULDN'T HAVE HAD ITS DELIBERATIONS DISTURBED...
...AND THE WORLD OUTSIDE THE WHEELERY MIGHT'VE GONE ON ITS MERRY WAY...
...WITHOUT BEING REMINDED OF THE FAGGOT WHO'D ONCE POPPED UP ON THE SIX O'CLOCK NEWS...
...JUST BEGGING FOR SOME FINE TOWNSMEN TO DROP BY AND HANG HIM.
I WALKED THROUGH THE SAN FRANCISCO HILLS FOR HOURS AFTER LEAVING ORLEY...
...WHILE SCENES AND EMOTIONS FROM MY CLAYFIELD DAYS FLASHED BACK AT ME IN MORE DETAIL THAN I WOULD'VE EVER THOUGHT POSSIBLE.
I'D LOGGED A LOT OF MILES SINCE THEN...
...BUT IT WAS STILL A REAL QUICK TRIP BACK TO KENNEDYTIME.

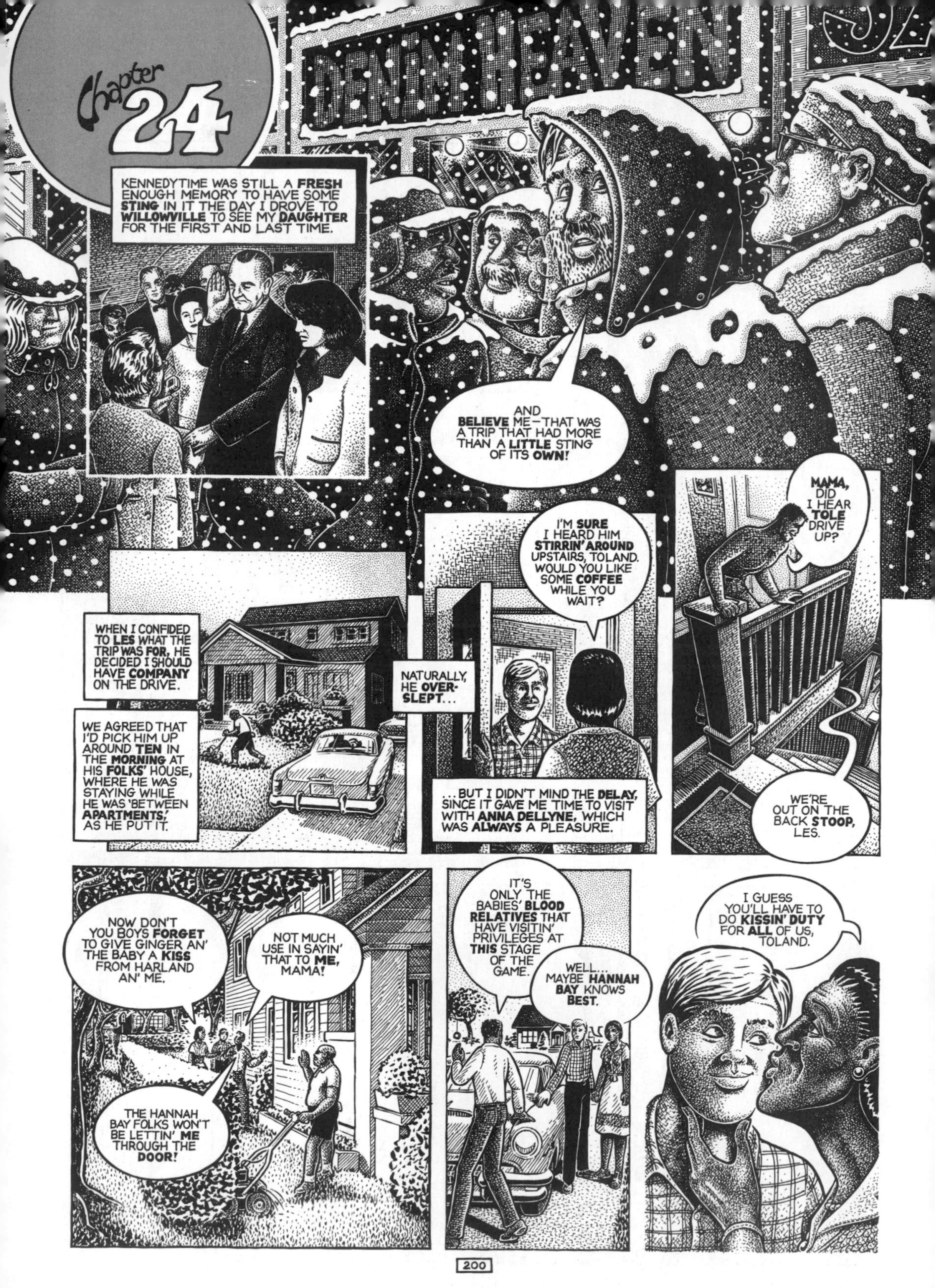
Chapter 24
DENIM HEAVEN
KENNEDYTIME WAS STILL A FRESH ENOUGH MEMORY TO HAVE SOME STING IN IT THE DAY I DROVE TO WILLOWVILLE TO SEE MY DAUGHTER FOR THE FIRST AND LAST TIME.
AND BELIEVE ME—THAT WAS A TRIP THAT HAD MORE THAN A LITTLE STING OF ITS OWN!
WHEN I CONFIDED TO LES WHAT THE TRIP WAS FOR, HE DECIDED I SHOULD HAVE COMPANY ON THE DRIVE.
WE AGREED THAT I'D PICK HIM UP AROUND TEN IN THE MORNING AT HIS FOLKS' HOUSE, WHERE HE WAS STAYING WHILE HE WAS 'BETWEEN APARTMENTS,' AS HE PUT IT.
NATURALLY, HE OVER-SLEPT...
I'M SURE I HEARD HIM STIRRIN' AROUND UPSTAIRS, TOLAND. WOULD YOU LIKE SOME COFFEE WHILE YOU WAIT?
...BUT I DIDN'T MIND THE DELAY, SINCE IT GAVE ME TIME TO VISIT WITH ANNA DELLYNE, WHICH WAS ALWAYS A PLEASURE.
MAMA, DID I HEAR TOLE DRIVE UP?
WE'RE OUT ON THE BACK STOOP, LES.
NOW DON'T YOU BOYS FORGET TO GIVE GINGER AN' THE BABY A KISS FROM HARLAND AN' ME.
NOT MUCH USE IN SAYIN' THAT TO ME, MAMA!
THE HANNAH BAY FOLKS WON'T BE LETTIN' ME THROUGH THE DOOR!
IT'S ONLY THE BABIES' BLOOD RELATIVES THAT HAVE VISITIN' PRIVILEGES AT THIS STAGE OF THE GAME.
WELL... MAYBE HANNAH BAY KNOWS BEST.
I GUESS YOU'LL HAVE TO DO KISSIN' DUTY FOR ALL OF US, TOLAND.

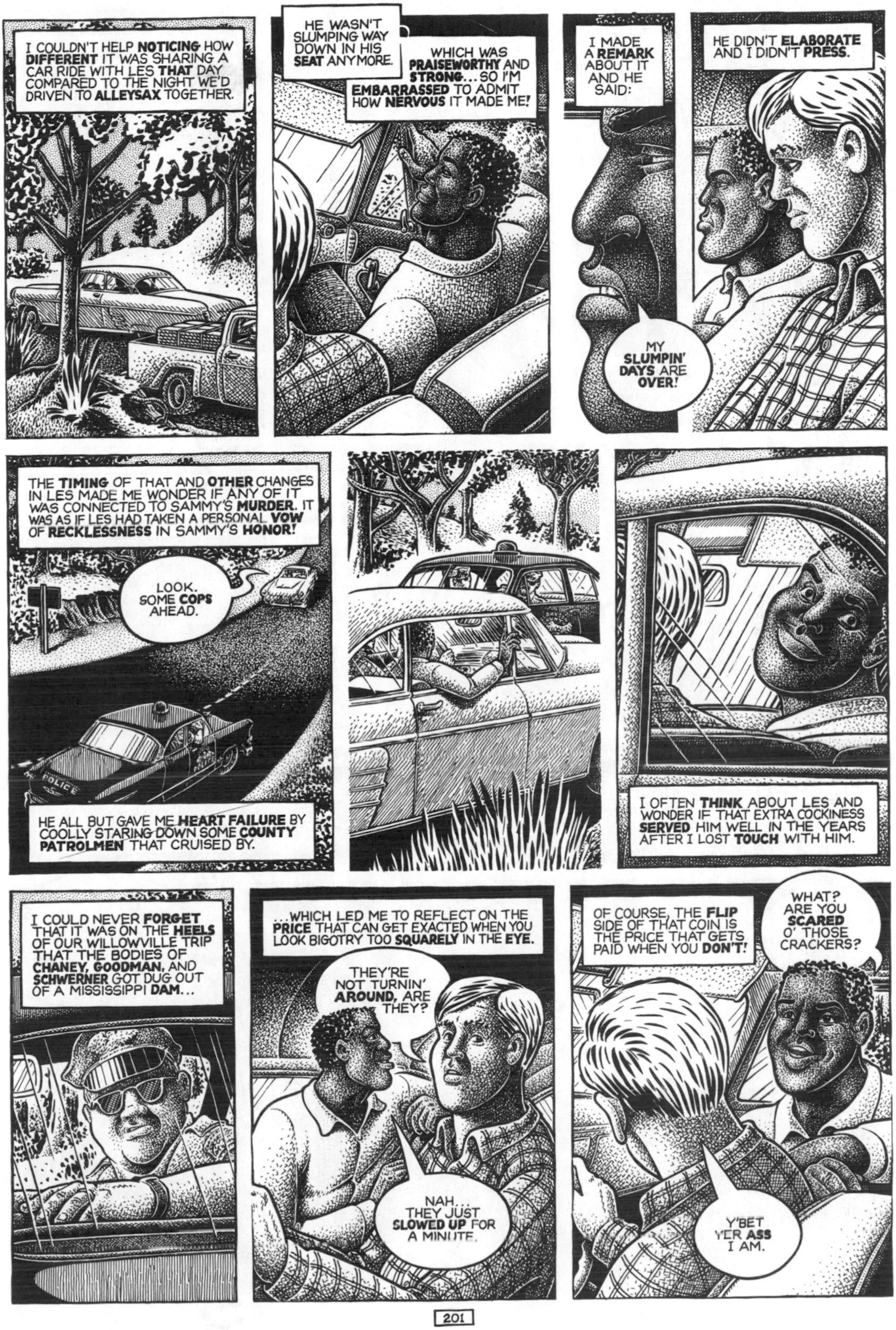

I COULDN'T HELP NOTICING HOW DIFFERENT IT WAS SHARING A CAR RIDE WITH LES THAT DAY COMPARED TO THE NIGHT WE'D DRIVEN TO ALLEYSAX TOGETHER.
HE WASN'T SLUMPING WAY DOWN IN HIS SEAT ANYMORE.
WHICH WAS PRAISEWORTHY AND STRONG... SO I'M EMBARRASSED TO ADMIT HOW NERVOUS IT MADE ME!
I MADE A REMARK ABOUT IT AND HE SAID:
MY SLUMPIN' DAYS ARE OVER!
HE DIDN'T ELABORATE AND I DIDN'T PRESS.
THE TIMING OF THAT AND OTHER CHANGES IN LES MADE ME WONDER IF ANY OF IT WAS CONNECTED TO SAMMY'S MURDER. IT WAS AS IF LES HAD TAKEN A PERSONAL VOW OF RECKLESSNESS IN SAMMY'S HONOR!
LOOK. SOME COPS AHEAD.
POLICE
HE ALL BUT GAVE ME HEART FAILURE BY COOLLY STARING DOWN SOME COUNTY PATROLMEN THAT CRUISED BY.
I OFTEN THINK ABOUT LES AND WONDER IF THAT EXTRA COCKINESS SERVED HIM WELL IN THE YEARS AFTER I LOST TOUCH WITH HIM.
I COULD NEVER FORGET THAT IT WAS ON THE HEELS OF OUR WILLOWVILLE TRIP THAT THE BODIES OF CHANEY, GOODMAN, AND SCHWERNER GOT DUG OUT OF A MISSISSIPPI DAM...
...WHICH LED ME TO REFLECT ON THE PRICE THAT CAN GET EXACTED WHEN YOU LOOK BIGOTRY TOO SQUARELY IN THE EYE.
THEY'RE NOT TURNIN' AROUND, ARE THEY?
NAH... THEY JUST SLOWED UP FOR A MINUTE.
OF COURSE, THE FLIP SIDE OF THAT COIN IS THE PRICE THAT GETS PAID WHEN YOU DON'T!
WHAT? ARE YOU SCARED O' THOSE CRACKERS?
Y'BET YER ASS I AM.

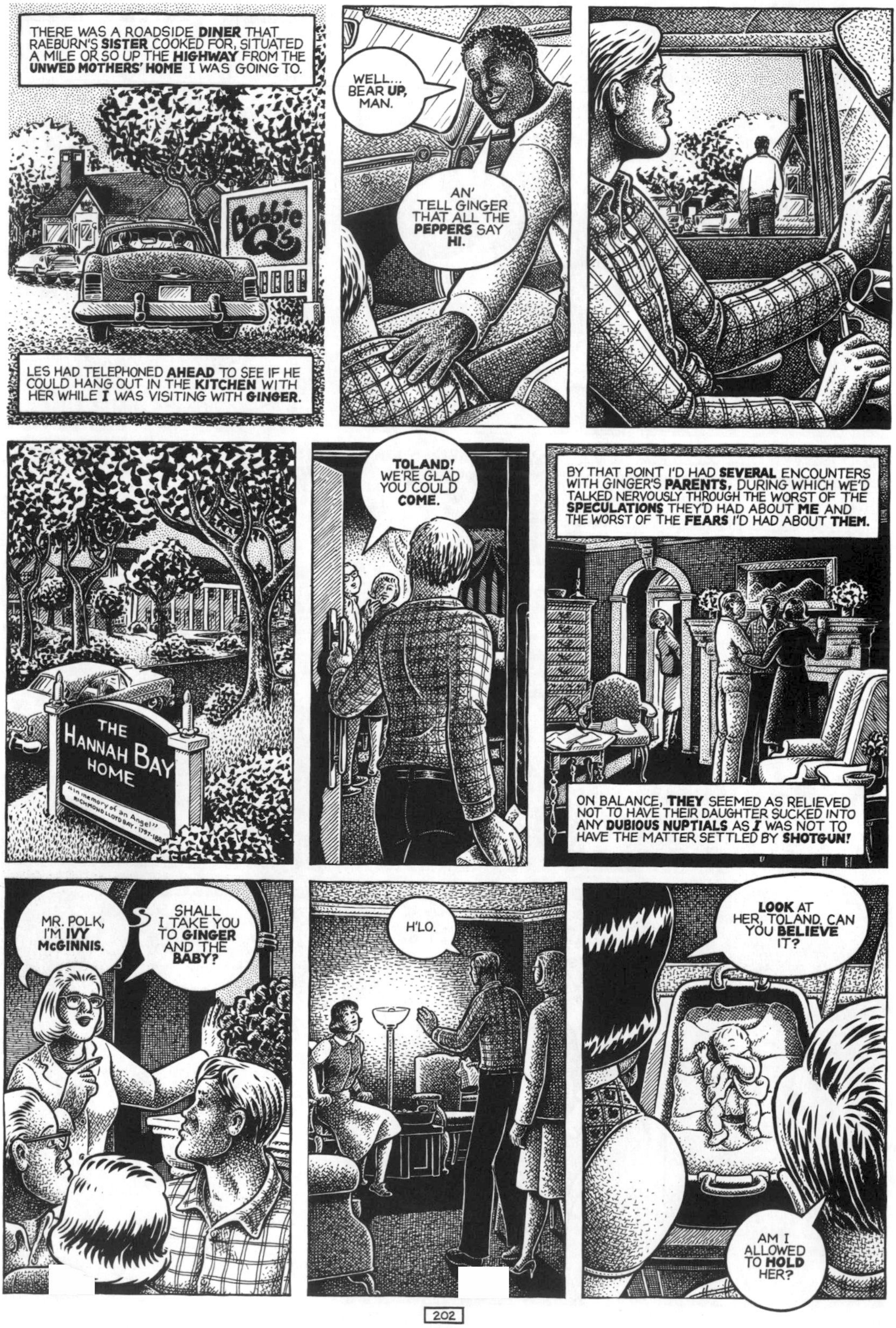
THERE WAS A ROADSIDE **DINER** THAT RAEBURN'S **SISTER** COOKED FOR, SITUATED A MILE OR SO UP THE **HIGHWAY** FROM THE **UNWED MOTHERS' HOME** I WAS GOING TO.
Bobbie Q's
LES HAD TELEPHONED **AHEAD** TO SEE IF HE COULD HANG OUT IN THE **KITCHEN** WITH HER WHILE **I** WAS VISITING WITH **GINGER**.
WELL... BEAR **UP**, MAN.
AN' TELL GINGER THAT ALL THE **PEPPERS** SAY **HI**.
THE HANNAH BAY HOME
TOLAND! WE'RE GLAD YOU COULD **COME**.
BY THAT POINT I'D HAD **SEVERAL** ENCOUNTERS WITH GINGER'S **PARENTS**, DURING WHICH WE'D TALKED NERVOUSLY THROUGH THE WORST OF THE **SPECULATIONS** THEY'D HAD ABOUT **ME** AND THE WORST OF THE **FEARS** I'D HAD ABOUT **THEM**.
ON BALANCE, **THEY** SEEMED AS RELIEVED NOT TO HAVE THEIR DAUGHTER SUCKED INTO ANY **DUBIOUS NUPTIALS** AS ***I*** WAS NOT TO HAVE THE MATTER SETTLED BY **SHOTGUN!**
MR. POLK, I'M **IVY McGINNIS**.
SHALL I TAKE YOU TO **GINGER** AND THE **BABY?**
H'LO.
LOOK AT HER, TOLAND. CAN YOU **BELIEVE** IT?
AM I ALLOWED TO **HOLD** HER?

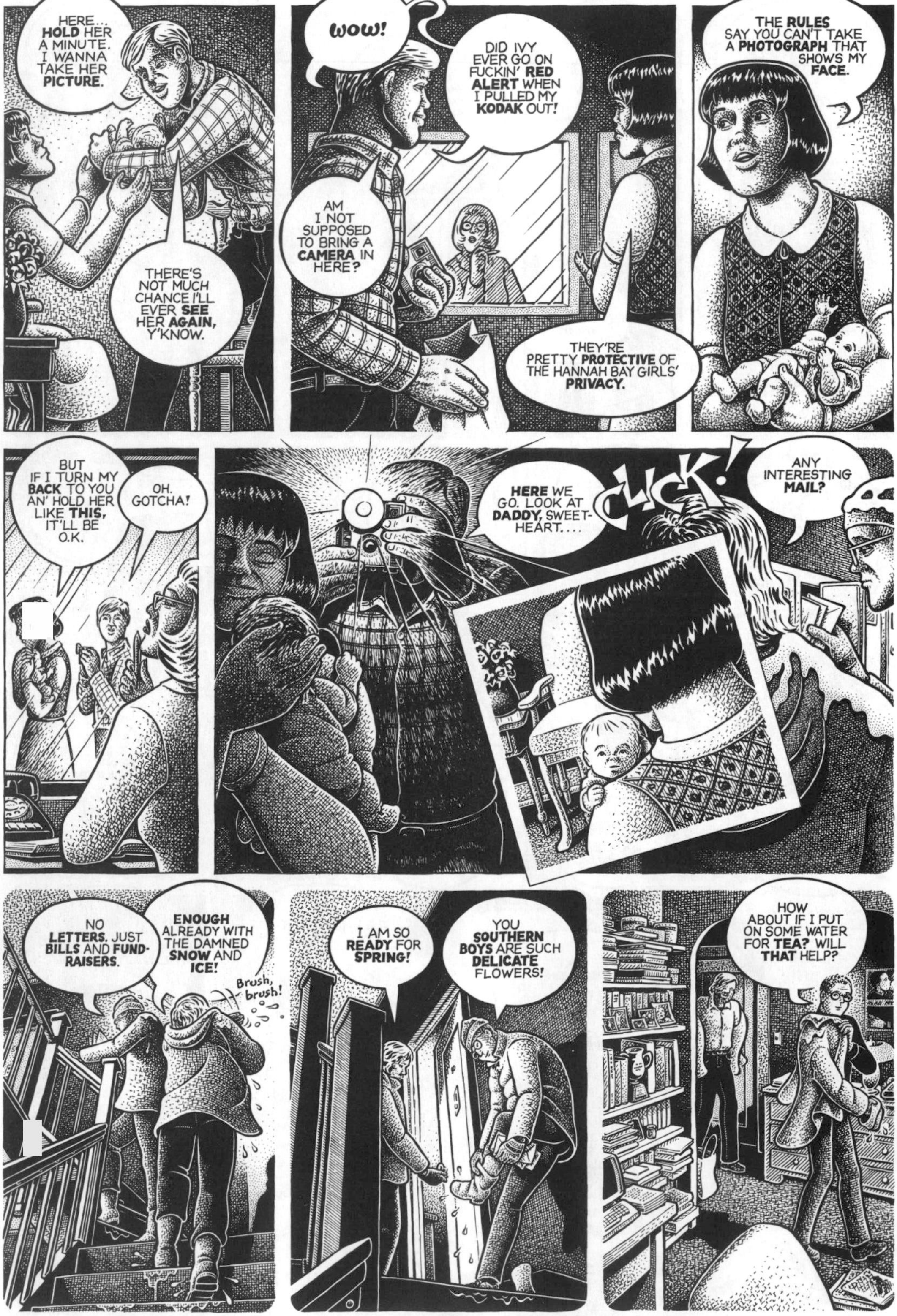
HERE... HOLD HER A MINUTE. I WANNA TAKE HER PICTURE.
THERE'S NOT MUCH CHANCE I'LL EVER SEE HER AGAIN, Y'KNOW.
WOW!
DID IVY EVER GO ON FUCKIN' RED ALERT WHEN I PULLED MY KODAK OUT!
AM I NOT SUPPOSED TO BRING A CAMERA IN HERE?
THEY'RE PRETTY PROTECTIVE OF THE HANNAH BAY GIRLS' PRIVACY.
THE RULES SAY YOU CAN'T TAKE A PHOTOGRAPH THAT SHOWS MY FACE.
BUT IF I TURN MY BACK TO YOU AN' HOLD HER LIKE THIS, IT'LL BE O.K.
OH. GOTCHA!
HERE WE GO. LOOK AT DADDY, SWEET-HEART....
CLICK!
ANY INTERESTING MAIL?
NO LETTERS. JUST BILLS AND FUND-RAISERS.
ENOUGH ALREADY WITH THE DAMNED SNOW AND ICE!
Brush, brush!
I AM SO READY FOR SPRING!
YOU SOUTHERN BOYS ARE SUCH DELICATE FLOWERS!
HOW ABOUT IF I PUT ON SOME WATER FOR TEA? WILL THAT HELP?

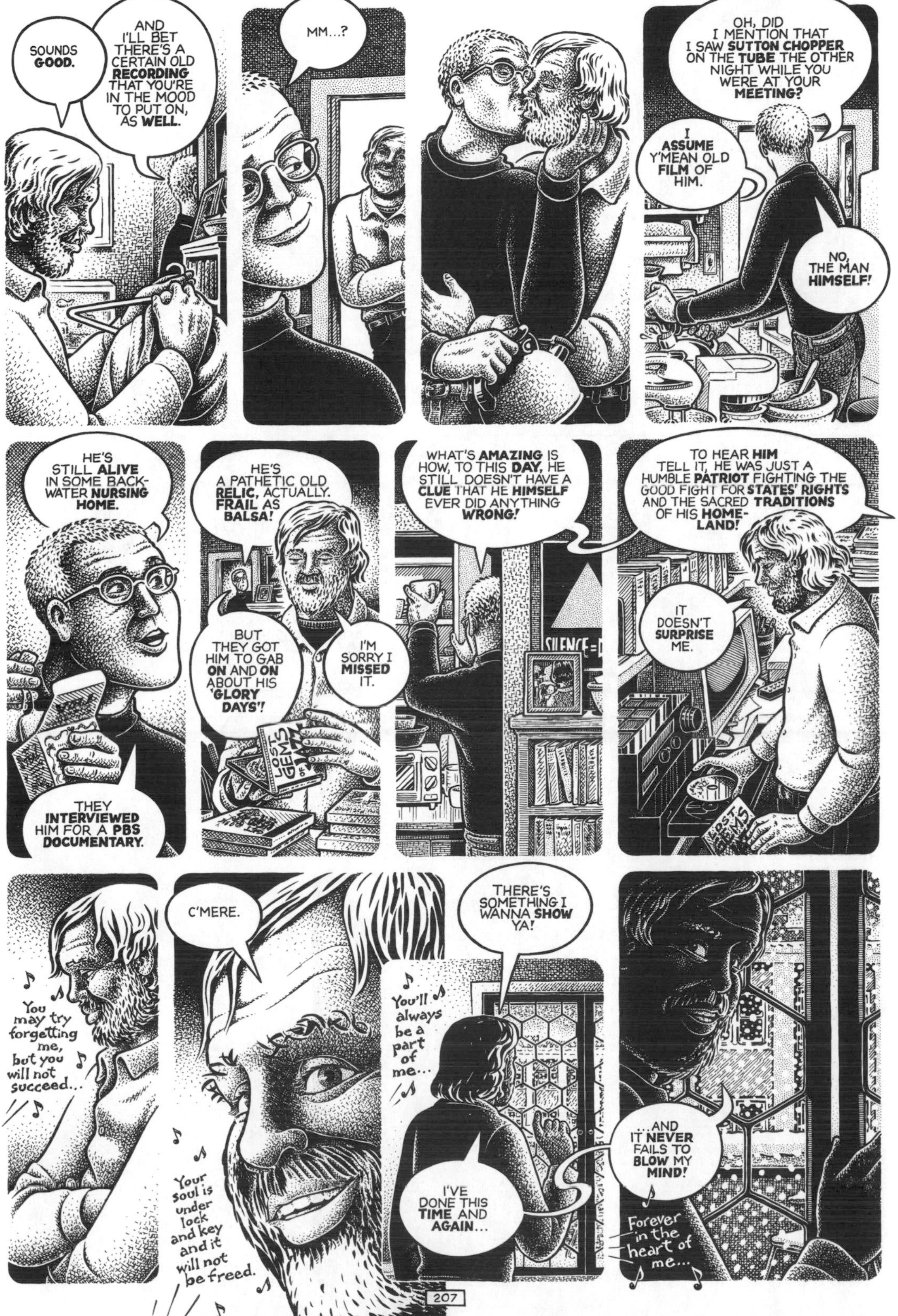
SOUNDS GOOD.
AND I'LL BET THERE'S A CERTAIN OLD RECORDING THAT YOU'RE IN THE MOOD TO PUT ON, AS WELL.
MM...?
OH, DID I MENTION THAT I SAW SUTTON CHOPPER ON THE TUBE THE OTHER NIGHT WHILE YOU WERE AT YOUR MEETING?
I ASSUME Y'MEAN OLD FILM OF HIM.
NO, THE MAN HIMSELF!
HE'S STILL ALIVE IN SOME BACK-WATER NURSING HOME.
THEY INTERVIEWED HIM FOR A PBS DOCUMENTARY.
HE'S A PATHETIC OLD RELIC, ACTUALLY. FRAIL AS BALSA!
BUT THEY GOT HIM TO GAB ON AND ON ABOUT HIS 'GLORY DAYS'!
I'M SORRY I MISSED IT.
LOST GEMS OF JAZZ
WHAT'S AMAZING IS HOW, TO THIS DAY, HE STILL DOESN'T HAVE A CLUE THAT HE HIMSELF EVER DID ANYTHING WRONG!
SILENCE=D
TO HEAR HIM TELL IT, HE WAS JUST A HUMBLE PATRIOT FIGHTING THE GOOD FIGHT FOR STATES' RIGHTS AND THE SACRED TRADITIONS OF HIS HOME-LAND!
IT DOESN'T SURPRISE ME.
You may try forgetting me, but you will not succeed...
C'MERE.
Your soul is under lock and key and it will not be freed.
THERE'S SOMETHING I WANNA SHOW YA!
You'll always be a part of me...
I'VE DONE THIS TIME AND AGAIN...
...AND IT NEVER FAILS TO BLOW MY MIND!
Forever in the heart of me...

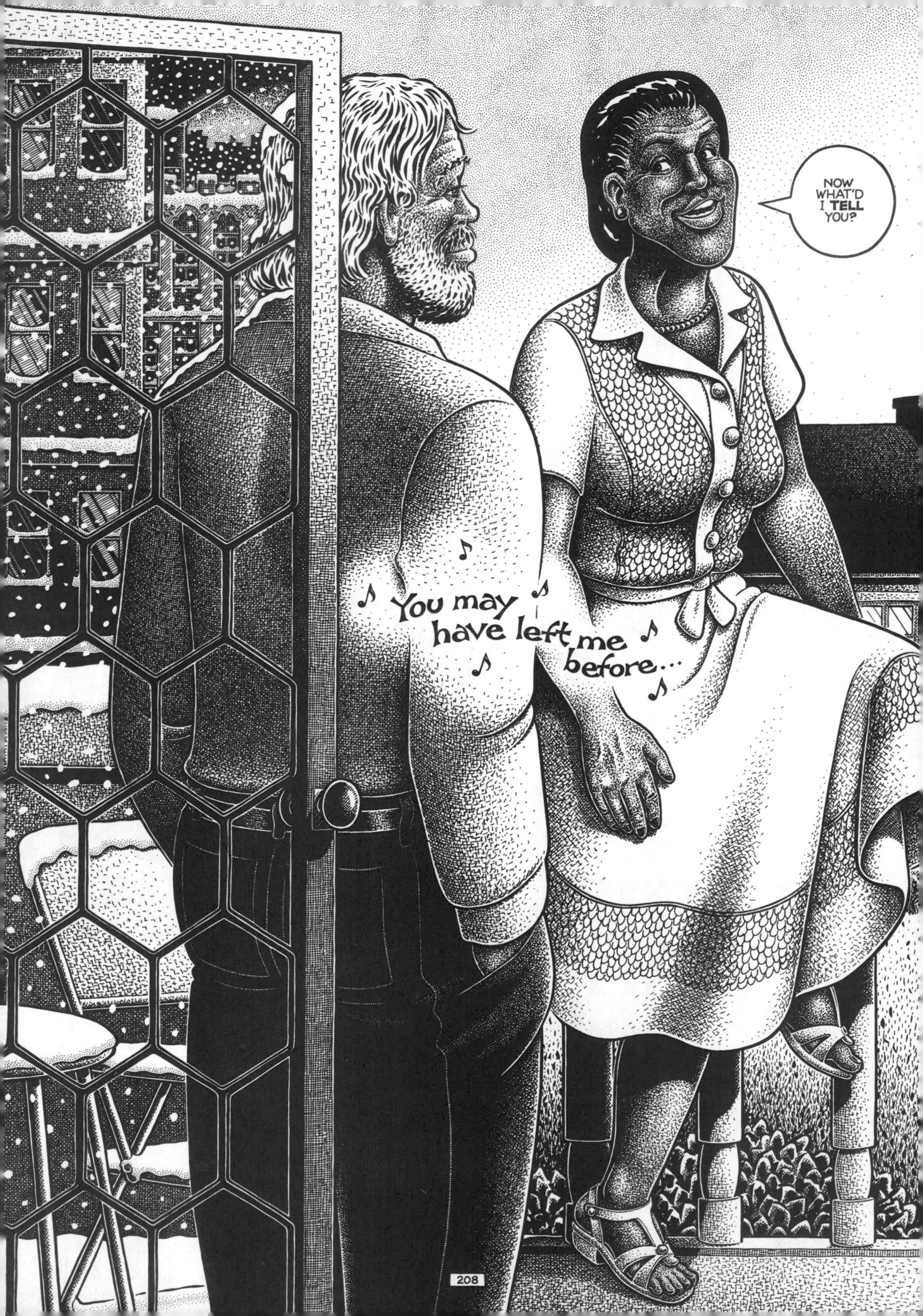
NOW WHAT'D I **TELL** YOU?
You may have left me before...

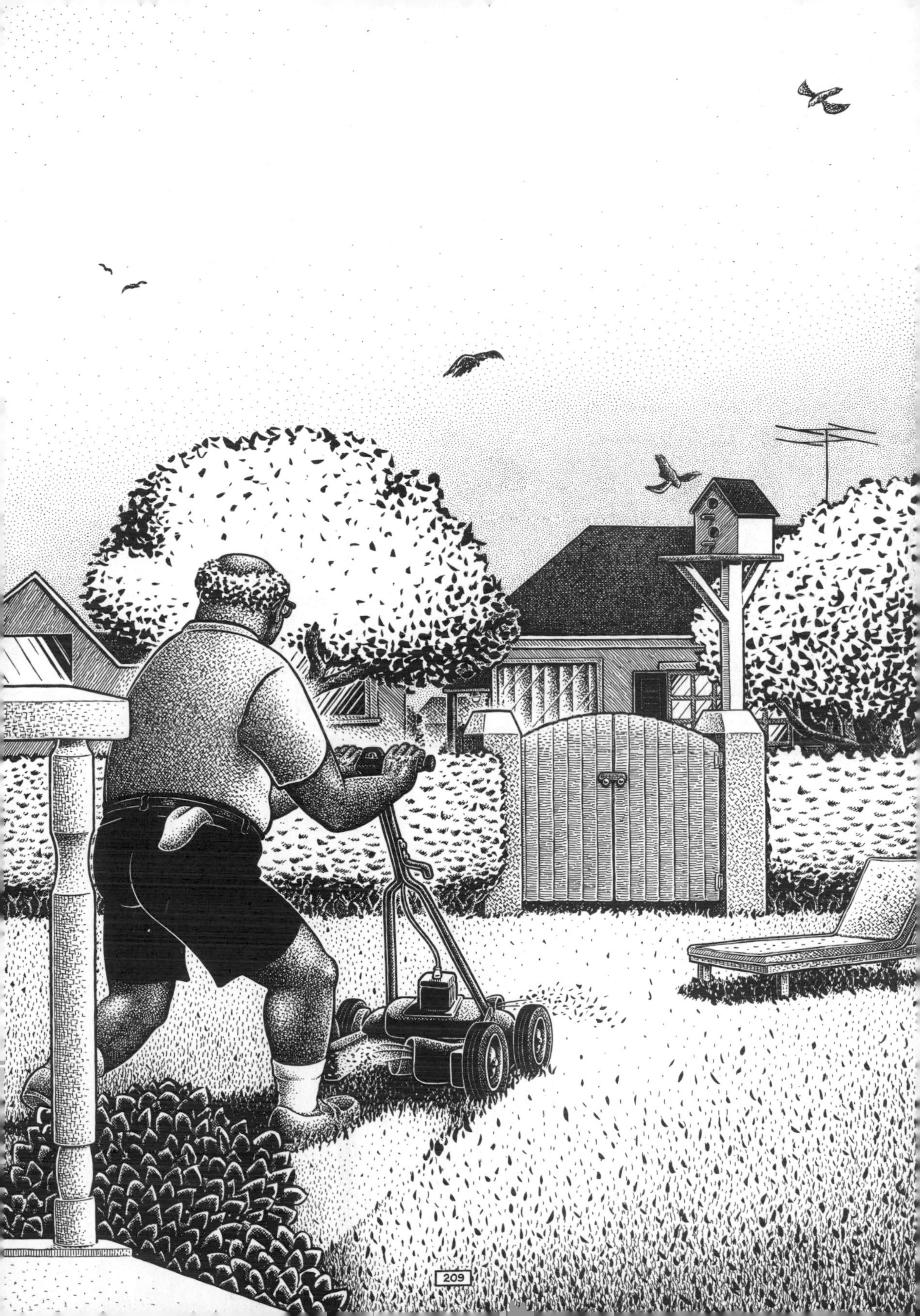

♪ ♪

...But you can't leave me behind. ♪

♪

♪

A C K N O W L E D G M E N T S

Stuck Rubber Baby is a work of fiction, not autobiography. Its characters are inventions of mine, and Clayfield is a make-believe city.

That said, it's doubtful I'd have been moved to write and draw this graphic novel if I hadn't come of age in Birmingham, Alabama, during the early '60s. My own experiences as well as those of old friends and new acquaintances who were kind enough to share their memories with me have served as springboards for various incidents in my narrative, as have the news accounts that I and a nation watched together. I'm grateful to the following individuals for setting aside time to tell me tales: Bob Bailey; Irene Beavers; Clyde and Linda Buzzard; Nina Cain; Dr. Dodson Curry; William A. Dry; John Fuller; Harry Garwood; Mary Larsen; Bill Miller; Bertram N. Perry; Cora Pitt; Perry Schwartz; Jim and Eileen Walbert; Jack Williamson; and Thomas E. Wrenn.

Let me emphasize that none of the individuals cited above had any hand in the actual development of my storyline nor any opportunity to evaluate the liberties I've taken in bringing my own point of view to the fictional incidents loosely inspired by their accounts. Any errors of history or perceived wrong-headedness of interpretation should be laid at my door, not theirs.

Others have aided me, too, in varying ways. Much help was provided at the outset by Marvin Whiting, the Birmingham Public Library's distinguished archivist. I have turned for enlightenment on technical points of law to David Fleischer and to David Hansell. Ed Still provided background on the history of Jim Crow laws. John Gillick helped me with guns; Diana Arecco provided architectural reference; and Murdoch Matthew and Gary Gilbert instructed me on Episcopalian matters. Mary McClain, Stephen Solomita, Dennis O'Neil and John Townsend also provided important nuggets of information.

I'm grateful to Harvey Pekar for answering my questions about jazz lore and to Wade Black of Bozart Mountain/Jade Films for letting me photograph his old movie cameras for reference. And it's by the good graces of Morton J. Savada of Records Revisited in Manhattan that Anna Dellyne's record labels and sleeves have a touch of authenticity.

I'm especially indebted to Leonard Shiller of the Antique Auto Association of Brooklyn, Inc., for cheerfully escorting me from garage to garage in his borough as I photographed not only classic cars but also his fascinating cache of gas pumps, washing machines, vacuum cleaners, scooters, bicycles, beverage trucks, fire engines and other collectibles from a bygone era.

I owe thanks to those who admitted me into their private domains so I could snap reference photos of old furniture, appliances, and representative bits of architecture: Arthur Davis and Ellen Elliott; David Nimmons and David Fleischer; Howie Katz; Elyse Taylor and Leonard Shiller; and Tony Ward and Richard Goldstein. And I'm grateful as well for the special contributions of Grady Clarkson, Tim J. Luddy, and David Hutchison.

I want to thank Andrew Helfer and Bronwyn Taggart, respectively the group editor and editor of Paradox Press, for supporting *Stuck Rubber Baby* unwaveringly during its extended incubation and for allowing me great artistic autonomy in its execution. I'm indebted to Mark Nevelow, the founding editor-in-chief of Piranha Press (Paradox's predecessor), who said yes in 1990 to my proposal for a graphic novel embodying themes that might have tempted a less adventurous editor to stand back, and whose subsequent feedback contributed to a sturdier narrative; and to Margaret Clark, Ms. Taggart's predecessor as editor, for her helpfulness while in that position. My agent, Mike Friedrich of Star*Reach Productions, Inc., has been an effective problem solver and a valued advisor with regard to both pictures and text. And I'm especially grateful to my longtime friend Martha Thomases, publicity manager of DC Comics, for the help she has provided on too many fronts to mention here, as well as for her seminal insistence, in the face of my initial skepticism, that space might exist at the House of Superman for an underground cartoonist's pursuit of a labor of love.

When I started *Stuck Rubber Baby*, I thought I could do it in two years. It took four. Thus was precipitated a personal budgetary crisis of unnerving proportions, one that forced an unwelcome diversion of energy into the search for enough supplemental funds to cover two unanticipated years of full-time drawing.

Accustomed as I am to creating art in relative solitude, it's been disorienting to find myself so dependent on assistance from others. But dependent I've been, and it's with deep gratitude that I catalog here the varied ways that friends and creative colleagues have gone to bat for me during difficult times.

Most of the forms I filled out in applying for foundation grants asked for letters of endorsement from individuals of creative accomplishment. The following people wrote such letters in my behalf: Stephen R. Bissette; Martin Duberman; Will Eisner; Harvey Fierstein; Richard Goldstein; Maurice Horn; Scott McCloud; Ida Panicelli; and Harvey Pekar.

When things seemed most precarious, a fundraising tactic was devised by which individuals could become "sponsors" of this book through the purchase of original artwork from it — at higher than market value and in advance of its even being drawn. In support of this tactic, a letter of endorsement for *Stuck Rubber Baby* was drafted and signed by fifteen writers, artists, film and TV producers, and other cultural leaders. Those who signed that letter were: Michael Feingold; Matt Foreman; David Frankel; Richard Goldstein; Arnie Kantrowitz; Tony Kushner; Harvey Marks; Lawrence D. Mass; Jed Mattes; Armistead Maupin; Michael Musto; Robert Newman; John Scagliotti; Randy Shilts; and John Wessel. Crucial technical tasks related to fundraising were performed by Tony Ward, Jennifer Camper, Robert Hanna, and Suk Choi of Box Graphics, Inc. I appreciate the willingness of Paul Levitz, the executive vice-president and publisher of DC Comics, to sanction the bending of some normal company practices in the assembly of our fundraising prospectus.

I am deeply grateful to the individual sponsors themselves, whose advance purchases of original art from this graphic novel made the completion of *Stuck Rubber Baby* possible. They are:

Fred Adams
Allan Cruse
Kevin Eastman
Richard Goldstein
Tony Kushner
Stanley Reed
Martha Thomases and John R. Tebbel
Bob Wingate

Additional support for this project was provided by:

Joan Cullman
Glenn Izutsu
Chopeta Lyons
The Anderson Prize Foundation

Let me finish by thanking Ed Sedarbaum, my companion of sixteen years, for his unshakable belief in me and in the merits of this graphic novel; for the concrete help he offered when practical problems loomed; and for the encouragement and thoughtful feedback he has provided as successive chapters have been offered for his assessment.

Howard Cruse
July 1995

ABOUT THE AUTHOR

Howard Cruse, creator of *Barefootz* and *Wendel* and the founding editor of *Gay Comix*, is an Alabama preacher's kid who counted *The Baptist Student* among his cartoon markets while still in high school. Since then his comic strips and cartoon illustrations have appeared in dozens of national magazines, underground comic books, and anthologies as well as in four book collections of his own. Since 1979 he has shared his life in New York City with book editor and political activist Ed Sedarbaum.